Social Information Technology:
Connecting Society and Cultural Issues

Terry Kidd
University of Texas Health Science Center School of Public Health, USA

Irene L. Chen
University of Houston Downtown, USA

INFORMATION SCIENCE REFERENCE

Hershey • New York

Acquisitions Editor:	Kristin Klinger
Development Editor:	Kristin Roth
Senior Managing Editor:	Jennifer Neidig
Managing Editor:	Jamie Snavely
Assistant Managing Editor:	Carole Coulson
Copy Editor:	Angela Thor
Typesetter:	Sean Woznicki
Cover Design:	Lisa Tosheff
Printed at:	Yurchak Printing Inc.

Published in the United States of America by
Information Science Reference (an imprint of IGI Global)
701 E. Chocolate Avenue, Suite 200
Hershey PA 17033
Tel: 717-533-8845
Fax: 717-533-8661
E-mail: cust@igi-global.com
Web site: http://www.igi-global.com

and in the United Kingdom by
Information Science Reference (an imprint of IGI Global)
3 Henrietta Street
Covent Garden
London WC2E 8LU
Tel: 44 20 7240 0856
Fax: 44 20 7379 0609
Web site: http://www.eurospanbookstore.com

Library of Congress Cataloging-in-Publication Data

Social information technology : connecting society and cultural issues / Terry Kidd and Irene Chen, editors.

    p. cm.

  Summary: "This book provides a source for definitions, antecedents, and consequences of social informatics and the cultural aspect of technology. It addresses cultural/societal issues in social informatics technology and society, the Digital Divide, government and technology law, information security and privacy, cyber ethics, technology ethics, and the future of social informatics and technology"--Provided by publisher.

  Includes bibliographical references and index.

  ISBN-13: 978-1-59904-774-4 (hardcover)

  ISBN-13: 978-1-59904-776-8 (e-book)

  1. Information society--Social aspects. 2. Information technology--Social aspects. 3. Social change. I. Kidd, Terry. II. Chen, Irene.

  HM851.S64 2008

  303.48'33--dc22

               2007037399

British Cataloguing in Publication Data
A Cataloguing in Publication record for this book is available from the British Library.

Table of Contents

Section III
International Social Information Technology Practices

Section IV
Online Social Information Technology Applications

Section V
Implications of Social Information Technology in Education

Detailed Table of Contents

Section I
Implications of Social Information Technology

Leigh uses the philosophical lens of Critical Race Theory to shed light upon the vast inequalities in access to information technologies that exists among racial, ethnic, and socioeconomic groups; a phenomenon that has come to be known as the digital divide. The primary focus is on how the digital divide has played out for African Americans and the use of CRT to explain the history of inequalities and why significant differences in educational opportunities have persisted into the 21st century.

The chapter explores gender differences in three key areas: computer attitude, ability, and use. The author indicates that males and females are more similar than different on all constructs assessed, for most grade levels and contexts. However, males report moderately more positive affective attitudes, higher self-efficacy, and more frequent users. Females are slightly more positive about online learning and appear to perform somewhat better on computer-related tasks. Finally, a model is proposed to understand and address gender differences in computer-related behaviour.

The author offers an overview of how technology is central to modern development, how technology has been conceptualized, and how virtual development is yet another frontier best captured in the notion of technopolis and/or technocity as contextual factors that sustain social technologies. The pervasiveness of technology, the factors that affect the technological experience besides the rhetoric of infallibility, and the taken-for-granted delivery of utility and efficiency will also be explored. By looking at the criticisms voiced against urban and virtual development about the loosening of social ties, the author argues for a fluid interaction that considers the possibilities for additional and different, if not new, social relations that both physical and virtual interactions afford to urbanites: technosociability.

Section II
Geo-Political Practices

The authors describe a comparative study that examined Web sites of Peace Movement Organizations (PMOs) in Japan and Israel. Collective action frame is used as a theoretical framework to analyze 17 Web sites, identifying the similarities and differences in the ways that online PMOs frame their activities. The findings indicate that these organizations employed various strategies to develop resonance, highlighting the importance of cultural resonance in framing online PMOs in different countries.

The chapter considers the utility of Clarke's worst-case planning by examining Y2K preparations at twosociogovernment agencies, the Bureau of Labor Statistics and the Federal Aviation Administration. The chapter concludes that the thoroughness of worst-case planning can bring much needed light to the subtlety of critical complex and interdependent systems. But such an approach can also be narrow in its own way, revealing some of the limitations of such a precautionary approach.

The chapter assesses how the USA Patriot Act protects US national security and through self-censorship over privacy concerns may affect sociopolitical and cultural diversity in cyberspace.

Chapter VII

The concept of health is universal culturally, and informatics disciplines are emerging fields of practice characterized by indistinct boundaries in terms of theory, policy, and practice. Various ethnographic and cultural associations are made by Jones in the chapter "Exploring Serres' Atlas, Hodges' Knowledge Domains and the Fusion of Informatics and Cultural Horizons." Jones also explores the extent to which selected writings of French philosopher Michel Serres and a health care model created by Brian Hodges in the UK can augment and inform the development of social informatics. Central to the chapter is the notion of holistic bandwidth, utilizing Hodges' model as a tool to develop and disseminate sociotechnical perspectives.

Chapter VIII

The chapter discusses open source as a most significant institutional disruption to the way software and digital content in general evolves and dissipates through society. On the one hand, less formal kinds of credits than money and the like often provide for a relatively efficient and viable way of accounting for credits in the development of large and complex software and technology projects. On the other hand, at the intersection of developer communities with end users there is a distinct need for formal money-based interactions, because informal contracts and credit redemption do work well in communities, but less so in anonymous market contexts.

Chapter IX

Hébert starts with describing the crisis over copyright and control of music distribution that has been developing. The outcome of this crisis has tremendous implications not only for the fate of commercial and creative entities involved in music, but for the social reproduction of knowledge and culture more generally. This chapter introduces the concept of "concretization," and demonstrates how it can be applied on the lives and work of the people using modern media. It can also give us not only a detailed description of the relations of various groups, individuals, and modern media technologies, but also a prescriptive program for the future maintenance and strengthening of a vibrant and radically democratized sphere of creative exchange. Critical theories of technology are used in addressing these implications.

Chapter X

The author observes that current information security strategies tend to focus on a technology-based approach to securing information. However, this technology-based approach can leave an organization vulnerable to information security threats, which in turn puts society at risk to potential losses due to inadequate security by the organizations they do business with. Humans operate, maintain, and use information systems. Their actions, whether intentional or accidental, are the real threats to organizations. The author argues that information security strategies must be developed to address the social issue.

Chen and Tarn claim that the use of electronic monitoring tools in the workplace has grown dramatically because of the availability of inexpensive but powerful monitoring systems, and the wide use of information and communication technologies in today's workplace. However, existing research pays little attention to the pervasive use of electronic monitoring systems on IT at work. This chapter draws theories in international and organizational cultures, and concludes four hypotheses on privacy concerns of employees and their perceived trust to the management when being electronically monitored.

Section III
International Social Information Technology Practices

The authors describe how exploratory research was conducted into the assessment and measurement of information systems' success by small- and medium-sized enterprises in Samoa, and the effect on IT investment. It was found that information quality, system quality, use, user satisfaction, and financial impacts were the main dimensions according to which success was assessed while intention to use, and cultural impacts were not usually assessed.

Sharma and Mishra discuss the deployment of e-learning technologies regarding how they are helping towards preserving and disseminating knowledge on Indian cultural heritage. An analysis has also been offered as regards how the culture impacts e-learning initiatives, design issues within online courses and programmes. This chapter makes an attempt to understand and frame Indian culture and experience through e-learning practices, and how the differentiated learning needs of multilingual and multinational consumers are addressed.

Fielden proposes that the New Zealand Family Court is an ideal public sector application for social informatics. In a study investigating ICT-assisted communications, which was conducted with multiple court stakeholders, paradoxical results emerged. This chapter encompasses private/public space, sense of self, emotional energies, and digital citizenship in the field of social informatics. This theoretical framework provides grounding for results within and across disciplines revealing deeply engrained behaviours, emotional states, customs, workplace cultures, and the problems associated with solving private problems in public spaces.

The chapter investigates one of the most common technology access points, Internet Cafés, by focusing the missions of these places regarding Internet use and game play and their roles in Ankara, capital city of Turkey. Data are collected by giving a questionnaire including demographic information about users and their Internet Café habits. Also, observation reports are employed while they are using Internet and playing computer games in these places. In the study, it is aimed to select Internet Cafés from both low and high socioeconomic regions in the city so that Internet Cafés and their roles in the society can be easily investigated by comparing different factors like socioeconomic status.

Section IV
Online Social Information Technology Applications

The chapter introduces search assistants and underlines their evolution toward social information. Thanks to the "new Web," the Web 2.0, personal search assistants are evolving using social techniques such as social networks and sharing-based methods. Due to the high amount of information and the diversity of human factors, searching for information requires patience, perseverance, and sometimes luck. To help individuals during this task, search assistants feature adaptive techniques aiming at personalizing retrieved information.

Chapter XVII

Meng-Fen Grace Lin, University of Houston, USA
Curtis J. Bonk, Indiana University, USA
Suthiporn Sajjapanroj, Indiana University, USA

Lin, Bonk, and Sajjapanroj investigate the emergence and growth of two participatory environments: the highly popular Wikipedia site and its' sister project, Wikibooks. Wikipedia has grown out of trends for free and open access to Web tools and resources. While Wikipedians edit, contribute, and monitor distinct pieces of information or pages of documents, Wikibookians must focus on larger chunks of knowledge, including book modules or chapters as well as entire books. Several key differences between these two types of wiki environments are explored. In addition, surveys and interviews conducted with Wikibookians shed light on their challenges, frustrations, and successes.

Section V
Implications of Social Information Technology in Education

Chapter XVIII

Christine Simard, Télé-université (TÉLUQ), Canada
Josianne Basque, Télé-université (TÉLUQ), Canada

Simard and Basque discusses how cultural variables can be taken into account when designing computer-based learning environments (CLE). Its purpose is to identify concrete recommendations to guide instructional engineering of computer-based learning for diverse cultures through a review of the literature on the subject. First, this chapter describes the context in which such recommendations have emerged, and identifies some of the issues underlying instructional design for diverse cultures. Then the chapter introduces models and guidelines on how cultural variables can be taken into account when designing CLEs. Specific recommendations are organized using a method of instructional engineering for CLEs called MISA, as a frame of reference. This is followed by a discussion on future trends that may affect how cultural variables guide instructional engineering over the next decade.

Chapter XIX

Maggie McPherson, University of Leeds, UK
Miguel Baptista Nunes, University of Sheffield, UK
John Sandars, University of Leeds, UK
Christine Kell, University of Sheffield, UK

McPherson, Nunes, Sandars, and Kell describe the potential of Social Information Technologies (SITs) for online continuing professional education (CPE), and identify the main driving forces in UK. The authors highlight the important findings from their experience and research of online CPE, particularly within the health service. In fact, the authors' motivation in writing this chapter was, in part, to raise awareness of the importance of the major differences between policy and the reality of the context of professional practice and online CPE, and to propose recommendations that can inform future policy and practice. Thus, although the illustrations will be largely based on the authors' studies of CPE for healthcare professionals in the UK, The authors believe that their study and findings can be generalized to other professions and to other contexts.

Chapter XX

The chapter states that in the nursing field in UK, 6 years after the Guidelines for Networked Learning in Higher Education were published, levels of students' skills and engagement with ICT remain problematic, which undermines attempts to deploy networked learning. Johnson argues that for such initiatives to succeed, more foundational connections need also to be promoted. He focuses on some of the factors that contribute to student nurses' ICT non-engagement: gender, caring, professional identity, and knowledge work. Finally, the author explains how some of the barriers identified can be overcome through integrating ICT.

Chapter XXI

The chapter describes three models of distributing education to achieve different social missions: a distance teaching university (The UK Open University), a multicampus higher education institute servicing remote and rural areas in the Highlands and Islands of Scotland (UHI Millennium Institute), and a new university in Greece spread over five small islands (University of the Aegean). The chapter considers the different social missions and the ways in which the choice of technologies supports distributed teaching and research. International activities are also described and future trends considered.

Chapter XXII

The chapter introduces CompILE as a sociotechnical "comprehensive interactive learning environment" system for personal knowledge management and visualization that represents the growing collective knowledge an individual gathers throughout his or her lifespan. A network of intelligent agents connects the user and his or her inhabited knowledge space to external information sources and a multitude of fellow users. Following a brief perspective on educational technology, concepts of human-computer interaction, and a description of CompILE, this chapter describes CompILE as a sociotechnical system supported by an enriched design process. From an educational perspective, CompILE can bridge the digital divide by creating community, embracing culture, and promoting a learning society.

Bopry and Cunningham describe an alternative to the cognitive and neo-behavioral views of learning that currently dominate the field of instructional design and development. Founded in the work of Chilean biologists Humberto Maturana and Francisco Varela, this view questions the fundamental notions that the environment can actually be "instructive" and that instruction can be prescribed to change learners in predictable ways. Instead, they offer a proscriptive model of instructional design, one that embeds the process in the basic foundation that learners are organizationally closed, structurally determined, and coupled with their environment.

Pivec and Panko analyzed three main aspects of instructional design (online learning communities, learning styles, and digital games) on the basis of gender preferences. Pivec and Panko noted the visible differences between males and females when interacting with technology, and reviewed the available literature in these areas. Pivec and Panko conducted a survey on males and females with an average age of 21 years, highlights the preferences between genders when related to the use and playing of computer games. The resulting conclusions were summarized to form part of the suggested guidelines for gender neutral and gender specific instructional design. Pivec and Panko hopes that with these guidelines, appropriate instructional design can open the area of learning equally to both sexes and foster equal participation of males and females in traditionally male dominated topics.

Foreword

SOCIAL IMPLICATIONS OF INFORMATION AND COMMUNICATION TECHNOLOGIES: A FEW INTERDISCIPLINARY THOUGHTS

At the risk of beginning my comments with an overstatement, it seems that all humans are influenced by social and cultural issues. By virtue of the fact that humans interact with other humans at one level or another on a daily basis, whether indirectly or directly, through words, actions, ideas, or consequences, social and cultural issues are implicated in our daily decisions, practices, and experiences. Some social and cultural issues are more overtly political in nature and on display while others are more personal and guarded. Interaction among humans at a social or cultural level takes many forms, among the most pervasive and vibrant are various forms of communication and the transmission or transferrance of information from one person to another.

Over the centuries, humans have developed a range of means through which they have, and continue to, communicate with each other, such as written and spoken language, music, dance, and other art forms, rituals and formal practices, codified texts and mythologies, and a host of other embodied symbolic representations. Such forms of communication seem to share the core purpose of transferring information from one person to another. The simplist form of interpersonal communication requires the participation of two people through verbal, visual, or symbolic transfer of ideas. In order to share important ideas with larger numbers of people, humans have devised numerous forms of social communication. These forms of social communication may have originated with the first symbols pressed into clay tablets, and progressed to the advent of moveable type, to the first telegraph and then telepone calls, and then to sending and receiving faxes and e-mail messages, reading, writing, and contributing to wikis and blogs and broadcasting Web cam and streaming videos. Indeed, forms of sharing information can range from intimate one-on-one exchanges to larger, social, and more participatory practices. That is, varying degrees of personal, cultural, and social interaction have been part of the rich history of humans who have invented, adopted, modified, and shared their various forms of communication with each other.

Ostensibly, this collection, Social Information Technology: Connecting Society and Cultural Issues, centers on issues within the social and cultural realms of information and communication technologies. As such, these concerns fall under a broader realm known as social informatics. An interdisciplinary field of study comprised of scholarship, issues, and practices that have bearing on "the design, uses and consequences of information and communication technologies (ICTs)" (Sawyer & Rosenbaum, 2000, p. 89), social informatics is a complex field comprised of numerous interests and interested parties. Kling (1999) notes that social informatics is "a body of research that examines the social aspects of computerization" (np), and helps put some perspective on the term by stating,

It is a field that is defined by its topic (and fundamental questions about it) rather than by a family of methods, much like urban studies or gerontology. Social informatics has been a subject of systematic analytical and critical research for the last 25 years. This body of research has developed theories and findings that are pertinent to understanding the design, development, and operation of usable information systems, including intranets, electronic forums, digital libraries and electronic journals. (np)

In short, social informatics is an interdisciplinary and transdisciplinary field that belongs to a larger body of socioeconomic research concerned with information and communications technology. This text, Social Information Technology, fits well within this interdisciplinary and transdisciplinary field as its contributors collectively shed light on various arenas within and across fields concerned with information and communications technology.

Contemporary information technology is more than the computer software and hardware that enable information and other data to be stored, transmitted, and translated. Information technology is also concerned with related forms of electronic communication, issues and practices related to how information is used, distributed, and secured. Recently, the areas of information technology and communication technology have moved to the center of a variety of social contexts including education, research, and leisure.

Within the past few decades, the majority of the world's population has become accustomed to one or more means of sharing information with their own cultural and social circles through some form of mediated practice, be it spoken or written language, newpapers, radio, television, telegraph, fax, e-mail, text messaging, or the World Wide Web. Withought doubt, these inclusive forms of communication media are means of sharing information and as we consider contemporary technologies used for sharing and presenting cultural and social information, such inclusive considerations of the terminology should also be applied.

Divided into five sections, Social Information Technology offers readers a structure with which to gain access into the complex overlapping territories of social informatics, information technology, and communication technology. The chapters of this book demarcate useful points of entry and means of engagement into and within such a rich discourse: Implications of Social Informatics; Sociocultural Practices; Geo-Political Practices; International Informatics Practices; Online Social Information Technology Applications, and Implications of Social Information Technology. These "practices" are applicable and of interest to a range of disciplines and also function as important interdisciplinary discourses and contexts. The collection offers a modest attempt to include a global perspective as it embraces viewpoints about these technology issues from scholars housed in various parts of the world. Such attention to an inclusive disussion regarding social informatics is a strength of this collection. In essence, Social Information Technology provides insights into information and communication technologies with respect to social, cultural, political, global, and pedagogical contexts while at the same time, maintains the integrity of particular disciplinary practices in the process.

So, how might scholars, students, and others who are concerned with such interdisciplinary pursuits begin to consider the social implications of information and communication technologies? With respect to information and communication technology, the simple answer, as Social Information Technology suggests, is that there are indeed no simple answers. During (2005) observes and warns, "The difficulty with technoculture is that no one knows exactly where it is heading or indeed exactly what it is" (p. 137). As is the nature of any interdisciplinary field, new developments spawn other new developments and render any degree of predictablility inaccurate and ineffective. Such uncertainty and evolution encourages meaningful interdisciplinary growth and discovery. Collectively, the authors of this book emphasize such explorations, analyses, interpretations, and commentary regarding the influences of information and communication technologies on society.

From my perspective, Social Information Technology, should prove an excellent foundational text for students, educators, and others who are interested in the complexities and interdisciplinary ramifications of information and communication technologies. This text helps shed light on the breadth and depth of social informatics as it plays the multifacited role of a collection of scholarship, documentation, and cultural criticism regarding social informatics. To some quite useful degree, the contributors to this book play the collective role of cultural critic in much the same way Johnson (1997) claims "part of a cultural critic's role is to make us think twice about experiences that are second nature to us" (p. 10). Readers whose professional, social, cultural, political, and other lives are directly and indirectly influenced by information and communication technologies often experience social informatics as second nature. And as online social networking and communications technologies such as MySpace, Facebook, YouTube, Second Life, and others become more and more popular, the interdisciplinary study of social informatics as explored through the contributions in Social Information Technology will prove to be essential models for those of us interested in the critical analysis of the uses of this technology for various social, cultural, educational, and other purposes.

REFERENCES

During, S. (2005). Cultural studies: A critical introduction. London: Routledge.

Johnson, S. (1997). Interface culture: How new technology transforms the way we create and communicate. New York: Basic Books.

Kling, R. (1999). What is social informatics and why does it matter? D-Lib Magazine, 5(1).

Sawyer, S. & Rosenbaum, H. (2000). Social informatics in the information sciences: Current activities and emerging directions. Informing Science, 3(2), 89-95.

B. Stephen Carpenter II, PhD is an associate professor of Art Education and Visual Culture at the Texas A&M University. He is past editor of Art Education (2004-2006) the journal of the National Art Education Association, assistant editor for The Journal of Curriculum and Pedagogy, and a member of the editorial boards of The Journal of Cultural Research in Art Education and Studies in Art Education. Carpenter is the author or coauthor of several book chapters, journal articles, and essays on cultural studies through visual inquiry, hypertext curriculum theory and design, visual culture, and ceramics criticism. He is a coauthor of Interdisciplinary Approaches to Teaching Art in High School, and a coeditor of Curriculum for a Progressive, Provocative, Poetic and Public Pedagogy. In 2001 and 2003, he exhibited his assemblage artwork in the 3rd and 4th Biennale Internazionale dell'arte contemporanea (Florence Biennale) in Florence, Italy.

Preface

As you have gleamed from the title, this book concerns itself with connecting social and cultural issues with our increasing use of information and communication technologies.

History has shown that the introduction of any significant innovation is followed by a period during which the public assesses it, adopts it, and becomes used ot its existence. After the initial period of saturation and use, the new technology can now be considered assimilated into one's society and culture.

The topic of social information technology has received an immense amount of coverage in recent years, with the media, law enforcers, and governments worldwide all doing their bit to bring the issue to our attention. For those unfamiliar with the term, the concept of social informatics is the study of information and communication tools in cultural or institutional contexts (Kling, Rosenbaum, & Sawyer, 2005). A more formal definition given by the past Rob Kling from the Center for Social Informatics at the Indiana University indicates that social information technology is "the interdisciplinary study of the design, uses and consequences of information technologies that takes into account their interaction with institutional and cultural contexts" (Kling, 2000).

Social information technology is broad and *transdisciplinary*. It is a field that is defined by its topic and fundamental questions raised by researchers. To understand the significance of the technology, society, and culture, it is important to appreciate the context in which they exist. The contextuality of social information technology looks at the larger framework, of which technology development relates to the overall framework of culture and society. Social information technology focuses on the economic, technological, social, cultural, educational, and organizational conditions. Social information technology investigates the relations between systems development on the one hand, and decision making, power structures, legislation, learning effects, organizational aspects, and media influence on the other. However, social information technology also takes careful consideration to specify contexts and situations.

The key word of social information technology is relevance, ensuring that technological innovations are socially driven rather than technology driven. Design and implementation processes need to be relevant to the actual social dynamics of a given aspect of social practice, and the substance of design and implementation need to be relevant to the lives of the people they affect.

This book helps make these ideas accessible to non-specialists, as well as to strengthen communication among specialists, and to strengthen the dialogs between communities of designers and social analysts.

ORGANIZATION

This book communicates ideas of social information technology that are relevant to scholars and the information technology professional community. The contributing authors examine key thoughts of the field, including educational issues. The text is divided into five major sections with a total of 24 chapters. These chapters serve as a brief introduction to the themes and issues of social information technology. The reference section in each chapter includes numerous reference sources to help interested readers readily identify comprehensive sources and additional information. A brief description of the sections and chapters are as follows:

SECTION I: The Implications of Social Information Technology

One key idea of social information technology research is that the social context of information technology development and its use plays in influencing the ways in which people use information and communication technologies, and how information and communication technologies affects the organizations, social and cultural relationships.

In "Historical Perspectives on Analog and Digital Equity: A Critical Race Theory Approach," the author uses the philosophical lens of Critical Race Theory to shed light upon the vast inequalities in access to information and communication technologies that exist among racial, ethnic, and socioeconomic groups; a phenomenon that has come to be known as the digital divide. The primary focus is on how the digital divide has manifested itself in the communities of people of color. The author uses Critical Race Theory to explain the history of inequalities that have persisted into the 21st century.

The chapter "Exploring Gender Differences in Computer-Related Behaviour: Past, Present, and Future" explores gender differences in three key areas: computer attitude, ability, and use. The author indicates that males and females are more similar than different on all constructs assessed, for most grade levels and contexts. However, males report moderately more-positive affective attitudes, higher self-efficacy, and more-frequent use. Females are slightly more positive about online learning and appear to perform somewhat better on computer-related tasks. Finally, a model is proposed to understand and address gender differences in computer-related behaviour.

"The Reversal of Technology" offers an overview of how technology is central to modern development. This chapter looks at how technology has been conceptualized, and how virtual development is yet another frontier best captured in the notion of technopolis and/or technocity as contextual factors that sustain social technologies. The pervasiveness of technology, the factors that affect the technological experience besides the rhetoric of infallibility, and the taken-for-granted delivery of utility and efficiency will also be explored. By looking at the criticisms voiced against urban and virtual development concerning the loosening of social ties, the author argues for a fluid interaction that considers the possibilities for additional and different, if not new social relations, that both physical and virtual interactions afford to urbanites: technosociability.

SECTION II: Geo-Political Practices

Section II emphasize the discussion of social information from the standpoint of public policy and public affairs. Questions about the consequences of new technologies are often posed in a very black and white manner. For instance: What demographic of people are not participating in the voting process, and will e-voting rectify the situation? People expect a straightforward black and white answer. However, there are no clear-cut answers. It is important to get involved in public debates, because the debates about the social roles of technologies sometimes ignore relationships that are recognized as being very important by social analysts. This allows those with a vested interest to dominate public debate about technology, since the most powerful voices in debates about computerization are the designers, sellers, and government agencies directly involved. Computerization can raise questions about social choices and value conflicts that the participants do not always seem to understand; thus, the contribution of scholars is to articulate these social choices.

The chapter "The Impact of the USA Patriot Act on Social Diversity in Cyberspace" assesses how the USA Patriot Act protects US national security and, through self-censorship over privacy concerns, may affect sociopolitical and cultural diversity in cyberspace.

In "A Comparative Analysis of Online Peace Movement Organizations," the authors take us on a journey into a comparative study that examines Web sites of Peace Movement Organizations (PMOs) in Japan and Israel. The collective action frame is used as a theoretical framework to analyze 17 Web sites, identifying the similarities and differences in the ways that online PMOs frame their activities. The findings indicate that these organizations employed various strategies to develop resonance, highlighting the importance of cultural resonance in framing online PMOs in different countries.

In "Planning for the Worst, Bringing Out the Best? Lessons from Y2K," the author considers the utility of Clarke's worst-case planning by examining Y2K preparations at two US government agencies, the Bureau of Labor Statistics and the Federal Aviation Administration. The chapter concludes that the thoroughness of worst-case planning can bring much needed light to the subtlety of critical complex and interdependent systems. However, such an approach can also be narrow in its own way, revealing some of the limitations of such a precautionary approach.

Since the concept of health is universal and culturally relevant, and the field of informatics is an emerging practice characterized by indistinct boundaries in terms of theory, policy, and practice, various ethnographic and cultural associations are made in the chapter "Exploring Serres' Atlas, Hodges' Knowledge Domains and the Fusion of Informatics and Cultural Horizons." The author explores the writings of French philosopher Michel Serres, and presents a health care that integrates development of social information systems. Central to the chapter is the notion of holistic bandwidth, utilizing Hodges' model as a tool to develop and disseminate sociotechnical perspectives.

In "The Social Glue in Open Source: Incomplete Contracts and Informal Credits," the author discusses open source as a most significant institutional disruption to the way software and, digital content evolves and is dissipated through society. On the one hand, less formal kinds of credits than money and the like often provide for a relatively efficient and viable way of accounting for credits in the development of large and complex software and technology projects. At the intersection of developer communities with end users, there is a distinct need for formal, money-based interactions, because informal contracts and credit redemption do work well in communities, but less so in anonymous market contexts.

With "Musique Concrètization: Music, Technology and Critical Constructivism," the author starts with a description of the crisis over copyright and control of music distribution that has been developing. The outcome of this crisis has had tremendous implications not only for the fate of commercial and creative entities involved in music, but for the social reproduction of knowledge and culture. This chapter introduces the concept of "concretization," and demonstrates how concretization can be applied on the lives and work of the people using modern media. In addition, the author gives us not only a detailed description of the relations of various groups and modern media technologies, the chapter also provides a prescriptive program for the future maintenance and strengthening of a vibrant and radically democratized sphere of creative exchange. Critical theories of technology are used in addressing these implications.

In "The Social Side of Security," the author argues that current information security strategies tend to focus on a technology-based approach to securing information. However, these technology-based approaches can leave an organization vulnerable to information security threats, which in turn put society at risk to potential losses, due to inadequate security by the organizations with which they do business. Humans operate, maintain, and use information systems. Their actions, whether intentional or accidental, are the real threats to organizations. Information security strategies must be developed to address the social challenge of security.

In "The Cultural Factors in Electronic Monitoring," the authors claim that the use of electronic monitoring tools in the workplace has grown dramatically due to the availability of inexpensive, yet powerful monitoring systems, including the widely used information and communication technologies in today's workplace. However, existing research pays little attention to the pervasive use of electronic monitoring systems on ICT at work. This chapter draws theories in international and organizational cultures, and concludes four hypotheses on privacy concerns of employees and their perceived trust to the management when being electronically monitored.

SECTION III: International Social Information Technology Practices

The effective use and infusion of information technology (IT) can either increase or decrease the "digital divide." Recent studies have indicated that the information technology investments have improved the productivity of national economies and organizations. As described in the four chapters included in this section, developing nations, such as Samoa, India, New Zealand, and Turkey, have been able to leverage national development with advances in IT.

In "Measuring IS Success in Small and Medium Sized Enterprises in Samoa," the author describes how exploratory research was conducted to assess and measure the success of information systems by small- and medium-sized enterprises in Samoa. The study also reveals the effects on IT investments both in terms of social and cultural capital.

In "Technology and Culture: Indian Experiences," the author discusses the deployment of e-learning technologies as it relates to preserving and disseminating knowledge of the Indian cultural heritage. An analysis has also offered insight on how culture impacts e-learning initiatives, design issues within online courses, and programs. This chapter makes an attempt to understand and frame the Indian culture and experience through e-learning practices, and how the differentiated learning needs of multilingual and multinational consumers are addressed.

In "ICT-Enabled Communication in the New Zealand Family Court: A Multistakeholder Study," the author proposes that the New Zealand Family Court is an ideal public sector application for social information technology. In a study investigating ICTs within multiple venues such as court stakeholders, paradoxical results emerged. This chapter encompasses private and public space, sense of self, emotional energies, and digital citizenship in the field of social informatics. This theoretical framework provides grounding for results within and across disciplines, revealing deeply engrained behaviours, emotional states, customs, workplace cultures, and the problems associated with solving private problems in public spaces.

"Technology Access Points in Turkey: A Case Study on Internet Cafés and their Roles in the Society" investigates one of the most common technology access points, Internet Cafés, by focusing the missions to regard Internet access and use as well as game play. Data was collected by giving a questionnaire, including demographic information about users and their Internet Café habits. In addition, observation reports were used while they were using the Internet and playing computer games in these places. The study aimed to select Internet Cafés from both low and high socioeconomic regions in the city so that Internet Cafés, and their roles in the society, can be easily investigated by comparing different factors like socioeconomic status.

SECTION IV: Online Social Information Technology Applications

Information and communication technologies are potentially transformative. The changes in society have occurred because of the implementation of new and complex Web 2.0 software tools. There is great speculation concerning the changes that might arise in society when new social software technologies become widespread. In the past few years, researchers of social information technology have developed findings that are pertinent to understanding the development and operation of usable information systems, including intranets, electronic forums, digital libraries, and electronic journals. The new Web 2.0 and wiki systems described in "Web Information Retrieval: Towards Social Information Search Assistants" and "Twin Wiki Wonders? Wikipedia and Wikibooks as Powerful Tools for Online Collaborative Writing" are also expected to work well for people and help support their work and collaboration, rather than make it more complicated.

"Web Information Retrieval: Towards Social Information Search Assistants" introduces search assistants and underlines their evolution toward social information. Thanks to the "new Web," the Web 2.0, personal search assistants are evolving using social techniques such as social networks and sharing-based methods. Due to the high amount of information and the diversity of human factors, searching for information requires patience, perseverance, and sometimes luck. To help individuals during this task, search assistants feature adaptive techniques aiming at personalizing retrieved information.

In "Twin Wiki Wonders? Wikipedia and Wikibooks as Powerful Tools for Online Collaborative Writing," the authors investigate the emergence and growth of two participatory environments: the highly popular Wikipedia site and its sister project, Wikibooks. Wikipedia has grown out of trends for free and open access to Web tools and resources. While Wikipedians edit, contribute, and monitor distinct pieces of information or pages of documents, Wikibookians must focus on larger chunks of knowledge, including book modules or chapters as well as entire books. Several key differences between these two types of wiki environments are explored. In addition, surveys and interviews conducted with Wikibookians shed light on their challenges, frustrations, and successes.

SECTION V: Implications of Social Information Technology in Education

One key area of social information technology is within the area of education. There is an increasing emphasis on the integration of information and communication technology to enhance the teaching and learning process within education. These effects are focused on the way in which participants interact with new technologies, and how the technologies aid in reshaping the society in medium- and long-term use through better education and training. Social information technology is a sustained method in understanding educational and training issues in ways that do help improve the learning outcomes.

In "How Can Cultural Variables Guide the Instructional Engineering of Computer-Based Learning?", authors discuss how cultural variables can be taken into account when designing computer-based learning environments. Its purpose is to identify concrete recommendations to guide instructional engineering of computer-based learning for diverse cultures through a review of the literature on the subject. This chapter describes the context in which recommendations have emerged and have identified the issues underlying instructional design for diverse cultures. Then, the chapter introduces models and guidelines on how cultural variables can be taken into account when designing CLEs. Specific recommendations are organized using a method of instructional engineering for CLEs, called *MISA,* as a frame of reference. This is followed by a discussion on future trends that may affect how cultural variables guide instructional engineering over the next decade.

Often, the main drive for technology-enhanced education has resulted in national policies that are supported by the government, such as the recent e-learning strategy that has been proposed for the National Health Service in the United Kingdom (UK). In "Technology and Continuing Professional Education: The Reality beyond the Hype," the authors describe the potential of Social Information Technologies (SITs) for online continuing professional education (CPE), and identify the main driving forces in UK. The authors highlight the important findings from our experience and research of online CPE, particularly within the health service. In fact, the authors' motivation in writing this chapter was in part to raise awareness of the importance of the major differences between policy and the reality of the context of professional practice and online CPE, and to propose recommendations that can inform future policy and practice.

The author of "Investigating and Encouraging Information and Communications Technology (ICT) Engagement amongst Student Nurses" states that in the nursing field in UK, 6 years after the Guidelines for Networked Learning in Higher Education were published, levels of students' skills and engagement with ICT remain problematic, which undermines attempts to deploy networked learning. The author argues that for such initiatives to succeed, more foundational connections need also to be promoted. Factors that contribute to student nurses' ICT non-engagement: gender, caring, professional identity and knowledge work are explored. Finally, the author explains how some of the barriers identified can be overcome through integrating ICT.

"Social Implications of Three Different Models of Distributed Learning" describes three different models of distributing education to achieve different social missions. A distance learning university (The UK Open University) is profiled as a multicampus higher education institute servicing remote and rural areas in the Highlands and Islands of Scotland (UHI Millennium Institute). A new university in Greece spread over five small islands (University of the Aegean) is another distance-learning university profiled to discuss the social implications of distributed learning. The chapter considers different social missions and the ways in which the choice of technologies supports distributed teaching and research. International activities are also described and future trends considered.

In "Instructional Design: Sex Driven?" the author analyzed three main aspects of instructional design (online learning communities, learning styles, and digital games) on the basis of gender preferences. The author noted the visible differences between males and females when interacting with technology, and reviewed the available literature in these areas. Maja conducted a survey on males and females, with an average age of 21 years, that highlights the preferences between genders when related to the use of playing computer games. The resulting conclusions were summarized to form guidelines for gender neutral and gender specific instructional design. Further, the author hopes these guidelines will assist appropriate instructional design to open the area of learning equally to both sexes, and foster equal participation of males and females in traditionally male-dominated topics.

The chapter "Sociotechnical System Design for Learning: Bridging the Digital Divide with CompILE" introduces CompILE as a sociotechnical "comprehensive interactive learning environment" system for personal knowledge management and visualization that represents the growing collective knowledge an individual gathers throughout his or her lifespan. A network of intelligent agents connects the user and his or her *inhabited knowledge space* to external information sources and a multitude of fellow users. Following a brief perspective on educational technology, concepts of human-computer interaction, and a description of CompILE, this chapter describes CompILE as a sociotechnical system supported by an enriched design process. From an educational perspective, CompILE can bridge the digital divide by creating community, embracing culture, and promoting a learning society.

In "Structural Coupling as Foundation for Instructional Design," the authors describe an alternative to the cognitive and neo-behavioral views of learning that currently dominate the field of instructional design and development. Founded in the work of Chilean biologists Humberto Maturana and Francisco Varela, these theories view questions of the fundamental notions that the environment can actually be "instructive" and that instruction can be prescribed to change learners in predictable ways. Instead, the research in this chapter offers a proscriptive model of instructional design, one that embeds the process in the basic foundation that learners are organizationally closed, structurally determined and coupled with their environment.

REFERENCES

Kling, R. (2000). Learning about information technologies and social change: The contribution of social informatics. *The Information Society, 16*(3), 217-232.

Kling, R., Rosenbaum, H., & Sawyer, S. (2005). *Understanding and communicating social informatics: A framework for studying and teaching the human contexts of information and communications technologies.* Medford, NJ: Information Today.

Terry T. Kidd is a PhD candidate from the Texas A&M University and is the Director of Instructional Development and Support Services at the University of Texas Health Science Center School of Public Health. He has presented at international conferences on designing technology-rich learning environments, Web-based instruction, and issues dealing with faculty and staff development. His research interests include designing technology-based learning environments, instructional design strategies for Web-based instruction, and the sociocultural aspect of information communication and technology as they relate to social change and community building.

Dr. Irene L. Chen received her Doctor of Education in Instructional Technology from University of Houston in 1998. Currently, she is an Associate Professor in the Department of Urban Education at the University of Houston Downtown. Dr. Chen has diverse professional experiences. Previously, she was instructional technology specialist, learning technology coordinator, and computer programmer/analyst. She has taught numerous courses in instructional technology and curriculum and instruction, and delivered many training and professional development activities for school teachers, university staff and faculty members. Her research interests include technology and culture, business education, multicultural education, and social informatics.

Acknowledgment

Terry T. Kidd: Completing a project of this magnitude is a great challenge and an opportunity many chose never to undertake. It is with the help of many individuals who have inspired me to complete the journey that lied ahead.

I would first like to take this opportunity to acknowledge the considerable time and effort the authors have invested in their respective publications in this book. The authors presented within this book are intelligent and well seasoned in their practice and respective areas. Without the hard work, dedication, and in some cases sacrifice, this book would not have been made into reality without the assistance of the authors. Thank you for being gracious and patient under fire and for accepting my comments and ideas on your chapters. I would like to send a special acknowledge and thanks to Dr. Stephen Carpenter, II from the Texas A&M University and to Ms. Taresa Mikle at the Baylor College of Medicine for assisting me during this project.

Gratitude and acknowledgements must go to the reviewers who spent countless hours reading, proofing, and articulating their comments from the proposal stage to the final chapter revisions.

Special thanks also must go to the IGI Global team, in particular, Ms. Deborah Yahnke and Ms. Meg Stockings, for their continued administrative support and hard work in helping me bring this vision to a reality. Without them, this would not have been made possible.

I would also like to acknowledge and thank Dr. Carolyn Ashe and Dr. Chynette Nealy from the University of Houston-Downtown for their encouragement and advice. I would also like to thank my co-editor Dr. Irene Chen for her hard work and diligence while working on this project.

Lastly, I would like to thank and acknowledge my two great friends, Mr. Demetrius Dougar for his wisdom in a time of need and Mr. Dennis Aaron Washington for being a close friend, lending his ear of reason to my insanity. It's a great honor to have such people as these two in one's life.

In closing, I wish to pay a special tribute to my nephew Zavion DeMarcus Lillie, who shows me it is good to be a kid sometimes and to my dear sister Ms. Brenda Kidd who works hard to reach the limits in the sky. This is dedicated to them.

Irene L. Chen: We would like to express our appreciation to the number of people that have contributed in some way to this publication. These include the chapter authors as well as the editors and designers from IGI Global, without whom this publication would not have been possible.

We also appreciate the following reviewers for their input and suggestions: Taresa Mikle of Baylor College of Medicine, and Robert Johnson, Shelley McIntosh, and Louis Evans, all with the University of Houston Downtown.

Section I
Implications of Social Information Technology

Chapter I
Historical Perspectives on Analog and Digital Equity:
A Critical Race Theory Approach

Patricia Randolph Leigh
Iowa State University, USA

ABSTRACT

In this chapter, the author uses the philosophical lens of critical race theory (CRT) to shed light upon the vast inequalities in access to information technologies that exist among racial, ethnic, and socioeconomic groups; a phenomenon that has come to be known as the digital divide. The primary focus is on how the digital divide has played out for African Americans and the use of CRT to explain the history of inequalities and why significant differences in educational opportunities have persisted into the 21st century. The author adopts the term "analog divide" to refer to all the non-computer/telecommunications-based educational inequities that African Americans have experienced for decades and even centuries. She further purports that one cannot understand or begin to rectify the digital divide unless one is willing to fully confront and attack the problem of the analog divide that preceded it and continues to persist.

INTRODUCTION

In this chapter, I use the philosophical lens of critical race theory (CRT) to shed light upon the vast inequalities in access to information technologies that exists among racial, ethnic, and socioeconomic groups; a phenomenon that has come to be known as the digital divide. I focus primarily on how the digital divide has played out for African Americans, and use CRT to explain the history of inequalities and why significant differences in educational opportunities have persisted into the 21st century. I adopt the term "analog divide" to refer to all the non-computer/telecommunications-based educational inequities that African Americans have experienced for decades and even centuries. I further purport that one cannot understand or begin to rectify the digital divide unless one is willing to fully confront and attack the problem of the analog divide that preceded it and continues to persist. Furthermore, the analog divide, with its resultant structural inequalities, demonstrates not only how social and cultural factors shape technology, but also illuminates the nature of technology and human interaction and how this interaction is shaped by these same factors.

The major tenets of CRT used to examine these divides are the claims that: a) racism is ingrained in the fabric of American society to the extent that it is invisible to most, and racist behaviors and attitudes therefore seem normal to the average citizen and b) the perspectives and stances of marginalized groups are many times best represented in the form of narratives, storytelling, and counter-storytelling. (Delgado, 1995)

In this chapter, I utilize counter-storytelling by presenting the reader with an original allegory entitled, "Crossing the Great Divide: A Tale of Analog and Digital Inequity." In this tale one finds two groups of troll-like beings, with one group dominating and enslaving the other. As the story unfolds, the reader sees how the oppressed become caught in a cycle of poverty and stuck in a land that weakens them and deprives them of the energy to cross over the great divide into more fertile fields. The dominant group, having given up their brutally overt oppressive ways after crossing the divide into lands where slave labor is no longer needed, soon forget why they had the energy and fortitude to cross the divide whereas the enslaved group did not. In fact, because of the hybrid food crop (knowledge) that the oppressed have been forced to ingest, they too have forgotten why they have been left behind and stuck in a cycle of backbreaking work and struggle. The tale ends with a group of concerned amnesiac leaders holding council concerning ways and means to bring more of the weakened

and impoverished across the divide into the rich soil of the northern region.

HISTORICAL BACKGROUND AND PERSPECTIVES

Critical race theory maintains that racism is endemic and pervasive in American society to the extent that all but the most blatant, egregious racist behaviors and attitudes are considered normal. Thus, critical race theorists, most notably Derrick Bell (1987) and Richard Delgado (1995), have used storytelling to bring into focus issues of race and racism in American society. The use of allegory allows the reader to view all too familiar issues and situations from new angles and perspectives. In "Crossing the Great Divide" I use allegorical storytelling to illuminate issues of racial inequality in the United States and to explain why the gaps in educational opportunities, including access to information technology, persist into this century. In this story, the oppressed are faced with these insurmountable gaps in the form of a vast and expansive chasm. This chasm represents the enormous inequalities in access to information technologies that exist between racial, ethnic, and social-economic groups; a phenomenon that has come to be known as the digital divide. "[T]he digital divide is conceived as," in van Dijk's (2005) work, "a social and political problem, not a technical one. Physical access is portrayed as only one kind of (material) access among at least four: motivational, material, skills, and usage" (p. 3). Moreover, the chasm or Great Divide in the tale is also a symbol of the many inequities that began and were nurtured long before the information or digital age. This immense chasm represents an "analog divide" wherein historically disadvantaged racial groups, specifically Black Americans, have been denied equal access to economic and educational opportunities. The analog divide simply refers to differential accesses to non-computer-related material resources or opportunities that are experienced by various groups in American society. The analog divide includes, but is not limited to, unequal access to up-to-date school books, science laboratories, challenging and engaging school curricula, adequately funded schools, adequately maintained school buildings and facilities, qualified teachers, safe communities, and adequate and sufficient housing, food, and health care. In examining these divides, I focus upon the disparities experienced by historically underserved native minority children, specifically African American children, as compared to what is experienced by children in the dominant culture. Mack (2001) contends, "meaningful education for the masses of [B]lack people was intentionally sacrificed to protect the interests of [W]hites and preserve the caste system.... As the economy shifted from agriculture to industry, the profound inequality in the allocation of educational resources meant that [B]lacks were extra-ordinarily ill-prepared to take part in the burgeoning industrial revolution" (p. 64).

Prior to the information age, discriminatory and racist attitudes and policies continued and assured that African American children, in particular, would have limited access to quality schools and educational opportunities. This analog divide set the stage for the digital divide and, given our history, it should be no surprise to us that African American children form a large portion of the "have nots" in our digital divide metaphor. Furthermore, using a critical race theory perspective, the racist attitudes and policies that gave rise to the analog divide have been woven into the fabric of our society, and have resulted in structural inequalities that serve to maintain these divides. Again, it is these previous injustices and resulting structural inequalities that we must address and find solutions to before we can adequately address the issue of the digital divide. Mack (2001) states, "...the largest and most noteworthy differential is developing between [B]lacks and [W]hites, two groups that have been divided on myiad bases

throughout the course of history. Thus, in many respects, it is as if this historical divide is repeating itself on the technology landscape" (p. xiii). In other words, the stage was set for the digital divide, which widened the gap or compounded the problem, once this nation and globe passed into this age of information technology.

THE ALLEGORICAL TALE

Crossing the Great Divide: A Tale of Analog and Digital Inequity

Long ago in a faraway, harsh, and barren land lived two groups of troll-like beings known as the Binefs and the Uninefs. How these creatures came to inhabit this land had long been forgotten, and the history of how the Binefs came to rule over the Uninefs was similarly lost to both groups. The feeling was, especially among the Binefs, that this was how things always were and how things should, in fact, be. The two-headed Binefs believed themselves to be superior in every way to their one-headed "cousins," the Uninefs. This inferiority myth was passed on from generation to generation and was widely accepted by both groups of Nefs. In fact, inferiority myth justified many things, especially the enslavement of the Uninefs by the Binefs.

The land inhabited by the Nefs was hard and rocky and required brutally intense labor and much sweat and toil to prepare the soil for food production. The Uninefs worked in the fields year after year, generation after generation, planting and harvesting food for their masters, receiving only leftovers for themselves. This food, called knowledge, had in fact been altered under the direction of the Binefs and a hybrid was created. Hybrid knowledge food could only be easily digested by the Binefs, and since it was the only legally produced food in the land, it left the Uninefs in danger of starvation. The enslaved Uninefs did manage to sustain themselves, but their inability to fully digest the food took a toll on their physical abilities. Even those Uninefs who had not fully accepted their alleged inherent inferiority, were weakened after years of compromised nourishment and were unable to effectively resist and win out over the Binefs.

The ancient land of the Nefs lay south of an enormous chasm referred to as the Great Divide. Nef mythology held that the northern border of their land marked the end of the world for physical beings and further claimed that the lush, green land on the other side was occupied by gods and goddesses. Many Uninefs had plunged themselves into the chasm in attempts to escape their oppressive existence, while numerous Binefs perished in their attempts to discover a means of crossing the divide. However, after countless failed attempts, the Nefs were successful in developing a mechanism for reaching the mythical lands. Of course the tools needed to make such a journey were initially available only to the wealthiest of Binefs and to none of the enslaved Uninefs. After all, there was no reason to provide for the escape of the ruling Nefs' free labor. In addition, because of their compromised diet, the enslaved Nefs were physically weaker than their masters and unable to endure the long, arduous journey across the Great Divide.

The Binefs were truly amazed at what they found in the mythical land of the northern region. To them, the fertile rich soil was truly enchanting and magical. With little effort they grew fields and fields of their hybrid knowledge crops and the new settlers flourished without the help or need of slave labor. They became comfortable and fat. The passing years brought new groups of Nefs to the region and, in addition, many generations were actually born in the land north of the great chasm. Most Nefs of any means had long ago escaped the southern region, leaving that harsh land primarily to the Uninefs who, incidentally, had been freed from slavery as a result of the massive migrations of their masters. A few Uninefs did manage to make it across by hook or crook, but for the most

part, though free, the Uninefs were physically too weak to make the journey and still lacked access to the mechanisms, regardless of how rudimentary or advanced, necessary to venture across the chasm. The small number of superior Binefs that remained in the harsh southern region did so also because of economic reasons. After all, not all ancient Binefs had been wealthy slave owners, just most.

The Nefs that tilled the rich soil of the northern region began to take pride in their labor and accomplishments and soon forgot how they eschewed such work in their ancient lands. These new generations of Binefs, in fact, put a high value on hard work and rugged individualism. Moreover, they publicly claimed to have put aside their feelings of superiority over the few Uninefs that were living among them or the many that remained in the barren southern region. Furthermore, they claimed no responsibility for how their ancestors had enslaved the Uninefs and had treated them badly. The fact that generations of Uninefs, though few in number compared to the Binefs, were flourishing as their neighbors was evidence that past enslavement or ill treatment was no longer of any consequence. Even the Binefs that held on to the ancient inferiority myth had come to believe that it was wrong to enslave fellow Nefs. Besides, according to those Binefs, "all that is in the past and this is a new time and day." It was widely believed that any Nef with the wherewithal could escape the southern region and was free to work the rich soil across the divide. In fact, for those who still held fast to the inferiority myth, the large numbers of Uninefs that failed to make the journey or who perished in their attempts was further proof of their inherent inferiority.

Even after Uninefs on either side of the divide were free to produce food crops of their choosing, they continued to plant and harvest only the hybrid knowledge food. This was all they knew. Even though this food was still not easily digested by the northern Uninefs, over time their systems began to accommodate it more readily. Having adequate amounts of food that the rich soil so graciously yielded and being released from the rigors of slavery allowed these Uninefs to gain physical strength. Those who had an abundance of hybrid knowledge food did, however, discover some side effects not reported by their enslaved ancestors. After ingesting a full meal of hybrid knowledge, they would experience hallucinations wherein negative, grotesque, and often demeaning images of themselves and fellow Uninefs would appear. At other times they would recall or have visions of life south of the divide as being just, democratic, and ideal. Still yet, if they overate or indulged in extremely rich varieties of the food knowledge, they would have bouts of amnesia about the past life of Uninefs and forget about their brothers and sisters still residing south of the Great Divide. When they relayed these strange incidents to their neighboring Binefs they found that, generally speaking, the Binefs felt and thought that way much of the time. Binefs viewed the negative visions and images of Uninefs and the altered recollections of the past (or the lack of recollections) as normal and healthy. In fact, they credited the food knowledge for keeping things in perspective and for keeping their thinking in line with reality. In any case, the Binefs believed that the past was not so bad after all and, even so, why dwell on the negative.

Hybrid knowledge crop production became as important in the northern region as it had been in the south. It continued to be the economic base for Nef societies and ultimately gave rise to experts who, in later years, began to focus their attention on the tools and means of crossing the divide. After all, it was obvious to all, crop experts included, that the rich northern soil produced the hardiest crops. Yet many Nefs remained stranded in the ancient lands and needed to avail themselves of the opportunities that awaited them elsewhere. The most radical of northern Binefs and Uninefs wanted to close the divide altogether. They believed that the ravages of slavery, poverty, and/or poor diet and health had taken its toll on the south-ern Nefs, especially the Uninefs, leaving them unable to recover well enough to cross the divide. However, this was a radical view held only by a small number of northern Nefs who had not been affected so profoundly by the amnesia inducing knowledge. They remembered the strength-sapping labor that most ancient Uninefs endured, and acknowledged the fact that no Nef would have had the strength or resources to cross the divide and explore the mythical lands without the benefit of slave labor. They argued that all generations of Nefs owed a great debt to the enslaved Uninefs of past ages and believed one way to repay the debt was to close the divide, making the journey to the fertile northern lands easy for the feeblest of southern Nefs. But because the Great Divide was ever so expansive, their ideas were dismissed as illogical, impractical, and, most of all, too labor intensive. Most of the northern Nefs, on the other hand, who voiced concerns about their brethren in the southern region looked for other ways to allow them to share in their bounty. Special groups of these crop experts across the northern region would travel miles and miles to council meetings concerning the theory and practice of crossing the Great Divide. However, despite their best rhetoric, nothing really changed from year to year. This is not to say that some Nefs did not benefit from the concerns and efforts of their cousins to the north and succeeded in journeying over the chasm. The overwhelming majority of Uninefs remained in the harsh land of the south while more of the unfortunate southern Binefs were able to make their escape. In either case, the most robust of the Binefs and Uninefs were able to take advantage of the opportunities and aid offered by the northern council. The departure of the strongest Nefs increasingly left the burden of southern crop production on the weakest Nefs. The Uninefs that were repeatedly left behind because of their lack of physical strength continued to struggle with the unrelenting soil to produce the hybrid knowledge food that, unknown to them, served to keep them in a weakened state. Their systems never had a chance to adapt so they were unable to gain the strength that the fortunate few northern Uninefs enjoyed. But despite the lack of progress in remedying the situation and because of the historical amnesia that flourished in the northern lands, the Nef council continued to meet year after year and talk about the unfortunate conditions that continued and were worsening in the ancient lands, proposing new and innovative means of transporting the southern Nefs across the Great Divide.

DECONSTRUCTING THE DIVIDE

One cannot understand why the Uninefs in this allegory are unable to cross the divide without understanding their history of oppression. By the same token, one cannot effectively address issues digital inequity as it pertains to African Americans without understanding the history of their oppression and how that oppression initiated and continues to support and foster inequalities in educational opportunities and achievement. One cannot, in fact, offer viable, long-lasting solutions to the digital divide without seriously looking to alter attitudes and institutions in the general society. There is little hope of closing the digital divide while leaving the analog divide untouched.

The hybrid knowledge food in this tale represents a dominant epistemology that is riddled with theories of inferiority and consists of a body of "knowledge" and "truths" that support the superiority of the dominant group. African Americans have had a steady diet of education grounded in this dominant epistemology that has served to influence their views of themselves. In *The White Architects of Black Education*, William Watkins (2001) describes the role of philanthropies in the establishment of Black educational institutions not long after slavery was abolished. He maintains that some of the most influential philanthropic organizations served to maintain the social order that

found Blacks at the bottom. Black schools were used as instruments of social engineering wherein the curriculum prepared students for occupancy of the lower layers of society only. Furthermore, the curriculum was absent of any African history or experiences that would engender a sense of pride in the African American student. In his work concerning reparations, Randall Robinson (2000) states:

Far too many Americans of African descent believe their history starts in America with bondage and struggles forward from there toward today's second-class citizenship. The cost of this obstructed view of ourselves, of our history is incalculable. How can we be collectively *successful if we have no idea or worse, the wrong idea of who we were and, therefore, are? We are history's amnesiacs fitted with the memories of others.... America's contemporary racial problems cannot be solved, racism cannot be arrested, achievement gaps cannot be fully closed until Americans*—all Americans—*are repaired in their views of Africa's role in history.* (p. 14)

Like the Uninefs in the tale, African American children know little about their history beyond enslavement and therefore cannot truly understand the predicament in which they find themselves. Their history and even their oppression is blatantly left out of American art and history. There is little to comfort them in their struggles. There is no past to take pride in or to foster self-esteem. Furthermore, they have little to counteract the negative images of themselves and their innate abilities that have been ingrained for decades, even centuries, by means of their educational experiences. Robinson further states, "Blacks and no less whites, need to know that in centuries preceding that Atlantic slave trade and the invention of a virulent racism to justify it, the idea of black inferiority did not exist" (p. 17). However, a dominant epistemology that supports racism and inferiority theory severely alters and omits the accomplishments of those from oppressed groups and the history of their oppression that would explain why they fall short in almost every measure of economic and educational achievement. Many Black Americans are trapped in the most impoverished urban areas in this nation without truly understanding the ongoing effects of slavery and the social and economic discrimination that followed slavery and prevented the escape of all but a relative few. William Julius Wilson (1996) states, "[o]ne of the legacies of historic racial and class subjugation in America is a unique and growing concentration of minority residents in the most impoverished areas of the nation's metropolises" (p. 15). He further explains that "[i]f large segments of the African-American population had not been historically segregated in inner-city ghettos, we would not be talking about the new urban poverty" (p. 23). However, according to Wilson, segregation alone does not explain the emergence of what he defines as the new urban poverty. "I mean poor, segregated neighborhoods in which a substantial majority of individual adults are either unemployed or have dropped out of the labor force altogether" (p. 19). Job discrimination, residential segregation, public policy that allowed for the concentration of low income housing, in addition to the absence of effective labor-market policy, have all contributed to the blight of the inner city and the continued entrapment of the ghetto resident. Like the weakened Uninefs who were unable to journey into the mythical northern regions, many African Americans are living in a cycle of poverty without the resources or strength to pull themselves up the socioeconomic ladder. They attend poorly funded schools, with poorly trained teachers, and with uninspired curricula. They are not told that they are the victims of decades of institutional racism that created their dire situations. Rather they are told to look to the growing Black Middle Class as proof that it is possible to "be anything you want to be." The message is that failure to achieve means one is

inherently unable to achieve. How else would one explain the incredible numbers of African American children that find themselves in impoverished homes and who fail or drop out of school. If a history of racism and truncated opportunities do not account for the schools described in Jonathan Kozol's (1991) *Savage Inequalities*, then inferiority theory must. That is the message that poor African American children are ingesting and internalizing daily. "There is an invisible layer of prejudices toward those who have not succeeded in our society," states Solomon and Allen (2003), "…. Anyone can lift himself or herself by the bootstraps can succeed. If you do not, you have only yourself to blame" (p. xx). The analog divide must be faced for what it is and American institutions challenged to accept responsibility for closing gaps that they were complicit in creating. The fact remains that most minority children attend schools with high minority enrollments and limited and often scandalously absent resources. Educators and practitioners in leadership positions who are interested in closing the digital divide for some of America's poorest and most despised children should perhaps first look at the true source and nature of the problem. If one cannot or will not get to the root cause of a problem, it is unlikely that one will uncover the most effectual solution.

CONCLUSION: GETTING AT THE ROOT OF THE PROBLEM

Van Dijk (2005) poses three questions:

- Are the observed divides simply a byproduct of old social inequalities?
- Is digital technology intensifying these inequalities in some way or another?
- Or are new inequalities appearing in the context of the information and network society? (p. 5-6)

He answers these same questions in stating, "Divides *are* byproducts of old inequalities, digital technology *is* intensifying inequalities, and new inequalities *are* appearing. Both old and new inequalities are shown to be working, and it becomes clear that digital technology has its own enabling and defining role to play" (p. 6)

In getting to the root of the problem, I suggest that we begin by examining an old and major structural inequality that has survived into the 21st century and shows no signs of weakening: school funding. The fact that school district funding is determined largely by the tax base of surrounding communities ensures inequalities among districts and moreover ensures that inner-city schools will always suffer with insufficient resources (Corbett, Wilson, & Williams, 2002; Darling-Hammond, 1997; Divers-Stammes, 2002; Meier 1995; Noguera, 2003).

School funding thus has created the digital inequalities of today and the analog divides that preceded them. Low socioeconomic schools have significantly less access to computers and informational technologies and are less able to attract exemplary computer using teachers. Solomon and Allen (2003) concur and go on to state, "Inequity further exists in the way technology is used with different kinds of students" (p. xxi). Even though Mack (2001) outlines many of the benefits of integrating technology into poor urban schools, she nevertheless does not ignore the impact that history has had on computer access and use in economically disadvantaged environments. She concurs with the findings of the US Department of Education's Universal Service Fund for Schools and Libraries (E-Rate) Study and reports, "Although computer technology is an essential component of the 21st century classroom, the E-Rate Study acknowledges that current efforts to integrate technology in the classroom are limited by the same socioeconomic realities that have played a role in creating impoverished school systems" (p. 78).

Henry Becker (2000) reports on extensive data gathered concerning the digital divide in an article entitled, "Who's Wired and Who's Not: Children's Access and Use of Computer Technology." He found that "...students' use of computers varied according to their teachers' judgments about class ability levels. For example, across all subjects, classes categorized as low achieving used substantially more drill-and-practice exercises, whereas classes categorized as high achieving used more spreadsheet/database and e-mail software." (p. 55) He goes on to report,

...data indicate that computer use in low-SES schools often involved traditional practices and beliefs about student learning, whereas computer use in high-SES schools often reflected more constructivist and innovative teaching strategies. For example, teachers in low-SES schools were more likely than those in high-SES schools to use computers for 'remediation of skills' and 'mastering skills just taught' and to view computers as valuable for teaching students to work independently. In contrast, teachers in high-SES schools were more likely to use computers to teach students skills such as written expression, making presentations to an audience, and analyzing information. (p. 55)

Why is this important? It is a commonly held belief that differences in instructional practices and school curricula render significant differences in students' acquired skill sets and therefore account for differences in students' post-K-12 job and/or educational opportunities, such as college entrance. Therefore, disparities that children experience in schools reinforce their current socioeconomic status and help assure limited movement along this socioeconomic ladder in their adult lives. The social, political, economic, and cultural factors that impinge upon inner-city classrooms also work to shape the technologies developed and used in those settings and directly affect the nature of the teacher-student-technology interactions. Such dynamics give insight to van Dijk's (2005) claim that the "...digital divide is deepening where it has stopped widening" (p. 2). In other words, the fictional Uninefs may have faced an overwhelmingly wide and treacherous chasm initially but as time went on, the council in the northern region may have been successful in narrowing the chasm at some strategic points only to find that it had deepened to such an extent to assure that the slightest misstep would lead to certain death. Perhaps attempts to close the digital divide without addressing the historical root causes has contributed to its deepening.

FUTURE RESEARCH DIRECTIONS

In this chapter, I examined the concept of the digital divide within the context of the history of Black and White race relationships within the US. However, the digital divide is an international, global phenomenon that negatively affects groups beyond this nation's border. There is a need for further research and exploration of the historical, political, sociological, and economic factors that engender global inequities. Using critical social theories to examine the creation and maintenance of structural inequalities and analog divides, particularly in developing countries, could illuminate the nature of the digital divide in a global context. Such research has promise for uncovering the ways in which social and cultural factors serve to not only shape technology, but also the nature of technology and human interaction. Examining differential access and use of technology in countries around the world and by people in various social identity groups is central to the analysis of this phenomenon called the digital divide. The books and articles in the "Additional Readings" section are suggested to support research in this direction.

REFERENCES

Becker, H. J. (2000). Who's wired and who's not: Children's access to and use of computer technology. *The Future of Children* (Fall/Winter), 44-75. Retrieved from http://www.futureofchildren.org

Bell, D. (1987). *And we are not saved: The elusive quest for racial justice.* New York: BasicBooks.

Corbett, D., Wilson, B., & Williams, B. (2002). *Effort and excellence in urban classrooms: Expecting—and getting—success with all students.* New York, NY: Teachers College Press.

Darling-Hammond, L. (1997). *The right to learn: A blueprint for creating schools that work.* San Francisco, CA: Jossey-Bass Publishers.

Delgado, R. (Ed.) (1995). *Critical race theory: The cutting edge.* Philadelphia: Temple University Press.

Divers-Stamnes, A. C. (2002). Oppression and resultant violence in the inner city: Causes, effects on students, and responsibilities of educators. In L. A. Catelli & A. C. Diver-Stamnes (Eds.), *Commitment to excellence.* (pp. 267-286). Cresskill, NJ: Hampton Press Inc.

Kozol, J. (1991). *Savage inequalities: Children in America's schools.* New York: Crown.

Mack, R. L. (2001). *The digital divide: Standing at the intersection of race & technology.* Durham, NC: Carolina Academic Press.

Meier, D. (1995). *The power of their ideas.* Boston, MA: Beacon Press.

Noguera, P. A. (2003). *City schools and the American dream.* New York, NY: Teachers College Press.

Robinson, R. (2000). *The debt: What America owes to Blacks.* New York: Dutton.

Solomon, G., & Allen, N. J. (2003). Introduction: Educational technology and equity. In G.

Solomon, N. J. Allen, & P. Resta (Eds.), *Toward digital equity: Bridging the divide in education.* (pp. xvii-xxiv). Boston, MA: Pearson Education Group, Inc.

van Dijk, J. A. (2005). *The deepening divide: Inequality in the information society.* Thousand Oaks, CA: Sage Publications, Inc.

Watkins, W. H. (2001). *The White architects of Black education: Ideology and power in America, 1865-1954.* New York: Teachers College Press.

Wilson, W. J. (1996). *When work disappears: The world of the new urban poor.* New York, NY: Vintage Books.

ADDITIONAL READING

Abbott, J. (Ed.) (2004). *The political economy of the Internet in Asia and the Pacific: Digital divides, economic competitiveness, and security challenges.* Westport, CT: Praeger.

Chandra, S. (2002). Information in a networked world: The Indian perspective. *International Information & Library Review, 34*(3), 235-246.

Day, P., & Schuler, D. (Eds.) (2004). *Community practice in the network society: Local action/ global interaction.* New York, NY: Routledge.

Dragulanescu, N. (2002). Social impact of the "Digital Divide" in a central-eastern European country. *International Information & Library Review, 34*(2), 139-151.

Fahmi, I. (2002). The Indonesian Digital Library Network is born to struggle with the digital divide. *International Information & Library Review, 34*(2), 153-174.

Gibson, D., Heitor, M. & Ibarra-Yunez, A. (Eds.) *Learning and knowledge for the network society.* West Lafayette, IN: Purdue University Press.

Guillen, M., & Suarez, S. (2005). Explaining the global digital divide: Economic, political and so- ciological drivers of cross-national Internet use. *Social Forces, 84*(2), 681-708.

Johnson, P. (2002). New technology tools for human development? Towards policy and prac- tice for knowledge societies in Southern Africa. *Compare, 32*(2), 381-389.

Jussawalia, M., & Taylor, R. (Eds.) (2003). *Information technology parks of the Asia Pacific: Lessons for the regional digital divide.* New York, NY: M. e. Sharpe.

Kagami, M., Tsuji, M., & Giovannetti, E. (Eds.) (2004). *Information technology policy and the digital divide: Lessons for developing countries.* Northhampton, MA: Edward Elgar.

Keniston, K., & Kumar, D. (Eds.) (2004). *IT experience in India: Bridging the digital divide.* Thousand Oaks, CA: SAGE Publications.

Kozma, R., McGhee, R., & Quellmalz, E. (2004). Closing the digital divide: Evaluation of the World Links program. *International Journal of Educa- tional Development, 24*(4), 361-381.

Latham, R., & Sassen, S. (Eds.) (2005). *Digital formations: IT and new architectures in the global realm.* Princeton, NJ: Princeton Univer- sity Press.

Lax, S. (Ed.) (2001). *Access denied in the infor- mation age.* New York, NY: Palgrave.

Mossberger, K., Tolbert, C., & Stansbury, M. (2003). *Virtual inequality: Beyond the digital divide.* Washington, D.C.: Georgetown Univer- sity Press.

Norris, P. (2001). *Digital divide: Civic engagement, information poverty, and the Internet worldwide.* New York, NY: Cambridge University Press.

Nulens, G. (Ed.) (2001). *The digital divide in developing countries: Towards an information society in Africa.* Brussels: VUB Brussels Uni- versity Press.

Parayil, G. (Ed.) (2006). *Political economy and information capitalism in India: Digital divide, development and equity.* New York, NY: Palgrave Macmillan.

Perrons, D. (2004). *Globalization and social change: People and places in a divided world.* New York, NY: Routledge.

Rahman, H. (Ed.) (2006). *Enpowering marginal communities with information networking.* Hershey, PA: Idea Group Publishing.

Singh, J. (2002). From atoms to bits: Consequences of the emerging digital divide in India. *International Information & Library Review, 34*(2), 187-200.

Taylor, W., & Yu, X. (Eds.) (2003). *Closing the digital divide: Transforming regional economies*

and communities with information technology. Westport, CT: Praeger.

Tiene, D. (2002). Addressing the global digital divide and its impact on educational opportunity. *Educational Media International, 39*(3-4), 211-222.

Tiene, D. (2004). Bridging the digital divide in the schools of developing countries. *International Journal of Instructional Media, 31*(1).

Valentine, S. (2004). *E-powering the people: South Africa's Smart Access Project.* Washington, D.C.: Council on Library and Information Resources. Retrieved from http://www.clir.org/pubs/reports/pub125/pub125.pdf

Warschauer, M. (2003). *Technology and social inclusion: Rethinking the digital divide.* Cambridge, MA: MIT Press.

Chapter II
Exploring Gender Differences in Computer–Related Behaviour:
Past, Present, and Future

Robin Kay
University of Ontario Institute of Technology, Canada

ABSTRACT

This chapter explores gender differences in three key areas: computer attitude, ability, and use. Past research (10-25 years ago) is examined in order to provide a framework for a more current analysis. Seventy-one studies and 644 specific measures are analysed with respect to overall patterns, time, education level, and context. Males and females are more similar than different on all constructs assessed, for most grade levels and contexts. However, males report moderately more positive affective attitudes, higher self-efficacy, and more frequent use. Females are slightly more positive about online learning and appear to perform somewhat better on computer-related tasks. The results must be interpreted with caution because of methodological limitations in many studies reviewed. Finally, a model is proposed to understand and address gender differences in computer-related behaviour.

INTRODUCTION

A reasonable argument could be made that computers are integrated into every major area of our lives: art, education, entertainment, business, communication, culture, media, medicine, and transportation. It is equally reasonable to assume that considerable power and success rests with understanding how to use this technology meaningfully and effectively. Many children start interacting with computers at three to four years of age, however, gender-based socialization begins much earlier when someone asks, "Is it a boy or a girl?" (Paoletti, 1997). A critical question arises as to whether computer behaviour is influenced by gender. Given the prominent role that computers play in our society, it is vital that males and females have equal opportunity to work with and benefit from this technology.

Numerous studies have investigated the role of gender in computer behaviour over the past 20 years (see AAUW, 2000; Barker & Aspray, 2006; Kay, 1992; Sanders, 2006; Whitley, 1997 for detailed reviews of the literature) and the following conclusions can be made. First, most studies have looked at computer attitude, ability, and use constructs. Second, clear, reliable, valid definitions of these constructs are the exception, rather than the rule. Third, roughly 30% to 50% of the studies report differences in favour of males, 10% to15% in favour of females, and 40% to 60% no difference. Fourth, differences reported, while statistically significant, are small. Overall, one could say there is a persistent pattern of small differences in computer attitude, ability, and use that favours males; however, considerable variability exists and has yet to be explained.

There are four main objectives for this chapter. First, past research on computers and gender will be summarized by examining the results of five previous literature reviews. Second, a more current analysis of gender and technology will be provided by looking at a comprehensive set of studies done over the past 10 years. Technology changes quickly, so might the attitudes and abilities of people who use this technology. Third, a clear emphasis will be placed on examining the impact of contextual issues (e.g., type of technology used, age group, setting, culture) in order to explain some of the variability observed in past research. Finally, a model for understanding gender differences in computer behaviour will be proposed to help set an agenda for future research.

BACKGROUND

At least five comprehensive reviews have been done examining various aspects of gender and the use of computers (AAUW, 2000; Barker & Aspray, 2006; Kay, 1992; Sanders, 2006; Whitley, 1997). Each review is well worth reading and of-fers detailed, insightful information about gender and technology. I offer a brief synopsis of key insights these authors make that help frame the ideas presented in this chapter.

Whitley Review

In 1997, Whitley did a metaanalysis involving 82 studies and 40,491 American and Canadian respondents from 1973 to 1993. Regarding computer attitudes, it was found males had more positive affective attitudes toward computers. Mean effect sizes ranged from .08 for grammar school students, .22 to .24 for college students and adults, and .61 for high school students. Note that Cohen (1988, 1992) suggests that an effect size of .10 is small, .30 is medium, and .50 is large. This means that gender did play a moderate to significant role with respect to liking computers in the early period of computer use in North America.

General cognitive attitudes or beliefs about computers appeared to show little gender bias, with effect size ranging from .04 (college students) to .20 (grammar school). However, when focusing on computer-based stereotypes or sex biases, males were substantially more biased in their attitudes with effect size ranging from .44 (college students) to .67 (grammar students).

Self-efficacy toward computers followed a similar pattern to affective attitudes. Effect size was not substantial for grammar school students, but favoured males in high school and beyond ($r=.32$ to .66). Even though males reported more confidence in using computers, effect size for computer experience was relatively small ($r=.15$ to .23). Finally, it appears that males used computers more often than females for all ages groups ($r=.24$ to .40), although this effect size range would be considered moderate according to Cohen (1998, 1992).

In summary, Whitley offers a statistical snapshot of male-female differences in computer attitude, ability, and use for North Americans prior to 1993.

Sanders Review

Sanders (2006) took a markedly different approach to reviewing the literature on gender and technology. Over 200 articles were examined, covering an approximate time period from 1990 to 2001, but the goal was to offer possible explanations for why women were so under represented in the field of Computer Science. The review, while not statistically rigorous, offers a multicultural, rich perspective on the potential factors that contribute to gender biases in computer-based behavior.

Sanders discusses in some detail the influence of society (e.g., parents, media, SES), age, attitude, ability, use patterns, and the classroom. Regarding attitude, ability, self-efficacy, and use, her results are consistent with Whitley. In addition, she offers the following observations:

- Stereotypes can start with parents
- The media portrays computers as a male domain
- High SES is associated with greater promotion of computers in girls
- Stereotyped use of computers starts at pre-school
- Gender differences tend to increase with age
- Males enroll in more computer-based courses
- Males play more computer games
- Differences between males and females in the area of online learning are not as prominent as in other areas
- The computer curriculum in high school favours male interests

This review generated some very interesting and provocative reasons for why males are far more actively involved in the field of Computer Science. Perhaps the most profound statement that Sanders made was that even with sizeable gender differences observed in attitude, ability, and use, almost no effort was being made to in-vestigate possible interventions that could level the proverbial "computer" playing field.

Barker and Aspray Review

Barker and Aspray (2006) provide a methodical and detailed analysis of research on girls and computers. Their approach is similar to that of Sanders (2006) in that they offer a rich discussion on factors that inhibit girls from pursuing careers in information technology. Their findings on computer attitude and use, dating from 1992 to 2004, are aligned with those reported by Whitley (1997) and Sanders (2006). They deliberately chose not to look at differences between girls and boys in computer literacy or ability.

A number of noteworthy observations were articulated in this review. First, elementary teachers, who are primarily females, have limited computing skills and therefore act as poor role models for young girls. Second, the gender gap with respect to computer access and use has narrowed rapidly over the past 5 years. Third, boys still use computers more than girls at home, although each sex uses computers for different reasons. Boys use games, educational software, and the Internet more, whereas girls use computers for e-mail and homework. Finally, the culture of computing is largely driven by males, and females begin to reject this culture starting in early adolescence. Females favour careers in more socially oriented fields such as medicine, law, or business and see computer-based occupations as boring and menial. Ultimately, it may do little good to give females extra resources designed to increase expertise in computers, when they find the IT curriculum to be "out of touch" with their experiences and interests.

American Association of University Women (AAUW), 2000

The AAUW (2000) did an extensive review of the research on gender and technology with the primary goal of identifying changes needed in the current computer culture to make it more appealing to girls and women. They agree with Barker and Aspray (2006) that girls reject the violence and tedium of computer games and would prefer to use technology in a meaningful manner. They summarize this position by stating that many girls have a "we can, but don't want to" attitude about technology.

The AAUW (2000) offers a poignant explanation of why a commitment to lifelong technology learning is important. They note that being successful in working with technology involves the ability to adapt to rapid changes, to critically interpret the morass of electronic information available, and to experiment without fear.

Kay Review

In 1992, Kay summarized the results of 98 articles looking at gender and computer attitude, ability, and use. The familiar pattern of male prevalence in these areas was observed. Of course, these results are dated now, but the final conclusion of this study is still valid. In the vast majority of studies analyzed in the past, clear, reliable, valid, and consistent measures of attitude, ability, and use constructs are rarely offered. Unfortunately, measurement problems are still substantial. Out of 644 measures used to analyze gender differences in this chapter, 24% offered estimates of reliability and 18% examined validity. The uncertainty and lack of cohesion with respect to constructs used to establish gender differences undermines the process of understanding and addressing gender differences and technology.

In general, when asked which sex is more positive toward computers, more apt at using computers and more likely to use a computer, one would best be advised to answer, 'It depends.' It depends on what attitudes you are measuring, what skills you are assessing and what the computer is being used for. (Kay, 1992, p. 278)

Objectives of this Chapter

The goal of this chapter is to build on previous research in order to provide a current and cohesive perspective on gender and technology. This goal will be achieved by:

- Collecting the most recent empirical data available after Whitley's (1997) review
- Focusing on the broader intent of creating technologically thoughtful, effective, risk takers (AAUW,2000), as opposed to IT professionals (Barker & Aspray, 2006; Sanders. 2006;)
- Determining how current data support the richer, contextual patterns noted by Sanders (2006) and Barker & Aspray (2006)
- Proposing a model to explore gender differences
- Discussing how a coherent model might advance an intervention program that Sanders (2006) notes is clearly lacking
- Examining methods and strategies that can help improve the quality and impact of information that is needed to develop a more comprehensive understanding of gender and technology (Kay, 1992)

Note that the term computer and technology will be used interchangeably. I realize that "technology" has a broader focus, but with respect to research involving gender differences, the sole area investigated involves computers.

Data Analysis

Seventy-one refereed (see Appendix for full list) papers were reviewed for this chapter spanning a decade of research (1997-2007). Each paper was coded for measures of attitude, ability, self-efficacy, and use. Each of these constructs was divided into subcategories to illustrate the wide range of computer behaviours assessed. This process resulted in 644 tests of gender differences involving more than 380,000 people, from 17 different countries. Computer behaviour was looked at from four main settings: home, school, the workplace, and online communication. Eight distinct populations were examined including kindergarten, elementary school (Grade 1-5), middle school (Grade 6-8), high school (grade 9-12), undergraduates, preservice teachers, graduate students, and adults. Each of the 644 tests of gender difference was rated according to whether there was a significant male advantage, a significant female advantage, or no difference.

In summary, every attempt was made to flesh out as much context as possible with respect to results reported; however, speculation was kept to a minimum when there was not enough evidence to make a firm conclusion. It is also important to recognize that while an attempt will be made to find patterns in gender differences with respect to attitude, ability, and use, the analysis will be compromised by the multitude measures used to address these constructs and the limited reliability and valid statistics available.

CURRENT RESEARCH ON GENDER AND COMPUTERS (1997-2007)

Computer Attitudes: Affect and Cognition

Computer attitudes accounted for 31% (n=202) of all gender-technology comparisons assessed for this chapter. It is a daunting task, though, to sort out the numerous types of attitudes assessed. Two principle constructs, based on Ajzen and Fishbein's (1988) theory of attitude measurement, provide a schema for understanding the numerous attitude scales.

The first construct is based on affect and, to date, encompasses two basic emotions: anxiety and happiness. Samples of affective attitudes are computer anxiety, computer enjoyment, comfort level, software and activity preferences, liking,

motivation, fun, and sense of achievement. The second construct looks at cognitions or a person's beliefs about computer-related activities and environments. Some examples of cognitive attitude are stereotyping, importance, perceived usefulness, trust, and acceptance.

When looking at studies measuring affective attitudes, males had more positive feelings 33% (n=30) of the time, females had more positive feelings 15% (n=14) of the time, and there were no differences 52% (n=64). There appears to be a moderate male bias with respect to affective attitude toward computers. The situation, though, is different for cognitive attitude where males had more positive thoughts about computers 23% (n=26) of the time, females more positive thoughts 20% (n=21) of the time, and no differences were reported 58% (n=64) of the time. Males and females do not appear to differ with respect to computer-based cognitions.

Digging into the attitude data a little deeper reveals several patterns. First, there appears to be no obvious change in male-female differences in overall attitudes over the past 10 years. While there is some fluctuation in favour of males or females on a year-by-year basis, males are slightly more positive than females when it comes to feelings about computers. One might expect that as the technology becomes more accessible, easier to use, and more diverse in application, that computer attitudes might level out between the sexes. This appears not to be the case. In fact, the most recent studies (2005-2007) show a strong male bias for both affective and cognitive attitude (40% favour males, 15% favour females, 45% show no difference).

A second pattern looks at the relationship between grade and gender differences with respect to overall computer attitudes. In elementary school (grades 1-5), females appear to have slightly more positive attitudes about computers, although the number of tests was small (n=9). In middle school, females and males have similar attitudes toward computers, but in high school males show more positive attitudes, a bias that continues in university. Male and female preservice teachers and graduate students have similar attitudes toward computers, but the general adult population shows a strong male bias. This pattern is consistent with previous reviews of gender and technology. Males and females do not start out with different feelings and thoughts about computers, they emerge over time and seem to be influenced by education level and culture. Nonetheless, it is absolutely critical to keep these findings in perspective. Most females or males do not follow this pattern. Even in the most extreme case (high school), male bias means males had more positive attitudes in about 40% of all tests done. Another way of stating this result is that females have more positive attitudes or there is no difference in of 60% of the cases observed.

The third pattern observed with respect to male-female differences in attitude involves the setting or context where computers are used. Surprisingly, not one study out of the 71 reviewed for this chapter looked at attitude toward home use of computers. When looking at gender differences in school, males reported more favourable attitudes 46% of the time, females were more positive 16% of the time, and no difference in computer attitude at school was observed 38% of the time. However, when one shifts to an online context, the picture is decidedly different. In this context, females were more positive 21% of the time, no difference was observed 76% of the time, leaving males with having more favorable attitudes only 3% of the time. When context was not mentioned at all, gender differences in attitude were marginal (27% favour males, 18% favour females, 55% no difference).

This analysis of context tells us that setting is important when looking at attitude toward computers, although a finer granularity is needed in future research. It is concerning that males are more positive toward computers in a school setting, but it is unclear what they are positive about games, educational software, presentations, word process-

ing? Azjen and Fishbein (1988) note that the more specific one is about the object of an attitude, the higher the predictive value. On the other hand, it is encouraging that females respond equally if not more positively to an online environment. Again, it is important to investigate the explicit nature of these attitudes in order to understand dynamics of gender-technology interaction.

In summary, the current analysis of gender and attitude toward computers offers the following conclusions. First, computer attitudes appear to be biased in favour of males with respect to affect but not cognition. Second, this bias typically means that males are more positive 30% to 40% of the time, females are more positive 15% to 25% of the time, and there is no difference 45% to 55% of the time. Third, differences do not appear to be attenuating over time, but are influenced by education level and the setting in which computers are used. Finally, more precise definitions of attitude and context are needed in order to develop a more comprehensive understanding of gender differences in computer technology.

Computer Ability and Self-Efficacy

I have put computer ability and self-efficacy in the same section because gender-computer researchers have not been precise when defining these terms. The rating of one's actual computer ability and one's confidence or belief in being able to perform a computer-related task (computer-self-efficacy) is often blurred. I will discuss each construct independently, but until operational definitions, reliability, and validity are reported more regularly, a sizeable overlap may exist between the two.

Ability

Differences between males and females regarding computer ability were looked at 93 times (14% of the total sample). Definitions of ability included general knowledge, games, application software, online tools, programming, and performance. Overall, males rated themselves higher in computer ability 47% of the time, females rated themselves higher just 9% of the time, and both sexes reported equal ability 44% of the time. This difference between males and females is accentuated if one removes actual performance estimates of ability. When looking at self-report measures, males rate themselves as having higher ability 60% of the time. However, if one looks at performance measures alone, females exceed males in computer ability. Five percent of the time males are better, 24% of time females are better, and 71% of the time there is no difference. Males have decidedly greater ability than females when self-report measures are used, but when actual performance is assessed, females appear to have the advantage. This anomaly calls into question the reliability and validity of using the self-report technique. More work needs to be done validating the accuracy of assessment tools used to evaluate computer ability.

It appears that estimates of computer ability from 1997 to 2007 are fairly stable (45% favour males, 10% favour females, 45% show no difference). One might expect that previously reported differences in favour of males would lessen over time given the increased ease of using a computer, but this expectation is not supported. On the other hand, the stability may simply mean that males continue to have inflated ratings of their computer ability.

It is particularly informative to look at computer ability across grade levels. Computer ability is essentially equal for all grade levels except university students and general working professionals, where males show significantly higher levels. It is unclear what happens at university or in the workplace that might cause this difference. What is clear is that most of the research on gender disparities in computer ability has focused on subjects who are 18 years or older. Without a broader representation of the total population, it is challenging to give a more informed analysis

with respect to the impact of gender on computer ability.

Self-Efficacy

Only 6% (n=38) of the gender tests focused on self-efficacy; therefore, a detailed analysis of this construct is not possible, nor reliable. Not surprisingly, the overall pattern for computer self-efficacy is almost the same as that for self-report measures of computer ability. Fifty-three percent of males felt more confident than females; the reverse scenario was observed only 5% of the time. Forty-percent of the time, males and females reported equal self-efficacy. As stated earlier, because of limitations in research methodology, self-rating of computer ability may be synonymous with self-efficacy. That said, one should not underestimate the influence of self-efficacy. It is entirely reasonable that feelings of confidence can influence computer behaviour and use. Even though there is evidence to suggest that females are as good if not better at using computers, self-efficacy could be holding them back. The relationship among self-efficacy and actual computer use has not been examined in detail; however, it should be placed on future research agendas.

Computer Use: Frequency

One could argue convincingly that the ultimate goal of understanding and addressing gender differences in computer–related behaviour is to ensure that males and females have the same choices and opportunities to use computers. This section will look at both frequency of use and actual computer behaviours.

Twenty-seven percent (n=172) of tests analysed for this chapter looked at computer use. This construct covered a number of domains: general use, access to computers, application software, entertainment, programming, and the Internet. Regardless of the domain, males used computers more often than females 40% of the time, females used computers more than males 5% of the time, and no difference in use was reported 56% of the time. Use of application software (74% no difference) and having access to computers (67% no difference) were the least gender-biased activities, whereas using the computer for entertainment (31% no difference) and general activities (43% no difference) were the most gender biased. Identifying the precise area of use, then, is important. Using computers for games, for example, may be an activity that is dominated by males, but participation will not necessarily be advantageous with respect to learning new software or making informed choices using technology. On the other hand, if females had significantly less access to a computer, which does not seem to be the case, that would be cause for concern because both opportunity and choice would be restricted.

An encouraging pattern with respect to use is the trend of decreased gender bias in computer use over the past 10 years. From 1997 to 2000, males reported using computers more than females 62% of the time. This decreased to 37% from 2001 to 2004 and 29% from 2005 to 2007. With respect to context, general (51% males report more use) and home (55% males report more use) use indicated significant male advantages, although no differences were observed at school or online. Interestingly, gender bias with respect to home and general use appears to be decreasing over time. Use in these two settings was strongly sex biased with 86% of males reporting significantly more use from 1997 to 2000, but from 2005 to 2007, male dominance dropped to 45%.

A closer look at the school context reveals that while no differences between males and females exist for elementary school students with respect to computer use, this pattern changes abruptly for all other education levels including middle school and university (38% male dominance), high school (51% male dominance), and the workplace/general population (60% male dominance). If one takes into account time and education level, high school and university male students continue to

exceed their female counterparts (between 33% and 44%), but not at the same level as previous years. Middle school use of computers, unfortunately, has not been studied in the past 3 years with respect to gender.

The results regarding computer use and gender difference offer a somewhat complicated picture. Clear gender differences in that appeared between the years of 1997 to 2000, attenuated markedly from 2005 to 2007. Areas of concern still exist for home and general use as well as high school and university settings, but even for these hotspots, a decreasing gender gap is a promising trend.

Actual Behavior

Actual computer behaviour has been studied far less than frequency of computer use, yet it is specific behaviour that can help uncover clues and nuances with respect to gender differences. While 14% (n=89) of the total sample of tests forged into an analysis of how males and females behave while using computers, only 6% (n=37) presented formal comparisons. No fewer than eight categories of behaviour were identified including cognitive activities, collaboration, communication, learning, teaching, problem solving, use of software help, and same vs. mixed-sex behaviour. Overall, no significant differences were reported with respect to specific computer behaviours 76% of the time. This does not mean that males and females do not behave differently with respect to computers, because the vast majority of studies on computer behaviour are qualitative and present rich descriptions of highly contextualized situations.

There are some interesting and potentially informative observations made with respect to actual behaviour. For example, in an online environment there is some evidence to suggest males are more authoritative and assertive (Fitzpatrick & Hardman, 2000; Guiller & Durndell, 2006) in online discussions, but are more flexible in a face-to-face conversation. Females, on the other hand, change their opinions more in an online than face-to-face environment. Another study indicated that girls accounted for nearly twice the number computer-based interactive behaviours than boys did (e.g., helping another student, asking questions) in an elementary school class (Waite, Wheeler, & Bromfield, 2007). Some researchers have examined the dynamics that occur in same vs. mixed-sex groups. Both males and females appear to do better with their same sex peers (Fitzpatrick & Hardman, 2000; Jenson, deCastell, & Bryson, 2003; Light, Littleton, Bale, Joiner, & Messer, 2000). Finally, some boys may not take girls seriously in terms of computer knowledge. Jenson et al. (2003) reported that even when girls were trained and had superior knowledge, boys tended to rebuff their attempts to help and guide.

These computer behaviour results have to be interpreted cautiously, as they are often detailed, but isolated examples collected from small samples. However, the kind of insight provided by rich qualitative investigation is critical to develop an effective, workable model to explain the interaction between gender and technology. We want males and females to have choice in using computers, but we do not want to undermine the learning process, for example, where it may be the case each sex reacts differently to online discussions. We certainly want to create an atmosphere of mutual respect and support in a computer-based classroom, although, there is some evidence to suggest that effective knowledge building may be undermined by gender prejudice. In short, while it is important to examine computer attitude, ability, self efficacy, and use, it is challenging to build a cohesive and informative model of gender and technology using only survey methodology.

FUTURE TRENDS AND RESEARCH DIRECTIONS

It is clear that more effort needs to be directed toward developing a model for interpreting and addressing gender differences in computer-related

behaviour. Isolated studies in this area have taken place for over 30 years. Solid reviews of the literature are helpful, but there is an overwhelming need to organize this data into a more coherent whole. I propose the model in Figure 1 to help organize and understand future research. The model is not empirically supported, but takes into account the full range of factors that have been studied to date.

The model is premised on the following assumptions. First, the major components including computer-based attitudes, ability, self-efficacy, use, and behaviour, occur in a context. The context may be an elementary or high school classroom, a business, an online discussion board. This means there could be slightly or drastically different dynamics in different environments. The more that one describes a given context, the more effective the model will be in predicting and

Figure 1. A model for understanding gender and computer-related behaviour

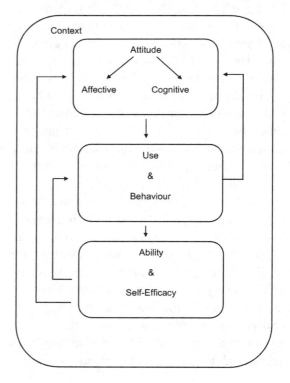

understanding behaviour. Second, attitude needs to be divided into at least two main constructs: affect and cognition. This division has been shown to be meaningful in the present analysis. It is speculated that attitudes, depending on whether they are positive or negative, lead to acceptance, neutrality, or rejection of computers. This, in turn, will prompt an individual to avoid or learn more about computers. If the context permits adequate access to computers, then a user can begin to develop computer ability and self-efficacy. Once a person begins using a computer, the type of use and specific behaviours experienced will have a direct effect on attitude. If a person experiences successful use of computers he/she will use a computer more, develop more positive affect and cognitions, and increased skills. If a person experiences challenges and significant barriers, attitude may become increasingly negative to the point of non-use. This model offers opportunities for future research with respect to improving methodology, addressing context, shifting focus, and developing intervention strategies. Each of these will be discussed in more detail.

Improving Methodology

What is blatantly clear is that researchers need to be more precise in operationally defining their constructs, and providing estimates of validity and reliability. A considerable leap of faith was taken, perhaps recklessly, in analyzing and reporting gender and technology research for this study. Only 17 out of the 71 studies discussed validity and offered reliability estimates of .70 or better. This accounted for only 9% (n=64) of all the data. In 1992, (Kay, 1992) I made the exact same plea to improve the quality of research simply because it is difficult to be confident in the results reported. While most research methodology is flawed in some way, developing solid assessment tools is fundamental to advance our knowledge on gender and technology.

Another suggestion, partially based on the next section on context, is to make scales domain specific. General measures give us watered-down estimates of attitude, ability, self-efficacy, and use. The results of the current review suggest that context is very important. For example, it was reported that males have more positive affective attitude toward computers. A closer look over a broad range of studies reveals that males may be very positive about using computers for entertainment, whereas females seem to prefer e-mail and using computers for a meaningful task. A general measure of computer affect would not uncover these important differences.

One final idea is to study multiple constructs simultaneously. Many studies focus on one or two areas of interest, but the ideal study should examine all of the key areas: attitude, ability, self-efficacy, and use. This way a statistical analysis can be done to examine the relationships among constructs. This kind of analysis is critical for model building.

Addressing Context

Models for understanding gender and technology need to start from a specific context. There is growing evidence, for example, that females are responding very positively to online environments, sometimes more positively than males. In high school and university settings, males continue to display more favourable computer attitudes, ability, and use. Sanders (2006) and Barker and Aspray (2006) speculate as to why these differences emerge, but more systematic research and evidence is needed to discover the mechanisms of bias. Detailed research looking at a wide range of behaviours over an extended time period will help reveal contextual complexities.

Shifting the Focus

The current research menu for investigating gender differences and technology over past decades needs to be altered in at least four fundamental areas. First, more effort needs to be directed toward understanding computer ability. Self-report measures do not align well with actual performance on computers. More effort needs to be directed to distinguishing self-efficacy from ability and gathering data that represents an accurate estimate of skill.

Second, researchers need to actively collect data from younger populations. Most of the current data is based on university students and the general population, age 18 years or older. This approach may promote the reporting of gender biases, simply because the subjects involved are older and may not be reflective of the current computer culture. Computer use for elementary school students today is far different than it was for university students 10 to 15 years ago. To get the most current snapshot of potential gender disparities, students from K to 8 need to have a stronger presence. Trends of computer use reflecting a reduced gender gap support the need for this shift.

Third, a research program focusing on gender and technology with respect to preservice and experienced teachers needs to be developed. Only 3 out of the 71 studies analysed for this chapter looked at the preservice population and no studies examined in-service teachers. Educators, though, are probably a primary influence, both indirect and direct, on students' behaviours toward computers. If a single teacher has a negative attitude toward computer use and is unable or unwilling to integrate computers in the curriculum, it can affect numerous students over an extended time period.

Finally, there is a clear need for richer, qualitative research all on key areas of computer behaviour. Qualitative research accounted for just 2% of the data points collected in this chapter (Goldstein & Puntambekar, 2004; Jenson et. al., 2003; Voyles & Williams, 2004; Waite et al., 2007). We have relatively clear overall patterns of attitude, ability, and use, but the only way

we are going to understand and address gender differences is to conduct interviews and observe actual behaviour. The wealth of survey data has left us at the mercy of speculation, some of which may be true, but little of which is supported by empirical data.

Developing Intervention Strategies

While no comprehensive model exists to explain the dynamics of gender and technology, the proposed model in Figure 1, provides a starting point for intervention research. Only 2 of the 71 studies (Jenson et al., 2003; Kay, 2006) examined how gender biases might change. Kay (2006) provided evidence that an 8-month, ubiquitous laptop program eliminated computer attitude, ability, and use differences in favour of males. Establishing a meaningful, supportive culture of computer use may be a substantial step toward producing effective intervention.

As Sanders (2006) suggests, more intervention studies are needed, and data from the last decade indicate that modifying affective attitudes and self-efficacy in middle school, high school, and university are reasonable areas to start. Of course, one could argue that more information on what causes gender differences is needed to create effective intervention. On the other hand, intervention research can provide useful feedback for understanding and addressing the computer gender gap in specific areas.

CONCLUSION

As with any large-scale review of the literature, more questions than answers are generated. In this specific review of gender and computer-related behaviour over the past decade, the following conclusions were made:

• Males have significantly more positive affective attitudes toward computers, particularly in high school, university, and the general workplace

- Gender bias in attitudes toward computers is affected by context – males have more positive attitudes in school, but females have more positive attitude in an online environment
- Gender differences with respect to computer attitude have remained relatively stable for the past 10 years
- Males in a university or general workplace setting have consistently reported stronger computer skills for the past 10 years, however, these differences disappear when one looks at actual computer performance
- Males report significantly higher computer self-efficacy than females
- Males report higher computer use, however, this gender bias has decreased markedly over the past 10 years
- Males report more computer use at home, but not in school
- When looking at computer behaviour, males and females appear to act differently, but there appear to be no significant advantages for either sex

It is important to note that when we are talking about gender bias, even in the most extreme case, there are no differences between males and females 50% of the time. In short, male and female computer attitudes, ability, self-efficacy, and use are more similar than different.

Only two studies (Anderson & Haddad, 2005; Ong & Lai, 2006) looked toward developing a model to understand and explain gender differences. A model was proposed in this chapter to help understand current findings and to direct future research efforts. The new research agenda needs to improve and expand methodology, include underrepresented populations, consider the context of computer use, and explore intervention strategies.

The importance of investigating gender and technology is best illustrated from a comment made by one of the girls who learned in a same-sex environment in Jenson et al.'s (2003) study. She said:

When you taught us, it was simple. And I think one of the parts about ... you ... teaching us is that it feels nice when people go 'oh you are so smart, you know how to do this' ...But like... if you ask a boy, 'oh could I have some help here,' they kind of laugh at you and say 'You don't know that?' ... You are like giving us an opportunity where we ... can say 'hey this is good maybe I will get into computers. (p. 569)

If what this girl felt is representative of the larger high school population where mixed sex education is the norm, then we cannot start early enough in rectifying this kind of prejudice. Ultimately, we need to create supportive environments that do not inhibit learning or choice with respect to using computers. It is also revealing that when efforts are made to create technology-rich environments that emphasize constructive, collaborative, problem-based learning, looking at authentic activities, no differences are reported between males and females with respect to attitude, self-efficacy, use, and performance (Mayer-Smith, Pedretti, & Woodrow, 2002). Perhaps, when technology is not the main focus but naturally and effectively integrated into a learning environment, gender biases are reduced or eliminated.

REFERENCES

Adrianson, L. (2001). Gender and computer-mediated communication: Group processes in problem solving. *Computers in Human Behaviour, 17*, 71-94.

Ajzen, I., & Fishbein, (1988). *Attitudes, personality, and behavior.* Chicago, IL: Dorsey Press.

American Association of University Women (2000). *Tech-savvy: Educating girls in the new computer age*. Washington, DC: American Association of University Women Foundation. Retrieved Dec 1, 2006 from http://www.aauw.org/member_center/publications/TechSavvy/TechSavvy.pdf

Anderson, D. M., & Haddad, C. J. (2005). Gender, voice, and learning in online course environments, *JALN, 9*(1), 3-14.

Atan, H., Sulaiman, F., Rahman, Z. A., & Idrus, R. M. (2002). Gender differences in availability, Internet access and rate of usage of computers among distance education learners. *Education Media International, 39*(3/4), 205-210.

Aust, R., Newberry, B., O'Brien, J., & Thomas, J. (2005). Learning generation: Fostering innovation with tomorrow's teachers and technology. *Journal of Technology and Teacher Education, 13*(2), 167-195.

Barker, L. J., & Aspray, W. (2006). The state of research on girls and IT. In J. M. Cohoon & W. Aspray (Eds.), *Women and information technology* (pp. 3-54). Cambridge, MA: The MIT Press.

Barrett, E., & Lally, V. (1999). Gender differences in an online learning environment. *Journal of Computer Assisted Learning, 15*, 48-60.

Bronson, M. (1998). The impact of psychological gender, gender-related perceptions, significant others, and the introducer of technology upon computer anxiety among students. *Journal of Educational Computing Research, 18*(1), 63-78.

Brosnan, M., & Lee, W. (1998). A cross-cultural comparison of gender differences in computer attitudes and anxieties: The United Kingdom and Hong Kong. *Computers in Human Behaviour, 14*(4), 559-577.

Broos, A. (2005). Gender and information and communication technologies (ICT) anxiety: Male self-assurance and female hesitation. *Cyberpsychology & Behavior, 8*(10), 21-31.

Broos, A., & Roe, K. (2006). The digital divide in the playstation generation: Self-efficacy, locus of control and ICT adoption among adolescents. *Poetics, 34*, 306-317.

Christensen, R., Knezek, G., & Overall, T. (2005). Transition points for the gender gap in computer enjoyment. *Journal of Research on Technology in Education, 18*(1), 23-37.

Cohen, J. (1988). *Statistical power analysis for the behavioural sciences* (2nd edition). New York: Academic Press.

Cohen, J. (1992). A power primer. *Psychological Bulletin, 112*(1), 155-159.

Colley, A. (2003). Gender differences in adolescents' perceptions of the best and worst aspects of computing at school. *Computers in Human Behaviour, 19*, 673-682.

Colley, A., & Comber, C. (2003). Age and gender differences in computer use and attitudes among secondary school students: what has changed? *Educational Research, 45*(2), 155-165.

Comber, C., Colley, A., Hargreaves, D. J., & Dorn, L. (1997). The effects of age, gender and computer experience upon computer attitudes. *Educational Research Volume, 39*(2), 123-133.

Crombie, G., Abarbanel, T., & Trinneer, A. (2002). All-female classes in high school computer science: Positive effects in three years of data. *Journal of Educational Computing Research, 27*(4), 383-407.

Durndell, A., & Haag, Z. (2002). Computer self efficacy, computer anxiety, attitude towards the Internet and reported experience with the Internet, by gender, in an east European sample. *Computers in Human Behaviour, 18*, 521-535.

Durndell, A., Haag, Z., & Laithwaite, H. (2000). Computer self efficacy and gender: a cross cultural study of Scotland and Romania. *Personality and Individual Differences, 28*, 1037-1044.

Durndell, A., & Thomson, K. (1997). Gender and computing: A decade of change. *Computers & Education, 28*(1), 1-9.

Enoch, Y., & Soker, Z. (2006). Age, gender, ethnicity and the digital divide: University students' use of Web-based instruction. *Open Learning, 21*(2), 99-110.

Fan, T., & Li, Y. (2005). Gender issues and computers: College computer science education in Taiwan. *Computer & Education, 44*, 285-300.

Fitzpatrick, H., & Hardman, M. (2000). Mediated activity in the primary classroom: Girls, boys and computers. *Learning and Instruction, 19*, 431-446.

Garland, K. J., & Noyes, J. M. (2004). Computer experience: A poor predictor of computer attitudes. *Computers in Human Behaviour, 20*, 823-840.

Goldstein, J., & Puntambekar, S. (2004). *Journal of Social Science Education and Technology, 13*(4), 505-522.

Guiller, J., & Durndell, A. (2006). "I totally agree with you": Gender interactions in educational online discussion groups. *Journal of Computer-Assisted Learning, 2*(5), 368-381.

Jackson, L. A., Ervin, K. S., Gardner, P. D., & Schmitt, N. (2001). Gender and the Internet: Women communicating and men searching. *Sex Roles, 44*(5), 363-379.

Jenson, J., deCastell, S., & Bryson, M. (2003). Girl talk: Gender, equity, and identity discourses in a school-based computer culture. *Women's Studies International Forum, 26*(6), 561-573.

Joiner, R. W. (1998). The effect of gender on children's software preferences. *Journal of Computer Assisted Learning, 14*, 195-198.

Joiner R., Gavin J, Brosnan M, Crook C., Duffield, J., Durndell A., Maras P., Miller J., Scott, A. J., & Lovatt P. (2005). Gender, Internet identification, and Internet anxiety: Correlates of Internet use. *Cyberpsychology and Behavior, 8*(4), 373-380.

Karavidas, M., Lim, N. K., & Katsikas, S. L. (2005). The effects of computers on older adult users. *Computers in Human Behaviour, 21*, 697-711.

Kay, R. H. (1992). An analysis of methods used to examine gender differences in computer-related behaviour. *Journal of Educational Computing Research, 8*(3), 323-336.

Kay, R. H. (2006). Addressing gender differences in computer ability, attitudes and use: The laptop effect. *Journal of Educational Computing Research, 34*(2), 187-211.

Kimborough, D. R. (1999). Online chat room tutorial – An unusual gender bias in computer use. *Journal of Science Education and Technology, 8*(3), 227-234.

King, J., Bond, T., & Blandford, S. (2002). An investigation of computer anxiety by gender and grade. *Computers in Human Behaviour, 18*, 69-84.

Lanthier, R. P., & Windham, R. C. (2004). Internet use and college adjustment: The moderating role of gender. *Computers in Human Behaviour, 20*, 591-606.

Lee, A. C. K. (2003). Undergraduate students' gender difference in IT skill and attitudes. *Journal of Computer Assisted Learning, 19*(4), 488-500.

Leonard, J., Davis, J. E., & Sidler, J. L. (2005). Cultural relevance and computer-assisted instruction. *Journal of Research on Technology in Education, 37*(3), 263-284.

Li, N., & Kirkup, G. (2007). Gender and cultural difference in Internet use: A study of China and the UK. *Computers & Education, 48*, 301-317.

Light, P., Littleton, K., Bale, S., Joiner, R., & Messer, D. (2000). Gender and social comparison effects in computer-based problem solving. *Learning and Instruction, 10*, 483-496.

Lightfoot, J. M. (2006). A comparative analysis of e-mail and face-to-face communication in an educational environment. *Internet and Higher Education, 9*, 217-227.

Mayer-Smith, J., Pedretti, E., & Woodrow, J. (2000) Closing of the gender gap in technology enriched science education: A case study. *Computers & Education, 35*, 51-63.

McIlroy, D., Bunting, B., Tierney, K., & Gordon, M. (2001). The relation of gender and background experience to self-reported computing anxieties and cognitions. *Computers in Human Behaviour, 17*, 21-33.

Mercier, E. M., Baron, B., & O'Connor, K. M. (2006). Images of self and others as computer users: The role of gender and experience. *Journal of Computer Assisted Learning, 22*, 335-348.

Miller, L. M., Schweingruber, H., & Brandenburg, C. L. (2001). Middle school students' technology practices and preferences: Re-examining gender differences. *Journal of Educational Multimedia and Hypermedia, 10*(2), 125-140.

North, A. S., & Noyes, J. M. (2002). Gender influences on children's computer attitudes and cognitions. *Computers in Human Behaviour, 18*, 135-150.

O'Neill, R., & Colley, A. (2006). Gender and status effects in student e-mails to staff. *Journal of Computer Assisted Learning, 22*, 360-367.

Ong, C., & Lai, J. (2006). Gender differences in perceptions and relationships among dominants of e-learning acceptance. *Computers in Human Behavior, 22*, 816-829.

Ono, H., & Zavodny, M. (2003). Gender and the Internet. *Social Science Quarterly, 84*(1), 111-121.

Ory, J. O., Bullock, C., & Burnaska, K. (1997). Gender similarity in the use of and attitudes about ALN in a university setting. *JALN, 1*(1), 39-51.

Osterweigel, A., Littleton, K., & Light, P. (2004). Understanding computer-related attitudes through an idiographic analysis of gender- and self-representations. *Learning and Instruction, 14*, 215-233.

Paoletti, J. (1997). The gendering of infants' and toddlers' clothing in America. In K. Martinez & K. Ames (Eds.), *The material culture of gender/ the gender of material culture.* Wilmington, DE: Henry Francis du Pont Winterhur Museum.

Papastergiou, M., & Solomonidou, C. (2005). Gender issues in Internet access and favourite Internet activities among Greek high school pupils inside and outside school. *Computers & Education, 44*, 377-393.

Passig, D., & Levin, H. (1999). Gender interest difficulties with multimedia learning interfaces. *Computers in Human Behaviour, 15*, 173-183.

Price, L. (2006). Gender differences and similarities in online course: Challenging stereotypical views of women. *Journal of Computer Assisted Learning, 22*, 349-359.

Ray, C. M., Sormunen, C., & Harris, T. M. (1999). Men's and women's attitudes towards computer technology: A comparison. *Office Systems Research Journal, 17* (1), 1-8.

Sanders, J. (2006). Gender and technology: A research review. In C. Skelton, B. Francis, & L. Smulyan (Eds.), *Handbook of Gender and Education.* London: Sage.

Sax, L. J., Ceja, M., & Teranishi, R. T. (2001). Technological preparedness among entering freshmen: The role of race, class, and gender. *Journal of Educational Computing Research, 24*(4), 363-383.

Schumacher, P., & Morahan-Martin, J. (2001). Gender, Internet and computer attitudes and experiences. *Computers in Human Behaviour, 17*, 95-110.

Shapka, J. D., & Ferrari, M. (2003). Computer-related attitudes and actions of teacher candidates. *Computers in Human Behaviour, 19*, 319-334.

Shashaani, L., & Khalili, A. (2001). Gender and computers: Similarities and differences in Iranian college students' attitudes toward computers. *Computers & Education, 37*, 363-375.

Shaw, G., & Marlow, N. (1999). The role of student learning styles, gender, attitudes and perceptions on information and communication technology assisted learning. *Computers & Education, 33*, 223-234.

Smeets, E. (2005). Does ICT contribute to powerful learning environments in primary education? *Computers & Education, 44*, 343-355.

Solvberg, A. (2002). Gender differences in computer-related control beliefs and home computer use. *Scandinavian Journal of Educational Research, 46*(4), 410-426.

Sussman, N. M., & Tyson, D. H. (2000). Sex and power: Gender differences in computer-mediated interactions. *Computers in Human Behaviour, 16*, 381-394.

Thayer, S. E., & Ray, S. (2006). Online communication preferences across age, gender, and duration of Internet use. *CyberPsychology & Behavior, 9*(4), 432-440.

Todman, J. (2000). Gender differences in computer anxiety among university entrants since 1992. *Computers & Education, 34*, 27-35.

Todman, J., & Day, K. (2006). Computer anxiety: The role of psychological gender. *Computers in Human Behavior, 22*, 856-869.

Tsai, C., Lin, S. S. J., & Tsai, M. (2001). Developing an Internet attitude scale for high school students. *Computers & Education, 37*, 41-51.

Volman, M., Eck, E., Heemskerk, I., & Kuiper, E. (2005). New technologies, new differences. Gender and ethnic differences in pupils' use of ICT in primary and secondary education. *Computers & Education, 45*, 35-55.

Voyles, M., & Williams, A. (2004). Gender differences in attributions and behaviour in a technology classroom. *Journal of Computers in Mathematics and Science Teaching, 23*(3), 233-256.

Waite, S. J., Wheeler, S., & Bromfield, C. (2007). Our flexible friend: The implications of individual differences for information technology teaching. *Computers & Education, 48*, 80-99.

Whitley, B. E., Jr. (1997). Gender differences in computer-related attitudes and behaviors: A metaanalysis. *Computers in Human Behavior, 13*, 1-22.

Wu, D., & Hiltz, S. R. (2004). Predicting learning from asynchronous online discussions. *JALN, 8*(2), 139-152.

Young, B. J. (2000). Gender differences in student attitudes toward computers. *Journal of Research on Computing in Education, 33*(2), 204-216.

Yuen, A. H. K. (2002). Gender differences in teacher computer acceptance. *Journal of Technology and Teacher Education, 10*(3), 365-382.

Zhang, Y. (2005). Age, gender, and Internet attitudes among employees in the business world. *Computers in Human Behaviour, 21*, 1-10.

ADDITIONAL READING

American Association of University Women (2000). *Tech-savvy: Educating girls in the new computer age*. Washington, DC: American Association of University Women Foundation. Retrieved December 1, 2006 from http://www.aauw.org/member_center/publications/TechSavvy/TechSavvy.pdf

Barker, L. J., & Aspray, W. (2006). The state of research on girls and IT. In J. M. Cohoon & W. Aspray (Eds.), *Women and information technology* (pp. 3-54).Cambridge, MA: The MIT Press.

Kay, R. H. (1992). An analysis of methods used to examine gender differences in computer-related behaviour. *Journal of Educational Computing Research*, *8*(3), 323-336.

Kay, R. H. (2006). Addressing gender differences in computer ability, attitudes and use: The laptop effect. *Journal of Educational Computing Research*, *34*(2), 187-211.

Sanders, J. (2006). Gender and technology: A research review. In C. Skelton, B. Francis, & L. Smulyan (Eds.), *Handbook of Gender and Education*. London: Sage.

Whitley, B. E., Jr. (1997). Gender differences in computer-related attitudes and behaviors: A metaanalysis. *Computers in Human Behavior*, *13*, 1-22.

APPENDIX

List of Papers Reviewed for this Chapter

Authors	Location	Val	Rel	Education	n	Context	Constructs
Anderson & Haddad, 2005	US	Yes	Yes	University	109	Online	Att, Abil, SE, Beh, M
Andriason, 2001	Sweden	No	No	Graduate	60	Online	Att, Beh
Atan et. al., 2002	Malaysia	No	No	University	315	Home	Use
Aust et. al., 2005	US	No	Yes	Preservice	265	School	Abil
Barrett & Lilly, 1999	US	No	NA	Graduate	14	Online	Att, Beh
Broos & Roe, 2006	Belgium	Yes	Yes	Grade 9 -12	1145	School	Att, SE
Broos, 2005	Belgium	Yes	Yes	Gen Pop	1058	General	Att, Abil
Brosnan & Lee, 1998	HK	No	No	University	286	School	Att, Abil
Brosnan, 1998	UK	No	No	University	119	School	Att, Beh, Use
Christensen et al., 2005	US	Yes	Yes	Grade 1 - 5	308 to 4632	School	Att
Colley & Comber, 2003	UK	No	Yes	Grade 7 & 11	344 to 575	General	Att, SE, Use
Colley, 2003	UK	No	No	Grade 7 & 11	213 to 243	General	Att
Comber et. al., 1997	UK	No	Yes	Grade 9-12	135-143	General	Att, Abil, SE, Use
Crombie et al., 2002	Canada	No	Yes	Grade 9-13	187	SG	Att, Abil, SE, Beh,
Durndell & Haag, 2002	Romanian	No	Yes	University	150	School	Att, SE, Use
Durndell & Thomson, 1997	UK	No	No	University	165	Home	Use
Durndell et. al., 2000	European	Yes	Yes	University	348	General	SE
Enoch & Soker, 2006	Israel	No	No	University	36430	General	Use
Fan & Li, 2005	Tawain	No	NA	University	940	School	Ability
Fitzpatrick & Hardman, 2000	UK	No	No	Grade 1-5	120	School	Att, Abil, Beh
Garland & Noyes, 2004	UK	No	Yes	University	250	School	Attitude
Goldstein & Puntambekar (2004)	US	No	Yes	Grade 6-8	159	School	Att, Abil, Beh
Graham et. al., 2003	Canada	No	No	Grade 9 -12	2681	School	Use, Beh
Guiller & Durndell, 2006	UK	No	No	University	197	Online	Behaviour
Jackson et. al., 2001	US	No	Yes	University	630	General	Use
Jenson et. al., 2003	Canada	No	No	Grade 6-8	54	SG	Abil, Intervention
Joiner et al., 2005	UK	No	Yes	University	608	Online	Att, Use
Joiner, 1998	UK	No	No	Grade 6-8	32	School	Attitude
Karavidas et. al., 2005	US	No	Yes	Gen Pop	217	General	Abil, Use
Kay, 2006	Canada	Yes	Yes	Preservice	52	School	Intervention
Kimbrough, 1999	US	No	No	University	92	Online	Abil, Use, Beh
King et. al., 2002	Australia	Yes	No	Grade 6-12	314-372	General	Attitude
Lanthier & Windham, 2004	US	No	Yes	University	272	General	Att, Use, Beh
Lee, 2003	HK	No	No	University	436-2281	School	Att, Abil
Leonard et al., 2005	US	No	No	Grade 1-5	73	School	Abil, Use, Beh
Li & Kirkup, 2007	UK & China	No	Yes	University	220	General	Att, Abil, Use
Light et. al., 2000	UK	No	No	Grade 6-8	62	SG	Att, Abil, Beh
Lightfoot, 2006	US	No	No	University	596	Online	Behaviour

continued on following page

Mayer-Smith et al., 2000	Canada	No	No	Grade 9 -12	81	School	Abil, SE, Use
McIlroy et. al., 2001	UK	Yes	Yes	University	193	General	Att
Mercier et al., 2006	US	No	Yes	Grade 6-8	86-102	General	Att, Abil, SE
Miller et. al., 2001	US	No	No	Grade 6-8	568	Home	Att, Abil, Use, Beh
North & Noyes, 2002	UK	No	No	Grade 6-8	104	General	Att
O'Neill & Colley, 2006	UK	No	No	Graduate	136	Online	Beh
Ong & Lai, 2006	Tawain	Yes	Yes	Gen Pop	156	General	Att, SE, M
Ono & Zavodny, 2003	US	No	No	Gen Pop	50000	General	Use
Oosterwegel et. al., 2004	UK	No	No	Grade 6-8	73	General	Att, SE
Ory et al., 1997	US	No	No	University	1118	Online	Att, Abil, Use, Beh
Papastergiou & Solomonidou, 2005	Greece	No	No	Grade 9 -12	340	School	Use
Passig & Levin, 1999	Israel	No	No	Kindergarten	90	School	Abil, Beh
Price, 2006	UK	No	No	University	268	School	Abil
Ray et. al, 1999	US	Yes	Yes	University	62	General	Att, Use
Sax et al., 2001	US	No	No	University	272821	General	Use
Schumacher et al., 2001	US	No	No	University	225	General	Abil, Use
Shapka & Ferrari, 2003	Canada	No	Yes	Preservice	56	School	Att, Abil, Use
Shashani & Khalili, 2001	Iran	No	No	University	375	Family	Att, SE
Shaw & Marlow, 1999	UK	No	No	University	99	General	Att, Beh
Smeets, 2005	Netherlands	No	No	Gen Pop	331	School	Beh
Solvberg, 2002	Norway	No	No	Grade 6-8	152	Home	SE, Use
Sussman & Tyson, 2000	US	No	Yes	Gen Pop	701	Online	Beh
Thayer & Ray, 2006	US	No	Yes	University	174	Online	Attitude
Todman & Day, 2006	UK	Yes	Yes	University	138	General	Attitude
Todman, 2000	UK	No	Yes	University	166-202	General	Attitude
Tsai et. al., 2001	Tawain	Yes	Yes	Grade 9 -12	753	Online	Att, SE
Volman et. al., 2005	Netherlands	No	No	Grade 1 -5	94-119	School	Att, Abil, Use
Voyles & Williams, 2004	US	Yes	No	Grade 7-8	57	School	Abil, SE, Beh
Waite et al., 2007	UK	No	No	Grade 1-5	7	School	Behaviour
Wu & Hiltz, 2004	US	Yes	Yes	University	116	School	Att, Abil
Young, 2003	US	No	No	Grade 7-8	462	General	Att, Abil, SE, Use
Yuen & Ma, 2002	HK	Yes	Yes	Preservice	186	General	Attitude
Zhang, 2005	US	No	Yes	Gen Pop	680	General	Attitude

Chapter III
The Reversal of Technology

Julia Nevárez
Kean University, USA

ABSTRACT

Cities are technological artifacts. Since their massive proliferation during the industrial revolution and their transformation of sites for both physical and virtual connectivity during globalization, cities afford the possibility for propinquity through different interest groups and spaces including the distant-mobile relationships of a society where technology and movement predominates. This chapter will offer an overview of how technology is central to modern development, how technology has been conceptualized, and how virtual development (in terms of both access to the virtual world and the development of the infrastructure to provide this access) is yet another frontier best captured in the notion of technopolis and/or technocity as contextual factors that sustain social technologies. The pervasiveness of technology, the factors that affect the technological experience besides the rhetoric of infallibility and the taken-for-granted delivery of utility and efficiency will also be explored. By looking at the criticisms voiced against urban and virtual development about the loosening of social ties, I argue for a fluid interaction that considers the possibilities for additional and different, if not new social relations, that both physical and virtual interactions afford to urbanites: technosociability. This technosociability should be considered in light of a critical reading of the contextual factors and conditions that support it.

ON TECHNOLOGY AND CITIES

Many concepts have been used to convey the intersection between cities and technology: "technocity" and "technopole" are some of the most distinct. Even though "city" and "technology" should not be used interchangeably, cities can be considered technological machines.

Technology—extensions, forms of life, tools, or affordances—mediates our relationships with our surroundings, and the social relations supported by it. Since most of the human population lives in cities, the juncture between cities and technology as it has developed through industrialization and globalization deserves a closer analysis. The relationship between cities and technology is complex and one that needs to be unpacked from different angles. Accordingly, definitions and approaches to technology need to be addressed in debates about technology and society. The context in which technologies and cities emerged (industrialization and globalization, modernity and postmodernity, respectively) serves to indicate the historical connection between these two moments in urban development including the notion of the technocity. The way virtual development is received resembles antagonistic views also voiced against urban living. The argument about the loosening of social ties during industrialization and the death of distance during globalization will help explore the kinds of sociabilities technology affords and future trends. Other aspects about technology not usually addressed, such as the rhetoric of technology and the instances in which it fails to deliver what it promises, are important considerations for a fuller understanding of technological discourses in their contemporary context.

The plausible division between technology and the social could be considered to be false since, as I argue throughout this chapter, modern cities, technology, and the social are embedded in a web of relations that is fluid. In a somewhat similar vein, Rothenberg asserts that technology "shape our relations to the world that surround us, modifying it into something that can be used and manipulated to submit to our needs and desires" (1993, p. xii). Since the birth of the industrial city, technology has been the driving force of modern development. More recently, the categories used to provide an understanding of the cultural aspects of globalization are still being debated. From postmodernity to a second modernity, the culture of globalization is for many an intensification of modernity's foundations and the next major economic and social shift after industrialization (Best & Kellners, 2001). From industrialization to globalization, the underlying principles that guide urban development have been anchored in a strong technological base. This chapter describes the foundations of urban development and technol-

ogy to better understand some of the social issues they generate. Broader issues regarding cities and technology serve to better frame our expectations of and disappointments with technology as well as to better articulate concerns. Technology has been addressed positively, to account for what it promises, but rarely has it been addressed to account for what it fails to provide. Critical approaches to technology emerged during the civil rights and other social movements of the 1960s and early 1970s. Different from the zero-sum game and cornucopia paradigms on technological growth, Best and Kellners (2001) argue instead for a "discourse of limits" in which technology is paired with social evolution and where scientific development, human beings, natural surroundings, and life context can coexist harmoniously.

Debates about technology, however, usually fall within the restrictive rhetoric of the modern impulse for progress and development. Many consider science and technology interchangeable, one incomplete without the other, and have coined the term technoscience to refer to this intersection. Modernity, concerned as it has been, with systems of order and control over the human world through technology came to be considered a problem solver. There lies the implicit construction of a concern, problem, or issue to be tackled. An ideological reading of control and efficiency presupposes a chaotic and out-of-control world. Framed by notions of hierarchy, standardization, centralization, expertise bureaucracy, and management, modernity offered a dominant ideology regarding how a modern and developed society should function. Rationality, order, and control as the bases of the modern ideology function to monitor, count, assess, and manage (Scott, 1998, pp. 81-82, in Bergerson, 2006, pp. 45). Likewise, logic, order, rule, and objective reasoning are part of the ideological foundations of the modern project (Coyne & Wiszniewski, 2000). Specialization, formalization (the use of rules, regulations, and standard operating procedures), and hierarchical authority are for Volti (2001) presupposed in technology. Prevalent assumptions, such as technology, being value free disregard social, cultural, and/or political factors that frame the design, production, and implementation of technologies. Moreover, there is the generalized expectation that technology will fix and solve everything (the technological fix). The determinism and overreliance on technology is ideological in that it is dismissive of the social relations, economics, and political processes that conform the technological experience, use, and production. The modern view of technology as an independent force out of our control carries both, technological contradictions, and unintended consequences. When looked at as a singular and monolithic mechanism, the complexities of technology are ignored. In solving a problem or improving a task, not much regard is placed to the social, political, and other ramifications that such a task could entail. Even the modern aesthetic is translated into slimness, simplicity, and increasingly small size of new tools.

When regarded as a threat to humans, technology is understood as an independent force extricated from humanity, when it could be otherwise considered an extension of the human presence in the world (Rothenberg, 1993). Technology is often thought to be better equipped to exert control over nature. Most criticisms however, do not make a clear distinction between different kinds of technologies, without recognizing the different risks different technologies pose, some may carry a larger risk than others (for instance, a watch vs. nuclear power) (Volti 2001). Even though machines do not have volition, we seem to assume that they do, which not only reveals their power of functionality but how technology changes us as we interact with it, thus, changing the way we experience things. Generally, tools are also developed faster than our capacity to make sense of them. Technology mirrors the complexity of our world. Even though there are different perspectives and understandings about technology, the fact still remains that most dominant criticisms

against technology refer back to the notion of the machine brought about by industrialization.

According to Hornborg (2001), machines hold power over the production of goods, power over other people, and over our minds. Hornborg demonstrates how the material existence of the modern, industrial infrastructure ultimately relies on specific cultural notions about production and exchange, and on the uneven flows of resources masked and reproduced by these same processes. Machines function by the global terms of trade and the "fetishism of the machine" implies that the machine is social and embedded in the "inverse observation, that our modern social system functions like a machine" (Hornborg, 2001, p. 5). It is during industrialization and the urban revolution when the city was expected to function like a machine at all levels: economic, political, social, and cultural. For Marcuse (2004):

Technology, as a mode of production, as the totality of instruments, devices and contrivances which characterize the machine age is thus at the same time a mode of organizing and perpetuating (or changing) social relationships, a manifestation of prevalent thought and behavior patterns, an instrument for control and domination. ...Technics by itself can promote autoritarianism as well as liberty, scarcity as well as abundance, the extension as well as the abolition of toil. (p. 63)

Marcuse (2004) provides a parallel between the new rationality of technoscience and what he calls new standards of individuality. The machine and patterns of mechanical labor socializes individuals to a matter-of-factness characteristic of a technical approach (Marcuse, 2004). The mechanical world offers expedience, convenience, and efficiency and for Marcuse, matter-of-factness "teaches reasonable submissiveness and thus guarantees getting along in the prevailing order" (2004, p. 68). A slightly different approach is offered by Welman et al (Welman, Quan-Haase, Boase, & Chen, 2003), for them networked individualism refers to the increased use of computer-mediated communications to individually design the specific ways in which to participate in networks and approach information. I would argue that an over-emphasis on networked individualism could prevent fuller forms of cooperation.

Winner (1986) conceptualizes technologies as forms of life, as ways of bringing order to our world through the activities in which we engage on an everyday basis. Technology falls within the realm of what could be called promiscuous utility, an over-reliance on the capacity of the machine to be useful. For Volti (2001):

Individual habits, perceptions, concepts of self, ideas of space and time, social relationships, and moral and political boundaries have all been powerfully restructured in the course of modern technological development. (p. 9)

These approaches to technology tend to define technology broadly and to focus on the dangers, keeping quite a fixed level of interpretation between technology and society. The relationship between technology and society seems to be instead rather changing. Technology and society mediate each other by the different political, economic, spatial, and social circumstances and moments, but are in flux nonetheless. From the effective and fast to the slow, ineffective, and sometimes useless applications of different kinds of technologies, there is an interchange among social, cultural, spatial, and technological dynamics. This technosocial flux is often hard to predict and control, despite efforts in the design of technology that imply the contrary. Technology might move ahead, but other aspects in society might lag behind. The ideology of ubiquitous access assumes that technology is everywhere and everyone has access to it. However, differential access in terms of class, ethnicity, and area of development separates those who make fuller use of technological advantages and those who

do not. Moreover, different levels of technological development and different brands of the same product deliver more or less quality according to purchasing power. Volti (2001) acknowledges:

Access to the Internet is not distributed equally. Ninety percent of Internet users reside in the industrialized countries, and more than half of the total live in the United States. ...Substantial disparities also exist within the economically developed world, where access to the Internet reflects existing social and economic divisions. According to the National Telecommunications and Information Adminsitration of the US Department of Commerce, in 1997 only 26.3 percent of households earning less than $35,000 annually had online access. In contrast, households earning more than $75,000 have nearly twice the ratio of online access, 50.3 percent. Racial membership also affected access to the Internet; 21.2 percent of white households had online access, but only 7.7 percent of black and 8.7 percent of Hispanic households did. Level of education also affects Internet availability; generally, the greater a person's education, the greater the likelihood that he or she has Internet access.... In the absence of parallel social changes, the Internet may intensify rather than diminish social inequalities. (p. 213)

Technology according to Coyne and Wiszniewski (2000), especially the Internet, is mostly accessible to a population of highly educated and economically better-off individuals, groups, and nations. This group conforms what Bauwens (2005) refers to as the "mass intellectuality" of the digital era or the distribution of human intelligence through the relations the Internet afford. Generally referred to as the "digital divide," Warschauer (2003) argues that it is a misnomer in that it assumes a condescending stance towards minorities, women, and poor people. Moreover, Warschauer argues that the overemphasis on access to technology implied in the notion of the "digital divide" clouds broader issues that affect social inclusion, therefore ignored (2003).

Notwithstanding, as more cultures become familiar with new technologies, their everyday life most likely will be interpreted by similar beliefs and values. This convergence theory (Volti, 2001) accompanied by the corresponding strong ethics of flexible labor and flexible time that technology facilitates, would affect and influence cultures in similar ways, normalizing practices and discourses. In this context, convergence can be understood as Westernization. As a development issue, then, modernization, industrialization, and the widespread use and increasing access and enhancement of technologies are Western values.

Everyday life is embedded within technology. The use of machines, techniques, and systems engenders patterns of activities and expectations that become habitual and ingrained in our own rhythms and patterns of behaviors. Technology is designed for convenience, ease of handling, and customer comfort to a wide group of customers. Similar assumptions could be attributed to the city.

TECHNOLOGY ON OVERDRIVE: FROM THE INDUSTRIAL CITY TO THE TECHNOCITY

The juncture at which technology and the city meet has a historical trajectory that began with industrialization. The purpose of this section is to trace this route up until the present globalization. The city as a machine gave shape to the industrial era. Factories, the assembly line, the elevator, the train, and other transportation technologies developed cities in an unprecedented manner. Likewise, this development brought many new residents as workers to the city. The city became a "living machine" (Harvey, 1990, p. 31). Rationality shaped the machine, the factory, technology, and the social relations that supported them. Fordism

and the assembly line not only produced goods, but also implemented a logic of anticipating outcomes, of organizing production, and the time allotted for productive and reproductive activities in and outside of work. The labor base required for this economic activity altered the social composition of cities and accentuated the function of the city as places for work and dwelling. Along came other technologies in transportation, such as the net of railroads, electricity, and the elevator, giving city buildings depth and height, allowing the city grow vertically to accommodate both businesses and city dwellers. The industrial revolution meant an intense and massive reordering of urban space. The next major change after following modernism's impulse to re-create itself as something new is now constituted by the advanced technologies of globalization. According to Hardt and Negri (2000),

In the passage to the information economy, the assembly line has been replaced by the network as the organizational model of production, transforming the forms of cooperation and communication within each productive site and among productive sites. (p.295)

Short and Kim (1999) argue that the network of global communications growth could be equated to the impact of previous technologies during industrialization, the building of railways, and during the postwar boom, manufacture of automobiles. The shift from the urban factory during industrialization is now the widespread global factory produced by globalization. According to Harvey (1990):

Technological change, automation, the search for new product lines and market niches, geographical dispersal to zones of easier labour control, mergers, and steps to accelerate the turnover time of their capital surged to the fore of corporate strategies for survival under general conditions of deflation. (p. 45)

Figure 1. Stadfresser/CITY Devourer, No place 2005.Markus Bader & Jan Liesegang with Anne -Claire Deville

The machine of the future, the "City Devourer" turns the uneconomic and obsolete city into an economically oriented city. The robot absorbs existing urban material, dismantles and reorganizes its components, and uses them to construct a "plot" city, modeled exclusively on the needs of the real estate market.

To a large extent, technologies have allowed capitalism to develop flexible accumulation in labor processes, labor markets, products, and patterns of consumption (Harvey, 1990). For Harvey, flexible accumulation,

is characterized by the emergence of entirely new sectors of production, new ways of providing financial services, new markets, and above all, greatly intensified rates of commercial, technological, and organizational innovation. It has entrained rapid shifts in the patterning of uneven development, both between sectors and between geographical regions, giving rise, for example to a vast surge in so-called 'service-sector' employment as well as to entirely new industrial ensembles in hitherto underdeveloped regions. (Harvey, 1990, p.147)

Through globalization, the world has become a single place. The debate has been polarized between "globalization from above" and "globalization from below," the latter especially anchored on a discourse of resistance to the homogenizing tendency of globalization (Bergerson, 2006, p. 145). Coyne and Wiszniewski (2000) point out the intentionality and design of globalization's technological buttressing:

The claims of egalitarian access and the necessity, inevitability and desirability of growth in computer systems conceals other agendas: the growth of big business, globalization, control and the preparation of a yet more compliant consumer culture. (Coyne & Wiszniewski, 2000, p. 2)

For Hornborg (2001), technologies develop, evolve, and interact, further complementing the development of new technologies. Advanced capitalist societies and their urban centers have assumed the role of providing services in the financial, advertising, and legal sectors, among others based on an informational economy sustained by the Internet. According to Sassen (1991), a few cities have become headquarters for transnational corporations and centers that coordinate finance at the global level. These global cities represent one of the most prominent indications of the restructuring that globalization has produced. And it is in the global city where "the production of financial innovations and the making of markets, [*are*] both central to the internationalization and expansion of the finance industry" (Sassen, 1991, p. 5). The information superhighway and wireless technologies have produced the information revolution through which the global city exerts its function as a headquarter center that coordinates global transactions.

Basically, urban sites within globalization are developed resting on the modern dyad of science and technology, to which the most recent advance is the management of information. Globalization has pushed forward a technological revolution based on information technologies in a global economy that tends to homogenize capital, management, labor, technology, information, and markets in real time. Castells and Hall (1994) calls some of this kind of growth the informational city that is an industry that relies in the generation of new knowledge and the access, appropriation, and management of information. The term "technopole" is then the most physical manifestation of efforts to transform cities into planned development to house the informational economy, mostly devoted for research and innovation in high technology (Castells & Hall, 1994). According to Mosco (2000), technopoles are new forms of cultural representation. In the technopole, infrastructure, the economic base, and labor power are all connected through technology (Castells & Hall, 1994; Mosco, 2000). Life in the technopole is mediated by a technology infrastructure. The city's openness to change, where new technologies strive and the limits of technology tested, also offers an infrastructure developed to attract information technology industries. Porter (1998) also articulates the notion of cluster development, and is more specific in indicating the many factors that are synchronized (such as housing, research institutions, retail, and information technology wiring) to attract new businesses and residents. Cities represent the central core for most of the information and communication technologies that generate dispersal because they provide, at different levels, the ability to telecommute. The problem of the "last mile" is, according to Dyson (2003), the challenge for information technologies of "connecting home and families, wherever they happen to be, with the nearest Internet terminal" (p. 136). This is likely the experience of the professional class in the service sector of immaterial labor within the informational economy. This professional class works mostly with the manipulation of information, what Hardt and Negri refer to as "knowledge workers" in the spheres of communication, cooperation, and the production and reproduction of affects and care work (Hardt & Negri, 2000, Slater, 2006). This is the group that tends to inhabit the technopole and other urban centers that control the global economy, such as the global city, that development initiatives target.

An example, among many others, of the technopole as an urban development initiative, is Harlem. There has been cluster development in the form of enterprise zone where one of the main components (in addition to retail, wiring, and real estate) mentioned in the enterprise zone plan is the development of a technology incubator:

Silicon Valley in California, Silicon Alley in the New York City's Lower East Side and Hi-Way 125 in Harlem all share in common development around advanced information technologies. Hi-Way 125 stands for Harlem Internet Way. This is the name for the technology district envisioned by the Empowerment Zone located on 125th Street from Second to 12th Avenues. Also equipped by a 'technology incubator,' Hi-Way 125 in Harlem developed an 8,000 sq. ft. of space to house eight to twelve companies. It is structurally prepared to offer competitive Internet technology, fiber optics, highspeed copper wire, turnkey maximum bandwidth, connectivity, state-of-the-art voice,

video and data transmission, as well as advanced telecommunications and data security. Educational institutions also buttress the technology district. Columbia University and City College of New York are to provide expertise and technology transfer á la Silicon Valley in Hi-Way 125. (Nevárez, 2005, p. 51)

Short and Kim (1999) point to the presence of advanced information technologies as responsible for the "future-oriented information-intensive industries" and as important components in efforts to foster urban economic development:

Intelligent buildings, teleports, fiber optic cables and other leading edge technologies have become part of the emerging infrastructure for the informational city. (Short & Kim, 1999, p. 36)

This has produced flexibility in how regions and cities adapt to "the changing conditions of markets, technology and culture" (Castells & Hall, 1994, p. 480). Moreover, technology itself responds to flexible patterns of technological innovation. Embedded in capitalism is technological dynamism, mainly because of the "coercive laws of competition and the conditions of class struggle endemic to capitalism" (Harvey, 1990, p. 105). Despite the ideology of rationality and control characteristic of modernism and even its postmodern condition, Harvey identifies capitalist modernity with a tendency towards an anarchical flux, change, and uncertainty (1990). Harvey argues that this instability happens simultaneously with the hyperrationalization entrenched within capitalism and ubiquitous technology. This constant flux becomes habitual and considered to be normal (Harvey, 1990, p. 106). Moreover, this technological dichotomy of flux and order also happens not only at the level of production of urban space but also in terms of the social relations supported by it.

TECHNOLOGIES OF MOVEMENT AND URBAN DEVELOPMENT: THE LOOSENING OF SOCIAL TIES

The technological sublime engulfs all areas of human activity. Physical and virtual movement are conditions of our times. Moreover, access to information and wireless technology is offered as an attractive feature of urban development in the form of the technopolis or informational city, discussed in the previous section. This technological ubiquity offers an unprecedented access to mobility, physical and virtual, through communication that has an impact on the ways social relations are maintained and developed. For mostly the professional class of the service sector industry, the urban spaces of connectivity are results of urban and virtual development initiatives produced by and for globalization. Social relations are sustained through the connectivity the technocity provides. The movement from the "village" to the "metropolis" as the movement from urban to virtual space and the use of computer-mediated communications and mobile technologies are changes that have triggered concerns about sociability.

The manner in which the Chicago School of Sociology depicted urban development during industrialization mostly emphasized the negative effect of urbanization: the loosening of social ties. The loosening of social ties argument has parallels to the criticisms of what I like to call "virtual development," the development of physical infrastructure that hosts access to virtual technologies and the relationships they support. During industrialization, the Chicago School of Sociology conceptualized and studied the intense changes taking place then, including massive urbanization. They focused, however, on social problems, urban anomie, and social disorganization triggered by the urban revolution when compared with previous modes of living including the preceding agricultural village life. Wirth (1996) defined urban living as increase

in population size, density, heterogeneity of the ethnicity of city dwellers, and changes in group life. In comparison to prior "village life," urban living posed the challenge of dealing with larger numbers of people in everyday interactions who were not necessarily members of the individual's extended family or blood relatives. The relationships that emerged were largely based on interest groups rather than kinship or family bonds. According to the Chicago School, even though cities could provide anonymity and the expression of individuality and creativity, the urban environment could also trigger alienation and social and psychological disorganization. Urbanism was then looked on,

as a form of social organization – substitution of primary to secondary contact, weakening of bonds of kinship, declining social significance of the family, disappearance of the neighborhood, and the undermining of the traditional basis of social solidarity...and the individual members pursue their own diverging interests in their vocational, educational, religious, recreational, and political life. (Wirth, 1996, p. 196)

Traditional ties of social relations, according to Wirth and the Chicago School, weaken. There is more independence between people and,

a more complicated, fragile, and volatile form of mutual interrelations over many phases of which the individual as such can exert scarcely any control....in the city we can only project the general pattern of group formation and affiliation, and this pattern will display many incongruities and contradictions. (Wirth, 1996, p. 196)

Wirth and many Chicago School urban ecologists considered that the diverse ways urbanites develop personality, status, and career does not provide for consistency and integrity of personality. This obviously involves a specific conception of personality, one that is coherent and integral.

Hence, "Personal disorganization, mental breakdown, suicide, delinquency, crime, corruption, and disorder might be expected under these circumstances to be more prevalent in the urban than in the rural community" (Wirth, 1996, p. 198). However, evidence shows that, at least in NYC, crime rates have dropped dramatically in recent efforts to make the global city safer for the professional class of residents and tourists. This fact is opposed to the social disorganization argument made by the Chicago School of Sociology.

Evidently, scholars who followed the Chicago School tradition in urban sociology did not consider alternative ways people band together to maintain and develop social networks, solidarity, and affinities. Many of those social possibilities were provided and afforded through technologies, such as the telephone, that allow overcoming distances and maintain contact between family members and friends. The emphasis of their analysis (understandably, as it was based on a comparison to preceding forms of group organization in villages) was based on the kinds of traditional relations rural areas provided, not on the possibilities of urban life and the social support communication technologies afforded. Increased movement through transportation and the spatial dispersion of the metropolis challenged traditional ways to form and maintain social ties.

An increasingly dramatic development of communication and transportation since World War II has helped to connect groups, people, organizations, institutions, and regions in new ways (Lechner & Boli, 2004). Moreover, globalization is anchored on the ease with which people can travel to distant places, satellites that present world events to a global audience, and the Internet's ability to bring different interest groups together. This is a slightly different view from the one offered by the Chicago School if we compare the social connectivity (that even if virtual) the Internet affords when compared to its predecessor, the telephone in urban living. If connectivity and innovative ways of establishing social ties are accentuated

rather than the loosening of social ties and social disorganization, a different analysis of urban living is possible. Light (1999) recognizes but does not express disapproval of the disparity between the rhetoric of virtual communities, virtual public life, and the role of new technologies in people's everyday life, for its possible "inauthenticity and dislocation" (p.127). Light makes two important distinctions in a general critique of urban and virtual space (1999). First, the complexity of cities and of cyberspace is undermined with general assumptions that oversimplify what constitutes a city and cyberspace. Second, Light states that uses and perceptions of this new virtual technology change constantly, just like the perception of new technologies such as electricity, telephones, radio, and photography did at their pivotal historical moments (1999).

The development of new communication technologies and the mobility they afford fashioned the almost celebratory "death of distance" argument. The opportunity to overcome distances that new transportation and virtual technologies afford erroneously assumes that the physical is obsolete. The "death of distance" argument, according to Mosco (2000), looks at geography from a physical perspective only. The role meaning plays in our relationship to place does not rely merely on its physical attributes. Harvey (1990) delineates in his analysis a more fragmented landscape produced by transportation and communication technologies in which interactions happen in a highly differentiated way within the postindustrial information-based economies. Assumingly, our relations to place in his structural analysis, one could argue, also produce differentiated social relations and cultural meanings.

It is certainly true that rootlessness is another way of conceptualizing the impact of transportation and communication technologies in the highly mobile context of contemporary societies. The "non-place," devoid of cultural markers distinct from the corporate global culture, could also be considered unenthusiastic. The phenomenology of cyberspace is an outcome of the global expansion of urban landscapes. Opposite to the previous disapproving arguments towards a sense of place and urban development, a different tone and perspective is apparent in the notion of "portable roots" that refers to the "freedom from place but an embrace of commitment" towards social relations with others, usually displayed in virtual environments (Kreiling & Sims in Fernback, 2007). For Beamish (2004):

Urban sprawl, motorisation and the decline of informal and public spaces in U.S. cities have directly forced people to search for these opportunities in online worlds. Online participation allows for a more direct shape of the environment (even if virtual) than the less opportunities to shape the physical environments of the cities they inhabit.

Moreover, Beamish argues that online constructed virtual worlds, cities, and communities afford people "new opportunities for sociability, creativity, and identity play" (2004, p. 273). The physical and virtual nomadism of urban life that could trigger the loosening of social ties could be related to the argument Volti (2001) made about the tendency towards privatization, the opportunity of retreat to the private, safe, rooted, stable, and secure realm of the home. Privacy can trigger loneliness, but instead of the pejorative way of judging communication technologies replacing traditional face-to-face interactions, he argues that these technologies provide other ways of connecting, with the potential of somehow dissipating the possible loneliness of the private. A new reconceptualization about loneliness, privacy, and uprootedness needs to be developed to accommodate the intervention of the virtual world in the privacy of the home. Likewise, wireless communication technologies afford the movement of the home to the street in terms of connectivity and sociability (Paulos & Jenkins, 2005). Varnelis (2006) argues that the contemporary city, what he calls the network city, sustains both virtual and physical networked publics. The built environment (streets, buildings, plazas, parks, etc.) is combined with the virtual (Web, e-mail, instant messaging, cell phones, wireless messaging, etc). Networked cities is the configuration of advanced capitalist societies and urban centers in developing countries.

Issues about communication and intimacy, real and virtual, dispersion and concentration point at the immediacy of issues and concerns that new technologies introduce. Moreover, they also point at the intersection of changing values in the ways of communicating, establishing, and maintaining relationships. For Varnelis, face-to-face interaction accompanied by the decentralization of the networked world (community with or without propinquity) will lead to a more intimate existence (2006). Only if it all worked at the same pace, and smoothly, would such desire for intimacy be accomplished, because technologies also fail to deliver what they promise. Fernack (2007) suggests that "community is an evolving concept, and that commitment is the truly desired social ideal in social interaction, whether online or off-line" (p. 49). Fernack's notion of community derives from one that "emphasizes the geographic space to a feeling or sense of collectivity" (p. 51) and describes Internet participation in groups as a new associational activity.

The idea of the city that supports a combination of physical and virtual systems of communication might not be completely new. The city has also offered information through screens or as a concentration of signs that provides a narrative to the actions, behaviors, and events that link the spaces of the city together. Therefore, it is not only in the shape of buildings, streets, and access to wireless technology that urban meaning emerges. DeCerteau developed the notion of the city as a text to be read to help understand the meanings of the urban matrix in the uses we make of it; in the way we inhabit the city (1985). The additional layers of understanding enhance the conceptualization of the city. Varnelis' notion of the network city as superimposed networks of virtual connectivity does offer, however, a more nuanced and complex perspective on the city itself. The many levels where information through networks is exchanged, this layering of networks is the augmented city. Social relations also overlap in the superimposition of the myriad of networks through which information travels.

The analysis of the city in terms of the possibilities for collaboration and solidarity rather than anomie and social disorganization can be evident in, for instance, the aftermath of September 11th in NYC where New Yorkers provided each other emotional support and solidarity (Erikson, 2005). In terms of technology, many systems failed, including the use of cellular phones during that time of crisis. Even though technology and the city offer opportunities to establish new and different forms of sociability, technological failures, the flux of the interactions, the direction of technological development, and the assumptions that guide technological design often pose obstacles and unfulfilled promises.

TECHNOLOGICAL LAG: THE OTHER SIDE OF TECHNOLOGY

Contemporary urban living and advanced technologies are in constant flux. The city seeks to locate itself within a vigorous economy through branding, cluster development, and the promise of ubiquitous access to the virtual world. The rhetoric of infallible and far-reaching technologies is, however, counterposed to the actual delivery of services. Interruptions, disconnections, and crashes, are part of the other side of technology. The reach for faster connections, for instance, leads to the expectation that connections and actual use of communication technologies can always be speeded-up. If that promise remains, this technological socialization stealthily moves and structures the ways we relate in face-to-face interactions. The fact that interruptions and disconnections happen might trigger impatience, or a more relaxed way of letting go when obstacles emerge. The length of communications might decrease due to constant movement; more brief but regular contacts might, at times, substitute for long conversations. Norman (1988) mentions that the frustration with technology, when it fails to deliver, will trigger other ways for technology to become more desirable. This is the "paradoxical hope." As one possible way in which technological change happens, the interruptions, disruptions, frustrations, and mishaps of technology can also rest on the assumption of reliance on the network and its continuity, despite these interruptions. Less effort might be made to reconnect, and there is a surrendering to the temporal impossibility of communication, to be reinstated at some other time in the future. Attitudes about technology then become transitional, both against and for technology. An intrinsic part of everyday life, technologies offer no other option than to rely on them, sooner or later. According to Harvey, technology is based on "disposability, novelty, and the prospects of instant obsolescence" (1991, p. 286). Technological gadgets tend to be designed around trivial aspects of their function (cell phone capabilities) and to be repetitive (different gadgets that can deliver similar service).

Comparatively, computer programming could lead us to believe that our minds function the same way. Many new communication-mediated technologies have been described as socializing users into instant gratification. For young people, technologies, such as cell phones, e-mail, and text messaging, can offer a sense of belonging to a network of peers. Despite the fact that such heavy reliance on technological gadgets, what Bronowski calls the "worship of gadgets" (1956, p. 113), could be seen as developing a community of "connected cocoons." It might offer, however, especially for adolescents, a less lonely search for identity. Accordingly, a lack of emphasis on fixed values that one could argue characterized previous generations, could provide the new ones with openness to new technologies. The sharing of a brand could translate into a sense of belonging, as superficial as that might sound for some people.

The myth that the Internet might cause loneliness is basically sustained by the fact that traditional face-to-face interactions are still privileged forms of social interaction. A study about chat rooms (Cooney, 2006) found that participants who scored as secure adults, in terms of personality, were more patient in waiting for others to arrive at the chat room, and their form of disclosure was reserved and short. In contrast, those who score as less secure were impatient and left the chat room if they did not find anyone there. But they disclosed more information about themselves and made more spelling mistakes when connected. This could be interpreted as the insecure people being lonelier or having fewer "real" friends. But yet another interpretation is possible. New technologies and technology-mediated communications might offer insecure people a vehicle to establish intimacy, while secure people might not choose the Internet as a way of establishing connections and even attachment with others. The secure and insecure traits, however, are not robust across all situations, and they depend on contextual factors as well. The Internet as a medium for social interaction could be considered, along with wireless and other technologically mediated means of communication, techno-affordances. They could provide anonymity similar to what cities provide in their heterogeneity and density. Shifting through different techno-affordances (e-mail, text messaging, cell phones) might help people to adapt to different personality and situational demands. Just holding the cellular phone or checking messages could be seen as a prompt or a way of dealing with social anxiety, showing that the person is in demand and/or popular. According to Wei and Lo (2006) in their study on cell phone use, people who were less socially connected adopted the cell phone late and used it less for social purposes (p. 70). They nevertheless used it as a marker of status, as fashion accessory, or a "second skin" (Katz, 2003; Katz & Askhus, 2002). As Les (2003 cited in Wei & Lo, 2006) states, cellular phones can function, "as a social prop," they can be considered "smart skins" for young people (p. 68).

Face-to-face interaction seems to remain a preferred way of establishing social relations for many, but there can be more variety in the selection of communication modes that technology affords. For instance, face-to-face interaction with friends and communities of interest might be complemented with e-mail and cell phone communication as extensions rather than substitutions (Wellman et al., 2003). Examples of the participation in the social affordances through the Internet are Myspace, Second Life, and other virtual environments. The confrontational aspect of a topic might be better dealt within an e-mail communication than with face-to-face interaction. The delayed response that e-mail provides could be preferred by people at their busiest moment rather than the immediate response a telephone call or in-person conversation might require. Different lifestyles might use these technologies differently to help structure schedules and make communications less intrusive. Moreover, they could also compensate for the limitations of day and night that face-to-face interaction might not easily accommodate. These technologies allow people to be always on the go, to be an urban nomad even if at home but connected to the Internet. There might be resistance against alternative technologies as part of the technological habitus already developed. Communication-mediated technologies are based on information sharing and collective learning (the notion that we all need to know the same in order to use technology). They are flexible in adjusting to time, schedules, and lifestyles, and entrepreneurial in being constantly molded to new and improved uses (even if these are dictated by the designers and manufacturing industries).

Even opting for less advanced technologies or those from a different price range and quality tells a story about the other side of technology that is rarely addressed. Moreover, the pervasiveness of technology in our lives and the kinds and quality of the communications we establish are mediated by context. Coyne et. al (2005) speaks about the design of spaces that help us think while using wireless technologies. Even though one might prefer to be in a library for quiet and calm, at other times work might require a more vivacious environment such as a café, or while on the move, a train or airport might be alternatively designed to provide adequate spaces for work and social exploration. Even though communication technologies are used as if substituting for physical space and allowing us to assume different identities, the fact remains that who we are virtually is still conditioned by the social, mental, and physical environment in which we are located. If an e-mail message is sent from bed, it might reflect a different tone than if it is sent from an office or from a park. Likewise, context could be hidden from a delivered communication.

Accordingly, the urban spaces that offer virtual opportunities are components of the next frontier, what might constitute the future technical and urban world. Predicting how these spaces provide for social interactions, and what kinds, is a challenge many have already considered.

FUTURE TRENDS

The shape and content of techno-social flux in the foreseeable future might depend on interventions here and now. The tendency toward miniaturization of technological devices might find answers in nanotechnology. Likewise, microprocessors, wireless technologies, mobile devices, data fields, and tracking systems are following a similar tendency. Moreover, the narrow scope of technological design might require a transformation to accommodate, as Scholz (2006) suggests, other

social issues and problems largely ignored by technological design, for instance, single motherhood and/or homelessness. Personal computing and the virtual world are being combined into network sociability, locative media, and responsive environments of the technopolis. Physical places and the city have been transformed into networks of objects, people, and spaces. Accordingly, technologies and the actions they trigger have become situated in the environments where they take place.

The changes still in store are contained within the cultural and social practices triggered by successes and failures of technology now. As Hannerz specifies regarding technologies and social change:

To a degree this may entail commoditizing meanings and cultural forms which were previously contained within the free-flow cultural economy of a form of life, but often this is only made possible through their incorporation into new syntheses with technology, organizational forms, and modes of expression drawn from the global flow of culture. (1997, p. 120)

There is an increasing tendency, at least among some researchers dealing with architecture and technology, to re-create situations and experiments that trigger effects different from those produced by the values of efficiency and applicability. Planning that is not guided by efficiency alone or the goal of determining a specific outcome. Even though these efforts sometimes border on the trivial, there is a serious effort to alter the generalized tendency towards efficiency. Moreover, technologies are also developed to directly affect, even if minimally, issues of social inequality. For instance, high brightness portable lights have been made available to indigenous people, which they have woven into their traditional bags (Kennedy, 2006). Scholz (2006) identified other areas ignored by technological development that could address social issues such as providing spaces for a more popular and democratic participation in the design of new technologies, which are usually in the control of corporations and the designers they hire. Likewise, making technology affordable for Third World and less-developed countries might contribute to an even plane of development, providing these new technologies the opportunity to be interpreted and used differently in different contexts (Rosenthal, 2005). Results based on research about the different uses and meanings of technology could be made available to broader audiences.

FUTURE RESEARCH DIRECTIONS

In the context of the city, technological interventions could be made that connect and extend physical and virtual space to be experienced by transitory and mobile subjects such as commuters, corporate nomads, tourists, itinerants, migrants, virtual workers, shoppers, and passersby, to account for both physical and virtual city dwellers. Research in these areas, such as the urban probes effort, might offer the kinds of information necessary to maximize technosociability and environments that provide for work, play, and a variety of social interactions preferred by technocity dwellers. Urban probes combine aspects of the physical environment, urbanism and urbanity, and virtual technology affordances with deep observation, interviewing, identifying patterns across space, and generating meaning(s) of space (Paulos & Jenkins, 2005). They could easily add the extra input of what kinds of communications are exchanged in terms of duration, content according to context, number of exchanges, and other relevant variables that shed light on the nature of social relations in the physical and virtual spaces of the technocity. From the social construction of technology approach, actors and their engagement in networks are the source for interpretations of how technologies are used, experienced, and understood (Kline & Pinch, 1999). This perspective

could help develop technological environments that are conducive to technosociability or different physical and virtual affordances for social interactions. Kline and Pinch (1999) emphasize the interpretive flexibility of an artifact, in which different social groups associate different meanings and uses. This method allows a better understanding of how social groups transform technology and of how the identities of social groups are reconfigured in the process (Kline & Pinch, 1999). Field-testing of new technologies can provide opportunities to imagine technologies and spaces that can support the needs and desires of increasingly varied and different forms of technosociability.

CONCLUSION: TECHNOSOCIABILITY

Mobility and sociability are not warranted through technologies alone, and they are also part of the ideological fabric of societies and its imaginaries, including the shape of space and the spaces of the city. Modern cities offer a fusion of superimposed networks, to which Varnelis (2006) refers as the augmented city, that challenges projections for future urban development. In the combination of virtual and physical city, the proper way of transmitting information to different nodes and the ability to still provide interesting urban centers that encourage Jacobs' (1961) notion of the street ballet and propinquity are important. The challenge is how to design spaces where people, objects, buildings, and information are in flow in an engaging way that eases functionality, facilitate connections, and allows for sociability. Since different technologies afford diverse ways of establishing and maintaining social relations, I argue for technosociability as a way of expressing this intersection of technology and sociability in contemporary societies and to help overcome the judgment that, in a simplistic way, might alternatively demonize or celebrate technology, without a careful examination of the social, political, and economic conditions in which it is used and understood. The critical analysis of how the physical, social, political, and economic aspects are organized in contemporary societies should be an important aspect to include in the analysis of technosociability. Bijker (1995) suggests a series of components to understand technology: identify the relevant social groups who use an artifact; interpretative flexibility that accounts for the different meanings an artifact might have for different groups; and the understanding of the technological frame in which tactical, conceptual, evaluative, and functional aspects of a specific technology are assessed. Assessing the way mediated communications support technosociability in the technopolis can provide a better understanding of the function and importance of establishing and maintaining social relations in the city.

REFERENCES

Bauwens, M. (2005). 1000 days of theory: The political economy of peer production. *CTheory*, td026. Retrieved April 1, 2007 from http://www.ctheory.net/articles.aspdx?id=499

Beamish, A. (2004) The city in cyberspace. In S. Graham (Ed.) *The cybercities reader* (pp. 273-281). NY: Routledge.

Bergerson, S. (2006). *Fragments of development: Nation, gender and the space of modernity.* Ann Arbor, MI: University of Michigan Press.

Best, S., & Kellners, D. (2001). *The postmodern adventure: Science, technology, and cultural studies at the Third Millenium.* NY: The Guilford Press.

Bijker, W. E. (1995). *Of bicycles, bakelites and bulbs: Toward a theory of sociotechnical change.* Cambridge, MA: MIT Press.

Castells, M., & Hall, P. (1994). *Technopoles of the world.* London: Routledge.

Cooney, E. (2006). *Communication in cyberspace: Attachment styles as a mediator of self-disclosure.* Dissertation defense presented at the Department of Developmental Psychology, Graduate Center, City University of New York, Friday, August 18, 2006.

Coyne, R., McMeel, D., & Parker, M. (2005) *Places to think with: Non-place and situated mobile working.* Edinburgh: Working Paper, Architecture ACE, The University of Edinburgh.

Coyne, R., & Wiszniewski, D. (2000). Technical deceits: Critical theory, hermeneutics and the ethics of information technology. *International Journal of Design Sciences and Technology*, 8(1), 9-18.

DeCerteau, M. (1985). Practices of space. In M. Blonsky (Ed.), *On signs* (pp.122-145). Baltimore, MD: The John Hopkins University Press.

Dyson, F. (2003). Technology and social justice. In M. E. Winston & R. O. Edelbach (Eds.), *Society, ethics, and technology* (pp. 126-136). Belmont, CA: Wadsworth Group, Thomson Learning.

Erikson, K. (2005). Epilogue: The geography of disaster. In N. Foner (Ed.), *Wounded city: The social impact of 9/11.* NY: Russell Sage Foundation.

Fernback, J. (2007). Beyond the diluted community concept: A symbolic interactionist perspective on online social relations. *New Media and Society*, 9(1), 49-69.

Hannerz, U. (1997). Scenarios for peripheral cultures. In A. King (Ed.), *Culture, globalization and the world-system: Contemporary conditions for the representations of identity* (pp. 107-128). Minneapolis, MN: University of Minnesota Press.

Hardt, M., & Negri, A. (2000). *Empire.* Cambridge, MA: Harvard University Press.

Harvey, D. (1990). *The condition of postmodernity.* Cambridge, MA: Blackwell.

Hasdell, P. (2002). *Mediated spaces*. Retrieved December 16, 2006, from http://www.arch.kth.se/mediatedspaces/mediatedspaces.pdf

Hornborg, A. (2001). *The power of the machine: Global inequalities of economy, technology, and environment*. New York: Altamira Press.

Jacobs, J. (1961). *The death and life of great American cities*. NY: Vintage Book.

Kennedy, S. (2006). *Small, smart, stealthy*. Paper presented at the Architecture and Situated Technologies Conference, The Urban Center, New York, NY.

Kline, R., & Pinch, T. (1999). The social construction of technology. In D. Mackenzie & J. Wajcman (Eds.), *The social shaping of technology* (pp. 113-115). Buckingham, UK: Open University Press.

Lechner, F. L., & Boli, J. (2004). *The globalization reader* (2nd. ed.). New York: Blackwell.

Light, J. (1999). From city space to cyberspace. In M. Crang, P. Crang, & J. May (Eds.), *Virtual geographies: Bodies, space and relations* (pp. 109-130). New York: Routledge.

Marcuse, H. (2004). Social implications of technology. In D. M. Kaplan (Ed.), *Readings in the philosophy of technology* (pp. 63-87). New York: Rowman & Littlefield Publishers, Inc.

Mosco, V. (2000). Webs of myth and power: Connectivity and the new computer technopolis. In A. Herman & T. Swiss (Eds.), *The world wide web and contemporary cultural theory* (pp. 37-60). New York: Routledge.

Nevárez, J. (2005). *Culture and empire in the global city: Urban development initiaves and the transformation of Harlem*. Retrieved November 13, 2007, from http://orsp.kean.edu/communications/documents/Denis%20Klein

Norman, D. A. (1988). *The design of everyday things*. New York: Basic Books.

Nye, D. (2006). *Technology matters: Questions to live with*. Cambridge, MA: MIT Press.

Paulos, E., & Jenkins, T. (2005). *Urban probes: Encountering our emerging urban atmospheres*. Retrieved December 5, 2006, from http://berkeley.intelresearch.net/Paulos/Pubs/Papers/Urban%Probes%20 (CHI%202005).pdf

Porter, M. (1998). Clusters and the new economics of competition. *Harvard Business Review, 76*(6), 77-91.

Rosenthal, C. (2005). Making science and technology results public: A sociology of demos. In B. Latour & P. Weibel (Eds.), *Making things public: Atmospheres of democracy* (pp. 346-348). Germany: ZKM/Center for Art and Media Karlsruhe & Cambridge, MA: MIT Press.

Rothenberg, D. (1993). *Hand's end: Technology and the limits of nature*. Berkeley, CA: University of California Press.

Sassen, S. (1991). *The global city: New York, London, Tokyo*. Princeton, NJ: Princeton University Press.

Scholz, T. (2006). *Overture, Architecture and Situated Technologies Conference*, The Urban Center, New York, NY.

Short, J. R., & Kim, Y. (1999). *Globalization and city*. Essex, England: Longman.

Slater, H. (2006). Towards agonism – Moishe's postpone's time, labour and social domination. *MuteBeta: Culture and politics after the net*. Retrieved November 16, 2006, from http://metamute.org/en/node/8081/print

Taipale, K. (1998). Technological change and the fate of the public realm. In K. Frampton (Ed.), *Technology, place and architecture* (pp. 194-199). The Jerusalem Seminar in Architecture, NY: Rizzoli International Publications.

Varnelis, K. (2006). *The network city: Emergent urbanism in contemporary life*. Retrieved November 6, 2006, from http://varnelis.net/books/networkcity/proposal

Volti, R. (2001). *Society and technological change*. New York: Worth.

Wei, R., & Lo, V.H. (2006). Staying connected while on the move: Cell phone use and social connectedness. *New Media and Society*, *8*(1), 53-72.

Wellman, B., Quan-Haase, A., Boase, J., & Chen, W. (2003). The social affordances of the Internet for networked individualism. *Journal of Computer Mediated Communication*, *8*(3). Retrieved November 12, 2006, from http://jcmc.indiana.edu/vol8/issue3/wellman.html

Winner, L. (1986). *The whale and the reactor: A search for limits in an age of high technology*. Chicago: University of Chicago Press.

Wirth, L. (1996). Urbanism as a way of life. In R. LeGates & F. Stout (Eds.), *The city reader* (pp. 189-197). London: Routledge.

ADDITIONAL READING

Achterhuis, H. (Ed.) (2001). *American philosophy of technology: The empirical turn*. Bloomington, IN: Indiana University Press.

Aranowitz, S. (Ed.) (1996). *Technoscience and cyberculture*. NY: Routledge.

Atton, C. (2004). *An alternative Internet: Radical media, politics and creativity*. Edinburgh: Edinburgh University Press.

Bijker, W. E. (1992). *Shaping technology/building society: Studies in sociotechnical change*. Cambridge, MA: MIT Press.

Bijker, W. E., Hughes, T., & Pinch, T. (Eds.) (1987). *The social construction of technological systems: New directions in the sociology and history of technology*. Cambridge, MA: MIT Press.

Bronowski, J. (1956). *Science and human values*. New York: Harper & Row.

Brown, B., Green, N., & Harper, R. (Eds.). (2001). *Wireless world: Social and interactive aspects of the mobile age*. Cologne: Springer-Verlag.

Brown, J. S., & Duguid, P. (2002). *The social life of information*. Boston: Harvard Business School Press.

Callon, M., Law, J., & Rip, A. (1996). *Mapping the dynamics of science and technology: Sociology of science in the real world*. Houndsmills, Basingstore, Hampshire: Macmillan.

Chant, C. (1999). *The pre-industrial cities and technology reader*. London: Routledge.

Dodge, M., & Kitchin, R. (2001). *Mapping cyberspace*. London: Routledge.

Dutton, W. H., Kahin, B., O'Callaghan, R., & Wyckoff, A. W. (Eds.). (2005). *Transforming enterprise: The economic and social implications of information technology*. Cambridge, MA: MIT Press.

Feenberg, A. (2002). *Transforming technology*. Oxford: Oxford University Press.

Fiske, A. P. (1993). *Structures of social life*. NY: Free Press.

Fortunati, L. (2002). The mobile phone: Towards new categories of social relations. *Information, Communications and Society*, *5* (4), 513-28.

Frampton, K., Spector, A., & Rosman, L. R. (Eds.). (1998). *Technology, place and architecture*. The Jerusalem Seminar in Architecture. NY: Rizzoli.

Gouchenour, P. H. (2006). Distributed communities and nodal subjects. *New Media and Society*, *8*(1), 33-51.

Graham, S. (Ed.) (2004). *The Cybercities Reader*. London: Routledge.

Graham, S., & Marvin, S. (2001). *Splintering urbanism: Network infrastructures, technological mobilities and the urban condition*. NY: Routledge.

Harding, S. (1998). *Is science multicultural? Postcolonialism, Feminism, and Epistemologies*. Bloomington: Indiana University Press.

Haraway, D. (1991). *Simians, Cyborgs, and Women: The reinvention of nature*. NY: Routledge.

Hayles, N. K. (1984). *How we became posthuman: Virtual bodies, in Cybernetics, Literature, and Informatics*. Chicago: University of Chicago Press.

Heeks, R. (1999). *Reinventing government in the information age: International practice in IT-tenable public sector reform*. NY: Routledge.

Illich, I. (1974). *Energy and equity*. London: Marion Boyars Publishers Inc.

Inglehart, R. (1989). *Culture shift in advanced industrial society*. Princeton, NJ: Princeton University Press.

Jenkins, T. L. (2003). Black Futurists in the information age. In A. H. Teich (Ed.), *Technology and the future*. Belmont, CA: Wadsworth/Thomson.

Katz, J. E. (Ed.). (2003). *Machines that become us: The social context of personal communication technology*. New Brunswick, NJ and London: Transaction Publishers.

Katz, J., & Askhus, M. (Eds.) (2002). The mobile phone: Towards new categories of social relations, Information. *Communication and Society*, *5* (4), 513-28.

Katz, J., & Askhus, M. (Eds.). (2002). *Perpetual contact: Mobile communication, private talk, performance*. Cambridge: Cambridge University Press.

Keeble, L., & Loader, B. (Eds.) (2001). *Community informatics: Shaping computer-mediated social relations*. London: Routledge.

Kellner, D. (Ed.). (1998). *Technology, war and fascism: Collected papers of Herbert Marcuse, Volume 1*. NY: Routledge.

Latour, B. (1993). *We have never been modern*. Cambridge, MA: Harvard University Press.

Latour, B. (1996). *Aramis or the love of technology*. Boston.: Harvard University Press.

Latour, B., & Wiebel, P. (2005). *Making things public: Atmospheres of democracy*. Cambridge, MA: MIT Press.

Law, J. (2002). *Aircraft stories: Decentering the object in technoscience*. Durham, NC: Duke University Press.

Lessing, L. (2004). *Free culture: How big media uses technology and the law to lock down culture and control creativity*. NY: Penguin.

Luke, T. (2004). The co-existence of cyborgs, humachines, and environments in postmodernity: Getting over the end of nature. In S. Graham (Ed.), *Cybercities reader*. London: Routledge.

Mitechell, W. J. (2003). *The cyborg self and the networked city*. Cambridge, MA: MIT Press.

Norman, D. A. (1988). *The design of everyday things*. NY: Basic Books.

Nye, D. (1994). *American technological sublime*. Cambridge, MA: MIT Press.

Nye, D. (1997). *Narratives and spaces: Technology and the construction of American culture*. UK: University of Exeter Press.

Poster, M. (1997). Cyberdemocracy: Internet in the public sphere. In D. Porter (Ed.), *Internet culture*. New York: Routledge.

Roberts, G., K., & Steadman, P. (1999). *American cities and technology: Wilderness to wired city*. London: Routledge.

Robins, K., & Webster, F. (1999). *Times of technoculture*. NY: Worth Publishers.

Ross, A. (1991). *Strange weather: Culture, science, and technology in the age of limits.* New York: Verso Books.

Ross, A. (1998). *Science wars.* Durham, NC: Duke University Press.

Surowiecki, J. (2005). *The wisdom of crowds.* NY: Anchor.

Teich, A. H. (2003). *Technology and the future* (9th ed.). London: Thomson Wadsworth.

Tenner, E. (2003). *Our own devices: The past and future of body technology* . NY: Vintage Books.

Tuomi, I. (2003). *Networks of innovation.* Oxford: Oxford University Press.

Virilio, P. (2000). *The information bomb.* London: Verso.

Warschauer, M. (2003). *Technology and social inclusion: Rethinking the digital divide.* Cambridge: MIT Press.

Wegner, E. (1996). *Communities of practice: Learning meaning and identity.* Cambridge: Cambridge University Press.

Wheeler, J., & Aoyama, Y. (Eds.). (1999). *Fractured geographies: Cities in the telecommunications age.* NY: Routledge.

Section II
Geo–Political Practices

Chapter IV
A Comparative Analysis of Online Peace Movement Organizations

Noriko Hara
Indiana University, USA

Pnina Shachaf
Indiana University, USA

ABSTRACT

The use of the Internet for civic engagement by the general public is becoming increasingly prevalent, yet research in this area is still sparse. More studies are particularly needed in the area of cross-cultural comparisons of online social movements or online peace movement organizations (PMOs). While it is possible that PMOs in diverse cultures differ in their collective action frames, it is unclear whether PMOs use collective action frames and, if so, how differently they are used. This chapter describes a comparative study that examined Web sites of PMOs in Japan and Israel. Collective action frame is used as a theoretical framework to analyze 17 Web sites, identifying the similarities and differences in the ways that online PMOs frame their activities. The findings indicate that these organizations employed various strategies to develop resonance, highlighting the importance of cultural resonance in framing online PMOs in different countries.

INTRODUCTION

The Internet has long been recognized for its ability to reduce initial barriers to transnational collective action, thus making it easier for the general public to participate (e.g., McCaughey &

Ayers, 2003). "Digital communication networks" have expanded mobilization of movements across cultural and national levels (Bennett, 2003). The advancement of information and communication technologies (ICTs) has become an indispensable part of daily life in the United States (Hoffman,

Novak, & Venkatesh, 2004) and other developed countries. The number of Internet users has increased from 30 million in 1995 to 900 million in 2004 (Nardi, Schiano, & Gumbrecht, 2004). In particular, the Internet has contributed to our field of study by facilitating collective action through resource distribution and the organization of forces (Bennett, 2003; McCaughey & Ayers, 2003).

Collective action involves organizing oppressed populations for the purpose of making positive changes in their social situations (Gamson, 1975; Tarrow, 1998). One collective action against the war in Iraq in 2003 was organized through the medium of the Internet. On February 15, 2003, peace demonstrations against the Iraq war were organized throughout the world, involving approximately 10 million people (Boyd, 2003). Apparently, the Internet played a pivotal role in facilitating the mobilization of this massive social action (Lee, 2003; Packer, 2003).

Internet use for civic engagement has been gradually increasing and, although social and political scientists have widely studied social movements for a number of years, the role of technologies to support the activities of these movements has rarely been investigated. Historically, technology has constructively influenced social movements, perhaps most famously in the use of the printing press by European social movements in the late eighteenth century (Tarrow, 1998). With the press, social movement organizers were able to widely distribute their ideas and better coordinate their activities. More recently, telephones, direct mailings, fax machines, and e-mails have commonly been used to disseminate information as well as mobilize critical mass (McCarthy & Zald, 1977; Porta & Diani, 1999). In a similar vein, ICTs have had a major impact on numerous recent social movements. While participation in social movements has traditionally been limited to so-called activists, today general citizens who may not consider themselves activists are participating in online civic engagement (e.g., Looney, 2004). Because of the wide use of the Internet, social movements are finding a way to reach the general public. As a result, it has become important for social movements to strategically frame their actions, in order to appeal to a wider audience.

Studies on the use of the Internet by social movements mostly examine a case or a single country. These studies have focused on feminist activists (Ayers, 2003); democratization activists in Burma (Danitz & Strobel, 1999) and Mexico, that is, the Zapatista Movement (Arquilla & Ronfeldt, 2001); and environmental activists (Galusky, 2003), emphasizing the important role that ICTs play within their movements. In the case of Burma, the ICT influences were indispensable at multiple levels: connecting freedom fighters all over the world, disseminating information quickly and cheaply, and gaining international support to organize boycotts and sanctions. While deep understanding of ICT use in a particular country is important, generalizations of findings from one country to another should be made with caution. Still, not a single study reports a cross-cultural analysis of collective action frame in online activism. Our study addresses this disparity and tries to identify the similarities and differences among countries through a cross-cultural comparative analysis of peace movement organizations' (PMOs) Web sites. This study describes how online PMOs who promote a similar cause, namely peace, in Japan and Israel differ from each other in framing their activities to encourage participation from the general public. Through the analysis of Web sites in these two countries, this study provides insight into how cultural diversity influences the way online PMOs frame their activities. Peace movements were deemed particularly appropriate for this international comparison of social movements as they promote a globally shared cause.

BACKGROUND: COLLECTIVE ACTION FRAME

In this comparative analysis, "collective action frame" is used to understand how the Internet was utilized to support PMOs in framing their activities to promote participation by the general public. Collective action frame is a theoretical framework that explains how social movement organizations facilitate developing collective cognitive frames to justify their activities and encourage wider participation. Collective action frames have been widely used to examine traditional (face-to-face) social movements. Benford and Snow (2000) define collective action frames as "action-oriented sets of beliefs and meanings that inspire and legitimate the activities and campaigns of a social movement organization" (p. 614). Their review of the literature on framing processes and social movements indicates this theoretical framework has been increasingly used over the years in studies of social movements.

Using Oliver and Johnston's (2000) characteristics of frame analysis, we focused on collective frames in this study and on the representations of frames. Oliver and Johnston define frames in terms of how individuals perceive phenomena, that is, as "individual cognitive structures" (p. 41). As such, these frames serve as the building blocks for the other three characteristics of the frame analysis. Though individually developed, frames, when united, have the potential to develop into resonated entities, eventually becoming collective frames. These collective frames become pivotal elements in supporting collective action and can be observed by examining representations of frames. For example, PMOs' Web sites are snapshots of representations of collective action frames. While frames can be analyzed as a snapshot of a stable cognitive framework, some prior studies have examined processes of developing frames (e.g., see the discussion of frame alight process examined by Snow, Rochford, Worden, & Benford, 1986). In this sense, structured frames

and framing processes should be distinguished from each other, the former serving as the primary focus in this study.

Collective action frames do not emerge spontaneously, but rather require processes of integration whereby individual frames of a movement are organized into a coherent and collective frame. Such integration enables collective action. "Frame alignment processes" are explained by Snow et al. (1986) as the processes necessary to link individual interpretation of a movement to the frame provided by social movement organizations. They further elaborate and explain four types of frame alignment processes: frame bridging, frame amplification, frame extension, and frame transformation. Snow et al. (1986) describe frame bridging as making a link between "two or more ideologically congruent but structurally unconnected frames regarding a particular issue or problem" (p. 467) while frame bridging is primarily executed by disseminating information through social networks, mass media, and other means. Frame amplification refers to strengthening a frame that supports a certain issue. Frame extension describes efforts to expand an existing frame to increase the number of supporters and participants. Finally, frame transformation occurs when the original framing is a misfit, which requires social movement organizations to readjust their frames. Snow et al.'s framework for the frame alignment process is useful when analyzing PMO Web sites.

Snow et al. (1986) suggest that one of the four characteristics, frame bridging, is best facilitated through new technologies, allowing social movement organizations to promote their own agendas. Hara and Estrada (2005), like other researchers (e.g., Hoffman et al., 2004; Kahn & Kellner, 2004), have shown how information and communication technologies (ICTs), such as e-mail, Web sites, and blogs, have helped mobilize not only hardcore activists, but socially conscious lay people. In the past, social movement organizations had limited means to promote their activities and ideologies, relying for the most part on the news media. The framing of the social movement organizations' activities by the news media was sometimes inconsistent with their own (see e.g., Gamson, Croteau, Hoynes, & Sasson, 1992). In fact, Almeida and Lichbach (2003) examined the reporting of worldwide protests for the World Trade Organization and found that activists' own Web sites had the most accumulative reporting of the protest events. Even the international news organizations did not extensively report on the protest events. The news organizations tend to cover sensational (e.g., violent and large) protests more than civil and peaceful protest events (Oliver & Maney, 2000). With the use of ICTs, social movement organizations now have a better way to reach the general public, and frame their movements to their advantage.

According to Benford and Snow (2000), collective action frames can best be differentiated from each other by observing how much resonance a movement can produce between a social movement organization and individuals. In their reading of resonance, defined as an act of producing an agreement with a presented frame, Benford and Snow have identified two factors influencing the degree of resonance: "credibility of the proffered frame and its relative salience" (p. 619). Credibility of the frame can be affected by consistency of messages sent by the social movement organization, the reality of the frame (whether it makes sense to the audiences), and persuasiveness of the frame (for example, strong leadership could provide credibility to a movement). Relative salience to the audience can be influenced by the significance of the issues presented by social movement organizations, the relevance of the presented frame, and the extent of cultural resonance produced by the presented frame.

Cultural resonance has the potential to enhance or inhibit the persuasiveness of social movements in general, and PMOs in particular. Cultural resonance is an incidence within which movement organizers develop a frame that is sensitive to cultural components, which, in turn, might influence the mobilization of movements, such as in the case of a student movement in Tiananmen Square of China (Zuo & Benford, 1995). This student movement originally tried to frame the movement to appeal to the Chinese government; it was only after a lack of governmental response that they changed their framing of activities to increase frame alignment with ordinary citizens, using three core Chinese traditions (Confucianism, communism, and nationalism). For example, the movement used a hunger strike as a tactic, which appealed to Chinese citizens because it aligned with the traditional Confucianist tenet of self-sacrifice. Further, Porta and Diani (1999) also emphasize the importance of culture in social movement research when stating, "culture provides the cognitive apparatus which people need to orient themselves in the world" (p. 68). Thus, different framing is necessary for people in different cultures. Though "peace" is often viewed as a universally desirable concept, interpretations of it vary greatly across different cultures. If the Eastern idea of peace connotes harmony, achieved internally as a state of mind, the Western idea of peace centers on victory, usually achieved externally through war (Ishida, 1969). By recognizing the inherent cultural differences in the meaning of peace, PMOs are more likely to produce cultural resonance with their frames; otherwise, they will not receive adequate support from the general public in their own countries. ICTs allow social movement organizations to have the control and legitimacy over content disseminated through the Internet (Garrett, 2006). As country-specific cases were investigated, this chapter presents a cross-cultural analysis of PMOs, illuminating the importance of cultural resonance in collective action frames.

RESEARCH METHODS

In order to ascertain how PMOs in Japan and Israel utilize the Internet for their activities, a comparative content analysis of the PMOs' Web sites has been applied. Content analysis of Web sites is a standard method through which to understand online activities, and other studies of online activisms, such as environmental advocacy (Sehmel, 2004), have used the method. Analysis of traditional social movements' collective action frame is rather difficult as activists do not advertise their framing to the general public, making it necessary for researchers to conduct interviews with these activists to identify and analyze their collective action frame (c.f. Snow, Rochford, Worden, & Benford, 1986). Web sites provide useful representations of frames for researchers when analyzing how PMOs frame their activities.

Data Collection

The study involved a comparative analysis of PMOs' Web sites from two countries that addressed the Middle East conflict in 2004. Japan and Israel were selected because both countries represent rare democracies in their geographical areas respectively; each of these two countries is the only democracy on its continent (Salter, 2003). In addition, because most of the studies on social movements have tended to focus on Western countries (Lee, 2003), analyzing Eastern countries is helpful in gaining a different perspective.

Because we could not find lists of PMO organizations in these two countries, the PMO Web site sample was based on searching Google and country specific Web-directories. We searched both Google.com and Google in each of the two countries: google.co.il for Israel and google.co.jp for Japan, using the term "peace" in Hebrew and Japanese, respectively. In addition, we examined Web directories in the two countries and used a pearl-growing searching technique, which involved following the external links that each of the PMO's Web sites provided. All in all, the sample included 17 Web sites: 6 Israeli Web sites, and 11 Japanese Web sites. A complete list of Web sites is presented in the Appendix.

The inclusion criteria for PMOs in this study were: (1) PMO's Web site's addressing the Middle East conflict (broadly defined); and (2) PMO's Web site's use of country-specific formal language (Hebrew for Israel or Japanese for Japan). Unlike other studies that utilized comparative analysis of Web sites in several countries (Cyr & Trevor-Smith, 2004), we found that a Web site's URL could not serve as an indication of country-specific PMOs. Cyr and Trevor-Smith (2004) analyzed governmental Web sites from Germany, the U.S., and Japan; in their study, these URLs were country specific. This method was not applicable to our study because PMOs are non-governmental grassroots organizations that use URLs that do not necessarily indicate the country of origin. Thus, a Web site's URL could not serve as an indication of country-specific PMOs. Our resolution was to identify country-specific PMOs' Web sites through the use of the formal language of the country. The chosen PMOs have created Web sites in Hebrew for Israel and Japanese for Japan. English Web sites of Israeli or Japanese PMOs were not included in our sample even when, for example, they were using Israeli URLs, and had contact information in Israel.

Data Analysis

Analysis of data began as the data were collected. After comparative content analysis was conducted on one PMO Web site from each country, a coding schema was developed, and then applied to other Web sites. We deployed an open coding approach, while collective action frame was used as a guide to develop the schema. As the coding evolved, additional codes emerged and were later integrated into the coding schema. We followed Westbrook's (1994) suggestion that "whatever theory or working hypothesis eventually develops must grow naturally from the data analysis rather than standing to the side as an a priori statement that the data will find to be accurate or wanting." (p. 245). Thus, the analysis was grounded in the data, and we identified emerging themes salient in collective action frame.

Limitations

The major limitation of this study is its sample size, which only focused on PMO Web sites in two countries, Israel and Japan. Transferability of these findings to other countries in the world must proceed tenuously. Future studies need to expand the sample size.

FINDINGS AND DISCUSSION

The nature and framing of PMOs' activities could appeal to the general public around the globe, at least as the concept of peace is universal. For that reason, the Internet could facilitate globalization of PMOs. The findings of the comparative analysis of PMOs illustrate "glocalization," or the coexistence of globalization and localization (Robertson, 2001) and not globalization alone. This process of glocalization is probably a result of the efforts of the activists to develop and emphasize "cultural resonance" (Benford & Snow, 2000) to fit a local population (of a specific country). The findings illustrate how the process of framing peace to increase cultural resonance changes depending on local cultures, languages, and the sociopolitical context in Japan and Israel. The findings are described along five themes, which emerged from the comparative analysis and the coding scheme: (1) scope of peace, (2) language use, (3) influence of culture and communication patterns, (4) leadership, and (5) online collective action. The first four focus on glocalization and the framing processes that aim to increase cultural resonance, while the fifth emphasizes the collective action frame in this sociopolitical context and describes how the framing of PMOs facilitates the promotion of PMOs' collective action.

Scope of Peace

One of the most prominent aspects of framing peace to increase cultural resonance is accomplished through the PMOs' presentation reflecting the local perspective on peace. On the one hand, the peace scope in Israel focused on the Israeli-Palestinian conflict and involved almost no references to the war in Iraq. This is an extremely domestic approach to peace in the Middle East. In Japan, on the other hand, the scope of peace involved not only domestic peace, but also a concern over the war in Iraq as well as information on the Israeli-Palestinian conflict. On the Japanese Web sites, the common domestic peace interests were a protest against U.S. military bases in Okinawa and the debate over the ninth clause in the Japanese constitution, a section established after World War II that prohibits Japan from using armed force to resolve conflicts. Although many different views exist, so long as the clause is in place, the Japanese government does not operate an official army. However, the Japanese Web sites did not focus solely on their domestic peace issues, but also provided peace information about conflicts in other countries across the globe. One of the most common issues discussed on Japanese Web sites was the Iraq war. The Israeli-Palestinian conflict, viewed primarily as a Middle Eastern concern, appeared to a far lesser extent on these Web sites. The Japanese perspective on peace seemed to reflect a global approach, as compared with the Israeli approach that focused on a solution to a local conflict. In both countries, however, this was an example of glocalizing peace.

To better understand modern peace movements in Japan and Israel, different perspectives on "peace" among various cultures were examined (Ishida, 1969). Israel is influenced by the Judeo-Christian perception of peace (Shalom or Brit-Shalom) while Japan is influenced by Confucian ethics (Heiwa). On the one hand, peace in Israel is conceptualized as negotiations within relationships, which need to be maintained over time. Peace, according to this approach, is achieved externally through war and involves the desire for justice. A militant, violent, and at times illegal attitude of Gush Shalom in Israel was an extreme interpretation of peace under the Judeo-Christian ethics. On the other hand, peace in Japan is conceptualized as a tranquil state of mind, which means harmony and adaptation to social order. This internal concept of peace involves interrelated notions of aesthetics and harmony in which social order and individual emotions are intertwined (based on the tradition of Shinto, where aesthetic factors were dominant). The Confucian influence on the 9Love Web site had a non-conflict and aesthetic, holistic approach. These disparate perceptions of peace greatly influenced the way each country framed its PMOs' activities to gain cultural resonance.

Language Use

The second aspect of framing peace to appeal to local audiences was to use languages. PMOs develop better cultural resonance by customizing the style of verbal messages for the local masses and by using local languages. This framing aspect was evident in two ways: (1) a dominant language used on the majority of a Web site. For example, on most of the Japanese Web sites, Japanese was more dominant than English; (2) a use of at least four different languages (Hebrew, Arabic, English, and Russian) in most of the Israeli Web sites. The use of four languages among Israeli Web sites reflected the diversity of languages used by the linguistically and culturally diverse Israeli population. However, in many of the Israeli Web sites, Hebrew was the most prominent language used. It should be stressed that the dominance of languages we found on the Web sites corresponds with the formal and foreign languages used in the two countries (CIA, 2004). For Japan, the *CIA's World Factbook* lists Japanese as the sole formal

language used in Japan, whereas, for Israel, it lists Hebrew as only one of several official languages. Arabic was listed for Israel as the second formal language because it is officially used by the Arab minority, and English was listed as the most frequently used foreign language. Russian is used extensively in Israel as a result of a mass immigration from Russia to Israel during the last decade.

Moreover, we found additional languages (aside from the formal languages) used on the Web sites in both Japan and Israel. In Japan, only 5 out of the 11 Japanese Web sites involved 1-2 additional languages. For example, the 9Love Web site was in Japanese only. This preponderance of Japanese-only sites was probably because of the Web site's content, as it focused on framing the scope of peace in domestic terms, such as the ninth clause of the Japanese constitution. Another reason for the use of one language (Japanese) on these Web sites was the homogeneous nature of the Japanese population, which overwhelmingly speaks Japanese. This Web site (9Love) exhibited other strong local features, influenced by Confucianism, including an emphasis on aesthetics and on references to other meanings of the number nine in Japanese culture. In the World Peace Now Web site (Japanese Web site), while English words were used on the Japanese pages, a shorter version of the Web site was provided in English. (In fact, the link to the English version was not hosted by the World Peace Now Web site.) The use of English pages probably reflected the site's global perspective frame, which aimed to achieve international visibility. Another Japanese Web site, Peace Boat, provided equal amounts of information in English and Japanese, making it the least localized Web site among the Japanese Web sites. This was in accordance with Peace Boat's conception of peace, which was more global in nature than most of the Japanese peace sites. Finally, the Peace Depot (Japanese) Web site used three languages: English, Japanese, and Korean, which represented the maximum number of languages used on any of the Japanese Web sites. It becomes easier to understand the increased incidence of Korean pages offered when we keep in mind that some members of the advisory board were Koreans.

In Israel, the use of multiple languages on PMOs' Web sites was more prevalent, as these sites use Hebrew, Arabic, English, and Russian. The first three were mentioned in the *CIA World Factbook* (CIA, 2004) as languages used frequently in Israel. Russian was used on these Web sites due to a large Russian immigration group in Israel, whose native language is Russian and who constitute about 25% of the Jewish population in Israel today. Thus, despite the fact that Russian is not an official language in Israel, it is, nonetheless, commonly used there. Furthermore, while Russian immigrants were traditionally considered to be unsupportive of the "left wing" and of the peace movements in the past, peace movements are now eager to attract immigrants of Russian descent. For instance, "Gush Shalom Seeks Dialog with the Russians" framed the campaign to target this particular group (see: http://www.gush-shalom.org/actions/action19-9-2004.html).

The use of four languages on the Israeli peace movements' Web sites was an example of the effort to create cultural resonance. Still, the use of 11 languages on the Neve Shalom (Israeli) Web site (most likely for public relations) provided the most global approach in terms of language use on Web sites in Israel or Japan. The use of multiple languages reflected Neve Shalom's idea of multicultural coexistence, practiced in daily life. Consequently, their use of multiple languages reflected, in contrast to the other peace movements, a desire to achieve global support for their actions and beliefs, rather than merely communicate with large local groups.

PMOs used languages on their Web sites to frame the boundary of their activities and the populations they reach. The use of a specific language that was spoken in only one country limited and defined participation in the organization's activities. For example, to participate in the discussions and activities of the 9Love Web site, the participants needed to understand Japanese. While none of the Israeli Web sites presented information exclusively in Hebrew, most of the Japanese Web sites presented information solely in Japanese.

In summary, local languages were primarily used for cultural resonance purposes and in order to frame group identity through excluding others. The use of multiple languages on PMO Web sites indicated frame extension in both countries to increase supporters. Israeli Web sites used frame extension through multiple language use more often than their Japanese counterparts. At the same time, the collective action frames in both countries did not target everyone who would like to promote peace, but rather only those who were able to understand the language(s). The choice of the languages used by the PMOs on their Web sites enabled or excluded potential global participation. In this respect, we can contend that the Japanese Web sites were the more exclusive, and thus more localized than the Israeli Web sites, although in both countries PMOs' Web sites were localized.

Influence of Culture and Communication Patterns

Another difference in attempts to increase cultural resonance was evident when analyzing culturally defined communication patterns. According to Hall's (1984) dichotomy, if Japan is more representative of what has been termed a "high context culture," Israel stands for a "low context culture." A high context culture focuses on processes, while a low context culture focuses on the results. In a high context culture, the focus is on the group, while in a low context culture, the focus is on the individual. In a high context culture, people communicate indirectly and rely on non-verbal messages. In contrast, in a low context culture, people communicate directly and do not rely heavily on non-verbal messages. If high context cultures conceive of communication as art where knowledge is embedded in the context, in low context cultures, communication is information exchange where knowledge is not context dependant. These differences in communication style between the two countries are evident on the PMOs' Web sites. When PMOs frame and justify their activities, they tend to follow culturally dependent communication styles.

Thus, a third cultural resonance aspect involves the influence of culture on communication and organizational dynamics. This was palpable, for example, in the case of the indirect style of communication (Gudykunst & Ting-Toomey, 1988) of the Japanese Web site, reflecting the Japanese high context culture (Hall, 1984). The Japanese PMOs did not clearly state their mission or goals on their Web sites. They did not directly try to influence the masses by justifying their support of peace actions. These goals and missions of the PMOs appeared to be well understood by the masses in Japan, based on shared understanding that did not need to be verbally communicated. The Japanese Web sites, even when written in English, presented the same indirect style of its high context culture. Unlike the Japanese PMOs, the Israeli PMOs did not assume any shared context. Thus, they clearly stated their mission and goals on their Web sites and made additional efforts to legitimize their actions by using photos of the PMOs' leaders. This direct communication style, reflecting their low context culture, was apparent in all the languages of each Israeli Web site.

Leadership

One of the factors influencing "frame resonance" is the empirical credibility of how a collective action frame is presented to its audiences (Benford & Snow, 2000). This empirical credibility is partially achieved through leadership. For Israeli PMOs, there was always a leader or two who founded the organization and provided empirical cred-

ibility for the collective action frame. To firmly entrench their peace movement, Israeli PMOs used leaders with political or military credentials, which provided credibility for the organization's existence and its activities. All the Israeli PMOs in this study, as evident from their Web sites, were leader-centered. While the Israeli Web sites centralized around their leaders, it appeared that the majority of the Japanese Web sites were "leaderless resistance." The Japanese PMO Web sites we analyzed did not explicitly articulate the identities of their leaders. Garfinkel (2003) noted, "Leaderless Resistance is a technique for fighting an incumbent government using self-organizing clandestine cells." Garfinkel contended that this type of resistance was observed in recent animal rights and environmental movements. Levin (2002) also argued that white supremacist organizations become leaderless resistance, suggesting its increased prevalence as a predominant form of social movements. While the Japanese PMO Web sites' leadership was more structured than this leaderless resistance concept, Japanese PMOs seemed to use a consensus-based leadership style. Based on the Japanese culture, it was speculated that the leaderless nature of Japanese PMOs was a default of collective action, which increases cultural resonance amongst the Japanese population. As a high context culture, Japanese sites tend to value group interests over individual (Hofstede, 1991). Nine of the Japanese peace Web sites did not mention individual names of leaders or organizers. World Peace Now was a rather extreme example of leaderless PMOs. Under "Contact Us," they did not provide physical address, names of activists, or their e-mail addresses, but listed a general e-mail address and phone numbers for participating organizations. The Web sites did not explicitly identify their organizers or the activists involved in their PMOs' activities.

Online Collective Actions

Although the PMOs we analyzed did not exist solely online, their online actions represented the framing of PMOs' activities, which reinforces their support for collective action. While participation in social organization activities has traditionally been off-line, we focused our attention on PMOs' participants' online actions and identified several distinct actions that have been appropriated by the use of the Internet. These online actions ranged in participation level from passive involvement, such as participants browsing through the information available online (e.g., World Peace Now), to more active involvement, such as participants signing a petition (e.g., Hamifkad Haleumi) or participating in online discussion forums (e.g., Gush Shalom). All of the PMOs also enabled interested parties to donate online, and most of them enabled online visitors to become more active members. These online actions were global ways of promoting collective action online; yet, Israeli Web sites provided a wider variety of online actions than did the Japanese Web sites.

This diversity of actions perhaps reflected the larger tendency of Israelis to share their opinions online. In general, Israelis tend to be verbally involved in writing comments in political (and other) discussion forums. This tendency spills over into discussions of any article in the main daily and weekly online newspapers, such as Maariv (http://www.nrg.co.il/) and Yediot Aharonut (http://www.ynet.co.il/). For example, an article on Arafat during the days he was in a coma attracted more than 500 posts from readers on the Maariv online Web site. Similarly, Gush Shalom had a very active discussion forum in Hebrew about the same topic. Although the English and Arabic versions of the Gush Shalom Web site provided the infrastructure for discussion forums, this type of online discussion forum was not used in these other languages. This participation could stem from culturally embedded behaviors. We have not identified a similar level of political involvement from readers of online newspapers in English, Japanese, or Arabic. However, it is worthwhile to note that before the U.S. started the Iraq war, MoveOn.org was involved in the anti Iraq war

movement, in which they used similar strategies, such as online petitions and discussion forums (Hara & Estrada, 2005).

In the analysis of online actions, one should make a distinction between two levels of argument about online actions: the infrastructure for online activity and the actual online actions. At the infrastructure level, it is clear that there was no infrastructure for discussion forums on most of the PMO Web sites in our sample. The only two Web sites that provided this infrastructure were Israeli sites, Neve Shalom and Gush Shalom. Yet, it was only on the Gush Shalom's discussion forum that active discussions were found, mostly in Hebrew (the infrastructure also supports English and Arabic). On the Neve Shalom discussion forum, only a few messages were submitted. The infrastructure was more like a bulletin board than a forum, which did not promote engaging in discussion.

Another unique type of online action with respect to Israeli Web sites was the option to sign a petition. This was probably unique to the particular goals of this PMO and the types of actions they were focusing on; therefore, this type of online action may not be useful for other PMOs.

A third online action available exclusively on one particular Israeli Web site, Neve Shalom, was the option to post a message to a guest book, just like a physical paper guest book for visitors in the actual Neve Shalom village.

Many of the PMOs' Web sites in both countries had information about donations on their first page and an option for subscribing to their e-mail list. Similarly, another online activity across all the Web sites was the reporting of current events planned by the organizations. As mentioned earlier, this was an advantage provided by the Internet to these organizations. PMOs can control the content on their Web sites, frame their own collective action, and reach a wider audience. These Web sites were updated at least once a week and sometimes more frequently. This reflects the nature of the Internet, a medium that requires constant updates; otherwise, users will not be loyal to that particular Web site (Farkas & Farkas, 2002). These Web sites did not appear to substitute for existing off-line peace movements' actions. The online actions took place in addition to the traditional peace movement actions: demonstrations, rallies, talks, and petitions. PMOs' Web sites, like other non-political online activities facilitated through the Internet, enabled additional non-traditional actions, such as geographically dispersed group discussions and information dissemination to larger audiences in shorter periods of time.

CONCLUSIONS AND FUTURE TRENDS

The PMOs' common purposes, which we found and analyzed, include massive mobilization, connecting people, widely disseminating information, and advocating their perspectives through collective action frames. These actions, evident on PMOs' Web sites in these two countries, are similar to other grassroots organizations that use the Internet. For example, it is widely reported that mobilization of protests for the World Trade Organization was facilitated by the Internet (e.g., Almeida & Lichbach, 2003; Vegh, 2003). The Internet helps connect people who have similar mindsets (e.g., Agre, 2002; Danitz & Strobel, 1999; Levin, 2002;) and helps grassroots organizations disseminate information with lower transaction costs (e.g., Bennett, 2003; Martinez-Torres, 2001). Previous research on online social movements has not explicitly addressed the notion of collective action frames in relation to cultural resonance and ignores the significant role culture plays in framing collective action. In this study, we examined how PMOs, as one type of social movement, advocate their perspectives by using collective action frames in two disparate contexts.

Specifically, this chapter described a comparative study that examined PMOs' Web sites in two non-western countries (Japan and Israel). Utilizing a framework of collective action frames to analyze 17 Web sites, the following themes emerged: scope of peace, language use, culture and communication, leadership, and online actions. Our findings show that these Web sites exhibit indicators for strong cultural resonance, or "glocalization," to frame a universal concept, peace, into their own cultural contexts. We also identified various communication patterns on the Web sites as well as online actions that underline the importance of collective action frame in increasing cultural resonance. It was apparent that these PMO Web sites carefully framed their motives and activities to align with cultural values and norms. This study demonstrates how culture influences collective action frames in the context of two countries. Further studies need to increase the number of countries used for analysis. Moreover, this study found that the Internet not only facilitates frame bridging, as others have previously claimed, but also supports frame extension for use of multiple languages on the examined Web sites.

As to whether online activism will continue to be more pervasive, there can be little question, yet the study of online activism is still in its infancy. We hope this study will serve as a starting point for future studies in this area.

FUTURE RESEARCH DIRECTIONS

Although many interesting cases examining the role that ICTs play in mobilizing grassroots activities have emerged in recent years, research in this area appears to be lagging behind, involving only a limited number of case studies, for example, the anti-WTO movement (e.g., Kahn & Kellner, 2004), Zapatista movement (e.g., Arquilla & Ronfeldt, 2001), and Indymedia (e.g., Kidd, 2003). So far, these case studies have focused attention mainly on Internet use without investigating mobile devices and other technologies that, in many cases, are more extensively utilized by social movements, such as the SARS crisis in China in 2003 (Castells, Fernandez-Ardevol, Qiu, & Sey, 2007) and April 10 Mobilization in 2006 by undocumented immigrants in the U.S. These kinds of studies have the potential to enhance the existing theoretical frameworks with novel perspectives.

Additionally, a range of other studies may shed further light on the diverse strategies used by ICT-driven movements, for example, frame alignment processes that these movements undergo. Currently, theoretical frameworks of ICT-driven mobilization are scarce. Some researchers, such as Bimber, Flanagin, and Stohl (2005) and Bennett (2003), attempt to address this research cavity. However, a disconnect between the traditional theories about social movements and the rising ICT-driven social movements is evident. As Garrett (2006) suggests, it would be fruitful to combine multiple methods to understand the ICT-driven phenomena. Once more case studies are available, it may facilitate the development and synthesis of various theoretical frameworks.

REFERENCES

Agre, P. E. (2002). Cyberspace as American culture. *Science as Culture, 11*(2), 171-189.

Almeida, P. D., & Lichbach, M. I. (2003). To the Internet, From the Internet: Comparative media coverage of transnational protests. *Mobilization: An International Journal, 8*(3), 249-272.

Arquilla, J., & Ronfeldt, D. (2001). Emergence and influence of the Zapatista social netwar. In D. Ronfeldt & J. Arquilla (Eds.). *Networks and netwars: The future of terror, crime, and militancy* (pp. 171-199). Santa Monica, CA: RAND.

Ayers, M. D. (2003). Comparing collective identity in online and off-line feminist activists. In M. McCaughey & M. D. Ayers (Eds.), *Cyberactivism: Online activism in theory and practice* (pp.145-164). New York: Routledge.

Benford, R. D., & Snow, D. A. (2000). Framing processes and social movements: An overview and assessment. *Annual Review of Sociology, 26*, 611-639.

Bennett, W. L. (2003). Communicating global activism: Strengths and vulnerabilities of networked politics. *Information, Communication & Society, 6*(2), 143-168.

Boyd, A. (2003). The Web requires the movement. *The Nation.* Retrieved October 31, 2006 from http://www.thenation.com/doc.mhtml?i=20030 804&c=1&s=boyd

Castells, M., Fernandez-Ardevol, M., Qiu, J. L., & Sey, A. (2007). *Mobile communication and society: A global perspective.* Cambridge, MA: MIT Press.

CIA, (2004). *The World FactBook,* Retrieved October 31, 2006 from https://www.cia.gov/cia/publications/factbook/index.html

Cyr, D., & Trevor-Smith, H. (2004). Localization of Web design: An empirical comparison of German, Japanese, and United States Web site characteristics. *Journal of the American Society for Information Science & Technology, 55*(13), 1199-1208.

Danitz, T., & Strobel, W. P. (1999). The Internet's impact on activism: The case of Burma. *Studies in Conflict and Terrorism, 22*, 257-269.

Farkas, D. K., & Farkas, J. B. (2002). *Principles of Web design.* New York, NY: The Allyn & Bacon.

Galusky, W. (2003). Identifying with information: Citizen empowerment, the Internet, and the environmental anti-toxins movement. In M. McCaughey & M. D. Ayers (Eds.), *Cyberactivism: Online activism in theory and practice* (pp. 185-205). New York: Routledge.

Gamson, W. (1975). *The strategy of social protest* (2nd ed.). Belmont, CA: Wadsworth Publishing.

Gamson, W. A., Croteau, D., Hoynes, W., & Sasson, T. (1992). Media images and the social construction of reality. *Annual Reviews of Sociology, 18*, 373-393.

Garrett, R. K. (2006). Protest in an information society: A review of literature on social movements and new ICTs. *Information, Communication & Society. 9*(2), 202-224.

Garfinkel, S. L. (2003). Leaderless resistance today. *First Monday, 8*(3), Retrieved October 31, 2006 from http://www.firstmonday.dk/issues/issue8_3/garfinkel/index.html

Gudykunst, W. B., & Ting-Toomey, S. (1988). *Culture and interpersonal communication.* Newbury Park, CA: Sage.

Hall, E. T. (1984). *The dance of life: The other dimension of time.* Garden City, N.Y., Anchor Press/Doubleday.

Hara, N., & Estrada, Z. (2005). An approach to analyse grassroots mobilization online: A case study. *Journal of Information Science, 31*(6), 503-514.

Hoffman, D. L., Novak, T. P., & Venkatesh, A. (2004). Has the Internet become indispensable? *Communication of the ACM, 47*(7), 37-42.

Hofstede, G. (1991). *Cultures and organizations: Software of the mind.* London: McGraw-Hill U.K.

Ishida, T. (1969). Beyond traditional concepts of peace in different cultures. *Journal of Peace Research, 6*(2), 133-145.

Kahn, R., & Kellner, D. (2004). New media and Internet activism: From the 'Battle of Seattle' to blogging. *New Media and Society, 6*(1), 87-95.

Kidd, D. (2003). Indymedia.org: A new communications commons. In M. McCaughey & M. D. Ayers (Eds.), *Cyberactivism: Online activism in theory and practice.* London. Routledge.

Lee, J. (February 23, 2003). Critical mass: How protesters mobilized so many and so nimbly. *New York Times,* WK 3.

Levin, B. (2002). Cyberhate: A legal and historical analysis of extremists' use of computer networks in America. *American Behavioral Scientists, 45*(6), 958-988.

Looney, S. (2004). Civic participation and the Internet. *LBJ Journal of Public Affairs, 14*, 49-61.

Martinez-Torres, M. E., (2001). Civil society, the Internet, and the Zapatistas. *Peace Review, 13*(3), 347-355.

McCarthy, J. D., & Zald, M. N. (1977). Resource mobilization and social movements: A partial theory. *American Journal of Sociology, 82*(May), 1212–1239.

McCaughey, M., & Ayers, M. D. (Eds.). (2003). *Cyberactivism: Online activism in theory and practice.* New York: Routledge

Nardi, B. A., Schiano, D. J., & Gumbrecht, M. (2004). Blogging as social activity, or would you let 900 million people read your diary? *Proceedings of the 2004 ACM conference on Computer Supported Cooperative Work*, 222-231.

Oliver, P. E., & Johnston, H. (2000). What a good idea! Frames and ideologies in social movement research. Mobilization: An international journal. 5(1), 37-54.

Oliver, P. E., & Maney, G. M. (2000). Political processes and local newspaper coverage of protest events: From selection bias to triadic interactions. *American Journal of Sociology, 106*(2), 463-505.

Packer, G. (March 9, 2003). Smart-mobbing the war. Eli Pariser and other young antiwar organizers are the first to be using wired technologies as weapons. *New York Times Magazine.* Section 6, p. 46.

Porta, D. D. & Diani, M. (1999). *Social movements: An introduction.* Oxford: Blackwell Publishing.

Robertson, R. (2001). *Comments on the "global triad" and "glocalization."* Retrieved October 31, 2006, from http://www2.kokugakuin.ac.jp/ijcc/wp/global/15robertson.html

Salter, L. (2003). Democracy, new social movements, and the Internet: A Habermasian analysis. In M. McCaughey, & M. Ayers (Eds.), *Cyberactivism: Online activism in theory and practice.* New York, NY: Routledge.

Sehmel, H. (2004). How a small environmental group uses the Web to inform and promote action: A content analysis. In A. Scharl (Ed.), *Environmental online communication.* London: Springer.

Snow, D. A., Rochford, B., Worden, S. K., & Benford, R. D. (1986). Frame alignment processes, micromobilization, and movement participation. *American Sociological Review, 51*(4), 464-481.

Tarrow, S. (1998). *Power in movement: Social movements and contentious politics* (2nd ed.). Cambridge: Cambridge University Press.

Vegh, S. (2003). Classifying forms of online activism: The case of cyberprotests against the World Bank. In M. McCaughey & M. D. Ayers (Eds.), *Cyberactivism: Online activism in theory and practice* (pp. 71-95). New York: Routledge.

Westbrook, L. (1994). Qualitative research methods: A review of major stages, data analysis techniques, and quality controls. *Library & Information Science Research, 16*(3), 241-254.

Zuo, J., & Benford, R. D. (1995). Mobilization processes and the 1989 Chinese democracy movement. *The Sociological Quarterly, 36,* 131-156.

ADDITIONAL READING

Bartlett, M. (2002). Paradigms of online peace activism. *Peace Review: A Journal of Social Justice, 14*(1), 121-128.

Benford, R. D., & Snow, D. A. (2000). Framing processes and social movements: An overview and assessment. *Annual Review of Sociology, 26,* 611-639.

Bimber, B., Flanagin, A. J., & Stohl, C. (2005). Reconceptualizing collective action in the contemporary media environment. *Communication Theory, 15*(4), 365-388.

Carty, V., & Onyett, J. (2006). Protest, cyberactivism and new social movements: The reemergence of the peace movement post 9/11. *Social Movement Studies, 5*(3), 229-249.

Castells, M., Fernandez-Ardevol, M., Qiu, J. L., & Sey, A. (2007). *Mobile communication and society: A global perspective.* Cambridge, MA: MIT Press.

Castells, M., Fernandez-Ardevol, M., Qiu, J. L., & Sey, A. (2007). *Mobile communication and society: A global perspective.* Cambridge, MA: MIT Press.

Diani, M. (2000). Social movement networks: Virtual and real. *Information, Communication and Society, 3*(3), 386-401.

Garrett, R. K. (2006). Protest in an information society: A review of literature on social movements and new ICTs. *Information, Communication & Society, 9*(2), 202-224.

Hands, J. (2006). Civil society, cosmopolitics and the net: The legacy of 15 February 2003. *Information, Communication & Society, 9*(2), 225-243.

Hess, D. J. (2005). Technology- and product-oriented movements: Approximating social movement. *Science, Technology & Human Values, 30*, 515-535.

Hunt, S. A., & Benford, R. D. (1994). Identity talk in the peace and justice movement. *Journal of Contemporary Ethnography, 22*(4), 488-517.

Johnston, H., & Klandermans, B. (1995). *Social movements and culture*. Minneapolis, MN: University of Minnesota Press.

McAdam, D., McCarthy, J. D., & Zald, M. N. (1996). Introduction: Opportunities, mobilizing structures, and framing processes—toward a synthetic, comparative perspective on social movements. In McAdam, McCarthy, and Zald (Eds.) *Comparative perspectives on social movements* (1-20). New York: Cambridge University Press.

McCaughey, M., & Ayers, M. D. (Eds.) (2003). *Cyberactivism: Online activism in theory and practice*. New York: Routledge.

Parvez, Z., & Ahmed, P. (2006). Towards building an integrated perspective on e-democracy. *Information, Communication & Society, 9*(5), 612-632.

Porta, D. D., & Diani, M. (1999). *Social movements: An introduction*. Malden, MA: Blackwell.

Postmes, T., & Brunsting, S. (2002). Collective action in the age of the Internet: Mass communication and online mobilization. *Social Science Computer Review, 20*(3), 290-301.

Ronfeldt, D., & Arquilla, J. (Eds.). (2001). *Networks and netwars: The future of terror, crime, and militancy*. Santa Monica, CA: RAND.

van de Donk, W., Loader, B. D., Nihon, P. G., & Rucht, D. (Eds.). (2004). *Cyberprotest: New media, citizens and social movements*. London; New York: Routledge.

Westby, D. L. (2002). Strategic imperative, ideology, and frame. *Mobilization, 7*(3), 287-304.

APPENDIX

Web Sites Analyzed for the Study

Japanese Web sites:

World Peace Now	http://www.worldpeacenow.jp/
Peace Boat	http://www.peaceboat.org/index_j.html
Bridge for peace	http://www.bfpj.net/
Peace Depot	http://www.peacedepot.org/
Japan Palestine Medical Association	http://www1.ttcn.ne.jp/~jpma/
Campaign for Children of Palestine	http://www32.ocn.ne.jp/~ccp/
Shion to no Kakehashi (Bridge to Zion)	http://www.zion-jpn.or.jp
Organization for Peace in Palestine	http://www.palestine-forum.org
Japan-Israel-Palestine Student Conference	http://www.jipsc.org
Women in Black	http://www1.jca.apc.org/fem/wib/index2.html
9Love	http://www.9love.org/

Israeli Web sites:

Gush Shalom (The Peace Bloc)	http://www.gush-shalom.org
Neve Shalom (Oasis for Peace)	http://nswas.com/hebrew/
Hamifkad Haleumi (The People's Voice)	www.mifkad.org.il
Shalom Achshav (Peace Now)	http://www.peacenow.org.il/site/he/homepage.asp
Ken Leheskem -Yozmat Geneva(The Geneva Accord) – PMO but not grassroots	http://www.heskem.org.il/default.asp
Kualitziat Nashim Leshalom (Coalition of Women for Peace)	http://coalitionofwomen.org/home/hebrew

Chapter V
Planning for the Worst, Bringing Out the Best?
Lessons from Y2K

Kevin Quigley
Dalhousie University, Canada

ABSTRACT

Organization theorist Lee Clarke (2005) argues when policy makers plan for disasters, they too often think in terms of past experiences and "probabilities." Rather, policy makers, when planning to protect the infrastructure, should open their minds to worst-case scenarios; catastrophes that are possible but highly unlikely. Underpinned by a precautionary principle, such an approach to the infrastructure would be more likely to produce "out of the box" thinking and in so doing, reduce the impact of disasters that occur more frequently than people think. The purpose of this chapter is to consider the utility of Clarke's worst-case planning by examining Y2K preparations at two US government agencies, the Bureau of Labor Statistics (BLS) and the Federal Aviation Administration (FAA). The data concerning Y2K come mostly from official US government sources, interviews, and media analysis. The chapter concludes that the thoroughness of worst-case planning can bring much needed light to the subtlety of critical complex and interdependent systems. But such an approach can also be narrow in its own way, revealing some of the limitations of such a precautionary approach. It potentially rejects reasonable efforts to moderate risk management responses and ignores the opportunity costs of such exhaustive planning.

INTRODUCTION

Critical Infrastructure Protection (CIP)—activities that enhance the physical *and* cyber-security of key public and private assets—is the focus of urgent attention among Western governments in light of recent power failures, computer viruses, natural disasters, epidemics and terrorist attacks, both threatened and realised (GAO, 2005). Government studies and popular analyses note the complex, interdependent, and fragile make-up of these infrastructures and the technologies that underpin them; one small failure can have a massive and unpredictable cascading effect. Consider the 2003 North American power outage: overgrown trees in Ohio helped trigger a power failure that affected 50 million people and cost the US economy anywhere from $4 billion to $10 billion (US-Canada Power System Outage Task Force, 2004). One critical question for policy makers is how do governments protect these fragile and interdependent critical infrastructures?

Organization theorist Lee Clarke (2005) argues that when policy makers plan for disasters, they too often think in terms of past experiences and "probabilities," that which is calculable. Problems are often structured by existing bureaucratic interests and routines rather than by the problems themselves. To Clarke, the approach is too limiting since it is the unimagined and the events considered "low probability" that often wreak havoc on society. Policy makers, when planning to protect the infrastructure, should therefore open their minds to worst-case scenarios, catastrophes that are possible but highly unlikely. Clarke argues such an approach, ideally underpinned by a **precautionary principle**[1], is more likely to "stretch the imagination," produce "out of the box" thinking, and in so doing, reduce the likelihood of these all-too-frequent catastrophes.

Clarke champions US reaction to **Y2K** (the Year 2000 computer bug), the date-related computer bug that threatened to bring systems down around the world at the turn of the century, as an instance of successful "**worst-case planning**" (Clarke, 2005, p. 73). He recalls the collective response from across all sectors that anticipated numerous scenarios and then guarded against them. To Clarke, this exhaustive effort averted a potential socioeconomic meltdown.

The purpose of this chapter is to consider the utility of Clarke's worst-case planning by examining Y2K preparations at two US government agencies, the Bureau of Labor Statistics (BLS) and the Federal Aviation Administration (FAA). First, the chapter situates Clarke's book in the relevant Organization Studies literature and summarizes Clarke's main argument for worst-case planning. Second, it recalls the Y2K case. Third, the chapter describes the Y2K directives that the Executive Office issued for government departments and agencies, and then employs the Hood, Rothstein, and Baldwin (2001) framework to compare the size, structure, and style of the BLS's and the FAA's approaches to Y2K. The chapter then considers the extent to which Y2K operations embodied the qualities that Clarke predicts for worst-case planning. The chapter concludes by asking, first, did the US government's response to Y2K constitute worst-case planning and, second, is worst-case planning an effective and desirable risk-management strategy? The data concerning Y2K come mostly from official US government sources, 34 in-depth, semistructured interviews, including 15 interview subjects from the specific agency case studies or their parent departments, and an analysis of media coverage from three leading US newspapers.[2]

Worst-case planning helps to bring to light the fragile, complex, and interdependent nature of critical infrastructure. While it can be expansive in one sense, however, worst-case planning can also be very narrow. Endless counterfactuals risk absorbing considerable resources without acknowledging the opportunity costs of such actions. Heady enthusiasm over eliminating all risk scenarios can also marginalize those who offer alternative, more-sceptical views. In such a context, worst-case planning can work against the very goals it seeks to achieve.

BACKGROUND: WORST CASES AND ORGANIZATION STUDIES

In *Worst Cases: Terror and Catastrophe in the Popular Imagination (2005)* Lee Clarke draws from, and contributes to, the debate in Organization Studies that is concerned with safety and reliability of complex technological systems. Broadly speaking, two schools define the field. Whereas **normal accidents theory** holds that accidents are inevitable in organizations that have social and technical interactive complexity and little slack (tight coupling), **high reliability organizations theory** states that hazardous technologies can be safely controlled by complex organizations if the correct design and management techniques are followed. (For a comparative discussion of the two theories, see Sagan, 1993. See Key Terms section for further references.) Clarke tends towards the former. Clarke sees disaster, or at least the potential for disaster, everywhere. He highlights our narrow understanding of complex systems, and laments the hubris that allows us to think we can control them. He challenges our present understanding of the critical infrastructure: a list of critical assets often reads like an engineer's inventory, he notes. It neglects equally important *social* systems, for instance.

Clarke argues that what we consider accidents, disasters—worst cases—are, in fact, quite normal. While he acknowledges that 9/11 has brought considerable attention recently to worst-case scenarios, he draws on examples from across countries, civilizations, and eras to demonstrate that they are more common than we think. Arguably, the only thing that is different in Western nations today is that our expectations for safety and security are higher.

His survey of disasters serves two purposes. First, he uses the illustrations to challenge our understanding of what we somewhat arbitrarily describe as a "worst case." Sometimes a "worst case" can be measured by the number of dead ("body count"); but other times it can be described by reference to one's proximity to the event, the amount of media coverage it receives, the age of the victims, or the manner in which they suffered, for instance. For Clarke, "worst cases" are, in fact, context sensitive; our understanding of a "worst case" is often motivated by our capacity to identify with the victims (Clarke, 2005, p. 19). Clarke also challenges the notion that such worst cases are random occurrences. Rather, they tend to mirror how people organize themselves (Clarke, 2005, p. 129). Typically, though not always, "worst cases" affect the people with the fewest resources and are therefore least able to cope with massive disruption (Clarke, 2005, p. 10). And, of course, what constitutes a worst case for some people creates opportunities for others. After all, careers can be built, or revitalised, on "disasters."

Second, and more critically for our purposes, Clarke argues that thinking carefully about worst cases can lead to greater understanding and control (Clarke, 2005, p. 1). Clarke argues that when policy makers plan for disasters, they too often think in terms of past experiences and probabilities (**probabilism**). This approach leads to collective imagination breakdown. Rather, policy makers should think in terms of that which is possible (**possibilism**).

Clarke offers only two rules with which to regulate possibilism. First, participants cannot "rewrite history." That is, participants cannot create a scenario that starts, "what if the Germans had won the war," for instance. Second, participants must restrict themselves to possibilities that are technically feasible. One cannot include a scenario that involves a "Star Wars" defence system that does not exist. Otherwise, Clarke encourages policy makers to open their minds and plan for all kinds of disasters.

Anticipating countless disasters—worst-case thinking—Clarke notes is a precautionary approach to CIP. For Clarke, a precautionary approach means more than simply a slow and careful plan. He writes, "the precautionary principle is a tool that can sometimes be used to make some of those interests consider worst-case possibilities. It can push policy makers to be explicit about the values they are pursuing, to specify the uncertainties in their decision processes, and to imagine alternatives that they might otherwise ignore" (Clarke, 2005, p. 180).

Specifically, the possibilism and counterfactuals ("what if" scenarios) of worst-case planning offer the promise of four outcomes: creativity, empowerment, effectiveness, and equity. Clarke argues the process empowers individuals to think "outside of the box." It disrupts routine thought patterns, stretches the imagination, and potentially produces creative solutions that reveal the true interdependence of systems and in so doing, allows us to make them more resilient. Moreover, the large scope and concern over protecting all systems rather than those that serve an economic elite make it a more socially just approach (Clarke, 2005, pp. 143-144). For Clarke, the Y2K operations embodied just such a strategy. We will consider the extent to which the FAA and BLS achieved the outcomes Clarke anticipates. First, we will recall the case.

Y2K RECALLED

Y2K, or the "millennium bug," referred to the fact that in computer programmes created in the 1950s and onwards, most year entries had been identified in two-digit shorthand, 1965, for instance, was entered as "65." Initially this shorthand was adopted to save on expensive computer memory. Through time, it simply became a commonly used practice. As the year 2000 approached, however, anxiety grew that systems would be unable to distinguish between twentieth century entries and twenty-first century entries (e.g., Would "01" be treated as "1901" or "2001"?). Such ambiguity, it was feared, would result in systems failing or producing inaccurate information. At the very least, it made information unreliable.

From the early nineteen nineties (when the first popular article about Y2K appeared) to the late nineteen nineties, the date-related computer glitch rose from relative obscurity to regular headline news. Between 1997 and 2000, for instance, three major American newspapers ran collectively over 500 articles on Y2K. In 1997, and prior to any significant government executive intervention in the economy, the tone of the media coverage was overwhelmingly alarming (Quigley, 2005). 1997 estimates of the worldwide cost of fixing Y2K-related problems ranged from $300bn to $1 trillion[3].

The Congress and the General Accounting Office (GAO; now the Government Accountability Office) were particularly aggressive in seeking out information about Y2K. IT consultants and Y2K specialists appeared before congressional committees frequently to testify about the potential consequences of the bug. Between 1996 and 1999, congressional committees and subcommittees held over 100 hearings on the subject and the GAO issued 160 Y2K reports and testimonials. Bruce Hall of Gartner, a leading Y2K/IT consulting firm, testified to a congressional committee: "we must accept that risk exists in *any* technology that was ever programmed by a human, examine such technology for possible failures, and form remediation strategies" (Hall, 1997; original emphasis). Gartner advised "plan not to finish" and advocated "active prioritisation and technology triage." Gartner predicted that 50% of organisations would not finish their Y2K plans. Ann Couffou, Managing Director at Giga Year 2000 Relevance Service, testified to Congress in 1997: "anything with an electronic component should be suspect. The rule should be *guilty until proven innocent*"(Coffou, 1997; original emphasis). She noted the following systems were susceptible to Y2K-related failures[4]: manufacturing control systems; elevators; telephone systems; medical equipment; stock markets; military messaging systems; radioactive material waste systems; fax machines, electronic time clocks; landscaping systems; vending machines; thermostats; and microwave ovens.

Clarke singles out Y2K as an example of successful "worst-case planning." Certainly it was a Herculean effort to manage a multifaceted threat that emerged from the present context: our perceived dependence on, and interdependence between, fragile and complex social and technological systems. After considerable negative and alarming publicity, most organizations, and all sizeable ones, implemented extensive Y2K plans. Planning usually entailed conducting a systems inventory, checking and renovating (or replacing) systems, and then testing them. There was also considerable effort vested in contingency planning and disaster recovery scenarios. Often the process ended with a third-party audit confirming organizations were Y2K compliant.

Budgeting for Y2K was done inconsistently and therefore, the actual cost of Y2K-related remediation remains elusive. Nevertheless, large companies claimed to spend anywhere from millions to tens of millions to hundreds of millions of dollars to manage the risks associated with the bug. The nine Wall Street firms that claimed to spend the most on Y2K, for example, reported that they spent $2.8bn collectively (Smith & Buckman, 1999).

Ultimately, Y2K was a damp squib: contrary to the build-up in the early media coverage, nothing apocalyptic happened. Depending on who one asks, one receives very different explanations as to why this was so. Was the problem oversold? Or was the effort to eradicate the threat so successful? One view suggests that the uncertainty surrounding the problem combined with the sizeable IT budgets and the considerable dependence on technology created incentives for Y2K specialists to oversell the problem. There is certainly

evidence to support such a claim. Y2K budgets were significantly greater in Anglophone countries, such the US, the UK, Canada, Australia, and New Zealand.[5] Many countries started much later and did considerably less than their Anglo-counterparts, yet these supposed "laggards" also experienced no significant systems failures[6]. Manion and Evan (2000) argue that most countries were less dependent on technology than countries like the US. They also argue that many countries made considerable progress in the last 6 months of 1999, learning as they went from the countries that had preceded them. Both points are no doubt true. *Most* countries are not as dependent on IT and *some* countries did make advances in those last 6 months. Nevertheless, if the bug had the bite that government publications, and particularly the earlier publications in 1997/98, proclaimed, one would still expect to see a disproportionately high number of failures in countries that prepared less. Instead, there are very few failures and almost no significant ones.

Nevertheless, there *were* Y2K-related failures, and Y2K specialists are quick to bring this fact to people's attention. Cap Gemini, a leading IT consultancy, in its ongoing survey of information technology executives at 161 companies and government agencies, reported in August 1999 that 75% had reported some Y2K-related failure (Hoffman, 1999). However, only 2% of the companies polled suffered business disruption because of the problem; most worked around the glitches. In the US Senate report, *Y2K Aftermath: Crisis Averted (Final Committee Report,* 2000), the committee appended 13 pages (283 examples) of Y2K-related glitches that actually occurred. The Senate report underscored that the extent of the problem would never be known because only a small fraction of the occurrences would ever be reported. As with most internal problems, organisations were likely to fix them and continue their operations unbeknownst to the general public (US Senate Special Committee on the Year 2000 Technology Problem, 2000, p. 37).

EXECUTIVE INTERVENTION: SIZE, STRUCTURE AND STYLE OF THE FAA AND BLS Y2K OPERATIONS

In January 1998, President Clinton signed Executive Order (EO) 13073, and in so doing, established a high standard by which all departments and agencies would be judged: department and agency heads were responsible to ensure that "no critical Federal program would experience disruption because of the Y2K problem." Prior to EO 13073, many members of Congress had argued that the Executive had been too slow to act. If it were so, EO 13073 represented a seismic shift in government efforts. All departments and agencies were expected to go through the standard five steps, as articulated by the GAO[7]: awareness; assessment; renovation; validation; and implementation. This process also included a mandatory third-party audit and the development of contingency plans. Office of Management and Budget (OMB) monitored departments' progress through their quarterly submissions, which were made public. Moreover, a special appropriation was approved by Congress to provide additional funding for department and agency Y2K operations. The following sections summarise the size, structure, and style of the two agency case studies.

Size

Size can be conceived of in two separate ways: (1) *Aggression*, the extent of risk toleration in standards and behaviour modification, and how far regulators go in collecting information about the risk; and (2) *Investment,* how much goes into the risk regulation regime from all sources (Hood, Rothstein, & Baldwin, 2001, p. 31).

IT staff within the BLS had been aware of the Y2K problem for years, but failed to advance any systematic manner of dealing with it. One director noted that the first time the BLS had to deal with a Y2K problem was in 1985, to fix the Employment Projection System. He recalls

issuing a memo on the potential consequences of the date-related problem in the early nineties, but it seemed to have had little effect. The lack of impact was not lost on Congress. In July 1996, in its first Year 2000 Progress Report Card, the Subcommittee on Government Management, Information and Technology (GMIT) issued an "F" to BLS' parent department, the Department of Labor (DOL), one of only four departments (out of 24) to receive the lowest grade. This grade was largely due to the lack of progress at BLS, an agency almost entirely dependent upon technology to perform its service. Systems had developed over years and at times in an ad hoc manner: there were no reliable inventories of systems; little prioritisation of systems or supply chains; and varying degrees of awareness about date-functionality of systems.

After continued criticism from Congress and the OMB, the Bureau of Labor Statistics slowly started to show progress. Following direct orders from the Department of Labor, in May 1997, BLS appointed a Y2K Project Manager who met monthly with the Department of Labor's CIO (GAO, 1998b, p. 4). Despite these initial steps and the Secretary of Labor declaring in a December 1997 memo that Y2K was a departmental priority, reports from GAO and OMB continued to show slow progress at the DOL and its agencies. By August 1998, for instance, only 11 out of 23 (48%) of the BLS mission-critical systems were considered compliant. (See, for example, OMB, 1997; OMB, 1998a; OMB, 1998b; GAO, 1998b.) Like all other departments, BLS eventually adopted an exhaustive system-by-system check that followed the GAO guidelines. No systems were exempt. In total, the DOL estimated it spent $60.4m on Y2K (OMB, 1999c, p. 53). Approximately 50% of this total was spent in 1999.

The FAA was even slower off the mark than the BLS. In January 1998, in response to a request made by Congress to audit the FAA's Y2K plan, the GAO reported: the FAA had no central Y2K programme management; an incomplete inventory of mission critical systems; no overall strategy for renovating, validating, and implementing mission critical systems; and no milestone dates or schedules (GAO, 1998a). In addition, until the aforementioned had been accomplished, the FAA's cost estimate $246m was unreliable. More importantly, the report concluded that "should the pace at which the FAA addresses its Year 2000 issues not quicken . . . several essential areas – including monitoring and controlling air traffic – could be severely compromised" (GAO, 1998a, p. 15). Following the GAO report and the FAA's appearance before the congressional subcommittee on Government Management, Information, and Technology, the FAA started its Y2K project *de rigueur*. It implemented almost immediately a vast and probing Y2K operation that satisfied GAO requirements. The FAA completed work on 424 mission-critical systems and 204 non-mission critical systems and was declared compliant by June 1999, less than 18 months after the GAO's highly critical report. Financial estimates are rough and broad. The US Department of Transportation, of which the FAA's Y2K costs were a part, spent $345.8 m on Y2K between 1996 and 2000 (OMB, 1999c, p. 51).

In sum, there was considerable uncertainty in both agencies about the scope of the problem. Systems had developed over time, and often in an ad hoc manner; they were not well documented. Y2K efforts in both agencies revealed critical systems, for instance, that the IT units did not even know existed. After slow starts, OMB and GAO prodded both agencies into detailed and exhaustive responses to Y2K, which included the following mandatory steps for all systems: awareness; assessment; renovation; validation; and implementation. The project foregrounded, in particular, the importance of IT, supply chains, and contingency plans to the agency's overall mission. Although a final sum remains elusive, Y2K efforts absorbed millions.

Structure

Structure overlaps with size to some extent. It refers to the way that regulation is organised; what institutional arrangements are adopted; and the way resources invested in regulation are distributed. Structure can be conceived of in at least two separate ways: (1) the extent to which regulation involves a *mix* of internal and external actors, including the use of intermediaries; and (2) how *densely* populated the regulatory space is by separate institutions, and how far the risk involves multiple, overlapping systems of regulation (Hood et al, 2001, p. 31).

The BLS Y2K operation was highly decentralised. The BLS had a Y2K committee but it met infrequently. Most direction was issued by e-mail directly from the DOL and with limited scope for input from the BLS. Therefore, the BLS Y2K staff (one director and one analyst) simply forwarded directions to individual programme areas. When Y2K IT staff received the results from the programme areas, they collated the reports, summarised them, and submitted them to the DOL.

There was considerable redundancy, institutionalised "double-checking," within Y2K projects in the form of audit. The BLS established and operated its own Internal Verification and Validation process (IV and V). In addition to the IV and V, the Department of Labor's Office of the Inspector General (OIG) contracted external auditors to carry out three audits at BLS.

From the time of the GAO report on the FAA, Administrator Garvey established a Y2K office and directed it to provide leadership, guidance and oversight, to FAA's seven Lines of Business (LOBs) and aviation industry partners. In the main, the FAA used contractors to get the work done and auditors to provide assurances. The Department of Transportation conducted its own audit of FAA Y2K readiness.

The FAA started to open itself up. Agency staff held meetings with key players and industry representatives as part of the US government's Y2K working group on transportation. The intention of the meetings was not to dictate plans to industry, but rather to allow people to share information about what their organisations were doing. The FAA also started having more press conferences and inviting its critics to visit the FAA and discuss its plans for compliance.

In sum, what started in both agencies as a largely internal operation transformed into something much more fluid, both horizontally and vertically. Guidelines were generated externally and were issued as top-down commands. The importance of supply chains meant that both agencies had to consult extensively with external parties to ensure their operations would be fully compliant. Moreover, the need to convince others, such as the lead department, OMB, GAO, and Congress, that the agencies were indeed compliant meant that these normally independent agencies had to open themselves up to allow external parties to test and validate the agencies' Y2K operations. Under considerable pressure from external parties, the FAA concentrated its Y2K authority into its Y2K team. The BLS, on the other hand, followed the directives of the DOL, but maintained a highly decentralised approach within the agency.

Style

Style overlaps with the other two descriptions of management. It can be conceived of in two ways: (1) how far regulation is *rule bound or discretionary*; and (2) the degree of *zeal* the actors show in pursuit of policy objectives. With style, culture and attitudes are important (Hood et al, 2001, p. 32).

There was a considerable amount of conflict between BLS staff and staff from outside the agency. The BLS staff noted repeatedly that the systems were too complex for outside auditors to understand and audit in a matter of weeks. On one occasion, the strife between the external auditors and the BLS staff was such that senior staff from the DOL had to come in to mediate the dispute. In another example, one director at the BLS recalled being pressured by the DOL into developing a work schedule that "showed progress." That is, that each quarterly report would show marked progress over the previous quarter. The staff member at DOL suggested that such a report would satisfy Congress's expectations. The director noted that he advanced the anticipated completion date in order to meet the DOL's (and OMB's) request. When the system was not ready in time, the BLS found itself criticised in the quarterly OMB report. Relations between the BLS and the DOL became strained, and eventually the head of the Y2K project at the DOL was replaced.

To a certain extent, the professionalism of the IT staff at the BLS was undermined not only by external auditors and staff at oversight agencies, but even executives within their own agency. The staff felt that their advice frequently fell on deaf ears. One interim strategy IT staff proposed was that they would focus Y2K efforts exclusively on those systems that were required to produce reports in January 2000. All other systems would be considered *non-critical*. (Many BLS reports are issued quarterly or semiannually.) This approach would have allowed BLS staff to delay any Y2K work on *non-critical* systems until after January 1, 2000, and then *only if* the system failed. BLS IT staff felt this was a balanced approach: fix those systems that were required for January 2000 outputs; and "wait and see" with the rest. In September 1998, the DOL informed the BLS it would be judged by the GAO guidelines, which made no such distinction, and therefore it was back to "audit, fix and test everything" by the deadline. In another example, one of the interview subjects for the International Price System noted that the system had been upgraded in 1995 and made Y2K compliant at that time. Despite making this point known within his chain of command, he was still directed to perform the Y2K audits. He estimates that a good part of 1 full year for him and his team was spent exclusively on Y2K, with little ever being found that was not compliant.

The intervention of Congress at the FAA marked a significant shift in style at the agency. Administrator Garvey started having weekly meetings specifically on Y2K with the Executive Committee at the agency. Garvey told the Y2K office that they should report to her directly, and insisted that they name individuals responsible if progress slipped. One interview subject noted it got some people angry and created some friction but the message was clear: people were going to be held to account. The entire approach to the problem changed. One interview subject noted, "it was removed from the realm of the IT geeks and moved to every corner of top management." It was also characterised as a political problem. The Deputy Secretary at the DOT informed his staff that if there were shortcomings it would make the President look bad at the start of an election year in which the "Technology" Vice President would be standing for election.

There was a sense of urgency that empowered area specialists to make decisions. According to every interview subject, money was not an object. The person that coordinated the FAA financial requests simply had to call the OMB and request the money. The FAA was never refused. One middle manager noted how, on one occasion, he signed personally for a $15 m upgrade during the 1998/1999 period, something that would have been unthinkable and organisationally unjustifiable a few months earlier.

When the FAA started to open itself up it was not simply a question of "structure" but also one of "style." The FAA wanted to show Congress, the media, and any other detractors that it was taking their criticisms seriously. Throughout 1999, it ran multiple "end-to-end" tests, "war game scenarios," and on one occasion simulated the "December 31-January 1" date change in real time. The FAA invited the GAO, the Office of the Inspector General (OIG), the FAA's Administra-

tor, and the press to all the events. The FAA also invited its most severe critics to its offices, Y2K management gurus such as Ed Yardeni and Peter De Jager, to explain what the FAA was doing to mitigate the risk. (DeJager eventually agreed to fly on a plane during the changeover, as did Administrator Garvey.) With respect to the aviation industry, one interview subject noted that organizations had been working in silos. By the end of 1998, the FAA was sponsoring industry days and having leading players in the industry present their Y2K plans to others; it helped to foster a cooperative spirit in the industry.

In sum, neither agency at the operational level, initially, took the problem as seriously as the oversight offices eventually did. Many were loath to break from their regular work routines. This resulted in false starts, inconsistent reporting, and delayed progress. As "outsiders" (i.e., OMB, GAO, OIG) began to infringe on their space—prescriptive orders, timelines, templates, audits—IT agency staff became aggravated. Y2K work was often boring, detailed, and tedious, supplemented by (sometimes) weekly detailed reporting requirements. In some cases, staff were confident either there were no Y2K-related problems or they could fix them as part of their normal processes, yet these observations went unheeded, particularly at the BLS. Like it or not, staff were corralled into large Y2K operations where risk *management* meant risk *elimination*. Eventually, the FAA IT staff thrived in such a context; the BLS staff did not.

WORST-CASE PLANNING AT THE FAA AND BLS

Clarke argues that worst-case planning encourages creativity, empowers participants, renders effective solutions, and achieves equity in those solutions.[8] The definition for each of these terms is subject to considerable negotiation. We offer a provisional, context-sensitive understanding of each term, and consider the extent to which worst-case planning at these agencies embedded these qualities.

Where it existed, *Creativity,* unconventional, "out of the box" ideas, tended to include either clever "work-around" solutions (e.g., how operations would recover in the event of failures) or lucid explanations as to why certain systems were *not* vulnerable to Y2K-related failures despite claims that all systems had to be checked. On the balance, however, the executives in neither agency encouraged creativity in operations. In fact, the opposite is true. Straying from GAO guidelines almost inevitably led to negative reports from auditors and unfavourable exposure within Congress. Staff at BLS in particular had alternative solutions dismissed by executives within the agency because of anxieties over relations with DOL, OMB, and Congress.

If we understand *empowerment* to mean giving someone influence and authority, then BLS IT staff lost power over the Y2K issue by early 1998. What seemed like its reluctance to cooperate with central Y2K directives led to power and influence seeping away to external parties. BLS staff note that despite having an excellent track record for maintaining their systems (a point corroborated by many external interviews), their advice was frequently ignored. Conflicts with external auditors sent in by DOL were common place. Ultimately, detailed and regular reporting requirements ensured IT staff never strayed from OMB/GAO central directives. Staff were not empowered; rather, they became at times combative; at times demoralised.

The FAA Y2K office was working under the same guidelines as BLS, yet the FAA IT staff felt empowered by them. The Y2K team had considerable support from an active Administrator who put Y2K at the top of the list of agency priorities. This support empowered the team to employ tactics in achieving Y2K compliance that would, under other circumstances, be considered inappropriate and perhaps career limiting. For instance, the

Y2K staff confronted agency executives at Y2K planning meetings when they failed to meet Y2K deadlines; Y2K staff authorised considerable spending on Y2K projects; they briefed members of Congress and the media. Many from the team describe Y2K as the highlight of their careers.

Ostensibly, both departments were equally *effective.* All systems were identified, fixed, tested, and audited. No systems failed as a result of the Y2K bug. Insofar as this was the goal, both agencies accomplished their missions. From a project management standpoint, however, there is again a distinction between the BLS and the FAA. The BLS started earlier than the FAA but became bogged down with conflicts between themselves and external agents. The FAA, on the other hand, started late but accomplished its mission in a relatively quick 18 months. The profile of Y2K, support from the Administrator, and strong sense of mission within the team had considerable impact at the agency. The Y2K staff worked long hours; they developed stretch targets; they celebrated together when they met them; and they felt a sense of collective defeat when they missed them. Because they were never refused funding, they never got bogged down in tedious budget debates; they got what they wanted, when they wanted it. Indeed, they felt they were doing important work. The BLS staff did not.

If we broaden our understanding of effectiveness to include value for money, however, evaluating Y2K efforts becomes much more problematic. Anything that might moderate the response, cost-benefit analyses, probability risk assessments, and arguably even professional judgement, were rarely incorporated into Y2K projects systematically in either agency. Indeed, the only limitation on efforts was the fixed deadline. As one FAA Y2K team member estimated, only about one in five systems at the FAA required Y2K-related work, but given the climate, it was simply not possible to tell Congress and the media that the FAA would not be looking at four fifths of its systems. Clearly, this approach increased the cost considerably with little or no discernible benefits from a systems standpoint.

Viewed through one lens, the Y2K plan seems to have achieved a sense of *equity*: all systems were checked and, if necessary, fixed, and therefore, all systems were treated equally. If one assumes that different people depend on different services and therefore, would prioritise systems differently, then, indeed, the Y2K plan did not serve some people's interests over others.

Again, however, if we assume a broader understanding of equity that views the Y2K project as only one initiative in agencies with limited resources and numerous competing projects, then the equity achieved within the agencies can be challenged. For over a year, Y2K projects were given a privileged status within government: reporting requirements were exhaustive and inflexible and there were virtually no limits on Y2K funding. The effort absorbed considerable resources and in so doing, neglected other priorities. As one IT manager at BLS noted, the opportunity cost of the project was rarely considered. One BLS executive went further: he felt Y2K diverted so many resources that it should be described a "failure of leadership, a dereliction of duty."

CONCLUSION

To finish, we will recall two central questions established at the outset of the chapter: First, did the US government's response to Y2K, as demonstrated at the BLS and the FAA, constitute worst-case planning? Second, is worst-case planning an effective and desirable risk management strategy?

The answer to the first question is almost certainly yes. The processes that supported the government's Y2K objective of "no disruption to service" were largely the same in both agencies, slow, detailed, and exhaustive. There were also significant overlaps in the form of mandatory third-party audits and contingency plans.

However, the agencies did not adopt, convincingly, the style of behaviour that Clarke attributes to worst-case planning. One agency was led through the process by strong and persuasive leadership, whereas the other was pitch-forked into doing its job, insulted and demoralised. Clarke's anticipated qualities of worst-case planning, creativity, empowerment, effectiveness, and equity, were only achieved occasionally and largely at the FAA. Somewhat ironically, this difference had little impact on either agency's capacity to achieve its goal of becoming fully compliant. Hence, while one might conclude that worse-case planning is possible, one cannot conclude that such planning would necessarily result in the organizational dynamics that Clarke predicts.

The second question is more contentious: is worst-case planning desirable? The absence of any moderating measures risks driving up costs and marginalizing the role of professional judgement. To start, Clarke skirts the issues of cost-benefit analyses and refutes the notion of probability risk assessments, even as heuristic devices. In the case of Y2K, there seemed to be few constraints acting on Y2K project teams other than organizational inertia and the fixed timeline, and therefore, with all the available funding and the pressure to become compliant, it was easier at the operational level simply to check and fix everything. As a result, relatively unimportant systems, as well as those that showed no discernible date-related risk, were subject to expensive, resource-intensive Y2K treatment. There were alternatives. Rather than simply measuring the extent to which systems were going through the standard process, more feedback loops could have helped detect the extent to which problems/failures were actually being identified, for instance. A more proactive effort at prioritisation of systems could also have helped focus efforts and limit resource expenditure.

Clarke also contends that probabilism protects the interests of the powerful. Again, he is not entirely persuasive. One might argue, for instance, that probabilism protects the majority, which is not necessarily impractical in a world of limited resources and unlimited potential for crises. In any event, it is unlikely that a precautionary approach would lead to addressing economic and social injustice. Powerful interests can just as easily manipulate precautionary approaches to ensure existing power structures are perpetuated, if not reinforced. Indeed, while there may have been inertia among many organizations not wanting to act on Y2K-related problems, the Y2K initiative was hardly a challenge to the status quo. In many respects, it was the opposite. EO 13073 directed agencies to ensure there would be no disruption to federal government programs. It also directed government departments to work with industry to help ensure the same standard. Y2K was a threat to "business as usual"; the government worked to ensure stability.

Clarke's precautionary approach is in fact selective in the reality it portrays. While in some ways he encourages policy makers to open their minds in fact, he simultaneously offers a very narrow view of the problem. Cass Sunstein (2005) astutely argues in his criticism of the precautionary principle that if one chooses to invest in mitigating the risks associated with one problem one almost certainly neglects *other* risks. How much spending on Y2K was too much spending? What projects went unfunded or under-resourced because of the insatiable appetite for Y2K work or the unwillingness to live with inconsequential failures? There are no answers to these questions, but that they were hardly considered is disconcerting. Clarke is silent on the drawbacks of such overreactions and the lack of transparency potentially at work in the process he advocates.

These problems do not lead to a complete indictment of worse-case planning. Whereas Sunstein alerts us to the trade-offs inherent within precautionary approaches, Clarke alerts us to the landmine of potential low probability/high consequence disasters that precautionary approaches

alone are likely to detect. As always, the art is in finding the appropriate balance, which is always the subject of power and negotiation.

FUTURE RESEARCH DIRECTIONS

The prevalence of disasters caused by the failures of complex systems keeps the normal accidents/high reliability organizations debate fresh and meaningful. This chapter has attempted to contribute to an aspect of this literature by examining the case of Y2K. Three broad and related sets of questions could benefit from serious scholarly research.

Question One: Learning from Disasters

First, how do we learn from disasters? What institutional arrangements are in place to gather information, set standards, and modify behaviour in light of past failures? Who interprets the failures? Ironically, government Y2K postmortems tend to reinforce starting assumptions rather than question them. After Y2K passed without incident, the UK government concluded, for instance, first, that its reaction to Y2K was an unqualified success, and second, that Y2K brought to light the significant extent to which economies depend on IT (Cm 4703, 2000). Few, if any, Y2K *postmortem* note the variation in dependence on IT across sectors or countries; nor do they note the ability of organisations and people to respond with flexibility and creativity to system failures. Rarely (if ever) does one see a serious investigation of the considerable resources allocated to minimizing the impact of the Y2K bug.

Y2K is one of the only preventative, pan-economic CIP initiatives on record. Many aspects of the initiative were successful. If we are going to learn from events such as Y2K, we have to look seriously at the assumptions that underpinned the planning and think more carefully about the extent to which it was a success and a failure and integrate those lessons into future planning. By this measure, Clarke's book is a valuable contribution.

Question Two: Cooperation

Second, given the perceived interdependence across sectors and political jurisdictions, how do governments and industries work together on these issues? 9/11, the 2003 power failure, and the 2005 tsunami, for instance, had significant global impacts. They necessitated cooperation across borders. While these crises require global collaboration, there are several technical, economic, cultural, and political barriers that prevent cooperation. In times of uncertainty, governments and industry can be reluctant or unable to disclose potentially sensitive information. Moreover, when governments do wish to cooperate, as many have since the advent of the "war on terror," how readily transferable is information? To what extent is information shaped by the institutional arrangements within each country? So, for instance, when the US government, representing a largely pluralist, federalist system, exchanges information with the UK government, representing a largely unitary, corporatist system, are they really exchanging the same types of information? Can these differences lead to incompatibility? How is this addressed? What are the implications?

Question Three: Implications of Differences

Third, if one anticipates different types of failures or one defines the critical infrastructure differently, how does this affect planning for and reaction to failure? What constitutes the *critical* infrastructure may seem universal at first blush, but it is almost certainly context sensitive: it is embedded in a specific geographic, cultural, economic, and political setting. Many countries are more concerned about natural disasters than ter-

rorism, for instance. Does this make a difference in their strategising about CIP? Many developing countries experience systems failures regularly. Does this inform how they prepare for and react to disasters? By the same token, if the levees in New Orleans had been sabotaged by an act of terrorism rather than resulted from a hurricane, would the US government's reaction have been different (better)? Would the American public have been more forgiving? We could benefit from serious scholarly investigation into these matters.

REFERENCES

Blitz, J., Hope, K., & White, D. (1999). Mediterranean trio see millennium bug as problem for manana. *Financial Times,* November 12.

Bowen et al (1999), Low tech culture may prove region's Y2K saviour. *Financial Times,* November 30.

Clarke, L. (2005). *Worst cases: Terror and catastrophe in the popular imagination.* Chicago: University of Chicago Press.

Cm 4703. (2000). *Modernising government in action: Realising the benefits of Y2K.* London: HMSO.

Couffou, A. (1997). Year 2000 risks: What are the consequences of technology failure? Statement of Hearing Testimony before Subcommittee on Technology and Subcommittee on Government Management, Information and Technology. March 20. Washington DC: GPO.

General Accounting Office. (1998a). *FAA computer systems: Limited progress on year 2000 issue increases risk dramatically.* GAO/AIMD-98-45. January 30. Washington, DC.

General Accounting Office. (1998b). *Year 2000 computing crisis: Progress made at labor, but key systems at risk.* GAO/T-AIMD-98-303. September 17. Washington, DC.

Government Accountability Office. (2005). *Critical infrastructure protection: Department of Homeland Security faces challenges in fulfilling cybersecurity responsibilities.* GAO-05-434. May. Washington DC.

Hall, B. (1997). *Testimony to Government Management, Information and Technology Subcommittee.* March 20.

Hoffman, T. (1999). Y2K failures have hit 75% of US firms. *Computerworld,* August 16, 33:33.

Hood, C., Rothstein, H., & Baldwin, R. (2001*). The government of risk: Understanding risk regulation regimes.* Oxford: Oxford University Press.

Jack, A. (1999). Level of Russian IT lessens year 2000 fears: Moscow has been late in putting together some moderate Y2K defences. *Financial Times,* November 26.

Kheifets, L. Hester, G., & Banerjee, G. (2001). The precautionary principle and EMF: Implementation and evaluation. *The Journal of Risk Research, 4*(2),113-125.

La Porte, T. R., & Consolini, P. (1991). Working in practice but not in theory: Theoretical challenges of high reliability organizations. *Journal of Public Administration Research and Theory,* 1, 19-47.

Manion, M., & Evan, W. (2000). The Y2K problem and professional responsibility: A retrospective analysis. *Technology in Society, 22*(3), 361-387.

Office of Management and Budget. (1997). *Progress on Year 2000 conversion.* Washington, DC: GPO. November 15.

Office of Management and Budget. (1998a). *Progress on Year 2000 conversion.* Washington, DC: GPO. May 15.

Office of Management and Budget. (1998b). *Progress on Year 2000 conversion.* Washington, DC: GPO. August 15.

Office of Management and Budget. (1999c). *Progress on year 2000 conversion.* Washington, DC: GPO. December 14.

Perrow, C. (1999). *Normal accidents: Living with high-risk technologies.* Princeton: Princeton University Press.

President's Council on Year 2000 Conversion. (2000). *The journey to Y2K: Final report.* Retrieved October 2004, from http://www.y2k. gov/docs/lastrep3.htm

Quigley, K. F. (2005). Bug reactions: Considering US government and UK government Y2K operations in light of media coverage and public opinion. *Health, Risk & Society,* 7(3), 267-291.

Sagan, S. (1993). *The limits of safety: Organizations, accidents and nuclear weapons.* Princeton: Princeton University Press.

Smith, R., & Buckman, R. (1999). Wall Street deploys troops to battle Y2K: Command centre, jets, extra toilets are at the ready. *Wall Street Journal,* December 22.

Sunstein, C. (2005). *Laws of fear: Beyond the precautionary principle.* Cambridge: Cambridge University Press.

Suzman, M. (1999), World is mostly ready for Y2K. *Financial Times,* December 30.

US-Canada Power System Outage Task Force. (2004). *Final report on the August 14 2003 blackout in the United States and Canada: Causes and recommendations.* Published jointly by the US Government and the Government of Canada. Retrieved October 2005, from http://reports. energy.gov

United States Senate Special Committee on the Year 2000 Technology Problem. (2000). *Y2K aftermath – A crisis averted* (Final Committee Report). Retrieved October 2004, from http:// www.senate.gov

Vaughan, D. (1996). *The Challenger launch decision: Risky technology, culture, and deviance at NASA.* Chicago: University of Chicago Press.

Weik, K., & Roberts, K. (1993). Collective mind in organizations: Heedful interrelating on flight decks. *Administrative Science Quarterly, 38*(3), 357-381.

ADDITIONAL READING

Beck, U. (1992). *Risk society.* London: Sage.

Bellamy, C., & Taylor, J. (1998). *Governing in the Information Age.* Buckingham: Open University Press.

Clarke, L. (2005). *Worst cases: Terror and catastrophe in the popular imagination.* Chicago: University of Chicago Press.

Cm 4703. (2000). *Modernising government in action: Realising the benefits of Y2K.* London: HMSO.

Finkelstein, A. (2000). Y2K: A retrospective view. Retrieved from http://www.cs.ucl.ac.uk/Staff/A.Finkelstein, originally published in *Computing and Control Engineering Journal, 11*(N4), 156-159.

Heeks, R. (1999), *Reinventing government in the Information Age.* London: Routledge.

Hood, C. (1996). Where extremes meet: SPRAT vs. SHARK in public risk management. In C. Hood and D. Jones (Eds), *Accident and design.* London: UCL.

Hood, C., Rothstein, H., & Baldwin, R. (2001). *The government of risk: Understanding risk regulation regimes.* Oxford: Oxford University Press.

House of Commons Library. (1998). *The millennium bug.* Research Paper: 98/72. London.

Jaeger, C., Webler, T., Rosa, E., & Renn, O. (2001). *Risk, uncertainty and rational action.* London: Earthscan.

Kheifets, L. Hester, G., & Banerjee, G. (2001). The Precautionary Principle and EMF: Implementation and evaluation. *The Journal of Risk Research, 4*(2), 113-125.

La Porte, T. R., & Consolini, P. (1991). Working in practice but not in theory: Theoretical challenges of high reliability organizations. *Journal of Public Administration Research and Theory, 1,* 19-47.

Margetts, H. (1999). *Information technology in government: Britain and America.* London: Routledge.

National Institute of Standards and Technology. (2001). *Risk management guide for information technology systems.* Special Publication 800-30. Washington DC: GPO.

Neustadt, R. E., & Fineberg, H. (1983). *The epidemic that never was: Policy-Making and the swine flu scare.* New York: Vintage Books.

Perrow, C. (1999). *Normal accidents: Living with high-risk technologies.* Princeton: Princeton University Press.

Power, M. (2004). *The risk management of everything.* London: Demos.

President's Council on Year 2000 Conversion. (2000). *The journey to Y2K: Final report.* Retrieved October 2004, from http://www.y2k.gov/docs/lastrep3.htm

Quiggin, J. (2005). The Y2K scare: Causes, costs and cures. *Australian Journal of Public Administration, 64*(3), 46-55.

Quigley, K. (2004). The Emperor's new computers: Y2K (re)visited. *Public Administration, 82,* 4.

Quigley, K. F. (2005). Bug reactions: Considering US government and UK government Y2K operations in light of media coverage and public opinion. *Health, Risk & Society, 7*(3), 267-291.

Rochlin, G. (1997). *Trapped inside the net: The unanticipated consequences of computerization.* Princeton: Princeton University Press.

Sagan, S. (1993). *The limits of safety: Organizations, accidents and nuclear weapons.* Princeton: Princeton University Press.

Sunstein, C. (2005). *Laws of fear: Beyond the Precautionary Principle.* Cambridge: Cambridge University Press.

Taylor-Gooby, P. (2004). *Psychology, social psychology and risk.* Working paper. Social contexts and responses to risk network, University of Kent at Canterbury. Retrieved from http://www.kent.ac.uk/scarr/papers/papers.htm

Vaughan, D. (1996). *The Challenger launch decision: Risky technology, culture, and deviance at NASA.* Chicago: University of Chicago Press.

Wahlberg, A., & Sjoberg, L. (2000). Risk perception and the media. *Journal of Risk Research, 3*(1), 31-50.

Weik, K., & Roberts, K. (1993). Collective mind in organizations: Heedful interrelating on flight decks. *Administrative Science Quarterly, 38*(3), 357-381.

KEY TERMS

Bureau of Labor Statistics (BLS): An independent national statistical agency that collects, processes, analyzes, and disseminates statistical data to the American public, the US Congress, other Federal agencies, State and local governments, business, and labor. The BLS also serves as a statistical resource to its parent department, the Department of Labor.

Critical Infrastructure Protection: Activities that enhance the physical *and* cyber-security of key public and private assets.

Federal Aviation Administration (FAA): Responsible for the safety of US civil aviation. The FAA regulates civil aviation, develops civil aeronautics, develops and operates air traffic control, researches and develops the National Airspace System and civil aeronautics, carries out programs to control aircraft noise and other environmental effects of civil aviation, and regulates US commercial space transportation. The FAA's parent department is the Department of Transportation.

Government Accountability Office: The Government Accountability Office (GAO) (formerly the General Accountability Office) is an agency that works for Congress. Congress directs GAO to study the programs and expenditures of the federal government. GAO, commonly called the investigative arm of Congress or the congressional watchdog, is independent and non-partisan. It studies how the federal government spends its money. GAO advises Congress and the heads of executive agencies about ways to make government more effective and responsive. GAO evaluates federal programs, audits federal expenditures, and issues legal opinions.

High Reliability Organizations Theory (HRO): Hazardous technologies can be safely controlled by complex organizations if the correct design and management techniques are followed, such as top-down commitment to safety, built-in organizational redundancies, the existence of a "safety culture" in the organization, including a commitment to learn from accidents. HRO is a response to Normal Accidents Theory. (See next entry.) Key contributors include LaPorte and Consolini, 1991 and Weik and Roberts, 1993.

Inspector General (Office of the Inspector General): The President appoints and Congress approves Inspectors General for each government department. The *Inspector General Act* (1978) gives the Office of the Inspector General (OIG) autonomy to audit the department (and related agencies) for which the Inspector General is responsible without interference.

Normal Accidents Theory (NAT): Accidents are inevitable in organizations that have social and technical interactive complexity and little slack (tight coupling). No management design can overcome this inevitability. NAT builds on Chaos Theory. Key contributors include Perrow, 1984, Sagan, 1993, and Vaughan, 1996.

Office of Management and Budget (OMB): Assists the President in overseeing the preparation of the federal budget and supervises its administration in Executive Branch agencies. OMB evaluates the effectiveness of agency programs, policies, and procedures, assesses competing funding demands among agencies, and sets funding priorities. OMB ensures that agency reports, rules, testimony, and proposed legislation are consistent with the President's Budget and with Administration policies.

Possibilism: Counterfactuals ("what if" scenarios). Thinking in terms of that which is possible rather than that which is probable.

Probabilism: Thinking in probabilities, drawing mainly from past experiences.

Size, Structure, and Style of Risk Regulation Regimes: Hood, Rothstein and Baldwin (2001) deploy the concept of "regimes" to explore and contrast variety in risk regulation across different policy areas. *Size* considers aggression and investment in risk regulation. *Structure* considers the mix of internal and external actors and how densely populated the regulatory space is. *Style* considers how far regulation is rule bound or discretionary, and the degree of zeal the actors show in pursuit of policy objectives.

Worst Case: According to Lee Clarke, a context-sensitive event, and is interpreted largely through our capacity to identify with the victims.

Worst-Case Planning: Devising plans based on counterfactuals ("what if" scenarios). The counterfactuals need only be possibilities; they need not be "likely" (in any calculable way) to occur.

Year 2000 (Y2K): Y2K referred to the fact that in computer programmes created in the 1950s and onwards, most year entries had been identified in two-digit shorthand, 1965, for instance, was entered as "65." Initially, this shorthand was adopted to save on expensive computer memory. Through time, it simply became standard practice. As the year 2000 approached, however, anxiety grew that systems would be unable to distinguish between twentieth century entries and twenty-first century entries (e.g., Would "01" be treated as "1901" or "2001"?). Such ambiguity, it was feared, would result in systems failing or producing inaccurate information. At the very least it made information unreliable. The US government eventually spent $8.5 billion to ensure government systems were compliant. The US government estimated that Y2K-related repairs cost the US economy $120 billion (President's Council on Year 2000 Conversion, 2000).

ENDNOTES

[1]   Kheifets, Hester, and Banerjee (2001) note there are several definitions for the precautionary principle, which can be grouped loosely into three trends. The three trends vary in emphasis and severity with respect to the evidence required to justify action as well as the action taken. Clarke's specific approach will be elaborated in the next section, "Background: Worst cases and organization studies."

[2]   *Wall Street Journal, New York Times,* and *USA Today.*

[3]   By the year 2000, the US Treasury estimated the cost to be $300bn worldwide.

4   Couffou was discussing the vulnerability of embedded systems. Embedded systems contain programmed instructions running via processor chips. The processor chips are similar to standalone computers buried inside various kinds of equipment

5   The Dutch government also had a sizeable Y2K operation in place.

6   For examples, see Blitz, Hope, and White (1999) on Italy, Spain, and Greece, Jack (1999) on Russia, Bowen (1999) on Latin America, and Suzman (1999) on Eastern Europe and Indonesia.

7   Based on preliminary work conducted by the CIO Council based at the Office of Management and Budget.

8   As noted earlier Clarke is supportive of how organizations reacted to Y2K. At the same time, Clarke notes his skepticism in *Worst Cases* about bureaucracies' capacity to respond in a crisis. He argues they are too inflexible. Certainly, this research would support such a claim. While on the one hand I share Clarke's skepticism about bureaucracies' capacity to respond in a crisis, I am less convinced by organizational responses to Y2K. This chapter attempts to make clear these concerns.

Chapter VI
The Impact of the USA Patriot Act on Social Diversity in Cyberspace

Marc Jung-Whan de Jong
University of Southern California, USA

ABSTRACT

The Uniting and Strengthening America by Providing Appropriate Tools Required to Intercept and Obstruct Terrorism Act (USA PATRIOT Act) of 2001 has increased the surveillance and investigative powers of law enforcement in the United States. While the Patriot Act serves to protect American society and interests abroad, critics suggest that it does not provide sufficient checks and balances to safeguard the civil liberties of U.S. citizens. This chapter assesses both of these claims: how the USA Patriot Act protects U.S. national security and through self-censorship over privacy concerns may affect sociopolitical and cultural diversity in cyberspace.

INTRODUCTION

The development of the Internet from a Cold War military communications protocol (Advanced Research Projects Agency Network - ARPAN) designed to withstand the force of potential Soviet nuclear attacks in the 1960s, to its current global form has been surrounded by utopian and dystopian views on its perceived social potential. Utopian views of the Internet see it as a powerful politically democratizing influence that is foundational to 21st century community and diaspora building and gives a voice to marginalized groups in society. Others view the rise of the Internet, or the information society in general, more somberly, and fear that its growing social importance contributes to an unbridgeable digital divide (Abbate, 1999; Castells, 2001); perpetuates the marginalization of socially oppressed groups (Chow-White, 2006); or point at governments' attempts to control and censor online content by using spyware[1], for example, in the Middle East (http://www.opennetinnitiative.com, 2006) or Asia (Gomez, 2002; Rodan, 1998).

In the United States, electronic privacy monitoring organizations, such as the Electronic Privacy Information Center (EPIC), have expressed concerns that the democratizing potential of the Internet may be threatened by the communication surveillance act H.R. 3162 (USA PATRIOT Act, 2001), better know as the Uniting and Strengthening America by Providing Appropriate Tools Required to Intercept and Obstruct Terrorism Act (USA PATRIOT Act). This chapter will not prove or disprove the validity of the aforementioned utopian and dystopian perspectives on the Internet. Rather, it assumes that like most new technologies, the Internet has both social advantages and disadvantages. It does have two objectives: to evaluate how (1) the USA PATRIOT Act works and (2) could affect Internet users' free speech and privacy rights, threatening sociopolitical and culture diversity in cyberspace.

In the aftermath of the terrorist attacks on September 11th, 2001, the USA PATRIOT Act was developed to protect U.S. citizens and American interests abroad against future attacks. The Act regulates how and when "suspicious" electronic communications and financial data can be monitored, intercepted, and used within the United States. To prevent misuse of these regulations, the USA PATRIOT Act provides several legal provisions that protect U.S. Internet users' constitutional First (free speech) and Fourth (privacy) Amendment rights. Yet critics have claimed that these provisions are too fragile and are concerned that the lack of judicial precedent involving free speech and privacy rights in cyberspace facilitates misinterpretations of the USA PATRIOT Act's regulations, and misuse of the intercepted communications and financial data. This chapter examines how these potential weaknesses, and the secrecy surrounding the legal use and types of data collected under the USA PATRIOT Act could deter some Internet users from freely expressing their political views in cyberspace. The first part

of this chapter briefly examines the history of and controversies surrounding electronic communication surveillance laws in the United States since the late1960s. Next, it discusses the social roles of the Internet within utopian and dystopian perspectives. Lastly, this chapter evaluates how the USA PATRIOT Act could threaten sociopolitical and cultural diversity in cyberspace.

BACKGROUND

With the abundance of political and scholarly attention lavished on to the USA PATRIOT Act since 2001, one could easily assume that government surveillance of communications and financial data is a distinctly 21st Century phenomenon. Western nations, however, have been intercepting communications data since the late19[th] century (Hills, 2006). In 1875, 17 countries came together to discuss and develop the St. Petersburg Convention, with the intention of regulating the interception of telegraph communications data for national security purposes (McDowell, 1998). The Convention's Article 7 authorized all signatory parties to hold the transmission of any private telegram they believed to pose a national security threat. Additionally, Article 8 allowed for the indefinite suspension of all incoming and outgoing telegraph services if this was deemed fundamental to the protection of a nations' social and moral order (International Telegraph Convention, 1875). The United States was one of the few western nations that did not adopt the Convention; in the nineteenth century, most U.S. telegraph companies were privately owned and therefore outside of the federal government's control (McDowell, 1998). In fact, it was not until 1968 that the Omnibus Crime Control and Safe Streets Act's Title III, as part of President Johnson's attempt to eliminate crime from America's streets, authorized law enforcement to intercept any electronic communications data it considered a threat to the stability of U.S. society.

The USA PATRIOT Act regulates the surveillance and interception of communications data from non-U.S. citizens in the United States for foreign and counterintelligence purposes. Because U.S. citizens are protected by the First and Fourth Amendments to the Constitution of United States, the Foreign Intelligence Surveillance Court (FISC), which oversees the issuance of surveillance warrants, seldom issues orders that may violate these civil rights, limiting law enforcement's communications surveillance powers to the interception and monitoring of routing data only. However, U.S. surveillance Acts have not always been as respectful of U.S. citizens' rights to freedom of speech and privacy as the Foreign Intelligence Surveillance Act (FISA), under which the FISC operates. The 1996 Communications Decency Act (CDA), for example, was heavily criticized for violating Internet users' First and Fourth Amendment rights. Critics argued that lawmakers had failed to take the Internet's unique information-dispensing character in to account; because of its global spread and public accessibility traditional obscenity laws should not be applied to Internet content (Petrie, 1997). The legal and political controversies that surrounded the CDA's development demonstrate the difficulty of expanding traditional communication surveillance and censorship laws to new communication technologies.

The CDA was created following United States v. Thomas (1994), a Six Circuit Court ruling on Internet users' rights to publish and distribute perceived obscene and indecent materials in and via cyberspace. The defendants, Robert and Carleen Thomas, had operated a California-based members-only Internet business that provided access to erotic chat lines, message boards, and downloadable pornographic image files. In 1993, a complaint about the pornographic nature of the business' online and off-line services was filed with the Tennessee United States Postal Services. A year later, a federal grand jury for the Western District of Tennessee indicted both defendants on violation of federal obscenity law and the improper use of a "means of interstate commerce" (telephone lines) to distribute obscene, computer-generated, downloadable materials. They were convicted on all counts of the indictment, clearing the way for the creation and enactment of the CDA. Around the time of the CDA's development and United States v. Thomas, the Internet had just become available to the general public. The increasing popularity of the Internet in the mid-1990s, particularly with children and teenagers, was accompanied by media reports and political commentary on the supposed psychological damage its accessibility to "cyberpornography" inflicted on young and impressionable users (McMurdo, 1997). In 1996, under increasing political and public pressure, the Clinton administration added Title V to the Telecommunications Act of 1995. Title V expanded the Telecommunications Act's indecency and obscenity regulations for cable television to Internet content, making it a criminal offense to distribute or release obscene or indecent Internet materials to anyone under the age of 21.

Title V, however, provided little specificity about the kinds of Internet content that could be defined as "indecent" or "obscene,'", merely stating "any comment, request, suggestion, proposal, image, or other communication that, in context, depicts or describes, in terms patently offensive as measured by contemporary community standards, sexual or excretory activities or organs, regardless of whether the user of such service placed the call or initiated the communication" (Title V, Section 223, 1996). Therefore, under Title V, content ranging from nudity in classic artworks to pictures of genitalia in medical or safe-sex educational texts could be deemed obscene or indecent if released to minors. Amidst First Amendment concerns, the American Civil Liberties Union and the American Liberty Association challenged the CDA's constitutionality. In the landmark Reno et al. v. ACLU et al. (1997), the U.S. Supreme Court issued its first opinion involving cyberspace, striking down the CDA and granting the Internet free speech protection.

In 2000, a Freedom of Information Act lawsuit filed by the Electronic Privacy Information Center (EPIC) forced the Federal Bureau of Investigations (FBI) to publicly confirm rumors surrounding its suspected use of Carnivore (later renamed DCS1000), an Internet data collection software filter system used to intercept electronic communications data (EPIC, 2000). EPIC believed that the secrecy surrounding the FBI's use of Carnivore (e.g., the types of data intercepted and its use in criminal investigations) infringed on Internet users' Fourth Amendment rights. They argued that Carnivore gave the FBI access to detailed personal and financial data of *all* subscribers to the Internet Service Provider (ISP) at which the Carnivore filter was installed, not just to that of Internet users under investigation. Congress demanded that further investigations were to be conducted[2], but these investigations had yet to be completed when the United States came under attack on September 11, 2001, diverting much of Congress' attention towards the USA PATRIOT Act.

How little was actually known about the scope of government sanctioned communications surveillance became evident in 2005, when the Bush administration admitted it had authorized the National Security Agency (NSA)[3] to establish a database consisting of billions of Americans' electronic communications data (international telephone calls and e-mail messages from U.S. citizens with suspected links to terrorists or terrorist organizations), most of which had been intercepted without FISC-issued warrants (USA Today, 2006). Though the FBI's use of the Carnivore filter was controversial and clouded in secrecy, unlike the NSA's surveillance program, Carnivore had been regulated by the FISC. In August 2006, a Federal Court ruled in ACLU et al. v. NSA et al. that the NSA's warrantless surveillance program was unconstitutional. Pending a possible NSA Supreme

Court challenge, more information gradually may become available about the scope and use of other electronic communications surveillance programs in the United States. This information may further effect sociopolitical organization and participation in cyberspace. Before elaborating on the potential deterring effects of electronic communications surveillance programs on Internet use, a more in-depth look at the USA PATRIOT Act is warranted.

THE USA PATRIOT ACT AND SOCIAL DIVERSITY IN CYBERSPACE

In the aftermath of the terrorist attacks on September 11, 2001, the USA PATRIOT Act was signed into law by President Bush, little over a month later. The USA PATRIOT Act (a re-worked version of the 2001 Anti-Terrorism Act which Congress had rejected as too far-reaching) consists of a series of additions and amendments made to existing surveillance Acts such as FISA, Title III (the Wire Tap Statute), the Computer Fraud and Abuse Act (CFAA) and the Electronic Communications Privacy Act (ECPA). The USA PATRIOT Act's main objective is to strengthen U.S. capabilities to detect and prevent future terrorist attacks against the United States. Specifically relevant to discussions on the potentially deterring effects of the USA PATRIOT Act on Internet use are its sections 210, 214, 216, 218, 219, 220, and 815.

Section 210 broadens the types of subscriber records law enforcement is authorized to collect, ranging from subscribers' financial information to their computers' IP addresses. Section 214 regulates FISC' issuance of pen register and trap and trace device orders. A pen register enables the coding or decoding of dialing, routing, or signaling information transmitted by communication devices such as telephones or computers that are connected to an ISP. Trap and trace devices enable authorities to trace wire or electronic communications back to their source (Smith et al., 2002). Section 216 expands law enforcement's authority to use trap and trace and pen register devices to retrieve and intercept real-time internet voice and data communications from computers located anywhere in the United States (Smith et. al, 2002). It also limits court-authorized officials' access to the intercepted data, stipulating that its content is protected by Fourth Amendment search and seizure requirements. Section 216 prohibits the unlimited interception of data (warrants specify the duration of the surveillance period) and requires that statutory exclusionary rules apply to any data collected using wire or pen trap devices. Data collected with wire or pen trap devices thus cannot be submitted in to evidence during criminal trial proceedings. Section 218 amended FISA to make it broader in scope, ordering that the interception of communications data serves a *significant* foreign or counter intelligence purpose, rather than this being its *sole* purpose. Lastly, Sections 219 and 220 decrease the amount of paper work involved in obtaining FISC-issued warrants, and Section 815 (under ECPA) limits ISPs' potential civil or criminal liabilities should these hold on to stored data at law enforcement's request.

The USA PATRIOT Act thus significantly expanded law enforcements' authority to intercept any electronic communications and financial data it perceived as potential threats to U.S. national security. Supporters of the USA PATRIOT Act maintain that its legal provisions sufficiently protect the rights of law abiding citizens and prevent federal misuses of the surveillance programs or intercepted data. Critics point at the legal controversies surrounding Carnivore or the NSA to suggest that the mere existence of legal provisions does not automatically prevent surveillance abuses, for example, warrantless data collection or the use of intercepted data content in criminal proceedings. While Section 216 requires that e-mail-content may not be retrieved without FISC-issued warrants, critics argue that the statutory definition of 'content' is unclear and

therefore subject to broad legal interpretations and speculations. Section 216 defines 'content' as "... any information concerning the substance, purport, or meaning of [the] telecommunication" (18 USC 2510), but does not consider the nature of information that can be captured electronically. URLs generated while using the Internet contain personal and financial data many times more revealing than that of, for example, intercepted telephone numbers.

The main question then is whether fears of potential surveillance abuses and misuse of data collected under the USA PATRIOT Act could influence how Internet users express themselves in cyberspace and if so, why? In order to answer this question, another brief look at the social impact of the Internet is needed. As mentioned in the introduction to this chapter, utopian views of the Internet tend to envision it as a thriving force behind the revitalization of the public sphere. Advances in communication technologies will enhance democratic political processes by providing the general public access to traditionally elite-controlled information, thus allowing people of all social backgrounds to participate in (online) political activism (Bimber, 1998; Lax, 2004). Cresser et al.'s (2001) study of women's use of electronic zines (e-zines), for instance, demonstrates how they use online magazines to share intimate every-day experiences with other women and, through these interactions, increase their self-esteem. Armstrong (2004) further notices how women's involvement with e-zines encourages and inspires other women and girls to become more familiar with the Internet and technology in general. The social importance of the Internet in identity-forming and community building processes is further illustrated by Campbell's (2004) examination of social interactions in gay chat rooms. Gay chat room users tend to construct and use online fictional personas as idealized extensions of their off-line selves. Like women's involvement with e-zine communities, these cyber-performances not only contribute to off-line self-esteem building but also to a sense of on and off-line collectivity, thus providing de-isolating functions.

Most utopian Internet scholars emphasize the ways in which online social interactions can lead to off-line self-esteem, community and network building, but not all scholars are convinced of the Internet's society-enriching potential. Hara and Estrada (2005), for instance, question the Internet's alleged positive influence on political processes. They believe that political organization and mobilization in cyberspace, for example, through organizations such as MoveOn.org, is ineffective if used by itself. Online political activism, they argue, needs to be conducted in conjunction with traditional off-line campaigning methods in order to have any serious impact on the off-line political landscape. Those involved in online political activism, Hara and Estrada argue, are more likely to be politically active off-line as well; political activism in cyberspace therefore may not necessarily reach those off-line electorates whose votes are necessary to shift the political balance. Other scholars are concerned that the growing social and economic importance of the Internet and the information society in general contributes to a digital divide (Couldry, 2004). The commodification of information and human services may level the social playing fields as it excludes the necessity to own natural resources. However, many Internet users may not be able to afford or are intellectually capable of keeping up with the latest software skill- requirements. Because Internet skills have become fundamental to human capital, those who financially benefit most from its use (that are particularly Internet-savvy) may be those who need these financial benefits the least (Beckles, 2001).

Chow-White (2006) argues that the Internet can be used in significantly anti-democratizing. His examination of sex-tourism message boards (where users rate their sexual encounters with sex workers in Asia) shows how the Internet facilitates the deepening of connections between the racialization, sexualization and commodification of disenfranchised sex workers' bodies and hegemonic (western) masculinity, contributing to deepening global social inequalities and structures of difference. Similarly, Adams (2005) observes how white supremacist groups' successfully use the Internet to build online global communities and social networks of racists, whose hate speech and political activities tend to spill over in to off-line societies. Lastly, Rodan's (1998) and Gomez's (2003) studies of the Singaporean government's attempts to monitor and censor political online content using spyware, as well as studies conducted by the OpenNet Initiative research consortium[4] (2006) and the Arabic Network for Human Rights Information[5] (2006), express concern about governments' too far reaching surveillance powers.

The aforementioned studies demonstrate that cyberspace's political and society enriching strengths lay in the alternative spaces it sets aside for expressions of counter-hegemonic political opinions (Warf & Grimes, 1997). The democratic character of these spaces is becoming increasingly restricted by threats of government surveillance, for example, through self-censorship or the use of privacy software to avoid possible data interception. The secrecy surrounding the scope and use of surveillance programs in the United States, may have significant deterring effects on groups which, historically, have been subjected to intense governmental scrutiny. For instance, during 1950s McCarthyism, communists and lesbians and gay men in civil service employment were actively monitored and persecuted by the federal government (Johnson, 2004). Parenti (2003) argues that, similarly, blacks have been subjected to governmental surveillance since slavery. Cyberspace serves as a space were like-minded, and often socially marginalized people freely exchange ideas, connect, and organize. Political groups that have experienced government scrutiny off-line may perceive the USA PATRIOT Act as yet another attempt to silence them.

FUTURE TRENDS

With the millions of Internet websites,[6] discussion boards, and chat rooms available to and visited by Internet users and Instant Messages sent on a daily basis, it is difficult to determine the actual effects of the USA PATRIOT Act, or other surveillance Acts for that matter, on the sociopolitical and cultural landscape in cyberspace. Yet, Internet studies increasingly acknowledge the social importance of the Internet for marginalized groups in society. In time, these same studies may take on the tall order of studying whether documented increases or decreases in Internet use among these groups are correlated with controversies surrounding surveillance programs such as the USA PATRIOT Act since the mid-1990s.

FUTURE RESEARCH DIRECTIONS

This chapter focused on the use of surveillance programs in the United States. Comparative research between the USA PATRIOT Act and similar surveillance programs in other countries could provides insight in to the global scope of communication surveillance and its social and global effects. Similarly, U.S. Internet users may use proxies to access and route information via Internet hubs in other countries, trying to avoid Internet use under U.S. jurisdiction and making legal data interception increasingly complicated. Studies therefore may start to focus on the use of privacy software (e.g., data encryption or the use of proxies), the privacy software industry (e.g., whether it is bound by legal limitations of the quality of data-encryption software it can provide to the general public), and the effects of such software on the socially democratizing potential of the Internet.

Lastly, as stated earlier, it is important to situate the potentially deterring effects of the USA PATRIOT Act on Internet use within the socio-historical experiences of marginalized groups in U.S. society. Studies focusing on how politically, socially, or culturally marginalized groups have been placed under government surveillance in the past, for example Parenti (2003), may provide further insight into these groups' possible aversion of present-day legalized communications surveillance in cyberspace.

CONCLUSION

In recent years, terrorist groups have increasingly turned to the Internet to plot terrorist attacks. Not surprisingly, the Internet has become an important focus in the United States' attempts to detect potential terrorist activities. The importance of surveillance of communications and financial data in detecting terrorist activities has created a legal and moral dilemma: how far can and should governments go in the surveillance of Internet data in order to protect public safety? It is difficult to determine when passionate online expressions of political bravura will translate into actual off-line actions that endanger U.S. society and under the USA Patriot Act, such determinations do not have to be (and perhaps cannot be) absolute. It is important to remember that the USA PATRIOT Act is not the first electronic communications surveillance program to exist and, as Kerr (2003) points out, did not add any major changes to existing laws and statutes. In fact, as Staples (1997) and Parenti (2003) suggest, Americans have lived under surveillance for quite some time: drivers' licenses, social security cards, mobile phones, e-mails, and credit cards are all digital tracers for surveillance.

The deterring effects of the USA PATRIOT Act then may partly rest in the Act itself. As previously discussed, critics have pointed at the broad interpretative nature of some of the Act's sections. However, it may also rest in the fact that the events of 9/11 and the subsequent political debates surrounding the enactment of the USA PATRIOT Act have made Americans more aware of government surveillance. This awareness, intensified by the secrecy and uncertainty surrounding the collection, storage, and use of communications data under the USA PATRIOT Act, could constitute the Acts' primary deterring effect: that of social control; the idea that "Big Brother" *could* be watching. It is this fear that ultimately may motivate some Internet users to find different modes of communication, networking, and community building in cyberspace.

REFERENCES

Abbate J. (1999). *Inventing the Internet*. Cambridge, MA: MIT Press

Adams, J. (2005). White supremacists, oppositional culture and the World Wide Web. *Social Forces, 84*(2), 759-778.

Armstrong, J. (2000, 2004). Web grrrls, guerrilla tactics: Young feminism on the Web. In D. Gauntlett & R. Horsley (Eds.), *Web.Studies* (pp.92-102). New York, NY: Oxford University Press.

Beckles, C.A. (2001). Africa: New realities and hopes. *Journal of Black Studies, 31*(3), 311-324.

Bimber, B. (1998). The Internet and political transformation: Populism, community, and accelerated pluralism. *Polity, 31*(1), 133-160.

Buckingham, D. (2000). *After the death of childhood: Growing up in the age of electronic media*. London, UK: Polity.

Campbell, J. E. (2004). *Getting it on online. Cyberspace, gay male sexuality and embodied identity*. Binghamton, NY: The Harrington Park Press.

Castells, M. (2001). *The Internet galaxy: Reflections on the Internet, business, and society*. New York, NY: Oxford University Press.

Chow-White, P. (2006). Race, gender and sex on the net: Semantic networks of selling and storytelling. *Media, Culture & Society, 28*(6), 883-905.

Couldry, N. (2000, 2004) The digital divide. In D. Gauntlett & R. Horsley (Eds.), *Web.Studies* (pp.185-194). New York, NY: Oxford University Press.

Cresser, F., Gunn, L., & Balme, H. (2001). Women's experiences of online e-zine publications. *Media, Culture & Society, 23*(4), 457-473.

Federal Bureau of Investigation, United States Department of Justice. (February 24, December 18, 2003). *Carnivore/DCS 1000 Report to Congress*.

Gomez, J. (2002). *Internet politics: Surveillance and intimidation in Singapore*. Singapore: Think Centre.

Hara, N., & Estrada, Z. (2005). Analyzing the mobilization of grassroots activities via the internet: a case study. *Journal of Information Science, 31*(6), 503-514.

Hills, J. (2006). What's new? War, censorship and global transmission. From the Telegraph to the Internet. *The International Communication Gazette, 68*(3), 195-216.

Johnson, D. K. (2004). *The Cold War persecution of gays and lesbians in the Federal Government*. Chicago, MI: University of Chicago Press.

Kerr, O. S. (2003). Internet surveillance law after The USA PARIOT Act: The big brother that isn't. *Northwestern University Law Review, 97*(2), 607-673.

Lawrence et al. v. Texas, 539 U.S. 558. (2003).

Lax, S. (2000, 2004). The Internet and democracy. In D. Gauntlett & R. Horsley (Eds.), *Web.Studies* (pp. 217-229). New York, NY: Oxford University Press.

McDowell, S. D. (1998). Regionalism and National Communications Policies: Canada and the United States in North American Telecommunications Governance. *Working Paper No. 9*. Retrieved December 1, 2006, from http://www.fis.utoronto.ca/research/iprp/publications/wp/wp9.html

McMurdo, G. (1997). Cyberporn and communication decency. *Journal of Information Science, 23*(1), 81-90.

Mosco, V. (2000). Webs of myths and power: Connectivity and the new computer technopolis. In A. Herman & T. Swiss (Eds.), *The World Wide Web and contemporary cultural theory* (pp.37-61). New York, NY: Routledge.

Omnibus Crime Control and Safe Streets Act of 1968 42 U.S.C. § 3789D

Parenti, C. (2003). *The soft cage: Surveillance in America from slavery to the war on terror.* New York, NY: Basic Books.

Petrie, S. J. (1997). Indecent proposals: How each branch of the federal government overstepped its institutional authority in the development of Internet obscenity law. *Stanford Law Review, 49*(3), 637-665.

Rackow, S. H. (2002). How the USA Patriot Act will permit governmental infringement upon the privacy of Americans in the name of intelligence investigations. *University of Pennsylvania Law Review, 150*(5), 1651-1696.

Reno, Attorney General of the United States et al. v. American Civil Liberties Union et al., 96 U.S. 511. (1997).

Rodan, G. (1998). The Internet and political control in Singapore. *Political Science Quarterly, 113*(1), 63-89.

Smith, M. S., Seifert, J. W., McLoughlin, G. J., & Moteff, J. DF. (2002). The Internet and the USA PATRIOT Act: Potential implications for electronic privacy, security, commerce, and government. *Congressional Research Service Report for Congress.* Retrieved December 1st, 2006, from http://www.epic.org/privacy/terrorism/usapatriot/RL31289.pdf

Staples, W. G. (1997). *The culture of surveillance: Discipline and social control in the United States.* New York, NY: St Martin's Press.

Uniting and Strengthening America by Providing Appropriate Tools Required to Intercept and Obstruct Terrorism (USA PATRIOT Act), HR 3162 RDS. (2001).

US Department of Justice, Office of Legislative Affairs, Office of the Assistant Attorney General, Washington, DC 20530. (2006). *Foreign Intelligence Surveillance Act 2005 Annual Report.*

USA Today. (2006). *Questions and answers about the NSA phone record program.*

Warf, B., & Grimes J. (1997). Counterhegemonic discourses and the Internet. *Geographical Review, 87*(2), 259-274.

ADDITIONAL READING

Bakardjieva, M. (2005). *Internet society: The Internet in everyday life.* Thousand Oaks, CA: Sage Publications.

Ball, H. (2004). *The USA Patriot Act: A reference handbook* (Contemporary World Issues). Santa Barbara, CA: ABC-CLIO.

Castells, M. (2003). *The oower of identity.* Malden, MA: Blackwell Publishing.

Davis, S., Elin, L., & Reeher, G. (2002). *The Internet's power to change political apathy into civic action.* Cambridge, MA: Westview Press.

Etzioni, A. (2004) *How patriotic is the Patriot Act?: Freedom vs. security in the Age of Terrorism.* New York, NY: Routledge.

Gerder, L. I. (Ed.). (2005). *The Patriot Act.* (Opposing Viewpoints Series). Farmington Hills, MI: Greenhaven Press.

Okin, J. R. (2005). *The Internet revolution: The not-for-dummies guide to the history, technology, and use of the Internet.* Winter Harbor, ME: Ironbound Press.

Scheppler, B. (2005). *The USA PATRIOT Act: Antiterror legislation in response to 9/11.* New York, NY: Rosen Central.

ENDNOTES

[1]   Spyware is a type of computer software that enables the collection of Internet users' personal information (e.g., websites they visited or content on their computers) without their consent.

[2]   Since 2001, the FBI has issued two reports to Congress which indicated it had used Carnivore 13 times between 2001 and 2004. The report, however, did not specify for what purpose and at what success rate. (FBI Reports, 2002, 2003)

[3]   The National Security Agency was founded in 1952 and is the U.S. government's main cryptology organization. The NSA encrypts U.S. foreign communications and collects and analyzes other nations' foreign communications data.

[4]   A research partnership between the Harvard Law School, the University of Toronto, Cambridge University, and the University of Oxford.

[5]   The Arabic Network for Human Rights Information (www.HRinfo.net) was founded in 2003 to monitor human rights developments and abuses in the Middle East and to provide a discussion forum of the latest information on human rights in the Middle East.

[6]   The Online Community Library Center estimated that there were 9,040,000 websites available on the Internet in 2002. http://www.oclc.org/research/projects/archive/wcp/stats/size.htm. Retrieved on December 10th 2006)

Chapter VII
Exploring Serres' Atlas, Hodges' Knowledge Domains and the Fusion of Informatics and Cultural Horizons

Peter Jones
Independent Scholar & National Health Service (NHS), UK

ABSTRACT

This chapter explores the extent to which selected writings of French philosopher Michel Serres and a health care model created by Brian Hodges in the UK can augment and inform the development of social informatics. The volume of Serres' output contrasts markedly with work devoted to Hodges' Health Career - Care Domains - Model. Since the concept of health is universal culturally, and informatics disciplines are emerging fields of practice characterised by indistinct boundaries in terms of theory, policy, and practice, various ethnographic and cultural associations will be made. Placing Hodges' model and Serres' work together is not intended to suggest direct equivalence, other than the common themes this author intends to bring to the attention of the social informatics community. Central to this is the notion of holistic bandwidth, utilising Hodges' model as a tool to develop and disseminate socio-technical perspectives.

INTRODUCTION

In 1986, whilst studying community mental health nursing, the author discovered a conceptual framework known as Hodges' Health Career-Care Domains-Model (hereafter referred to as h2cm).

Clinical experience, work in health informatics, and awareness of contemporary social informatics issues including access; community economic development; social cohesion; development and learning (Clement, Gurstein, Longford, et al., 2004) convinces the author of the value and potential utility of h2cm to the extended informatics community. This potential arises by virtue of the model's structure and four knowledge domains. As for any generic framework, Hodges' model can be used to address several issues; policy development, health promotion and education, intercultural matters, communication, research, public involvement, service development and evidence-based care, plus community informatics and e-government. This list is pragmatic, incomplete, and not meant to impress. While successful application of any tool ultimately depends on its users, the model's scope and the problems of the 21st century make the potential h2cm user base and beneficiaries immense.

Demographics are the dynamic that shapes health and social policy as well as population pyramids. Globalization, migration, ongoing humanitarian crises highlighted by Rieff (2002), superbugs, terrorism, and environmental degradation bring home the lesson of just how interconnected, interdependent, and vulnerable humanity has become. Commentators report on the digital divide, the increase in social and political exclusion, and the policy imperative to engage citizens in the political process. Citizens in turn are deluged with wave after wave of messages. While the majority are contentedly fully immersed and cannot be distracted, others play the part of King Canute and try to stop the tide. Where is the wisdom in the exponential growth in the volume of information produced, to sell it as knowledge, as intelligence, transactions completed in nanoseconds? Amid frequent calls for new tools, what might a framework like h2cm provide?

As social informatics emerges as a distinct discipline, it needs to define its boundaries and differentiate its content from other informatics disciplines to produce the social informatics curriculum. Social informatics is not unique in this regard, sharing this issue with other informatics practitioners. The author (Jones, 2004a) coined the term *holistic bandwidth;* an as yet loosely defined concept, this may nonetheless assist informatics curricula developers. Holistic bandwidth refers to the conceptual scope of a discipline. So in use, h2cm can help identify those issues and concerns that are truly unique, and those which overlap informatics fields.

Reading Serres' translated texts, this author was immediately struck, firstly, by the similarity of Serres' concerns to current informatics issues; secondly, the problems that led to h2cm's creation (which will be explained shortly); and finally, how well Hodges' model could represent both. This expressive power arises from h2cm's structure; a conceptual space created by diagrammatic representation of four pivotal concepts: *individual*, *group*, *humanistic*, and *mechanistic*. This construct leads to a conceptual framework with generic, and specific, broad and detailed capacities.

This chapter begins with brief introductions to the range and nature of Serres' ideas and Hodges' model. The main text then comprises a fusion of the two linked to informatics, culminating in a discussion of why this chapter matters. Common themes are epistemology, the relationship of the sciences to the humanities, space and time, noise, information, and interdisciplinarity. Researcher's attention to Serres and Hodges can be justified on several levels including integration of knowledge; the need to equip the civic population with tools to facilitate engagement and critique; to blend and balance analysis-synthesis, the quantitative and qualitative.

Despite the philosophical and metaphorical emphasis in this chapter, it is of significance to the social informatics practitioners on several levels:

- Health is a key determinant in quality of life outcomes.
- Demographic trends continue to highlight the health burden on communities, locally and globally (Lopez, Mathers, Ezzati, Jamison, Murray, 2006).

- There is an acute lack of political engagement and malaise within many electorates
- Public health professionals seek to assess and disseminate positive health and wellness messages in opposition to mass media and contradictory government policies.
- Tools to engage people individually and in groups are needed, with exposure early in an individual's educational career.
- While technology is frequently associated with the new; community development is about sustainable growth and regeneration.
- Tools to assist policy makers and bridge the humanistic-mechanistic divide are also needed to achieve sociotechnical synergy (Mumford, 1996).
- The advent of the semantic Web provides a coming of age for conceptual frameworks with the requirement for research into tools such as h2cm.

MICHEL SERRES

Born in 1930, Serres' formative years, study, and writing was influenced by conflict and the holocaust, leading him to his life's work. With more than 20 books published, Serres' output is subject to ongoing debate (Abbas, 2005; Assad, 1999). Science, as a tool, is not neutral, but was compromised in Hiroshima and Nagasaki. The values within applied science remain stark today in bioterrorism, the state of the biosphere, and how we can achieve sustainable societies. Serres believes it will take a fusion of knowledge from disparate disciplines for us to grasp what is at stake (Abbas, 2005, p.3). This means travelling through passages, exploration of relationships with each other, science and technology, God, nature, and time. Passage can also be afforded by time, a dynamical time.

Appointed to the Académie Française in 1990, Serres' position as one of France's most prominent intellectuals is assured. Tenure at Stanford University has brought Serres to the attention of the English-speaking world, with approximately half of his books translated to English. Viewed by some of his peers as a maverick, Serres is nonetheless unique; a provocative and unorthodox thinker. His encyclopaedic approach combines and connects seemingly disparate events, objects, and themes, from what are usually distinct disciplines. The resulting philosophy is kaleidoscopic, drawing upon the object-subject language debate, local vs. global and other antagonistic dichotomies, law and science, and the development of the social and political contract. These latter contracts are now challenged by the need for a *natural contract*. This dynamic mix disorientates the reader who anticipates a standard academic exposition.

Serres' tools and style variously provoke controversy, surprise, and admiration. The adopted approach differs markedly from what is accepted academe. This does not sit well with experts in their respective fields, denoted by an agreed (institutionalised) tool set. By reading Serres, we see that temporal distance does not matter; all authors should be treated as our contemporaries (Serres, 1995a). Consequently, Serres is accused of being a dabbler, an isolated thinker (Dale & Adamson, 1998-1999). His thought can be challenging (personally and academically) when, for example, cultural similarities are drawn between the space shuttle Challenger accident and human sacrifice within Carthaginian worship of Baal (Serres, 1995b). A highly emotive view, the impact is reinforced by the 2003 Columbia disaster. The West also hates children (Serres, 1995c). Despite such controversy, Serres' work is extraordinary in its disciplinary bandwidth. He provides a snapshot in a tantalising and marvellous way of the myriad of discoveries we see when several surfaces are scratched together, paper, stone, earth, fabric, cyberspace, and skin; possibilities born of every discipline and others yet to emerge.

Given the potential appeal of his work to the humanities, environmental, interdisciplinary, and informatics studies Serres is overlooked. He is a Janus-like figure, but in addition to looking simultaneously to the future and past, Serres stands on the bridge seeking to encourage traffic between the sciences and humanities. No less than to provide a means to unify thought in the sciences and humanities. Rather than looking one way only and commanding "you shall not pass" in a Tolkinesque tumult, Serres wants to alter the perspectives of these two encampments. Using the sciences and humanities, especially history, literature, politics, and myth, Serres develops ideas using tropes such as *noise*, the *multiple*, the *parasite*, *The Emperor of the Moon*, and others. The resulting messages ultimately translate into love and evil. For Serres, violence at a personal and atomic level is the key message. Myth, literature, and history can also inform everyday life and science.

Serres' texts are built around a central theme; although this may not be clear from the outset as the objects and subjects Serres presents include statues, angels, mythological figures, the five senses, Lucretius, and modern fluid dynamics (Serres, 1977). His books are highly individualised wanderings, a path that is erratic and appears littered with specious argument untouched by the sharp edge of logic, honed by Occam's razor. This does not mean that Serres output is unstructured, that he fails to explain, fails to achieve his goal. On the contrary, critics have identified development in his thought.

Communication and the more complex aspects of information theory inform the earliest works, in which Serres employs *Hermes,* the messenger of Zeus; and *angels* from the Greek word for messenger. *Hermes* is also an ideal trope to explore Hodges' model and informatics, being the *philosopher of plural spaces.* Hermes is equipped to navigate the passages between disciplines, between distinct epistemologies as explained by Assad (1999, p.9). While h2cm is generic, the plurality of conceptual spaces represented in Hodges' framework can lead us to other models within the health care sector germane to informatics. Zubin

and Spring's (1977) stress-vulnerability model explains illness and wellness with reference to an individual's social skills, coping skills, information, and information processing strategies. While the "World Health Organisation" extols *"health for all"*; information overload is a problem for all: mentally, physically, and digitally.

Les Cinq Sens published in 1985 explores language, signs, and the senses. Language is a screen; it acts as both a barrier to passage and facilitates passage. In health care, language is also a screen. People generally, and health professionals in particular, may use language to avoid difficult subjects and issues. Individuals are not only *screened* within disciplines, each with its own vocabulary and terms, but *to be screened* is to seek passage through gatekeeping services in order to access services. H2cm can ease this passage physically, emotionally, and cognitively? The book *Le Contract Natural* (1995) argues for a natural contract with the Earth, to bring order as the Social contract has brought order in how people relate to each other. *Le Contract Natural* deals with *the* issue of the 21st century: global environmental change. The text builds on previous work even if this is not referred to directly. If people fail to cooperate, accept discipline, and act as a team on board ship, they are imperilled. The planet Earth is our ship and we are all crew members.

HODGES' MODEL: A COGNITIVE PERIPLUS FOR LIFE-LONG LEARNING

Developed in the UK during the early 1980s, Hodges' model is a conceptual framework that is person centred and situation based. In structure, it combines two axes to create four care (knowledge) domains (as per Figures 1 and 2). Academics and practitioners in many fields create models that help support theory and practice (Wilber, 2000). Models act as a memory jogger and guide. Whereas in health education, theoretical frameworks are discipline related with specific and generic uses, community informatics emerged from university, corporate, and governmental environments without a model (Clement, et al., 2004). In health care, generic models can encourage holistic practice directing the user to consider the patient as a whole person and not merely as a diagnosis derived from physical investigations. Exposure of h2cm is limited to a small (yet growing) cadre of practitioners; several published articles (Adams, 1987; Hinchcliffe, 1989; Jones 2004a, b). In addition to a Web site (Jones, 1998), there is a blog and an audio presentation, both first published in 2006.

The best way to explain h2cm is to review the questions Hodges originally posed. To begin, who are the recipients of care? Well, first and foremost, individuals of all ages, races, and creed, but also groups of people, families, communities, and populations. Then Hodges asked what types of activities, tasks, duties, and treatments, do nurses carry out? They must always act professionally, but frequently according to strict rules and policies, their actions often dictated by specific treatments including drugs, investigations, and minor surgery. Nurses do many things by routine according to precise procedures, as per the stereotypical matron with machine-like efficiency. If these are

classed as mechanistic, they contrast with times when healthcare workers give of themselves to reassure, comfort, develop rapport, and engage therapeutically. This is opposite to mechanistic tasks and is described as humanistic; what the public usually think of as the *caring* nurse. In use, this framework prompts the user to consider four major subject headings or care domains of knowledge. Namely, what knowledge is needed to care for individuals, groups and undertake humanistic, mechanistic activities? Through these questions, Hodges' derived the model depicted in Figures 1 and 2.

Initial study of h2cm on the Web site has related Hodges' model to the multicontextual nature of health, informatics, consilience (Wilson, 1998), interdisciplinarity, and visualization. H2cm says nothing about the study of knowledge, but a great deal about the nature of knowledge is implied in Figures 1 and 2. This prompted two Web pages devoted to the structural and theoretical assumptions of h2cm (Jones, 2000a, b). Although the axes of h2cm are dichotomous, they also represent continua. This duality is important, as an individual's mental health status is situated on a continuum spanning *excellent* to *extremely unwell*. There are various states in between affected by an individual's beliefs, response to stress, coping strategies, epigenetic,

Figure 1. Health career model axes

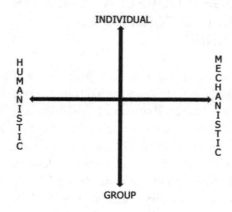

Figure 2. Health career model care domains

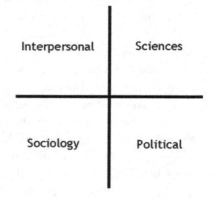

and other influences. H2cm was created to meet four educational objectives:

1. To produce a curriculum development tool
2. Help ensure holistic assessment and evaluation
3. To support reflective practice
4. To reduce the theory-practice gap

Since h2cm's formulation, these objectives have grown in relevance. The 1980s may seem remote, but these problems are far from archaic, as expansion of points 1-4 reveals. Student life is preparation for lifelong learning. Curricula are under constant pressure. Despite decades of policy declarations, truly holistic care (combining physical, mental, and pastoral care) remains elusive. The concept and practice of reflection swings like a metronome, one second seemingly de rigour, the next moment the subject of Web-based polls. H2cm can be used in interviews, outlining discussion and actions to pursue, an agenda, agreed and shared at the end of a session. The model is equally at home on paper, blackboard, flipchart, and interactive whiteboard. Finally, technology is often seen as a way to make knowledge available to all practitioners; the means to bridge theory-practice gap through activities such as e-learning, governance, and knowledge management.

The axes within h2cm create a cognitive space; a third axis projecting through the page can represent history; be that an educational, health, or other "career." It is ironic that an act of partition can simultaneously represent reductionism and holism. Reductionism has a pivotal role to play, which h2cm acknowledges in the sciences domain. What h2cm can do is prompt the expert (single domain) practitioner that there are three other pages to reflect and write upon.

SERRES AND HODGES: INFORMATICS INTERLOPERS OR INTEGRATORS?

If social informatics is to make a difference it must eschew the silo mentality that develops in many disciplines, limiting vision, reach, and action. Schools of informatics, such as health, genomics, social, community, medical, bioinformatics, and e-government, must cohere in order to amount to more than the sum of their sociotechnical parts. What this means for many infant or pubescent informatics disciplines and curricula is another debate. Where is the (cultural) centre of informatics? Is informatics built around the individual, the community, devices; or all combined? By opening our minds to possibilities, this chapter is a call for coherence. Wherever and however conceived, the various communities of practice using the label "informatics" must ensure they amplify each other. If not, they run the risk that they will interfere and cancel each other out; becoming yet another source of environmental and cultural noise. With the introduction completed, as you navigate what follows consider it an exploration: searching for the locus of informatics.

The Serres-cruciform motif is, of course, a fortunate coincidence of syntax, semantics, nomenclature, and form. When you look at Hodges' model what do you see; a crossroads, junction, or collision? Is there a gap between care domains, or do concepts gradually fuse with their neighbours in adjacent domains? It is always easier to ask questions, but several must be raised at this juncture. What exactly is a nurse, patient, carer, or citizen doing when they complete the h2cm matrix? Why do they place concepts into one domain rather than another? What consistency is there between users and are there any objective metrics to assist? Is there a way here, a crossroads,

Figure 3. H2CM-SERRES motif

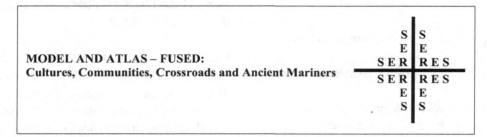

MODEL AND ATLAS – FUSED:
Cultures, Communities, Crossroads and Ancient Mariners

a way to represent, present, and share differing yet equally legitimate perspectives on the problems and issues that bind? How do we balance objective (mechanistic) and subjective (humanistic) health care? Are there only four domains? Who determines the number? Whatever our beliefs about the meaning of life, death, faith, and why we are all here, the pastoral-spiritual 5th domain is missing. It is there, all four domains combined plus one word. The biggest question of all: humanity, the plaintiff asks, why?

Serres endeavours to provide a comprehensive map, which he calls an atlas. This atlas is not aimed at a specific audience, such as an atlas of the heavens, but incorporates all disciplines. The purpose of the atlas is not recognisable at first. The key is not presented to us. Serres' work assaults the conventional academic senses. Like an explorer on a rope bridge, Serres runs the full length of the h2cm's axes, back and forth reaching into the knowledge domains. Getting to grips with Serres' thought means appreciating the uncertainty principle. We may know either the discipline where Serres currently resides, but not the instant of arrival or departure. As Serres wanders, quick, quick, slow; quantum leap, slow; such frenzied activity gives the impression of somebody lost, rather than following a predetermined agenda. The symbols and objects presented are instantly recognisable, but their juxtaposition makes them strangely alien. To be fully understood the familiar needs to be reappraised.

Gibson explores Serres' crossroads (Abbas, 2005, pp.84-98). Are crossroads merely a linear bisection? Or do travellers create a chiasmatic junction, moving like impulses flowing East-West and West-East to the optical centre, a nexus of communities and cultures? According to Cunliffe's (2001) book about the voyages of the ancient Greek explorer Pytheas, early mariners navigated using a text called a periplus. Providing some of the earliest recorded observational views of the world, the periplus described coastlines by landmarks, winds, and topography. Within care education, h2cm acts as a periplus for learners, an aide memoir, and reflective tool, a space to record those initial sightings and learning encounters. The model provides placeholders for knowledge, the exact position, content, and process of revision are not fixed. Hodges' model provides the coastline in template form; the context defines the topography; the landmarks.

In one sentence Serres (1997, p.20) conjoins the travels of mariners with their reliance on knots to modern graph theory and the need to explain complexity. Following the lessons of history and legend to solve a problem you might cut a knot. To fully understand it, you must untie it. This means entering the weft and weave of knowledge, back and fore in time, using hands and eyes: brain. Increasingly the disciplines are tied together because our problems are such that new knots are sought to repair and maintain the rigging. Conner notes Serres' observation that *"where topography is visual, topology is tactile"* (Abbas, 2005, p.158). Hodges' model helps us to see what is significant. Rigged together, the four vistas from the house of ideas have become our sail. In contact with individuals, communities, and cultures, h2cm can help us to recognise and address bias, prejudice, and the taunts of personal and ethnic histories. Only then, with memories and pain shared and understood, can we feel our way. In order to travel with someone you must both pass through the same crossroads and meet at the same portal.

ART AND SCIENCE: ACROSS THE GREAT DIVIDE

Whatever the situation interfaces abound. All inevitably have data, information, and knowledge in common. These concepts represent our age as no longer just real and imagined, but virtual as implemented in the World Wide Web. People interface using their senses. For Serres, touch is *the* interface. A computer *senses* through its interfaces about which Serres (1995b, p.70) observes:

Have you noticed the popularity among scientists of the word interface – which supposes that the junction between two sciences or two concepts is perfectly under control? On the contrary, I believe that these spaces between are more complicated than one thinks. This is why I have compared them to the Northwest Passage ... with shores, islands, and fractal ice floes. Between the hard sciences and the so-called human sciences the passage resembles a jagged shore, sprinkled with ice, and variable ... It's more fractal than simple. Less a juncture under control than an adventure to be had.

Hermes' travels are curtailed if creativity is stymied. If h2cm is to be a universal tool what does this mean in terms of *interface*? Information and communication technologies are not pure mechanism, developers of all tools must constantly acknowledge cultural and language differences. Does h2cm provide a template for an international interface combining left-right and right-left reading? From another perspective the human-computer interface literature asked readers how they would label four quadrants: as a *mathematician*, a *clock-watcher*, or a *book-reading clock-watcher* (McCabe, 1992)?

Although written at a time when the (first) Internet bubble was still inflating, Join-Lambert et al. (Join-Lambert, Klein, & Serres, 1997) throw light on the possible future directions of study and knowledge:

Intelligence is not about knowing axiomatically how to reason... The French 16th Century philosopher Montaigne already had dismissed the concept of a 'well-stuffed head.' The advent of the printing press made the memorization of Ulysses' travels and of folk tales - the support of knowledge at that time - redundant. Montaigne saw no longer use in memorizing a library that was potentially infinite. But does not the Internet ask for a 'well-endowed head'? Won't the best surfer be a 'Jack of all trades'? The fastest surfer is not going to be your typical Ivy-league super-titled philosopher: That guy's head will be simply too loaded to sort it out on the Net. So, there will be fresh opportunities for those who were viewed by society as laggards. It is a clean start with equal opportunities for all. [Online]

Serres' vision is not all conquering. Concern continues as to the quality of knowledge on the Web, especially health information, and the realisation of benefits from e-learning. Social exclusion, access to care services and education remain key political issues. Groups have mobilised to reduce the digital divide through digital communities furthering political, democratic, and environmental awareness using information technology under the aegis of social and community informatics. Access to information and communication technologies (ICT), education, and training provides early warning of obstacles; alternate passages through the system(s) become visible, whether for individuals, community groups, or global communities.

In addition to the gaps suggested by these interfaces, the void between theory and practice is a subject of ongoing debate within health care (Cody, 2003) and without (Northouse, 2003; Temperton et al., 2004). There is another; the mind gap. This refers to the "distance" an individual must traverse to access education (Join-Lambert et al., 1997). For many people this proves a complex negotiation, as well recognised in medical sociology. Parsons' (1951) seminal work on the sick role, explaining the sequence individuals pass through when a personal health problem reaches the point when expert help must be sought (however defined culturally). The formal step of going to the doctor must be sanctioned and initiated socially. Individuals, especially juniors, must frequently rely on the financial or emotional support of a family member if they are to pursue serious study; or their peers to engage in a community development programme. People need permission to be sick or clever(er).

Serres, Hodges, and others raise the question of whether there is a point midway between the sciences and humanities. Serres steps over the disciplinary boundaries; or rather he dismisses them as with an astronaut's view of Earth. He grasps the bottles stuffed with their messages [see forward of Genesis, Serres, 1995c] and smashes the bottleneck. Whatever the answer to this question, informatics can help overcome the barriers of time, distance, and social prejudices. The "home," the second seat of learning becomes a campus: but this is not a given.

The Frenchman finds *residence, belonging,* and claims for the *homeland* disturbing. In the book *Rome,* Serres (1981) explains how the foundation of civilization and culture is based on violence. When people become a mob, they raise the buildings to the ground exposing the

foundations. Serres is telling us to look again at the mosaics buried beneath our feet, wherever we are. Introducing anthropology, Eriksen (2001) describes the need to simultaneously allow for *emic* and *etic* accounts. Individuals and communities (patients and carers) must describe themselves in their own terms (*emic*), but this affects the way an encounter or situation is analysed (*etic*). Cultural relativism complicates our efforts to explain, and yet where there is contrast there is difference and an opportunity to learn.

It is no coincidence that the words *community* and *communication* are so similar. Brown (1999) explains how Serres repeatedly focuses on etymology, for example, complex from *plexus* that which is woven, but also from *plicare,* a fold. Physicists warp 2-D space, to explain hypothetical faster than light travel. In the mind of the user, h2cm warps a 2x2 matrix plus time, making concepts and disciplines neighbours; an act of folding surely? Serres also utilises the French language, *le temps,* with its dual meaning for time and weather. Global communities are becoming a homogenised temporal conurbation. Globalisation challenges not only our notions of subjective time, but unique cultural perspectives such as that of the Aymara people, who apparently have a concept of time opposite to all the world's studied cultures: the past is ahead of them and the future behind (Spinney, 2005). Hermes lays a taut golden thread. The tension is created by the need to communicate universally, without diluting cultural and community identities.

LANGUAGE TO CARE

When engaging with others we can remain safe, never venturing, never taking a risk for new experiences, new knowledge; Serres likens this to swimming a river and reaching halfway, a decision must be made, to continue or turn back Serres (1997). In the middle, choices become stark, a challenge, a rite of passage, when a venture becomes an adventure. Suddenly, inner resources must come to the fore, dare we rely on them, so many characteristics and attributes: handedness, gender, learning styles. Does a change of knowledge (care) domain or even a shift towards another domain signify change of contexts? Passing from one care domain to another is akin to reaching mid-river. An opportunity to reflect and (re)appraise this twist of the thread.

In conversation with Latour, Serres (1995a) questions the ascendancy of concepts above prepositions. Psychology and cognitive science have produced a wealth of research (Rosch, 1981) built using concepts as the fundamental unit. To bridge the disciplinary divide, to understand the role of noise, Serres argues that prepositions also have importance. Prepositions locate us in time and space: *with, before, after, until, during, on, later, across*. In caring and informatics, prepositions assume humanistic prominence, giving quality and meaning to goals, priorities. This is not just a question of whether concepts alone are sufficient for dialogue between the sciences and humanities. In community development and care programmes, the language used is critical to reaching out and fully engaging people, to overcome apathy, low self-esteem, alienation and, as Serres argues, a lack of 'travel.'

Our whole experience is grounded in time; hence, the mythic status of timelessness. In h2cm "career" refers to life chances defined by Hughes (1958, p.63):

... the moving perspective in which the person sees his life as a whole and interprets the meanings of his various attitudes, actions, and the things which happen to him.

The concept of *career* is future oriented, the idea of life chances having a direct correspondence to Serres' description of life and choice; freedom. As we get older there is less scope for our path to meander. Choices become fewer, windows of opportunity pass and may be grieved for such is the sense of loss that accompanies them. Time is of course embedded in each of the h2cm's domains: *interpersonally* in the subjective passage of time and healing of the psyche; in the *sciences* in chronological age vs. pathological age, and physical healing processes: life and death.

The primary objective of science is often described as *casting light on the dark, the unknown.* It is ironic that in casting light, it is our communities that shine brightly, dimming the stars that first made us wonder. In our wanderings we placed our myths in the night sky. Now our cities shine to such an extent that the significance of our situation is lost in the glare. In the popular 1980s TV series *Cosmos,* Carl Sagan linked us intimately with the stars. Serres (1997, p.10) notes that "under the cranial vault constellations twinkle." The human train continues: this miraculous combination of humanistic and mechanistic dance partners. Now the coupling falters the music inaudible. The dance is unidirectional, physically and temporally: "to the right!" The mechanistic march has set the bridge swaying. Who will break step and afford safe passage?

What step are informatics practitioners marching to? By definition, being *community* or *social* centred, this cohort are either leading or following the crowd. A sense of home, place, territory is involved. Beyond the professional codes of practice (British Computer Society, 2001) of information technology professionals and Kling et al. (2005, p.93) who observe that ICT is not value neutral, what values does social informatics hold?

In *Five Senses*, Serres does not overtly discuss mortality, loss, depletion, and omission (Connor, 1999). Management consultants advise that to succeed "think outside the box," but the population pyramid announces an ageing population and *the* box is frequently found full and yet empty? Plaques disconnect, disable the memory; the critical biological box no longer registers and connects. The noise that counts, the background bioelectrical hum is disrupted or absent. Memories once ready to roll downhill, surfing the wave of potential are inaccessible, if marshalled at all. Wither the neural crossroads; the *informatique* mote in Hermes' eye?

Our older people, those not yet ephemeral have become peripheral, their personal space an adjunct to furniture. New quantities in life, beg questions of quality, especially quality of care and what it means to care. The concept of self, personhood is a prime distinguishing factor in terms of describing the attitudes of cultures and communities to older adults and memory loss. In the developed nations the debate continues: is this the price of a long life, or a way of life? In our search for the locus: the sign on the door reads *deep informatics*. Listen carefully, as inside the seniors are cared for at home (touched) remotely courtesy of telecare solutions. The values here of course extend from inappropriate use of informatics to lack of access to such services (Barlow, Bayer, & Curry, 2006).

There are three records: the care record, the knowledge record now imbued in the Web, and the planet. It is strange, this obsession with risk and records: physically, cognitively, and computationally. Two obsessions, closely related, so hand-in-hand that incessant washing cannot erase evidence of this union. Now, the planet is humanities record. Through remote sensing our senses are extended; they are exosomatic (Medawar, 1984), but seeing more means recording more. Do we really understand more? We are still learning about the entities and attributes of this planetary record, some people argue that being incomplete it cannot be read. When is a record complete? Information already overflows the cup; but whether full of cappuccino or medicine, four (or five?) sugared domains will help wash it down.

Gaia taps our shoulder with increasing insistence. Who will turn around and look her in the eye? The dare increases in magnitude moment by year. Avoidance of Nature's gaze will not serve to protect, because we are already turning to shades of grey. People need to see the stars to see how transient they are, to wonder and respect as once

before. Comets were cast in the role of *Hermes*, the harbingers of tomorrow. Today, the appearance of contrails near the horizon is striking, so comet like, especially as they buzz the sun. In addition to finding h2cm there, what other messages are writ large in the sky?

CLOSING DISCUSSION

Since h2cm has never been fully developed in theory or practice, comparison with Serres' (translated) work is limited. Both are encyclopaedic, they share a psychohistorical objective in education, and in both, information can act as a unifying concept, but for what reason, why is this significant? Politics and philosophy suffer from a lack of public engagement. Citizenship is crucial in health and the environment and vice versa. Do we just sit and wait for synchrony to occur? Could the commercial notion of just-in-time processes apply in this instance, meaning that spontaneous citizen activism is possible? This would be revolutionary no less. Will Serres' *Natural Contract* emerge out of the political and social noise? People fear change because it so often means rupture. Can informatics prove the catalyst for a third way in terms of evolutionary vs. revolutionary change? Governance cannot, by definition, be unidirectional. There must be political equivalence with cross-party and governmental policy continuity termed "simultaneous policy" (Bunzl, 2001) on issues that affect us all, such as economics and global warming. Only then can issues be addressed nationally for translation into international objectives.

The scholastic 3Rs alone are no longer sufficient to equip youngsters for current and future challenges. Wither health literacy without digital, information, and visual literacy (accessibility issues acknowledged)? Carroll and Rosson (2007) recognise the moral imperative of participative design. If technology has the capacity to change, people must be involved in that change. Are governments granted the electorate they deserve? The ability to appreciate what lies between analysis and synthesis is the 21st century touchstone. In being educated to care for others, self, and the planet, there is a need for a generic model that can be taught globally, across curricula, cultures, and ethnic divides. Janus-like we must combine the local and global, achieving *glocal* perspectives (Erikson, 2001, chap. 19).

To manage this most complex of times, we must repeatedly cross Serres' middle, all knowledge domains must be accessible. Ironically, the ubiquity of information provides the scope to think not only out of the box, but in it as well. Midgley (2003) warns about the seductive properties of big ideas. Brainstorming alone does not a solution make? Although health is multicontextual, there is a danger that having all contexts means having none. We must, however, persevere. Now, health and the environment are like two pearls threaded on a fine cord called quality of life. What price to leave footprints that do not corrupt the mental, physical, and spiritual health of others, locally, globally, today, and tomorrow?

The philosopher Gadamer wrote of the *fusion of horizons* (Gadamer, 2004); however Gadamer is interpreted, as individuals we see one horizon at a time. Once we leave home the four points of the compass make their presence felt, or at least they used to. Now our journeys prompt mundane speculation on travel times, road works, fuel costs, expenses, and mobile communications. In combination Serres and Hodges provide an architectonic foundation for our knowledge. The act of twisting a single horizon to create a multitude imbues great potential. At a time when *fusion* is (desperately) sought as a solution to our energy needs, the fusion of ideas and action across disciplines, communities, and cultures is no less critical as we cross *the* middle and step into tomorrow.

ACKNOWLEDGMENT

I would like to express my sincere thanks to the editors for their interest; Steve Brown, Malte Ebach, Maurice Gledhill and Steve Marks for support and many very helpful comments on previous drafts of this chapter.

REFERENCES

Abbas, N. (2005). *Mapping Michel Serres*. Ann Arbor: University of Michigan Press.

Adams, T. (1987). Dementia is a family affair. *Community Outlook*, 7-8.

Assad, M. L. (1999). *Reading with Michel Serres: An encounter with time*. State University of New York Press.

Barlow, J., Bayer, S., & Curry, R. (2006). Implementing complex innovations in fluid multistakeholder environments: Experiences of "telecare". *Technovation*, *26*(3), 396-406.

British Computer Society. (2001). *Code of Conduct*, Version 2.0, MTG/CODE/292/1201.

Brown, S. D. (1999). *Caught up in the rapture: Serres translates Mandlebrot*. Retrieved May 12, 2007, from http://www.keele.ac.uk/depts/stt/cstt2/comp/rapture.htm

Bunzl, J. (2001). *The simultaneous policy: An insider's guide to saving humanity and the planet*. New European Publications.

Carroll, J. M. & Rosson, M. B. (2007). Participatory design in community informatics. *Design Studies*, *I*(3), 243-261.

Clement, A., Gurstein, M., Longford, G., et al. (2004). The Canadian Research Alliance for Community Innovation and Networking (CRACIN). *Journal of Community Informatics*, *1*(1), 7-20.

Cody, W. K. (2003). Nursing theory as a guide to practice. *Nursing Science Quarterly, 16*(3), 225-231.

Connor, S. (1999). *Michel Serres' five senses.* Retrieved May 12, 2007, from http://www.bbk.ac.uk/english/skc/5senses.htm

Cunliffe, B. (2001). *The extraordinary voyage of Pytheas the Greek.* Penguin.

Dale, C., & Adamson, G. (1998-1999). *A Michel Serres interview.* Retrieved May 12, 2007, from http://www.thepander.co.nz/culture/mserres5.php

Eriksen, T. H. (2001). *Small places, large issues.* Pluto Press.

Gadamer, H-G. (2004). *Truth and method.* London:Continuum Publishing Group.

Hinchcliffe, S. M. (Ed.). (1989). *Nursing practice and health care,* (1st ed. only). London: Edward Arnold.

Hughes, E. (1958). *Men and their work.* New York: Free Press.

Join-Lambert, L., Klein, P., & Serres, M. (1997). Interview. Superhighways for all: Knowledge's redemption. *Revue Quart Monde, 1,*163. Retrieved May 12 2007, from http://www.nettime.org/Lists-Archives/nettime-l-9810/msg00137.html

Jones, P. (1996). Humans, information, and science. *Journal of Advanced Nursing,* 591-598.

Jones, P. (1998). *Hodges' health career care domains model.* Retrieved May 12, 2007, from http://www.p-jones.demon.co.uk

Jones, P. (2000a). *Hodges' health career care domains model, structural assumptions.* Retrieved May 12, 2007, from http://www.p-jones.demon.co.uk/theory.html

Jones, P. (2000b). *Hodges' health career care domains model, theoretical assumptions.* Retrieved May 12, 2007, from http://www.p-jones.demon.co.uk/struct.html

Jones, P. (2004a). Viewpoint: Can informatics and holistic multidisciplinary care be harmonised? *British Journal of Healthcare Computing & Information Management, 21*(6), 17-18.

Jones, P. (2004b). *The four care domains: Situations worthy of research.* Conference: Building & Bridging Community Networks: Knowledge, Innovation & Diversity through Communication, Brighton, UK. Retrieved May 7, 2007, from http://www.comminit.com/healthecomm/planning.php?showdetails=318

Kling, R., Rosenbaum, H., & Sawyer, S. (2005). Understanding and communicating social informatics. *Information Today.*

Lopez, A. D., Mathers, C. D., Ezzati, M., Jamison, D. T., & Murray, C .J. L. (2006). Global and regional burden of disease and risk factors, 2001: Systematic analysis of population health data. *The Lancet, 367*(9524), 1747-1757.

McCabe, M. (1992). Human factors aspects of user interface design. *Engineering Computing Newsletter,* SERC #38, 4-5.

Medawar, P. (1984). *The limits of science.* Oxford, Oxford University Press.

Midgley, M. (2003). *Myths we live by.* Routledge.

Mumford, E. (1996). *Systems design ethical tools for ethical change.* Macmillan.

Northouse, P. G. (2003). *Leadership: Theory and practice.* Sage Publications Ltd.

O'Neil, D. (2002). Assessing community informatics: A review of methodological approaches for evaluating community networks and community technology centres. *Internet Research, 12*(1), 76-102.

Parsons T. (1951). *The social system*. Glencoe, IL: The Free Press.

Rieff, D. (2002). *A bed for the night, humanitarianism in crisis*. Vintage.

Rosch, E. (1981). *Prototype classification and logical classification: The two systems*. In E. Scholnick (Ed.), *New trends in conceptual representation*. Hillsdale, NJ: Erlbaum.

Serres, M. (1977). *The birth of physics*. Clinamen Press.

Serres, M. (1981). *Rome: The book of foundations*. Ann Arbor, MI: University of Michigan Press.

Serres, M. (1995a). *Conversations on science, culture, and time*. Ann Arbor, MI: University of Michigan Press.

Serres, M. (1995b). *The natural contract*. Ann ARbor, MI: University of Michigan Press.

Serres, M. (1995c). *Genesis*. Ann Arbor, MI: University of Michigan Press. p.6.

Serres, M. (1997). *The troubadour of knowledge*. Ann Arbor, MI: University of Michigan Press.

Spinney, L. (2005). How time flies. *The Guardian*.

Temperton, V. M. et al., (Eds.) (2004). *Assembly rules and restoration ecology: Bridging the gap between theory and practice*. Washington, Island Press.

Vidal, R. V. V. (2006). *Creative and participative problem solving – The art and the science, informatics and mathematical modelling*. Technical University of Denmark. Retrieved from http://www2.imm.dtu.dk/ vvv/CPPS/

Wilber, K. (2000). *Integral psychology: Consciousness, spirit, psychology, therapy*. Shambhala Publications.

Wilson, E. O. (1998). *Consilience: The unity of knowledge*. Abacus.

Zubin, J., & Spring, B. (1977). Vulnerability - A new view of schizophrenia. *Journal of Abnormal Psychology, 86*(2), 103-124.

Chapter VIII
The Social Glue in Open Source:
Incomplete Contracts and Informal Credits

Matthias Bärwolff
Technische Universität Berlin, Germany

ABSTRACT

Open source has, of late been discussed as a most significant institutional disruption to the way software and, indeed, digital content, in general, evolves and dissipates through society. Credits and their due redemption play a vital yet often underrated role in the development and dissemination of open source. While credits in open source development are often of a rather elusive and informal nature (goodwill, reputation, indirect effects), formal credits have their inevitable role, too. On the one hand, less formal kinds of credits than money and the like often provide for a relatively efficient and viable way of accounting for credits in the development of large and complex software and technology projects. On the other hand, at the intersection of developer communities with end users, there is a distinct need for formal money-based interactions, because informal contracts and credit redemption do work well in communities, but less so in anonymous market contexts.

INTRODUCTION

The importance and value of open source to society is now undisputed. It has, in due course, come to be a metaphor so vivid and laden with interpretative scope that we can barely contain the notion to a meaningful definition. Yet despite its evasive nature, it has valuably reminded us of the world of institutions aside from markets and firms in a time when economics clings largely unchallenged to superiority in the analysis and construction of our society.

Open source links technology and its progress with economics in a way that overturns much of the conventional wisdom about the institutions of capitalism (Weber, 2004). No more is capital and the employment of labour by capital the primary means of organising production and allocation of resources. Open source empowers people in an unheard of fashion to create their resources, share them with others, and build unimpededly on the work of others (Stallman, 1999). This novel mode of production is often more efficient than previous ones based on control and exclusion, even for public companies accountable to profit-seeking shareholders (Grand, von Krogh, Leonard, & Swap, 2004). And it goes beyond software: As the hype over open source settles, we have come to realise that *open innovation* may not only govern the production of software, but that of intangibles in general, most of which have invariably fallen within the realm of the Internet's all-encompassing digitalisation (Chesbrough, 2003; Ogawa & Piller, 2006).

The connection of people via the Internet is creating value in itself, synergies impossible to obtain by command-and-control structures, and entirely new opportunities for experimentation with technologies. Bertolt Brecht has mused on the value of such a system long ago:

The radio would be the finest possible communication apparatus in public life, a vast network of pipes [...] If it knew how to receive as well as transmit, how to let the listener speak as well as hear, how to bring him into a relationship instead of isolating him. (1932, emphasis added)

Today, we stand on the verge of a world in which any receiver may be a supplier, too, through the design and capability of our technologies, but also through the social forces that have overcome established practices of command and control.

It is not our objective here to work through all relevant issues raised by the dawning *democratisation of innovation, production, and consumption* (to paraphrase the metaphor introduced by Hippel, 2005), but to highlight one important, and often overlooked aspect, inherent to all such contexts:

the accounting for, and redeeming of, informal credits obtained in incomplete contracts settings. This is not to say that such transactions and according credit frameworks have never existed. Ever since people have started to specialise their efforts to raise the cumulative value of their work, they have had to devise means of accomplishing the due allocations. But we have, of late, become so preoccupied with the supremacy of money as a means of credit that we sometimes forget that money is but one kind of credit, and not always the most sensible one to employ as a means of mediating transactions. We believe that informal credits provide a valuable means of understanding open source and open innovation processes. The absence of price tags and the history of open source as a primarily social movement do not foreclose the existence and viability of credits. With our approach, we identify a promising angle from which to analyse open source practices of production and dissemination without having to resort to bold claims of open source being a completely novel mode of production distinct from market and firm. Thus we make a cautious step towards a deeper understanding of open source practices, and one that firmly relates to existing knowledge about credits, contracts, and incentives.

The chapter proceeds as follows. First, we will briefly look at the notion of open source, and the motivations behind contributions to such processes from the solid and well-researched microperspective. Then we will go on to consider the equally sound subject of informal credits and incomplete contracts in commerce in a general manner. By doing so, we have set the stage for a deeper understanding of the factors that make for the sustainability of open source practices, to be elaborated in the remainder of the chapter. Thus in section 3, we turn to the social institutions of open source, and introduce our credit approach to open source. At last, we provide a conclusion and further research directions.

BACKGROUND

Open Source and the Question of Incentives

The term open source has been championed by some of its proponents, namely a group headed by Eric S. Raymond, in order to capture the practice of attaching liberal open source licenses to software, and make it more accessible and attractive a choice for corporations (Raymond, 1999). Indeed, open source turns conventional intellectual property rights practices on their head. It makes use of a legal system originally insituted to strengthen the power of inventors, creators, and their principals over the commercial exploitation of their works, but it aims at achieving precisely the opposite effect: using the legal ownership like rights of a creator in order to ensure that his creation and all its derivatives remain once and for all in the public domain.

The innovation that gave rise to open source dates back to the free software movement in the 1980s when Richard Stallman developed a legally enforceable software license, the GNU General Public License (GPL), that granted far-reaching rights to a receiver of a software program put under such license.[1] In order for the receiver to enjoy those rights—"the right to run the program, for any purpose, [...] to modify the program, [...] to redistribute copies, either gratis or for a fee, [and] to distribute modified versions of the program" (Stallman, 1999), they will have to abide by the GPL provision stating that any modifications of the program must only be further distributed under precisely the same GPL license terms along with the program's source code.[2] The GPL freedoms attached to a software thus propagate irrevocably throughout society. If a receiver redistributes the software or a derivative work but fails to conform to the duties imposed by the GPL license, the rights granted therein become void, and elapse to the ordinary fair-use rights granted by copyright law. And those do not in general allow redistribution.

A second major open source license is the Berkeley Software Distribution License (BSD) developed at Berkeley University primarily to appreciate and give substance to the fact that most university research is publicly funded and shall thus be available to the public under the least restrictive terms. The BSD license is less restrictive than the GPL in that virtually any use of a software thus licensed is being permitted, including proprietary use. This feature makes BSD-licensed software very attractive for companies pursuing a strict proprietary software licensing model.[3]

The legal status and moral legitimacy of open source have not been undisputed by private parties that stand to lose from a proliferation of open source software.[4] However, as a social practice it is based on the widely accepted societal norm according to which anyone is and should be, by and large, free to pursue whatever objectives he wishes to as long as there are no convincing moral, legal, or economic arguments for the opposite. No one has, thus far, seriously suggested curtailing the freedom of people to contract over or let go off their intellectual property as they see fit, however, irrational and economically inefficient that may seem. Indeed, it is the very premise of pro-free-market arguments that the individual utility function of a person is beyond economic reasoning (Friedman, 1962). Thus we may safely state that open source is, in principle, compatible not only with our basic legal framework of intellectual property rights, but with our societal norms, too (Lessig, 2004).

The question remains as to why people other than tax-funded researchers would want to contribute their efforts in such an institutional setting where they are bound to waive the residual control normally granted by intellectual property rights law. Answering this question has, indeed, been at the center of scholarly work in the field of open source, and an enormous amount of due literature, both theoretical and empirical, has emerged in its quest.

The empirical evidence indicates that largely rational motivations of developers explain for most open source activities. Lerner and Tirole (2002) argue that most developers will be motivated by career considerations aiming to signal their skills to prospective employers. Most empirical studies support this view. First, in the large majority of projects, the bulk of development is done by relatively few people, often no more than two or three persons (Ghosh et al., 2006; Krishnamurthy, 2002). Second, those contributors often manage to obtain higher wages as a result of their achievements and visibility (Hars & Ou, 2001; Lee, Moisa, N., & Weiss, 2003). Today, many open source projects are sponsored directly by larger corporations, resulting in an accordingly large percentage of contributions by paid employees of those companies (Bärwolff, 2006).[5]

More adventurous theoretical approaches argue that intrinsic motivations on the part of developers explain for open source efforts (e.g., Osterloh et al., 2002). This view, however, is not easily supported with empirical results outside laboratory experiments. Dalle and David (2005) have put forward the hypothesis that the viability open source critically depends on both rational contributions and intrinsically motivated contributions. Their model building efforts and empirical results are still preliminary, though.

The problem with the answers provided thus far is that they do not conclusively explain what makes for the sustainability of open source development. The next section will thus digress to the issue of credits, more specifically, the feasibility of informal credits and incomplete contracts transactions. Equipped with an understanding of these issues, we may then turn to the question of open source sustainability in section 3, the main body of this chapter.

Informal Credits and Incomplete Contracts

The importance of the institution of credit, in general, and its different shapes, in particular, for the economic development of society can hardly be overstated. Credits are the foundation of any meaningful commerce amongst individuals and groups of people in a society, for they allow the reciprocation of services and goods in a delayed manner, thus, opening up a much wider horizon of transactions than would be possible in an idealised barter economy (Innes, 1914).

Today, we often tend to reduce the notion of credit to bank-issued and state-backed money, as well as its close relatives, denotable in pecuniary terms. Clearly, there is some value in realising, in money, the gains from trade ones efforts give rise to. Yet credits in social interactions have always taken a host of shapes ranging from tacit agreement between two individuals on delayed reciprocation, to such understandings made in public involving the threat of punishment by third parties in case of failure to reciprocate, to the bank-issued and state-controlled money so prominent in modern day transactions. Money is but one form of credit, and it is social in origin no matter how seemingly void of social meaning it has become.[6]

The reason for the variety of credit institutions is their respective difference in performance with regard to the transaction costs (Coase, 1937) they give rise to. Any system of credit accounting entails costs whose respective magnitude depends on the specifics regarding the interplay of law and norms, the economic environment, and the nature of assets to be transferred. While money, as arguably the most easily transferable and universal form of credit, plays a vital role in the history of capitalism (Ingham, 2004), it is important to realise that it need not always be the most efficient means of credit. There have always been areas in society where money credits play little to no role precisely because they entail higher transaction costs than other more informal means of credits.

Particularly, in settings with a sufficient level of trust and reciprocity, a system of tacit accounting economises on the transaction costs inevitably associated with the maintenance of a monetary system. Such settings are, in fact, more common than is generally assumed. In order to help sustain trust and reciprocity, there is often an institutional mix of social norms, legal threats, economic imparatives, and technical premises that goes well beyond the limited scope of complete contracts and formal money credit accounting (Bowles, 2004). One may object that informal accounting practices lack the very formality required to feasibly enforce agreements in a court of law. However, the same often goes for written contracts. Whenever the assets to a transaction are difficult to specify, knowledge and rationality of the participants are bounded, and the contingencies of a transaction may not be fully captured in all detail; we are inevitably left with incomplete contracts (Grossman & Hart, 1986; Hart & Moore, 1988). Due to their flexibility and low-cost enforcement, incomplete contracts and informal credit systems are an important institutional governance solution to a whole host of real-world contexts including that of distributed software development, as we shall see in the following sections.

MAIN FOCUS OF THE CHAPTER

Open Source: An Institutional Innovation in the Making

From the question of incentives section, we know that open source is an institutional practice that goes beyond publicly funded university research, and that there are rational incentives for developers to engage in the production of open source software. From the informal credits and incomplete contracts section, we also know that the absence of contracts tightly specified in writing and money credits do not, per se, entail an absence of commerce. Still, if software production gives rise

to gains from trade, which is no doubt the case, then open source should, in the long-term, come to fall within received economic categories of markets and firms, or remain a fringe phenomenon compared with the massive commercial software industry. This is apparently not the case given the high-profile success of Linux and other open source software projects. We shall in this section see why this is so.

The origin of open source has been a social practice, not economic efficiency considerations on the part of individual actors. Open source is thus primarily a social innovation, not a managerial one. Yet the first reason for its sustainability as a social practice is the legal framework set up by open source licenses that often prohibits the appropriation of modifications by receivers (see question of incentives section). The legal institution of open source licenses is so vital because it makes defection from community norms once subscribed to practically impossible. It increases trust in and credibility of participants' commitments. Thus open source can thrive in and extend to more anonymous and untrustworthy contexts where there are no more "frequently repeated, multifaceted, face-to-face situations" (Bowles, 2004, p. 258) that help sustain basic social norms of reciprocity. Here, the real threat of legal action against those that defect from social norms is a sensible means of ensuring cooperation. The second major reason for the success of open source as a social practice carried by ever more commercial enterprises is found in the structural complexity of software. Bessen (2005) notes that this complexity effectively forecloses the feasibility of complete contracts:

[T]he software code itself is the complete description of how the software will function in every circumstance and, consequently, writing a contract that covers every contingency costs roughly the same as writing the software itself. Practical contracts for software will thus not completely specify all details, interactions and contingencies. (p. 2)

The problem pointed out by Bessen applies both to the production and the distribution or sale of software. It is hard for users to specify their demand, it is hard for a manager to monitor work efforts of programmers; in fact, it is hard for anyone even to judge the state, the progress, and the quality of a software project (Brooks Jr., 1995; Rosenberg, 2007). Thus a substantial part of software development is not being conducted in competitive market contexts, but is instead either subject to monopolist practices or conducted in-house. Lock-in and network effects, the peculiarities of the software market that give rise to its decisively anticompetitive characteristics (Shapiro & Varian, 1999), may actually be traced back to the complexity of software. The inefficiencies of the software market are a consequence of the inevitable incompleteness of contracts following from the complexity of software.

The adverse effects of software complexity may, however, be alleviated. To this end, Bessen (2005) has proposed three principal optimisation strategies, one of which is to contribute ones code to an open source commons, waiving the exclusive ownership of ones investments and thus avoiding the resulting contractual hassles. This will be the more attractive the larger the existing commons. Not only does the open source solution reduce complexity by containing contractual contingencies, it also overcomes the "adversarial relationship" between vendors and users stemming from the opposing interests regarding control over a software product's source code and use (Assay, 2005). Alleviating this tension creates a significant social value in its own right that adds to the value from having access to and control over the source code and future modifications on the part of users. Also, the trust and goodwill for producers generated by this practice improves communication and feedback cycles between users and producers that again raises the value of the artefacts at hand (Demil & Lecocq, 2003). However, Bessen limits the scope of his considerations about complexity reduction to "more complex, 'geekier' applications" (p. 4) where users tend to be producers, too, for in his model there is no explicit room for conventional market relationships between contributors and users. Still, Bessen has identified an important instance in which open source as a social practice overcomes the resource allocation problem posed by the complexity of software.

Hippel (2005) has further extended the scope of these considerations beyond software to any context in which end users may sensibly get involved with the production of goods. His argument about open innovation, which is both positive and normative, builds on the premise that precise information about user demand often cannot be perfectly communicated to a potential supply side due to the transaction costs involved, again making for an absence of efficient markets. Thus it is in the face of prohibitive transaction cost structures more efficient for users, particularly lead users, to amend existing products according to their needs by themselves and freely reveal their innovation to others. It should be noted, however, that though Hippel identifies a number of instances where user innovation takes place, the empirical evidence behind his model is rather thin.

The interesting question is whether and how open source practices may be found in and applied to contexts in which producers and consumers are more disparate. We would argue that open source may, indeed, be a viable mode of production and dissemination beyond Bessen's "more complex, 'geekier' applications" or Hippel's user innovation contexts. Referring back to the previous section on incomplete contracts and informal credits we shall in the following section look closer at how contractual obligations and credits apply to open source practices, so as to reconcile them with more conventional commercial practices and sustainably extend them beyond negligible fringes and tax funded research contexts.

A Credit Approach to Open Source

We have seen that open source and open innovation practices create value beyond that generated in "adversarial" market relationships. On the one hand, this is due to the added value stemming from the shift of control and power over source code and software usage to users. On the other hand, there is a somewhat more intangible social value from the relationship between producers and consumers becoming non-adversarial. Thus far we have confined the feasibility of such practices to a relatively small subset of social and economic activities found in a society. The superiority of market- and firm-based resource allocation has not been challenged substantially, neither by theoretical nor by empirical accounts on open source and open innovation. In fact, proponents of a "third mode of production" such as Benkler (2006) have a hard time substantiating their bold claims about social processes void of commercial considerations, as Strahilevitz (2007) notes. We believe that applying our considerations about informal credits and contracts to open source and open innovation fills some of the gaps in our current understanding of such practices. This section provides some general ideas and approaches towards this end. Specifically, it is our claim that open source practices largely build on credit generation and redemption much like markets and firms, albeit in a profoundly different fashion so as to reduce the inherent inefficiencies of formal contracts and money-like credits.

Credits in the process of open source development transactions do not typically take the shape of money or other such credits.[7] Instead, they consist of little more than the mere mentioning of contributor names in the software itself as well as in communications regarding the same. The judging of the merits of individual contributions is a dynamic process both within the project itself and the adoption of the software by third parties that may, again, be observed by noninvolved parties. A contribution of high value will often find its way into a project subject to the scrutiny of other peers, while a useless contribution will simply not be adopted, much like low-quality goods will not easily be sold in a market for a reasonable price. There is, however, an important difference between conventional markets and open source markets regarding the credits and their generation. Credits in open source development, unlike those generated via money, are directly linked to the activities that create them. If money is the most anonymous and detached kind of credit, then open source credits are the ones most inextricably linked to the context in which they were created.[8]

It may at first seem curious to liken credits in open source projects, entries in the credits-file,[9] on the project Web site, in mailing lists, forums, and so forth, to credits in a capitalist economic system. Yet apart from denoting authorship, in a legal sense, this is *the* one vital function of credits in open source projects: to account for individual achievements in those projects. Without such an institution no one could easily claim any credits in open source development, something that, in fact, frequently happens. Those credits may then be redeemed, as we shall see in the following.

Priddat (2006) has interpreted the credits obtained by efforts in open source projects as a means of attaining higher status in those projects and related exclusive networks. Such status may not be bought with money whilst the commercial value of such status in unquestionable, involving easier access to central information and increased influence on project decisions. We may really speak of credit redemption here, since the credits will have to be renewed at some point in order to maintain the social position once achieved. Given the meritocratic nature of practically all successful open source projects, there is ample empirical evidence for this claim. In most projects, the founder becomes project leader, too, and important positions are occupied on the basis of merit often by means of democratic elections. For example, no one would seriously want to question the prominent position of Linus Torvalds in the Linux kernel project, given that he founded the project and has always remained an important contributor. Also, think of the Debian Linux distribution project that elects a project leader once a year.

Lerner and Tirole (2002), following the seminal work of Spence (1973), have argued that the credits obtained from open source efforts may serve as a means of signalling ones professional skills to prospective employers. Since it is costly for an employer to judge the skills of an applicant directly, he may depend on a more easily observable proxy to this end, such as the quality of his contributions to open source projects, and the status achieved therein. This, to Lerner and Tirole, is what the credits obtained in open source accomplish. Note, again, that those credits may not generally be obtained in exchange for money. And, again, the credits will lose some of their exchange value over time.

Generally, anyone who has risen to an important position in the social hierarchy of a bigger open source project has proven enough technical merit to be a natural target to be hired outright by a software company, sometimes continuing to work full time for their project. Examples include Linus Torvalds, founder of Linux, working for a long time for Transmeta, now working for Linux Foundation; Ian Murdoch, founder of Debian, now working for SUN Microsystems; and Daniel Robbins, founder of Gentoo Linux, working briefly for Microsoft, to name but a very few.

To sum up, the credits obtained by successfully contributing to an open source project generally translate into one of the following:

- Social status within the project and its wider community
- Goodwill with prospective clients or employers

The credits and their prospective redemption, laid out previously, may not only accrue to individuals but to companies, too. If a firm contributes their resources, typically paid software developers, to an open source project, it will gain in status within the community, but also with customers and other stakeholders. The former will give a firm some leverage over a project's future direction that may positively impact on a company's offerings in market contexts, and the latter will translate into an improved standing in the market, with respect to related commercial offerings. Someone who has proven intimacy with a certain software will more easily be trusted to perform well at providing related services (Grand et al., 2004). Think, for example, of Red Hat, who have managed to obtain a very favourable standing in the open source community by their active and forthcoming involvement in many upstream projects. Also, their merits make it easier for them to sell services related to their Linux distribution Red Hat Enterprise Linux (RHEL) such as subscriptions to updates, and so forth. When Oracle Corp. tried to directly imitate some of Red Hat's offerings, it did not succeed precisely because they lack the requisite credits with the community and potential customers.

The informal nature and the social meaning of the credits obtained through the involvement in open source is their very strength over more formal kinds of credits such as money, for they may be redeemed in social contexts where money would simply not be as efficient, or not even do at all. This, then, is what makes for their attractiveness to rationally incentivised parties who will link through their value chain conventional formal credits with informal credits in open source. The linking of formal and informal credits by companies is also vitally important in overcoming some of the inevitable limitations of informal credit accounting and redemption in open source. The limits to the viability of informal contract and credit systems in open source are shaped, particularly, by their costs relative to more formal governance systems. As Bowles (2004) has noted, there may be motivational reasons to prefer incomplete contracts over complete ones even with respect to goods or services that would permit more complete contracts. However, the requisite trust and reciprocity will not easily extend to anonymous and passive use contexts. Neither will there be feasible remedies based on community norms, nor legal remedies based on license obligations, in order to make for due redemption of informal credits. In short, there are areas in the field of, and closely related to, open source, where the informal system of contracts and credits laid out previously performs poorly compared with more formal systems. This is particularly true of areas where the expected discount to informal credits obtained from open source involvement is so heavy as to make their obtaining futile (Dalle & David, 2005). Also, wherever the costs of drawing more complete contracts are relatively low and the participants to the transactions in question are easily identified, a more formal credit system will become a more sensible strategy for all parties involved.

It is no coincidence that the most important business models to generate tangible revenue streams in open source are support, services, training, dual-licensing, and the offering of proprietary extensions ("secret sauce") that do not fall under the restrictive licensing obligations of the open source software they build on. All those models are based on formal contracts with customers and money payments, as well as the more informal credits obtained by involvement in the underlying open source projects.

Effectively, the revenues obtained from these models help fund some of the more neglected areas in open source. Most importantly, companies pursuing those business models, such as Novell with their Linux distribution, play a vital role in the productisation of open source software, for they can afford the substantial money payments involved in obtaining certification, financing weighty marketing efforts, and offering insurance and warranty to customers.

Ultimately, we find both informal and formal structures of contract and credit in the wider context of open source depending on their respective viability and relative performance. While rationally operating companies provide some important linkages between the two, it is mainly the informality of open source credits that creates the social glue that brings together the large variety of actors and their respective interests in open source. We have, in this section, drafted but a first approximation to this exciting extension of conventional value creation processes. Yet the credits perspective on open source is an important step towards modelling the processes within and around the production of open source software and open innovation artefacts, in general, in a manner that is more comprehensive than previous approaches.

CONCLUSION

Most of the information technology that surrounds us is social by its very nature. Social software is a collection of ever developing and changing artefacts that come to be used, appropriated, and modified in a host of different ways, evading any feasible central control and judgement, for it gives rise to interactions that will often generate value in ways that are impossible to anticipate duly. Thus formal contracts and money transactions are often inadequate means to obtain the full potential for users of those technologies to create such value by interacting with one another as they see or come to see fit. Notwithstanding the merits of a money-based credit system in market contexts, the social costs of formal systems of commerce will often exceed those of informal ones. The development of social technology is inevitably endogenous to the social processes they shape. The making of those technologies is thus itself a social process that will be governed best by informal and incomplete means, for they allow greater flexibility and appropriation of the technologies in ways unforeseeable to any single mind.

Consequently, open source has developed as a bottom-up solution to the problems posed by the complexity of software and the social implications of technology that often do not lend themselves to proprietary development practices. It is both the complexity and the social nature of technology that make for the superiority of informal credit accounting in the creation of software. This, in turn, is what we have come to call open source. Importantly, the informal credits generated in open source easily qualify as means of commerce in that they amount to credits with society at large, obtained through efforts put into open source. Thus open source can be construed as a way of commerce compatible with money-based exchange systems.

In open source, informal contractual relationships involving credits consisting of little more than public notes about respective individual involvements make for a surprising institutional framework built on three basic premises:

- The binding and enforceable prohibition of appropriation by way of open source licenses that govern the legal rights of all receivers of the software
- The prohibitive costs of complete contract and money credit institutions in the development of large complex software
- The feasibility of business models in the field of open source partly based on complete contracts and money payments

This model is particularly relevant with regard to the coding efforts involved in the development of open source. While the licensing terms are a vital means of foreclosing a proprietary direction of a project once it is open source, it is the relative superiority of informal relationships among a dispersed community of individuals in the development and use of open source software that makes the model so successful. Similarly, there are areas

in open source development where proprietary models fare better and tend to outperform efforts organised in an informal manner. Principally, this is the case where the work on and around open source interfaces with more traditional institutional business structures such as professional services, marketing and support.

The credit model put forward in this chapter provides us with a unified means of understanding and modelling a wide array of open source development efforts and the incentives behind those efforts. It illuminates the difference and the respective strengths of informal and more formal means of commerce in software development and dissemination. Also, it shows us, vividly, that there are viable informal means of social interaction to alleviate the divergence between private and public ends that is so often found in the context of information goods. Finally, it reminds us that those informal institutions often work very well if not better than complete contracts and credits in money terms.

FUTURE RESEARCH DIRECTIONS

First, the scope of redemption of open source credits may be limited to certain contexts. Also, they may not be enforceable in a court of law. Thus some of these credits may never be redeemed, in effect making them worthless. Consequently, we will have to add an appropriate discount rate plus a risk premium to the individual costs of operating in such a tacit credit accounting system, the magnitude of which lowers the relative efficiency of such system accordingly. This is an area where future quantitative research efforts will have to shed a more empirical light on the subject matter.

Second, it remains to be seen how open source and open innovation practices based on informal means of commerce further develop, given the high-profile involvement of corporations that has completely changed the face of the movement in recent years. We have noted that the term open source has been somewhat elusive, and there is some risk that its meaning becomes even more blurred by companies claiming to be "open source" when they are, in fact, not even subscribing to the very basic open source principles. Future research will have to look at the continued viability of, and possible amendments to, our model.

And, third, apart from possible changes in the validity of our model due to the dynamics in economics and society, it must be noted that we have based our discussion on existing literature, our personal experience with the subject area, and anecdotal evidences cited throughout the text. A more rigorous empirical backing may strengthen the reliability of our mostly theoretical contribution, and make for the due derivation of detailed policy implications. Here, we can only caution not to rush regulatory efforts to further behaviour we consider favourable given todays social environment. If there is one thing that open source teaches us, it is the incredible strength and creativity of bottom-up solutions to social issues. Open source shows us that the ways in which we as individuals interact with one another in the creation of commercial value depend not on perfect markets, nor perfect control in firms, but on a much richer institutional set of surprisingly informal yet amazingly powerful means.

REFERENCES

Assay, N. M. (2005). Open source and the commodity urge: Disruptive models for a disruptive development process. In C. DiBona, D. Cooper, & M. Stone (Eds.), *Open sources 2.0: The continuing evolution.* London: O'Reilly. Retrieved from http://www.open-bar.org/docs/matt_asay_open_source_chapter_11-2004.pdf

Bärwolff, M. (2006). Tight prior open source equilibrium. *FirstMonday, 11*(1). Retrieved from http://www.firstmonday.org/issues/issue11_1/barwolff/index.html

Benkler, Y. (2006). *The wealth of networks: How social production transforms markets and freedom.* Yale University Press. Retrieved from http://www.benkler.org/Benkler_Wealth_Of_Networks.pdf

Bessen, J. E. (2005). *Open source software: Free provision of complex public goods* (Working Paper). Research on Innovation. Retrieved from http://ssrn.com/abstract=588763

Bowles, S. (2004). *Microeconomics: Behavior, institutions, and evolution.* Princeton University Press.

Brecht, B. (1932). Der Rundfunk als Kommunikationsapparat. *Blätter des Hessischen Landestheaters*(16). (Excerpt of English translation titled "The Radio as an Apparatus of Communication." Retrieved from http://www.medienkunstnetz.de/source-text/8/

Brooks Jr., F. P. (1995). *The mythical man-month: Essays on software engineering – anniversary edition.* Reading: Addison-Wesley. (First published in 1975.)

Chesbrough, H. W. (2003). *Open innovation: The new imperative for creating and profiting from technology.* Harvard Business School Press.

Coase, R. H.(1937). The nature of the firm. *Economica, 4*, 386–405.

Dalle, J.-M., & David, P. A. (2005). Allocation of software development resources in open source production mode. *Perspectives on free and open source software* (pp. 297–328). Cambridge, MA: The MIT Press. Retrieved from http://mitpress.mit.edu/books/chapters/0262562278.pdf

Demil, B., & Lecocq, X. (2003). *Neither market nor hierarchy or network: The emerging bazaar governance.* Retrieved from http://opensource.mit.edu

Friedman, M. (1962). *Capitalism and freedom.* Chicago: The University of Chicago Press.

Ghosh, R. A., et al. (2006). *Economic impact of open source software on innovation and the competitiveness of the information and communication technologies (ICT) sector in the EU* (Final Report, Contract ENTR/04/112). UNU-MERIT. (Prepared for European Communities). Retrieved from http://ec.europa.eu/enterprise/ict/policy/doc/2006-11-20-flossimpact.pdf

Grand, S., von Krogh, G., Leonard, D., & Swap, W. (2004). Resource allocation beyond firm boundaries: A multi-level model for open source innovation. *Long Range Planning, 37,* 591–610.

Grossman, S. J., & Hart, O. D. (1986). The costs and benefits of ownership: A theory of vertical andlateral integration. *Journal of Political Economy, 94*(4), 691–719.

Hars, A., & Ou, S. (2001). *Working for free? motivations of participating in open source projects.* (Proceedings of the 34th Hawaii International Conference on System Sciences.) Retrieved from http://csdl.computer.org/comp/proceedings/hicss/2001/0981/07/09817014.pdf

Hart, O. D., & Moore, J. (1988). Incomplete contracts and renegotiation. *Econometrica, 56*(4), 755–785.

Hippel, E. Von. (2005). *Democratizing innovation.* Cambridge, MA: MIT Press. Retrieved from http://web.mit.edu/evhippel/www/democ.htm

Ingham, G. (2004). The emergence of capitalist credit money. In L. R. Wray (Ed.), *Credit and state theories of money: The contributions of a. mitchell innes* (p. 173-222). Cheltenham: Edward Elgar.

Innes, A. (1914). The credit theory of money. *Banking Law Journal, 31,* 151–168.

Krishnamurthy, S. (2002). Cave or community? An empirical examination of 100 mature open source projects. *First Monday, 7*(6). Retrieved from http://www.firstmonday.org/issues/issue7_6/krishnamurthy/

Lee, S., Moisa, N., & Weiss, M. (2003). *Open source as a signalling device: An economic analysis* (Discussion Paper No. 03-20). German Economic Association of Business Administration e. V. Retrieved from http://www.whu.edu/orga/geaba/Papers/2003/GEABA-DP03-20.pdf

Lerner, J., & Tirole, J. (2002). Some simple economics of open source. *Journal of Industrial Economics, 50*(2), 197–234. (The working paper from 2000 is available from http://www.people.hbs.edu/jlerner/simple.pdf)

Lessig, L. (2004). *Free culture: How big media uses technology and the law to lock down culture and control creativity.* Penguin Books. Retrieved from http://www.free-culture.cc/

Malinowski, B. (1922). *Argonauts of the western pacific: An account of native enterprise and adventure in the archipelagoes of melanesian new guinea.* London: Routledge & Kegan Paul.

Ogawa, S., & Piller, F. T. (2006). Collective customer commitment: Reducing the risks of new product development. *MIT Sloan Management Review, 47*(2), 65–72. Retrieved from http://sloanreview.mit.edu/smr/issue/2006/winter/14/

Osterloh, M., Rota, S., & Kuster, B. (2002). *Open source software production: Climbing on the shoulders of giants* (Working Paper). The University of Zurich. Retrieved from http://opensource.mit.edu/papers/osterlohrotakuster.pdf

Priddat, B. P. (2006). *Open Source als Produktion von Transformationsgütern.* In B. Lutterbeck, Bärwolff, M., & Gehring, R. A. (Eds.), *Open source jahrbuch 2006. Zwischen softwareentwicklung und gesellschaftsmodell* (pp. 109–121). Berlin: Lehmanns Media. Retrieved from http://www.opensourcejahrbuch.de

Raymond, E. S. (1999). The revenge of the hackers. In C. DiBona, S. Ockman, & M. Stone (Eds.), *Open sources: Voices from the open source revolution.* London: O'Reilly. Retrieved from http://www.oreilly.de/catalog/opensources/book/raymond2.html

Rosenberg, S. (2007). *Dreaming in code: Two dozen programmers, three years, 4,732 bugs, and one quest for transcendent software*. Crown Publishers.

Samuelson, P., & Scotchmer, S. (2002). The law and economics of reverse engineering. *The Yale Law Journal, 111*, 1575–1663.

Shapiro, C., & Varian, H. R. (1999). *Information rules: A strategic guide to the network economy*. Harvard: Harvard Business School Press.

Spence, A. M. (1973). Job market signaling. *Quarterly Journal of Economics, 87*, 355–374.

Stallman, R. M. (1999). The GNU operating system and the free software movement. In C. DiBona, S. Ockman, & M. Stone, (Eds.), *Open sources: Voices from the open source revolution* (pp. 53–70). London: O'Reilly. Retrieved from http://www.oreilly.de/catalog/opensources/book/stallman.html

Strahilevitz, L. (2007). Wealth without markets. *Yale Law Journal, 116*. Retrieved from http://papers.ssrn.com/sol3/papers.cfm?abstract_id=946479

Weber, S. (2004). *The success of open source*. Harvard University Press.

ADDITIONAL READING

Adler, P., & Kwon, S.-W. (2002). Social capital: Prospects for a new concept. *Academy of Management Review, 27*(1), 17–40. Retrieved from http://www.uky.edu/~skwon2/Social%20capital.pdf

Axelrod, R. (1984). *The evolution of co-operation*. London: Penguin Books.

Benkler, Y. (2002). Coase's penguin, or, Linux and the nature of the firm. *Yale Law Journal, 112*(3), 369–446.

Benkler, Y. (2004). Sharing nicely: On shareable goods and the emergence of sharing as a modality of economic production. *Yale Law Journal, 114*(2), 273–358. Retrieved from http://www.yalelawjournal.org/pdf/114-2/Benkler_FINAL_YLJ114-2.pdf

Boyle, J. (2000). Cruel, mean, or lavish? Economic analysis, price discrimination and digital intellectual property. *Vanderbilt Law Review, 53*(6), 2007–39.

Denning, P. J. (2004). The social life of innovation: The profession of IT. *Communications of the ACM, 47*(4), 15–19.

Ellickson, R. C.(1991). *Order without law: How neighbors settle disputes*. Harvard University Press.

Fehr, E., and Falk, A. (2001). *Psychological foundations of incentives* (Working Paper No. 95). Institute for Empirical Research in Economics of the University of Zurich.

Fehr, E., & Gächter, S. (2000). Fairness and retaliation: The economics of reciprocity. *The Journal of Economic Perspectives, 14*(3), 159–181. Retrieved from http://e-collection.ethbib.ethz.ch/ecol-pool/incoll/incoll_553.pdf

Frischmann, B. M. (2004). *An economic theory of infrastructure and sustainable infrastructure commons*. SSRN Electronic Library. Retrieved from http://papers.ssrn.com/sol3/papers.cfm?abstract_id=588424

Gehring, R. A. (2005). The institutionalization of open source. *Poiesis und Praxis, 4*(1), 54–73.

Merges, R. P. (2004). *A new dynamism in the public domain* (Boalt Working Papers in Public Law No. 65). UC Berkeley, Boalt Hall. Retrieved from http://papers.ssrn.com/sol3/papers.cfm?abstract_id=558751

Romer, P. M. (1990). Endogenous technological change. *Journal of Political Economy*, *98*(5), 71–102.

Stallman, R. (2007). Warum "Open Source" das wesentliche von "Freier Software" verdeckt. In Lutterbeck, B. Bärwolff, M., & Gehring, R. A. (Eds.), *Open source jahrbuch 2007. Zwischen freier software und gesellschaftsmodell,* (pp. 1–7). Berlin: Lehmanns Media. Retrieved from http://www.opensourcejahrbuch.de

Stallman, R. M. (1992). *Why software should be free.* Retrieved from http://www.fsf.org.philosophy/shouldbefree.html

ENDNOTES

1   The GPL is the most important of all open source licenses and has come to govern most of the world's open source software including the Linux kernel project.

2   A software program's source code is typically being written in a human-readable higher level programming language such as C or C++ and then translated into machine-readable code that is no more intelligible to humans. The source code of a software program may not as easily be inferred from the machine code. Reverse-engineering, the process of inferring the internals of a program, is typically a very costly and uncertain endeavour (Samuelson & Scotchmer, 2002).

3   For example, it is understood that Microsoft have been using a BSD Internet networking implementation for its Windows software. Also, Apple have been using a complete BSD operating systems kernel for their latest operating systems. Had these software programs been under GPL licenses, their derivative works had to be licensed under a GPL, too, making an adoption by proprietary software companies much less likely.

4   Microsoft have been somewhat notorious for claiming more or less blatantly that open source has an adverse effect on innovation and economic welfare. Courts have thus far withstood any attempts to ban open source as a mode of distribution or declare it illegal (e. g., Wallace v. IBM, No. 06-2454, 7th Cir., November 9, 2006, http://www.ca7.uscourts.gov/tmp/Z10LYHZ8.pdf).

5   Companies such as Red Hat, Novell, IBM, and HP are heavily involved in a number of open source projects. In many cases companies have become the driving forces behind open source projects. E. g., more than 65 percent of work on the latest Linux kernel comes from people working for companies (http://lwn.net/Articles/222773/). Some projects are even completely "owned" by companies to all intents and purpose, for they are the sole contributors to the project. One example is the popular MySQL database owned by the Swedish company MySQL AB.

6   Credit as a general means of accounting for debts and according credits is virtually as old as mankind itself. It is a common misunderstanding to reduce societies that dispense with a state regulated banking and money system to pre-economic systems barely capable of organising self-sufficient household economies. Most native societies have developed dedicated institutions of property rights and means of credits to sustain their economies (Malinowski, 1922).

7   The informal credits generated in the primary open source process may at subsequent or upstream stages translate into formal money credits. See below in this section when we consider the role of companies within open source projects. This secondary effect, however, does not change the primacy and material significance of informal credits in the production of open source software.

8 One may argue that trademarks have a similar effect. However, whilst trademarks do establish a brand with customers, they rarely serve to provide a linkage to the firm behind it, let alone individuals' contributions to the product. Understandably, most customers are completely indifferent about the firm or individual behind a certain brand, and this is so with open source software, too. However, the weath of information about individual contributions recorded and disseminated in open source is unlike any other production processes in proprietary software and ordinary market goods.

9 Typically, every open source software contains a file called *credits.txt* that lists all its contributors. Further information will often be available in a history-file and a changelog-file. Even the complete history of every single code change in an open source software is often available from a public version control system.

Chapter IX
Musique Concrètization:
Music, Technology and
Critical Constructivism

Jean Hébert
Simon Fraser University, Canada

ABSTRACT

For the past several years, a crisis over copyright and control of music distribution has been developing. The outcome of this crisis has tremendous implications not only for the fate of commercial and creative entities involved in music, but for the social reproduction of knowledge and culture more generally. Critical theories of technology are useful in addressing these implications. This chapter introduces the concept of "concretization" (Feenberg, 1999), and demonstrates how it can be mapped onto the field of current music technologies and the lives and work of the people using them. This reading of popular music technologies resonates strongly with themes arising out of current scholarship covering the crisis of copyright and music distribution. Reading music technology in this way can yield a lucid account of the diverse trajectories and goals inherent in heterogeneous networks of participants involved with music technologies. It can also give us not only a detailed description of the relations of various groups, individuals, and technologies involved in networks of music, but also a prescriptive program for the future maintenance and strengthening of a vibrant, perhaps less intensively commercialized, and radically democratized sphere of creative exchange.

INTRODUCTION

For the past several years, a crisis over copyright and control of music distribution has been developing. The outcome of this crisis has tremendous implications not only for the fate of commercial

and creative entities involved in music, but also for the social reproduction of knowledge and culture more generally. Various branches of scholarship have recently explored some of the contours of the current crisis, variously interpreting its historical significance (Lessig, 2002, 2004), measuring its economic impact (Leyshon, 2001; Leyshon, Webb, French, Thrift, & Crewe, 2005), and prophesizing future scenarios for the social role of music and the commercial industry structures that support and derive revenue from it.

The current crisis centers around a difficult dilemma: the prevalence of freely available technologies (audio recording software, the MP3 format, the Internet) that circumvent a traditional regime of monetized exchange of sound recordings over a wide geographical territory. The implications of this crisis are clear for those whose revenues and livelihoods are most affected by it: creators, recording companies, music publishers, and related industries (radio, television, retail, distribution, concert halls, and so on) whose revenues depend on these well-established networks of the business of music. But the crisis is making itself felt to many other parties as well. Certainly, lawsuits by the Recording Industry Association of America (RIAA) have criminalized and heavily penalized a number of Internet users, victims of a music industry desperate to preserve its traditional value chain via costly legal instruments. Software companies working in the areas of file-sharing platforms and audio compression technologies have felt the pinch, too, having either gone underground (e.g., eDonkey, BitTottent), or having been bought lock, stock, and barrel by one or more of the Big Four (such as happened to MP3.com, Emusic, and Napster), or having been incorporated into the design and marketing of related commercial products (ITunes Music Store/IPod).

Lawrence Lessig (2004) writes about this crisis of copyright as symptomatic of a more fundamental attempt to recover what he terms "read-write culture." In Lessig's view, knowledge and culture were primarily disseminated in Western liberal democracies via "read-only" media (radio, television, cinema) during most of the twentieth century; media regimes in which consumers were technically limited in their ability to manipulate and reuse cultural artifacts to create their own art. The ability of audiences to take part in using cultural artifacts for their own ends has always been contested (as observed in the historical legal battles over the VCR and over the rights of cable television providers to rebroadcast television signals). However, never before have the rights of audiences to do so been so restricted as they are now. Ironically, this takes place at a time when computer technologies have made it easier than ever to compose, copy, remix, and share music.

But there is an additional factor to be considered: one that transforms a simple crisis of copyright and piracy into a world-shaping crisis. The set of technologies used for the production of popular music have all but converged with the set of technologies used in music's reproduction and distribution. The networked personal computer has become a highly malleable locus of the most efficient and most closely converged set of music production, reproduction, and distribution technologies in history (Ebare, 2003). While it is true that much commercial music making is still embedded in conventional networks of production (recording studios, professional audio engineers, CD manufacturing facilities, and so forth [Leyshon et al., 2005; Théberge, 1997]), the blurring of production, reproduction, and distribution technologies is potentially destabilizing to conventional conceptions of what it means to be a creator or consumer. As the distinction between musical production and consumption recedes (or perhaps the appropriate phrase is "in remission"), the utility and relevance of technologies that support this distinction ("read-only" media) also fade from use. Technologies of "read-write culture" may herald the end of culture industries altogether, or at least their radical transformation; indeed, the enactment of culture as an "industry" depends on technologies designed to divide populations into content producers and content consumers.

The claims of Lessig and others [notably Benkler (2006)], that the growth of "read-write culture" has deep implications for the reproduction of knowledge and society (in Benkler's terms, the creation of a "networked information economy"), pose serious questions about how this set of circumstances came about, and whether (and how) such a radically new regime of technologized cultural production might be maintained or even strengthened.

But because technology is the fulcrum around which the crisis turns, we are well advised to turn to critical theories of technology to address these questions. In this chapter, I will introduce the concept of "concretization" (Feenberg, 1999), and demonstrate how it can be mapped onto the field of current music technologies and the lives and work of the people using them. This reading of popular music technologies will be seen to resonate strongly with themes arising out of the current scholarship covering this crisis of copyright and music distribution. Reading music technology in this way can yield a lucid account of the diverse trajectories and goals inherent in heterogeneous networks of participants involved with music technologies. It can also give us not only a detailed description of the relations of various groups, individuals, and technologies involved in networks of music, but also a prescriptive program for the future maintenance and strengthening of a vibrant, perhaps less intensively commercialized, and radically democratized sphere of creative exchange.

BACKGROUND

The topic of democratization and technology is nothing new in popular music scholarship. In fact, it is often a crucial theme, from Adorno (1981) to the present. But typically, analyses of the democratizing potential of technologies utilize an impoverished notion of democracy, whether that is represented by the mundane experience of democratized arts for which we suffer the loss of "aura" (Benjamin, 1986), whether the claim is that blank recordable media liberate the listener from dominant ideological programs (Frith, 1986) or some other permutation of what "democratic" might mean.

While more recent inquiries into technology and popular music have touched on some of the most important potentialities of the current musical technological assemblage (Internet, iPods, MP3s, software recording studios), none have taken a broader view of what is increasingly a unified sphere of musical activities (the blurring of producers and consumers). Additionally, and crucially, none have addressed the historical codependence of popular music and the technologies in which its practice is embodied. Only one theorist (Attali, 1985) has hinted (prophetically) at the wider implications of this sort of convergence, but his comprehension of social change is so rooted in the economics of music's exchange that he can offer no sustained critical account of technologies of music beyond the ways in which they embody market instrumentalities (yet another substantivist reading).[1] At any rate, none of these theories leads to a complete account for the intersection of contemporary networked computer technologies and musical practice in a satisfactory way.

A contemporary instrumentalist view of music and its relation to technology is summarized quite well in Leyshon *et al.* (2005). From the perspective of the business of bringing music to a market and selling it, the current relationship of the popular music industry with Internet technologies is readily conceived as a "crisis" to which various commercial enterprises are responding with a range of proposals intended to reinvigorate their flagging revenues and failing profit models. But this instrumental critique cannot sustain itself against even the most basic empirical realities with which it is faced. At first, the authors point out three trends in the areas of production and consumption (in which technological changes are heavily implicated): (1) the reversal of the value chain with respect to the economics and cultural capital of dance music (whereby live performance becomes the locus of exchange, rather than a promotional conduit for recorded media) (p.183); (2) the erosion of music as a primary commodity and its changing role as something marketable primarily in conjunction with other products (movies, games, etc.) (p.184); and (3) music's diminished role in the media ecology of the music industry's traditional imagined audience, who are more easily captivated by games, movies, and mobile phones (pp.184-5).

Despite offering a description of three fundamental changes facing the current encounter between music and technology that point to underlying social transformations, the authors turn to a very limited account of how music businesses of various types have responded to the crisis. The authors document several,

differing strategies in the face of the contemporary crisis of the musical economy. The major companies have sought to adapt to the challenges of software formats and Internet distribution systems through litigation, diversifying through multimedia, seeking to add new revenue streams (such as ring tones and merchandising) while promoting transparency so that people can see the value added by labels in the networks of the musical economy. Meanwhile, new business models…seek to reformulate the new musical economy by re-intermediating musical value chains. (p.201)

It is a strange turn indeed that while these authors acknowledge the emergence of such significant new parameters in the practices of music production and audition, their prescriptions for reconstituting existing value chains around the new technological assemblage do not transcend mere functional revisions of existing entertainment industry practices. These perspectives fail to apprehend the extent of the threat such radically changing habits and technologies of consumption pose to conventional notions of a music "industry." The "reintermediation of value chains," the most radical of their proposals for change, merely reinforces a logic of market instrumentality from the perspective of parasitic Internet startups vying to become the next generation of *Forbes* cover stories. As recounted by one of their interviewees, the manager of an online A&R service:

it's just going to take its time and eventually we're going to end up with this subscription streaming service, and all I'm doing is sitting here biding my time but perfecting what we do and refining it and making it better and building our brands, so that when the day comes and somebody needs to step up and be the J.D. Power [of the music industry], I'm there! (Interview 5, in Leyshon et al., 2005, p. 199).

The most radical program of change that the authors observe, then, is an uncritically deterministic, "wait-and-see" attitude toward current (Internet) technologies, with sheer commercial success and technical dominance as the explicit goal. While this attitude is unsurprising in the context of business, its uncritical echoing by academic observers leaves more unanswered questions than it purports to resolve. While taking note of how music audiences and producers alike make use of enabling, underdetermined technologies to recast their roles as listeners or performers, the authors reduce the problem to an account of how businesses attempt to inscribe themselves into these recrafted networks as profiteering intermediaries.

Not all perspectives on the reconfiguration of the economics of popular music are so one dimensional. Lessig (2004) takes a much more inclusive approach by revisiting more fundamental ideas about music, culture, and society. Lessig maintains that over the past 30 years, U.S. copyright law has been progressively reformulated to erode and prohibit noncommercial and transformative appropriation, and to all but terminate the existence of a public domain. The implications of this trend are far reaching and contrary to the fundamental precepts of Western liberal democracies. According to Lessig, one of the most important casualties of this increasingly strict legal regime is noncommercial creative appropriation or sampling, which is criminalized along with audio piracy. Combined with an increasingly concentrated corporate media landscape, the long-term prospects are grim, Lessig suggests, seeing that less and less cultural content will be available for reuse by fewer and fewer creators.

Lessig's view of the problem in terms of a balancing act at the intersection of law, architecture (physical infrastructure, code, networks), norms, and the market has some potential in leading us to a critical theory of popular music and technology. Lessig argues that in the current regime of copyright control, an overly strict legal code (embodied in industry sponsored initiatives such as the Digital Millennium Copyright Act and other measures) buttresses an unforgivingly use-prohibiting technical code (architecture), which reinforces the interests of a highly concentrated oligopoly of rights holders. Consumers lose out the most due to the bias within the latest technical code.

Furthering this argument, Lessig suggests some more fundamental ideas about creativity and the dissemination of art. The new technologies, writes Lessig, retrieve a freer culture of amateur production, as embodied in the remix, or in the mashup, or even in technological artifacts as seemingly innocuous as playlists. Lessig's view is on the whole more balanced than most analyses. It is also insightful, drawing our attention to how "read-write culture" is something ingrained in Western liberal traditions, including its legal traditions. In so formulating the current crisis, Lessig's analysis offers a reasoned counterpoint to the current litigious strategies of the RIAA and major recording and movie companies. And in previous works, he also acknowledges how the ethical codes of developers, of open structure, open design, and free code, are literally inscribed into the technologies they develop, including the very architecture of the Internet (1999). Lessig's

view clearly bears some informal resemblance to a critical constructivism of technology.[2]

But Lessig misses one crucial point: both the culture (and, to extend the argument, knowledge) and technology of modernity are mutually constitutive. Our notion of a musical "creator" is mediated by the technical environments in which creators and listeners are cast (and cast themselves). Similarly, a "recording artist" is technically distinguished from a "songwriter," who is technically distinguished from an "audience member," a "recording engineer," a "press agent," a "roadie," and so on. These instrumentalized divisions of labor are mediated by technical designs that inscribe difference and provide loci for differentiated skills and expertise to inhabit.

Elsewhere (Ebare, 2004), I have developed these ideas into an analysis of participation in music practice along a continuum of different degrees of engagement, giving support for the plasticity and interchangeability of musical action. More or less, music is increasingly becoming a participatory field, and technical designs mediate the extent to which that participatory characteristic is embodied in our social realities. But the increasingly participatory nature of popular music cannot be explained via instrumental or substantive theories, or theories that simply refuse to consider the *essential* imbrications of culture and technology.

CRITICAL CONSTRUCTIVISM, POPULAR MUSIC AND TECHNOLOGY

Critical constructivism breaks from former substantivist critiques in the philosophy of technology, reigning in influences from Actor-Network theory and cultural studies to socially contextualize technology. It also positions users of technology as having agency to influence technological design and, in turn, associated social outcomes.

Two recent works address the topic of contemporary music technologies using a critical constructivist frame of reference, one focusing on computerized technologies of music creation, and another concerned with online distribution. I will first discuss these attempts to frame the crisis in these terms and then, using Feenberg's concept of "concretization," I will try to draw these interpretations together into a more comprehensive account of our relation to this newly converged set of musical technologies.

Di Scipio (1998) applies the notion of "subversive democratization" (following Feenberg, 1995) to a political aesthetics of electronic music practice. He critiques Heidegger's substantive critique of technology, arguing against Heidegger's "narrow focus on technology": "technology (a)s an aid in our daily practical life … that … has no influence on our being comes from and leads to the belief that technology is a decontextualized, autonomous dimension" (Di Scipio, 1998, p. 7). In reading Heidegger's view on technology in this manner, Di Scipio invites the reader to consider the ability of technology users to participate in the production of technology, a process Feenberg would call a form of subversive rationalization. To apply subversive rationalization to the technologies of music composition, Di Scipio describes a scenario in which "artists, musicians among them, can be interpreters of technology, provided that they actively participate in the knowledge domain and the hermeneutic dimensions of the *technê* of music" (p.13). Clearly, a constructivist view of the technology of music practice describes the musician as a technical subject.

Longford (2005) draws out a more complex vision of the codes of meaning implied in contemporary technologies of Internet-based music distribution, and filesharing. Recognizing "the significant degree to which the terms and conditions of modern citizenship are laid down by technical codes embodied in the technologies and technical systems in which our lives are enmeshed," Longford describes "cybercitizenship

as embodied in the design of the early Internet" as it centers around values of open structure and wide collaborations. The challenge to the open code of cyberspace, Longford argues, comes from the advancement of proprietary code, Digital Rights Management (DRM) technologies, and the legal instruments utilized to prevent their circumvention. He offers a program of interpretation for future studies into Internet (and music) technologies as follows:

to interrogate the terms and conditions of digitally encoded citizenship. We must examine more fully the socio-technical means by which Internet users become citizens of cyberspace via subtle processes of enculturation, inducement and coercion, as well as how they resist and rearticulate, through their daily practices and social appropriation of the technology, the terms and conditions of citizenship imposed by its current configuration. (Longford, 2005).

Both Longford and Di Scipio have applied a critical constructivist framework to two discrete activity areas: music composition and recording, and music distribution and sharing, respectively. As I have argued previously, the emergence of remixing, mashups, and the like, signal an intensified blurring of these two areas of activity. Audiences are increasingly casting themselves as active participants in musical culture via the adoption of technologies that tend to offer them the option to edit, mashup, and share their creations. It follows that both fields of practice (creation and audition) are increasingly occupying the same space of interaction; they are increasingly becoming parts of the same encounter between culture, technologies, and human actors. Can they be productively analyzed as such?

CONCRETIZATION

It is possible. Andrew Feenberg's concept of *concretization* can help to broaden a constructivist critique of popular music technologies, as summarized previously. But to clarify my reading of this concept, I need to first explain it in the context of the framework with which Feenberg (1999) develops it.

Feenberg offers a theory of technology that highlights the possibilities of agency and under-determination in technical design and adoption. To achieve this, he describes two layers of instrumentalization, primary and secondary. Primary instrumentalizations refer to the "*functional constitution* of technical objects and subjects," whereas secondary instrumentalizations refer to the "*realization* of the constituted objects and subjects in actual networks and devices" (p.202). Here Feenberg is offering a critique of prior substantivist and instrumental theories of technology, which limited their analyses to merely the primary instrumentalizations of technology.

The two primary instrumentalizations, as Feenberg describes them, bear the mark of Heidegger's conception of the impact of technology on objects and subjects (Heidegger, 1977). Firstly, *decontextualization* refers to how technology reconstitutes natural objects and subjects as technical objects and subjects (Feenberg, 1999, p.203). Secondly, *reductionism* describes the process by which objects are purged of content that is technically useless, so that all that remains of them are aspects that can be enrolled in a network, as determined by a technical subject's program (p.203). Clearly, this order of rationalizations descends from Heidegger's concept of "Enframing" (*Ge-stell*), or the technical organization of nature (Heidegger, 1977, p.23) as "standing-reserve" (*Bestand*), a concept that accounts for the conversion of natural objects into technical resources, concealing what they are and how they came to be (p.17).[3]

Feenberg proposes two further primary instrumentalizations, *autonomization* and *positioning*, essentially refinements of concepts introduced by Jurgen Habermas (1971), that complete the account of a "basic technical relation" (Feenberg, 1999, p.205). *Autonomization* refers to the feature of technical action (or administrative action, in Habermasian terms), in which technology acts upon an object, achieving effects to which the object cannot or does not act reciprocally upon the technical subject. The concept of *Positioning* refers to the fashion in which technical subjects control objects according to the laws inscribed in objects (and not by changing or challenging those laws). *Positioning* is a strategic maneuvering of the manager or authority to utilize the technical codes written into objects for their own advantage (p.204).

The primary instrumentalizations account for substantive and instrumental interpretations of technology, but with the addition of Feenberg's secondary instrumentalizations, the primaries also demarcate the limitations of these views. Feenberg puts forward four secondary instrumentalizations to account for how technology becomes embodied in a network or device: *Systematization*, *Mediation*, *Vocation*, and *Initiative*.[4] *Systematization* accounts for the reintegration of decontextualized technical objects into a network or device (p.205), following (Latour, 1983). *Mediation* involves ethical and aesthetic features of the technical process in which technical objects are brought into line with moral or aesthetic imperatives among affected groups or groups of users (Feenberg, 1999, p.206). *Vocation* reflects how the technical subject is transformed by its actions, a tendency to reverse the effects of *autonomization* (p.206). And *Initiative* accounts for tactical (as opposed to strategic) actions by individuals subject to technical controls (p.207). While the primary instrumentalizations may be characterized as strategies that reinforce preexisting technical designs and imperatives (typically in accordance with the strategic interests of the technical subjects involved in their innovation), secondary instrumentalizations account for tendencies for ascribing meaning to and/or the adoption of technologies in (sometimes unexpected) ways that support the needs of groups and individuals who become entangled in interactions with (or uses of) technology. Clearly, this is a much more refined view of the cross-currents of agency and structure in a highly technologized society than that offered by instrumental and substantivist models.

This conceptual framework lays the foundation for the concept of concretization as a program for *democratic rationalization*s of technology. Concretization refers to strategies that "can adapt technology to the environment (and) the vocational self-development of its human operators," among other human needs (p.220). In contrast with processes of differentiation, "concretizing innovations adapt them(selves) to a variety of demands that may at first appear disconnected or even incompatible" (p.217), incorporating the needs of progressively more and more purposes, or more and more user groups. Examples include "a solar house that gets its heat from the sun rather than from burning fossil fuels…internaliz(ing) environmental constraints in its design (p.217). Concretization is a process of synergization of the functional characteristics of technologies with the relationship of technologies to their environment and social milieu (p.217). It is a reflexive process that can be built into technological design and innovation.

Feenberg observes concretization at work in several historical examples, including the development of the French MiniTel system, the environmental movement, and most substantially in the successful attempt by AIDS activists to achieve a degree of active participation in the medical milieu of doctors and research laboratories involved in developing experimental treatments for their shared condition. Presumably, we can extend the concept to the field of music technologies, too.

Concretization and Popular Music Technology

In previous sections, I have given a partial account of the crisis of popular music and network computing technologies. I have shown how

instrumentalist accounts (Leyshon et al., 2005) that are seemingly bounded by the prerogatives of one group of users (copyright holders and associated commercial entities that stand to profit from restrictions on Internet technologies) offer programs for reform (digital rights management, extended terms of copyright) that are undesirable by audiences, who require extensive bullying and propaganda to become convinced that such restrictive measures are a desirable path. I have also outlined the basis of a limited substantivist critique as embodied in Lessig's romanticism about "free culture" (2002; Lessig, 2004). This position fails to come to offer a complete view due to Lessig's apparent tendency to position culture in isolation from technology. With a critical constructivist view, we can correct these biases.

Following Longford (2005) and Di Scipio (1998), a generalized constructivist critique of the mutually constitutive relation of network computing technologies and popular music comes into view. As Di Scipio insists, the engagement of the artist with technology in creative practice is always a reshaping of technique, and a new composition of the artist as an aesthetic technician of sorts, a process of "subversive rationalization." And as Longford describes it, the same can be said of techniques of music distribution, sharing, and audition: listeners engage in a critical encounter with an underdetermined set of technical artifacts, in which they are partly free to inscribe their own codes and recast themselves as participants in culture and, referring to my own prior work, to recast the degree to which they engage actively *both* with technology *and* with the culture they consume. The overwhelming evidence that this indeed takes place is observed in the remarkable spread of remixing and mashup practices, among numerous other new forms of musical creativity entangled with network computing (DJing, podcasting, custom ringtone ripping, and so on). The broadening of the field of participants, and the inscription of codes of technical empowerment into technologies that enable the open manipulation and rewriting of prerecorded music, amount to something of a "democratization" of popular music.

Concretization opens this up even more. But a more or less complete illumination of concretization at work in this matrix of technologies, actors, and culture demands first a description of some of the more important activities that fall under Feenberg's various primary and secondary instrumentalizations. Firstly, consider some of the activities reflective of the primary instrumentalizations, which account for the basic technical relation in the construction of music technologies. The primary instrumentalizations of music technologies at present confront musicians and audiences on three fronts: (1) the rationalization of composition and recording technique, (2) the rationalization of space and acoustics, and (3) the rationalization of users roles as networked consumers (or, variously, pirates) of music and technologies of music.

- **Decontextualization:** The digitization of music rationalizes all sounds into computer code, which is an increased abstraction over analog recordings. Similarly, the composer and listener are recast in their roles as technicians, operators of digital technologies; they become technical subjects, embedded in a network of computer keyboard, mouse, screen, software, network, and headphones. The deauthoring effect of remix culture tends to transform creative engagement into technical engagement (Di Scipio, 1998).
- **Reductionism:** Putting audio production and reproduction software into a personal computing environment strips fixed physical sites for collaboration from creative practice. To be collaborative, each individual requires a computer connected to the network, and there are less incentives for shared physical consoles or interfaces. Technically useless or inefficient, these forms of creative collaboration are not included in new technical

designs. Reductionism may be observed also in the tendency to strip away errors and noise due to increasingly cost efficient and user friendly pitch correction and time stretch/ tempo matching tools (among many other intricately calculative software tools).

- **Autonomization:** Contemporary digital recording and audition technologies have less impact on the sonic environment and physical space than their historical predecessors. Personal studios inside personal computers do not require physical instruments or even audio recording equipment to create recordings. There is reduced impact on domestic and commercial recording space through reduced size and power consumption of recording equipment (laptops, which are smaller and consume less power than analog consoles and even digital sequencers of the past 20 years) have progressively less and less impact on their immediate environments (as object) with increased miniaturization (though the question becomes more complicated considering the environmental impact of computer technologies).
- **Positioning:** Positioning takes place in this milieu in an interesting way. Lessig writes that the more open networks are, the more susceptible they are to surveillance. File-sharing activities on the major networks are known to be monitored by the RIAA for the purposes of identifying people sharing music of which their member artists and companies own the rights. Rightsholders are taking advantage of the open code inscribed into the architecture of the Internet in order to meet their own ends (suing file sharers for exorbitant amounts to deter other filesharers). The basic technical relation, as defined by the primary instrumentalizations in realm of music technology, is countered by tendencies that exemplify the secondary instrumentalizations. These tendencies assert the autonomy of musicians and audiences,

and how they incorporate and accommodate technologies in their practices.

- **Systematization:** The systematization process can be observed in the adoption of digital recording and playback software into existing home studio environments. Where artists introduce software and the practice of remixing into their existing stable of techniques and creative habits, to an extent they reclaim their autonomy. At the same time, their lifeworld/network in which they interact with technologies absorbs the new technology into it.

- **Mediation:** Users inclined to rip the works of others and remix it inscribe the values of a vibrant participatory culture into technical designs. Developers respond by inscribing these values into new software designs (through open standard adoption, e.g., MP3 vs. AAC or WMF, and through making remix functions increasingly user friendly).

- **Vocation:** Once accustomed to technologies, users tend to incorporate their technical codes into their vocational identities. Use of particular software platforms, for recording or listening to music, breeds familiarity and personal custom, which in turn feeds into users' self-definitions as artists.

- **Initiative** can be observed in tendencies of users to tinker with the very software they are using in order to hack it for their own purposes. User groups intervene in the constitution of audio recording and playback software in this subversive way, too. The inclination to tinker with software not only improves its design in accord with user preferences, but it also increases users' freedom with relation to technology.

Remember that concretization refers to strategies that "can adapt technology to the environment (and) the vocational self-development of its human operators" (Feenberg, 1999, p.220). The concept accounts for how technologies increasingly meet an ever-widening set of needs by different social groups. Essentially referring to the tendencies classified under the rubric of secondary instrumentalizations, concretization occurs where users cause the technologies to adapt to them. In the present case, where the technical spheres of music production, dissemination, and audition merge into the same shared space (the networked computer studio), increasingly, efforts by originally divergent groups (audiences, remixers, artists, hackers) are drawn together to tackle problems affecting them all, which results in concretization of the technology. Examples include efficient means for compressing and decompressing MP3 files, and a generalized autonomy to manipulate code openly, though it can be presumed that many more lie on the horizon.

FUTURE TRENDS

One of the most important trends in scholarship on the topic of popular music and technology that can be reasonably expected to receive further attention is the revisioning of the relationship of technology and society, under the influence of the Actor-Network theory of scholars such as Bruno Latour, Michel Callon, Trevor Pinch, and others. In such an intellectual climate, the adaptation of conceptual schema from philosophers of technology such as Andrew Feenberg will likely gain wider appeal among popular music scholars.

Of course, the changing technical and political terrain of both the Internet and the field of popular music will likely have some impact on future trends in scholarship as well. The current political struggle over the open structure of the Internet brings to the attention of scholars the need for work that specifically advocates in the interests of the idea of the Internet as a public resource. The preferential treatment of commercial entities by Internet service providers (ISPs) has clear implications for the potential of the Internet as a site of "democratization," whether in the cultural production of music or in some other domain. And given the "walled garden" structure of many emerging mobile Internet environments, the sustainability of a democratized sphere of music production and reception is not guaranteed. This state of affairs calls for more crossover in this area with political economy studies, which would enable critical, philosophical engagement with concrete economic realities.

FUTURE RESEARCH DIRECTIONS

While the technologies of popular music production and consumption are converging in the space of the personal computer, the open structure of these technologies is not guaranteed. In this environment, new questions arise that attach to notions of authorship, creativity, digital media literacy, and empowerment that deserve scholarly attention and inquiry.

In an era where the popular imagination accepts and celebrates concepts such as "we" media and "read-write culture," the customary notion of authorship is under challenge. Where a musical work can be reshaped by numerous hands, with numerous recorded destinies or remixes, the act of taking part in the creation of a work invites new definitions of what a creative subject constitutes. If a musician is recast as a "contributor" "editor" rather than an "author" or "composer," then what are the implications for the role of (1) art and (2) artists in this environment?

Secondly, this discussion raises questions about the role of technology developers and marketers in the process of creating software and hardware that facilitate user modifications, or that are underdetermined (in critical constructivist parlance). What interest do developers have in creating such technologies? Are there mutual benefits to business and user communities in "read-write" media, or "read-write" technologies? How much user customization is practically useful, and how much is too much?

A third area of suggested research centers around the aesthetics of music mediated by network computers. While read-write media that center around knowledge-by-consensus (for example, Wikipedia, and Del.icio.us, among many others) have demonstrable benefits to public life and hold obvious emancipatory promise, it is still up for grabs whether an equivalent approach to art can be taken without sacrificing much of art's impetus. There is a sense in which artists risk losing intimacy with their own works. The idea of authoring collectives, adopted broadly, is as potentially problematic as it is promising, it seems. How can critical cultural studies, specifically popular music studies, contribute to this discussion?

CONCLUSION

What are the opportunities for democratization offered in the sphere of popular music? Clearly peer-to-peer technologies, creative commons licensing, online communities of practice, participatory design regimes as in the case of open software projects, and the reduced costs of tools of recording and remixing, offer more opportunities to more participants. But how do these map out in a wider analysis of democratization of music practice, and the potential for music to effect democratizing trends outside of its spheres of practice and audition? What is the state of the nation with music since the advent of the Internet, low-cost production software, and the proliferation of easy to use copy paste media tools?

Perhaps the most important opening for democratic rationalization, or technologically activist approaches to music and sound technology in practice, is in the space opened up by the convergence of media of production and consumption (and the coincident blurring between productive and consumptive practices evinced in mashups, amateur remixes, open source music software, IPod hacks, open format MP3s and free filesharing), the space where direct alliances between coders, artists, and audiences can be forged, and tactical initiatives that work in the interests of all of these groups can be enacted.

The *technê* of artist and audience are converging *onto* a technological platform, one which enables direct dialogue less encumbered (than prior music media) by commercial intermediaries, who may not be capable of reintermediating in this space between. The plasticity of recordable, rewriteable media usable by amateurs, professionals, and fans alike, is the primary space where the artist and the audience are reconfigured, and where technology and its roles in musical creation and audition will likely be rewritten.

With a nod to Jacques Attali,[5] is a new age heralded by the blurring of listener and creator, in which we might conceive of a new *networked creative subject*? The networked subject is a turn we might make to explain "free culture," mashups, and wiki communities.

It is arguable that the networked musical subject is a subject equally inscribed in and by technology as it is inscribed in and by music. It is clear that modern popular music and the technologies of the modern era are mutually constituted. And it is clear that there are a number of strategies (of *concretization*) that artists and audiences can adopt (or at least become cognizant of) in order to improve their autonomy in relation to the social structures written into the technologies they use. What is less clear is how this crisis will ultimately play out. The viability of a vibrant "free" or "read-write" culture of music (and, by extension, knowledge) depends, though, on participants' willingness and ability to face up to their identity as technical and aesthetic subjects embedded in technical and aesthetic networks of practice which they recast (and recast themselves in) each day they take part.

REFERENCES

Adorno, T. W. (1981). *Prisms* (1st MIT Press ed.). Cambridge, MA: MIT Press.

Attali, J. (1985). *Noise: The political economy of music*. Minneapolis: University of Minnesota Press.

Benjamin, W. (1986). The work of art in the age of mechanical reproduction (H. Zohn, Trans.). In H. Arendt (Ed.), *Illluminations*. New York: Harcourt Brace.

Benkler, Y. (2006). *The wealth of networks: How social production transforms markets and freedom*. Yale U Pr.

Di Scipio, A. (1998). Questions concerning music technology: From Heidegger's view to Feenberg's subversive rationalization. *Switch*, (4).

Ebare, S. (2003). *The computerization of practice in peripheral music communities*. Unpublished M.A., Simon Fraser University, Burnaby.

Ebare, S. (2004). Digital music and subculture: Sharing files, sharing styles. *First Monday, 9*(2).

Feenberg, A. (1995). Subversive rationalization: Technology, power, and democracy. *Technology and the Politics of Knowledge*, 3-22.

Feenberg, A. (1999). *Questioning technology*. London; New York: Routledge.

Feenberg, A. (2003). *What is philosophy of technology?* Lecture for the Komaba undergraduates, June, 2003. Retrieved January 20, 2007, from http://www-rohan.sdsu.edu/faculty/feenberg/komaba.htm

Frith, S. (1986). Art versus technology: The strange case of popular music. *Media, Culture and Society, 8*(3), 263-279.

Habermas, J. (1971). Technology and science as "Ideology" (J. J. Shapiro, Trans.). In J. Habermas (Ed.), *Toward a rational society; student protest, science, and politics* (pp. 81-122). Beacon Press.

Heidegger, M. (1977). *The question concerning technology, and other essays* (W. Lovitt, Trans. 1st ed.). New York: Harper & Row.

Latour, B. (1983). Give me a laboratory and I will raise the world. In K. D. Knorr-Cetina & M. J.Mulkay (Eds.), *Science observed* (pp. 141-170). Beverly Hills: Sage.

Lessig, L. (1999). *Code and other laws of cyberspace.* Basic Books.

Lessig, L. (2002). *The future of ideas: The fate of the commons in a connected world.* New York: Vintage Books.

Lessig, L. (2004). *Free culture: How big media uses technology and the law to lock down culture and control creativity.*

Leyshon, A. (2001). Time-space (and digital) compression: Software formats, musical networks, and the reorganisation of the music industry. *Environment and Planning A, 33*(1), 49-77.

Leyshon, A., Webb, P., French, S., Thrift, N., & Crewe, L. (2005). On the reproduction of the musical economy after the Internet. *Media, Culture & Society, 27*(2), 177-209.

Longford, G. (2005). Pedagogies of digital citizenship and the politics of code. *Techné: Research in Philosophy and Technology, 9*(1).

Mosco, V. (1996). *The political economy of communication: Rethinking and renewal.* London; Thousand Oaks, CA: SAGE Publications.

Théberge, P. (1997). *Any sound you can imagine: Making music/consuming technology.* Hanover, NH: Wesleyan University Press: University Press of New England.

ADDITIONAL READING

Bruckman, A. (2002). Studying the amateur artist: A perspective on disguising data collected in human subjects research on the Internet. *Ethics and Information Technology, 4*(3), 217-231.

Bull, M. (2004). Sound connections: An aural epistemology of proximity and distance in urban culture. *Environment & Planning D: Society & Space, 22(*1), 103-116.

Burkart, P. (2005). Loose integration in the popular music industry. *Popular Music & Society, 28*(4), 489-500.

deBeer, J. F. (2005). The role of levies in Canada's digital music marketplace. *Canadian Journal of Law & Technology, 4*(3), 15.

Deuze, M. (2006). Collaboration, participation and the media. *New Media & Society, 8*(4), 691-698.

Di Scipio, A. (1998). *Towards a critical theory of (music) technology. Computer music and subversive rationalization.* Retrieved from http://xoomer.alice.it/adiscipi/tct(m)t.htm

Feenberg, A. (2002). Democratic rationalization: Technology, power and freedom. *Dogma.* Retrieved November 26, 2006, from http://dogma.free.fr/txt/AF_democratic-rationalization.htm

Feenberg, A., & Feenberg, A. (2002). *Transforming technology: A critical theory revisited.* Oxford; New York, NY: Oxford University Press.

Felten, E. W. (2003). A skeptical view of DRM and fair use. *Communications of the ACM, 46*(4), 56-59.

George, C., & Chandak, N. (2006). Issues and challenges in securing interoperability of DRM systems in the digital music market. *International Review of Law, Computers & Technology, 20*(3), 271-285.

Gillespie, T. (2004). Copyright and commerce: The DMCA, trusted systems, and the stabilization of distribution. *Information Society, 20*(4), 239-254.

Gillespie, T. (2006). Designed to 'effectively frustrate': Copyright, technology and the agency of users. *New Media & Society, 8*(4), 651-669.

Gopinath, S. (2005). Ringtones, or the auditory logic of globalization. *First Monday, 10*(12).

Gresham-Lancaster, S. (1998). The aesthetics and history of the hub: The effects of changing technology on network computer music. *Leonardo Music Journal, 8*(1), 39.

Hennion, A. (1989). An intermediary between production and consumption: The producer of popular music. *Science, Technology, & Human Values, 14*(4), 400-424.

Hennion, A. (2001). Music lovers: Taste as performance. *Theory, Culture & Society, 18*(5), 1.

Jenkins, H. (2006). *Convergence culture: Where old and new media collide.* New York: New York University Press.

Jenkins, H., Seawell, B., & Thorburn, D. (2003). *Democracy and new media.* Cambridge, MA: MIT Press.

Jones, R. (2005). Entertaining code: File sharing, digital rights management regimes, and criminological theories of compliance. *International Review of Law, Computers & Technology, 19*(3), 287-303.

Jones, S. (2000). Music and the Internet. *Popular Music, 19*(2), 217.

Julien, O. (1999). The diverting of musical technology by rock musicians: The example of double-tracking. *Popular Music, 18*(3), 357.

Katz, M. (2004). *Capturing sound: How technology has changed music.* Berkeley, CA; London: University of California Press.

Kendall, G. (1999). Pop music: Authenticity, creativity and technology. *Social Alternatives, 18*(2), 25.

Latour, B. (1992). Where are the missing masses: Sociology of a few mundane artefacts. . In W. Bijker & J. E. Law (Eds.), *Shaping technology/building society: Studies in sociotechnical change* (pp. 225-259). Cambridge, MA: MIT Press.

Latour, B. (1993). *We have never been modern.* Cambridge, MA: Harvard University Press.

Madden, M. (2004). *Artists, musicians and the Internet: Pew Internet & American Life Project.*

Mansfield, J. (2005). The global musical subject, curriculum and Heidegger's questioning concerning technology. *Educational Philosophy & Theory, 37*(1), 133-148.

Marontate, J. (2005). Digital recording and the reconfiguration of music as performance. *American Behavioral Scientist, 48*(11), 1422-1438.

McCourt, T. (2005). Collecting music in the digital realm. *Popular Music & Society, 28*(2), 249-252.

Negus, K. (1992). *Producing pop: Culture and conflict in the popular music industry.* London; New York: E. Arnold.

Negus, K. (1995). Where the mystical meets the market: Creativity and commerce in the production of popular music. *Sociological Review, 43*(2), 316-341.

O'Hara, K., & Brown, B. (2006). *Consuming music together: Social and collaborative aspects of music consumption technologies* (K. O'Hara & B. Brown, Trans.). Dordrecht: Springer.

Oudshoorn, N., Pinch, T. J., & Books24x7 Inc. (2005). *How users matter: The co-construction of users and technology.* 1st MIT press paperback. From http://www.lib.sfu.ca/cgi-bin/validate/books24x7.cgi?bookid=12347

Pinch, T., & Bijsterveld, K. (2004). Sound studies: New technologies and music. *Social Studies of Science (Sage), 34*(5), 635-648.

Pinch, T. J., & Bijsterveld, K. (2003). Should one applaud? *Technology & Culture, 44*(3), 536.

Pinch, T. J., & Trocco, F. (2002). *Analog days: The invention and impact of the Moog synthesizer.* Cambridge, MA: Harvard University Press.

Reiffenstein, T. (2006). Codification, patents and the geography of knowledge transfer in the electronic musical instrument industry. *Canadian Geographer, 50*(3), 298-318.

Richards, R. (2006). Users, interactivity and generation. *New Media & Society, 8*(4), 531-550.

Székely, M. (2006). Pushing the popular, or, toward a compositional popular aesthetics. *Popular Music & Society, 29*(1), 91-108.

Theberge, P. (2004). The network studio: Historical and technological paths to a new ideal in music making. *Social Studies of Science, 34*(5), 759-781.

Woodworth, G. M. (2004). Hackers, users, and suits: Napster and representations of identity. *Popular Music & Society, 27*(2), 161-184.

ENDNOTES

[1] It goes without saying that Attali's analysis predated the growth of the Internet, and did not predict anything resembling it.

[2] Though Lessig's view is clearly reminiscent of Habermas' (1971) view of technology, in which the domains of technology is discrete from the realm of values and norms. I shall return to review the shortcomings of this view later.

[3] Clearly there are resonances with the Marxian concept of commodification here, via which objects packaged for markets conceal or mystify the exploitative social relations and processes by which they come to be (Mosco, 1996).The conceptual crossover here warrants theoretical work

[4] These derive largely from the Actor Network Theory of Latour and Callon.

[5] Keeping in mind Attali's prophecy that the age of Repetition (industrial mass production of music as a commodity) would give way in the late 20th Century to an era of Composition, in which musicians would evolve into creatures that make music for self enjoyment rather than market exchange (1985).

Chapter X
The Social Side of Security

Richard G. Taylor
University of Houston, USA

ABSTRACT

The introduction of new technologies to accumulate large amounts of data has resulted in the need for new methods to secure organizational information. Current information security strategies tend to focus on a technology-based approach to securing information. However, this technology-based approach can leave an organization vulnerable to information security threats. Organizations must realize that information security is not necessarily a technology issue, but rather a social issue. Humans operate, maintain, and use information systems. Their actions, whether intentional or accidental, are the real threat to organizations. Information security strategies must be developed to address the social issue.

INTRODUCTION

The only safe computer is one that is turned off, locked in a safe, and buried 20 feet down in a secret location. (Elsberry, 1999)

Times are a'changing. Long gone are the days when your television only had three channels and a cup of coffee cost 25 cents. Now, satellite and cable services deliver hundreds of channels to your home (and you do not have to go outside in the rain to adjust the antenna). Coffee chains offer five-dollar cups of coffee, which we gladly pay. Perhaps the greatest impact on society in the recent past has been the introduction of new

technologies. Vinyl records have been replaced by CDs or digital downloads, our cars can talk to us and give us directions, there are as many computers in homes as televisions, cell phones keep us connected anywhere we go, and the Internet has opened up a world of information and entertainment. I suppose Darwin would refer to this as evolution.

Technology has also entirely changed the landscape in businesses. Computers have become pervasive in the workplace; there is one at every desk. The affordability of data storage allows organizations to accumulate vast amounts of information about their own organization and about their customers. There has been more digital information amassed in the last 2 years than has been accumulated in the entire history of mankind (O'Rourke, 2005). This plethora of information has been of great use to organizations, allowing them to make more-informed decisions. This wealth of information has also created a new challenge for organizations. They must keep their information secured. Governmental legislation such as HIPAA[1] and GLBA[2] has mandated that organizations protect customer information. Failure to do so can result in large fines and sanctions.

Much as technology has changed the social and business landscape, it has also changed the views of information security. I recall working in the financial services industry in the late 1980s and early 1990s. The focus of information security was keeping the information physically secured by putting locks on doors and file cabinets and having security guards monitor the building. Another concern was the threat from internal employees. Internal fraud could lead to losses, and steps were taken to prevent it. However, in the mid-1990s something happened that changed the entire focus of information security. One single cable was plugged into an organization's network or mainframe, connecting them to the Internet, thus opening up their systems and information to the entire world. This created great concern for managers, as it should have. Organizations started spending significant amounts of money to secure their information from the outsiders who could access their system via the Internet. The focus of information security moved away from implementing procedures to prevent internal fraud and moved to implementing technology measures to keep unwanted intruders out of their systems. Information security was now considered a technology problem.

Though considered a technology problem, organizations must realize that information security is foremost a social and managerial issue. "Information security continues to be ignored by top managers, middle managers, and employees

alike. The result of this neglect is that organizational systems are far less secure than they might otherwise be and that security breaches are far more frequent and damaging than is necessary" (Straub & Welke, 1998, p. 442). With the advancements of solutions to address information security issues—firewalls, virus prevention software, biometric identification devices—one has to wonder why organizational information remains vulnerable. This chapter suggests that the primary cause of information vulnerability is that organizations tend to view information security as a technical problem, ignoring the social aspects. This technology-based view has altered the perception of managers regarding information security issues. The result of this current view can be seen in the increasing number of information security incidents.

In 2004, proceeds from information theft were estimated at $105 billion, greater than proceeds from illegal drug sales (Swartz, 2005). The trend has continued in 2005, with millions of people becoming victims of ID theft as a result of poor security. The Internet has become one of the primary threats to organizational information. In 1988, only six Internet incidents were reported; however, for the year 2003 that number had increased to 137,527 (CERT, 2004). The number of incidents was growing so rapidly, that the CERT[3] institute at Carnegie Mellon stopped tracking occurrences after 2003. These incidents, often publicized in the media, have caused an amplification of managers' fears, thus resulting in the implementation of additional technology-based solutions.

Other reports also show the continued information security problem. According to the annual CSI/FBI Computer Crime and Security Survey (Gordon, Loeb, Lucyshyn, & Richardson, 2005), 56% of the organizations surveyed reported an information security incident within their organizations in the previous 12 months.[4] These incidents included virus attacks, unauthorized access to computer-based systems, fraud, sabotage, and denial of service attacks. However, some organizations did not even know if their system had been compromised. Thirteen percent of the organizations participating in the survey stated they did not actually know if they had experienced any security incidents, indicating that the number of organizations reporting security incidents may be understated. "Better perimeter technologies are helping organizations fight against e-crime's depleting effect on time, money and resources; however, we're also seeing increased reports of 'harm to reputation' and 'lost current/future revenues" (CSO, 2006).

The private sector is not alone when it comes to information security problems. All 24 federal government agencies were graded over the past several years (OMB, 2006). The overall government-wide grade has only improved from an "F" to a "D+" from 2001 to 2005, revealing continued information security problems in the public sector. The Department of Homeland Security, which has the responsibility for insuring the security of critical infrastructure sectors, has received an "F" for the past 3 years.

Without a clear understanding of the causes of these information security problems, it becomes increasingly difficult to solve the problems. Therefore, an expanded view is necessary; a view that sees information security as more than just a technology problem.

TECHNOLOGY-BASED VIEW

From the book *Arabian Nights*, Scheherazade tells the tale of *Ali Baba and the Forty Thieves*. In the tale, there is a group of 40 thieves who keep an abundance of riches locked away in a cave. The entrance to the cave would magically open when a secret phrase, known only to the thieves, was spoken. While working one day in the forest, Ali Baba overheard the thieves speak their secret phrase: "Open Sesame." Ali Baba hid in the forest until the thieves had gone. He was then able to speak the secret phrase and enter the cave of riches, thus becoming a wealthy man.

The thieves believed that the security mechanism protecting their treasures was effective. From a technological standpoint, they were probably correct. However, the thieves failed to recognize the human and environmental aspects of their security. Since the secret phrase was known by all 40 thieves, there was a chance that one of the thieves could share the password with someone else. Or, as with Ali Baba, the thieves forgot to consider their environment. The cave of riches was located in a forest that provided ample places for anyone to hide and steal the password, unbeknownst to the thieves.

The same technology-based view of information security still exists today. To understand how to properly secure an information system, an understanding of an information system is necessary. Information systems themselves are social systems (Lee & Liebenau, 1996; Walsham, Symons, Waema, 1990). By definition, an *information system* consists of (1) technology, (2) people, and (3) the environment (Laudon & Laudon, 2004). For an information system to be successful, all three aspects must be considered.

Research examining past information systems failures (Lucas, 1975) indicates that most have failed because management has concentrated on the technical aspects and overlooked organizational behavior and social problems. Early research on information systems success showed that 40% of projects totally failed or did not achieve their intended goals. Of those failures, only 10% were attributed to technical problems. The other 90% were the result of human and/or social issues (Bikson & Gutek, 1984).

Logic would follow that successful information security should address all aspects of an information system. Much like Mumfords' (1995) suggestion of a sociotechnical approach to information system design, information security management must also consider both the social and the technical aspects of securing organizational information. Because of this, one can see that information security is not really a technical problem, but a social and organizational issue, because these technological systems must be operated and used by people.

Organizations, though, tend to focus primarily on technology solutions to keep their information secure. "Businesses today are experiencing a problem with managing information security. This is not only because of increased reliance of individuals and businesses on information and communication technologies, but also because the attempts to manage information security have been rather skewed towards implementing increasing complex technological controls" (Dhillon & Backhouse, 2000, p.13). It is evident that this approach is not always effective. One only has to pick up the daily newspaper or turn on the nightly news to find examples of organizations whose security has been compromised. With the level of technological expertise that is available, how is it that organizations still have security issues? To understand this, organizations must understand the real threat to information security. It is the human element that ultimately leads to organizational information security risks. Threats to information systems can be either technical-based or human-based (Loch, Carr, & Wartentin. 1992). Both technical- and human-based threats can have the same damaging effects on organizations, however, much less attention has been given to human-based information security threats.

A search of the literature found several references to human-based threats (Dhillon, 1999; Dhillon, 2001; Dhillon & Moores, 2001; Harrington, 1996; Straub, 1990; Straub & Nance, 1990; Straub & Welke, 1998), most often referred to as "*computer abuse*." Computer abuse is defined as "the unauthorized and deliberate misuse of assets of the local organizational information system by individuals, including violations against hardware, programs, data, and computer services" (Straub, 1990, p.257). To prevent computer abuse, organizations need to understand and identify the

vulnerabilities that exist within their organizations, both technology based and human based. Once identified, actions can be taken to correct or eliminate the vulnerabilities (Rosenthal, 2003). Those actions must address the human element.

Technological solutions can be impenetrable, however, if one employee gives out their system password, leaves confidential information unsecured on their desk, or throws sensitive information in the trash, then the organization's information has been put at risk. Technological solutions cannot address all of these issues. Even if they could, technological solutions must be developed properly (without design flaws), installed and configured correctly, and maintained and updated regularly to remain effective. All of which are the responsibility of people.

Research has begun to examine the social aspect of information security, focusing on information security as a social and organizational issue, as opposed to a technology issue (Dhillon, 2001; Dhillon & Backhouse, 1996, 2000; Dhillon & Torkzadeh, 2006). This research also supports the claim that current information security management tends to rely on the technology-based solutions and ignores human and environmental aspects. Technology-based solutions alone cannot protect an organization's information. These technologies are designed by people and operated/maintained by people, which in itself makes information security management a social and organizational issue (Dhillon, 2001). Therefore, information security management must be addressed as a social and organizational problem, not a technical problem (Dhillon & Backhouse, 2000).

This widespread use of technology as the primary method for securing organizational information has given rise to "security blindness" on the part of executives (Dhillon & Backhouse, 2000). Studies have shown that managers are aware of only a fraction of the possible actions that can be taken to reduce information security risks (Straub & Welke, 1998). The technology-based view has led to a lower level of managerial commitment to countermeasures (conducting security awareness training, instituting stronger deterrence measures, implementing more effective detection methods, administering more appropriate punishment for security violations, etc.) to reduce information security risks. The underlying problem is that many managers are not well versed on the nature of security risk, likely leading to inadequate protection (Straub & Welke, 1998). Another explanation is that information security risk has been a back-burner issue for decades, and it is difficult to change a perception.

PERCEIVED RISKS

Recall the story of the three little pigs. The mother pig sent her three little pigs to live on their own. The first pig built his house out of straw. The second pig built his house of sticks. The third pig built his house out of brick. Each pig was visited by a "big bad wolf." When the first two pigs refused to let the wolf enter their homes, the wolf huffed and puffed and blew their houses down. The wolf also called upon the third pig and, like his two brothers, he refused to let the wolf into his house. However, when the wolf tried to blow the pig's house down, he was unable to because the house was built of brick.

Their mother had warned the pigs of the wolf and told them to beware. However, the first two obviously did not perceive the threat to be real. Based on that perception, they built their houses accordingly. The third pig perceived the threat to be real and took the extra precaution to insure his security. The first two little pigs paid dearly for their misperception. Giddens (2002) supports this concept of misperception, writing that unless there is a real belief that a severe consequence can happen, little attention will be paid to it. Information security threats must be perceived as real or they too will be ignored.

Managers have differing perceptions about the real value of security. Without a major loss due to poor security, it may be that security concerns will generally be quite low. It may take a major loss to open the eyes of managers to information security risks. Managers may continue to be reluctant to commit resources to information security countermeasures until there is an actual loss (Keefe, 1983). Research has shown that the extent of an organization's current security effort is primarily the result of past information security incidents (Straub, 1990). The result is an ad hoc approach to information security, where the latest incident becomes the model for the next information security action (Rees, Bandyopadhyay, & Spafford, 2003). "[R]esults suggest that management needs to (1) become more informed of the potential for security breaches…(2) increase their awareness in key areas, …and (3) recognize that their overall level of concern for security may underestimate the potential risk inherent in the highly connected environment in which they operate" (Loch et al., 1992, p.185).

Manager's decisions are limited by bounded rationality; they make decisions without the all the necessary information (Cyert & March, 1963). Slovic (1987) has utilized the theory of bounded rationality to research the effects of perceptions of risk. He indicated that rational decision making is not always used "when judging probabilities, making predictions, or attempting to cope with probabilistic tasks" (Slovic, 1987, p.281). Instead, people tend to use judgmental heuristics when making decision. These heuristics may be valid in certain situations, but in others they can lead to biases that are "large, persistent and serious in their implications for decision making" (Slovic, Fischhoff, & Lichtenstein, 1976, p.36).

Initial research on perceived risks focused on hazards such as earthquakes, nuclear power, food preservatives, and so forth. Other research has taken these theories and applied them to subjects such as the perception of risks toward using seat belts (Slovic, Fischhoff, & Lichtenstein, 1978), adolescents' perceptions of risks from smoking (Slovic, 1998), and the risks of using a mobile phone while driving (White, Eiser, & Harris, 2004). Past research indicates that management's perceptions of risks have a direct impact on the decisions they make (Siegrist, Keller, & Kiers, 2005; Sjoberg 1999; Slovic 1987; Slovic, Fischhoff, Lichtenstein, 1979).

Slovic (1987) identified two psychological dimensions of perceived risks: (1) the severity of consequences, and (2) the probability of their occurrence (Slovic et al., 1976). The two dimensions can be applied to managers' perception of information security risks. It is suggested that management is primarily concerned with the severity of the consequences from technology-based information security threats and are not as concerned with the human-based threats. Management will also consider these human-based threats to be rare occurrences, therefore posing little risk and needing no attention (Taylor, 2006).

Management's perceptions of information security risks can lead to strategic decisions resulting in inadequate information security (Taylor, 2006). Misperception can lead to managers' being overly optimistic (Helweg-Larsen & Shepperd, 2001). The optimism has been identified at both the individual and group level, resulting in people rating their own risks as lower than other similar people or groups (Helweg-Larsen & Shepperd, 2001). Research has shown that managers perceive their organizations' level of information security to be high (Taylor, 2006). This perception interferes with the institution of countermeasures, such as information security policies and security awareness training, to address information security risks. Managers feel overly optimistic about their employees' awareness of information security policies and their employees' adherence to these policies (Taylor, 2006). This type of optimism can also be attributed to manager's perception that the organization's employees are part of a homogenous "in-group" whose behavior is based

on a positive exemplar, which is often the manager herself (Judd & Park, 1988). Therefore, since the manager reads and adheres to information security policies, they perceive that their employees will do the same. The concept of a homogenous "in-group" involves a high level of trust among employees within an organization.

IN-GROUP TRUST

Around 200 BC, a great wall was built in China to protect its borders from invading armies. The wall was fortified centuries later, in 1449 during the Ming Dynasty, after China's defeat of the Mongols. This fortified wall protected China from all invading forces. Around 1600, China faced another invasion attempt. However, the Great Wall held strong. The attacking armies tried every possible way to breach the Great Wall but were unsuccessful. However, in 1644, the army successfully entered China, seized Beijing, and thereby ended the Ming Dynasty. But how did the army get through the Great Wall? They did not climb over the wall, dig under the wall, or break through the wall. They simply bribed a Chinese border guard to open a gate and let them pass. The historical account should remind us that even the greatest security feature can be breached. In this case, the security feature performed as expected and kept away outsiders. However, it was the violation of trust by an insider that led to the security incident.

By understanding that security is a social issue, it becomes necessary to investigate behavioral issues that affect information security. Trust is one such issue that is a contributing factor to the level of information security risk. Managers trust that their employees will follow information security policies and that software developers will write programs that do not contain security holes. Employees trust that other employees will not do anything that will put the organization at risk, and that non-employees such as vendors, consultants, and the cleaning crew will not steal confidential information that has been left unsecured.

Trust has been defined as "confidence that one will find what is desired from another, rather than what is feared" (Deutsch, 1973, p.95). Understanding why people trust, and how that trust shapes social relations has been a focus for psychologists (Worchel, 1979), sociologists (Gambetta, 1988), political scientists (Barber, 1983), anthropologists (Ekeh, 1974), and organizational behavior researchers (Kramer & Tyler, 1996). The role of organizational trust has also appeared in management literature (Hosmer, 1995). Trust is important in many organizational activities, including teamwork, goal setting, leadership, performance appraisal, development of labor relations, and negotiation (Mayer, Davis, & Schoormann, 1995; Morris & Moberg, 1994). However, there is also growing concern about distrust and the violation and/or abuse of trust within organizations (Bies & Tripp, 1996; Giacalone & Greenberg, 1997; Lewicki & Bunker; 1996). The potentially greatest threat to modern organizations is not external agencies, but the betrayal of trust by organizational insiders who are "ambitious, selfish, deceitful people who care more for their own advancement than the mission of the organization" (Hogan & Hogan, 1994, p.94).

Loch et al. (1992) state that information security threats can be external or internal. Social and organizational issues require management to expand their view of information security to look beyond the external threats and realize that internal threats must also be addressed. As with the Great Wall of China, evidence also suggests "that the violation of safeguards by trusted personnel of an organization is emerging as a primary reason for information security concerns. Between 61% and 81% of computer related crimes are being carried out because of such violations" (Dhillon & Backhouse, 2000, p. 13). Threats from organizational insiders are grossly overlooked by management, and potentially represent the greatest threat to organizational information.

While investigating trust as it applies to information security, one can also look at literature related to bias. Bias literature explains the relationship between in-groups and out-groups (Allport, 1954; Brewer, 1979; Brewer, 1999; Sumner, 1906). Throughout history, societies have formed group relationships for the purpose of survival, thus creating an in-group. Those not associated with one's in-group were considered the out-group. "[M]embers of a group share a common outcome that is distinct from the outcome shared by members of the other group. Such a co-occurrence of group boundaries and common fate is one of the criteria for perceived 'entitivity' of social groupings" (Brewer, 1979, p.308).

The in-group/out-group distinctions can shape social interactions and opportunities for cooperation, imitation, and interdependence (Brewer, 1999). Past research on bias was primarily focused on societal level biases and centered on discrimination. However, these same principles can be applied to business organizations.

In-group/out-group sentiments surely exist within organizations today. Organizations attempt to create an atmosphere where all employees feel they are part of the organizational in-group. Within this organizational in-group, an atmosphere of trust soon develops. However, the creation of the in-group can be an area of concern in regards to information security. Who is allowed into this in-group? Obviously management and employees are included in an organizational in-group. But what about employee family members, vendors, consultants, customers, or even the cleaning crew? These are people that often have regular contact with the organization and may often be accepted into the organizational in-group. However, this inclusion may lead to increased information security risk. If the cleaning crew is included in this in-group, then it is possible that employees may leave confidential information unsecured after hours because of the high trust level employees have in the members of their in-group. Therefore, it is important that organizational in-group membership is clearly defined.

In-group trust also leads to out-group distrust. As mentioned, organizations still take technology-based approaches to securing an organization's information. Firewalls and intrusion detection systems are put in place for the primary reason of keeping the organizations' information protected from outsiders: the out-group. Organizations tend to do a good job protecting their information from the out-group; however, focusing only on the out-group has led to unwanted information security risks. Organizational focus on out-group distrust takes attention away from the internal focus.

Within the in-group, the trust relations that are developed among the members have the potential for creating information security risks because in-group members create "bounded communities of mutual trust and obligation that delimit mutual interdependence and cooperation. An important aspect of this mutual trust is that it is depersonalized, extended to any member of the in-group, whether personally related or not. Psychologically, expectations of cooperation and security promote positive attraction toward other in-group members, and motivate adherence to in-group norms of appearance and behavior that assure that one will be recognized as a good or legitimate in-group member" (Brewer, 1999, p. 433).

Employees are also susceptible to acts of "social engineering" based on their in-group trust. Social engineers attempt to gain access to a system by lying to employees to persuade them to reveal system passwords and other sensitive information. This is much easier than one might think. The key to convincing an employee to give up this information is by convincing the employee that the social engineer is a part of their in-group. Social engineers will pose as employees of the data processing department, vendors who work with the organization, or family members of other employees. Infamous hacker Kevin Mitnik claims that he was so successful in this line of attack

that he rarely had to result to a technology-based attack (Mitnick, 2003).

CONCLUSION

As businesses adjust to the changing times, they must alter their perception of information security to include the social aspect that can put organizational information at risk. Technological solutions to minimize information security risks are a necessity, but reliance on those solutions may lead to a neglect of the social side of security. This may prove to be very costly, resulting in tangible and intangible damages.

While all employees need to be aware of possible information security threats, it is management who are the key to successfully deterring, preventing, and detecting information security incidents as well as pursuing remedies and/or punishing offenders for abuse (Straub & Welke, 1998). Managers must address all information security needs of the organization. But as long as managers' perception of human-based information security risks remains low, employees will continue to contribute to information security risks; because employee awareness will, in turn, be low, punishment will be inadequate or nonexistent, and prevention and detection methods will be nonexistence or ineffective.

It all comes down to people. People design computer systems, people decide which information security countermeasures should be implemented, people do things that put organizational information at risk (often unbeknownst to them). Information systems are social systems; therefore, the security of information systems must also be a social issue. In closing, I refer back to infamous hacker, now turned consultant, Kevin Mitnick:

People are the weakest link. You can have the best technology; firewalls, intrusion detection systems, biometric devices…and somebody can call an unsuspecting employee. That's all she wrote, baby. They got everything. (Mitnick, 2003)

REFERENCES

Allport, G. W. (1954). *The nature of prejudice.* Cambridge, MA: Addison-Wesley.

Barber, B. (1983). *The logic and limits of trust.* New Burnswick, NJ: Rutgers University Press.

Bikson, T. K., & Gutek, B.(1984). *Implementation of office automation.* Santa Monica, CA: Rand Corporation.

Bies, R. J., & Tripp, T. M. (1996). Beyond distrust: Getting even and the need for revenge. In R. Kramer & T. Tyler (Eds.), *Trust in organizations: Frontiers of theory and research* (pp. 246-260). Thousand Oaks, CA: Sage.

Brewer, M. B. (1979). In-group bias in the minimal intergroup situation. A cognitive motivational analysis. *Psychological Bulletin, 86,* 307-324.

Brewer, M. B. (1999). The psychology of prejudice: In-group love or out-group hate?*Journal of Social Issues, 55*(3), 429-444.

CERT. (2004). *2004 E-Crime Watch Survey.* Pittsburg, PA: Carnegie Mellon University.

CSO. (2006). *2006 E-Crime Watch Survey from CSO magazine.* Retrieved February 10, 2007, from http://www2.csoonline.html/info/release.html?CID=24531

Cyert, R. M., & March, J.G. (1963). *A behavioral theory of the firm.* Englewood Cliffs, NJ: Prentice-Hall.

Deutsch, M. (1973). *The resolution of conflict: Constructive and destructive processes.* New Haven, CT: Yale University Press.

Dhillon, G. (1999). Managing and controlling computer misuse. *Information Management & Computer Security, 7*(5): 171-175.

Dhillon, G. (2001). Violation of safeguards by trusted personnel and understanding related information security concerns. *Computer & Security, 20*(2), 165-172.

Dhillon, G., & Backhouse, J. (1996). Risks in the use of information technology within organizations. *International Journal of Information Management, 16*(1), 65-74.

Dhillon, G., & Backhouse, J. (2000). Information system security management in the new millennium. *Communications of the ACM, 43*(7), 125-128.

Dhillon, G., & Moores, S. (2001). Computer crimes: Theorizing about the enemy within. *Computers & Security, 20*(8), 715-723.

Dhillon, G., & Torkzadeh, G. (2006). Value focused assessment of information system security in organizations. *Information Systems Journal, 16*(3), 391-392.

Ekeh, P. P. (1974). *Social exchange theory: The two traditions.* Cambridge, MA: Harvard University Press.

Elsberry, R. B. (1999). The spying game: How safe are your secrets? *Office Systems,* September.

Gambetta, D. (1988). *Trust: Making and breaking cooperative relations.* New York: Basil Blackwell.

Giacalong, R., & Greenberg, J. (1997). *Antisocial behavior in organizations.* Thousand Oaks, CA: Sage.

Giddens, A. (2002). The consequences of modernity. In Calhoun, Gerteis, Moody, Pfaff, & Virk (Eds.), *Contemporary sociological theory,* (pp. 244-255).

Gordon, L. A., Loeb, M. P., Lucyshyn, W., & Richardson, R. (2005). *2005 CSI/FBI computer crime and security survey.* Computer Security Institute.

Harrington, S. J. (1996). The effect of codes of ethics and personal denial of responsibility on computer abuse judgments and intentions. *MIS Quarterly, 20*(3), 257-278.

Helweg-Larsen, M., & Sheppard, J. A. (2001). Do moderators of the optimistic bias affect personal or target risk estimates? A review of the literature. *Personality and Social Psychology Review, 5*(1), 74-95.

Hogan, R., & Hogan, J. (1994). The mask of integrity. Pp. 107-125 In T. Sarbin, R. Carney, & C. Eoyang (Eds.), *Citizen espionage: Studies in trust and betrayal.* Westport, CT: Praeger.

Hosmer, L. T. (1995). Trust: The connecting link between organization theory and philosophical ethics. *Academy of Management Review, 20,* 379-403.

Judd, C. M., & Park, B. (1988). Out-group homogeneity: Judgments of variability at the individual and group levels. *Journal of Personality and Social Psychology, 54*(5), 778-788.

Keefe, P. (1983). Computer crime insurance available-for a price. *Computerworld, 31,* 20-21.

Kramer, R. M., & Tyler, T. R. (1996). *Trust in organizations: Frontiers of theory and research.* Thousand Oaks, CA: Sage.

Lee, H., & Liebenau, J. (1996). In what way are information systems social systems? A critique from sociology. *Proceedings of the First UK Academy for Information Systems Conference.* Cranfield School of Management, Cranfield, Bedford.

Lewicki, R. J., & Bunker, B. B. (1996). Developing and maintaining trust in work relationships. In R. Kramer & T. Tyler (Eds.), *Trust in organizations: Frontiers of theory and research,* (pp. 14-139). Thousand Oaks, CA: Sage.

Loch, K. D., Carr, H. H, & Wartentin, M. E. (1992). Threats to information systems: Today's reality, yesterday's understanding. *MIS Quarterly, 17*(2), 173-186.

Laudon, K, & Laudon, J. (2004). *Managing the digital firm* (8th ed.). Upper Saddle River, NJ: Prentice-Hall.

Lucas, H. C. 1975. *Why information systems fail.* New York: Columbia University Press.

Mayer, R., Davis, J., & Schoormann, F. D. (1995). An integrative model of organizational trust. *Academy of Management Review, 20,* 709-734.

Mitnick, K. (2003). *The art of deception.* New York, NY: John Wiley & Sons.

Morris, J. H., & Moberg, D. J. (1994). Work organizations as contexts for trust and betrayal. Pp. 163-187 In T. Sarbin, R. Carney, & C. Eoyang (Eds.), *Citizen espionage: Studies in trust and betrayal.* Westport, CT: Praeger.

Mumford, E. (1995). *Effective systems design and requirement analysis: The ETHICS approach.* Basingstoke, UK: Macmillan Press.

OMB. (2006). *Report to Congress on Federal Government Information Security Reform.* Office of Management and Budget.

O'Rourke, M. (2005). Data secured? Taking on cyber-thievery. *Risk Management,* Oct.

Rees, J., Bandyopadhyay, S., & Spafford, E. (2003). PFIRES: A policy framework for information security. *Communications of the ACM, 46*(7), 101-106.

Rosenthal, D. A. (2003). Intrusion detection technology: Leveraging the organization's security posture. *Information Systems Management, 19,* 35-44.

Siegrist, M., Keller, C., & Kiers, H. A. L. (2005). A new look at the psychometric paradigm of perception of hazards. *Risk Analysis, 25*(1), 211-222.

Sjoberg, L. (1999). Risk perception by the public and by experts: A dilemma in risk management. *Research in Human Ecology, 2*(2), 1-9.

Slovic, P. (1987). Perception of risk. *Science, 236*, 280-285.

Slovic, P. (1998). Do adolescent smokers know the risks? *Duke Law Review, 47*(6), 1133-1141.

Slovic, P., Fischhoff, B., & Lichtenstein, S. (1976). Cognitive processes and societal risk taking. Pp. 165-184 In J. S. C. J. W. Payen (Ed.), *Cognition and social behavior*. Potomac, MD: Lawrence Erlbaum Associates.

Slovic, P., Fischhoff, B., & Lichtenstein, S. (1978). Accident probabilities and seat belt usage: A psychological perspective. *Accident Analysis and Prevention, 10*, 281-285.

Slovic, P., Fischhoff, B., & Lichtenstein, S. (1979). Rating the risks. *Environment, 21*(3), 14-39.

Straub, D. (1990). Effective IS security: An empirical study. *Information Systems Research, 1*(3), 255-276.

Straub, D., & Nance,W. (1990). Discovering and discipling computer abuse in organizations: A field study. *MIS Quarterly, 14*(2), 45-60.

Straub, D., & Welke, R. (1998). Coping with systems risk: Security planning models for management decision making. *MIS Quarterly, 22*(4), 441-469.

Sumner, W. G. (1906). *Folkways*. New York: Ginn.

Swartz, J. (2005). 2005 worst year for breaches of computer security. *USA Today*.

Taylor, R. (2006). *Management perception of unintentional information security risks*. International Conference on Information Systems, Milwaukee, WI. December 10-13, 2006.

Walsham, G., Symons, V., & Waema, T. (1990). Information systems as social systems: Implications for developing countries. In S. Bhatnagar & N. Bjorn-Andersen (Eds.), *Information Technology in Developing Countries, (*pp. 51-61). Amsterdam: Elsevier Science Publishers.

White, M. P., Eiser, J. P., & Harris, P. R. (2004). Risk perceptions of mobile phone use while driving. *Risk Analysis, 24*(2), 323-334.

Worchel, P. (1979). Trust and distrust. In W. G. Austin & S. Worchel (Eds.), *The social psychology of intergroup relations*. Belmont, CA: Wadsworth.

ENDNOTES

[1]   Health Insurance Portability and Accountability Act requires that health providers keep patient information private and secured.

[2]   Gramm-Leach-Bliley Act requires financial institutions to insure the privacy and security of customer information.

[3]   Computer Emergency Response Team

[4]   In 2005, the CSI/FBI Computer Crime and Security Survey consisted of 700 organizations responding, representing various industries and organization sizes.

Chapter XI
The Cultural Factors in Electronic Monitoring

Jeng-Chung Victor Chen
National Cheng Kung University, Taiwan

J. Michael Tarn
Western Michigan University, USA

ABSTRACT

The use of electronic monitoring tools in the workplace has grown dramatically because of the availability of inexpensive but powerful monitoring systems and the wide use of information and communication technologies (ICT) in today's workplace. However, existing research pays little attention to the pervasive use of electronic monitoring systems on ICT at work. This chapter draws theories in international and organizational cultures and concludes four hypotheses on privacy concerns of employees and their perceived trust to the management when being electronically monitored.

INTRODUCTION

It is an inevitable trend today that businesses are reaching and interacting with international customers via the Internet. Thus, the issue on the privacy concerns of Internet consumers has been repeatedly discussed and widely researched (Hoffman & Novak, 1999; Milberg, Burke, Smith, & Kallman, 1995; Nord, McCubbins, & Nord, 2006; Wen & Gershuny, 2005). Nord, et al. (2006) examine the employer-employee workplace privacy relationship and identify the existing federal and state laws governing workplace privacy. Milberg et al. (1995) investigated the relationships among personal information privacy concerns, nationalities, cultural values, and information privacy regulations, and found that cultural differences play an important role on personal information privacy concerns. However, less attention has been paid on the company employees' privacy concerns while corporations are turning global, setting up foreign branches, and recruiting overseas employees. Moreover, the impact of the widely installed surveillance tools that monitor employees' computers and Internet connections has, yet been investigated further. Previous studies on the impact of these surveillance tools were focused on trust and privacy (Agre, 1994; Nord et al., 2006; Tabak & Smith, 2005; Westin, 1992) without considering employees' cultural differences. This chapter aims to discuss the relationship between employees' cultural differences and their privacy concerns under the electronic surveillance working environment.

TREND IN THE USE OF ELECTRONIC MONITORING

In this information era, employees use computers at work more often than before. According to the U.S. Department of Commerce's survey (2002), the number of employees 25 or older who used computers at work increased from 52% in 1998 to 57% in 2001. Nevertheless, the percentage of those who used the Internet and/or e-mail at work soared 22% from 1998 to 2001. An important finding of this survey is that many employees admitted that they went online at work for personal business. The employers, on the other hand, were worried about their employees being distracted from work, along with such issues as security concerns due to easy desktop Internet access (Noack, 1999; Urbaczewski & Jessup, 2002).

Not surprisingly, more and more organizations are monitoring their employees at the workplace. Simply observe the historical trend from 1997 to 2005 (AMA, 2001, 2005). In 1997, there were 35% of major American corporations that recorded and reviewed employees' communications and activities on the job. This figure climbed to almost 81% in 2001. There are many different types of surveillance tools that companies use such as monitoring telephone, e-mail, computer, video camera, and Internet connections. E-mail monitoring was the

type of surveillance with the sharpest increase in use from 1997 to 1999. From 2000 to 2005, the use of Internet connection monitoring increased from 54% to 76%. By observing the employees who were fired in 2005, it was found that 26% of them lost their jobs for misusing the Internet while 25% misused e-mail.

Schulman (2001) confirms that monitoring employees has become a worldwide trend. According to his research, 35% of employees in America and 27% of employees worldwide were monitored by monitoring software installed by their employers. In the U.S., a possible reason for the prevalent use of electronic monitoring at work is that ECPA 1986, the only frequently cited law in workplace privacy suits, gives little protection to employees in the workplace, especially when they use company-owned equipment. After the September 11 attack, the Patriot Act (or the Uniting and Strengthening America by Providing Appropriate Tools Required to Intercept and Obstruct Terrorism Act of 2001) has given the federal government more authority and power to monitor electronic communications such as e-mails and Internet activities.

As the focus of corporate monitoring is switching from telephone and video monitoring to e-mail and computer-based monitoring, employees being monitored are expanding from blue- to white-collar workers. More and more white-collar workers, such as managers, professionals and even university faculty, are being monitored (Allen, 1993).

There are many types of monitoring software or surveillance tools that can record keystrokes and browsed websites. For monitoring e-mail, special software is able to filter out e-mails which include words such as porn, sex, boss and others. To an extreme, employers can even track where their employees are via GPS technology using their cell phones. The management of electronic monitoring technology has become a critical issue.

MANAGING ELECTRONIC MONITORING TECHNOLOGY

According to Wen and Gershuny (2005), computer-based monitoring technology can be classified into six categories, as follows, based on monitoring capabilities:

- **Keystroke monitoring:** For example, maintaining a record of keystrokes along with the window they are typed in and time stamp and tracking computer idle time.
- **E-mails sent and received:** For example, screening e-mails for potentially offensive or inappropriate messages and scanning employee e-mails for questionable keywords predetermined by the employer.
- **Events timeline logging:** For example, logging all events users perform, and viewing them in an organized, chronologically ordered listing.
- **Application usage:** For example, monitoring and logging all applications ran by users or all Internet sessions and chat conversations made on a computer.
- **Window activity:** For example, recording documents and files opened and/or viewed by users or viewing a list of the current Internet connections on a desktop computer.

How a company employs these powerful and versatile monitoring tools to monitor its employees in the workplace becomes very arguable since both sides can justify whether electronic monitoring is economic, legal, or ethical (Wen & Gershuny, 2005). Nevertheless, much evidence shows that more and more employees use their desktop computers to do Internet activities including instant messaging, online shopping, downloading music, watching videos, and so forth, which eventually would distract them from their work and decrease their productivity (Nord et al., 2006). According to an interesting study by Ara (2006), a software company's employees in Florida spent an average of 75 minutes a day in doing online gaming, gambling, or shopping on office computers. It is estimated that it will result in a $300,000 annual loss for a 50-employee company.

From an employer's perspective, the installation of electronic monitoring systems may be simply to constrain employees' attempts to surf the Internet for their personal businesses at work. In other words, many employers believe that by installing the monitoring system, their employees will become more disciplined and self-controlled. However, it is argued that monitoring technologies may not discipline employees but violate the human privacy right instead.

In this sense, managing electronic monitoring will eventually have to deal with the employer-employee relationship, in which similar conclusions were reached by both earlier and recent research studies. For example, in his case study on the Federal Express Corporation's telecommunication call centers, Westin (1992) found that employees usually found it unfair that employers use surveillance tools to monitor them at work. The biggest concern of employees was their loss of privacy rights. Later, the management decided to abandon the surveillance tools because they were harmful to employer-employee relationships. Today, managing electronic monitoring has become even more complicated after the emergence of mobile technology because this could easily change the nature of the supervisor-employee relationship. Schlosser (2007) observes the management's use of mobile technologies in the working environment to communicate and supportively monitor salesperson performance. He concludes that how salespersons perceive their supervisors' monitoring using mobile technology will influence their perceptions of the supervisor-employee relationship. In other words, perceptions of quality management-employee relationships are indeed important to retaining and motivating employees. This discussion has triggered a difficult task about how to seek a balancing point between managing an effective electronic monitoring and maintaining a good employer-employee relationship. Employee privacy, which will be discussed in the following section, is one of the most critical factors that need to be addressed.

EMPLOYEE PRIVACY

From the technological standpoint, there is less privacy for employees. For example, most employees thought their passwords would protect their e-mail account from monitoring, and they could delete e-mails to eliminate any evidence. However, the employer has access to all passwords, and backups of e-mails are stored in servers.

Although the U.S. Constitution warrants the right of privacy, there is still little legal protection from electronic monitoring. Under most circumstances, electronic monitoring is, in fact, legal (De Pree & Jude, 2006). There are many reasons that support an employer's decision to monitor employees (Dary, Tipton, & Jeretta, 2006). For instance, an e-mail system is owned by the employer, who must take responsibility for its management and security. If employees' e-mails from their corporate e-mail accounts include pornographic, racial, sexual, or inappropriate words, it is likely that someone may file a lawsuit against the company (Nadeem, Ramin, & Jitka, 2006).

However, many employees believe that privacy is a right in the work place. Indeed, the rights of the employer and employee related to privacy and monitoring could be defined by several laws as follows:

- The Federal Criminal Codes (18 U.S.C. §2510 and §2511) discuss interception of wire, electronic, and oral communication. According to these laws, it must define clearly what the company's property is and what the personal property is for the right of electronic privacy in the work place.

- The Civil Rights Act 1964 supports an employee's position if he or she perceives being discriminated because of the corporate use of electronic monitoring.

- The Fourth Amendment, which protects U.S. citizens against unreasonable search and seizure by the government, does not guarantee a right of privacy in the workplace. Because private firms are not the government, this law does not protect private employees against electronic monitoring in the workplace.

- The Electronic Communications Privacy Act 1986 (ECPA) is closely related to the privacy of the employee. Under this act, it is a federal crime for an individual to intentionally conduct activities such as intercepting, accessing, disclosing, or using another's wire, oral, or electronic communication. However, this act does not apply to workers in a private business.

- The Notice of Electronic Monitoring Act establishes how often employers must inform their employees of electronic monitoring.

The electronic communication area has just been developed in recent years, which explains the reason that most situations in this area have not been applied to the current laws and regulations. Therefore, there is an urgent need to develop new laws in the related field to assure the privacy right in the workplace between employers and employees.

PRIVACY AND CULTURE

As discussed earlier, privacy plays an important role for the implementation of electronic monitoring. When the privacy issue is shifted to an international environment or a diversified workplace, it is deemed as not a simple independent but complex cultural phenomenon. As confirmed by Shah,

White, and Cook (2007), differences in cultures have resulted in many difficulties in establishing global standards and legislations to ensure privacy. Nevertheless, the research on the relationship between privacy and culture is not new, but well explored. Although many researchers consider monitoring technology as surveillance, Agre (1994) argues that there are indeed two models of privacy involved, surveillance and capture. In his viewpoint, the surveillance model comes from cultural phenomenon, while the capture model comes from Fordism or Taylorism, which focuses on training disciplined employees. Based on Agre's theory, the Foucauldian framework of discipline belongs to the capture model.

Ogburn's culture lag theory (1966) was proposed long before Agre's surveillance model of privacy and cultural phenomenon. This theory suggests that a social crisis will emerge if people's old culture does not catch up with the use of the new technologies, which are treated as material culture. Because of the rapid advance in technology or material culture, there is always a significant gap in terms of the advancement between the material technologies and non-material technologies (i.e., ethical values), which is defined as a cultural lag. Further, if there is no wide-emerging consensus formed by people on any new modern technology, a social conflict will occur. People will not feel comfortable if their enjoyment of embracing new technologies does not match with the ethical values of old, non-material culture. In short, privacy is not simply a technical phenomenon, could be difficult to manage from a technical aspect, and should be embedded in social and cultural contexts (Dourish & Anderson, 2006).

Westin (1967) found that every society values privacy. However, the ways that different societies express privacy vary significantly. Altman and Chemers (1980) also found that privacy is a universal culture. They identify cultural practices, verbal behavior, nonverbal behavior, and environmental behavior as the four major components that comprise the privacy regulation. They further define the components of the cultural practice as "a variety of customs, rules, and norms which communicate openness or closeness to others and which are readily understood by most people in a particular culture."

On the other hand, Hofstede (1980) identified four dimensions of culture: collectivism/individualism, power distance, masculinity, and uncertainty avoidance. Among them, collectivism/individualism is the one being studied most. According to Hofstede (1980), people in countries with high scores on the dimension of individualism mainly focus on their personal lives. People in those countries expect that everyone has the right to have a private life. In contrast, people in countries with high scores on the dimension of collectivism (or low individualism) are more tolerant to invasion of private life or personal privacy. In other words, people who are from Western (European and American) countries that have high individualism scores respect privacy more than their counterparts from Eastern countries (e.g., Japan, China, and Korea). Hofstede's theory has been applied by many recent research studies (Dinev, Bellotto, Hart, & Russo, 2006; Lu, 2006; Soares, Farhangmehr, & Shoham, 2007).

Furthermore, different cultures not only share similar privacy concerns, but also differ to a great extent (Soares et al., 2007). Cultural values are associated with differences in privacy concerns (Bellman, Johnson, Kobrin, & Lohse, 2004). According to Newell's (1998) experiment, a general observation was that all cultures agreed on the need for privacy. When observing differences, it was found that participants from Senegal had more difficulty in obtaining privacy when they required it, while most American and Iris participants noted that they could usually obtain privacy when required. This finding can explain why Western countries respect privacy more than other countries.

In addition, most Chinese people had the tendency to be intimate while they were with members of their group with collective cultures

(Lu, 2005). In other words, the Chinese would be in higher level of self-disclosure with members from collective cultures. On the other hand, most Americans are with superficial acquaintances where high levels of self-disclosure are not expected. According to these rationales, the following hypotheses are formed:

- **Hypothesis 1:** The privacy concerns of employees vary in different countries when they are being electronically monitored at work.
- **Hypothesis 2:** Employees in Eastern Asian countries have less privacy concerns than employees in Western countries when they are being electronically monitored at work.

TRUST AND CULTURE

While privacy is a passive factor, trust is an active component. In addition to examining the relationship between privacy and culture, the relationship between trust and culture needs be justified. Urbaczewski and Jessup (2002) apply both Theory X and Theory Y to predict employees' behavior and satisfaction in their first study of electronic monitoring conducted in the classroom. They found that both Theory X and Theory Y are supported in terms of performance or productive behavior (supporting Theory X) and satisfaction (supporting Theory Y). In the second study conduced in a controlled lab environment, they further found that people who are more motivated and high performing would accept the electronic monitoring more than those who are less motivated and low performing. However, they acknowledged that individual differences along with other factors should be measured in future studies. In today's international working environment, employees' differences in workplaces may be a result of the four (Hofstede, 1980) or five (Hofstede, 1991) dimensions of cultural differences.

Trust is an important factor in management because it is considered as social capital (Fukuyama, 1995). Trust being treated as social capital reflects that it is a culturally dependent asset that people inherit from their forefathers. According to Fukuyama (1995), trust is an important factor when explaining the different levels of economic development among countries that are similar, culturally or geographically. An example is Japan vs. other neighboring Confucius countries, for example, Taiwan and South Korea. Japan enjoys higher economic development because it is a high-trust country compared to other Eastern Asian countries, even though they are all influenced by Confucianism. Based on Fukuyama (1995) and Hofstede's theories (1991), Doney et al. (Doney, Cannon, & Mullen, 1998) argued that the formation of trust is dependent on cultural differences. Collectivist people (mostly from Eastern Asian countries) would be more likely to trust people via prediction, intentionality, and transference processes while individualist people would trust others via calculative and capability processes. In other words, collectivist people trust others mostly based on their "belonging" to the trustee, but individualist people trust the trustee mostly based on "exchange" or "negotiation" processes. Kramer and Wei (1999) suggested that people mostly do not have to verify or negotiate trust if identity-based exists. Other empirical research confirmed that trust is essentially relational and identity based but not calculation based.

Early literature on the relationship between monitoring and trust can be tracked back to Strickland's research (1958), which found that observers who use surveillance tools tend to distrust those who they are watching. The surveillance itself will increase an observing person's belief that those who are being watched are not truthful. The finding is questionable because people, by nature, tend to monitor distrusted people. The effect observed by Strickland only appeared in the initial settings where no other factors were considered. Aiello (1993), on the other hand, looked at how employees reacted to the use of electronic monitoring. He suggested several potential moderating factors that could exist once a monitoring system is implemented. His first suggestion was the type of organizational climate that currently exists for employees. He argued that employees may be more integrated into a cohesive workgroup or detached from their coworkers if monitoring systems are installed in a Theory X type of environment. Zuboff's case studies (1988) show that managers who are able to monitor employees tend to depersonalize social relations. Zuboff concludes that the employees' mistrust toward their managers would emerge as long as a surveillance tool is installed. The observation was that "This mistrust was not rooted in a perception of evil or malicious intent … It was, indeed, the feeling evoked in the silent dance of the observer and the observed" (Zuboff, 1988, p.344).

Trust undermined by surveillance equipment has been identified for many decades since Strickland's research. The situation of monitoring employees is much more popular today than it is used to be because technology has been integrated into people's daily life and work. Kramer (Kramer & Wei, 1999) identified that trust is an enduring issue in organizations but surveillance tools could undermine trust. In his opinion, systems that are used to enhance trust, ironically, make it worse in an organization, because honest and well-behaved employees may feel immoral when the regulations designed to increase trustworthy performance encourage perverse behaviors instead. Cialdini (1996) uses "tumor" to describe the structure of organizational dishonesty, which explains the reason that an organization will experience a set of costly consequences if it allows the use of dishonest, influential tactics. One of the tumors is the cost of surveillance in work climate. Cialdini identified three reasons that surveillance could undermine trust in an organization; that is, evident lack of trust in employees, the undermining of desirable behavior, and the exaggerate causality of surveil-

lance. The latter means that managers tend to believe that exemplaric behavior of the employees they are monitoring is caused by the surveillance, even though such behavior might have occurred anyway. Based on these discussions, the following hypotheses can be presented:

- **Hypothesis 3:** Employees' confidence in their managers varies in different countries when they are being electronically monitored at work.
- **Hypothesis 4:** Employees in Eastern Asian countries have more faith in their managers than employees in Western countries when they are being electronically monitored at work.

CONCLUSION

The four hypotheses, based on two famous theories in sociology and management, are very much culture oriented. While Hofstede's theory is prevalent in the field of management, many researchers in other disciplines might consider culture as a "soft" matter. However, we live in a connected world where people frequently mingle with those of other cultures. When an international enterprise expands its business to a country, its first mission is definitely to learn the local culture. The importance of culture has been recognized in the field of marketing and information systems. For example, it has been proven in marketing that an advertisement is much more powerful and persuasive if it embeds more with local culture values (Zandpour, Campos, Catalano, Chang, Cho, Hoobyar, et al., 1994).

It has been recognized in the field of management that culture is an important factor in an organization. Privacy is probably one of the most important areas when technology and culture/society interact with each other. The business activities of an international enterprise are heavily impacted by different cultures and local laws. Future empirical tests on the four developed hypotheses will provide a more thorough understanding on how the culture factor affects people's privacy concerns in an organization. When studying the use of electronic monitoring technology in organizations, privacy concerns must be investigated over a broad range of organizational activities.

Since trust is treated as a valuable asset in an organization, electronic monitoring tools that could undermine organizational trust should be carefully evaluated before installation. However, most organizations in industry have not seen possible negative impacts yet. This chapter, in addition to discussing the use of electronic monitoring tools and its impact on privacy concerns, raises another important issue: trust. Like privacy concerns that are mostly raised by employees, trust is an important managerial issue that every organization should deal with seriously. This chapter concludes that first, employers are encouraged to treat and be cautious with their employees' privacy concerns, and, secondly, management should carefully evaluate the negative impacts of electronic monitoring on organizational trust. Understanding cultural issues and concerns, managers in multinational corporations or in well-diversified workplaces should carefully employ the prevalent electronic monitoring technology to support corporate activities.

FUTURE RESEARCH DIRECTIONS

This chapter emphasizes the cultural factors in electronic monitoring, which discuses the privacy concerns and trust when using electronic monitoring as managerial tools in organizations, and its impacts on the relationships between the employers and employees. Future research beyond cultural factors and privacy of employees at the workplace and the relationships between employers and employees are encouraged especially in ethics, security, and morality. Differences among different industries, for example, engineering, IT, or nonprofit businesses, are also worth studying. Recent advances in social issues, cyberspace, or cybertechnology-related fields also pay much attention to this issue. Researchers from other related fields can definitely provide different insights to the issue. As for the industry, employers may be interested in finding the relationship of the use of any kinds of monitoring systems and other managerial functions such as human resource, personnel training, corporate intangible assets, strategies, …and so forth.

In addition, the issue of privacy can be further investigated considering the social issues, security means, efficiency of information retrieval or filtering, and regulations. In the so called "information age," organizations are recognizing the importance of privacy and hence, are initiating new important executive positions called Chief Privacy Officer (CPO), who is responsible for defending their consumers' privacy rights. The newly created position also serves to declare to the public that the organization is serious about their stakeholders. Take banking industry as an example; CPO's job nowadays is getting critical when more and more of their customers are switching to online banking service. How to ensure their valuable online consumers' privacy rights while maintaining good relationships with the customers through the newly born panoptic information technology has become a big challenge. Online banking customers, on average, do frequent business transactions with larger amount of money. However, these customers are more concerned about their personal information. What CPO can do to better serve their valuable customers can be a new research line.

REFERENCES

Agre, P. E. (1994). Surveillance and capture: Two models of privacy. *The Information Society*, *10*(2), 101-127.

Aiello, J. R. (1993). Computer-based monitoring: electronic surveillance and its effects. *Journal of Applied Social Psychology, 23*(7), 499-601.

Allen, J. (1993). Groupware and social reality. *Computers and Society, 2,* 23-28.

Altman, I., & Chemers, M. (1980). *Culture and environment.* Monterey, CA: Brooks/Cole Publishing.

AMA. (2001 & 2005). 2001 and 2005 *AMA survey: Workplace monitoring and surveillance.* Retrieved from www.amanet.org/research/archive_2001_1999.htm

Ara, C. T. (2006). To spy, or not to spy. *National Underwritter Life & Health.* Aug. 21/28, 58.

Bellman, S., Johnson, E., Kobrin, S., & Lohse, G. (2004). International differences in information privacy concerns: A global survey of consumers. *Information Society, 20*(5), 313-324.

Cialdini, R. B. (1996). Social influence and the triple tumor structure of organizational dishonesty. In D. M. Messick & A. E. Tenbrunsel (Eds.), *Codes of conduct: Behavioral research into business ethics* (pp. 44-58). New York: Russell Sage Foundation.

Daryl, G. N., Tipton F. M., & Jeretta, H. N. (2006). E-monitoring in the workplace: Privacy, legislation, and surveillance software. *Communications of the ACM, 49*(8), 73-77.

De Pree Jr., C., & Jude, R. (2006). Who's reading your office e-mail? Is that legal? *Strategic Finance, 87*(10), 45-47.

Dinev, T., Bellotto, M., Hart, P., & Russo, V. (2006). Privacy calculus model in e-commerce - A study of Italy and the United States. *European Journal of Information Systems, 15*(4), 389-402.

Doney, P. M., Cannon, J. P., & Mullen, M. R. (1998). Understanding the influence of national culture on the development of trust. *Academy of Management Review, 23,* 601-620.

Dourish, P., & Anderson, K. (2006). Collective information practice: Exploring privacy and security as social and cultural phenomena. *Human-Computer Interaction, 21*(3), 319-342.

Fukuyama, F. (1995). *Trust: The social virtues and the creation of prosperity.* New York: Macmillan.

Hofstede, G. (1980). *Culture's consequences: International differences in work-related values.* Newbury Park, CA: Sage.

Hofstede, G. (1991). Culture and organizations: Software of the mind. *Journal of Applied Social Psychology, 23*(7), 499-507.

Hoffman, D. L., & Novak, T. P. (1999) Marcos Peralta, building consumer trust online, *Communications of the ACM, 42*(4), 80-85.

Kramer, R. M., & Wei, J. (1999). Social uncertainty and the problem of trust in social groups: The social self in doubt. In T. M. Tyler & R. M. Kramer, & O. P. John (Eds.), *The psychology of the social self* (pp. 145-168). Mahwah, NJ: Lawrence Erlbaum Associates.

Lu, L. T. (2006). The relationship between cultural distance and performance in international joint ventures: A critique and ideas for further research. *International Journal of Management, 23*(3), 436-446.

Lu, Y. H. (2005). Privacy and data privacy issues in contemporary China. *Ethics and Information Technology, 7*(1), 7-15.

Milberg, S. J., Burke, S. J., Smith, H. J., & Kallman, E. A. (1995). Values, personal information privacy, and regulatory approaches. *Communications of the ACM, 38*(12), 65-74.

Nadeem, M. F., Ramin, T., & Jitka, S. (2006) E-mails in the workplace: The electronic equivalent of 'DNA' evidence. *The Journal of American Academy of Business, 8*(2), 71-78.

Newell, P. B. (1998). Across-cultural comparison of privacy definitions and functions: A systems approach. *Journal of Environmental Psychology. 18*, 367-371.

Noack, D. (1999). *Nearly a third of firms monitor works online*. Retrieved from http://www.apbnews.com/safetycenter/business/1999/11/11/vaultsurvey1111_01.html

Nord, G. D., McCubbins, T,. & Nord, J. H. (2006). E-monitoring in the workplace; privacy, legislation, and surveillance software. *Communications of the ACM, 49*(8), 72-77.

Ogburn, W. F. (1966). *Social change with respect to cultural and original nature*. New York: Dell.

Schlosser, F. (2007). Can managers use handheld technologies to support salespeople? *Qualitative Market Research, 10*(2), 183-198.

Schulman, A. (2001). *One-third of U.S. online workforce under Internet/e-mail surveillance*. Retrieved from http://www.privacyfoundation.gov/workplace/technology/extent.asp

Shah, J., White, G., & Cook, J. (2007). Privacy protection overseas as perceived by USA-based professionals. *Journal of Global Information Management, 15*(1), 68-82.

Soares, A., Farhangmehr, M., & Shoham, A. (2007). Hofstede's dimensions of culture in international marketing studies. *Journal of Business Research, 60*(3), 277-284.

Strickland, L. H. (1958). Surveillance and trust. *Journal of Personality, 26*, 200-215.

Tabak, F., & Smith, W. (2005). Privacy and electronic monitoring in the workplace: A model of managerial cognition and relational trust development. *Employee Responsibilities and Rights Journal, 17*(3), 173-189.

Urbaczewski, A., & Jessup, L. (2002). Does electronic monitoring of employee Internet usage work? *Communications of the ACM, 45*(1), 80-84.

U.S. Department of Commerce. (2002). *A nation online: How Americans are expanding their use of the Internet*. Retrieved from http://www.ntia.doc.gov/ntiahome/dn/

Wen, H. J. & Gershuny, P. (2005). Computer-based monitoring in the American workplace: Surveillance technologies and legal challenges. *Human Systems Management, 24*(2), 165-173.

Westin, A. F. (1967). *Privacy and freedom*. New York: Atheneum.

Westin, A. F. (1992). Two key factors that belong in a macroergonomics analysis of electronic performance monitoring: Employee perceptions of fairness and the climate of organizational trust or distrust. *Applied Ergonomics, 23*(1): 35-42.

Zandpour, F., Campos, V., Catalano, J., Chang, C, Cho, Y, Hoobyar, R., Jiang, H., Lin, M, Madrid, S., Scheideler, P., & Osborn, S. (1994). Global research and local touch: achieving cultural fitness in TV advertising. *Journal of Advertising Research, 34*(5), 35-63.

Zuboff, S. (1988). *In the age of the smart machine: The future of work and power*. New York: Basic Books.

ADDITIONAL READING

Adam, A. (2004). Gender and computer ethics. In R. A. Spinello & H. T. Tavani, (Eds.), *Readings in cyberethics* (2nd ed.) (pp. 67-80). Sudbury, MA: Jones and Bartlett.

Amstrong, P. (1999). Information privacy concerns, procedural fairness and impersonal trust: An empirical investigation. *Organ, Sci., 10*(1), 105-121.

Baasa, S. (2003). *A gift of fire: Social, legal, and ethical issues in computing* (2nd ed.). Upper Saddle River, NJ: Prentice Hall.

Berscheid, E. (1977). Privacy: A hidden variable in experimental social psychology. *Journal of Social Issues, 33*(3), 85-101.

Birsch, D. (2004). Moral responsibility for harm caused by computer system failures. *Ethics and Information Technology, 6*(4), 233-245.

Bolter, J. D. (1984). *Turing's man: Western culture in the computer age.* Chapel Hill, NC: University of North Carolina Press.

Bowyer, K. (Ed). (2001). *Ethics and computing: Living responsibility in a computerized world* (2nd ed.). New York: IEEE Press.

Brey, P. (Ed.). (2005). *Surveillance and privacy.* Special Issue of *Ethics and Information Technology, 7*(4). Dordrecht, The Netherlands: Springer.

Brey, P. (2005). Freedom and privacy in ambient intelligence. *Ethics and Information Technology, 7*(3), 157-166.

Cambridge Reports. (1989). Technology and consumers: Jobs, education, privacy. *Bulletin on Consumer Opinion,* (157).

De George, R. T. (2003). *Ethics of information technology and business.* Malden, MA: Blackwell Publishers.

Diettrich, D., & Himma, K. E. (2005). Active response to computer intrusion. In H. Bidgoli (Ed.), *The handbook of information security.* Hoboken, NJ: John Wiley & Sons Inc.

Duska, R. (1991). Whistle-blowing and employee loyalty. In D. G. Johnson (Ed.), *Ethical issues in engineering* (pp. 241-247). Englewood Cliffs, NJ: Prentice Hall.

Fried, C. (1990). Privacy: A rational context. In M. D. Ermann, M. B. William, & C. Gutierrez (Eds.), *Computers, ethics, and society* (pp. 51-67). New York: Oxford University Press.

Gotterbarn, D. (1995). Computer ethics: Responsibility regained. In D. G. Johnson & H. Nissenbaum (Eds.), *Computers, ethics and social values.* Englewood Cliff, NJ: Prentice Hall.

Heinssen, R. K., Glass, C. R., Knight, L. A. (1987). Assessing computer anxiety: Development and validation of the computer anxiety rating scale. *Comput. Human Behavior, 3*(2) 49-59.

Kelvin, P. (1973). A socio-psychological examination of privacy. *British Journal of Social Clinical Psychology, 12*(3), 248-261.

Kizza, J. M. (2003). *Ethical and social issues in the Information Age* (2nd ed.). New York: Springer-Verlag.

Ladd, J. (1989). Computer and moral responsibility: A framework for ethical analysis. In C. Gould (Ed.), *The information Web: Ethical and social implications of computer networking.* Boulder, CO: Westview Press.

Ladd, J. (1991). Collective and individual moral responsibility in engineering: Some questions. In D. G. Johnson (Ed.), *Ethical issues in engineering* (pp. 26-39). Englewood Cliffs, NJ: Prentice Hall.

Laufer. R. S., & Wolfe, M. (1997). Privacy as a concept and a social issue: A multidimensional developmental rheory. *Journal of Social Issues, 33*(3), 22-41.

Mason, R. O. (1986). Four ethical issues of the Information Age. *MIS Quarterly, 10*(1), 4-12.

Milberg, S. J., Burke, S. J., Smith, H. J., & Kaliman, E. A. (1995). Values, personal information, privacy concerns, and regulatory approaches. *Communications of the ACM, 38*(12), 65-74.

Miller, A. (1982). Computers and privacy. In W. M. Hoffman & J. M. Moore (Eds.), *Ethics and the management of computer technology.* Cambridge, MA: Oelgeschlager, Gunn, and Hain Publishers, Inc.

Nissenbaum, H. (1998). Protecting privacy in an Information Age. *Law and Philosophy, 17,* 559-596.

Orlikowski, W. J., & Baroudi, J. J. (1991). Studying information technology in organizations. *Information Systems Research, 2*(1), 1-28.

Parasuraman, S., & Igbaria, M. (1990). An examination of gender differences in the determinants of computer anxiety and attitudes toward microcomputers among managers. *Internal J. Man-Machine Stud., 2*(3), 327-340.

Rachels, J. (1995). Why privacy is important. In D. G. Johnson & H. Nissenbaum (Eds.), *Computers, ethics, and social values* (pp. 351-357). Englewood Cliffs, NJ: Prentice Hall.

Reid, R. C., & Pascalev, M. (2002). Strategic and ethical issues in outsourcing information technology. In A. Salehnia (Ed.), *Ethical issues of information systems* (pp. 232-248). Hershey, PA: IRM Press.

Smith, H. J. (1994). *Managing privacy: Information technology and organizational America.* Chapel Hill, NC: University of North Carolina Press.

Smith, H. J., Milberg, S. J., & Burke, S. J. (1996). Information privacy: Measuring individuals' concerns about organizational practices. *MIS Quart. 20*(2), 167-196.

Smith, H. J., Milberg. S. J., & Kallman, E. A. (1995). *Privacy practices around the world: An empirical study.* Working paper. Washington, D.C.: Georgetown University.

Stahl, B. (2004). *Responsible management of information systems.* Hershey, PA: Idea Group Publishers.

Stewart, K. A., & Segars, A. H. (2002). An empirical examination of the concern for information privacy instrument. *Information Systems Research, 13*(1), 33-49.

Stone, D. L. (1986). Relationship between introversion/extraversion, values regarding control over information, and perceptions of invasion of privacy. *Perceptual and Motor Skills, 62*(2), 371-376.

Stone, E. F., Gardner, D. G., Gueutal, H. G., & McClure, S. (1983). A field experiment comparing information-privacy values, beliefs, and attitudes across several types of organizations. *Journal of Applied Psychology, 68*(3), 459-468.

Stone, E. F., & Stone, D. L. (1990). Privacy in organizations: Theoretical issues, research findings, and protection mechanisms In K. M. Rowland & G. R. Ferris (Eds.), *Research in personnel and human resources management, 8,* 349-411. Greenwich, CT: JAI Press.

Straub, D. W., Jr., & Collins, R. W. (1990). Key information liability issues facing managers: Software piracy, proprietary databases, and individual rights to privacy. *MIS Quarterly, 14*(2), 142-156.

Thompson, P. B. (2001). Privacy, secrecy, and security. *Ethics and Information Technology, 3*(1), 22-35.

Tolchinsky, P. D., McCuddy, M. K., Adams, J., Ganster, D. C., Woodman, R. W., & Fromkin, H. L. (1981). Employee perceptions of invasion of privacy: A field simulation experiment. *Journal of Applied Psychology, 66*(3), 308-313.

Vedder, A. H. (2004). KDD, privacy, individuality, and fairness. In R. A. Spinello & H. Tavani (Eds.), *Readings in cyberethcis* (2nd ed.) (pp. 462-470). Sudbury, MA: Jones and Bartlett.

Warren, C., & Laslett, B. (1977). Privacy and secrecy: A conceptual comparison. *Journal of Social Issues, 33*(3), 43-51.

Williams, & Shauf, M. S. (Eds.). *Computers, ethics, and society* (2nd ed.) (pp. 3-19). New York: Oxford University Press.

Section III
International Social Information Technology Practices

Chapter XII
Measuring IS Success in SMEs in Samoa

Filifotu Vaai
Victoria University of Wellington, New Zealand

Val Hooper
Victoria University of Wellington, New Zealand

ABSTRACT

Information technology (IT) can either increase or decrease the 'digital divide.' Developing nations, such as Samoa, can leverage their economies with investment in IT, but investment is often determined by past information systems (IS) success. Exploratory research was conducted into the assessment and measurement of IS success by small and medium sized enterprises in Samoa, and the effect on IT investment. It was found that information quality, system quality, use, user satisfaction and financial impacts were the main dimensions according to which success was assessed, while intention to use, and cultural impacts were not usually assessed. Culture acted more as a moderator of the assessment. Measurements focused more on system related measures. Assessment on all dimensions impacted on future investment in IT.

INTRODUCTION

Information technology (IT) can drive and leverage the economic success of a country, but it can also either increase or decrease the "digital divide" between developed and developing nations (Purcell & Toland, 2002). The South Pacific island nations can be considered developing nations. Encompassing some 1.8 million people who are culturally diverse and scattered over 32 million square miles of ocean, they are isolated from world economic markets (Purcell & Toland, 2002) and lag behind the rest of the developed world in terms of IT uptake (Pacific Enterprise Development Facility & International Finance Corporation, 2003).

For IT, or information systems (IS), to provide economic leverage, it requires both investment and some measurement of its success because, it could be assumed, investment in IT would be largely driven by the success of past IT investments. However, irrespective of whether in developed or developing nations, investment often occurs without measurement of its success, and this has led to a "productivity paradox" that questions whether the productivity returns brought about through IS investment justify the resources being supplied to it (Ives, 1994). Measuring the success of IS is, therefore, an issue for organizations everywhere. This is even more the case for developing nations like those in the South Pacific, where investment in IS/IT can mean investment in minimizing the digital divide.

Small- and medium-sized enterprises (SMEs) make up the bulk of the economies of the South Pacific nations, and the livelihood of their economies is much dependent on the success of their SMEs (Pacific Enterprise Development Facility & International Finance Corporation, 2003). Measurement of the success of IS in these SMEs thus becomes an important step towards providing evidence of return on investment in IT and thus support for further investment. However, it has been noted that the impact of investment in IT in the Pacific region is difficult to quantify (International Finance Corporation, 2002; Olutimayin, 2002; Pacific Enterprise Development Facility and Corporation, 2003).

The measurement of the dependent variable or success of IS at the organizational level has proven to be an elusive and challenging task. The plethora of measures, frameworks, and models that attempt to define and measure IS success evidences this. However, these studies have focused mainly on large organizations in developed countries, and the measures developed might not be entirely appropriate for SMEs, and even less so for those in developing countries.

This study thus set out to explore the measurement of IS success in SMEs in the South Pacific, and its impact on future IT/IS investment.

BACKGROUND

Measuring IS success, or effectiveness, is a well-explored area. A number of frameworks exist that synthesize past research and guide future research. One of the most widely cited pieces of research and resultant framework is that of DeLone and McLean (1992), in which they found that most measures fell into one of six dimensions: System Quality, Information Quality, Use, User Satisfaction, Individual Impact, and Organizational Impact.

Acknowledging the rapid changes brought about by developments such as the Internet, in 2003, DeLone and McLean presented their updated model, which incorporated some refinements to the original model, based on the previous decade's research. In particular, they added Service Quality as a measure of assurance, empathy, and responsiveness of IS services. They also aggregated individual and organizational impacts into Net Benefits at the group, industry, and national level. The model is a causal model, and many of the interrelationships between the variables have been empirically tested and validated by other researchers (Rai, Lang, & Welker, 2002).

Another model that reviews and categorizes previous literature was proposed by Grover, Jeoung and Segars (1998) in the form of a conceptual framework for IS evaluation. They found that research seemed to fall into the four main areas: criteria demonstration research, measurement research, criteria relationship research, and antecedents of IS effectiveness research. Six effectiveness classes, based on evaluative referent, unit of analysis, and evaluation type, were defined. Most of these classes represent a similar success variable to those of DeLone and McLean (1992), although they viewed System Quality as an antecedent, rather than as a dimension of IS effectiveness.

Smithson and Hirschheim (1998) also developed an IS Success framework that categorized the evaluation of IS effectiveness into three zones, efficiency, effectiveness, and understanding, but their focus was more on the measurement of the variables, as opposed to the identification of variables and their interrelationships (DeLone & McLean, 2003).

However, Seddon, Staples, Patnayakuni, and Bowell (1999) proposed an IS effectiveness matrix which posits that different measures are appropriate in different contexts. The matrix contains two dimensions: the type of system studied and the stakeholder in whose interests the system is being evaluated (Seddon et al., 1999). In 2003, DeLone and McLean stated that context is indeed important, and that selection of variables is often a function of the objective of the study and the organizational context. As context also includes cultural background, the latter becomes an important factor to be recognized.

With regard to the measurement of IS success in SMEs, Cragg and King (1993) found that computing "growth," with data recording actual use and reports by management, was used. This seemed to correlate with DeLone and McLean's (2003) category of Use. DeLone (1988) found improvement in receivables collections, inventory control, and maintaining adequate records, were used as indicators of IS success. They all seemed to point to DeLone and McLean's (2003) category of Information Quality. DeLone (1988) also found improved service and financial impact (increased sales, return on computer investment) to be means of assessment (and measurement). These correspond with DeLone and McLean's (2003) category of Service Quality and DeLone and McLean's (1992) category of Financial Impacts. Seibt (1979) suggested the effect of IS on cash flow would be an appropriate measure, while Raymond (1987) extended an instrument of Bailey and Pearson (1983) that examined user satisfaction as a measure of Management IS success in the SME context.

With regard to developing countries, there do not appear to have been any studies that have directly addressed IS success assessment and measurement in SMEs in the South Pacific region, although Roztocki and Weistroffer (2004) examined financial impacts in terms of activity-based costing as a means of evaluating IT in developing countries. However, an area that might provide some insight is the impact of IT on culture. Culture and IT seem to be competing for a position of importance and power in the Pacific nations, and it is suggested that while IT has helped these nations in their social development, this progress comes at the expense of culture (Olutimayin, 2002; Purcell, 1999).

CONCEPTUAL MODEL

Because of the comprehensive coverage and depth of DeLone and McLean's model (2003), as well as the validation and rapport it has received to date, it was regarded as the most appropriate point of departure for this study, although it is acknowledged that it is not exhaustive. Additional dimensions are included and one is excluded, and all the paths lead directly to Future Investment in IT. The underlying reason for these changes was the relatively simple nature of IT development and consequently, assessment of success in the South Pacific and the focus of the study on future IT investment. The conceptual model, or research framework, is presented and briefly outlined in Figure 1.

System Quality refers to the desired characteristics of the system. The most common criteria used to measure it include the reliability of the computer system; (online) response time; data accuracy (DeLone & McLean, 1992); accuracy and consistency of software estimates; and effectiveness of communication between e-mail and face-to-face as measures (Mukhopadhyay, Vicinanza, & Prietula, 1992; Seddon et al., 1999; Zack, 1993).

Information Quality considers the quality of the IS output. However, obtaining an objective measurement of this variable is problematic

Figure 1. Research framework

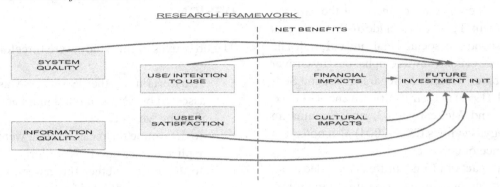

RESEARCH FRAMEWORK

due to its relatively subjective nature (DeLone & McLean, 2003). Common success measures include the perceived importance and usability of information output; and system related items such as information accuracy, output timeliness, reliability, completeness, and currency (Bailey & Pearson, 1983).

Although Pitt, Watson, and Kavan (1995) highlighted the importance of Service Quality, and DeLone and McLean (2003) subsequently added this dimension in their updated model, Service Quality did not emerge as an area that has been assessed by SMEs in studies to date. A possible reason might have been the limited size and resources of SMEs that might not extend to focusing on any more than the core products/services manufactured/sold. It was, thus, excluded as a dimension.

Use refers to the recipient's consumption of the output of an information system (DeLone & McLean, 1992). Seddon (1997) distinguished between perceived usefulness of future use and the actual use of the IS. Actual use is one of the most frequently reported measures, and entails, for example, observing microcomputer monitors and self-reported actual use (DeLone & McLean, 1992; Shayo, Guthrie, & Igbaria, 1999). Use can be mandatory or voluntary; therefore, actual use is only an indicative measure if use is voluntary (DeLone & McLean, 1992). If Use is mandatory,

User Satisfaction is a better measure (Seddon et al., 1999; Shayo et al., 1999). It is from this notion that the Intention to Use dimension was included in DeLone and McLean's (2003) model.

User Satisfaction is an important means of measuring the success of the interaction by users with the information system (DeLone & McLean, 1992). It is one of the most popular measures for IS Success, and includes criteria such as subjective self reports of content, format, accuracy, ease of use, and timeliness (Doll & Torkzadeh, 1988).

Net Benefits refers to the system impacts of IS, examined at both the organizational and individual level. At the individual level, one measure that has been used is to assess managerial performance, productivity, and job satisfaction (Blili, Raymond, & Rivard, 1998). At an organizational level, financial impacts of IT is a criterion given that IT in business is primarily profit driven (DeLone & McLean, 2003; Seddon, 1997). Seddon et al. (1999) included sales growth, labour productivity, productivity and consumer surplus, reduced inventory holding costs, and general cost savings as ways of measuring financial impacts. With regard to SMEs, the focus seems to have been on the financial impacts of IT as a measure of IS Success. This is not surprising, given that small firms can ill afford costly mistakes. Thus, the Financial Impacts of IS was specifically selected as a measure of IS success.

Context, or environment, as a success dimension, encompasses elements of the external environment. These can include different aspects such as economic, social, legal, and cultural. The importance of context was emphasized by Grover et al. (Grover, Jeoung, & Segars, 1998) and Seddon et al. (1999) in their IS Effectiveness Matrix. DeLone and McLean (2003) and Sugumaran and Arogyaswamy's (2003/2004) also noted the importance of context.

The impact of IT on culture is regarded as an important factor in information and communication technology (ICT) adoption in the South Pacific (Purcell, 1999). It could quite possibly also be an important factor in IS success determination. Consequently, context would be considered in terms of Cultural Impact in this study.

The effect of IS success measurement on future investment in IT is not an area that appears to have been directly explored. However, Dos Santos (2003) suggested that financial analysis provides insight to help managers to make investment decisions. It may be considered implicit in assessing and measuring IS success that it will impact on future investment. In view of the importance placed on IT investment as a way of bridging the digital divide (International Finance Corporation, 2002), it was included as an extra dimension to explore.

The scope of this study was such that it did not examine the relationships between the dimensions or their relative importance. Rather, it looked specifically at identifying which of these dimensions is valid in SMEs in the South Pacific, and determining how each of these areas is measured. Also, and perhaps more importantly, it examined whether and how this assessment and measurement affected future investment in IT.

RESEARCH OBJECTIVES AND DESIGN

The objectives of this study were threefold:

- To ascertain whether IS success was being assessed by SMEs in the South Pacific and if so, by what criteria.
- To determine the measures that were being applied to measure those criteria.
- To ascertain whether this assessment and measurement affected future investment in IT and if so, in which way.

Because the research was exploratory but based on well-accepted theories, it adopted a post-positivist approach (Creswell, 2003). It was decided that the most suitable means of data collection would be a survey of a relevant official within each SME sampled. The survey would take the form of a questionnaire administered personally by one of the researchers. However, the administration would be conducted more like an interview because it was suspected that a certain amount of clarification and probing might be necessary in order to elicit appropriate responses. The questionnaire was based on the research objectives and the research framework. Each of the following dimensions was examined with regard to each of the three objectives: System Quality, Information Quality, Use/Intention to use, User Satisfaction, Financial Impacts, and Cultural Impacts. A number of demographic questions were also included.

Once the questionnaire was finalised, it was precoded as far as possible so as to allow for easy capture of the collected data. However, as many of the questions were open-ended, only provisional precoding of these could be done.

SAMPLE

Because of the geographically dispersed nature of the South Pacific islands and because this study was only exploratory, it was decided to select one country in which to conduct the research. The proviso, though, was that it should be sufficiently similar to the other nations of the region to be regarded as representative of them. South Pacific nations share similar size, economic structure and development, culture, and ICT development (Olutimayin, 2002; Pacific Enterprise Development Facility & International Finance Corporation, 2003; Purcell & Toland, 2002). On this basis, and because one researcher was Samoan, Samoa was selected as that country.

Contrary to many developed nations, in the South Pacific, SMEs are determined by the number of employees being 50 or less. As in the rest of the South Pacific region, the majority of businesses in Samoa are classed as SMEs, with 58% being regarded as medium-sized firms employing more than 20 but less than 50 employees, and 42% being regarded as small firms employing fewer than 20 people (Purcell, 1999).

Countries of the Pacific share many cultural characteristics and most of them fall into Hofstede's (1991) high power distance category (Olutimayin, 2002). Such nations have a high degree of acceptance of inequality among the population of that culture (Hofstede, 1991). This is evident in Samoans as they have been described as very tradition-oriented, very steeped in a complex set of social hierarchies, courtesies, and customs that regulate their social, religious, and political life (Bennet, Swaney, & Talbot, 2003). The emphasis on tradition and customs in everyday life highlighted the value of exploring the Cultural Impacts as a measure of IS success.

The population in this study were thus Samoan-based businesses employing 50 or fewer staff and that use some IS in their business operations. (Some 82% of the population had adopted some form of IT (Pacific Enterprise Development Facil-

ity & International Finance Corporation, 2003)). In particular, the sample consisted of those people within the population organizations that had a knowledge of IS and any assessment of its success within the organization; typically the Chief Executive Officer (CEO), Managing Director, or IT manager/specialist.

A list of registered SMEs, the nature of their business, and the contact details of their respective CEO's was obtained from the Inland Revenue Department of Samoa. As no list was available for those SMEs in Samoa that used IS, organizations drawn randomly from the complete list of SMEs were approached to first determine whether or not they used IS before they were asked to participate. This contact was initially made by e-mail from New Zealand.

The survey was administered by the Samoan researcher in Samoa over a 2-week period. While recording the responses in the questionnaires, the researcher also took note of some qualitative comments made by respondents in order to aid interpretation of the data collected. Of the 15 organizations approached, 12 respondents agreed to participate. The response rate of 80% was therefore relatively high.

The three non-respondent firms were in the newspaper/communications, IT, and consultancy industries. There were no obvious reasons to attribute response bias to these industries as they were well represented in the respondent pool. The reason provided by all for not participating was a lack of time to do so.

FINDINGS

The average number of employees in SMEs in the respondent pool was 13 employees, with the largest (Respondent 10) having 42 employees and the smallest (Respondent 6) having just one employee. The industries represented were mainly the IT and telecommunications industry, and the tourism industry. Two respondents were in the consulting industry, and one was in real estate. The average length of operation of the businesses was 10.5 years, with Respondent 10 having been operational for 27 years. The majority (75%) of the respondents were in general management roles, with a few being specifically in the management of IT.

The following subsections present the findings with respect to each specific IS success dimension. The tables include only those measures that were indicated as measures of IS success by more than one respondent. However, where multiple single responses were forthcoming, this is noted in the relevant sections.

Information Quality (see Table 1)

The majority of respondents indicated that they assessed Information Quality. Most of this was done informally. A significant percentage (75%) of respondents claimed that Information Quality assessment affected their future investment in IT. However, two respondents indicated that although they assessed Information Quality, their assessment did not affect future investment. Each of these respondents represented businesses that employed fewer than five people and had been in operation for less than 2 years. What this might show is that their approach might still be to as-

Table 1. Information Quality and System Quality: Assessment and measurement

Respondent	1	2	3	4	5	6	7	8	9	10	11	12
Measures of information quality												
Usability		x									x	
Client and user feedback on site appearance		x	x									
Timeliness of information			x	x	x		x		x		x	
Usefulness for clients			x	x						x		
Completeness of information				x	x						x	
Accuracy of information				x			x			x	x	
ISP pricing plan - value for money										x		x
Effect on future investment												
Indicate whether IQ needs investment	x	x	x	x								
Indication of quality			x		x							
Indicate type of investment required			x								x	
System quality decreases, investment increases					x		x		x			
Measures of system quality												
Reliability		x	x		x							
Response time		x	x	x	x	x						
Connection Speed								x	x		x	
Effect on future investment												
Indicates whether to increase investment	x			x		x						
Indicate type of investment required		x								x		

sess return on investment, rather than to consider future expenditure. At that relatively early stage, there would also still need to be consideration for start-up costs, rather than consideration for ongoing maintenance and expansion.

While there were many single measures of information quality, the most prominent was timeliness of information, followed by information accuracy, completeness of information, and its usefulness for clients/users. Both businesses that identified the pricing plan of Internet service providers as a measure of success operated in the IT industry.

The assessment of Information Quality affected the future investment of a significant number of businesses by way of indicating which areas of Information Quality required attention and investment. It was also a common cry that this was especially the case in small firms that were required to compete on quality rather than scale. Both firms that indicated that measuring Information Quality had the effect of indicating what type of future investment was required, operated in the consultancy industry. There were no other obvious correlations in terms of the size or industry of the respondents and the reported effect of measurement on future investment.

System Quality (see Table 1)

The findings with regard to the assessment of System Quality were very similar to those of Information Quality, with the majority of respondents indicating that they assessed System Quality and that the assessment was largely informal. However, several respondents that assessed System Quality did not take this assessment into account in their future investment of IT. In contrast to Information Quality assessment, where the firms in which assessment had no effect on future investment in IT were all young SMEs, the firms in which the assessment of Systems Quality had no effect on future investment did not seem to share any demographic characteristics.

There were a number of single measures of system quality. However, the measures that were frequently mentioned were response time, reliability, and connection speed.

The assessment of System Quality seemed to affect the future investment of these firms in the same way the Information Quality assessment did in that it indicated whether investment was required, and areas where it was required in order to increase or maintain an acceptable standard of System Quality.

Use (see Table 2)

All but one respondent measured the Use of the IT/IS resources. This was done in a largely informal manner, with a few businesses employing formal measures as well. There do not seem to have been any characteristics that linked the organizations that assessed formally or those that assessed informally, and this would suggest that it was purely a matter of choice.

All but one organization stated that their assessment of the use of IS affected their future investment in IT.

The most commonly mentioned measures were formal Internet and phone bills, as well as informal measures such as general observation and random checks of Internet use, or the number of hits on a Web site. All of the measures tended to reflect the quantity of use. There do not seem to have been any measures that specifically measured the type of use.

Of the multiple effects identified by the respondents, the most prominent way in which the assessment of Use affected future investment in IT was by encouraging investment in technologies that have a high usage. In addition, it allowed for informed decisions to be made about ways to improve business. This suggests an indirect assessment of IT value, and that Use of IS affects not only future investment in IT, but the general future direction of the business.

Table 2. Use and Intention to Use: Assessment and measurement

Respondent	1	2	3	4	5	6	7	8	9	10	11	12
Measures of use of IS												
No. of bookings from Web site	x						x					·
No. of good positive feedback from comment sheets	x	x										
No. of hits on Web site		x			x							
No. of e-mails sent and received			x				x					
Indicated on Internet Bill - No. of hours online, Co$t…				x	x		x		x	x	x	
Observation of general computer use				x		x	x					
Cell phone bills - hours and cost						x	x		x	x		
Log-in records hours								x	x	x		
Amount of work you have done online								x			x	
Effect on future investment												
High usage encourages investment	x			x	x	x	x					
Informs decision about ways to improve business			x		x					x		
Low usage requires investment to increase it								x	x			
Measures for intention to use												
Noting no. of refusals by certain people to use IT or features			x									
Observation of levels of internet use by people			x									
Effect on future investment												
Discussions about need to address low usage			x									

Intention to Use IS (see Table 2)

Intention to Use IS was not an area that was measured by most of the respondents. This was possibly because use was largely mandatory. In the one organization that did assess Intention to Use, use was voluntary, and informal measures were used.

The informal measures were general observations of non-usage by team members and discussions about it amongst the team. This assessment affected future investment in IT in terms of discussions of how to address or increase people's intention to use certain technologies. It was discovered in the administration of the questionnaire that this was important because the lack of use by one or a few members of the team affected the productivity of the entire team. It was also interesting to note, in the same firm, that the adoption of new hardware or software was driven, not necessarily on a needs basis, but by a desire to appear tech-savvy amongst leaders in the community.

User Satisfaction (see Table 3)

User Satisfaction was assessed by all but one organization. Most of the assessment was informal, with only two respondents indicating that they employed formal measures.

The most frequently mentioned measures of User Satisfaction were ease of use in navigation

Table 3.   User Satisfaction: Assessment and measurement

Respondent												
	1	2	3	4	5	6	7	8	9	10	11	12
Measures of user satisfaction												
Presentation of the Web site - people like pictures	x				x		x					
Efficiency for task		x	x		x							
Reliability for task			x			x						
Ease of use of site					x	x	x					
Good or bad reaction of customer									x			x
No. of formal complaints										x		x
Effect on future investment												
High US encourages investment			x	x	x			x		x		
Increase compatibility with clients			x				x			x		x

of a Web site, efficiency of the IT for a task, and the presentation of the interface. Other less prominent measures included reliability of IT, and the number of formal complaints.

All but one of the respondents that assessed and measured User Satisfaction stated that this assessment impacted on future investment in IT. The most frequently mentioned effect was that high User Satisfaction in certain IS encourages investment in them. Another frequently noted effect was that the assessment identified areas that needed attention in order to increase the business's compatibility with clients.

Financial Impacts (see Table 4)

Most of the respondents indicated that the Financial Impacts of their IT were assessed. Unlike all the previous sections, assessment was done in a significantly formal manner, with 50% of respondents stating that they used formal measures.

A mixture of measures was used, and these included the amount of sales generated from the Web site or enabled by IT. Reduction of operating costs was identified as a measure of the Financial Impacts of IS, which is indicative of the early manifestation of IT benefits. An interesting

response among the respondents was that it was a given that all revenue was generated in some way from IT. This is also an indication of the acknowledgment of the indirect benefits derived from IT/IS.

The assessment of the Financial Impacts of IS affected the future investment in IT in all but one business. The most frequently mentioned effect was for the business to continue to invest in areas in which there were currently significant Financial Impacts. Other frequently mentioned effects were informing the investment decision with information on costs and expected future revenues, and identifying areas of opportunity for the future.

Cultural Impacts (see Table 4)

Contrary to expectations, only two respondents indicated that they assessed the Cultural Impacts of IS, and they did this in an informal manner.

Only one measure of the Cultural Impacts of IS was common to both respondents. This was the extent of communication through IT, which was seen as a main purpose of IT amongst respondents generally. The communication was required to be culturally sensitive, as well as a

Table 4. Financial Impacts and Cultural Impacts: Assessment and measurement

Respondent												
	1	2	3	4	5	6	7	8	9	10	11	12
Measures of financial impacts												
Sales generated from the Web site	x			x	x		x					
Reduction of operating costs		x		x							x	
Additional revenue earned		x	x									
It is a given, all revenue is generated from IT						x	x	x			x	
Effect on future investment												
Higher sales encourages investment	x			x	x	x						
Costs & expected revenues considered in investment		x				x	x					
Opportunities & areas that req. finance are identified								x		x		
Measures of cultural impacts												
Extent of communication that must be culturally correct			x							x		
Effect on future investment												
Service delivery needs to be culturally correct									x			
Training is tailored to cultural needs of clients									x			
Invest in filtering content to be culturally sensitive										x		

reflection of culture in business approach and in Web site appearance.

Both firms indicated that this assessment did impact on their future investment in IS, primarily through having to deliver service or products that were culturally sensitive or in a culturally sensitive manner.

Many of the respondents commented that while the direct impact of IT on culture was not an area they assessed specifically, being sensitive to the Samoan culture was central in their approach to business and dealing with customers.

DISCUSSION

The first objective was to determine whether or not IS success was being assessed and if so, according to which criteria. From the findings, it was evident that IS success was being assessed and that Information Quality, System Quality, Use, User Satisfaction, and Financial Impacts were

the criteria applied in most cases. This accords with the findings of most IS success studies, for example, Bailey and Pearson (1983), DeLone (1988), DeLone and McLean (2003), and Seddon et al. (1999), in terms of some of the criteria.

Most assessment was informal, although the assessment of Financial Impacts was much more of a formal nature. This was probably prompted by the obligations of companies to keep detailed, formal financial records, and the resultant focus on return on investment. Intention to Use and Cultural Impacts do not appear to have received much attention. In the first instance, it could have been because in most firms, Use was mandatory. DeLone and McLean (2003) had indicated that in such a case, User Satisfaction was a better indicator than Use of IS. However, this did not appear to have been the case with more formal measures being allocated to Use than to User Satisfaction. With regard to Cultural Impacts, the findings are at odds with the literature, for example, Olutimayin (2002) and Purcell (1999), which indicated that it might be a factor considered in IS success. This suggests that it might be more appropriate to explore the impact of IT on culture, as opposed to it being interpreted as a measure of IS success.

The second objective was to determine the measurements being used to assess the criteria. With regard to Information Quality, most of the measures were systems related, such as accuracy of information, timeliness of information, and usefulness, all of which had been identified by the literature, for example, Bailey and Pearson (1983) and DeLone & McLean (1992). Completeness was another measure also previously identified by Bailey and Pearson (1983) and DeLone (1988).

System Quality measures included reliability of the system, its response time and connection speed, and accuracy and effectiveness of communication, all of which are similar to DeLone and McLean's (2003) findings.

Similarly to Cragg and King's (1993) findings, Use was measured in terms of actual usage measures such as that recorded in phone bills. Measures tended to be formal and addressed the frequency rather than the type of usage.

User Satisfaction was a popular dimension of assessment and many measures emerged. The more frequently noted ones were with regard to systems features such as efficiency of the IS for the task, reliability, and ease of use. These echoed the findings of Bailey and Pearson (1983) and Doll and Torkzadeh (1988).

Financial Impacts emerged as a dimension that was often assessed formally. The measures that were more prominently used were sales growth, sales generated from e-mail or through the Web site, and reduction of operating costs. Each of these measures had been identified in IS success measurement studies in both large and small organizations (DeLone, 1988; DeLone & McLean, 2003; Seddon et al., 1999). An interesting common response was that Financial Impacts were not measured because it was a given that IT had a great financial impact.

The 25% of respondents that did measure the Cultural Impacts did so according to the extent to which formal communication needed to be culturally sensitive. Other measures included the reflection of culture in Web sites, and the uptake of cell phones by customers and society. This agrees with Olutimayin (2002), who recognized the impact of IT on culture. Although Cultural Impacts did not appear to be an area that was measured by many respondents, it appeared to be an area important for consideration in general business rather than as a measure of IS success. This would suggest that it acts more as a moderator, rather than a dependent variable.

The third objective sought to determine whether these assessments affected future investment in IT and, if so, in which way. From the findings, it became evident that future investment in IT appears to be informed largely by Use, User Satisfaction, and Financial Impacts. While Information Quality and System Quality were areas that were heavily measured, a significant number of respondents (25%) did not regard this assessment as important in directly informing their future investment decisions. By and large, the role of most of the assessment in informing future investment decisions seemed to have been in helping to indicate what areas in IS required investment. Although not assessed by many SMEs, the majority of those that measured it did so to inform their business rather than to informing future IT investment.

FUTURE TRENDS

The assessment and measurement of IS success is an ongoing challenge. Models abound and different emphases seem to indicate that different aspects take on a higher level of importance, depending on the organization that is assessing the success of IS. However, what has become clear is that traditional models of assessment focussed on internal organizational users or aspects. That was the main target of the deployment of IS. Nowadays, though, organizations, irrespective of size, are seeking to embrace a wider domain, predominantly by means of the Internet and the Web, so that assessment takes much more than the internal organizational context into account. The external context has, and will, become a much more important influence (Rai et al., 2002).

With regard to the development of IS applications in the South Pacific region, the leverage that can be provided to national economies by means of e-commerce cannot be denied. The Asia-Pacific region has received significant attention in this regard, and both the global forces that drive the readiness of businesses to participate in these developments and national policies as enablers of that development need attention (Javalgi, Wickramasinghe, Scherer, & Sharma, 2005).

More and more, countries will be required to participate in the regional and global activities prompted by IT and IS developments, and a means of assessing and measuring the success of any investment in this area will become all the more crucial (Javalgi et al., 2005).

FUTURE RESEARCH

Given the findings of the research and the future trends of investment in IT to leverage economic growth, the importance of ascertaining how IS success is measured and assessed in developing nations cannot be overstated. Relatively little research has been conducted in such contexts. However, it cannot be assumed that similar methods and metrics, as in developed nations, will be applied. In addition, the cultural context can exert a significant influence on the application of IS and its success. It thus becomes imperative to obtain some understanding of this area of IS. Although this research has focussed on a South Pacific nation, and the automatic expansion of the research would be into other South Pacific nations,

similar studies in other developing regions would provide further enriching insights.

Furthermore, while most studies on IS success have been conducted on large organizations, the majority of organizations in developing countries such as the South Pacific nations, are small and medium sized. This also provides a different context in which the IS is applied and its success measured. Given the preponderance of SMEs in many countries, research in this area promises to be rewarding.

CONCLUSION

The findings of this research suggest that Information Quality, System Quality, Use, User Satisfaction, and Financial Impacts are the main dimensions according to which IS Success in SMEs in the South Pacific is assessed. Of these, only Financial Impacts is measured in a formal manner to any significant extent. With regard to measurement, system-related measures, such as accuracy, response time, and reliability, were frequently mentioned as measures for all the dimensions. Intention to Use and Cultural Impacts are not generally regarded as dimensions of IS Success in SMEs in Samoa. Rather, Cultural Impacts is seen as an area important for consideration in general business rather than as a measure of IS Success, and acts more as a moderator of the assessment.

Most of the assessment and measurement of IS success did affect organizations' future investment in IT. This was largely the same across all dimensions in that it helped to identify areas that required investment. It also helped to inform the investment decision in terms of what sort of investment was required.

It would appear that the focus of assessment and measurement is on the financial impact of the IS, and implicitly on how the system is providing a desirable return on that investment. IT investment, in turn, is guided by that same focus, that is, the identification of areas where that return can be greatest. This is not surprising, given that for most SMEs, the main challenge is one of financial survival. It could be expected that as the SME matures, a greater focus would be placed on other dimensions of IS success.

The findings of this research both supported and contradicted much of the existing literature The latter might be due to the uniqueness of the South Pacific as a context previously unexplored in IS success scholarship. As an exploratory study, this research has paved the way for further research into IS success in SMEs in the South Pacific. It offers some insights into the differences that might exist between developed and developing countries, and the areas where more formal attention might yield greater benefits in the long run. If IT is to be used to bridge rather than intensify the digital divide more research into, and attention to, the measurement of IS success in developing countries is warranted.

REFERENCES

Bailey, J. E., & Pearson, S. W. (1983). Development of a tool for measuring and analysing computer user satisfaction. *Management Science, 29*(5), 530-545.

Blili, S., Raymond, L., & Rivard, S. (1998). Impact of task uncertainty, end-user involvement, and competence on the success of end-user computing. *Information & Management, 33*, 137-153.

Cragg, P. B., & King, M. (1993). Small firms computing: Motivators and inhibitors. *MIS Quarterly, 17*(1), 47-60.

Cresswell, J. B. (2003). *Research design: Qualitative, quantitative, and mixed methods approaches* (2nd ed.). Thousand Oaks, CA: Sage.

DeLone, W. H. (1988). Determinants of success for computer usage in small business. *MIS Quarterly, 12*(1), 51-61.

DeLone, W. H., & McLean, E. R. (1992). Information systems success: The quest for the dependent variable. *Information Systems Research, 3*(1), 60-94.

DeLone, W. H., & McLean, E. R. (2003). The DeLone and McLean Model of Information Systems success: A ten-year update. *Journal of Management Information Systems, 19*(4), 9-30.

Doll, W., & Torkzadeh, G. (1988). The measurement of end user computing satisfaction. *MIS Quarterly, 12*(2), 259-274.

Dos Santos, B. L. (2003). Information technology investments: Characteristics, choices, market risk and value. *Information Systems Frontiers, 5*(3), 289-301.

Grover, V., Jeoung, S. R., & Segars, A. J. (1998). Information systems effectiveness: The construct space and patterns of application. *Information & Management, 31*(4), 177-191.

Hofstede, G. (1991). Levels of culture. In *Cultures and organizations. Software of the mind* (pp. 3-18). London: McGraw-Hill.

International Finance Corporation. (2002). *E-commerce readiness assessment of selected South Pacific economies*. International Finance Corporation.

Ives, B. (1994). Probing the productivity paradox. *MIS Quarterly, 18*(2).

Javalgi, R. G., Wickramasinghe, N., Scherer, R. F., & Sharma, S. K. (2005). An assessment and strategic guidelines for developing e-commerce in the Asia-Pacific region. *International Journal of Management, 22*(4), 523-531.

Mukhopadhyay, T., Vicinanza, S. S., & Prietula, M. J. (1992). Examining the feasibility of a case-based reasoning model for software and effort estimation. *MIS Quarterly, 16*(2), 155-171.

Olutimayin, J. (2002). Adopting modern information technology in the South Pacific: A process of development, preservation, or underdevelopment of the culture? *The Electronic Journal of Information Systems in Developing Countries, 9*(3), 1-12.

Pacific Enterprise Development Facility, & International Finance Corporation. (2003). *SME Business Survey, Country Report - Samoa. Summary of Findings.*

Pacific Enterprise Development Facility, & International Finance Corporation. (2003). *SME Business Survey. Pacific Region. Summary of Findings and Country Reports.*

Pitt, L. F., Watson, R. T., & Kavan, C. B. (1995). Service quality: A measure of information systems effectiveness. *MIS Quarterly, 19*(2), 173-188.

Purcell, F. (1999). *E-commerce adoption and SMEs in developing countries of the Pacific. An exploratory study of SMEs in Samoa.* Unpublished exploratory case study, Victoria University of Wellington, Wellington.

Purcell, F., & Toland, J. (2002). *Information & communications technology in the South Pacific: Shrinking the barriers of distance.* Foundation for Development Cooperation.

Rai, A., Lang, S. S., & Welker, R. B. (2002). Assessing the validity of IS success models: An empirical test and theoretical analysis. *Information Systems Research, 13*(1), 50-69.

Rai, A., Patnayakuni, R., & Patnayakuni, N. (1997). Technology investment and business performance. *Association for Computer Machinery. Communications of the ACM, 40*(7), 89-97.

Raymond, L. (1987). Validating and applying user satisfaction as a measure of MIS success in small organizations. *Information & Management, 12*, 173-179.

Roztocki, N., & Weistroffer, H. R. (2004). Evaluating information technologies in emerging economies using activity based costing. *Electronic Journal of Information Systems in Developing Countries, 19*(2), 1-6.

Seddon, P. B. (1997). A respecification and extension of the DeLone and McLean model of IS success. *Information Systems Research, 8*(3), 240-253.

Seddon, P. B., Staples, S., Paynayakuni, R., & Bowtell, M. (1999). Dimensions of information systems success. *Communications of AIS, 2*(3).

Seibt, D. (1979). User and specialist evaluation of system development. In Sijthoff & Nordhoff (Eds.), *Design and implementation of computer-based information systems* (pp. 24-32). Germantown, MD.

Shayo, C., Guthrie, R., & Igbaria, M. (1999). Exploring the measurement of end user computing success. *Journal of End User Computing, 11*(1), 5.

Smithson, S., & Hirschheim, R. (1998). Analysing information systems evaluation: Another look at an old problem. *European Journal of Information Systems, 7*(3), 158-174.

Sugumaran, V., & Arogyaswamy, B. (2003/2004). Measuring IT performance "contingency" variables and value modes. *The Journal of Computer Information Systems, 44*(2), 79-86.

Zack, M. A. (1993). Interactivity and communication mode choice in ongoing management groups. *Information Systems Research, 4*(3), 207-239.

ADDITIONAL READING

Ballantine, J., Levy, M., & Powell, P. (1998). Evaluating information systems in small and medium sized enterprises: issues and evidence. *European Journal of Information Systems, 7*(4), 241-251.

Baroudi, J. J., & Orlikowski, W. J. (1988). A short-form measure of user information satisfaction:

A psychometric evaluation and notes on use. *Journal of Management Information Systems, 4*(Spring), 44-59.

Beal, T. (2000). SMEs and the World Wide Web: Opportunities and prospects. In A. M. A. (Ed.) *Small and medium enterprises in Asia Pacific; Vol. III: Development prospects* (pp. 102-134). Nova Science, Commack, New York.

Bennet, M., Swaney, D., & Talbot, D. (2003). *The Samoan Islands*. Retrieved 11 November, 2004, from http://www.lonelyplanet.com/destinations/pacific/american_samoa/culture.htm

Bentz, V. M., & Shapiro, J. J. (1998). Quantitative and behavioural inquiry, action research, and evaluation research. In *Mindful inquiry in social research* (pp. 121-127). Thousand Oaks: Sage.

Bridges.org. (2003/2004). *Spanning the digital divide: Understanding and tackling the issues.* Retrieved 31/10/2004, from http://www.bridges.org/spanning/summary.html

Brynjolfsson, E. (1993). The productivity paradox of information technology. *Association for Computer Machinery. Communications of the ACM, 36*(12), 67-71.

Brynjolfsson, E. (1996). Paradox lost? Firm-level evidence on the returns to information systems spending. *Management Science, 42*(4), 541 - 558.

Davis, F. D. (1989). Perceived usefulness, perceived ease of use, and user acceptance of information technology. *MIS Quarterly 13*(September), 318-340.

Dutta, A. (1999). The physical infrastructure for electronic commerce in developing nations: Historic trends and the impacts of privatization. *International Journal of Electronic Commerce, 2*(1), 63-82.

Economic Intelligence Unit. (2001). Pyramid research e-readiness rankings. Retrieved from http://www.ebusinessforum.com

Elliot, G., & Starkings, S. (1998). Information systems and infomation technology. In G. Black & S. Wall (Eds.), *Business information technology systems, theory and practice* (pp. 16-19). London: Longman.

Galliers, R. D. (1992). Choosing information systems research approaches. In R. D. Galliers (Ed.), *Information systems research: Issues, methods and practical guidelines*. Oxford: Blackwell Scientific Publications.

Harris, S. E., & Katz, J. L. (1991). Firm size and the information intensity of life insurers. *MIS Quarterly, 15*(3), 333-352.

Hussin, H., King, M., & Cragg., P. (2002). IT alignment in small firms. *European Journal of Information Systems, 11*(1), 108-127.

International Finance Corporation. (2004). *SME definition*. Retrieved 12 March 2004, from http://www2.ifc.org/sme/html/sme_definitions.html

Javalgi, R.G., & Ramsey, R. (2001). Strategic issues of e-commerce as an alternative global distribution system. *International Marketing Review, 18*, 376-391.

Kaplan, B., & Duchon, D. (1988). Combining qualitative and quantitative methods in information systems research: A case study. *MIS Quarterly, 12*(4), 362-377.

Keen, P. G. W. (1980). *Reference disciplines and a cumulative tradition*. Paper presented at the International Conference of Information Systems.

Kim, K. K. (1989). User satisfaction: A synthesis of three different perspectives. *Journal of Information Systems, 3*(Fall), 1-12.

Kimberly, J. R., & Evanisko, M. J. (1981). Organizational innovation: The influence of individual, organizational, and contextual factors on hospital adoption of technological and administrative innovations. *Academy of Management Journal, 24*(4), 689-713.

Lee, C. S. (2001). Modeling the business value of information technology. *Information & Management, 39*(3), 191-210.

Locke, L. F., Spirduso, W. W., & Silverman, S. J. (1992). Research proposals: Function and content. In R. D. Galliers (Ed.), *Information systems research: Issues methods and guidelines*. Oxford: Blackwell Scientific Publications.

Oxley, J. E. & Yeung, B. (2001). E-commerce readiness: Institutional environment and international competitiveness. *Journal of International Business Studies, 32*(4), 705-723.

Panagariya, A. (2000). E-commerce, WTO and developing countries. *The World Economy, 23*(8), 959-978.

Pervan, G. P., & Klass, D. J. (1992). The use and misuse of statistical methods in information systems research. In R. Galliers (Ed.), *Information systems research: Issues, methods and practical guidelines*. Oxford: Blackwell Scientific Publications.

Purcell, F., & Toland, J. (2004). Electronic commerce for the South Pacific: A review of e-readiness. *Electronic Commerce Research, 4*, 241-262.

A Report Prepared for Asia Pacific Foundation. (2002). *Asia-Pacific e-commerce: B2B & B2C*. Retrieved from http://www.gii.co.jp/english/em11033_asia_ec_toc.html

Thong, J. Y. L., Yap, C.-S., & Raman, K. S. (1993). *Top management support in small business information systems implementation: How important is it?* Paper presented at the Special Interest Group on Computer Personnel Research Annual Conference. Conference on Computer Personnel Research, St. Louis, Missouri, USA.

Thong, J. Y. L., Yap, C-S., & Raman, K. S. (1996). Top management support, external expertise in information systems implementation in small businesses. *Information Systems Research, 7*(2), 248-267.

Venkatraman, N. (1997). Beyond outsourcing: IT resources as a value center. *Sloan Management Review*, 51-64.

Chapter XIII
Technology and Culture:
Indian Experiences

Ramesh C. Sharma
Indira Gandhi National Open University, India

Sanjaya Mishra
Indira Gandhi National Open University, India

ABSTRACT

This chapter discusses the deployment of e-learning technologies in the context of how they are helping towards preserving and disseminating knowledge on Indian cultural heritage. An analysis has also been offered as regards how the technologies like e-learning initiatives have their impact on sociocultural settings within Indian context. This chapter attempts to understand and frame Indian culture and experiences through ICT and e-learning practices, and how the differentiated learning needs of multicultural society can be addressed.

INTRODUCTION

Culture has been important, perhaps one of the most important concepts, of anthropology. A surviving culture is always dynamic in nature; it evolves over time and, at the same time, maintains its identity. Matsumoto (1996, p. 16) defined culture as, "the set of attitudes, values, beliefs, and behaviours shared by a group of people, but different for each individual, communicated from one generation to the next." It is these values and beliefs which make a culture that can survive against all odds.

Indian civilization is one of the oldest civilizations of the world (dates back to more than 5,000 years). In spite of various foreign invasions and dominations, visits by scholars in search of knowledge, India's cultural own identity has been maintained. It has adopted the good from them while rejecting those that might have destroyed its unique unity in diversity feature. This nation has witnessed many social, economic, political, and technological changes. Here, science and spirituality both exist. Indian architecture, festivals, dance forms, painting, sculptures, cuisine, literature, and teacher-taught relations, all have different dimensions of extraordinary variety. This cultural heritage has been passed onto from generation to generation by appropriately preserving, promoting, and disseminating modes be it oral, written, or now electronic.

INFORMATION COMMUNICATION TECHNOLOGY (ICT) IN INDIA

The government of India has accorded high priority to the deployment of ICT for social and community development. Since early 1970s, India has witnessed constant growth in the area of telephone density, Internet penetration, establishment of radio and television stations, broadband connections, and affordable computers and peripherals. These have become within easy reach of the educational institutions, businesses, and individuals and so forth.

Starting with nearly a thousand Internet users in 1992, over 5 million users were enjoying Internet in 2000 (GOI, 2003). TRAI (Telecom Regulatory Authority of India, 2005) reported that there were 105,000 Internet cafes in India; telephone density was 0.6 % in 1991, which increased to 11.7% in 2006.

Telephone, radio, and television has been widely used in educational settings in India (Sharma, 2002; Vyas, Sharma, & Kumar, 2002a, 2002b). One-way-video two-way-audio teleconferencing is quite effective for content presentation, learner-expert interactions, and learner-supported activities (Mishra, 1999). In addition satellites have also been considered to be useful in catering to the educational needs of the society. For example, EDUSAT is the first Indian satellite designed and developed exclusively to meet the demand for an interactive satellite-based distance education system for the country (Sharma, 2006).

All these different instruments of ICT, like radio, television, teleconference, satellite, Internet, have contributed to the community development under various schemes of the government.

ICT FOR CULTURAL HERITAGE

Different measures for the preservation, transmission, and advancement of languages and culture have been adopted by the communities. With the physical expansion of the world, different cultures and languages have realized the increasing importance of having dynamic and vibrant mechanisms that can help them maintain their identity and foster progress in a multicultural learning environment. Odasz (n.d.) states, "The world's diverse cultures jointly represent the full cultural genome of humankind's search for individual and group identity and meaning" and exert pressure to record this important "shared story of humankind." The sooner actions are taken to save the cultural knowledge of our ancestors, the better will be, as it is feared that nearly half of the world's 6,000 languages may disappear in one lifetime. Odasz (n.d.) recommends, "The vast cultural knowledge of our elders must be recorded via multimedia storytelling for preservation while they (our elders) are still with us."

The use of ICT to the cause of culture has been best exemplified through different kinds of technological tools (radio, television, Internet, etc.) being heavily used by Indian communities to maintain or to create new relations. The social networking tools, like MySpace (http://www.myspace.com); Ning (http://www.ning.com); Second Life (http://www.secondlife.com) or Orkut, are connecting people across different cultural and social backgrounds. Cellular phones have become an integral part of common people, due to slashing of rates prompted by the entry of many players and due to the Government of India's intention to reach to the masses through telephone network. SMS poll is nowadays a common phenomenon in case of any national event where the viewpoint of masses has a say. This is becoming a cultural bonding technology even in some cultural events when the contestants request the people to vote for them through SMS like reality shows on television. Cole and Crawford (2007) consider ICT tools as an effective means of enhancing communication among communities, building peace and facilitating better understanding of each other. A culture is what we think, what understanding we have for others, and how we behave. Manjul (2005) reported an "alternate media," in the form of a rural newsletter that was initially launched as a communication channel among the women themselves, but by the impact it had on the sociocultural issues, it evolved into a mechanism whereby it addresses the community as a whole, and a great tool for women empowerment.

TECHNOLOGICAL INITIATIVES AND CULTURE

ICT applications in India have been used for educational, economic, and social development of scheduled castes, other backward classes, and minorities, as well as protection of rights and opportunities for the welfare of disabled persons, children in distress, victims of drug addiction, and the senior citizens. Establishing a telephone help line for disabled persons in Mumbai has been a significant achievement. Similarly, a toll-free telephone service, "Childline," provides help to children in distress or by adults on behalf of such children. This facility was significantly beneficial to Tsunami affected areas during 2005, like Kanyakumari, Nagapattinam, Kanchipuram, Cuddalore, Kollam, and PortBlair and so forth.

Although many religious communities in India possess a strong, gender-related norms, situation is comparatively serious in Muslim community. Girls are not encouraged to leave home without a veil, education is low priority, early child marriage is common. Sharma and Maindiratta (2005)

reported an interesting case, where the effort by Datamation Foundation Trust to establish an ICT centre at Babool-Uloom Madrasa (a religious residential school providing learning opportunities to boys from poor families) in a densely populated and low income area of New Delhi initially met with cold response. The Trust wanted to set an ICT centre to address urban poverty and increase women empowerment, and the project was initiated, keeping in view local cultural values. Internet was also used (using eNRICH, a local Web-based browser) to encourage local talent and cultural heritage. Cross-cultural experiences were made available to them to learn about the communities in other countries. Slowly, the results showed their effects and the centre started gaining popularity. This was most conspicuous during the month of Ramadan, when the center was to be closed for the month. The girls convinced the concerned authorities successfully to let the centre remain open for some time. That was unimaginable before, as the girls are not allowed to have such a dialogue. This clearly establishes the impact of the ICT on the cultural values.

Governmental Agencies in India and Projects

In India, technological mechanisms are being used for maintenance and conservation of the country's heritage, ancient monuments, and historic sites; promotion of literary, visual, and performing arts; administration of libraries, museums, and institutions of anthropology; maintenance, preservation, and conservation of archival records and archival libraries; research and development in the conservation of cultural property; and promotion of institutional and individual initiatives in the field of art and culture. Technology is helping out in generating cultural awareness at the grassroots level to promote cultural exchanges at an international level. Detailed information is also made available on Indian history, literature, philosophy, religions, Sufism, art, architecture, astronomy, astrology, mathematics, medicines, and physical sciences.

Some of the important organizations and agencies in India dealing with preservation, conservation, and spreading awareness of culture are:

- Archeological Survey of India, New Delhi
- National Archives of India, New Delhi
- National Council of Science Museum, Kolkata
- Nehru Memorial Museum & Library, New Delhi
- Sangeet Natak Akademi, New Delhi
- Sahitya Akademi, NewDelhi
- Lalit Kala Akademi, New Delhi
- National School of Drama, New Delhi
- Centre for Cultural Resources & Training, New Delhi
- Gandhi Smriti & Darshan Samiti, New Delhi
- Asiatic Society, Kolkata
- Salar Jung Museum, Hyderabad
- National Institute of History of Art Conservation & Museology, New Delhi
- Indira Gandhi National Centre for the Arts, New Delhi (www.ignca.gov.in)

Cultural Informatics Laboratory

Cultural Informatics Laboratory (CIL) establishes a synergy between the disciplines of art and information technology leading to usage, development, and demonstration of new technology and cultural documentation.

Kalasampada

The project is sponsored by Ministry of Communications and Information Technology, Govt. of India, (MCIT) under *digital library initiative (DLI)*–India. The prime focus of this project is to develop a databank of cultural heritage housing over 4.5 million pages of manuscripts, 4,000 photographs, and 200 hours of audio and video.

Content Creation and IT Localisation – Network (COIL-NET)

Sponsored by the Ministry of Communications and Information Technology, Govt. of India, a Web site on "Cultural Heritage Digital Library" has been developed in Hindi with special focus on Hindi Speaking region mainly states of Uttar Pradesh, Uttaranchal, Madhya Pradesh, Chattisgarh, Bihar, Jharkhand, and Rajasthan.

Manuscripts Digitization Projects

The digitization of rare manuscripts written in archaic languages and scripts such as Arabic, Persian, Sanskrit, Hindi, Urdu, Turkish, and Pushto, and so forth, is an important step towards preservation of Indian cultural heritage.

Ajanta - In-house CD-ROM Project

This CD-ROM project provides wide-ranging knowledge and visual experience (in the form of 1,500 illustrated images, articles from eminent authorities, Bibliography, Glossary, etc.) on Ajanta, a major heritage site of India, included in the UNESCO's list of World Heritage monuments.

Eternal Gandhi – Multimedia Exhibition

The Eternal Gandhi is state-of-the-art digital multimedia exhibition, which deals with information on the historical events of the life and message of Mahatma Gandhi. The exhibition also presents a wide spectrum of information technology visions inspired by the thought and teachings of Mahatma Gandhi.

National Multimedia Resource Centre (NMRC) project

The National Multimedia Resource Centre (NMRC) project (launched in 1998 and sponsored by the Department of Information Technology, Ministry of Communications & Information Technology, Government of India) identifies and disseminates cost-effective applications of multimedia among the masses.

Indian Heritage Portal

The Indian Heritage Portal developed by C-DAC (Centre for the Development of Advanced Computing) provides information on Indian scriptures like the Vedas, Bhagavad-Gita, Mahabharata, and Dhyaneshwari and so forth.

E-LEARNING FOR CULTURAL ISSUES

E-learning is increasingly considered as a means of greater access to education and development (Mishra & Sharma, 2005). Such projects have their impact on rural, illiterate, or women populations, the upliftment of whom is of prime importance. These have greater impact on the cultural issues also. E-learning practices have been found to be an important tool in preserving, promoting, and advancing cultural heritage. The initiatives taken by Kerala Government through its e-tourism have generated a world wide interest. Another successful example is Tamil Virtual University (http://www.tamilvu.org/) established as an Internet-based resource that provides details on the history, art, literature, and culture of the Tamils. This project is very popular among those Tamils who have settled in various parts of world, and interested in knowing about the cultural heritage of Tamil community. Indian Tobacco Company (ITC) is one of India's leading private companies, and has initiated an e-Choupal effort (http://www.echoupal.com/) that places computers with Internet access in rural farming villages (http://www.digitaldividend.org/case/case_echoupal.htm). A "Choupal" is a local village gathering place where the villagers gather and discuss their problems or issues.

Culture and Language Instructional Context

Many cultures (like rural folk in Gujarat and Rajasthan State in India) use narration and storytelling as a way of passing on the information from past to the present generation. Narration enables the learners to participate in the process and becomes the core of experiential and contextual approach to learning.

FUTURE TRENDS

Different technologies have different characteristics and thus, impact differently on the cultures (Idrus & Sharma, 2007). A radio or a television may impact differently than Internet. It depends on the nature of technology, that is, be it one-way or two-way/synchronous or asynchronous, how the cultural issues are going to be affected by it. It would be significant to understand in what way innovative ICT approaches can maximize the impact of different technologies by integrating them (Girard, 2005; Mathison, 2005). For example, in the Kothmale Community Radio Internet Project in SriLanka (http://www.kothmale.org) Internet is used to search the information and radio to disseminate it. Also, the listeners can send the questions to the radio station either by post or calling through telephone. Then the team at Radio Station uses Internet to search for needed information, translates it in local language, and broadcasts the answer.

Further, the research on measuring the impact of ICT on community development is still in its infancy in India. There is a strong need to undertake microdata analysis to identify the extent to which ICT changes the performance of small and medium enterprises in developing countries.

FUTURE RESEARCH DIRECTIONS

Future research directions must address the issues like how do the technology programmes deal with different communities and different cultures and languages? Which interventions need to be customized? To what extent is a programme effective in a specific community? Is there any supportive culture for using ICT for bringing out community development?

CONCLUSION

India is a vast country covering wide geographic area, divided into numerous cultures and languages. Over 700 million Indians live in rural areas. Of these, around 190 million live below poverty line. India has perhaps the largest number of poor people in the world. The situation further aggravates, as 84% of our illiterates live in villages. The diversity and magnitude of these problems create huge challenges for the ICT channels, which appear to be disorganized and with little effectiveness for communication and resource sharing. We need to have an in-built feedback mechanism and supporting research studies to showcase the indigenization of culture through ICT.

Culture of a place is reflected through group behaviour, social norms, how the group thinks, behaves, reacts, and responds to a situation. ICT can be an effective tool by encouraging cross-cultural exchanges, while at the same time bringing out positive social changes, by developing mutual respect for each other's culture, sharing of opinion. Proper networking of different agencies in a planned way would tackle sociocultural issues. The public-private partnership involving government would create innovative solution for society's need. The invention of the simputer in India is an example.

Issues that may arise while developing culturally sensitive instructional material are values and attitudes, ethical perspectives diversity within groups, historical perspectives, socioeconomic perspectives, social roles, social networks, learner expectations, learning styles, and opportunities for interactions (Collis 1999; Dunn & Griggs, 1995; Mcloughlin, 1999; Powell, 1997; Reeves, 1997and). Gjedde (2005, p. 104) suggested that issues, such as social and cultural backgrounds and gender-specific interests, must be considered when developing meaningful content and creating narrative e-learning environments. Singh (2003, p. 100) suggested steps to deal with problems faced during the development of e-learning in India viz. the diversified geographical spread; the use of different languages in different states and regions; the communication infrastructure; and the illiteracy. The language problem is being tackled on many fronts. The Microsoft XP desktop operating system has the ability to support nine Indian languages. Modular Infotech Pvt. Ltd., a Pune (Maharastra)-based company, is actively working on the language front. It has partnered with Microsoft to develop various keyboard handlers for Indian languages.

The Government of India has urged upon private-sector companies to make a commitment to rural areas. India is looking forward to establishing a "Universal Service Fund" to service the rural IT plan. The Government of India has reduced telephone call rates to promote the use of the Internet and make the Internet and telephone services affordable to the general public. The Ministry of IT holds regular meetings to promote the concept of e-learning. The fast developments in information technology and products have revolutionized the ways of teaching and learning across different cultures. The content generated with IT applications acts as a vehicle for knowledge that is well-suited to many cultures and languages across the globe. The Internet tools in the form of Web-logs or pod-casting provide great opportunities for the preservation, expression, strengthening, and dissemination of cultural identities and languages (Mishra & Sharma, 2004).

REFERENCES

Cole, R. S., & Crawford, T. (2007). *Building peace through information and communications technologies.* Retrieved on June 22, 2007 from http://www.idealware.org/printable.php?page=/articles/peace_through_ICTs.php

Collis, B. (1999). Designing for differences: Cultural issues in the design of the WWW-based course-support sites. *British Journal of Educational Technology, 30*(3), 201-215.

Dunn, R., & Griggs, S. A. (1995). *Multiculturalism and learning style: Teaching and counseling adolescent.* Westport, CT: Praeger.

Girard, B. (2005). Internet, radio and network extensioin. In A. K. Mohan & W. H. Melody (Eds.), *Stimulating investment in network development: Roles for regulators.* Report on the World Dialogue on Regulation. Retrieved from http://www.regulateonline.org

Gjedde, L. (2005). Designing for learning in narrative multimedia environments. In S. Mishra & R. C. Sharma (Eds.) *Interactive multimedia in education and training*, (pp. 101 – 111). Hershey, PA: Idea Group.

GOI. (2003). *v2020: Vision 2020 report.* Retrieved from http://planningcommission.nic.in/reports/genrep/bkpap2020/1_bg2020.pdf

Idrus, R. M., & Sharma, R. (2007). *Leveling the information field via interactive technologies.* Paper presented at the Academic Conference on Information Revolution and Cultural Integration in East Asia, 25-26 January 2007, Vietnam National University, Ho Chi Minh City, Vietnam

Manjul. T. (2005). *From women's media to rural media.* Retrieved June 24, 2007, from http://www.indiatogether.org/2005/jun/med-rurmedia.htm

Mathison, S. (2005). *Digital dividends for the poor.* ICT for Poverty Reduction in Asia. Global Knowledge Parternership.

Matsumoto, D. (1996). *Culture and psychology.* Pacific Grove, CA: Brooks/Cole Pub. Co.

McLoughlin, C. (1999). Culturally responsive technology use: Developing an online community of learners. *British Journal of Educational Technology, 30*(3), 231-243.

Mishra, S. (1999). An empirical analysis of interactivity in teleconference. Indian *Journal of Open Learning, 8*(3), 243-253.

Mishra, S., & Sharma, R. C. (2004). Multimedia: Meeting the challenge of cultures and languages. *Distance Learning Link.* Retrieved September 28, 2004, from http://www.idea-group.com/downloads/pdf/DLL.pdf

Mishra, S., & Sharma, R. C. (2005). Development of e-learning in India. *University News, 43*(11), 9 – 15.

Odasz, F. (n.d.) *Realizing cultural sovereignty through Internet applications.* Retrieved October 14, 2004, from http://lone-eagles.com/sovereignty.htm

Powell, G. C. (1997). On being culturally sensitive instructional designer and educator. *Educational Technology, 37*(2), 6-14.

Reeves, T. C. (1997). An evaluator looks at cultural diversity. *Educational Technology, 37*(2), 27-31.

Sharma, C., & Maindiratta, Y. R. (2005). Reconciling culture and technology in India. Retrieved on 24 June 2007 from http://www.centerdigitalgov.com/international/story.php?docid=92645

Sharma, R. (2006). EDUSAT: Taking Indian distance education to new frontiers. *Distance Learning Link*, Jan-June 2006, 6-8.: Information Science Publishing.

Sharma, R. C. (2002). Interactive radio counselling in distance education. *University News, 40*(10), 8-11.

Singh, K. P. (2003). *Multimedia and e-learning: A new direction for productivity* (pp. 96-100).

Vyas, R. V., Sharma, R. C., & Kumar, A. (2002a). Educational radio in India. *Turkish Online Journal of Distance Education, 3*(3). Retrieved from http://tojde.anadolu.edu.tr/tojde7/articles/educationalradio.htm

Vyas, R. V., Sharma, R. C., & Kumar, A.. (2002b). Educational television in India. *Turkish Online Journal of Distance Education, 3*(4). Retrieved from http://tojde.anadolu.edu.tr/tojde8/articles/educationaltv.htm

ADDITIONAL READING

Akbar, M. J. (2003). *India, the siege within: Challenges to a nation's unity.* New Delhi: Rolli.

Bandyopadhyaya, J. (1987). *The making of India's foreign policy.* New Delhi: Allied Publishers Private Ltd.

Basham, A. L. (1967). *The wonder that was India.* London: Sidgwick & Jackson.

Castells, M. (1999). *Information technology, globalisation and social development.* Geneva: The United Nations Research Institute for Social Development .

Chen, A.Y., Mashhadi, A., Ang, D., & Harkrider, N. (1999). Cultural issues in the design of technology-enhanced learning systems. *British Journal of Educational Technology, 30*(3), 217-230.

Fischer, L.. (1989). *Life of Mahatma Gandhi.* Norwalk, CT.: Easton Press.

GOI. (1999). *National Task Force on Information Technology and Software Development: IT Action Plan Part III – Long Term National IT Policy.* New Delhi: Government of India. Retrieved from http://it-taskforce.nic.in/actplan3/

Gunawardena, C. N., Wilson, P. L., & Nolla, A. C. (2003). Culture and online education. In M. G. Moore & W. G. Anderson (Eds.), *Handbook of distance education.* Mahwah, NJ: Lawrence Erlbaum Asso.

Hickey, H. (2007). *Mobile phones facilitate romance in modern India.* Retrieved on June 23, 2007 from http://uwnews.org/article.asp?articleid=30477

Jasola, S., & Sharma, R. (2005). Open and distance education through wireless mobile Internet: A learning model. *International Journal of Instructional Technology and Distance Learning, 2*(9), 35-47. Retrieved from http://www.itdl.org/Journal/Sep_05/article04.htm

Kawachi, P. (2005). Computers, multimedia and e-learning. In Reddi, U. V. & Mishra, S. (Eds). *Perspectives on distance education: Educational media in Asia* (pp. 97-122). Vancouver: Commonwealth of Learning.

Kawachi, P., Sharma, R. C., & Mishra, S. (2004). E-learning technologies in Asia. Asian Journal of Distance Education, 2(2). Retrieved from http://www.asianjde.org/

LeLoup, J. W., & Ponterio, R. (1998). Using WWW multimedia in the foreign language classroom: Is this for me? *Language Learning & Technology, 2*(1), 4-10. Retrieved from http://llt.msu.edu/vol2num1/Onthenet/

Nehru, J.. (1946). *The discovery of India* (Calcutta: The Signet Press). (Reprint. New Delhi, Oxford University Press), 2003.

Pruitt-Mentle, D. (2003). *Cultural dimensions of multimedia: Design for instruction.* Presentation made at NECC conference, Seattle. Retrieved from http://edtechoutreach.umd.edu/Presentations/NECC2003/2003_presentation_v2.ppt

Yoshii, R., Katada, F., Alsadeqi, F., & Zhang, F. (2003). Reaching students of many languages and cultures. *Proceedings of the EDMEDIA Conference*, AACE.

Yúdice, G. (2003). The expediency of culture. Raleigh, NC: Duke University Press.

ONLINE RESOURCES

- Association for Progressive Communications: http://www.apc.org/
- Bytes for All: http://www.bytesforall.org/
- Content Creation and IT Localisation – Network (COIL-NET) (http://www.tdil.mit.gov.in/coilnet/ignca/welcome.html)
- Culture and development. Unesco: http://www.unesco.org/culture/development/briefings/html_eng/.
- Doors Delhi Web site http://doors8delhi.doorsofperception.com/
- Education Development Center: http://main.edc.org
- Global knowledge partnership: http://www.globalknowledge.org/
- Indian Heritage Portal http://www.cdac.in/html/ihportal/index.asp
- National Multimedia Resource Centre (NMRC) http://www.cdac.in/html/nmrc/about.asp
- OneWorld: http://www.oneworld.net/
- Sarai, The New Media Initiative Delhi India: http://www.sarai.net
- The Center for Knowledge Society: http://www.ict4d.info
- Worldbank: http://www.worldbank.org/

Chapter XIV
ICT–Enabled Communication in the New Zealand Family Court:
A Multistakeholder Study

Kay Fielden
Unitec, New Zealand

ABSTRACT

The New Zealand Family Court is an ideal public sector application for social informatics. In a study investigating ICT-assisted communications that was conducted with multiple court stakeholders, paradoxical results emerged. This research is positioned within a five-fold layered theoretical framework encompassing: private/public space; sense of self; emotional energies; digital citizenship; and Sawyer's (2005) five common observations about research in the field of social informatics. This richly textured theoretical framework provides grounding for results within and across disciplines revealing deeply engrained behaviours, emotional states, customs, workplace cultures, and the problems associated with solving private problems in public spaces.

INTRODUCTION

A study of the impact on ICT-enabled communication within the New Zealand Family Court (NZFC) was initiated in 2004. In this study, current trends and issues relating to the social side of technology within the New Zealand Family Court were monitored. This research has only been possible because of the widely differing skills and knowledge that the research team bring to the project. In-depth knowledge of family court policies and practices from the viewpoint of an experienced family-court counsellor, combined with the perspective of an academic researching the field of social informatics, have enabled this research project to proceed. Data collected from separating families, including children, was only possible through the services of the court counsellor.

This chapter explores first the theoretical and philosophical field of social informatics that is relevant both within New Zealand and a global context. Next five philosophical arenas of private/public space; sense of self; emotional energies; digital citizenship; and Sawyer's five common observations about research in the field of social informatics are discussed, and placed within a single framework (Figure 1) that provides a means of positioning the multiple effects of ICT-enabled communication within the New Zealand Family Court.

Sawyer (2005) suggests that there are five observations about computerization that he believes to be the core common findings for social informatics because they have been noted in many social informatics publications. These are that:

1. Uses of ICT lead to multiple and sometime paradoxical effects. In this chapter, the way in which ICT-enabled communications have been used by NZFC stakeholders suggest that there are multiple and paradoxical effects including: fears as well as acknowledgement of benefits; and the ability to use ICT-enabled communications to provide multiple emotional distances between stakeholders.

2. Uses of ICT shape thought and action in ways that benefit some groups more than others. People live and work together in powered relationships. Thus, the political, economic, and technical structures they construct include large-scale social structures of capital exchange, as well as the microstructures that shape human interaction. An examination of power often shows that a system's implementations can both reinforce the status quo and motivate resistance. That is, the design, development, and uses of ICT help reshape access in unequal and often ill-considered ways.

3. The differential effects of the design implementation and uses of ICT often have moral and ethical consequences.

4. The design implementation and uses of ICT have reciprocal relationships within a larger social context. From the 2001 New Zealand census, it can be seen that one-parent families with children and single adults have a lower socioeconomic standing than two-parent families with children.

5. The phenomenon of interest will vary with the level of interest.

Scope, stakeholder, research method, data gathering, analysis, and discussion of this multi-stakeholder follow the discussion on the theoretical framework. Implications for the wider context of the ever-changing effects of ICT-enabled communications on separating families, especially those affected by complex and traumatic situations, are discussed. Implications for cultural and societal issues in social informatics technologies that address deeply ingrained behaviours within families are also addressed. Finally, possibilities for future research in this are presented.

BACKGROUND

In New Zealand there is a high incidence of family violence, particularly within Maori and Pacifica families. New Zealand statistics reveal that it is from these ethnic backgrounds that most trauma is experienced when there is family conflict, and it is from these ethnic backgrounds that conflict elevates into violence, usually against women and children. These are the cases that come to the media's attention, and occupy a large proportion of family court processing.

It has also been discovered that within these communities, it is most likely that families have the latest mobile technology, in favour of landline phones (Weatherall & Ramsay, 2006). In a recent case involving the death of 3-month-old twin boys, the family member interviewed by the media on a number of occasions was seen conducting the interview on a mobile phone. The New Zealand

Family Court is trialling a special court to deal with family violence to deal with such cases, (see Box 1).

It is at these times when private lives collide with the legal domain and when private matters become public; when emotional energies are in a chaotic and highly charged state; and when individual sense of self flounders for appropriate role models in moving from one family private domain into the legal domain (described by Habermas (1996) as public authority) where this research on the impacts of ICT-enabled communications is situated. When the public/private space metaphor underpinning the philosophical stance adopted by this research is enriched by individual sense of self; the difference in emotional energies experienced in fractured private spaces, and public authority represented by the New Zealand Family Court; and the marked differences that are exhibited in

digital citizenship by stakeholders in this domain, surprising results emerge, especially when they are framed in Sawyer's (2005) five observations on multiple research projects carried out within the field of social informatics (Figure 1). Sawyer's (2005) five observations are emergent and differing results when multiple stakeholders are considered in public/private spaces affected by ICT-enabled communication; inequity issues arising from the uptake of ICT within the domain; multiple ethical implications resulting from ICT within the domain; multilayered social context; and differing results dependent on the layers, levels, and depth of the analysis carried out within the domain.

An ongoing research project situated within the New Zealand Family Court looking at the issues associated with ICT-enabled communications for multiple stakeholders has highlighted some

Box 1.

Hearing the Child

Hearing their voices, seeing their faces
  loving their souls in communal space

Losing their voices, missing their faces
  still loving their souls no common spaces

No voice to be heard intermediaries talking
  deciding for them where they should be

Hearing their voices seeing their faces
  loving their souls in virtual spaces
                              (Fielden, 2005)

Absent from Home

Where do I go, to whom do I talk

Download the forms - too hard for me
  written in lingo I've never seen

Damned if I do, lost if I don't

Now where do I live when I have walked out
  leaving behind the blood on the floor

Where do I go, to whom do I talk
                              (Fielden, 2006)

Me and the Kids

I'm glad that he's gone- it's best for the kids
  The lawyers will fix this mess up for me

I'll email him when he sees the kids
  Or txt if I want for the pickup tonight

I'll see him in court and we will be fine
  I'm glad that he's gone- it's best for the kids
                              (Fielden, 2006)

From the Court
We only talk to those that we see
Then we advise to download from the net

We cannot say how they are to talk
We deal with the forms and the attendance in court
We don't make the laws just fill out the forms

Yes, we use the net at work – not for play
They shouldn't txt or email to us
Please lodge your forms in the time honoured way
Then we can help you get out of court
                              Fielden (2006)

Figure 1. Spaces in the NZFC communication domain (Based on Habermas, 1996)

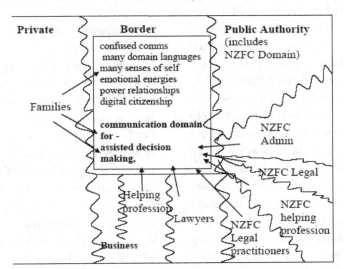

important aspects that impact on the digital divide that affect all stakeholders in a variety of ways. Research, to date, suggests that there is a lack of ICT knowledge within the helping profession, which has implications for recommendations made to separating families on how they can keep in touch; an unwillingness by the legal profession to make formal recommendations for ICT-enabled communications between child and non-custodial parent; and the separate arenas in which various stakeholders operate. There appears to be a need for ICT-enabled communication between legal practitioners and the helping profession as intermediaries to expedite the NZFC process. If the multiple communication channels that exist between different helping professionals, legal practitioners, government agencies, and custodial and non-custodial parents and their children could be streamlined and simplified by the use of interoperable ICT communication systems, the processes in the NZFC may be able to provide quicker and more sustainable solutions for families and their children. It is also envisaged that a set of guidelines for ICT-enabled communications for all stakeholders will be produced.

Participants included legal practitioners, psychologists, counsellors, social workers, government agencies, family court administrators, and separating families, including children. Data was gathered on ICT skills, knowledge of the impact on ICT-enhanced communication within the wider community. It is within the border between the private arena and public authority (Habermas, 1996) that communication between NZFC stakeholders becomes complex. Sawyer's (2005) social informatics framework, overlaid on this border, shows how the multiple dimensions afforded by ICT-assisted communication assume multiple and paradoxical roles. These multiple dimensions include stakeholder digital citizenship; sense of self within the border; power relationships that emerge between stakeholders in the border; and emotional energies that accompany ICT-assisted communication.

DIGITAL CITIZENSHIP

Amongst the stakeholders involved in helping families reach decisions that will enable them to reframe their lives, there are widely varying levels of digital citizenship (Fielden & Malcolm, 2006; Prensky, 2001). There are also differing views on the appropriateness of ICT-assisted communication within the border. Private legal practitioners, acting on behalf of separating family members, have well-developed ICT knowledge and skills, and are aware of how these can help them to run their business more effectively. There is less awareness, however, of how advances in technology can assist separating families (Fielden & Goldson, 2005). Members of the helping professions are usually late adopters of ICT. They accept that ICT is a normal part of working life, and that e-mail is a more convenient way of communicating with clients. There is almost unanimous agreement (Fielden & Goldson, 2005) that e-mail is good for logistics for separating families in conducting asynchronous communication in an emotionally charged situation. The lack of knowledge and skills in the helping professions means that the advice given to separating family members on how ICT can help is limited. Within the NZFC, there are also differing levels of digital citizenship. NZFC administrators are the first contact point for separating family members who cannot afford private legal advice. From the data gathered, NZFC administrators are also late adopters of technology, with the accompanying lack of ICT knowledge and skills about ICT. It is interesting to note that the NZFC chief judge is an enthusiastic supporter of ICT-assisted communication who can see the benefits of streamlining court administrative procedures. His digital citizenship status is clearly different from most administrators contributing to this research project. However, he presides over an administrative system that is mired in traditional bureaucracy, where administrators have a very clear view of their professional role. There are also clearly drawn lines about the use of cell phones, which, according to administrators, are not for use in the public domain when dealing with clients.

DOMAIN-SPECIFIC LANGUAGE

The "language" of NZFC is set in legal and bureaucratic terms that are echoed on the NZFC Web site. This is a language style that is usually unknown to separating family members. Each stakeholder acting on behalf of separating families uses domain-specific professional language. For NZFC-appointed stakeholders, the language is situated within a legal use of English with specific and precise use of terms, most of which are unfamiliar to separating family members. NZFC administrators' language is also set within a bureaucratic system bounded by legal rules and regulations. Court-appointed helping professionals add to this their own set of therapeutic terms. These subsets of English, on the whole, are unfamiliar to separating family members.

SENSE OF SELF

The only stakeholder within the border operating from a fractured sense of self is the separating family member (SFM). Every other stakeholder operates as a professional familiar with her/his particular role. SFMs move from decision making and communication within a single family unit in the private arena, to the border with public authority in which decision making is either assisted by other stakeholders, or decisions are made for them. SFMs go from being in charge and communicating about their private lives with the family to being disenfranchised by unfamiliarity with the variety of language subsets, private matters becoming public, and by being in an emotional state that is different from all other stakeholders (Goffman, 1967).

EMOTIONAL ENERGIES

SFMs enter the border between previously private family life and the NZFC public domain at an emotionally charged time. They are the only stakeholders in the system not operating in a calm and rational manner. Being emotionally charged colors the way in which communications take place between other stakeholders. Highly charged emotions also affect the ability to make rational decisions that affect them personally in moving into rearranged family settings. Emotionally charged states also affect the power balance between stakeholders (Collins, 1981).

POWER RELATIONSHIPS

Emerging from the data collected (Fielden & Goldson, 2005) is evidence of imbalances in power relationships between stakeholders. Whilst family law in New Zealand is moving towards mediated solutions for separating families, ultimate responsibility for the way in which decisions are reached, and what these decisions are, rests with NZFC judges. Private legal practitioners, in their role as SFM advisers, have more power than most other NZFC stakeholders because of their role status and because of their considerable knowledge of the law. Court administrators, on the other hand, know what their role is, which is to advise SFMs to make sure that forms are completed and lodged correctly. They know it is not their role to advise SFMs what to do with their lives.

Fielden and Goldson (2005) found that children as "digital natives" (Prensky, 2001), with their knowledge and skill levels of ICT, overcame communication barriers when confronted with them. One child knew how to gain access and use any device, whether it was mobile phone, landline, or computer, no matter where it was located and who owned the device. This particular child had regained control of his own communications with both parents, despite power and control issues clouded by emotional and psychological issues.

THE COMMUNICATION DOMAIN

This border system, therefore, is a domain in which the likelihood of communications becoming confused for SFMs is high. The advantages offered by ICT-assisted communications are many. However, the disadvantages, often fueled by lack of knowledge and fear, loom large. Catalysts for each stakeholder group in adopting ICT to assist families rearrange their private lives in a sustainable manner appear to be different, and in many cases, are seen to be possible only on a case-by-case basis (Fielden & Goldson, 2005) .

THE COMMUNICATION DILEMMA AFTER SEPARATION

Not only does communication become more difficult for the separated family with emotional, psychological, financial, and legal issues, but also there are different living arrangements in multiple spaces that may or may not be geographically distant. When the family separates, a child's ability to communicate with the non-custodial parent is reduced. Power and control issues relating to time, place, and form of communication are changed for the child.

SOCIOECONOMIC FACTORS

Households consisting of a couple with children were more likely to report having Internet access, compared with all other household types, as shown in Figure 2. By comparison, two-parent families with dependent children were about twice as likely as sole-parent families (50% compared to 25%) to have Internet access.

Other factors affect family dynamics (and hence, communication patterns). A cognitive mas-

Figure 2. Internet access (Source: Statistics New Zealand, 2001 Census of Population and Dwellings)

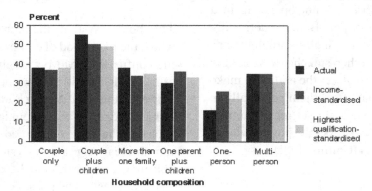

tery of disruptive events gives the child a resilience that stems from a right to participate (Jensen & McKee, 2003; Scanlan, Robinson, Douglas, & Murch, 2003; Taylor, Smith, & Tapp, 2001).

Another issue that affects family dynamics is the reduction in disposable income for both parents (often it is the custodial parent with the greatest income reduction, which in turn increases the income differential between the parents), access to ICT between the two homes, disparity of ICT knowledge of the respective parents, and differential parent/child communication between the custodial and the non-custodial parent. The child is less likely to communicate with the non-custodial parent. Inevitably, these communication barriers are compounded by the emotional and psychological issues that arise after separation.

STAKEHOLDER POSITIONING

Often, an early stakeholder to enter the scene on separation is a counselor. In New Zealand, separating couples are given up to 6 hours of state-funded counseling in an effort to assist the couple to find matters of conciliation. It has been found (Fielden & Goldson, 2005) that members of helping professions, such as counselors, are less technologically skilled than other external

stakeholders who influence family decisions at this time. This, in turn, impacts on the range of options for postseparation communication between family members. It was also found that members of the legal profession are more skilled with ICT. They are more aware of how ICT can assist the practice of law than with how technology can assist separated families. All external stakeholders act in the role of intermediaries (Castells, 2000) acting on behalf of the family either in their separate identities or as the reconstituted separated family units. Without child focused or child inclusive counseling practice (Goldson, 2004), there is a real risk of the child's voice being lost in the welter of adult concerns.

ENABLERS FOR ICT-ASSISTED COMMUNICATION

In their ICT-assisted communications with their children, both custodial and non-custodial parents are disadvantaged by their lower digital citizenship. Fielden and Goldson (2005) found that some parents who participated in their study could send text messages (but most preferred not to). Most parents preferred to use the landline phone at home to talk to other family members. Text messages were for making logistical arrangements. They were not for conversation. One custodial parent endeavored to get his child to have conversations with the non-custodial parent in preference to sending a text message "so that there was dialogue happening with her mother."

For most parents, the main concern was the cost of the communication, either real or perceived. Communication with the other parent should be "paid for by him/her not by me." Most non-custodial parents used whatever ICT-assisted communication that was available. Most custodial parents stated that they preferred to talk on the phone at home. It is interesting to note that this statement did not line up with reported communication experiences of the other parent, who found that home phone numbers were withheld, e-mails unanswered, and cell phones not used.

Most legal practitioners regarded themselves as experienced ICT users. They could see the benefits of having recorded communication by the use of e-mail (Table 1). They could also see that the act of writing an e-mail message could mean that more thought was put into the communication. One legal practitioner reported that e-mail messaging was less intrusive than phone calls and therefore, less likely to cause conflict. Issues were more likely to be resolved in a less stressful virtual space where there was no direct contact between the parties. The speed with which NZFC business could be conducted was cited both as an enabler and a barrier for ICT-assisted communication; an enabler because solutions could be found more quickly and a barrier because some separated parents require time "to settle down" before solutions can be found. Whilst some legal practitioners acknowledged children's skill with ICT-assisted communication, only a few were incorporating ICT-enabled communication in formal recommendations for separated families.

Members of the helping professions, counselors, psychologists, youth workers, and family therapists, also agreed that ICT-assisted communication meant that families communicated in a "more measured" way. One counselor sug-

Table 1. ICT enablers for family court stakeholders

Enablers Stakeholders	Communication	Conflict	Time	Skill	Empowerment
Legal	Permanent record, More measured, Less intrusive	Reduced, Issues resolved, No direct contact	Speed	Children have ICT skill	
Helping	More measured, Mutually agreed guidelines, More comms channels	Psychological presence			For family
Govt	Permanent record, More comms channels		More time to access info		
Non-cust parent	More comms channels				For some
Custodial parent	More comms channels				For some
Child	More comms channels				For children

gested that the mutually accepted communication guidelines were necessary for the effective use of ICT. Most helping professionals agreed that more communication channels meant a greater likelihood of messages being received and family conflict being resolved. One counselor noted that virtual communication space allowed for a "psychological presence," another mentioned that e-mail communications between visits to the counselor could obviate misunderstanding and crises. One youth worker identified the benefits of virtual space for "conducting conversations privately, not publicly."

One member of a government agency, who acted as a family coordinator whose role it was to bring stakeholders together for the benefit of separated families, noted that the permanent record from a collection of e-mails was an added cheap resource, enabling her to spend more time with the communication record in order to facilitate effective solutions.

BARRIERS TO ICT-ASSISTED COMMUNICATION

The biggest differentiating barrier for ICT within separated families is the lack of ICT knowledge. Not only do children know more about ICT, the differential between parents is likely to increase when the family separates. No longer are they one family unit with shared resources including ICT knowledge and skills. Children, however, do not have the financial resources to provide their own infrastructure to support ICT-assisted communication. The financial differential between custodial and non-custodial parents increases and at the same time, the disposable income of both parents decreases. The combination of lack of

Table 2. ICT barriers for family court stakeholders

Barriers Stakeholders	Fears	Skill	Comms guidelines	Attitude to ICT
Legal	Virus threat, Information safety, Online chat fears, Confidentiality	Lack of ICT Knowledge, Ease of use,	No Formal recommendations made, Intrusive phone calls, ICT for all parties	Cost of ICT, E-mail abuse
Helping	Virus threat, Information safety, Online chat fears	Lack of ICT Knowledge, Ease of use	No Formal recommendations made, No communication guidelines	-ve attitude Cost of ICT, E-mail abuse
Govt	Virus threat	Lack of ICT Knowledge, Ease of use	Each case considered, ICT for all parties	-ve attitude
Non-cust parent		Lack of ICT Knowledge, Ease of use		-ve attitude Cost of ICT
Custodial parent		Lack of ICT Knowledge, Ease of use	ICT for all parties	Some, Cost of ICT
Child		Availability of ICT		Cost of ICT

knowledge and cost of ICT contribute to attitudes that create a barrier to the effective use of ICT.

Legal practitioners regard the negative factors regarding ICT, threat of virus, information safety, fears associated with chat rooms, and lack of confidentiality, as barriers to effective use. These barriers impinge on their willingness to incorporate ICT-assisted communication in formal recommendations for separated families.

For the helping professional, information safety and online chat fears were regarded as barriers that affected recommendations to families about adopting ICT-assisted communication. The absence of ICT communication guidelines was seen as a barrier as well. Most helping professionals regarded themselves as "inexperienced users." This, in turn, has an impact on perceptions and views that enter the guided space when separated families seek help. Counselors are only too aware of the financial status of the separated families with whom they interact ,and see this as a barrier to effective adoption of ICT. They also regard the opportunity for separated parents to trade abusive e-mails as a barrier to effective use of ICT.

For government agency staff members, the main barrier appears to be a lack of ICT knowledge. ICT is regarded as hard to use, and introduces the risk of virus attack. This, in turn, affects the attitudes that they bring to family sessions to solve communication dilemmas.

MULTIPLE COMMUNICATION SPACES

After families separate, shared virtual private space offers benefits not afforded anywhere else. Separated families find their communications taking place in public spaces, mediated by one or more NZFC stakeholders. Discussions that would have been conducted previously in a mutual private arena are now shared in the murky space that borders public authority (Figure 1). More importantly, the child's voice is less likely to be heard directly. There is no single, shared, private arena for separated families. ICT-assisted communication allows not a single, private arena, but rather multiple, private, conversation spaces. These multiple, private and virtual communication channels provide an avenue for children's voices. When we consider that the highest ICT skill level and the highest motivation to communicate is demonstrated by children, it is as if the need to be heard has been achieved. ICT-assisted communication provides a series of vehicles for children to be heard directly.

It is no surprise that cost is a common barrier to the adoption of ICT-enabled communication for separated families. As reported in the Social Report, 2004, in New Zealand, it is three times more likely that a single-parent family with dependent children will be below the poverty line than a two-parent family with children (anon, 2004).

It is also no surprise that lack of ICT knowledge was considered a barrier by separated parents within this pilot study. Not only did the economic status of both parents decline, the ICT knowledge base within the family is no longer shared between the parents.

Goldson (2004) points to the need for a stable family environment upon separation. Increasing the number of ICT-enabled communication channels for the separated family is one factor contributing to family stability.

The gaps that have been identified for ICT-assisted communication in the NZFC are:

- A lack of ICT knowledge within the helping profession. This has implications for recommendations made to separating families on how they can keep in touch.
- An unwillingness by the legal profession to make formal recommendations for ICT-enabled communications between child and non-custodial parent.
- The separate arenas in which various stakeholders operate. There appears to be a need

for ICT-enabled communication between the legal practitioners and the helping profession as intermediaries to expedite the NZFC process. If the multiple communication channels that exist between different helping professionals, legal practitioners, government agencies, and custodial and non-custodial parents and their children could be streamlined and simplified by the use of interoperable ICT communication systems, the processes in the NZFC may be able to provide quicker and more sustainable solutions for families and their children.

- A set of guidelines for ICT-enabled communications for all stakeholders.

FUTURE TRENDS

In this research conducted in the NZFC, ICT-assisted communication channels pose both dilemmas and benefits to future trends. Looking to the future suggests a greater emphasis be placed on training and education for all stakeholders, especially in developing a deeper understanding of other points of view in the NZFC. It is also important to consider the wider implications for not only access to, but also understanding of the relevance and timeliness of access to e-information.

FURTHER RESEARCH DIRECTIONS

These wider implications for access to e-information could be conducted for future studies on the economic benefits of earlier intervention in family crises, assisted by easy-to-access and understand information at the greatest time of need; possibly a one-stop Web site and/or cell phone number. Research could also involve an investigation of policies and procedures within schools to provide Internet access for children to keep in touch with the non-custodial parent; and information Web

pages on separation processes and procedures for children so that they have direct access to information. Currently in New Zealand there is no national policy or guidelines on Internet access for children when they are at school. Whilst there have been structural changes within the NZFC, instigated by the chief family court judge, more research into acceptance of these changes involving ICT-assisted communication needs to be conducted. Entrenched bureaucratic attitudes appear to be impeding progress at present. There is a need to up-skill all stakeholders in ethical and effective use of ICT-assisted communication.

CONCLUSION

Findings from this research, conducted within the NZFC, provide valuable information to continue further research in this domain. The qualitative research conducted also adds to the total knowledge pool about how ICT-assisted communication can improve and empower separated families through a deeper understanding of cultural and socio-economic factors from all stakeholders' views. The impacts of this study are both immediate and applicable in the foreseeable future. As ICT becomes cheaper, more separated families can make better use of the technology available

As families rearrange themselves on separation, the dilemmas posed by changed and more complex communication can be addressed, at least in part, by the effective use of ICT. This chapter has explored the concept of ICT-enabled communication for separated families that have come under the jurisdiction of the Family Court in New Zealand (NZFC). In exploring the wider issues of whether ICT can be utilised to provide effective communication within separated families and between families and the Family Court, it seems likely that children (as digital natives) in such situations are more likely to have a higher skill level with ICT-enabled devices than their parents.

Whilst the underlying philosophy of the NZFC is to primarily represent children's interests, their voices are rarely heard directly throughout protracted and difficult negotiations. Significantly too, research indicates that it is not just in the legal arena that children do not feel heard and acknowledged, but also in the private spaces during and following their parents' separation(Smith, Taylor, & Gollop, 2000). Subsequent to separation, the family no longer has a "single private space," but rather multiple private spaces interacting with the public sphere and with public authority. Within these multiple private spaces, financial, custodial, and technological inequalities are likely to exist. Results to date for this research project suggest that the main empowering catalyst for children is their higher ICT skill level. Results to date also suggest that technically assisted communication is valued by members of the legal profession who represent families within the NZFC to facilitate running their own legal organization, and this empowering catalyst for children is not recognized by members of the legal profession. Early results also indicate that members of the helping professions, counselors, social workers, and government employees, who are often the first port of call for separating families, do not possess high ICT skill levels, and do not advocate the use of technically-assisted communication as an empowering catalyst for children. This research, which is ongoing, utilizes (Habermas, 1987) communicative action theory, and Habermas's (1996) structural transformation in the public as a theoretical and philosophical base.

This study highlights the need for a more open approach to the development of closer links and alignment of aims and objectives for ICT-assisted communications between the various stakeholders within the NZFC. This study has also revealed diverse interests and divergent enablers and barriers for the stakeholders considered. Future directions point to the need for different NZFC structures, culture, training, and engagement by all stakeholders.

ACKNOWLEDGMENT

This research project would not have been possible without the assistance of Jill Goldson, family court counselor, researcher, friend, and colleague. The invaluable assistance of Andy Williamson in the initial stages of the project is also acknowledged. Thanks go to Bianca Wilson for her assistance with data entry and assessing literature sources. I am also very grateful to his Honor Principal Judge of the New Zealand Family Court, Peter Boshier, for his endorsement of the project. Acknowledgement also goes to the Family Court Association for their assistance in gathering data for this research. Acknowledgement is also given to Unitec's Research and Advanced Practice research grant which funded this research.

REFERENCES

anon. (2004). *The social report*. Wellington, New Zealand.

Castells, M. (2000). Towards a sociology of the network society. *Contemporary Sociology, 29*(5), 693-699.

Collins, R. (1981). On the microfoundations of macrosociology. *American Journal of Sociology, 86*, 948-1014.

Fielden, K., & Goldson, J. (2005). *Hearing their voices: ICT-enabled communication in the Family Court*. Paper presented at the CIRN2005: The second annual conference of the Community Informatics Network, Capetown.

Fielden, K., & Goldson, J. (2005).*Hearing their voices: ICT-enabled communication in the Family Court*. Paper presented at the CIRN2005: The second annual conference of the Community Informatics Network, Capetown.

Fielden, K., & Malcolm, P. (2006). *Feasibility and evaluation: Critical early research steps*. Presented at the 3rd Qualit Conference, Brisbane.

Goffman, E. (1967). *Interaction ritual: Essays on face-to-face behavior.* New York: Pantheon Books.

Goldson, J. (2004). Children's voices: Optimizing the opportunities for inclusion. *Social Work Now, January,* 5-9.

Habermas, J. (1987). *The theory of communicative action, Volume 2, System and lifeworld: A critique of functionalist reason.* Boston, MA: Beacon Press.

Habermas, J. (1996). *The structural transformation of the public sphere: An inquiry into a category of bourgeois society.* Great Britain: Polity Press.

Jensen, A., & McKee, L. (2003). *Children and the changing family: Between transformation and negotiation.* London: RoutledgeFalmer.

Johnson, R. (2005). *The evolution of family violence criminal courts in New Zealand.* Police Executive Conference, Nelson. Retrieved December 18, 2006, from http://www.police.govt.nz/events/2005/ngakia-kia-puawai/johnson-on-evolution-of-family-violence-courts-in-nz.pdf

Prensky, M. (2001). Digital natives, digital immigrants. *On the Horizon, 9*(5).

Sawyer, S. (2005). Social informatics: Overview, principles and opportunities. *Bulletin of the American Society for Information Science and Technology, 31*(5).

Scanlan, Robinson, Douglas, & Murch. (2003). *Divorcing children: Children's experience of their parents' divorce.* London: Jessica Kingsley Publishers.

Smith, A., Taylor, N., & Gollop, M. (Eds.). (2000). *Children's voices. Research, policy and practice.* Auckland, NZ: Pearson Education.

Taylor, N. J., Smith, A. B., & Tapp, P. (Eds.). (2001). *Childhood and family law: The rights and views of children.* Dunedin: Children's Issues Centre.

Weatherall, A., & Ramsay, A. (2006). *New communication technologies and family life.* Wellington: Blue Skies Fund. Retrieved December 18, 2006, from http://www.nzfamilies.org.nz/download/blueskies-weatherall.pdf

ADDITIONAL READING

Allen, K., & Rainie, L. (2002). Parents online. *Pew Internet & American life project.* Retrieved 12 October 2004, from http://www.pewinternet.org/

Baker, E. (2000). *Child residency litigation: Processes and effects.* Paper presented at the Family futures: issues in research and policy 7th Australian Institute of Family Studies Conference, Sydney, July.

Brignall, T. W., & Valey, T. V. (2005). The impact of Internet communications on social interaction. *Sociological Spectrum, 25,* 335-348.

Brown, J. S. (Ed.). (1997). *Seeing differently: Insights into innovation.* Cambridge, MA: Harvard Business Review Book.

Brown, J. S., & Duguid, P. (Eds.). (2000). *The social life of information.* Cambridge, MA: Harvard Business School Press.

Brunt, L. (2006). *Mapping NZ family violence research.* Social Science Research Centre, University of Canterbury.

Buie, J. (Date unknown). *Virtual families and friends.* Retrieved 23 September, 2004, from http://www.virtualfamiliesandfriends.com/

Burby, L. N. (2001). *Together time.* Retrieved 25 September, 2004, from http://www.divorceinteractive.com/consumer/RelationshipArticle.asp?ID=50

Cashmore, J. (2003). Chidren's participation in family law matters. In C. Hallett & A. Prout (Eds.), *Hearing voices of children* (pp. 158-176). London: RoutledgeFalmer.

Deflem, M. (1996). Introduction: Law in Habermas's Theory of Communicative Action. In M. Deflem (Ed.), *Habermas: Modernity and law* (pp. 1-20). London: Sage.

Gurstein, M. (2003). Effective use: A community informatics strategy beyond the Digital Divide. *Firstmonday.* Retrieved 10 February 2004, from http://www.firstmonday.dk/issues/issues8_12/gurstein/

Hallett, C., & Prout, A. (Eds.). (2003). *Hearing the voices of children: Social policy for a new century.* London: RoutledgeFalmer.

Jackson, M. (2002). Using technology to add new dimensions to the nightly call home. *New York Times,* 22 October.

Lamb, R., & Kling, R. F. (2002). *From users to social actors: Reconceptualizing socially rich interaction through information and communication technology.* Retrieved January 23, 2004, from http://www.slis.indiana.edu/CSI/WP/WP02-11B.html

Maclean, C. (2005). Family violence court at Manukau is called both 'therapeutic and punitive.' *Auckland District Law Society Newsletter.*

Martin, S. (2003). Working online - developing online support groups for stepfamilies. In *Australian Institute of Family Studies Conference.* Canberra.

McIntosh, J. (2000). Child inclusive divorce mediation: Report on a qualitative study. *Mediation Quarterly, 18*(1), 55-69.

Meredyth, D., & Ewing, S. (2003). Social capital and wired communities: A case study. In *Australian Insititute of Family Studies Conference.* Canberra.

Payne, P. (2002). *Long-distance Mom.* Paper presented at the AFCC Conference: New Horizons for Families, Courts and Communities.

Pidgeon, J. (2003). *Family pathways - Towards an integrated family law system in Australia.* Paper presented at the Children's Issues Centre's Fifth Child and Family Policy Conference: Joined Up Services; Linking Together for Children and Families, Dunedin.

Prior, J., & Rodgers, B. (2001). *Children in changing families: Life after parental separation.* Oxford: Blackwell.

Putnam, R. D. (2000). *Bowling alone: The collapse and revival of American community.* New York: Simon & Schuster.

Rheingold, H. (2000). *Tools for thought: The history and future of mind-expanding technology.* Cambridge, MA: MIT Press.

Schultz, J. (2001). *Long distance families · Discussion on how to use the Internet to maintain and nurture long-distance relationships.* Retrieved 23 September, 2004, from http://groups.yahoo.com/group/longdistancefamilies/message/152

Sheikh, S. (2004). *In the place of the public sphere? Or the world of fragments.* Lecture given at the Multicultural Centre, Botkyrka.

Smith, B. (2004). *Parent-child contact and post-separation parenting arrangements* Canberra: Research Report No.9 Australian Institute of Family Studies.

Tapp, P., & Henaghan, M. (2000). Family law: Conceptions of children and children's voices- the implications of Article 12 of the United Nations convention on the rights of the child. In A. Smith, N. Taylor & M. Gollop (Eds.), *Children's voices. Research, Policy and Practice.* (pp. 132-145). Auckland, New Zealand: Pearson Education.

Wray, R. (2004). Mobiles to let parents keep a track on children. *The Guardian, 25 September.*

Chapter XV
Technology Access Points in Turkey:
A Study on Internet Cafés and Their Roles in the Society

Yavuz Inal
Middle East Technical University, Turkey

Zehra Akyol
Middle East Technical University, Turkey

Orhan Erden
Gazi Univesity, Turkey

ABSTRACT

Purpose of the study is to examine one of the popular Internet access places, Internet cafés, in Turkey by focusing the missions of these places regarding gameplay, computer use, Internet use, and their roles in the society. In the study, 71 Internet cafés, existing in 8 different districts in Ankara, capital city of Turkey, were examined during 4 weeks. Data were collected by giving a questionnaire including demographic information about users and their Internet café habits. Internet café users' observation patterns were reported while they were using Internet and playing computer games. Besides, interviews were conducted with volunteer users in terms of their preferences, such as surfing, chatting, doing homework, or playing computer games, to collect deep information regarding aims of the research. Results of the study revealed that one of the main missions of the Internet cafés in the society is that they are seen as places for game play, because majority of the Internet café users preferred playing computer games. It was found that there are certain differences among café users from low and high socioeconomic districts and gender in terms of Internet café frequency, use habits, and use aims. In addition, parental control on Internet café use showed significant differences among café users. Although there are prejudices and negative considerations on Internet café use in the society, they are not harmful places to the majority of the participants.

INTRODUCTION

Internet has been an active part of social life since the mid-1990s, influencing several aspects of the daily lives such as business, military, health, education, or engineering (Gurol & Sevindik, 2007). In today's world, it has been available for public use at home, in Internet cafés, university campuses, libraries, airports, and so on. In Turkey, it has been accepted and reached wide use since last decade, when it appeared first in the society (Yesil, 2003), and nowadays, there are more than 7 million Internet users in the country (Cagiltay, 2005).

People prefer using Internet frequently, both in daily lives and work places, in order to make their activities easier, more effective and more efficient. Besides, to reach a large amount of information without any or limited restriction, Internet is very appropriate due to its characteristics. For instance, Press (2000) cited in Mwesige (2004) stated that "a more optimistic hypothesis is that the Internet's flexible, low-cost communication may lead to improved economic productivity, education, health care, entertainment, awareness of the world, and quality of life in development nations and pockets of poverty within nations, thus reducing disparity" (p.84). Also, Leagran (2002) stated "Internet is seen as a cultural medium to the wider world, opening paths for new impulses" (p.157).

Because of the characteristics of the Internet and its widespread use, the needs for Internet have been increasing speedily, and people need to reach Internet via some places. Internet cafés, one of the popular places allowing people to use Internet technologies, have been reaching wide use and gaining significance for the societies. In order to provide easy access to the virtual worlds, Internet cafés were founded (Gurol & Sevindik, 2007), and they meet the necessities of the people in terms of using Internet, chatting, surfing, reaching information, or playing computer games. Since several young people prefer spending most of their time without any limitations while using computer in these places, studies investigating Internet cafés and their missions are gaining significance.

Internet cafés have been playing important roles in sociocultural and socioeconomic issues in Turkish culture. Allowing people access to computer and Internet technologies easily without facing any restrictions have been making Internet use an active and inevitable factor of social life, depending on it for shopping, banking, registering societies, paying bills, and the like. In the future, it might be expected that Internet use becomes an inevitable part of social life, and will reach a large amount of acceptance and popularity among people in order to make their daily lives easier. Internet cafés have been showing tremendous developments and reaching a large number of users from day-to-day. This has been influencing not only the social and cultural aspects of the society, but also economic and political issues as well.

According to Gurol and Sevindik (2007), "using Internet as the means, customers can surf the Web, communicate via e-mail, do online shopping, have access to knowledge, do educational or personal research, and do all these while a quick snack and a soda" (p.60). Internet Cafés have been diffusing all over the country rapidly, and several people, especially youngsters, prefer using Internet and playing computer games in these places in Turkey. Also, for some of the people, Internet cafés were the unique places that provide them use of computer technology easily. In addition, it is obvious that for each society, Internet cafés have different roles and missions. For instance, in Turkey, according to the previous studies (e.g., Baran & Kuloglu, 2001, cited in Gurol & Sevindik, 2007) focusing on Internet cafés and their use, it is seen that males prefer going to these places rather than females, and playing computer games is one of the most popular aims among people in terms of going to Internet cafés.

Gurol and Sevindik (2007) stated in their study that David Tonge has stated "the number of Internet cafés per population is highest in Turkey than in any other country in the world." Because of the unlimited Internet access and limited controlled possibilities of the Internet cafés and their characteristics of the audience (mostly students in age between 15 and 25), Turkish government started to take some legal precautions to restrict Internet café use in Turkey. However, although government made some arrangements about Internet café use in Turkey, keeping under control of these places is still being very difficult for authorities.

Research focusing on Internet cafés, their missions, and roles in the societies are gaining much importance in order to draw a framework in terms of technology use among people, because "there is little literature on the digital divide within the national borders of developing countries" (Mwesige, 2004, p.84), Internet use is growing enormously in Turkey (Cagiltay, 2005), and Internet cafés are very popular among people, especially young ones, in the country (Gurol & Sevindik, 2007). In the society, there are some prejudices related to Internet cafés, and they are seen as places where youngsters prefer entering illegal Web sites. They are also seen as places that cause failures of students in schools, and waste of time for them. However, in spite of such negative considerations among the society, it is seen from the studies that nearly half of the Internet users prefer using Internet cafés (Andic, 2002).

Under the light of the aforementioned considerations, in the present study, one of the popular Internet access places, Internet cafés, in Turkish society, by focusing the missions of these places regarding gameplay, Internet use, and their roles in the society were examined. It was aimed to select Internet cafés from both low and high socioeconomic districts in the city so that Internet cafés and their roles in the society can be easily examined by comparing different factors such as socioeconomic status.

METHODOLOGY

In the present study, both qualitative and quantitative data collection and analysis methods were used to examine one of the popular Internet access points, Internet cafés, in Turkish society. In the study, 71 Internet cafés existing in 8 different districts in Ankara, capital city of Turkey, were examined in 2006 summer. Totally, 310 females and 1,162 males, who ranged in age from 7 to 45, used Internet in these places during the study. Observation of Internet users lasted 218 hours during 4 weeks.

In order to collect data, Internet users were given a demographic questionnaire including 21 items. Three hundred and thirty of the volunteer café users responded to fill the questionnaire. There were 232 males and 98 females filling the questionnaire. Items of the questionnaire were regarding users' preferences of computer use, Internet café use, habits and use aims, parental controls on Internet café use, and their opinions on Internet cafés in the society. Internet café users' activity patterns were reported while they were using Internet and playing computer games.

During the observation, numbers of users in terms of their gender and activities were reported. In addition, unstructured interviews were conducted with volunteers, during the observations, according to their Internet use preferences, such as surfing, chatting, doing homework, playing computer games, to collect in-depth information. Moreover, some of the Internet café owners also participated voluntarily to indicate their ideas about Internet use of their customers. These data were also used in order to triangulate the results obtained from questionnaires, observations, and unstructured interviews.

Demographic data were coded and frequency calculations were obtained using SPSS version 11. Results of the analysis on collected data were represented descriptively, and Crosstabs analysis conducted in order to get detailed information.

RESULTS

Seventy-one Internet cafés existing in eight different districts were examined. There were differences recognized among the Internet cafés with regard to their districts. The Internet cafés located in high socioeconomic status areas obey the age restriction and provide separation for smokers and non-smokers. In these places, it was observed that individuals under the age of 15 come to the cafes with their parents and their parents take them later. The cafe owners stated that they do not allow children to come in if their parents are not with them. Also, these cafes were cleaner and more comfortable compared to the Internet cafés located in districts with low socioeconomic status.

In most of the Internet cafés in low socioeconomic status, there was not a physical separation of smokers and non-smokers. Smoking and slangy talk were encountered more frequently in these Internet cafés compared to ones in high socioeconomic districts.

Demographics of the Internet Café Users

It was observed that in total, 310 females and 1,162 males, who ranged in age from 7 to 45, used Internet in such places during the study. Three hundred and thirty of the volunteer café users responded to fill the questionnaire. There were 232 males and 98 females filling the questionnaire. The mean of the males' ages is 18.78 and the mean of females' ages is 19.35. Although it is legally forbidden for individuals under the age of 15 to enter Internet cafés, approximately one third of observed individuals and 59 of the questionnaire respondents were under the age of 15.

Table 1 shows the number of respondents in terms of their gender and educational level. Compared to the primary and secondary school graduates, high school and university graduates were more frequent Internet café users both in males and females.

One hundred and seventy-four of the respondents have computer at home, whereas 156 respondents do not have. A two-way contingency table analysis was undertaken to assess whether an association existed between Internet café use and the status of having a computer at home. It was found that the individuals, who do not have computer at home, spent more time on Internet cafés $(X^2(2, N=326)=26.66, p<.001)$. Two hundred and twenty-two respondents stated that they have direct access to Internet. The most cited Internet access point by the respondents was Internet café (n=213), and the others were home (n=104), school (n= 22), dormitory (n=12), and other places such as office (n=10), respectively.

Internet Cafés as Technology Access Points

There are also significant differences on the time that individuals spent on being in these places with respect to their educational level. Crosstabs analysis yielded that hours of Internet use in Internet

Table 1. Number of males and females in terms of educational level

	Male	Female	Total
Primary and Secondary School	64	14	78
High School	84	49	133
University	84	31	115
Total	232	94	326

cafés decrease as the educational level of individuals increase (X^2(4, N=321) =23.46, p<.001). This is related to the role of Internet cafés in the society in terms of technology access. Mostly individuals having low educational level prefer Internet cafés for accessing Internet applications and playing games rather than individuals with high educational level. Table 2 shows the number of individuals according to their educational level and hours of Internet use per week in cafes.

The Crosstabs analysis to assess whether there are differences between males and females according to their weekly computer use, Internet use and Internet café use yielded some differences. Table 3 shows the number of males and females according to the time spent on computers, Internet, and Internet café, and frequency of Internet café use. It was found that the number of male respondents increases according to the time spent on computers, whereas the number of female respondents

Table 2. Number of participants in terms of educational level and time spent in Internet cafés

| | | Educational Level | | | |
		Primary & Secondary School	High School	University	Total
Hours of internet use per week	1-5 hours	37	60	83	181
	6-10 hours	23	46	16	85
	More than 10 hours	16	27	13	56
Total		**76**	**133**	**112**	**321**

Table 3. Distribution of computer, Internet, Internet café use, and Internet café frequency according to gender

		Males	Females	Total
Hours of computer use per week	1-5 hours	48	34	**82**
	6-10 hours	83	36	**119**
	More than 10 hours	100	27	**127**
	Total	**231**	**97**	**328**
Hours of internet use per week	1-5 hours	88	34	**122**
	6-10 hours	67	41	**108**
	More than 10 hours	74	22	**96**
	Total	**229**	**97**	**326**
Frequency of internet café use	Seldom	123	67	**190**
	Few days in a week	47	18	**65**
	Everyday	59	12	**71**
	Total	**229**	**97**	**326**
Hours of Internet café use per week	1-5 hours	123	60	**183**
	6-10 hours	58	28	**86**
	More than 10 hours	47	9	**56**
	Total	**228**	**97**	**325**

decreases as the hours on computer use increase (X^2(2, N=328) =9.80, p=.007). This is mostly related to differences between males and females with regard to Internet café use aims. Because majority of males prefer using Internet cafés for playing games, their Internet café frequencies were higher than female users.

A significant difference on the time spent on Internet cafés according to the districts they were located in were also found (X^2(2, N=325) =7.81, p=.02). The results showed that the individuals living in districts with low socioeconomic status preferred spending more time compared to the individuals living in districts with high socioeconomic status. Individuals having low socioeconomic status might find chance to use Internet applications and play games only in Internet cafés due to low rates of having computers at home among them.

Patterns of Internet Café Use

In order to investigate patterns of Internet café use, the respondents were asked the reasons of Internet café use. The analysis of the questionnaire and the observations revealed that respondents used Internet café mostly for chatting and games. The response rates of activities for which individuals prefer Internet café were 136 for gaming, 124 for chatting, 87 for information gathering, 63 for mailing, 52 for doing homework, and 8 for shopping. Internet use aims showed differences according age groups of individuals. It is observed that playing computer games was mostly preferred by teenagers and some adolescents under the age of 18, whereas the individuals over the age of 18 seemed to prefer other activities, especially chatting.

Respondents were asked whether they play computer games or not. Two hundred and nineteen respondents (189 male, 30 female) stated that they play computer games for enjoyment (n=130), avoiding stress (n=54), spending leisure time (n=43), mental development (n=14), and socialization (n=14). On the other hand, the individuals (n=109, with 41 males and 68 females) who do not prefer playing games pointed out the reasons for their preferences such as being not interested in (n=58), not knowing how to play games (n=23), seeing as a time-consuming activity (n=20), and

Table 4. Number of respondents with their reasons of game play preferences

The Reasons of Preferences	Playing Games
Avoiding from stress	54
Spending leisure time	43
Mental development	14
Enjoyment	130
Socialization	14
Total	**219 (189 males, 30 females)**

The Reasons of Preferences	Not Playing Games
Being not interested in	58
Not knowing how to play games	23
Seeing as a time consuming activity	20
Not having time for playing games	14
Total	**109 (41 males, 68 females)**

not having time for playing games (n=14) (see Table 4).

Similar to Internet access point, the most favorite places for games were Internet cafés (n=129), and the others were respectively home (n=95), school (n=6), and other such as a friend's house or office (n=11). Preferring playing games with their friends and avoiding their family's control were two main reasons indicated by individuals.

Most of them stated that they prefer playing games in Internet cafés with their friends; thus, they prefer MMORPGs (Massively Multiplayer Online Role-Playing Games) to play. Males preferred playing online games mostly when they were compared to females. Whereas 115 males play games with their friends on Internet, only 12 females prefer playing.

Results also revealed that more than 50 different games are being played by people in such places. The most favorite games that respondents preferred to play were, respectively, FIFA (n=78), Counter Strike (n=75), Need for Speed Underground (n=52), GTA Vice City (n=33), Call of Duty (n=30), Championship Manager (n=21), Knight Online (n=19), Serious Sam (n=17), and Age of Empires (n=10). It is seen that game preferences of individuals show similarities in the whole respondent group. Individuals in districts with both low and high socioeconomic status prefer using similar computer games in Internet cafés. This may be due to the global attributes of games.

Second most applied activity was online communication using such programs as ICQ, MSN, or MIRC. Almost all age groups were seen as chatting, but mostly 16-23 age groups were heavily chatting during the observations in Internet cafés. The main reasons of chatting indicated by the individuals were avoiding stress and meeting with new people. There were also individuals downloading some programs, clips, videos, movies, or sounds during the cafe observations. Very few individuals were seen as searching the Internet or using office programs such as Word. This may be due to the fact that the observations

were held during summer after the schools were closed. Some of the café owners expressed that the percentage of individuals who do homework or research increase during the school term.

Parental Control on Internet Café Use

Parental control towards Internet café use is also important in order to examine impacts of Internet cafés in the society. Therefore, the attitudes of respondents' parents towards both the games and Internet café use, and which factors may influence their attitudes, were investigated. 47.9% of the respondents' parents give permission for Internet café use, 21.6% indicated that their parents did not know about their Internet café use, 21% of the parents were found as against high usage, and 3% of the individuals indicated that their parents never gave permission.

There were 222 respondents who play computer games. 26.1% of these respondents indicated that their parents allowed them to play, 12.4% indicated their parents did not know, 32.4% indicated their parents were against spending much time for games, and only 4.1% indicated that their parents never allowed them to play computers games.

Generally, as the individuals get older, the parents are more likely to give permission or their control on individuals about games and Internet café use disappears. With regard to the game play, the mean of individuals' age whose parents give permission is 19.4, whereas the mean of individuals' age whose parents never give permission is 14.8. Similarly, the mean of individuals' age whose parents give permission for Internet café use is 20.4, whereas the mean of individuals' age whose parents never give permission is 14.8. Most of respondents over 23 (for gameplay) and 25 (for Internet café use) years old indicated that their parents had no control over themselves. The distributions of parental control on gameplay and

Table 5. Distribution of parental control on game play and Internet café use according to the educational level

		Parental Control on Gameplay					Total
		Allow	Do not know	Against much	Never allow	Others	
Educational Level	Primary and Secondary School	11	19	31	6	0	67
	High School	43	14	22	1	5	85
	University	31	8	17	2	9	67
	Total	85	41	70	9	14	219
		Parental Control on Internet café Use					Total
		Allow	Do not know	Against much	Never allow	Others	
Educational Level	Primary and Secondary School	15	30	25	7	1	78
	High School	62	28	35	2	6	133
	University	77	13	8	1	14	113
	Total	154	71	68	10	21	324

Internet café use, according to the educational level of respondents, are displayed in Table 5.

Crosstabs analyses were conducted in order to assess whether there are any associations between parental control and gender, and between parental control and Internet café districts. It was not found a significant difference on parental control on game play or Internet café use in terms of respondents' gender. However, the analysis yielded significant differences according to Internet café districts ($X^2(4, N=328)=18.32, p=.001$). The results indicated that the parents living in districts with high socioeconomic status allowed more than the parents living in districts with low socioeconomic status. Moreover, it is found that the number of individuals whose parents did not know their Internet café use was more in low socioeconomic districts than the high socioeconomic districts. It is believed that the physical and social conditions of Internet cafés may also influence parents' attitudes, as they differ according to the districts.

The Internet and its Impacts: Considerations of the Respondents

One of the questions in the survey was whether the individuals think Internet cafés are harmful. 20.9% of the respondents (n=69) indicated that they found Internet cafés as harmful, whereas 79.1% of the respondents (n=261) did not find as harmful. A two-way contingency table analysis was undertaken to assess whether an association existed between perception of harmfulness and gender, and between perception of harmfulness and educational level. The analysis did not yield a significant difference for the gender factor. However, it is found that the individuals perceive harmfulness of Internet cafés differently according to their educational level ($X^2(2, N=326) =11.69, p=.003$). The analysis showed that the number of individuals who think that Internet cafés are harmful increases as their educational level increases. As Table 6 shows, 10% of the primary- and secondary-school graduates (n=8), 19.5% of high-school graduates (n=26) find the

Table 6. The number of respondents in terms of their perceptions of harmfulness and educational level

		Educational Level			
		Primary & Secondary School	High School	University	Total
Are Internet cafés harmful?	Yes	8	26	35	69
	No	70	107	80	257
Total		78	133	115	326

Internet cafés, and 30% of the university graduates (n=35) find Internet cafés as harmful.

Fifty-eight of the individuals who viewed Internet cafés as harmful also explained the reasons for their views. Twenty-eight respondents indicated that Internet cafés are harmful for children and young individuals for their health and mental development. Written expressions of the respondents showed that most of them thought that children and teenagers are at risk because of indoor smoke. Some of them indicated that school children waste their time in Internet cafés by playing games instead of studying. The slangy talk and smoke are the ones most frequently complained about by the respondents. Eight individuals expressed their complaints about entrance of harmful sites such as pornographic sites. There were also dissatisfactions about physical conditions of the Internet cafés; crowdedness and dirtiness as well as indoor smoke were indicated as negative aspects of the environments, causing dissatisfaction.

DISCUSSION

Internet applications have been available for public use at home, in Internet cafés, university campuses, libraries, airports, and so on. In the future, it might be expected that Internet use becomes an inevitable part of social life, and will reach wide acceptance and popularity among people in order to make their daily lives easier.

Considering the profile of Internet café users in Turkish context, it was found that a high percentage of Internet café users were comprised of young males. It is consistent with the previous findings that youngsters are the main Internet café users not only in Turkish society, but also in many other countries like Uganda (Mwesige, 2004), Norway (Lægran, 2002), Kuwait (Wheeler, 2003), and China (Hong & Huang, 2005). This might be the result of the popularity of the Internet use among young people in all countries. For instance, Hong and Huang (2005) stated that majority of the Internet users in China are under the age of 30. Another possible reason of this use rate might be the result of the ability to use Internet and computer technologies. Uribe and Marino (2006) concluded that there is a clear relationship between Internet use and ability to use it. It might be claimed that young people growing in the information era have more ability and tendency to use computer and Internet technologies rather than adults.

Similarly, in Turkey, generally, the Internet café users ranged in age from 7 to 45, and majority of the users were youngsters, according to the results of the present study. Although there is an age restriction for individuals under the age of 15, legally, many individuals under this age were observed using Internet cafés. This issue is akin to results of the previous studies. For instance, Gurol and Sevindik (2007) concluded that "Although it is legally forbidden for customers under the age of 15 years to enter Internet cafés, most of the customers are under this age" (p 67).

The reasons for this might be the fact that these individuals do not have computer at home, or they cannot play computer games at home due to the parental control, because the results pointed out that the main role of Internet cafés in the society is perceived as the most preferred places for game play as well as Internet, and individuals under the age of 15 were observed playing games in Internet cafés. Baran and Kuloglu (2001) (as cited in Gurol & Sevindik, 2007) found that approximately half of the Internet café users prefer playing computer games in these places. Similarly, Gurol and Sevindik (2007) investigated profile of Internet café users in Turkey, and they concluded that one third of the Internet café users prefer games.

In order to understand the role of Internet use and Internet café in the social lives of the individuals, individuals' weekly use of computer, Internet, Internet café were also investigated. Analysis yielded that only one third of individuals were heavy Internet users spending more than 10 hours. One of the interesting findings regarding time spent in Internet cafés was that as the educational level of individuals increased, the hours they spent in Internet cafés decreased. It is supposed that this result might be due to the differences of Internet café use aims and different perceptions of impact of Internet cafés on society. It was observed that the individuals with higher educational levels did not prefer game play, and the analysis revealed that they perceive Internet cafés more harmful compared to others.

In Turkey, playing computer games is one of the most popular leisure time activities among youngsters, especially boys (Inal & Cagiltay, 2005). Similarly, Internet cafés were found as the most frequent access points for Internet and games by the individuals. The observation did not yield differences on game genres in terms of Internet café districts. Generally, sport games (e.g., FIFA, Championship Manager), first person shooter (e.g., Counter Strike, Doom), and car race games (e.g., Need for Speed Underground, Formula 1) were preferable ones among individuals.

It was found in the previous findings that similar to aforementioned games were mostly favorable among players (e.g., Akgunduz, Oral & Avanoglu, 2006; Hong & Huang, 2005). Therefore, it is supposed that game preference did not make a sense of difference for Turkish context, as these games are also the most favorite ones in the world game markets.

Other activities, such as information gathering, doing homework, and shopping, were less preferable by the individuals. The low percentage of information gathering and doing homework might be due to the fact that the data were collected in the summer. The café owners also indicated that during the school terms, the number of individuals doing homework or researching increases. Because shopping through Internet could not reach widespread use in the society up to now, Internet café use aims on shopping was the lowest among all. Moreover, another reason for low shopping in Internet cafés might be that individuals might not find computers in cafés secure enough to send personal information and passwords for shopping.

Apart from games and communication, the use of Internet café for educational purposes or other activities has a small percentage found in similar studies related to Internet cafés and Internet café use. For example, Baran and Kuloglu's (2001) (as cited in Gurol & Sevindik, 2007) study, conducted in Ankara, Turkey, yielded that 81.2% of the Internet café clients use e-mail and read, 62.4% chat, 50.6% play games, whereas 43.3% do research. Gurol and Sevindik (2007) also found that among most of the individuals in the Internet cafés in Elazığ (a city in Turkey), only 22% of the users prefer educational purposes at Internet cafés. These findings are seen not only in Turkey, but also other countries. Studies conducted in other countries also indicated low application of such activities. For example, in the study of Wahid et al. (Wahid, Furuholt, & Kristiansen, 2006) conducted in Indonesia about patterns of Internet café use, the authors found that most of the individuals use Internet café for communication (chat and e-mail use), and compared to other categories of use, very few Internet café customers who were older and more highly educated used it for more serious purposes (seeking information, research, reading online news).

Omotayo's (2006) study in Nigeria with undergraduates about Internet access and use revealed that e-mail was the most frequent reason for the use of Internet. Papastergiou and Solomonidou (2005) also found that pupils in Greece mostly use Internet for entertainment (playing games, downloading games, videos, music, logos, etc.) and for their personal interests inside and outside of school. Similarly, in the study of Mwesige (2004) in Uganda, e-mail was the most frequent category of use, with 85% saying they used it regularly. Forty percent said they regularly surfed, while 35% said they regularly carried out online research.

With regard to parental control on Internet café use, one of the important factors that yielded difference was Internet café districts. The results indicated that the parents living in districts with high socioeconomic status allowed more than the parents living in districts with low socioeconomic status. Better physical conditions of Internet cafés in districts with high socioeconomic status might have a positive impact on parents' attitudes towards these places.

However, parental control on Internet café use of individuals from districts with low socioeconomic status showed an increase. It is found that the number of individuals whose parents did not know their Internet café use was more in districts with low socioeconomic status than the districts with high socioeconomic status. Families who do not allow might see Internet cafés as places leading to time consuming for their children and avoiding them from school contexts. However, the low prices of Internet café use in Turkey, majority of individuals coming from low socioeconomic districts might enter these places easily without getting permission from their parents. This situa-

tion confirms the findings of Gurol and Sevindik's (2007) study that not only high income groups, but also the low income groups have been using the Internet cafés in Turkey.

General views of individuals about the impact of Internet cafés on the society were investigated as well. Results yielded that majority of the individuals do not consider that Internet cafés are harmful. However, an important difference was found on this view according to educational level of individuals; the number of individuals who think that Internet cafés are harmful increases as their educational level increases. Written expression of these respondents indicated that they found Internet cafés as harmful, especially for children and young individuals for their health and mental development.

Two of the negative sides that individuals' complained most frequently were the slangy talk and smoke. The physical conditions of the Internet cafés, such as crowdedness and dirtiness as well as indoor smoke, were indicated as negative aspects of the environments causing dissatisfaction. Gurol and Sevindik (2007) also investigated what the users do not want in the Internet cafés. The results of their study indicated that 73.5% of the users did not want the consumption of alcohol, 46.7% are against smoking, 60.7% are bothered by the loud noise, and 44.6% are against 15-year olds' and younger customers' entrance to Internet cafés.

However, as Akyay (2004) indicated, all these negative aspects can be eliminated in Internet cafés that are surrounded well in terms of technical, environmental, and social and that are managed by higher-level educated people. Akyay also suggests that regular controls should be in terms of both technical and educational aspects. Especially, he emphasizes that there should be trainings and regular activities for the café owners including both technical and social topics to serve better. Moreover, he states that Internet cafés should be organized places that the parents and teachers can also visit. This may also decrease the number of parents who do not know their children use of Internet cafés and increase the trust and satisfaction level of parents towards the Internet cafés. Given the fact that individuals think Internet cafés are harmful for children because of indoor smoke and slangy talk, there could be separate Internet cafés for children and adults. Also, the games played by children at cafés might be chosen by their parents, teachers, or psychologists, to help their mental development. Wahid et al. (2006) indicated schools in Turkey and other developing countries could play an important role in cultivating attitudes and skills for social utility of Web use and Internet café use by educating young people.

FUTURE RESEARCH DIRECTIONS

Internet café use is very popular and shows importance for many societies depending on their social, cultural, political, and economic attributes. In the future, it might be expected that because of the inevitable use of Internet for social lives among societies, using Internet will be one of the main requirements and needs for people. Places allowing people use of Internet and its applications will become important. Therefore, further studies focusing on Internet cafés should be conducted by investigating their use aims, frequencies, demographics of users, attitudes of society toward these places, and parental control on café use.

REFERENCES

Akgunduz, H., Oral B., & Avanoglu, Y. (2006). Bilgisayar oyunlari ve internet sitelerinde sanal şiddet öğelerinin değerlendirilmesi. *Milli Eğitim Dergisi, 71*, 67-82.

Akyay, S. (2004). Internet kafelerin çocuklar üzerine etkileri, *Çağın Polisi Dergisi, 3*(32).

Andic, Y. (2002). *İnternet cafeler nereye gidiyor?* VIII. "Türkiye'de Internet" Konferansı, İstanbul, Turkey.

Cagiltay, K. (2005). *Türkiye intenet'i büyüme eğilimleri.* X. "Türkiye'de Internet" Konferansı, İstanbul, Turkey.

Gurol, M., & Sevindik, T. (2007). Profile of Internet café users in Turkey. *Telematics and Informatics, 24*, 59–68.

Hong, J., & Huang, L. (2005). A split and swaying approach to building information society: The case of Internet cafes in China. *Telematics and Informatics, 22*, 377–393.

Inal, Y. & Cagiltay, K. (2005). *Turkish elementary school students' computer game play characteristics.* BILTEK 2005 International Cognition Congress, Eskişehir, Turkey.

Lægran, A. S. (2002). The petrol station and the Internet café: Rural technospaces for youth. *Journal of Rural Studies, 18*, 157–168.

Mwesige, P. G. (2004). Cyber elites: A survey of Internet café users in Uganda. *Telematics and Informatics, 21*, 83–101.

Omotayo, B. O. (2006). A survey of Internet access and usage among undergraduates in an African university. *The International Information & Library Review, 38*, 215–224.

Papastergiou, M., & Solomonidou, C. (2005). Gender issues in Internet access and favourite Internet activities among Greek high school pupils inside and outside school. *Computers & Education, 44*, 377–393.

Uribe, S., & Marino, R. J. (2006). Internet and information technology use by dental students in Chile. *Eur J Dent Educ, 10*, 162–168.

Wahid, F., Furuholt, B., & Kristiansen, S. (2006). Internet for development? Patterns of use among Internet café customers in Indonesia. *Information Development, 22*(4), 278-291.

Wheeler, D. L. (2003). The Internet and youth subculture in Kuwait. *Journal of Computer-Mediated Communication, 8*(2).

Yesil, B. (2003). Internet café as battlefied: State control over Internet cafés in Turkey and the lack of popular resistance. *The Journal of Popular Culture, 37*(1), 12-127.

Section IV
Online Social Information Technology Applications

Chapter XVI
Web Information Retrieval:
Towards Social Information Search Assistants

Guillaume Cabanac
Institut de Recherche en Informatique de Toulouse (IRIT), France

Christine Julien
Institut de Recherche en Informatique de Toulouse (IRIT), France

Max Chevalier
Institut de Recherche en Informatique de Toulouse (IRIT), and Laboratoire de Gestion et de Cognition (LGC), France

Chantal Soulé-Dupuy
Institut de Recherche en Informatique de Toulouse (IRIT), France

Claude Chrisment
Institut de Recherche en Informatique de Toulouse (IRIT), France

Pascaline Laure Tchienehom
Institut de Recherche en Informatique de Toulouse (IRIT), France

ABSTRACT

Nowadays, the Web has become the most queried information source. To solve their information needs, individuals can use different types of tools or services like a search engine, for instance. Due to the high amount of information and the diversity of human factors, searching for information requires patience, perseverance, and sometimes luck. To help individuals during this task, search assistants feature adaptive techniques aiming at personalizing retrieved information. Moreover, thanks to the "new Web" (the Web 2.0), personal search assistants are evolving, using social techniques (social networks, sharing-based methods). Let us enter into the Social Web, where everyone collaborates with others in providing their experience, their expertise. This chapter introduces search assistants and underlines their evolution toward Social Information Search Assistants.

INTRODUCTION

Searching for information is commonly an individual task that aims at solving any information need. To do that, one may go to a library, or go surfing the Web in order to find relevant information. Indeed, due to the large amount of available documents, the Web has become a favorite information source for solving daily information needs. An issue remains; the Web is in perpetual evolution; so the problem is less the existence of relevant information rather than the way users find it. One may compare searching for information on the Web with "looking for a needle in a haystack." Thus, searching the Web suffers from many limits that can be reduced by using a search assistant. Such an assistant helps the user to find relevant information on the Web. At the beginning, those assistants were principally helping each user individually. Nowadays, we are witnessing the rise of social approaches in such systems. Those latter systems help users to find relevant information by using other users' experience, shared information ... Therefore, each user is helped thanks to the mass crowd. This chapter underlines the evolution of these search assistants. It is organized as follows: section 1 introduces the underlying concepts and limits of traditional information search process and its application to the Web. Section 2 explains the search assistant concept by detailing its evolution from individual to social approaches. Sections 3 to 5 present current approaches that search assistants may use to help any user to query and browse the Web as well as to improve search-related activities. To conclude, future trends for Web information assistants are discussed.

BACKGROUND

Searching for information can be achieved through two specific modalities: querying and browsing (Agosti, 1996). Querying consists in using a specific tool, such as a search engine, in order to find relevant information. Browsing consists in navigating the Web thanks to hyperlinks that exist in Web pages; that is the reason why the Web is then considered as a hyperdocument. Moreover, searching for information is also correlated with many activities that must be taken into account because they are achieved during the search process. These activities are active reading, memorizing, and organizing information, as well as sharing information. Moreover, it is essential to underline that the efficiency and success of a search process depend also on specific human factors.

HUMAN FACTORS

Human factors are essential in any information searching process. Thus, as it is the case for any software, its success is conditioned by context, human factors, and capabilities (Shneiderman, 1998). More precisely, in the information-seeking context, two knowledge types are implied: "practical" knowledge and "domain" knowledge, so, the success of any search process depends on both of them. The use of this twofold knowledge is underlined by the GVU study (1998) and by Hölscher and Strube (2000). This latter study underlines the behavioral difference between experts and newbies when seeking information according to these two types of knowledge:

- **Practical knowledge:** A user who wants to search for information needs to know how the Internet works and how to handle the Web itself. Thus, he/she has to know how to formulate and interpret a URL (Uniform Resource Locator), how to view and handle documents, how to use tools implied in the seeking process (search engine query language...).
- **Domain knowledge:** The most important knowledge that affects the information seeking process is domain knowledge. Indeed,

it is a bit contradictory, but to successfully achieve an information search process a user must know what he/she is searching for or, at least, the "semantic space" of the search topic. Thus, domain knowledge is involved at two levels of the information seeking process (Pejtersen & Fidel, 1998):

o When the user expresses his/her information need by transforming his/her mental information need representation into a formal query that consists (sentence or keyword)

o When the user evaluates the relevance of a retrieved document, that is, how much the document corresponds to his/her information need.

Therefore, the information searching process efficiency depends on these human factors in addition to the way users master the search process itself. To master this process, users must know how to query and browse the Web, which are the two main modalities of the search process.

Information Searching Modalities

Searching for information relies on two modalities identified by Agosti (1996): querying and browsing. These two modalities are interwoven: on the Web, a user unconsciously switches from one to the other; so, when searching for information, a user browses, queries a search engine, browses again and so on ...

Querying the Web

Querying the Web consists of using a specific tool that returns relevant information according to the queried search engine in response to a specific information need. Two approaches can be considered, namely *pull,* which is mostly spread on the Web, and *push* (Belkin & Croft, 1992). These approaches share main concepts but are different

in the way the user interacts with systems during his/her search process.

Pull Approaches

Querying the Web, thanks to a pull approach (Figure 1), is very usual, as it consists in using a common search engine. From the user's point of view, querying a search engine is a twofold task. First, he/she has to formulate his/her query. To do that, he/she must translate his/her mental information need into a formal query made up of words. The difficulty of this exercise is related to the way he/she chooses words. Indeed, words that are too general may produce results too big to be easily managed. Furthermore, words being too specific may provide no result at all, that is, the search engine does not find any document at all. Thus, the user must have a good knowledge of what he/she is looking for to choose the best words to use in a query for a search engine. To sum up: the better the domain knowledge is, the more adapted the query is, and the better the search result is. Then, the user has to manage the search results to identify the set of retrieved documents that really match his/her information need. This latter activity implies the user's domain knowl-

Figure 1. A search engine's common architecture

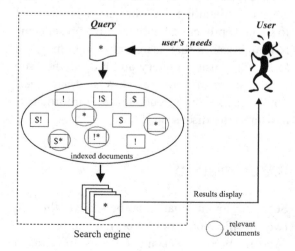

edge that helps him/her to distinguish relevant information from no relevant one.

To achieve their task, search engines traditionally index documents that are generally retrieved from the Web by crawlers. The aim of crawlers is to find documents on the Web that are not yet indexed by the search engine, or that have been modified since the last indexation. To achieve that, a crawler follows hyperlinks to discover documents. Due to the hypertextual structure, search engines can only index documents that compose the so-called "visible Web" (i.e., documents that are directly accessible via an URL). The visible Web has to be opposed to the "invisible Web," which is composed of documents that are "hidden" behind a database or a form that cannot be filled in by crawlers. Bergman (2001) points out that the invisible Web is 400 times greater than the visible Web. Indexing commonly relies on specific information retrieval models and follows many specific steps (Baeza-Yates & Ribeiro-Neto, 1999). Thanks to the index from indexed documents, a search engine computes a similarity value between a user's query and any document contents. This similarity value is used to identify documents that are considered relevant according to the point of view of the search engine. Traditionally, relevant documents are displayed to the user through a ranked results list.

Web information retrieval is based on traditional pull IR techniques that have been adapted in order to improve Web search efficiency. This adaptation relies on Web characteristics such as its hypertextual structure, its size … So two pull approaches can be identified: *i*) traditional pull approaches that consider a "large" volume of documents that remain "reasonable" to handle, as well as *ii*) pull approaches, implemented for the Web, whose volume is hard to handle. On the one hand, for traditional IR pull approaches, a collection is well defined and generally corresponds to a homogeneous set of documents gathered on a known medium. On the other hand, for most new IR pull approaches, for example, on the Web, the collec-

tion is less and less easy to encompass. Documents or granules of documents are scattered, often in different formats. This characterizes heterogeneity of structure and level of abstraction. It really is the hyperlink concept that makes it possible to aggregate granules and to prevent the contents of each granule from dispersion, duplication, and heterogeneity. Nowadays, the intuitive step that consists in considering that a link between two documents expresses a semantic relationship is possible thanks to hyperlinks (Hetzler, Harris, Havre, Whitney, 1998). This assumption has sparked specific research focused on the Web, but also on Digital Libraries via the "citation" concept. The structuring of collections simplifies the problem of granules determination and the characterization of collections. In addition, the Internet and Web-related scale factor implies that even if the user knows more or less what he/she is searching for, the exploited collection is only a subset of the available one (i.e., crawlers only cover a small part of the visible Web). Moreover, search results are proved to be generally larger than in any traditional approach. The hypertext concept and its underlying structure were defined for breaking sequentiality in order to approach texts on any level. First of all, it allowed the implementation of the "hyperdocument" concept, through traditional hypertexts. Then it has encouraged its application and its wide-scale deployment in Web context. The deployment of this structure may be explained today by two essential motivations:

- Bringing additional information on top of a document. An author always defines a hyperlink for a particular reason. Either, he/she wishes to propose a page that he/she regards as being a reference in the field, or a page pertaining to the same site, or more generally, a page containing information on the same subject, and so forth. However, the link is generally syntactic only: determining its related semantics is a commonly encountered problem. Answering this question is one of the main IR concerns and also one of the Semantic Web interests (http://www.w3.org/2001/sw/).

- Capacity for sharing information and for navigating "with its own way" while following the hyperlinks. A user can be interested in a document, in a page or in a URL because of their contents or because of the documents, pages, or URL they reference. This document then constitutes a starting point for navigation.

Various works have been focused on hyperlinks exploitation when searching for information, their main aim being to produce better search results. There are two kinds of approaches: the first one integrates the hyperlink concept *a priori*, that is, at the indexing level; the second one uses links *a posteriori* to widen the result set or to better target this unit, as well as to reformulate the query. Work completed in this second category generally aims to one of the following objectives:

- To reorder the documents retrieved in response to a query by taking into account the incoming/outgoing links as well as their relevance, computed according to the relevance of the linked documents
- To use links as an alternative to the standard IR process and to propagate the activation of relevant documents towards connected documents
- To be useful for a classification and for a categorization of a document collection.

To carry out these goals, there are two possible strategies: either to use mechanisms only based on the enumeration of incoming and/or outgoing links, or to use jointly incoming and/or outgoing links and textual contents of the connected documents, that is, complete text or part of text surrounding the link. Initially, however, it should be noted that IR works that exploit hyperlinks strongly took as a starting point the studies made

on scientific citations in the bibliometric field, which relates to the study of written documents connected to each other by means of citations. Various works were focused on the use of citations in order to estimate the importance or the popularity of scientific articles (Liu, 1993). The assumption underlying this type of work is that bibliographical references give credit to quoted work because they clearly influence the quoting paper. Thus, the basic idea is that citations represent judgments that authors implicitly express: if a document's author quotes another document, then he/she thinks that it contains useful information related to the topic developed in his/her document. To estimate a scientific article's importance, Garfield (1972) proposed a measure called "impact factor." This factor represents, for a given year, the relationship between the number of citations on the number of articles published by a newspaper, over one reference period of 2 years. It thus measures the average frequency with which the set of a newspaper's articles of this newspaper is quoted during a definite length of time. Citations analysis, as introduced by Garfield, was criticized by many authors (Hauffe, 1994), mainly owing to the fact that groups tend to quote the ones rather the others for respect-related reasons rather than for relevance. Indeed, the major disadvantage of the impact factor is that it is only based on incoming citations count. In addition, it would be necessary to take into account the context of use of citations, and to make a distinction between those that argue a thesis and those that refute it. However, none of the suggested models treats this aspect.

Other measures were then proposed. They consider that citations have not the same importance, and that their influence varies according to the impact factor of the newspaper in which they appear.

However, criticisms related to Garfield's impact factor remain specific to the bibliometric field. Indeed, as Bharat and Henzinger (1998) argued, these problems occur less in Web context because the community is various and distributed, and the right of publication cannot be restricted within groups.

Citation indexing brings several advantages, compared to traditional keyword-based indexing (Savoy & Picard, 2001):

- It is independent of the terms and of the language; thus making it possible to mitigate ambiguity issues related to natural language
- Terms or sentences that describe the semantic contents of a document are prone to scientific or technical obsolescence
- It is easier to automate because it follows a more precise syntax, for example, URL syntax on the Web.

Regarding citation as a means of substituting or representing the contents of a document is not always objective, and several motivations can invalidate the basic assumption leading to this type of practice. However, as underlined by Liu (1993), the motivations for using citations can be more complex: on top of the author's motivations; it is necessary to add the editors' and referees' ones. Works on citations were largely applied to the Web. In particular, hypertext analysis has been primarily used as an alternative to the standard keyword-based IR process (Bharat & Henzinger, 1998; Carrière & Kazman, 1997; Kleinberg, 1998; Savoy & Picard, 2001). Thus, various algorithms for relevance evaluation on the Web use the underlying Web hypergraph (Agosti & Melucci, 2000). In most of these approaches, traditional IRS (information retrieval systems) techniques are used to index documents (keywords) and to compute their relevance for a given query. The hyperlinks of a retrieved document set are used *a posteriori* to reformulate or to rerank the result. Then we may distinguish two types of approaches, according to whether one considers only the links or that one combines the textual analysis of the documents with the analysis of

the hypertext structure. The aim of Carrière and Kazman (1997) is to reorder retrieved Web pages; it is mainly based on incoming and outgoing links enumeration. The rank of a page can be interpreted as a popularity (or quality) value based on the links surrounding this page, for example, the sum of its incoming links and its outgoing links. It is thus a measure similar to Garfield's (1972) impact factor. On the other hand, Brin and Page consider that links surrounding a page should not be taken into account in the same way. It is the case in particular for the Google search engine (http://www.google.com), which implements an algorithm that exploits the hyperlinks of the Web in a very simple way, according to the *PageRank* algorithm (Brin & Page, 1998; Savoy & Picard, 2001). As in the bibliometry context, this principle consists in taking into account the fact that a page is the target of "many" hyperlinks (i.e., is often referred by other pages): the more numerous hyperlinks point at a page, the more this page will constitute a good reference document. The rank of a page, called *PageRank* (Brin & Page, 1998), is computed by using a common iterative algorithm that corresponds to a principal vector of eigenvalues of the normalized matrix of the links of the Web. Savoy and Picard (2001) also proposed a method of reevaluation of the rank of a retrieved document based on a probabilistic approach. In comparison, the algorithm proposed by Kleinberg (1998) restricts the result to the set of the retrieved pages in response to a query, that is augmented with pages pointed by (or which point at) these pages. Kleinberg defines two concepts: *Authority* page and *Hub* page. A Hub page is a page that contains links towards relevant pages; an Authority page is a page whose contents are relevant. There is thus a mutual reinforcement link between hub pages and authority pages: a good hub page is a page that points to many authority pages; a good authority page is a page pointed by good central pages. Transitively, the more a hub page points to good pages, the better it will be. In the same way, the more one authority page is pointed by good hub pages, the better it will be. One of the differences between Brin and Page's algorithm and Kleinberg's one is that, for the first one, the quality (or authority) of a page passes directly from authority pages to other authority pages, without interposing a concept of hub.

Thanks to pull approaches, the user has to query information sources each time he/she wants to find relevant documents. A more automated way to obtain information can be seen in push approaches.

Push Approaches

Push approaches are relatively different from pull ones notably concerning user interaction. For pull approaches, the user has to query the system each time he/she wants to find documents. For push systems, the user expresses his/her

information needs only once, and the system finds automatically and regularly new incoming relevant information. Thus, in push systems, the user is informed about new relevant information each time the system finds it.

In addition, push systems rely on the same concepts as those developed in pull approaches (e.g., indexing, measuring query-document similarity). Indeed, they make use of the same aforementioned algorithms to index and match queries with documents. Concretely, differences between pull and push approaches (Belkin & Croft, 1992) are summed up in Table 1.

More generally, push approaches are commonly implemented through *filtering/routing* or *recommender* systems. Filtering is usually based on decision rules that select relevant documents and reject non-relevant ones, see Figure 2. Then,

Table 1. Pull approaches vs. push approaches

Criteria	Pull approaches	Push approaches
Information need	short time	long time
Required User Interaction	high	low

Figure 2. A common recommender system architecture

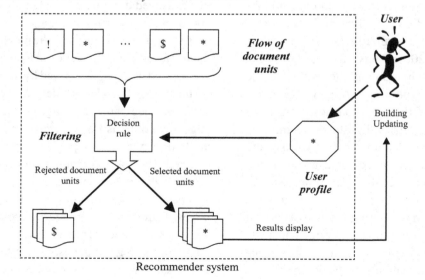

documents that are both relevant and selected constitute the recommendation set.

Push approaches require either the definition of a recurrent query or, more generally, the use of users' profiles. These profiles may integrate the result of the analysis, for instance, of previous searches that can be considered as "preferences." A training stage is then necessary to build this profile, which is used to personalize the search process.

Browsing the Web

The second modality of searching for information is *browsing*. This modality is based on the hypertext concept (Agosti, 1996). A hypertext consists of a network of documents linked by anchors. The hypertext on the Web is built on HTTP (HyperText Transfert Protocol) and on HTML anchors. When browsing the Web, a user does not know *a priori* the structure of the hypertext he/she browses. To achieve successfully a search process by browsing, a user must have, in addition, a good practical knowledge to manipulate the Web (anchors, URLs) the best way.

Searching the Web is not so easy. It is not limited to these two modalities; it also implies many other activities detailed in the next section.

Information Searching Related Activities

Beside previous Information Retrieval modalities, many related activities are practiced during the information search process: active reading, memorizing, organizing information, spreading/sharing information. These activities are important for allowing the user to achieve a good information retrieval task.

Active Reading

The concept of active reading has been identified by Adler and van Doren (1972). When browsing

documents or reading the snippet (e.g., keywords in context) of a retrieved document from a search engine, one has to decide whether a document is relevant or not regarding his/her information need. To achieve this task, a user may carry out "active reading." Indeed, active reading consists in discussing the document contents (formulating remarks, summing up the document contents ...), critical thinking, and learning while reading. It can principally be supported by commentaries written down on documents. This activity directly implies the user's domain knowledge because to be effective, active reading must be as objective as possible. Thus, the better domain knowledge is, the better the evaluation of the relevance of a document is.

Memorizing and Organizing Documents

Memorizing relevant information is a starting point and an ending point of the information search process. Indeed, a user can start the process from an already known document (search engine, portal ...) and can memorize new documents for further use. This activity is not limited to the information search process. For instance, when dealing with paper documents, Kaye et al. (Kaye, Vertesi, Avery, Dafoe, David, Onaga et al., 2006) have shown that people archive documents for many reasons, one of the most important being the need to find interesting documents later again. This field study does not reveal a universal organizational practice: everybody has his/her own strategy that works for him/her. Therefore, personal paper archives are organized in many ways. This observation can also be applied to digital documents.

These memorized documents may also be used as a starting point: a user can start browsing from a specific and already known document or from the result of a search engine.

Spreading/Forwarding Documents

When searching for information, one related activity consists in spreading encountered documents. Indeed, each time a user finds a document, he/she may suppose that one of his/her friends or colleagues may be interested in it. Thus, the user may spread or forward documents to specific users. This activity is difficult because it must not be intrusive for any user. Furthermore, this activity implies that the user who wants to spread information knows other users' information needs or up-to-date interests. Finally, this activity is highly resource consuming (in time, for instance) because spreading documents is commonly achieved manually *via* e-mail sending. This activity is important because it can be considered as a supplement to the information searching process (Table 3).

Limits of Information Searching on the Web

Searching for information suffers from many limitations that have been identified following many IRS fails (Baeza-Yates & Ribeiro-Neto, 1999; GVU, 1998). These main limits are:

- The impossibility of finding relevant documents
- The difficulty of querying a search engine
- The difficulty of using the search engine query language
- The fact that only the visible Web is really indexed

Table 3. How a user arrives on a Web site? – CommerceNet/Nielsen Media – July 1997

71.0 %	Via search engines
9.8 %	Proposed by friends or colleagues
8.5 %	Quotidian books
8.4 %	A link in another Web page
8.1 %	Randomly, via browsing
3.6 %	TV advertisement
3.3 %	Books referencing Web pages

- The difficulty of managing retrieved documents from a search engine
- The impossibility of finding a document that has already been encountered
- The impossibility of returning to a visited document (history)
- The impossibility of knowing where the user is located in the hypertext (disorientation)
- The impossibility of visualizing the hypertext structure
- The cognitive overload occurring when browsing the Web caused by the hypertext structure memorization
- The difficulty of organizing memorized documents when they get numerous.

To limit these issues, many solutions have been proposed in order to help the user to search for relevant information. Such approaches are implemented in search assistants. The next section presents such systems while underlying the rise of collective/social approaches that aim at helping users searching the Web.

Search Assistants: Towards Social Information Search Assistants

Searching the Web via previously traditional approaches is not fully efficient because they do not solve the user's confusion issue when facing the flooding mass of available information. Thus, to help any user to find relevant information on the Web, search assistants have to take into account:

- The users' interests through the concepts of "profile" and "context"
- The users' specific wishes concerning preferences for documents that may be exploited by a relevance feedback algorithm, for instance
- The users' behavior. Based on search engines uses and users' practices, for instance, statistical analyses may be carried out. They

aim at characterizing the users and their needs as closely as possible (Jansen, Spink, & Saracevic, 2000). On the Web nowadays, it is possible to observe users' behaviors in a relatively simple way and in real time. For example, it is easy to take into account:

o   The most frequent queries for a search engine

o   The average time that a reader spends on a page or a document

o   The navigation paths followed from a page or a given document

o   The language used by the users to formulate their queries, as well as the language of the documents that they read …

These practices are very frequent for the e-marketing domain or for direct marketing to target potential customers. They may, however, be of a great interest for IR itself, for example:

•   Query analysis makes it possible to characterize the closest user or a group of users'

•   Frequency of result selections enables to penalize documents that are not often, even not at all, selected, and thus allows one to optimize the relevance of the other turned over results

•   Each net surfer's navigation analysis through statistics makes it possible to define "interest areas" by computing similarities between sites (competitor or not), and to suggest new destinations likely to interest users.

In fact, users' behavioral analysis may be a base for profiles definition, that is, users' representation. So the "user profile" notion is detailed in the next section. Indeed, to help the user to find relevant information on the Web, these approaches take into account the user, his/her activity, and his/her information needs. Then, specific approaches aiming to help a user to improve the search process

are presented, meanwhile focusing on the rise of social/collective approaches.

A REQUIRED STEP: USER PROFILING

As users' satisfaction is the main goal of search assistants, describing the users precisely, the most faithfully and with details is a key step towards that goal. Generally, a user profile is described by a set of characteristics that identifies or represents him/her. User profiling can be studied under various aspects: *profiles representation models*, *profiles definition methods*. The description of a user profile generally follows a given model. We discern two widely used models for users' profiles representation: the *attribute-value model* and the *hierarchical model*.

The *attribute-value model* describes a user profile by a set of independent attributes bounded to an atomic value (string, numeric, date …). For instance, one may describe a user's demographic data with the attribute-value model as follows: *(name, Peter), (gender, male), (age, 18), (job, student)*. The first element of each previous pair represents the attribute and the second element describes the value bounded to this attribute. The attribute is considered as a key, so in an attribute-value model, two attributes with the same name cannot exist at the same time.

The *hierarchical model* organizes various characteristics (or attributes) of a user profile as a tree, where leaves are bounded to values representing the contents of the profile. The hierarchy is a way of defining a relationship between the different characteristics. Hence, each non-leaf node represents a class of attributes. Moreover, in a hierarchical model, two attributes with the same name but with different access paths in the hierarchy can exist at the same time.

More specifically, there are *contents representation models* of profiles that somehow define their exploitation framework. Generally, contents of users' profiles are represented by a *list of atomic values* or by a *list of weighted values* (Korfhage, 1997). Atomic values lead to a form of database matching when comparing different attributes, while weighted values allow a fuzzier matching that evaluates a degree of similarity between different attributes instead of a binary similarity value. Weighted values are mostly used in IR, and the cosine formula is generally used to measure interprofile or query-profile similarities (Baeza-Yates & Ribeiro-Neto, 1999)…

Manual methods are often used to define profiles; to do that, a user generally fills in a form. On the other hand, automatic or semiautomatic methods may also be used to define attribute contents of profiles such as indexing, clustering, profiling, and stereotypes approaches:

- **Indexing** consists in selecting the keywords that best characterize a text (document, query …). For each keyword, a weight is calculated by using *tf.idf* -like formulas (Baeza-Yates & Ribeiro-Neto, 1999); so, one may define the given user's interests by indexing the set of documents that he/she has visited, saved, or judged (Godoy & Amandi, 2006).
- **Clustering or machine learning** (Leouski & Croft, 1996) consists of identifying object classes based on similarity of their characteristics. Clustering tries to minimize variance inside a given class, and to maximize this variance between classes. Clustering result is then a set of heterogeneous classes with homogenous contents. Hence, one may create users' profiles by applying clustering methods on the set of document contents they saved, judged, or visited, in order to discover a user's interests or topics.
- **Stereotypes** (Shapira, Shoval, & Hanani, 1997) consist of predefining classes and characteristics of these classes. Documents

or users are automatically bounded to a given class according to their content. The stereotypes approach is a kind of clustering, and is mainly used for defining users' groups.
- **Profiling** (Cho, Kyeong, & Kim, 2002) consists of tracking the user during his/her different log sessions, and in analyzing his/her behavior. Profiling helps to find documents saved or judged by a user. Therefore, profiling is mostly used in electronic commerce in order to identify which kinds of products a user is looking for, and then recommend him/her items that meet these needs. For that purpose, profiling generally analyzes clicks on products, products saved in a shopping basket, purchase of products …

Note that the analysis on users' profiles (classification of users' profiles, associated generic models, contents representation models, defining profiles methods) is the same for either individual user profiling or for users' group profiling.

Thanks to this representation of users, search assistants can implement algorithms that assist the user during his/her search process. Two types of search assistants are considered in this paper:

- **Individual search assistants** that help a single user by exploiting information concerning this user only,
- **Social or collective search assistants** that help a single user or a group of users by exploiting information concerning the user in addition to information about other users (experience, shared information …). For such systems, each user is benefiting from the mass crowd.

The actual rise of social search assistants can be explained by the evolution of the Web as a whole. The new Web, also called "Web 2.0," encourages such types of systems.

The New Web: The Rise of Collective Search Assistants

We, nowadays, attend the birth of a new Web that is meant to be more open, as an evolution of the previous "Web 1.0." Tim O'Reilly in 2005 named it "The Web 2.0." Concretely, this new Web goes beyond its initial role of "a worldwide electronic library" as it shifts to an alive, dynamic, and interactive space where people may get involved and benefit from it. Actually, Web users go from a passive reader state to an active role of contributor. In fact, this change of era is twofold: a technical facet and a social one characterize it. On the one hand, the Web 2.0 may be perceived as a replacement of the Web 1.0 techniques by services-oriented techniques. On the other hand, it represents a new network made up of social interactions. The blogs, RSS (Really simple Syndication) feeds, the wikies ... belong to this tendency. People also call this new Web "The Read/Write Web" to color the fact that it is no more exclusively oriented towards publication, but also supports a strong collaboration between their users (http://www.readwriteweb.com/). This Web 2.0 repositions the user and the relationships he/she has with others at the heart of the Internet. According to Tim O'Reilly, the key to success in this evolution of the Web lies in "the Collective Intelligence." Moreover, the economic stake seems important, since many industrialists and leaders on the market of data processing also seem to be interested in the fact that people are more efficient when they work collectively. For example, it is the case for Microsoft, which has published, in France, a document about collective effectiveness that gathers analyses, testimonies, and reflections carried out by experts of the domain (http://www.ec2006.blogs.com/). In less than 10 years, we passed from static Web pages to a Web made up of objects, people, and services, bound by a central aggregator: the individual.

In this context, information searching techniques have also evolved. Indeed, the information retrieval task was first approached as an individual step. Each new IR task was regarded as a long time as an isolated act. But today, the collaborative aspects in the processes of information retrieval attract a growing interest. Indeed, if one observes the most frequent situations where users need to seek information, one realizes that they are generally in social, organizational, or professional contexts. In these contexts, users act as groups, and need to share their experience, as well as to retrieve information (Fidel, Bruce, Pejtersen, Dumais, Grudin, & Poltrock, 2000; Karamuftuoglu, 1998; Talja, 2002). Therefore, these observations guide a new research aiming at helping users in a setting of information seeking and so, in real-life environment (e.g., communities of academics, scientists, engineers ...).

More recently, Hansen and Järvelin (2005) showed that collaborative IR is very frequent, even more frequent than expected. Thus, they give the following preliminary definition of Collaborative Information Retrieval (CIR):

CIR is an information access activity related to a specific problem solving activity that, implicitly or explicitly, involves human beings interacting with other human(s) directly and/or through texts (e.g., notes, figures, documents) as information sources in a work task related information seeking and retrieval process either in a specific workplace setting or in a more open community or environment.

Moreover, they analyzed IR activities according to how and what collaborative activities are involved. They identified two types of collaboration in IR activities:

- **Document-related collaborative activities:** This concerns creation, sharing, or reuse of documents. These activities include:
  - Sharing and reusing documents (created or retrieved in the same community)

- o Creating, sharing, and reusing contextual relationships (annotations, citations, references)
- o Sharing and reusing judgments, decisions or opinions (objective or subjective ones)
- o Sharing representations of information need (query terms, query structures …)
- o Sharing the history of information objects, such as logs, links, bookmarks, or documents themselves.

- **Human-related collaborative activities:** This concerns the use of knowledge possessed by other humans (individuals or groups). These activities can be explicit or implicit, and most of the time they are in verbal form. Among those activities we can quote:
  - o Sharing tasks (cooperation) and/or sharing subtasks (division and distribution of tasks);
  - o Sharing search strategies, search terms, or classification codes …
  - o Sharing or asking for external and/or internal expertise. Users of a same group (or having the same goal) may be asked for domain specific knowledge, as well as for information retrieval specificities;
  - o Sharing internal experience;
  - o Communicating and sharing advices, personal and subjective opinions …

In the same way, various studies undertaken in the information science domain come to corroborate these aforementioned observations (Prepok, 2002; Sonnenwald & Pierce, 2000). It is then obvious today that the information retrieval related activities may be improved by only taking into account the fact that any user may profit and benefit from any form of collaboration within the framework of given activities. Moreover, it is argued that "the fundamental intellectual problems of IR

are the production and consumption of knowledge. Knowledge production is fundamentally a collaborative task, which is deeply embedded in the practices of a community of participants constituting a domain" (Karamuftuoglu, 1998). From now on, current advances in networked systems cross the boundaries of researches on IR: they do not only concern technical problems, but also human and intellectual aspects, and then, a better understanding of the social aspects of information retrieval.

In this context, it is interesting to underline different approaches that can be implemented to help the user to improve his/her search process via search assistants. In the next sections, these approaches are detailed, taking into account each type of assistant, that is to say, individual and social assistants. The next sections follow the different search process steps to present different search assistants.

Querying Web Assistants

Pull-Based Assistants

Individual Pull-Based Assistants
To help a user to query an IRS, many approaches may be implemented at each step of the querying process: a search engine selection, the formulation of the information need (query), the management of search results. Thus, the provided help concerns the important steps that condition the quality of the search process.

Selecting the suitable search engine. On the Web, there are many search engines: some of them are domain specific, others are generalists. When searching for information, a user has to select the right search engine to get the most relevant documents. For instance, *GlOSS* (Gravano, Garcia-Molina, & Tomasic 1999) indexes several search engines. When searching for information, a user can first query *GlOSS* to find the most adapted search engine. Then, the user can directly query the selected search engine. The limit of such an approach is that *GlOSS* must have access to the search engines' contents. Moreover, search engines suffer from the limited overlap between search results for the same query. That is to say, for the same query, different search engines may not retrieve the same document set. To limit this issue, metasearch engines have been implemented.

Selecting multiple search engines. Metasearch engines aim at querying multiple search engines for the same query and to synthesize search results. *MetaSearch* (http://www.metasearch.com), *InternetSleuth* (http://www.isleuth.com), or the well-known *Copernic* (http://www.copernic.com) are examples of tools that use such an approach. A user first selects the list of search engines he/she wants to query. Then, the metasearch engine queries each search engine while eventually adapting the query. Lastly, search results are synthesized and displayed in a single ranked list.

Dreilinger and Howe (1997) propose a mixed approach that features search engine selection associated with metasearch.

Even if these approaches allow the user to query the most suitable search engines, a main difficulty remains: query formulation.

Formulating a query. Helping users to formulate their queries is gaining a great importance, more particularly in Web context. When the user formulates his/her information need by a query, the chosen terms for his/her query have an influence on the response of the system. However, generally, the user formulates his/her queries with its own vocabulary, which may not strictly correspond to the one used to index the relevant documents of the queried collections. Therefore, some approaches like *WebCluster* (Mechkour, Harper, & Muresan 1998) offer query formulation via a mediating system. Such systems display the user many sets of documents. Then, the user selects the set of documents that corresponds to his/her information needs. Thanks to this set of documents, the system automatically generates a query according to the indexing terms contained in these documents. Then the user may use the generated query to interrogate any search engine. Thanks to this query or thanks to his/her own query, a user is assisted while adapting or reformulating his/her query in order to find what he/she is really searching for.

Reformulating a query. In order to select the maximum of relevant documents while limiting the noise (i.e., too many no relevant documents retrieved), the user should choose known relevant terms from the indexing language. This task proves to be difficult insofar as, in general, on large corpus, it is impossible to know the indexing language used. Indexation, and in particular its exhaustiveness, thus have a direct incidence on the quality of the answers of the system. One can conclude from it that, taking into account increasing volumes of the collections, to find relevant information by using only the initial query is a quasi-impossible operation. The automatic reformulation of the initial request of the user is a means of mitigating the problem and of helping the user to target his/her need. The query reformulation is a process aiming at generating a new query more adequate than the one initially formulated by the user. This reformulation makes it possible to coordinate the language of research (used by the user in its query) and the indexing language. Consequently, it limits the noise and silence due to a bad choice of the index terms in the expression of the query on the one hand, and the gaps of the indexing process on the other hand. We distinguish mainly two approaches to reformulate queries, (1) according to whether they use predefined term associations, or (2) the relevance and not relevance of the documents retrieved in response to an initial query. The two principal techniques used are respectively query expansion and relevance feedback.

1. Query expansion is based on the following principle: the simple comparison between the contents of the query and the documents

of the collection does not make it possible to have all the documents corresponding to a given query; so, some relevant documents remain not retrieved. Research tasks proposed to reformulate the initial query by the addition of the semantically close terms. Those terms may result from:

- Studies on the natural language (morphological alternatives …). It is thus possible to add to the query the morphological alternatives of the various terms employed by the user. The goal of this mechanism is to ensure the restitution of the documents indexed by alternatives of the terms composing the query. Within this framework, one uses stemming and truncating algorithms.
- Statistical studies and analyses on the contents of the documents of the base. One can thus choose to add a certain number of the most relevant terms of the selected documents, or to preserve of it only one number limited among the initial and added terms.

In the same way, another method proposes to add terms close to or terms associated with those of the query. It is a question of seeking interterms associations. In this direction, various research tasks were undertaken. One distinguishes the manual methods, using, for example, predefined thesaurus (directed indexing) and methods entirely automatic such as:

- The computation of the contextual links between terms
- The computation of correlation matrix between terms
- The automatic classification of terms
- The automatic classification of documents.

These associations are generally created automatically and based on the co-occurrence of the terms in the documents. The interterms links reinforce the concept of relevance of the documents compared to the queries. Manually established associations generally represent relations of synonymy and hierarchy. The manually built thesauri are an effective means for the query expansion. However, their construction, and the maintenance of semantic information that they contain, are expensive in time, and require the recourse to experts of the considered fields. Currently, the most used terminological resources, as well on the Web as on dedicated systems, are the *SynSets* of *Wordnet* (http://wordnet.princeton.edu/).

2. Relevance feedback takes into account the user's relevance judgments on the documents that have been retrieved in response to its initial query. The user can provide judgments of relevance with regard to the retrieved documents by stating those that it considers relevant and those that it considers not relevant. These judgments are then used to reformulate the query. The fundamental principle of relevance feedback is to use the initial query to start research, then to modify this one starting from the judgments of relevance and/or non-relevance of the user, either for reweighting the terms of the initial query, or to add to it (resp. to remove) other terms contained in the relevant (resp. nonrelevant) documents. The new query, obtained at each feedback iteration, makes it possible to correct the direction of research in the direction of the relevant documents. The approach described in Rocchio (1971) proposes to repeatedly derive the optimal query starting from operations on the relevant documents and non-relevant documents. The idea is that the relevant documents have terms associated with the terms of the initial query; their semantic weights are then increased by the addition of the relevant document terms. Conversely, the weights of the terms contained in the nonrelevant documents are decreased. In

the same way, the terms absent from the initial query are added. Then Rocchio's work was extended by Ide (1971) to develop two other strategies that appeared more powerful according to various studies (Salton & Buckley, 1990). The first strategy is the basic Rocchio's formula without standardization taking into account the numbers of relevant documents and non-relevant documents. The second strategy is similar to the first one, but makes it possible to limit the feedback starting from the no-nrelevant documents by using only the k first non-relevant documents in the ordered list.

At this stage, the user must be able to judge retrieved documents. Therefore, he/she needs to know how to handle and manage search results.

Managing search results. When querying a search engine, an important step is to manage the search results. To do this, the user has to analyze search results to identify which documents are relevant to his/her information need. To help the user to identify what he/she is searching for, a single, ranked list may not be suitable enough. Indeed, this ranked list is not efficient when the number of retrieved documents is too important,

or when a global view of the retrieved documents is necessary. To help the user to identify relevant information, various visualizations have been proposed. These visualizations are also called Visual Information Retrieval Interfaces (VIRI). A classification of such interfaces has been proposed in Zamir (1998). Figure 3 shows an example of VIRI extracted from the *Easy-DoR* software (Chevalier, Chrisment, & Julien, 2004) that represents retrieved documents in a 3-D space. Each colored plot corresponds to a set of retrieved documents having the same combination of query keywords.

In addition to such visualizations, clustering approaches, like *Scatter/Gather* (Cutting, Karger, & Pederson, 1993), may be applied to limit the number of displayed documents and to make search results more interpretable.

Social Pull-Based Assistants

The large majority of social assistants concern distributed IRS and peer-to-peer (P2P) networks. The guiding principles are based on the fact that it is more judicious and easier to create and share knowledge at a local level, in a definite context, where the relevance of information is better controlled (Jin, Ning, & Chen, 2006; Klemm & Aberer, 2005; Kwok, 2006; Wu & Aberer, 2004).

Figure 3. VIRI proposed in EasyDoR

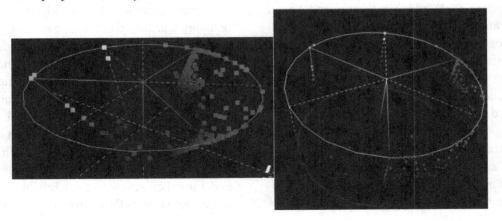

These works all focus on decentralized IR and integrate contextual information sources.

Peer-to-peer information retrieval, like *HumanLinks* (Memmi & Nérot, 2003), is increasingly receiving attention (Kwok, 2006; Yang & Garcia-Molina, 2002). Indeed, like peer-to-peer systems, P2P information retrieval systems have emerged as an appropriate way to share and reuse huge volumes of documents. Yang and Garcia-Molina defined P2P systems as "distributed systems in which nodes of equal roles and capabilities exchange information and services directly with each other." According to Milojicic et al. (Milojicic, Kalogeraki, Lukose, Nagaraja, Pruyne, Richard, 2002), the main benefits of a P2P approach include: "improving scalability by avoiding dependency on centralized points; eliminating the need for costly infrastructure by enabling direct communication among clients; and enabling resource aggregation."

To sum up, information seeking and retrieval can benefit from P2P systems' features in order to bring some help to information seekers and to optimize their tasks. Information searching is then decentralized, and realized either locally or routed (duplicated) towards other peers. Each peer must maintain an information repository available for sharing. Several studies report different experiences in P2P information retrieval. In a social context, the most significant work is discussed in what follows. Kwok (2006) describes some queries and searching trends in P2P networks. Wu and Aberer (2004), and then Klemm and Aberer (2005) and Jin et al. (2006) study different strategies for searching, they have implemented and experimented them on P2P networks. The main problem remains: whatever the basic strategy on each peer, the aggregation of the partial results obtained on each peer in a global result (global ranking or global relevance evaluation) is quite difficult to implement.

Wu and Aberer (2004) revisit the *PageRank* algorithm to apply its principle in a decentralized way. They propose to compute a *SiteRank* on the pages of each site, and then to aggregate the rankings from multiple sites. They argue that while decomposing the task of global page-ranking computation to distributed participating servers (in a decentralized search system), their strategy can overcome the missing of a global view. Moreover, spamming becomes very difficult with *SiteRank* computation.

Later on, Klemm and Aberer (2005) study a full-text retrieval strategy on P2P technology. Each peer acts as an independent IRS with its own collection, its own indexes (local term vocabulary). Local term frequencies can be computed, and then global term frequencies can be inferred.

Jin et al. (2006) propose an information retrieval strategy based on semantic small world in an unstructured P2P document sharing system. In such architecture, each peer maintains its own semantic representation. The computation of the similarity between two peers is based on a formula derived from the cosine measure. Short-range links and long-range links are identified to construct a semantic small world, as well as to reduce network traffic.

In another way, several works were interested in the semantic description of the sources in distributed systems or in P2P systems, among them Haase et al.'s studies. Haase et al. (Haase, Stojanovic, Sure, & Völker, 2005) proposed to organize knowledge (as metadata description) within communities by the use of ontologies. They have extended the *Bibster* system by integrating an ontology learning process. The ontology is built on each peer from the users' local repositories. Thus, each ontology reflects the personal interests of local users. Such learned ontologies allow systems to create personalized classification and then personalized information retrieval. So in a social point of view, the common point of these decentralized strategies, and their main advantage too, is that users (and by extension, peers) may limit their search to some reliable sites. The target can be sites they already have identified, or sites that were recommended to them. In that way, the main help that can be brought to any user is to guide him/her in his/her search step, by providing local terminological resources, as well as topological maps of search spaces. It is still necessary to take into account the collaborative and social aspects to construct and to broadcast these semantic resources.

Collective pull approaches can also use semantics stored in annotations. Thus, Fraenkel and Klein (1999) argue that it is worth exploiting such human-contributed contents to improve Information Retrieval. Merging annotations corresponding to a given query is proposed in Sannomiya et al. (Sannomiya, Amagasa, Yoshikawa, & Uemura, 2001). More recently, in the Digital Library area, Agosti and Ferro (2005) have been considering people's annotations for reranking results of search engines. Collective annotations are also considered valuable by Frommholz and Fuhr (2006); they even model exchanged e-mails as discussion threads for the TREC Enterprise Track.

From the user's point of view, the management of search results can be improved, thanks to collective aspects. A relevant example is illustrated in the system *VR-Vibe* (Benford, Snowdon, Greenhalgh, Knox, & Brown, 1995), which proposes a collaborative space containing all queries and search results of a group of users. Users can interact together via annotations associated with retrieved documents.

Push Approaches: Filtering or Recommender Systems

Individual Recommender Assistants

Filtering or recommending information is a passive task, since the user does not explicitly express his/her needs through a query formulated in a more or less structured natural language (as it is the case for pull-based search engines). User's needs are stored in his/her profile and are then compared to available information in order to find which one best corresponds to him/her. For an individual access to information, filtering is generally content based.

Individual content-based filtering uses the description of information contents in order to determine to which individual users' needs profiles they corresponds. Their recurrent interests are described by a list of weighted keywords (Korfhage, 1997), see section on users' profiles. These profiles are obtained by indexing users' information saved or judged, for instance (Bottraud, Bisson, & Bruandet, 2003).

On the other hand, one can also recommend a given user a document similar to another one, previously judged interesting by this user. In this particular case, the user profile is described by his/her judgments passed on several documents, and the comparison or matching process is performed between two information descriptions, where one has been judged by the user and the other one is the new candidate information (not yet judged) for recommendation.

Content-based recommendation may also be based on parts of documents. For instance, one may use parts of documents that contain words of the user's information needs in order to find other relevant documents (Teevan, Dumais, & Horvitz, 2005). All the same, parts of documents that have been highlighted by a user can also be used for finding and recommending documents that correspond to him/her (Price, Schilit, & Golovchinsky, 1998).

Suitor (Maglio, Barrett, Campbell, & Selker, 2000) is a representative system that studies the user's environment and actions to build his/her profile. The approach innovates by various functionalities. In particular, it uses a scrolling window, making it possible to post the information suggested by *Suitor* on the bottom of the screen. It proposes especially a system enabling to follow the user's glance via a camera in order to identify parts of the screen that he/she is looking at.

Social Recommender Assistants

There are several types of collaborative filtering or collaborative recommending (Malone, Grant, Turbak, Brobst, & Cohen, 1987; Montaner, Lopez, & Rosa, 2003;), such as social filtering, demographic filtering, and content-based collaborative filtering.

Social filtering. Social filtering uses judgments (or feedbacks) of a set of users about a set of documents in order to perform recommendations. To do that, a similarity measure is computed between the users' judgments (Goldberg, Nichols, Oki, & Terry, 1992; Konstan, Miller, Maltz, Herlocker, Gordon, & Riedl, 1997). This measure may help to determine if a judged document corresponds to a given user. In social filtering, the description of document contents is completely ignored.

Demographic filtering. Demographic filtering uses demographic data (gender, age, profession, address, etc.) in order to create groups of users and make recommendations within a given group (Krulwich, 1997). To do that, personal judgments are classified according to individuals' demographic data. This categorization allows determining which type of information is appreciated by a given type of user. The categorization either may be manual or based on users judgments, for instance, in order to deduce the type of users (or group of users) to which information corresponds (Pazzani, 1999).

Hybrid filtering or content-based collaborative filtering. The previous collaborative filtering methods are not exclusive and can then be combined. Therefore, different hybrid methods have been developed by combining different kinds of filtering methods (Good, Schafer, Konstan, Borchers, Sarwar, Herlocker et al., 1999; Pazzani, 1999). The use of hybrid approaches improves the results' relevance of the various filtering systems introduced previously by mitigating their limits (Balabanovic & Shoham, 1997), which are over-specialization in individual content-based filtering; users' judgments on a document, which is a very time-consuming task …

Hybrid filtering methods may also be called content-based collaborative filtering, since they generally combine content-based filtering with social or demographic filtering as follows:

- Users' similarities can be deduced thanks to their profiles needs constructed with the information contents that they have already judged (Pazzani, 1999); so, in order to identify groups of users, one may no longer consider similarity between users' judgments only. The point of this type of hybrid filtering is that it allows making recommendations to a new user by determining his/her group from his/her profile needs. In pure collaborative filtering, one should have to wait until this new user had made enough judgments on information in order to associate him/her to a given group and then recommend him/her some documents. This is called the "cold start problem" of pure collaborative filtering systems.
- All the same, documents similarities can be deduced by comparing their respective contents instead of comparing judgments made on these documents (Yager, 2002). Hence, one can recommend information if its description is similar to another one that has been already validated (judged interesting) by the user. An interest of this approach is that it is possible to recommend information that has not yet been judged; whereas in pure collaborative filtering, an information has to be judged at least once to be recommended.

In point of fact, collaborative filtering has as a principle of exploiting the evaluations made by a group of users upon certain documents in order to recommend these same documents to another group of users. All the users of a collaborative filtering system can benefit from the evaluations of the others by receiving recommendations for which the closest users gave favorable (positive) judgments. That does not require that the system has a process of extraction of the document contents. Moreover, the user is able to discover various interesting fields, because the principle of collaborative filtering is absolutely not based on the thematic dimension of the profiles, and so it is not subject to the funnel effect. Another advantage of collaborative filtering is that the judgments of the users integrate not only a thematic dimension, but also other factors relating to the quality of the documents, such as diversity, the innovation, the adequacy with the public concerned, and so on.

Collaborative filtering is mainly based on the principle of communities. A community represents a set of users who share the same centers of interests. A collaborative filtering system exploits communities to generate the best recommendations; so the management of the communities (their creation, their evaluation, their perception) in collaborative filtering systems takes an important part because the quality of the recommendations sent to the users depends basically on the quality of the communities formed by the system. It exists as different approaches to create communities. Most of the time the communities are generated from the computation of users proximity according to the history of their evaluations. The most popular approach to build the community of a user is that of the closest neighbors (Breese, Heckerman, & Kadie, 1998; Herlocker, Konstan, Borchers, & Riedl, 1999).

Many systems of recommendations are based partially or completely on filtering collaborative (Herlocker et al., 1999; Herlocker, Konstan, Terveen, & Riedl, 2004; Jin, Chai, & Si, 2004). The experiments carried out with these systems proved the effectiveness of collaborative filtering and the help brought to the users by the recommendations generated (usefulness of these recommendations). At all events, the positioning of new users within communities is not obvious and must be the subject of studies to come.

Other collaborative recommender systems.
Many other approaches propose alternative recommendation systems. For instance, Siteseer (Rücker & Polanco, 1997) or Easy-DoR (Chevalier et al., 2004) recommend documents to users according to the contents of their bookmark hierarchies. The main difference between these two approaches is that the second one takes into account the hierarchical organization of bookmarks.

Fab (Balabanovic & Shoham, 1997) or Groupmark (Pemberton, Rodden, & Procter, 2000) propose recommender systems based on groups of users, namely communities. Fab queries external search engines to find and recommend information to user groups built according to their information needs. Groupmark recommends to users the groups that are adapted to him/her. A group can be considered as an information need. An alternative can be seen via ReferalWeb (Kautz, Selman, & Shah, 1997), which relies on the word-to-mouth principle.

In addition to pull-based assistants, assistants have been developed to improve the second modality of the search process: browsing.

Browsing Assistants

The main lacks of browsing come from the cognitive effort that it implies. Indeed, the user does not know the hypertext structure, and should remind which path he/she follows to reach a specific document: this commonly implies a cognitive overload. Moreover, the user has to identify which links are relevant to his/her information need. Nevertheless, when the number of links rises, this judgment is less easy. Navigation suffers mainly from problems coming from the architecture on which it is based, that is, on the hypertext concept. These problems are cognitive overload and disorientation. For both of them, we present the approaches that aim at limiting these problems.

Individual Browsing Assistants

Cognitive Overload

In order to limit the cognitive effort induced by the hypertext, various tools were implemented to keep a trace of the visited documents.

Navigation "history" list. Navigation history is a basic browser feature pioneered by Mosaic in autumn, 1993. Concretely, the browser automatically stores addresses of documents visualized by the user in a chronological order of visit. Thus, the user can retrieve an encountered document at any time, provided the fact that he/she remembers the date of visit. This requirement makes the exploitation for a navigation history cognitively expensive. Traditionally, documents pertaining to a user's navigation history are represented by their title and URL in a widget list, as in Internet Explorer, for example. However, such a representation is hard to exploit, in particular when searching for a document. People rather have a visual memory of a document than its title, *Bookmap* (Hascoët, 2000). This project is interesting because it uses "thumbnails" (reduced images of the visited documents) instead of traditional URLs or titles of the documents. Thanks to this hint, the user may visually have a direct outline of a document, which facilitates its evaluation. Unfortunately, the user must nevertheless provide a high cognitive effort during his/her navigation because the various documents are presented independently. Navigation visualization systems try to limit this issue.

Navigation visualization. Navigation visualization systems can be considered as an evolution of the navigation history list. It makes it possible to graphically represent the visited documents as well as the possible links between these documents. We can give as example *WebMap* (Dömel, 1994). Thanks to such tools, the user can visualize not only the documents that he/she has previously visited, but also the organization of these documents.

Disorientation

Disorientation is caused by the fact that the user loses the progression of his/her navigation. This is due to the fact that he/she does not understand the organization of the local hypertext anymore. To avoid that, mapping the local hypertext has been proposed. Instead of only presenting the visited documents, these cartographies aim at presenting the documents visited within their local hypertext. Thus, the visited documents appear with the documents bound by hypertext links so that the user can have a global vision of the "local" hypertext in which he/she is located. As an example of cartography tools, we can give *Hyperspace* (Wood, Drew, Beale, & Hendley, 1995) or *Internet Cartographer* (http://www.inventix.com/).

Thanks to the various approaches suggested in the literature, the navigation task can be carried out under better conditions, but information retrieval on the Web also requires a research task. The following section presents the approaches aimed at improving the research task.

Letizia (Lieberman, 1995) uses the visited documents to initialize the user's profile. This latter is built starting from the terms that result from the visited documents and the actions of the user. During a document visit, *Letizia* downloads the contents of all the documents related to the active document in order to evaluate the matching with the user profile. The links towards relevant documents are presented to the user by means of an additional window.

These systems only tell the user potentially relevant documents for navigation in progress. However, it is also interesting to inform the user that the document he/she is visiting is relevant (or not relevant) for the topics that interest him/her. The *Syskill & Webert* (Pazzani, 1996) system aims at filling this task. The user can create as many topics as necessary. The topics must be organized in a non-hierarchical list. Each time he/she finds a relevant (or non relevant) document for the topics he/she has created, the user announces it to the system. Then this one updates a profile corresponding to the topic. During navigation, the system indicates to the user whether the document he/she visits is relevant (or not relevant) for his/her topics.

In a more general way, agents can also take into account the user's search environment (collection of applications) to deduce his/her needs, and to recommend documents to him/her that are not necessarily connected (by hyperlinks) to the visited documents. *WBI* (Barrett, Maglio, & Kellem, 1997), for example, studies the user's actions ,and organizes the visited documents into classes representing the user's needs. From these needs, *WBI* queries research tools to propose the search result to the users. It moreover proposes functionalities of history management, notification (announces the modifications in the contents of a document), and shortcuts generation (if the user daily follows the same sequence of bonds to reach a document everyday). This approach is based on a multiagent architecture, and the interface of *WBI* is integrated into Web documents.

The *Watson* system (Budzik & Hammond, 1999) innovates concerning the identification of regular expressions in the visited documents (as the addresses for example) in order to propose contextual services to the user. For an identified address, *Watson* generates an urban map, allowing the user to locate it.

To limit user's disorientation, an alternative of such recommender systems can be seen in *Topic Maps* (Le Grand & Soto, 2005), which can produce a topic-based navigation of the document set.

Social Browsing Assistants

Social assistants that help a user to browse the Web can also be called browsing accelerators. They recommend the user links that the system considers as relevant for the user's navigation.

Webwatcher (Armstrong, Freitag, & Joachims, 1995) used the user's information needs, which can be considered as a query, to recommend the user relevant hypertext links. A user may judge each document he/she visits. For each relevant document, the system stores the user's relevance judgment. The system uses this information to identify links that are relevant for the user's information needs. To do this, the system prefetches the entire document that is linked to the visited one, and uses all stored information about each document associated with, as well as the user's information needs, to compute the relevance of each document. The hyperlinks corresponding to relevant documents are indicated via specific icons added by the system within the visited document.

Broadway (Jaczynski & Trousse, 1997) is based on the same idea. It relies on the hypothesis that two users visiting the same documents in the same order implies that they are looking for the same information. The user profile corresponds to a user's navigation path associated with many behavior characteristics (e.g., reading time). The system stores all profiles to identify relevant information for a new user. To identify these documents, *Broadway* is based on a case-based reasoning algorithm that identifies the paths similar to a specific user's ones within store navigation. When similar navigation paths are found, *Broadway* recommends some documents found in retrieved navigations that the user will probably visit. It allows the user to accelerate his/her navigation by going directly to the required information.

Rather than recommending documents, some approaches (social navigation systems) offer users a shared space or a virtual world in which documents are displayed.

For instance, *FootPrints* (Wexelblat & Pattie, 1999) displays the browsing behavior of users in a 2-D interface. Anyone can see others' navigation paths as well as documents that have been the most visited one ...

CoBrow (Sidler, Scott, & Wolf, 1997) is a system that displays the hypertext structure in which visited documents occur. It also features communication functionalities between users visiting the same documents, thus transforming the Web into a virtual space where people meet on Web pages.

A more sophisticated system is illustrated by *StarWalker* (Chen, 1999), which offers a 3-D virtual environment dedicated to a document collection browsing where users can interact, for example, by exchanging information, communicating.

To help the user to improve his/her search process as a whole, he/she needs to be assisted during search-related activities.

Improving Other Search-Related Activities

Individual-Based Improvement

Systems provide individual help to achieve both modalities of information search: browsing and querying. Moreover, activities such as document storing, document active reading, and document sharing are taken into account to improve users' experience and knowledge "capitalization." The following sections describe how systems intend to improve these activities.

Active Reading Individual Assistants
In past centuries, when books were rare and personal possessions, readers used to annotate and share their own copies (Jackson, 2002). Nowadays, annotating books borrowed from a library is considered defacement, since they are public materials. However, some people still seek for the "dirtiest," that is, most annotated copy available, because they find previous readers' annotations valuable (Marshall, 1998). Now that documents are digitized, annotation value is reconsidered and introduced into the digital library through software called "annotation systems."

Currently, documents tend to be drawn up using word-processing software, and are mainly spread through networked computers. It is noticed that reading documents on-screen is less comfort-

able, slower, and less persuasive than reading paper. Moreover, according to an experiment recounted by Sellen and Harper (2003), readers feel frustrated at not being able to annotate digital documents.

The need to annotate digital documents was soon understood by researchers and companies that have been developing annotation systems since the early 1990s, consider for example *Commentor* (Röscheisen, Mogensen, & Winograd, 1994). Concretely, people consulting a digital document can select a passage, create an annotation using the appropriate software function, and then type in a comment. Once the annotation is created, it is generally displayed in context, as close as possible to its anchor, that is, the selected passage, like in *Amaya* (Kahan, Koivunen, Prud'Hommeaux, & Swick, 2002).

Document Management Individual Assistants
Nowadays, people have to manage huge amounts of digital documents that they receive or for which they have searched. Moreover, these digital documents can be multimedia, combining texts, pictures, sounds, and videos. With the advent of handy and user-friendly software, people can also easily produce their own documents. Furthermore, they are able to publish them on the Web so as others can retrieve them. Actually, organizing digital material is a key issue for being able to share and to find them later, as is the case for paper documents. Jones et al. (Jones, Phuwanartnurak, Gill, & Bruce, 2005) have observed that people prefer to organize documents themselves rather than to trust in a personal search engine. In fact, they feel that searching by querying makes them lose control of their personal data, as they do not rely on the system's performance. Indeed, we now present three facilities for storing encountered documents.

Navigation history list. In Web context, browsers have soon allowed people to reach encountered documents again by keeping their navigation histories. Actually, the browser automatically fills the user's navigation history with every visited Web page. However, a very restricted subset of these documents may really interest the user. That is the reason why browsers also provide a bookmarking feature that enables users to store interesting documents, in a more active way.

Personal bookmarks. In paper document setting, "bookmarking a page" refers to the act of locating a specific page thanks to a thin marker, commonly made from paper or leather. Nowadays, people more and more work with digital documents; therefore, bookmark facility has naturally been transposed from paper to the digital world. The browser's bookmarking feature enables readers to keep traces of an interesting document by storing its URLs. Bookmarks are organized in a hierarchy similar to a file system: it is a tree whose nodes are folders, and leaves are pointers to documents.

Concretely, a Web user that wants to keep a document for future use may insert it into his/her hierarchy. Back in 1998, users were already storing an average of three bookmarks per navigation session; experience showed that they create folders when their whole bookmarks do not fit anymore into the screen (Abrams, Baecker, & Chignell, 1998). Actually, users mostly structure their bookmarks in an incremental fashion, corresponding to their use. Bookmarks are nowadays widely used, as they are integrated into any browser. However, they suffer some limits that may be swept away by the use of annotations, as discussed in the following section.

Digital annotations. Annotating a paper is an activity commonly practiced, mostly involved in active reading. On paper, an annotation is more informative than a bookmark for at least two reasons. First, the reader associates his/her annotation to a particular location within the document. This anchoring point usually represents the annotation's function, for example, writing phrases in the header of a document may sum it up, whereas crossing text out may express refutation. Secondly, an annotation may consist of a

comment, expressed in the reader's own verbal representations, that reflect his/her understanding of the document.

Such differences can also be noticed on digital documents. Indeed, software called "annotation systems," such as *Amaya* (Kahan et al., 2002), provides an annotation feature on documents of the Web or even on everything displayable—users annotate screen shots—thanks to *ScreenCrayons* (Olsen, Taufer, & Fails, 2004). Once created, annotations can be stored in the user's personal annotation repository, which is usually a hierarchy. Later on, a user can directly retrieve a particular annotation and its related document by browsing his/her annotation hierarchy, or by querying the system with keywords.

Social-Based Improvement

Nowadays, modern systems do not consider that users act alone any longer. Indeed, they are viewed as community members that can benefit from an identified group, and *vice versa*. Systems that are aware of such links between people can improve users' activities by providing specific tools. In this section, we describe how activities identified in the Information Searching Related Activities section are improved this way.

Active Reading Social Assistants
Annotation systems enable readers to formulate annotations such as comments about Web page contents. Annotations are attached to specific locations called "anchoring points," for example, a word or a paragraph. When they are stored on a dedicated annotation server, as in *Amaya* (Kahan et al., 2002) or *Pharos* (Bouthors & Dedieu, 2000), for example, they can be retrieved along with documents. Regarding privacy, users can specify annotations' visibility, for example, private, public, and restricted to some defined groups. Marshall and Brush (2004) have shown that public annotations are private ones at first. In fact, annotators have to reformulate them before

their publication. Indeed, provided that they have appropriate grants, readers can both read documents and associated annotations.

In their slightest form, annotations only consist in highlighted passages of documents. Considering that these passages reflect n users' interests, Marshall (1998) defines the "n-way consensus": it is a new document obtained by extracting the passages commonly highlighted by almost n readers. By relaxing the constraint on n, a user can progressively view passages that have been highlighted by less and less people. Therefore, users' annotations can be useful for identifying passages that have been judged as important by previous readers.

Considering a collective use, Wolfe and Neuwirth (2001) observed that annotations allow readers to provide feedback to writers or promote communication with collaborators, as well as to address remarks directed to future readers while authoring. Now, one may consider a comment of an annotation as subjective because it expresses the annotator's point of view. In order to allow readers to discuss documents in context, systems treat annotations as annotatable contents. Therefore, an annotation system can support asynchronous discussions within "discussion threads." A discussion thread is a hierarchy of annotations that is ordered by their timestamps, and rooted to its anchor, that is, a document.

Concretely, argumentative discussion can take place in the context of a document, thanks to argumentative annotations. Such annotations reflect readers' opinions, such as gradual confirmation or refutation. For example, annotations in the *Collate* project have been used by scientists for collaborative interpretation and indexation of movies (Thiel, Brocks, Frommholz, Dirsch-Weigand, Keiper, & Stein, et al., 2004). Since traditional visualization of annotations, by a specific icon, can clutter widely annotated documents, Cabanac et al. (Cabanac, Chevalier, Chrisment, & Julien, 2005) propose to evaluate the consensus of discussion threads for adapting their visualiza-

tion. Thus, users can ask for visually emphasized confirmed annotations rather than refuted ones, for example. Therefore, they can focus on ongoing conversations or on confirmed propositions that have been validated by people.

Document Management Social Assistants

Regarding personal bookmarks as a collective source of information has early been proposed by Keller et al. (Keller, Wolfe, Chen, Rabinowitz, & Mathe, 1997) with the *WebTagger* system, for example.

A new way for storing encountered documents is called "social bookmarking," as it also enables users to share them on the Internet. Indeed, we currently attend the growth of such numerous online services (Hammond, Hannay, Lund, & Scott, 2005), such as *OneView* (http://beta.oneview.de), the very popular *del.icio.us* (http://del.icio.us), or *Flickr* (http://www.flickr.com), for instance. Such services enable Internet users to store online documents' URLs along with a comment and one or more *tags*. A "tag" is a free-form text of the user's choosing; it aims at describing the document contents, for example, "chapter" and "social IR" may be used for describing this chapter.

In traditional library settings, indexing process consists in identifying a resource with a proper call number based on content. In contrast with this, social bookmarking users produce numerous labels for each resource, which can be content-based, usage-based, and so forth. The "social" aspect of these systems allows people to view *tags* associated to a particular document; they can also view every document associated to a given *tag*. For example, one can retrieve each document that people tagged with "computer science" via the http://del.icio.us/tag/computer+science URL. In fact, one can find interesting documents by browsing users' tags.

Social Document Sharing Assistants

Social bookmarking is a simple but effective way for sharing documents. In order to improve the efficiency of this approach, systems encourage users to reuse previously defined *tags*. Moreover, Golder and Huberman (2006) show that people tend to make uniform the names of the tags they create by employing singular words rather than plurals, for example. They also learn from others' naming patterns, leading them to employ tags that are often used, for example, "web2.0" *vs* "The Web 2." As a consequence, this kind of "tag convergence" helps users to find nuggets of information more easily.

"Collective intelligence" is a key concept of Web 2.0 that relies on information sharing within a community. However, general social book-marking services are too open for that; in order to gather contributions related to specific topics, community-based services have been needed. The most famous example may be the *Connotea* service (http://www.connotea.org) provided by the *Nature Publishing Group* since 2005. It has been designed for sharing scientific references between researchers (Lund, Hammond, Flack, & Hannay, 2005). For an industrial context, the *DogEar* system (Millen, Feinberg, & Kerr, 2006) allows employees at I.B.M. to tag and share resources, helping them to find experts on certain domains.

As seen before, more and more related activities are being developed in the field of information searching to help users, but most of the issues still concern future trends and need to be experimented.

CONCLUSION AND FUTURE TRENDS

Information seeking is based on many activities requiring many capabilities to be effective. Information retrieval systems are the main and the most powerful tools to find a needle in the haystack that corresponds to the Web. Indeed, the volume, the structure, the granularity, the validity of available information on the Web, cannot be manually handled. However, we can notice that many approaches have been provided to help a user during his/her search process. In the Web 2.0 context, collaborative tools that benefit from other users' experience progressively replace individual search assistants. The aim of the current Web 2.0 is to gather applications, services, and collective intelligence. While this evolution is not totally mature and widespread enough—one may describe it as a "beta" version—the next step of Web evolution is, according to Markoff (2006), already envisioned: the Web 3.0. New generation systems may harness semantics (such as ontologies) for understanding data, logics for deducing facts, users' profiles for personalized reasoning, extracting accurate data rather than documents from the Web ... This evolution joins the Semantic Web concepts mentioned since 1999 by Tim Berners-Lee, the creator of the original World Wide Web.

Unfortunately, most search assistants are not enough spread on the Web or even not accepted by users. Indeed, the information seeking process is split into multiple tools that do not communicate together, for example, a browsing accelerator, an external annotation system. Thus, users, who may not care for using many different tools together to find relevant information, are only interested in tools that quickly return a result, even if it is approximate or incomplete or sometimes non-relevant. However, the sole use of an information retrieval system without associating related activities like active reading, memorization ... may not be really effective because it is incomplete.

Therefore, integrated search assistants should not only mix query and browsing features, but also should incorporate annotating, memorizing, and sharing features. This limit is not really solved in the Web 2.0 context. Even if the Web is nowadays supporting more and more social or collective applications, the whole of activities in the search process are still independent and considered separately. The Web 2.0 evolution has also some limits. Social bookmarking systems, for instance, are based on users' active participation. Such participatory systems suffer from "free-riding" behaviors: when people only benefit from systems without really contributing to them. In order to limit this issue, observations of social psychology studies may be considered. For example, Ling et al. (Ling, Beenen, Ludford, Wang, Chang, Li et al.,2005) show that a person contributes more when he/she is aware that his/her contributions *i*) are judged useful by others and *ii*) are special, that is, nobody else could have contributed that way. Moreover, Wu et al. (Wu, Zhang, & Yu, 2006) underlines some limits of folksonomies, like the need to organize them when their number rises … One interesting drawback of such approaches is also the trend to uniformity. Indeed, to share information or tags, users have to use intelligible words and so, use the same terms as other users. For instance, a document may be tagged by the term "database" and not "db." This implies that systems should respect the user's point of view while providing powerful sharing capabilities. As a solution, such systems should manage two distinct user's "views" in order to respect these two aspects: a personal view and a social view. The personal view may be limited to the user who should be allowed to manage it as he/she likes.

Therefore, social approaches should not limit the user to any "social" correct way of thinking: a kind of single thought. Any user has its own "right to think" that is shared with others in the same or in a different form. Moreover, social approaches may motivate users to participate (Beenen, Ling, Wang, Chang, Frankowski, Resnick, et al., 2004), and may lead to limit "free-riding" penalizing behaviors.

Despite these drawbacks, social information retrieval must be developed to allow anyone to benefit from other users' experience. For instance, newbies should profit and learn from experts' experience. The modality is not really defined and everything is possible. To do that, users and their behavior have to be more detailed in users' profiles that represent the basis of search

assistants, being either individual or collective. On top of the accurate description of users, along with their needs, profiles may also integrate users' constrains. Indeed, the future of search assistants may be based on an improved adaptability of the search process. The adaptability may be seen at multiple levels. For example, the assistant must be task-oriented, and must take into account the time the user can spend for his/her search process. Moreover, it should adapt retrieved information to user's incapacities, language constraints, format constraints … Thus, in addition to be retrieved, relevant information will have to be adapted, transformed (e.g., from Microsoft Word's format to Adobe's PDF one), and extracted, to be really and efficiently exploited by the user. A first solution to such an adaptation may be seen through the widespread of Web services or more generally, services specifically selected in addition to the search engine to complete its capabilities. It may adapt the search process itself or the results to a specific user. As a conclusion, adaptation methods associated with the Semantic Web concepts could provide an open architecture through which, for instance, one could offer and describe services in the same way as it is done today for information.

REFERENCES

Abrams, D., Baecker, R., & Chignell, M. (1998). Information archiving with bookmarks: Personal Web space construction and organization. In *CHI '98: Proceedings of the SIGCHI Conference on Human Factors in Computing Systems* (pp. 41-48). New York, NY: ACM Press/A-W Publishing Co.

Adler, M. J., & van Doren, C. (1972). *How to read a book*. NY: Simon & Shuster.

Agosti, M. (1996). An overview of hypertext. In M. Agosti & A. F. Smeaton, *Information retrieval and hypertext* (pp. 27–47). Dordrecht: Kluwer Academic Publishers.

Agosti, M., & Ferro, N. (2005). Annotations as context for searching documents. In *CoLIS '05: Proceedings of the 5ᵗʰ International Conference on Conceptions of Library and Information Sciences* (pp. 155-170). *LNCS, 3507.* Springer.

Agosti, M., & Melucci, M. (2000). Information retrieval on the Web. In M. Agosti, F. Crestani, & G. Pasi (Eds.), *ESSIR 2000, Lecture Notes in Computer Science 1980* (pp. 242–285). Berlin: Springer Verlag.

Agosti, M., & Smeaton, A. F. (1996). *Information retrieval and hypertext.* Dordrecht: Kluwer Academic Publishers.

Armstrong, R., Freitag, D., & Joachims, T. (1995). Webwatcher: Machine learning and hypertext, In *Proceedings of the 1995 AAAI Spring Symposium on Information Gathering from Heterogeneous, Distributed Environments.* Palo Alto, CA: Stanford University.

Baeza-Yates, R., & Ribeiro-Neto, B. (1999). *Modern information retrieval.* Addison Wesley.

Balabanovic, M., & Shoham, Y. (1997). Fab: Content-based, collaborative recommendations. *Communications of the ACM, 40*(3), 66–72.

Barrett, R., Maglio, P. P., & Kellem D. C. (1997). How to personalize the Web. In *International ACM Conference on Human Factors and Computing Systems (CHI)*, Atlanta Georgia (pp 75-82).

Beenen, G., Ling, K., Wang, X., Chang, K., Frankowski, D., Resnick, P., & Kraut, R. E. (2004). Using social psychology to motivate contributions to online communities. In *CSCW '04: Proceedings of the 2004 ACM conference on Computer Supported Cooperative Work* (pp. 212–221). New York, NY: ACM Press.

Benford, S., Snowdon, D, Greenhalgh, C., Knox, I., & Brown, C. (1995). VR-Vibe: A virtual environment for cooperative information retrieval. *EuroGraphics, 14*(3), 349–360.

Bergman, M. K. (2001). The Deep Web: Surfacing the hidden value. *Journal of Electronic Publishing from the University of Michigan.* Retrieved January 10, 2007, from http://www.press.umich.edu/jep/07-01/bergman.html

Belkin, N. J., & Croft, W. B. (1992). Information filtering and information retrieval: Two sides of the same coin? *Communication of the ACM, 35*(12), 29-38.

Bharat, K., & Henzinger, M. (1998). Improved algorithms for topic distillation in a hyperlinked environment. In *Proceedings of the 21ᵗʰ Annual International ACM SIGIR Conference on Research and Development in Information Retrieval, Distributed Retrieval* (pp. 104-111).

Bottraud, J. C., Bisson, G., & Bruandet, M. F. (2003). An adaptive information research personnal assistant. In *Proceedings of the Workshop AI2IA (Artificial Intelligence, Information Access and Mobile Computing) IJCAI.*

Bouthors, V., & Dedieu, O. (1999). *Pharos, a cooperative infrastructure for Web knowledge sharing.* Technical report num. 3679, Institut de Recherche en Informatique et en Automatique (INRIA).

Breese, J. S., Heckerman, D., & Kadie, C. (1998). Empirical analysis of predictive algorithms for collaborative filtering. In *Proceedings of 14ᵗʰ Conference on Uncertainty in Artificial Intelligence (UAI'98)*, Wisconsin (pp. 43-52).

Brin, S., & Page, L. (1998). The anatomy of a large-scale hypertextual Web search engine. In *Proceedings of the 7ᵗʰ International World Wide Web Conference* (WWW7) (pp. 107-117).

Budzik, J., & Hammond, K. (1999). *Watson: Anticipating and contextualizing information needs.* Annual Meeting of the American Society for Information Science (ASIS), Washington.

Cabanac, G., Chevalier, M., Chrisment, C., & Julien, C. (2005). A social validation of collaborative annotations on digital documents. In J.-F. Boujut (Ed.), *International Workshop on Annotation for Collaboration* (pp. 31-40). Paris: Programme société de l'information, CNRS.

Carrière, J., & Kazman, R. (1997). WebQuery: Searching and visualizing the Web through connectivity. In *Proceedings of the 6ᵗʰ International World Wide Web Conference* (WWW6) (pp. 701-711).

Chen, C. (1999). The StarWalker virtual environment - An integrative design for social navigation. *Human-Computer Interaction: Communication, Cooperation, & Application Design, Proceedings of HCI International'99, the 8th International Conference on Human-Computer Interaction, 2* (pp. 207-211).

Chevalier, M., Chrisment, C., & Julien, C. (2004). Helping people searching the Web: Towards an adaptive and a social system. In P. Asaias & N. Karmakar (Eds.), *IADIS/WWW Internet 2004*.

Cho, Y. H., Kyeong, J., & Kim, S. H. (2002). A personalized recommender system based on Web usage mining and decision tree induction. *Expert System with Applications, 23*(3), 329 –342.

Cutting, D. R., Karger, D. R., & Pederson, J. O. (1993). Constant interaction-time scatter/gather browsing of very large document collections. In *14ᵗʰ International ACM SIGIR Conference on Research and Development in Information Retrieval* (pp 121-131).

Dömel, P. (1994). Webmap - A graphical hypertext navigation tool. *2ⁿᵈ International World Wide Web Conference* (pp. 785-798).

Dreilinger, D., & Howe, A. E. (1997). Experiences with selecting search engines using metasearch. *ACM Transactions on Information Systems, 15*(3), 195 –222.

Fidel, R., Bruce, H., Pejtersen, A. M., Dumais, S., Grudin, J., & Poltrock, S. (2000). Collaborative information retrieval (CIR). *The New Review of Information Behaviour Research* (pp. 235-247).

Fraenkel, A. S., & Klein, S. T. (1999). Information retrieval from annotated texts. *J. Am. Soc. Inf. Sci., 50*(10), 845-854.

Frommholz, I., & Fuhr, N. (2006). Probabilistic, object-oriented logics for annotation-based retrieval in digital libraries. In *JCDL '06: Proceedings of the 6ᵗʰ ACM/IEEE-CS Joint Conference on Digital Libraries* (pp. 55-64). New York: ACM Press.

Garfield, E. (1972). Citation analysis as a tool in journal evaluation. *Science, 178*(4060), 471-479. Retrieved from http://www.garfield.library.upenn. edu/essays/V1p527y1962-73.pdf

Godoy D., & Amandi A. (2006). Modeling user interests by conceptual clustering. *Information Systems, 31*(4), 247–265.

Goldberg, D., Nichols, D., Oki, B. M., & Terry, D. (1992). Using collaborative filtering to weave an information tapestry. *Communication of the ACM, Information Filtering, 35*(12), 61–70.

Golder, S. A., & Huberman, B. A. (2006). Usage patterns of collaborative tagging systems. *Journal of Information Science, 32*(2), 198-208.

Good, N., Schafer, J., Konstan, J., Borchers, A., Sarwar, B., Herlocker, J., & Riedl, J. (1999). Combining collaborative filtering with personnal agents for better recommendations. In *Proceeding of AAAI, AAAI Press, 35*, 439-446.

Gravano, L., Garcia-Molina, H., & Tomasic, A. (1999). GloSS: Text-source discovery over the Internet. *ACM Transactions on Database Systems, 24*(2), 229-264.

GVU. (1999). *10th WWW user survey. Graphic, visualisation & usability center (GVU)*. Retrieved January 10, 2007, from http://www.gvu.gatech. edu/user_surveys/survey-1998-10/

Haase, P., Stojanovic, N., Sure, Y., & Völker, J. (2005). On personalized information retrieval in semantics-based peer-to-peer systems. In *Proceedings of the BTW-Workshop "WebDB Meets IR."* Retrieved January 10, 2007, from http://www.aifb.uni-karlsruhe.de/WBS/ysu/publications/2005_webdbir.pdf

Hammond, T., Hannay, T., Lund, B., & Scott, J. (2005). Social bookmarking tools (I): A general review. *D-Lib Magazine, 11*(4).

Hansen, P., & Järvelin, K. (2005). Collaborative information retrieval in an information-intensive domain. *Information Processing & Management Journal, 41*(2005), 1101–1119.

Hascoët, M. (2000). A user interface combining navigation aids. In *Proceedings of the 11th International ACM Hypertext Conference* (pp 224-225).

Hauffe, H. (1994). Is citation analysis a tool for evaluation of scientific contributions? In *13th Winterworkshop on Biochemical and Clinical Aspects of Pteridines*. Retrieved January 10, 2007, from http://www.uibk.ac.at/ub/ueber_uns/publikationen/hauffe_is_citation_analysis_a_tool.html

Herlocker, J. L., Konstan, A. J., Borchers, A., & Riedl, J. (1999). An algorithmic framework for performing collaborative filtering. In *Proceedings of the 22nd International ACM Conference on Research and Development in Information Retrieval* (SIGIR'99) (pp. 230-237).

Herlocker, J. L., Konstan, A. J., Terveen, L., & Riedl, J. (2004). Evaluating collaborative filtering recommender systems. *ACM Transactions on Information Systems (TOIS), 22* (1), 5-53.

Hetzler, B., Harris, W. M., Havre, S., & Whitney P. (1999). Visualizing the full spectrum of document relationships. In *5th International Conference of the International Society for Knowledge Organization (ISKO)* (pp. 168–175).

Hölscher, C., & Strube, G. (2000). Web search behavior of Internet experts and newbies. In *Proceedings of the 9th International World Wide Web Conference on Computer Networks: The International Journal of Computer and Telecommunications Networking* (pp. 337-346). Amsterdam: North-Holland Publishing Co.

Ide, E. (1971). New experiments in information retrieval. In G. Salton, (Ed.), *The SMART retrieval system – Experiments in automatic document processing* (pp. 337–354). Englewood Cliffs, NJ: Prentice Hall, Inc.

Jackson, H. J. (2002). *Marginalia: Readers writing in books*. Yale University Press.

Jaczynski M., & Trousse B. (1997). Broadway: A World Wide Web browsing advisor reusing past navigations from a group of users. In *Proceedings of the 3rd UK Case-Based Reasoning Workshop (UKCBR'97)*.

Jansen, B. J., Spink, A., & Saracevic. T. (2000). Real life, real users and reals needs: A study and analysis of users queries on the Web. *Information Processing & Management Journal, 36*(2), 207–227.

Jin, H., Ning, X., & Chen, H. (2006). Efficient search for peer-to-peer information retrieval using semantic small world. In *Proceedings of the 15th International Conference on World Wide Web* (pp. 1003-1004). NY: ACM Press.

Jin, R., Chai, J. Y., & Si, L., (2004). An automatic weighting scheme for collaborative filtering. In *Proceedings of the 27th International ACM Conference on Research and Development in Information Retrieval*. SIGIR'04 (pp. 337-344).

Jones, W., Phuwanartnurak, A. J., Gill, R., & Bruce, H. (2005). Don't take my folders away!: Organizing personal information to get things done. In *CHI '05: CHI '05 extended abstracts on Human factors in computing systems* (pp. 1505-1508). New York, NY: ACM Press.

Kahan, J., Koivunen, M.-R., Prud'Hommeaux, E., & Swick, R. R. (2002). Annotea: An open rdf infrastructure for shared Web annotations. *Computer Networks, 32*(5), 589-608.

Karamuftuoglu, M., (1999). Collaborative information retrieval: Towards a social informatics view of IR interaction. *Journal of the American Society for Information Science, 49*(12), 1070–1080.

Kautz, H., Selman, B., & Shah, M. (1997). ReferralWeb: Combining social networks and collaborative filtering. *Commun. ACM, 40*(3), 63–65.

Kaye, J. J., Vertesi, J., Avery, S., Dafoe, A., David, S., Onaga, L., Rosero, I., & Pinch, T. (2006). To have and to hold: Exploring the personal archive. In *CHI '06: Proceedings of the SIGCHI conference on Human Factors in computing systems* (pp. 275-284). New York, NY: ACM Press.

Keller, R. M., Wolfe, S. R., Chen, J. R., Rabinowitz, J. L., & Mathe, N. (1997). A bookmarking service for organizing and sharing URLs. In *Selected papers from the 6th International Conference on World Wide Web* (pp. 1103-1114). Essex, UK: Elsevier Science Publishers Ltd.

Kleinberg, J. M. (1999). Authoritative sources in a hyperlinked environment. In *Proceedings of the 19th Annual ACM-SIAM Symposium on Discrete Algorithms* (pp. 668-677).

Klemm, F., & Aberer, K. (2005). Aggregation of a term vocabulary for peer-to-peer information retrieval: A DHT stress test. In *Proceedings of the Third International Workshop on Databases, Information Systems and Peer-to-Peer Computing* (DBISP2P 2005).

Konstan, J. A., Miller, B. N., Maltz, D., Herlocker, J. L., Gordon, L. R., & Riedl, J. (1997). Grouplens: Applying collaborative filtering to usenet news. *Communications of the ACM, 40*(3), 77–87.

Korfhage, R. R. (1997). *Information storage and retrieval.* Wiley computer publishing.

Krulwich, B. (1997). Lifestyle finder: Intelligent user profiling using large-scale demographic data. *AI Magazine, 18*(2), 37-45.

Kwok, S. H. (2006). P2P searching trends: 2002-2004. *Information Management and Processing Journal, 42*(1), 237-247.

Le Grand, B., & Soto, M. (2005). Topic maps, RDF graphs and ontologies visualization. In V. Geroimenko & C. Chen (Eds.), *Visualizing the semantic Web* (2nd ed.). Springer.

Leouski, A. V., & Croft, W. B. (1996). *An evaluation of techniques for clustering search results, Technical Report IR-76.*

Lieberman, H. (1995). Letizia: An agent that assists Web browsing. *In Proceedings of the IJCAI* (pp. 924-929).

Ling, K., Beenen, G., Ludford, P., Wang, X., Chang, K., Li, X., Cosley, D., Frankowski, D., Rashid, L. T. A. M., Resnick, P., & Kraut, R. (2005). Using social psychology to motivate contributions to online communities. *Journal of Computer-Mediated Communication, 10*(4), 10.

Liu, M. (1993). The complexities of citation practice: A review of citation studies. *Journal of Documentation, 49*(4), 370–408.

Lund, B., Hammond, T., Flack, M., & Hannay, T. (2005). Social bookmarking tools (II): A case study - Connotea. *D-Lib Magazine, 11*(4).

Maglio, P. P., Barrett, R., Campbell, C. S., & Selker, T. (2000). SUITOR: An attentive information system. *International ACM Conference on Intelligent User Interfaces (IUI)* (pp. 169-176).

Malone, T. W., Grant, K. R., Turbak, F. A., Brobst, S. A., & Cohen M. D. (1987). Intelligent information sharing systems. *Communications of the ACM, 30*(5), 390–402.

Markoff, J. (2006). Entrepreneurs see a Web guided by common sense. *The New-York Times*, November 12, 2006.

Marshall, C. C., (1999). Toward an ecology of hypertext annotation. In *HYPERTEXT '98: Proceedings of the 9th ACM conference on Hypertext and hypermedia* (pp. 40-49). New York, NY: ACM Press.

Marshall, C. C., & Brush, A. J. B. (2004). Exploring the relationship between personal and public annotations. In *JCDL '04: Proceedings of the 4th ACM/IEEE-CS Joint Conference on Digital Librarie*, (pp. 349–357). New York, NY: ACM Press.

Mechkour, M., Harper, D. J., & Muresan G., (1999). The Webcluster project: Using clustering for mediating access to the World Wide Web. In *Proceedings of the 21st International ACM SIGIR Conference on Research and development in Information Retrieval* (pp. 357-358), August 24-28, 1998.

Memmi, D., & Nérot, O. (2003). Building virtual communitites for information retrieval. In Favela & D. Decouchant (Eds), *GroupWare: Design, implementation and use.* Berlin: Springer.

Millen, D. R., Feinberg, J., & Kerr, B. (2006). Dogear: Social bookmarking in the enterprise. In *CHI '06: Proceedings of the SIGCHI Conference on Human Factors in Computing Systems* (pp. 111-120). New York, NY: ACM Press.

Milojicic, D. S., Kalogeraki, V., Lukose, R., Nagaraja, K., Pruyne, J., Richard, B., Rollins, S., & Xu., Z. (2002). *Peer-to-peer computing.* Technical Report HPL-2002-57, HP Lab.

Montaner, M., Lopez, B., & Rosa, J. L. D. L. (2003). A taxonomy of recommender agents on the internet. *Artificial Intelligence Review, 19*, 285-330.

Olsen, D. R. J., Taufer, T., & Fails, J. A. (2004). ScreenCrayons: Annotating anything. In *UIST '04: Proceedings of the 17th Annual ACM symposium on User Interface Software and Technology* (pp. 165-174). New York, NY: ACM Press.

Pazzani, M. (1999). A framework for collaborative, content-based and demographic filtering. *Artificial Intelligence Review, 13*(5-6), 393-408.

Pazzani, M., Muramatsu, J. and Billsus, D., (1996). Syskill & Webert: Identifying interesting Web sites. In *Proceedings of the Thirteenth National Conference on Artificial Intelligence* (pp. 54-61).

Pejtersen, A. M., & Fidel, R. (1999). *A framework for centred evaluation and design: a case study of information retrieval on the Web.* Working paper for mira workshop, Grenoble, France. Retrieved January 10, 2007, from http://www.dcs.gla.ac.uk/mira/workshops/nancy/amprf.html

Pemberton, D., Rodden, T., & Procter, R. (2000). GroupMark: A WWW recommander system combining coopérative and information filtering. In *Proceedings of the 6th ERCIM Workshop "User Interfaces for All"*.

Prekop, P. (2002). A qualitative study of collaborative information seeking. *Journal of Documentation, 58*(5), 533–547.

Price, M. N., Schilit, B. N., & Golovchinsky, G., (1999). Xlibris: The active reading machine. In *CHI '98 Conference Summary on Human Factors in Computing Systems* (pp. 22-23). ACM Press.

Rocchio, J. J. (1971). Relevance feedback in information retrieval. In G. Salton (Ed.), *The SMART retrieval system - Experiments in automatic document processing* (pp. 313-323). Englewood Cliffs, NJ: Prentice Hall, Inc.

Röscheisen, M., Mogensen, C., & Winograd, T. (1994). *Shared Web annotations as a platform for third-party value-added, information providers : Architecture, protocols, & usage examples.* Technical report CSDTR/DLTR, Stanford, CA.

Rücker, J., & Polanco, M. J. (1997). Siteseer: Personalized navigation for the Web. *Communications of the ACM, 40*(3), 73–75.

Salton, G., & Buckley, C. (1990). Improving retrieval performance by relevance feedback. *Journal of the American Society for Information Science, 41*(4), 288–297.

Samulowitz M., Michahelles F., & Linhoff-Popien C. (2001). Capeus: An architecture for context-aware selection and execution of services. In *New developments in distributed applications and interoperable systems* (pp. 23–39).

Sannomiya, T., Amagasa, T., Yoshikawa, M., & Uemura, S. (2001). A framework for sharing personal annotations on Web resources using XML. In *ITVE '01: Proceedings of the Workshop on Information Technology for Virtual Enterprises* (pp. 40-48). Washington, DC: IEEE Computer Society.

Savoy, J., & Picard, J. (2001). Retrieval effectiveness on the Web. *Information Processing & Management Journal, Elsevier Science, 37*(4), 543–569.

Sellen, A. J., & Harper, R. H., (2003). *The myth of the paperless office.* Cambridge, MA: MIT Press.

Shapira, B., Shoval, P., & Hanani, U. (1997). Stereotypes in information filtering systems. *Information Processing & Management, 33*(3), 273–287.

Shneiderman, B. (1999). *Designing the user interface.* Addison-Wesley.

Sidler, G., Scott A., & Wolf H. (1997). Collaborative browsing in the World Wide Web. In *Proceedings of the 8th Joint European Networking Conference.*

Sonnenwald, D., & Pierce, L. G. (2000). Information behaviour in dynamic group work contexts: Interwoven situational awareness dense social networks and contested collaboration in command and control. *Information Processing and Managemnt. 36*(3), 461–479.

Talja, S. (2002). Information sharing in academic communities: Types and levels of collaboration in information seeking and use. *New Review of Information Behaviour Research,* 3, 143-159.

Teevan, J., Dumais, S. T., & Horvitz, E. (2005). Personalizing search via automated analysis of interests and activities. In *Proceedings of the 28th Annual International ACM SIGIR Conference on Research and Development in Information Retrieval* (pp. 449-456). ACM Press.

Thiel, U., Brocks, H., Frommholz, I., Dirsch-Weigand, A., Keiper, J., Stein, A., & Neuhold, E. J. (2004). COLLATE - A collaboratory supporting research on historic European films. *Int. J. Digit. Libr.,* I(1), 8-12.

Wexelblat, A., & Pattie M. (1999). Footprints: History-rich tools for information foraging. ACM SIGCHI Conference on Human Factors in Computing Systems. In *CHI'99 Proceedings.* ACM Press.

Wolfe, J. L., & Neuwirth, C. M. (2001). From the margins to the center - The future of annotation. *Journal of Business and Technical Communication, 15*(3), 333–371.

Wood, A., Drew, N., Beale, R., & Hendley, B. (1995). Hyperspace: Web browsing with visualisation. In *Proceedings of the 3rd International World Wide Web Conference (WWW3)* (pp. 21-25).

Wu, J., & Aberer, K. (2004). Using SiteRank for decentralized computation of Web document ranking. In *Adaptive hypermedia and adaptive Web-based systems, LNCS 3137*: 265-274.

Wu, X., Zhang, L., & Yu, Y. (2006). Exploring social annotations for the semantic Web. In *WWW '06: Proceedings of the 15th International Conference on World Wide Web* (pp. 417–426). New York, NY: ACM Press.

Yager, R. R. (2002). Fuzzy logic methods in recommender systems. *Fuzzy sets and Systems, 136*(2), 133–149.

Yang, B., & Garcia-Molina, H. (2002). Improving search in peer-to-peer networks. In *Proceedings of the 22nd International Conference on Distributed Computing Systems* (pp. 5-14).

Zamir, O. (1999). *Visualisation of search results in document retrieval systems.* General Examination, University of Washington, 1998.

ADDITIONAL READING

Axelrod, R. (Ed.) (1997). *The complexity of cooperation.* Princeton University Press.

Baeza-Yates, R., & Ribeiro-Neto, B. (1999). *Modern information retrieval.* Addison Wesley.

Bair, J. H., (1989). Supporting cooperative work with computers: Addressing meeting mania. *IEEE Computer*, (4), 208-217.

Baum, E. (1989). A proposal for more powerful learning algorithms. *Neural Computation, 1,* 201-207.

Booker, L., Goldberg, D., & Holland, J. (1989). Classifier systems and genetic algorithms. *Artificial Intelligence Journal, 40,* 235-282.

Chen, C. (2006). *Information visualization – Beyond the horizon.* Springer.

Dewan, P. (1999). A technical overview of CSCW. Tutorial. *ACM Computer-Supported Cooperative Work* (CSCW'98), Seattle.

Engel, A., & Van Den Broeck, C. (2001). *Statistical mechanics of learning.* Cambridge University Press.

Hammond, T., Hannay, T., Lund, B., & Scott, J. (2005). Social bookmarking tools (I): A general review. *D-Lib Magazine, 11*(4).

Hansen, P., & Järvelin, K. (2005). Collaborative information retrieval in an information-intensive domain. *Information Processing & Management Journal, 41*(2005), 1101 –1119.

Lauwers, J. C., & Lentz, L. A. (1990). Collaboration awareness in support of collaboration transparency: Requirements for the next generation of shared Windows systems. In *Conference on Computer Human Interaction CHI'90* (pp. 303-311).

Montaner, M., Lopez, B., & Rosa, J. L. D. L. (2003). A taxonomy of recommender agents on the Internet. *Artificial Intelligence Review, 19,* 285-330.

Salton, G., & Buckley, C. (1990). Improving retrieval performance by relevance feedback. *Journal of the American Society for Information Science, 41*(4), 288–297.

Savoy, J., & Picard, J. (2001). Retrieval effectiveness on the Web. *Information Processing & Management Journal, 37*(4), 543–569.

Tindale, R. S., & Kameda, T. (2000). "Social sharedness" as a unifying theme for information processing in groups. *Group Processes & Intergroup Relations, 3*(2), 123-140.

Wasserman, S., & Faust, K. (1994). *Social network analysis – Methods and application.* Cambridge University Press.

Zamir, O. (1999). *Visualisation of search results in document retrieval systems.* General Examination, University of Washington, 1998.

KEY TERMS

Annotation: Composed of metadata, that is, objective information (author, publication date, anchor ...) and subjective information (formulated by users for instance). A commentary, a critique can be considered as annotations.

Browsing: A search modality. When browsing, users discover documents through the hyperlinks they follow. They do not know how the information is organized.

Collective Intelligence: Emerges from a collective work through which everyone participates and gains from the group. It can also be called "Community of practice."

Collective Search Assistants: An evolution of search assistants. Techniques used are "social," that is to say that expertise and knowledge are shared between users. Everyone gains from the mass crowd (i.e., collaborative filtering). See also *Collective Intelligence*.

Document: It is one kind of knowledge supports. It stores knowledge that is articulated through information.

Querying: When querying the Web, users have to transform their information needs into a synthetic list of terms: a query. Thanks to this query, the search engine displays most relevant information to the user. A search engine can only return information that has previously been indexed.

Search Assistant: Features adaptive functionalities in order to help a user to achieve a more effective information search task. Individuals are using search engines like Google, Yahoo! … to query the Web.

User Profile: Can be considered as a user's model. It characterizes user behaviors, information needs, relationships with others … It is used by adaptive techniques that make it evolve in order to keep it up to date.

Chapter XVII
Twin Wiki Wonders?
Wikipedia and Wikibooks as Powerful Tools for Online Collaborative Writing

Meng-Fen Grace Lin
University of Houston, USA

Curtis J. Bonk
Indiana University, USA

Suthiporn Sajjapanroj
Indiana University, USA

ABSTRACT

Web 2.0 technologies empower individuals to contribute thoughts and ideas rather than passively survey online content and resources. Such participatory environments foster opportunities for community building and knowledge sharing, while encouraging the creation of artifacts beyond what any single person could accomplish alone. In this chapter, we investigate the emergence and growth of two of such environments: the highly popular Wikipedia site and its sister project, Wikibooks. Wikipedia has grown out of trends for free and open access to Web tools and resources. While Wikipedians edit, contribute, and monitor distinct pieces of information or pages of documents, Wikibookians must focus on larger chunks of knowledge, including book modules or chapters as well as entire books. Several key differences between these two types of wiki environments are explored. In addition, surveys and interviews, conducted with Wikibookians, shed light on their challenges, frustrations, and successes.

INTRODUCTION

Thomas Friedman, in his 2005 book, *The World is Flat*, talks about 10 forces that have flattened the world in terms of economic globalization. The word "flat" acts as a metaphor to symbolize the "leveled" playing field on a global scale. In Friedman's (2005) view, when the playing field is leveled, everyone can take part. And he means everyone! Talking from a business perspective, Friedman charts the progress of globalization from what he describes as 1.0 to 3.0. Globalization 1.0 focused on country to country relationships, such as treaties and trade. In Globalization 2.0, such relationships moved down to a company-to-company level. We are now entering an age of Globalization 3.0, where the rise of the individual comes into focus. It is in this third phase of globalization, wherein individuals obtain new powers and freedoms to participate socially, economically, politically, and educationally with others around the world. *Time Magazine* recognized this trend, and in 2006 named "You" as the person of the year (Time Magazine, 2006/2007). In effect, the Year 2006 signified the trend toward empowering technology users with what was called Web 2.0 technologies, which allowed individuals to generate ideas online instead of just reading and browsing through someone else's Web pages (Grossman, 2006/2007a, 2006/2007b).

Lessig (2005) called this phenomenon the "read-write Web," to contrast the read-only Web, where users were merely passive consumers of information. Most fundamentally, the read-write Web dramatically enhances the power of individuals, and fosters a participatory culture of building, tinkering, learning, and sharing (Brown, 2006). Typically included in Web 2.0 technology lists are wikis, podcasts, blogs, online photo albums, and virtual worlds such as Second Life. In particular, wikis offer an innovative mechanism of computer-supported collaboration. This highly unique social phenomenon utilizes armies of volunteers who work without pay, recognition, or much acclaim to continually contribute, update, or edit resources online (Lin, 2006).

In this chapter, we primarily offer insights into the recent emergence of two wiki developments; namely, Wikipedia and Wikibooks. First, we detail what a wiki is. Subsequently, we briefly review existing wiki-related research, and then document the emergence and growth of what is the most popular wiki today; Wikipedia. After presenting our research findings in Wikibooks, we compare and contrast some of the underlying principles and features of Wikipedia to those found in Wikibooks.

BACKGROUND

Brandon Hall (2006) defines a wiki as "a collection of Web pages that can be easily viewed and modified by anyone, providing a means for sharing and collaboration." These are open-ended, generative, and unstructured environments (Honegger, 2005; Leuf & Cunningham, 2001; Lio, Fraboni, Leo, 2005). Pioneered by Ward Cunningham in 1995, wikis are online spaces for recording information, sharing knowledge, typically in collaboration with others. Each modification is recorded as the history of a document. The history page records the time of change, the person who made the change, and the changes that were made. Such a mechanism not only permits page retraction by anyone, it also behaves as a podium for reputation management. In addition, the history page permits open examinations of each revision, allowing each version to be compared and contrasted by anyone.

Many universities have picked up the wiki fever and started using its functions for information sharing. For example, Stanford has an institutionalized wiki wherein students can contribute information on places to eat, workout, study, socialize, and so forth. (Campus Technology, 2006b). As this Web site indicates, there is now a wave of student-contributed wiki resources. Similarly, MIT has created the Center for Collective Intelligence, where people from around the planet could come and solve huge scientific, social, and business problems (Campus Technology, 2006a). The underlying belief of these wiki projects indicates that, collectively, the human race can act more powerfully than it can at an individual level. As a prime example of this principle, in early February, 2007, Penguin books announced "*A Million Penguins,*" a Web site "where people from around the planet will help write a novel" (Reuters, 2007). Similarly, in the academic world, faculty at MIT and Wharton School of Business invited thousands of individuals or potential authors to help write a collaborative online textbook at the site "*We are Smarter than Me*" (Campus Technology, 2007).

There is scant academic research on wiki technology and resources even though we are in the midst of a proliferation of wiki-based projects. In particular, the research on Wikibooks, which emerged with much enthusiasm in 2003 (Wikibooks, 2007a), is particularly thin. Some Wikipedia-related research has explored the accuracy of the content (Lih, 2004; Rosenzweig, 2006), historical flow visualizations of contributions (Viegas, Wattenburg, & Dave, 2004), the formality of the language used (Emigh & Herrring, 2005), hackers and trolls (Schachaf & Hara, 2006), contributions within collaborative authoring environments (Korfiatis, Poulous, & Bokos, 2006), differences between experts and novices (Bryant, Forte, & Bruckman, 2005), and cultural differences in Wikipedia contributions and editing behaviors (Pfeil, Zaphiris, & Ang, 2006). Such studies are, of course, just the starting point for a long line of research on wikis.

A BRIEF HISTORY OF THE BRIEF HISTORY OF WIKIPEDIA

Wikipedia is a free online encyclopedia to which anyone can contribute. Created in January 2001,

Wikipedia started out as a side experiment of a failing project called Nupedia.com, created by Larry Sanger and Jimmy Wales, that also aimed to create a free online encyclopedia. However, Nupedia.com employed a traditional prepublishing review process that demanded an elaborate and often long procedure of coordination among submission, reviewing, and negotiation. Few articles were published as a result of this arduous process. Wikipedia was created as an experiment to bypass this prepublishing review process and empower the postpublication, real-time, peer-review procedure among volunteer collaborators (Ciffolilli, 2003; Voss, 2005).

Today, Wikipedia is perhaps the largest instance of a wiki. With easy to explore and open technology at its core, Wikipedia quickly became an online volunteer community with its devotion to the creation of a free encyclopedia where the division of labor is facilitated by information technology. That volunteer community now includes more than 50,000 individuals who have made at least 10 contributions to Wikipedia (Rosenzweig, 2006).

According to Alexa, a Web ranking service, as of February 7th, 2007, Wikipedia had become the 12th most visited Web site across all languages (alexa.com, 2007). During the past 6 years, Wikipedia has enjoyed tremendous, if not exponential, growth in terms of registered users, number of articles, and number of languages. Not surprisingly, Wikipedia quickly overshadowed Nupedia.com and caused Nupedia.com to close in 2002. As of February 2007, the combined Wikipedia site included articles in 250 languages, 6.4 million articles, and almost 3.5 million contributors (Wikipedia, 2007d). The English language version of Wikipedia continues to be the largest site at more than 1,624,000 articles, while some other language versions remain quite small (Wikipedia, 2007b, Wikipedia, 2007c). There are more than 300,000 articles in German, French, Polish, and Japanese languages, with the German Wikipedia site now pushing over 500,000. This is an impressive amount of work to accomplish since inception 6 years ago. It is also quite obvious that a vast number of willing volunteers awaited just such an opportunity to contribute their time and knowledge.

Wikipedia's exceptional growth was perhaps best captured and described by Voss (2005), who conducted one of the first quantitative analyses of the structure of Wikipedia. From the elaborated numbers, charts, and mathematic formulas, Voss presented a comprehensive picture of the overall Wikipedia community. As would be expected, Wikipedia experienced a period of linear growth, while the more spiked or exponential growth that is often alluded to in the media did not occur until about 15 months after inception in April 2002. Since that time, the number of new articles in Wikipedia has increased at various speeds among different languages. Even though anyone with Internet access on this planet is invited to contribute to Wikipedia, according to the Voss study, the average number of authors per article remains four to five, a number that is perhaps much lower than most people would assume. Even more interesting is that about half (48%) of the articles had less than five authors and about one-third (28%) of the articles in German Wikipedia had only been edited by one author. In addition, one-third of the Wikipedia authors had only contributed one article, and just one in five Wikipedians had been involved in more than 16 articles. Granted that Voss excluded anonymous edits in his calculation, these numbers indicate that not everyone will contribute, or at least continue to contribute, just because they can.

In summary, then, the Wikipedia community has the following characteristics. It is a volunteer-based project to which everyone can contribute. Wiki technology facilitates certain divisions of labor, enables the ease of contributing and participation, and records all change histories for easy examination and recovery. It is a rapidly growing community where authority is gained through individuals' active participation. Its social structure does not necessarily recognize people based on their expertise, even though it does employ a promotion mechanism for various roles in the community. Positioning itself as an encyclopedia, Wikipedia inherits the perception of being a reliable reference source. However, its credibility continues to be questioned.

WIKIBOOKS AND OTHER WIKI SITES

Sister projects to Wikipedia coordinated by the Wikimedia Foundation include Wikibooks, mentioned previously, as well as Wikispecies, Wikiquote, Wikinews, Wikiversity, Wiktionary, Wikisource, Commons, and Meta-Wiki. Wiktionary, for instance, is a free, community created online dictionary and thesaurus with more than 300,000 entries in nearly 400 different languages (Wiktionary, 2007). Wikiquotes contains an index of thousands of quotations from famous people from Laozi, William Shakespeare, Aristotle, Hellen Keller, and Martin Luther King, as well as from literacy works, television shows and movies, news pages, and other creative efforts (Wikiquotes, 2007). Wikinews, like other online news services, contains current events making headlines. But as folks like Rosenzweig (2006) point out, it often can break leading stories before the other news services since its reporters cover the planet.

In our own work, Wikibooks has been the primary focus. The Wikibooks Web site, originally named the Wikimedia Free Textbook Project and Wikimedia Textbooks, was initiated on July 10, 2003 (Wikibooks, 2007a). It was the brainstorm of Karl Wick, who was searching for a place to host his books on organic chemistry and physics as a means to bring such educational resources to the people of this planet while addressing the high costs and other limitations of existing books and materials on these topics. By the end of that month, there were 123 modules or chapters posted and

47 registered users at that site. Two months later, there were 530 modules and 150 registered users. Since it began, controversies and criticisms have been posed regarding the scope of the Wikibook project, copyright and licensing issues, the quality of the books posted, and the large number of unfinished book projects.

The coordinator of one or more Wikibook projects is called a Wikibookian. Given that in less than 4 years Wikibooks has become a collection of over 1,000 free online book projects containing more than 20,000 modules or chapters (Wikibooks, 2007b), there are many active Wikibookians. The Wikibooks Web site contains collaboratively written textbooks and nonfiction books, study guides, and booklets are socially negotiated documents. There are both books for adult learners as well as the more recent emergence of junior books for younger learners, ages 8 to 11 (Wikibooks, 2007c) (see Figure 1). The junior Wikibooks site is currently creating full-color booklets on topics such as bugs, big cats, the kings and queens of England, and dinosaurs.

Such environments offer hope for someday providing access to educational books, study guides, and other documents to every connected learner and in any language. Nevertheless, there are myriad issues, questions, and problems related to online collaboratively authored books, such as those found at the Wikibooks site, that need to be better understood. Figure 2 depicts the key aspects of the Wikibook environment.

Studying Wikibookians

During a 4-month period in early 2006, we observed how Wikibookians communicated and shared ideas with each other. Based on our observations and literature review, we designed a close-ended survey that encompassed basic demographic data, as well as a set of questions geared toward issues involved in the process of

Figure 1. Screen shot of the Wikibooks Web site.

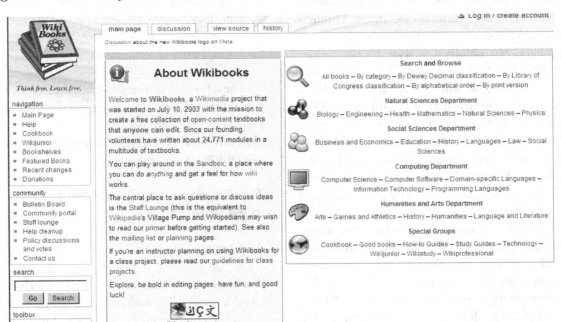

Figure 2. The Wikibook environment

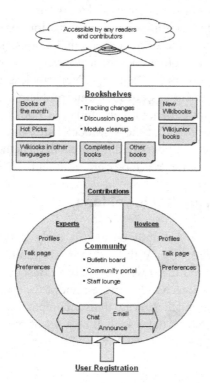

After tallying the surveys, we randomly selected 15 people from the survey respondents for follow-up e-mail interviews. The e-mails were sent in July 2006, and eight Wikibookian participants joined this part of the study. Participants were asked to answer a 12-question e-mail interview related to how they had started in Wikibooks, previous experiences in such an online collaboration process, the future of Wikibooks, advantages and disadvantages of this environment, whether an online book could ever be complete, and suggestions for improvement.

FINDINGS

The survey and interview data helped us understand the challenges, frustrations, and successes of Wikibookians. From the 8 participants and 12 e-mail interview questions, five key themes emerged. These themes were as follows:

1. The expression of authority in Wikibooks
2. The nature of collaboration process in Wikibooks
3. Completeness and success of one's Wikibook project
4. Advice to Wikibook wannabes
5. The future of Wikibooks

The following sections describe the themes and present the different views participants offered. Based on these findings, as well as existing wiki literature, we offer a comparison of the Wikipedia and Wikibook environments.

The Expression of Authority in Wikibooks

Authority

Working on a wiki as an editable Web platform could be rewarding and challenging at the same time. The number one critique of Wikipedia has

creating a Wikibook from a sociocultural point of view (Bruns & Humphreys, 2005). Through communication channels frequented by active members, we obtained a user list providing around 45,000 Wikibookian's names who had previously registered an account at the Wikibook Web site. Using this list, in the spring of 2006, we randomly sent survey invitations to around 1,500 Wikibookians whose status was shown as active via the contacting function found at the Wikibook Web site. We used an online survey tool, SurveyShare, to distribute the survey and collect the data. We received 80 responses to our survey. Ninety percent of the survey respondents had been active in Wikibooks for more than 6 months, 72% for more than one year, and nearly one-third for 2 years or more. In addition, 82% were under age 35, 97% were men, and more than half did not have a four-year college degree (Sajjapanroj, Bonk, Lee, & Lin, 2007).

been its authoritative value. It is not surprising that such questions and concerns about authority also appeared in our Wikibook findings. Some participants seemed to disregard the traditional view of an "expert" or authority:

...people can work together on a wiki and come up with a result that is better than something written by one or a couple of "experts." ...There is not one person in charge who can make the hard decisions that everyone will respect. (Participant 1)

Nevertheless, some seemed to also demand the skill of "experts" in order to create a good quality book:

I expected it to be not very effective, as it's hard to let people work together at all, especially on this large amount, and even more when it's spread over multiple pages with a special subject. You should need at least two specialists, as both have to understand the subject very good. That appeared to be hard indeed. (Participant 6)

Wikibookian views about community or multiple contributor authority over the knowledge of "experts" revealed the nontraditional belief that each one of us possesses our unique knowledge that could contribute to the creation of a Wikibook. On the other hand, there seemed to be a demand for such knowledge to be able to qualify at an acceptable level as an expert.

Control

If looking at the issue of authority at a deeper level, we further discovered the concerns regarding control over contribution. Who has the right to contribute? Who can decide who has the right to contribute? Who can decide whose contribution is superior to others? In other words, is it true that in the world of Wiki, everyone stands equally? Certainly some did not believe so:

The biggest problem I see are the control guilds that have sprung up. They can be the Christian groups, or the anti-metaphysicists that go around labeling everything pseudoscience because they lack the ability to see the difference between the two. (Participant 2)

Most participants addressed the issue about control over contribution from the perspective of being able to monitor changes. For instance, Participant 7 wrote to us about the importance of being able to "track the contributions and changes of each contributor." Participant 3 elaborated further:

I think the fact that Administrators monitor the content and make sure that if it is inaccurate or copyright protected that it cannot be posted is a very important aspect of WikiBooks/Wikipedia that should be emulated by others. (Participant 3)

One other aspect of control over contributions surfaced as well. As shown in the following quote, Participant 6 expressed the desire to create a temporarily safe environment during the creation of a Wikibook:

Make a special area where one set group of people can take over a book for a time, for example, to enable one class or one group of professors [to] develop materials in a protected environment where, at least for a time, they have the final authority of whatever happens in that area. (Participant 6)

As indicated, Participant 6 believed that having authority even for a period of time was deemed important. Participant 4 shared that "the biggest disadvantage is a sacrifice in control over the direction of the book," which seemed to indirectly echo Participant 6's point. Here, the control issue seems to center on setting the overall goal of the book and the initial creation of the first draft.

As demonstrated, even though most participants did not directly bring up the question about control, through interview excerpts, we observed how multiple dimensions of authority were realized among Wikibookians. Our survey data indicated that an overwhelming majority of the surveyed Wikibookians believed that Wikibooks promote individual accountability in terms of one's contributions to an online book project (15% strongly agree, 54% agree). However, still 31% of them disagreed that individuals could be held accountable for the accuracy of contents contributed. It is not surprising to see that Wikibookians wrestled with these questions, which leads to the next section about how Wikibookians collaborate.

The Nature of Collaboration Process in Wikibooks

Coordination

Working in a Wikibook project requires coordination, communication, an understanding of the collaborative writing process, and a great deal of time management. In particular, Participant 4 shared many of his perspectives about the inner workings of a Wikibookian and the process of Wikibook creation:

Development has been slower than expected. I expect to be able to finish the book…in about two years.

My experience has been that Wikimedia projects promote much more formal rules of etiquette, but a much less structured writing process.

Maintaining a wiki is much more a challenge for social issues than for technological issues. Above all, a collaborative writing community must have a common vision, specifically a vision to create a written work.

Interestingly, he suggested that software be created that makes it easy to post a positive contribution and more difficult to post something negative.

Communication

Clearly, issues about communication stood out in many of the Wikibookian observations and suggestions. Some of the comments included:

Coordination is key. So [is] communication between editors, contributors, etc. is important. It must also be easy to use, fast and one must quickly be able to see what was changed, who changed the document and if necessary, change it back. (Participant 8)

Collaboration

The concept of a wiki assumes a collaborative process. While many participants clearly showed their agreement, two indicated their disappointment when no other took interest in their book:

I also hoped that collaborators would take an interest in the book as it developed. Although there have been isolated contributions, no one else has taken an interest in making a real investment in the book. I still hope this will eventually happen. (Participant 4)

My expectation was to help create a free, collaboratively written textbook. At this point I have done almost all of the work on the book. Admittedly, word about the book hasn't gotten out, but hopefully once it does others will begin to contribute. Until that happens, my expectations will not, technically, have been met. (Participant 7)

Resolving Disagreements

Even though some seemed to be lone writers, disagreements are bound to happen when working with strangers from around the world. We asked the Wikibookians about how they resolved differences. Again, communication provided the bridge to reconcile different opinions, including mechanisms such as the talk page, a mediator, private message, or revert the changes. However, Wikibookians differed in how they would approach or resolve the differences. As the following quotes indicate, some would revert the changes, some would discuss them first, and still others did not know since they had yet to experience such situations:

So revert it :) It's a Wiki, so everybody can edit it. When s.o.'s edit doesn't apply to my standards, I can revert it. And that person can revert me too. When we both find it important, we can start talking through the talkpage, and in the end, maybe get a mediator, or ask the community what they think about it. (Participant 1)

This happens frequently. I usually either talk to them via the "Talk" pages or send them a private message regarding the change(s) if they are not an anonymous user. I leave or qualify their changes if they are correct, but if not, I may revert them back to their original form. (Participant 3)

Perhaps such quotes reflect the degree of expertise of the Wikibookian. Byrant, Forte, and Bruckman, (2005), for example, found that expert Wikibookians have a policy not to revert changes or additions in Wikipedia if at all possible. They tend to post their concerns to the talk page first.

From the nature of the collaboration process, we see the complexity of not only the communication process among authors, but a philosophical question about the definition of a finished Wikibook emerged. As an emerging phenomena, Wikibooks draw interest and attention, especially for their education and self-learning value.

Completeness, Success, and Happiness Regarding One's Wikibook Project

Wikibook Completion

Given the comments and concerns about the quality of Wikibooks and length of time to complete them, it was important to ask Wikibook contributors about Wikibook completion and overall successes experienced. Using all the methods mentioned here, will the revision process ever be completed? In other words, will a Wikibook ever be finished? We raised this question to all of our participants and had rather interesting findings. In our survey responses, nearly 60% of Wikibookians indicated that a Wikibook could be completed. However, as the following quotes exemplify, respondents to our interview questions were quite varied in their opinions regarding online book completion:

It will probably depend on the subject. When you will try to explain a limited subject, it can theoretically be complete. However, it will be hard to have it finally completed indeed. (Participant 1)

No wiki is ever complete, because it is ever evolving. That's one of the best things about wikis. I personally think that paper is dead and in many ways the ideas contained within them too. I want my ideas and thoughts evolved and allowing others to improve them makes the work alive. (Participant 2)

Wikibooks can eventually become "complete," when the authors decide that there is no more to write...so a book is substantially complete once the last "proper" author leaves....It is by dedicated writers that books are written, not casual one- sentence contributors or people who drop in for an afternoon. (Participant 4)

As demonstrated, some Wikibookians thought that completion of the book would naturally be indicated by participant interest in the topic or the scope of the project. One Wikibookian explained that "I think a Wikibook becomes complete when the participants loose interest in the topic." On the other hand, another Wikibookian suggested that a Wikibook could be complete if all the relevant information on a topic was included or known such as the "Iran-Contra scandal of the early to mid 1980s." Overall, however, there was some agreement that a Wikibook is not as a product but a process, because a Wikibook is always evolving and "allowing others to improve them makes the work alive." From this notion, a more refined question surfaced: who decides whether a Wikibook is finished? Can we say a Wikibook is finished when nobody is contributing to it anymore?

Wikibook Success and Happiness

According to our online survey, most Wikibookians felt that their Wikibook was a success (see Figure 3). We did not, however, ask what determines that success. This issue relates back to the previous one regarding completion; if Wikibookians focus on the process and not the final product, then success is an extremely fleeting concept. At the very least, success is then focused on social interaction and collaboration processes, instead of simply on the quality and use of the final document.

Some Wikibookians seem truly inspired by the Wikibook process and working in any type of wiki environments. For example, Participant 1 simply stated, "Go rockin' on!" when asked for additional comments, while Participant 2 noted, "I love wikis they're truly the closest example of the purest form democracy."

Advice to Wikibook Wannabes

Technology Skills and Realistic Goals

Obviously, a Wikibookian needs to have the necessary technology skills to operate within a wiki environment. Beyond technological savvy, understanding the magnitude of creating a book and setting realistic goals could help start one on the right foot:

A little bit is better than nothing, it can always be improved later. Often times there is no book for a topic because everyone thinks "Oh, someone else will make it." (Participant 6)

Figure 3. Wikibookians perceptions of Wikibook success.

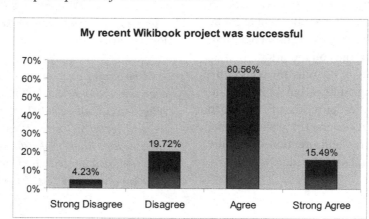

Get help. Don't try to do it on your own, it's a too big amount of work and you will definitely loose the overview. (Participant 1)

Wikibooks are Demanding

As the following quote from Participant 5 indicates, experienced Wikibookians also warned us about the difficulty of chapter organization:

I'd suggest getting several coauthors from the get go and deciding on a template for the book chapters so it is uniform from the beginning. It's bound to change over time, but you may as well start with a plan. Also, I'd mention that, for the most part, they shouldn't expect many people to contribute to the book. Writing a book is challenging; most people will never attempt it. (Participant 5)

In addition to getting the flow and direction of the book, Participant 4 advised us the importance of understanding the book-writing process. In this opinion, joining an existing book might be the best way to become involved in Wikibooks:

I would first offer a warning that writing can be very difficult. Writing a textbook is an involved task, demanding the full scope of your expertise, and requiring a substantial investment before any payoff can be realized. Yet it's extremely rewarding.......I would encourage users to consider working on an existing book rather than starting a new one. Starting off with a more manageable goal will let a user test the water without making a big commitment. (Participant 4)

Wikibooks are Different from Wikipedia

Most Wikibookians seem to have initial wiki backgrounds from editing or contributing to Wikipedia. They may have shifted to Wikibooks on the advice of others that their textbook-related ideas belonged in Wikibooks not in Wikipedia.

Still, their prior history in Wikipedia shaped their expectations. Among all the suggestions, Participant 5 brought up the idea that involvement with a Wikibook is different from working on a piece of an article in Wikipedia:

I think authors have to make concepts before they write a book and think about it, because it's not only an article like in Wikipedia. (Participant 5)

As a result of this difference, in order to work in a Wikibook, more communication, organization, and compromise is required. Participant 3 shared with us his view about how Wikibooks are different from other collaborative productions:

I expected WIKIBOOKS to be more in-depth about specific subject areas and to provide more details than Wikipedia articles. In the case of video games, for example, I expected WikiBooks to provide background stories and walkthroughs. (Participant 3)

Future studies might explore the need for additional planning processing and tools within Wikibooks. Would outlining and planning tools, for instance, enhance the final product and the percentage of Wikibooks that are, in fact, completed? These and other differences between Wikipedia and Wikibooks are explored later on in Table 2.

The Future of Wikibooks

We were interested in how these experienced Wikibookians viewed the future of their Wikibook work. Based on their experience, did Wikibooks even have a future? And what tools and features might enhance it? As Participant 6 rightfully pointed out, the spirit of a wiki aims to "make the world a juster place by putting the tools of education into the hands of every person."

Future Growth and Success of Wikibooks

Some seemed concerned about the lack of reader interests at this early stage of Wikibooks:

It's difficult to tell at this stage. Wikibooks is faced with a sort of "chicken and egg" problem -- it needs readers to attract writers and writers to attract readers. The project will recruit more and more talented writers as it picks up steam, and will have better and better books in its library. ... But Wikibooks may never take off at all. ... (Participant 4)

The so-called "chicken and egg" issue was shared by Participant 1, who believed Wikibook will be either successful or die. As he stated, "There is no 'some people will use it.' Because when you want your book to become used, it has to be used by a large amount of people, not by a few." He also felt that a single dedicated person could make a huge difference in determining the ultimate success or failure of Wikibooks. "Now that is some incentive to participate!"

Then the next logical question arises. Why do few people use the books at the Wikibook Web site? Is it because "there has not been an example yet of a book that goes all the way through and is put into use" or perhaps it is because "People have not seen it work enough for them to believe in it, and there are not mechanisms in place that convince educators of the value of Wikibooks as a teaching or learning tool?"

Academic Acceptance

In their responses to our online survey questions, Wikibookians seemed to strongly believe in Wikibooks as an online library (64%), a learning tool (40%), and a supplement to classroom or training resources (36%). In addition, it was a place for communities of writers (60%) and learners (34%) to form. However, making Wikibooks a teaching and learning tool and enabling the educational community to embrace it proved a difficult task. Academics might be the largest potential users of Wikibooks; they might hold the key to Wikibooks' success. The following quotes indicate the shared concerns and hopes of Participant 6 and 7:

I don't think the concept will catch on except among small niches until there are some very well-developed textbooks available on the site. If academics turn to using it regularly for free introductory textbooks, Wikibooks could explode with interest. But we aren't there yet. Maybe in the next 5 years or so. (Participant 7)

This is a very valuable project with very important goals, and any educator who is able to contribute a bit or to draw his or her students or colleagues into the process will be doing groundbreaking work in education which is worthy of praise. Things can only continue to go up from here. (Participant 6)

FUTURE TRENDS

Each of the previously mentioned themes provides interesting data for further wiki-related research and development; especially that related to Wikibooks. Table 1 summarizes our major findings according to the five themes.

COMPARING WIKIPEDIA AND WIKIBOOKS

As indicated in the literature review, there are many distinct differences between Wikipedia and Wikibooks. As shown in Table 2, they differ in terms of the types of communities that they foster, the resources created, size of user community, technology supports required, the goals and needs of both experts and novices, and many other variables.

Table 1. Key themes from interviews with Wikibookians

Theme 1: The Expression of Authority in Wikibooks	
Authority: Each one of us possesses unique knowledge that could contribute to the creation of a Wikibook.	"not one person in charge" "need at least two specialists, as both have understand the subject very good"
Control: Some liked to be able to monitor changes and most believed in personal accountability.	"When a lone writer is trying to open people's minds to the reality of things and closed minded indoctrinated individuals that in all reality could be a 13 yr old who has been given admin powers can be judge and jury over your work.."
Theme 2: Collaboration Process in Wikibooks	
Coordination: Writing a Wikibook together might be more of a social issue than a technical one.	"Above all, a collaborative writing community must have a common vision"
Communication: Communicating among writers proved essential.	"…requires communication in order to get the project off the ground and into something tangible…"
Collaboration: Finding someone else who is also interested in your book might not be so easy.	"…there have been isolated contributions, no one else has taken an interest in making a real investment in the book…"
Resolving Disagreements: One would revert the changes, some would discuss them first, and still others did not know since they had yet to experience such situations.	"I usually either talk to them via the 'Talk' pages or send them a private message regarding the change(s) if they are not an anonymous user."
Theme 3: Completion, Success, and Happiness Regarding One's Wikibooks	
Completion: Agreement seemed to be that a Wikibook is not a product but a process because a Wikibook is always evolving.	"No wiki is ever complete, because it is ever evolving. " "Wikibooks can eventually become 'complete,' when the authors decide that there is no more to write"
Success and Happiness: Success is then focused on social interaction and collaboration processes.	"Go rockin' on!" "I love wikis they're truly the closest example of the purest form democracy."
Theme 4: Advice to Wikibook Wannabes	
Technical Skills and Realistic Goals: Be realistic regarding your skill level and writing goals.	"Don't try to do it on your own, it's a too big amount of work and you will definitely loose the overview."
Wikibooks are Demanding: Writing a book chapter is a difficult task.	"Writing a textbook is an involved task, demanding the full scope of your expertise, and requiring a substantial investment before any payoff can be realized."
Wikibooks are Different from Wikipedia.	See Table 2 for comparison.
Theme 5: The Future of Wikibooks	
Growth and Success: Lack of readership at early stage.	"it needs readers to attract writers and writers to attract readers."
Academic Acceptance: Academics might be the largest potential users of Wikibooks; they might hold the key to Wikibooks' success.	"…educator who is able to contribute a bit or to draw his or her students or colleagues into the process will be doing groundbreaking work in education which is worthy of praise."

FUTURE RESEARCH DIRECTIONS

After their birth in 1995, wikis proliferated quickly into the mainstream of human life. From users' perspectives, wikis offer common knowledge resources, whether they be dictionaries, ency- clopedias, books, or sets of morals, fables, and quotes. At a basic knowledge level, then, wikis provide community-driven access to informa- tion resources when needed. From a contributing writers' viewpoint, on the other hand, wikis are a penultimate example of collaboratively writ-

Table 2. Comparison of Wikipedia and Wikibook environments

Issue or Characteristic	Wikipedia	Wikibook
1. Date Launched	January 15, 2001	July 10, 2003
2. Community	Wikipedia is a community of practice for millions of people. There are myriad subcommunities within it for different languages, topics, resources, and tools.	Wikibooks has communities of practice for each book project. There is also an overall community of Wikibookians at the staff lounge within Wikibooks.
3. Resources Created	Wikipedia is an information resource for people to look up. It is comprised of many linked, yet individual pieces.	Wikibooks creates usable texts, guidebooks, and reference materials. The final product should be coherent.
4. Historical Statistics (as of February 9, 2007):	7,483,939 pages 6.4 million articles 1,629,257 articles in English 250 languages 110,836,256 edits 14.81 edits per page 700,001 media files 3,511,411 registered users 1,111 system administrators (Wikipedia, 2007d).	67,399 pages 23,790 modules or chapters Over 1,000 books, the largest category in English 120 languages 759,033 page edits 11.26 edits per page 50,582 registered users, 33 system administrators (Wikibooks, 2007b).
5. Views of Contributors	"One could think of the Wikipedians as a global ant colony, except that there is no queen, and users choose their own roles." Some Wikipedians welcome newcomers, while others determine awards, upload images, clean article grammer, work on article histories, revert vandalism, and so forth. (Wikipedia, 2007e).	A Wikibookian is someone who coordinates or contributes to a Wikibook project.
6. Goals and Focus	Wikipedians are concerned with the quality of Wikipedia. They maintain or monitor a set of "watch" pages (Bryant, Forte, & Bruckman, 2006).	Wikibookians are concerned with the quality of the particular books and study guides that they are preparing.
7. Participation or Contribution Criteria	Enter Wikipedia site with generalized knowledge but add specific pieces of information.	Enter book project with specialized knowledge.
8. Technology Tools, Features, and Resources	Tools for tracking the history of document changes, talk pages, edit pages, hyperlinking, lounges, site statistics, and so forth.	Same tools as Wikipedia but could also use book planning, outlining, and overview tools, enhanced discussion tools, mark-up and commenting tools, enhanced tracking of book contributions and contributors, and ways of fostering collaboration and interaction among those in a Wikibook project.
9. User Community	Massively millions.	Extensive yet far more limited membership than Wikipedia
10. Qualification and Participant Filters	None, open to all to contribute or edit a document.	None, open to all to contribute or edit a document.

continued on following page

Table 2. continued

11. Novices	Wikipedia is more of a collection of articles with random people adding information here and there, then as a way to communicate, collaborate, and protect good work (Bryant, Forte, & Bruckman, 2005).	Wikibooks is a collection of books to which one can contribute to or read.
12. Experts	Wikipedia is a community of coauthors who use their talents to help establish and maintain the quality of Wikipedia; Wikipedia is more important than any single article or set of articles or resources (Bryant, Forte, & Bruckman, 2005).	Wikibooks is a place wherein one can coordinate a book project that can contribute to the movement of making open knowledge more accessible.
13. Generation, Distribution, and Maintenance of Ideas	Many to many.	One to many as well as many to many.
14. Speed of Content Development	Tends to be fast. Assisted by a huge army of volunteer contributors as well as by news and media features or stories. Tends to be fast.	Tends to be relatively slow. Book projects take longer than Wikibookians often expect; many incomplete or unfinished books and resources (Sajjapanroj et al., 2007).
15. Ownership	Free. No one owns.	Free. No one owns.

ten and socially negotiated texts. Contributions in a wiki can be small pieces of information or media for a presentation, train schedules for a trip to the UK, places to eat at the riverwalk in San Antonio during a conference, and synonyms for a word being defined in Wiktionary. At the same time, they might also be entire chapters or modules of a book or an entire book as in the case of Wikibooks.

As the scope of wiki-work increases from an informational focus at the word, sentence, or paragraph level, as is often the case in Wikipedia or Wikiquotes, to something much more substantive, as in the case of Wikibooks or other online book sites, the problems, issues, and challenges also significantly change. The same wiki tools, approaches, and procedures that work so effectively for Wikipedians may not to be sufficient for Wikibookians. In addition, the level of expertise required to help write a book is at a higher level of specificity and depth than most arriving at a wikibook type of site would likely have. At the same time, the communities of practice that form around such a book have to negotiate issues of

chapter coherence, book organization, and topical relevance that those in other types of wiki-related sites do not typically need to consider. Such issues place serious challenges as well as opportunities in the face of wiki researchers as well as designers of new generations of wiki-related technologies.

CONCLUSION

As we pointed out in this chapter, wikis offer a unique window into knowledge negotiation and collaboration processes. The coming decade will undoubtedly witness new tools and resources to track and better understand such negotiation and interaction processes. Now is the time to begin organizing a set of research initiatives, agendas, and questions that will allow for responsive research that helps in the formation of new tools, as well as enhances understanding of the power of wikis. Wikpedia and Wikibooks and many other wiki sites are wondrous tools and resources for twenty-first century working, learning, and living. With these wiki wonders, YOU can now all participate in the human race in new and exciting ways! Engage.

REFERENCES

Alexa. (2007). *Results for Wikipedia*. Retrieved February 7, 2007, from http://www.alexa.com/search?q=wikipedia

Brown, J. S. (2006). *Relearning learning—Applying the long tail to learning*. Presentation at MIT iCampus. Retrieved February 9, 2007, from http://www.mitworld.mit.edu/video/419

Bruns, A., & Humphreys, S. (2005). *Wikis in teaching and assessment: The M/Cyclopedia project*. Paper presented at the WikiSym 2005. Retrieved February 5, 2007, from http://www.wikisym.org/ws2005/proceedings/paper-03.pdf

Bryant, S. L., Forte, A., & Bruckman, A. (2005). Becoming Wikipedian: Transformation of participation in a collaborative online encyclopedia. In M. Pendergast, K. Schmidt, G. Mark, & M. Acherman (Eds.), *Proceedings of the 2005 International ACM SIGGROUP Conference on Supporting Group Work*, GROUP 2005, Sanibel Island, FL, November 6-9 (pp. 1-10). Retrieved February 7, 2007, from http://www-static.cc.gatech.edu/~aforte/BryantForteBruckBecomingWikipedian.pdf

Campus Technology (2006a, October 10). News Update: MIT launches center for Collective (Wiki) intelligence. *Campus Technology*. Retrieved February 2, 2007, from http://campustechnology.com/news_article.asp?id=19384&typeid=150

Campus Technology (2006b, October 10). News update: Stanford debuts Wiki of all things Stanford. *Campus Technology*. Retrieved February 2, 2007, from http://campustechnology.com/news_article.asp?id=19384&typeid=150

Campus Technology (2007, January 30). News update: MIT, Wharton to publish collaborative textbook by Wiki. *Campus Technology*. Retrieved February 2, 2007, from http://campustechnology.com/news_article.asp?id=20096&typeid=150

Ciffolilli, A. (2003). Phantom authority, self-selective recruitment and retention of members in virtual communities: The case of Wikipedia [Electronic Version]. *First Monday, 8*(12). Retrieved February 10, 2007, from http://firstmonday.org/issues/issue8_12/ciffolilli/index.html

Emigh, W., & Herring, S. C. (2005). Collaborative authoring on the Web: A genre analysis of online encyclopedias. *Proceedings of the 38th Hawai'i International Conference on System Sciences (HICSS-38)*. Los Alamitos: IEEE Press. Retrieved February 3, 2007, from http://ella.slis.indiana.edu/~herring/wiki.pdf

Evans, P. (2006, January/February). The Wiki factor. *BizEd*, 28-32.

Friedman, T. L. (2005). *The world is flat: A brief history of the twenty-first century*. NY: Farrar, Straus, and Giroux.

Grossman, L. (2006/2007a). You: Time Magazine Person of the Year. *Time Magazine, 168*(26), 38-41. December 25, 2006/January 1, 2007.

Grossman, L. (2006/2007b). Power to the people. *Time Magazine Person of the Year, 168*(26), 42-47, 50, 53-56, 58.

Hall, B. (2006). Five innovation technologies. *Chief Learning Officer, 5*(7), 13. Retrieved February 2, 2007, from http://www.clomedia.com/content/templates/clo_article.asp?articleid=1443&zoneid=190

Honegger, B. D. (2005). *Wikis – A rapidly growing phenomenon in the German-speaking school community*. Paper presented at the WikiSym 2005. Retrieved February 5, 2007, from http://www.wikisym.org/ws2005/proceedings/paper-10.pdf

Korfiatis, N., Poulos, M., & Bokos, G. (2006). Evaluating authoritative sources using social networks: An insight from wikipedia. *Online Information Review, 30*(3). Retrieved February 4, 2007, from http://www.korfiatis.info/papers/OISJournal_final.pdf

Lessig, L. (2005). Creatives face a closed net. *Financial Times*. Retrieved February 14, 2007, from http://www.ft.com/cms/s/d55dfe52-77d2-11da-9670-0000779e2340.html

Leuf, B., & Cunningham, W. (2001). *The Wiki way: Quick collaboration on the Web*. Addison Wesley Longman.

Lih, A. (2004). *Wikipedia as participatory journalism: Reliable sources? Metrics for evaluating collaborative media as a news resource*. Paper presented at the 5th International Symposium on Online Journalism, April 16-17, UT Austin.

Lin, M. (2006). *Sharing knowledge and building community: A narrative of the formation, development, and sustainability of OOPS*. Unpublished dissertation, University of Houston, Houston, TX.

Lio, E. D., Fraboni, L., & Leo, T. (2005). *TWiki-based facilitation in a newly formed academic community of practice*. Paper presented at the WikiSym 2005. Retrieved February 5, 2007, from http://www.wikisym.org/ws2005/proceedings/paper-09.pdf

Pfeil, U., Zaphiris, P., & Ang, C. S. (2006). Cultural differences in collaborative authoring of Wikipedia. *Journal of Computer-Mediated Communication, 12*(1), article 5. Retrieved February 7, 2007, from http://jcmc.indiana.edu/vol12/issue1/pfeil.html

Reuters (2007). Publisher launches it's first "wiki" novel. *Yahoo News*. Retrieved February 5, 2007, from http://news.yahoo.com/s/nm/20070201/tc_nm/penguin_wiki_dc_4

Rosenzweig, R. (2006). Can history be open source: Wikipedia and the future of the past. *The Journal of American History, 93*(1), 117-146. Retrieved February 4, 2007, from http://chnm.gmu.edu/resources/essays/d/42

Sajjapanroj, S., Bonk, C. J., Lee, M., & Lin, M.-F. G. (2007). *The challenges and successes of Wikibookian experts and Wikibook novices: Classroom and community perspectives*. Paper presented at the American Educational Research Association, Chicago, IL.

Schachaf, P., & Hara, N. (2006). *Beyond vandalism: Trolls in Wikipedia*. Presentation at the Rob Kling Center for Social Informatics, School of Library and Information Science, Indiana University, Bloomington, IN.

Time Magazine. (2006/2007). *Time Magazine Person of the Year, 168*(26), December 25, 2006/January 1, 2007.

Viégas, F. B., Wattenberg, M., & Dave, K. (2004). Studying cooperation and conflict between authors with history flow visualizations. In E. Dykstra-Erickson & M. Tscheligi (Eds.), *Proceedings from ACM CHI 2004 Conference on Human Factors in Computing Systems* (pp. 575-582). Vienna, Austria. Retrieved February 3, 2007, from http://web.media.mit.edu/~fviegas/papers/history_flow.pdf

Voss, J. (2005). Measuring wikipedia [Electronic Version]. *Proceedings for International Society for Scientometrics and Informetrics*. Retrieved February 10, 2007 from http://eprints.rclis.org/archive/00003610/01/MeasuringWikipedia2005.pdf

Wikibooks (2007a). *Wikibooks: History of Wikibooks*. Retrieved February 9, 2007, from http://en.wikibooks.org/wiki/Wikibooks:History_of_Wikibooks

Wikibooks (2007b). *Wikibooks: Statistics*. Retrieved February 9, 2007, from http://en.wikibooks.org/wiki/Special:Statistics

Wikibooks (2007c). *Wikibooks: Wikijunior*. Retrieved February 16, 2007, from http://en.wikibooks.org/wiki/Wikijunior

Wikipedia (2007a). *Wikipedia: Larry Sanger.* Retrieved February 7, 2007, from http://en.wikipedia.org/wiki/Larry_Sanger

Wikipedia (2007b). *Wikipedia: List of Wikipedias.* Retrieved February 7, 2007, from http://meta.wikimedia.org/wiki/List_of_Wikipedias#All_Wikipedias_ordered_by_number_of_articles

Wikipedia (2007c). *Wikipedia: Main page.* Retrieved February 7, 2007, from http://en.wikipedia.org/wiki/Main_Page

Wikipedia (2007d). *Wikipedia: Statistics.* Retrieved February 9, 2007, from http://en.wikipedia.org/wiki/Special:Statistics

Wikipedia (2007e). *Wikipedia: Wikipedians.* Retrieved February 4, 2007, from http://en.wikipedia.org/wiki/Wikipedia:Wikipedians

Wikiquotes (2007). *Wikiquotes: Main page.* Retrieved February 16, 2007, from http://en.wikiquote.org/wiki/Main_Page

Wiktionary (2007). *Wiktionary: Main page.* Retrieved February 16, 2007, from http://en.wiktionary.org/wiki/Main_Page

ADDITIONAL READING

Bargh, J. A., & McKenna, K. Y. A. (2004). The Internet and social life. *Annual Review of Psychology, 55,* 573-590.

Bezroukov, N. (1999b). A second look at the cathedral and the bazaar [Electronic Version]. *First Monday, 4*(12). Retrieved March, 15, 2007, from http://firstmonday.org/issues/issue4_12/bezroukov/index.html.

Bonk, C. J. (2001). *Online teaching in an online world.* Bloomington, IN: CourseShare.com.

Bonk, C. J., & Cunningham, D. J. (1998). Searching for learner-centered, constructivist, and sociocultural components of collaborative educational learning tools. In C. J. Bonk & K. S. Kim (Eds.), *Electronic collaborators: Learner-centered technologies for literacy, apprenticeship, and discourse* (pp. 25-50). NJ: Erlbaum.

Bonk, C. J., & Kim, K. A. (1998). Extending sociocultural theory to adult learning. In M. C. Smith & T. Pourchot (Ed.), *Adult learning and development: Perspectives from educational psychology* (pp. 67-88). Lawrence Erlbaum Associates.

Bonk, C. J., Wisher, R. A., & Nigrelli, M. L. (2004). Learning communities, communities of practice: Principles, technologies, and examples. In K. Littleton, D. Miell & D. Faulkner (Eds.), *Learning to collaborate, collaborating to learn* (pp. 199-219). Hauppauge, NY: Nova Science Publishers.

Brown, J. S. (2006, December 1). *Relearning learning—Applying the long tail to learning.* Presentation at MIT iCampus. Retrieved February 9, 2007, from http://www.mitworld.mit.edu/video/419

Cole, M., & Engestrom, Y. (1997). A cultural-historical approach to distributed cognition. In G. Salomon (Ed.), *Distributed cognitions: Psychological and educational considerations* (pp. 1-46). Cambridge, UK: Cambridge University Press.

Coles, R. (1993). *The call of service: A witness to idealism.* Mariner Books.

Desilets, A., Paquet, S., & Vinson, N. G. (2005). *Are Wikis usable?* Paper presented at the WikiSym 2005. Retrieved February 26, 2006, from http://www.wikisym.org/ws2005/proceedings/paper-01.pdf

Evans, P. (2006). The Wiki factor. *BizEd.* Retrieved April 1, 2006, from http://www.aacsb.edu/publications/Archives/JanFeb06/p28-33.pdf

Fichter, D. (2006). Using Wikis to support online collaboration in libraries. *Information Outlook, 10*(1), 30-31.

Garlick, M. (2005). A review of Creative Commons and Science Commons. *EDUCAUSE Review, 40*(5), 78-79.

Giles, J. (2005). Internet encyclopaedias go head to head [Electronic Version]. *Nature, 438,* 900-901. Retrieved December 15, 2005 from http://www.nature.com/nature/journal/v438/n7070/full/438900a.html

Hayes, J. R., & Flower, L. S. (1986). Writing research and the writer. *American Psychologist, 41*(10), 1106-1113.

Howe, J. (2006/2007). Your Web, your way. Time Magazine Person of the Year. *Time Magazine Person of the Year, 168*(26), 60-61. Lamb, B. (2004). Wide open spaces: Wikis, ready or not. *EDUCAUSE Review, 39*(5), 36-48. Retrieved February 26, 2006, from http://www.educause.edu/ir/library/pdf/erm0452.pdf

Langer, J. A., & Applebee, A. A. (1987). *How writing shapes thinking.* Urbana, IL: National Council of Teachers of English.

Lave, J., & Wenger, E. (1991). *Situated learning: Legitimate peripheral participation.* Cambridge, UK: Cambridge University Press.

Lin, M., & Lee, M. (2006).E-learning localized: The case of the OOPS project. In A. Edmundson (Ed.), *Globalization in education: Improving education quality through cross-cultural dialogue* (pp. 168-186). Hershey, PA: Idea Group.

Mann, C., & Stewart, F. (2000a). *Internet communication and qualitative research: A handbook for researching online.* Thousand Oaks, CA: Sage Publication.

Matsuhashi, A. (Ed.). (1987). *Writing in real time: Modelling production processes.* Norwood, NJ: Ablex Publishing Corporation.

McHenry, R. (2004). *The faith-based encyclopedia.* Retrieved February 10, 2005, from http://tcsdaily.com/article.aspx?id=111504A

McKierman, G. (2005). WikimediaWorlds Part I: Wikipedia. *Library Hi Tech News, 22*(8), 46-54.

Neuwirth, C., Kaufer, D., Chimera, R., & Gillespie, T. (1987). *The notes program: A hypertext application for writing from source texts.* Paper presented at Hypertext '87, Chapel Hill, NC.

Orlowski, A. (2005). Wikipedia founder admits to serious quality problems [Electronic Version]. *The Register.* Retrieved February 10, 2006 from http://www.theregister.co.uk/2005/10/18/wikipedia_quality_problem/

Palloff, R., & Pratt, K. (2005). *Collaborating online: Learning together in community.* San Francisco, CA: Jossey-Bass.

Pea, R. D. (1996). Practices of distributed intelligence and designs for education. In G. Salomon (Ed.), *Distributed cognitions: Psychological and educational considerations* (pp. 47-87). New York: Cambridge University Press.

Raymond, E. S. (2000). *The cathedral and the bazaar.* Retrieved March 10, 2007, from http://www.catb.org/~esr/writings/cathedral-bazaar/cathedral-bazaar/

Raymond, E. S. (2001). *The cathedral and the bazaar: Musings on Linux and open source by an accidental revolutionary.* Cambridge, MA: O'Reilly.

Rheingold, H. (2000). *The virtual community: Homesteading on the electronic frontier.* Cambridge, MA: MIT Press.

Rogoff, B. (1990). *Apprenticeship in thinking: Cognitive development in social context.* New York, NY: Oxford University Press.

Salomon (Ed.). (1993). *Distributed cognitions: Psychological and educational considerations* (pp. 47–87). New York: Cambridge University Press.

Salomon, G. (1988). AI in reverse: Computer tools that turn cognitive. *Journal of Educational Computing Research, 4*(2), 123-139.

Sanger, L. (2004). *Why Wikipedia must jettison its anti-elitism*. Retrieved February 10, 2006, from http://kuro5hin.org/story/2004/12/30/142458/25

Scardamalia, M., & Bereiter, C. (1986). Research on written composition. In M. C. Wittrock (Ed.), *Handbook of research on teaching.* (3rd ed.), (pp. 778-803). New York: Macmillan Education Ltd.

Schrage, M. (1990). *Shared minds: The technologies of collaboration.* New York: Random House.

Souzis, A. (2005). Building a semantic Wiki. *IEEE Intelligent Systems, 20*(5), 87-91.

Utne, L. (2006). To wikifinity and beyond! [Electronic Version]. *Utne Magazine.* Retrieved April 29, 2006 from http://www.utne.com/issues/2006_133/view/11894-1.html

Wagner, C., & Bolloju, N. (2005). Supporting knowledge management in organization with conversational technologies: Discussion forums, Weblogs, and wikis. *Journal of Database Management, 16*(2), i-viii.

Wenger, E. (1998). *Communities of practice: Learning, meaning, and identity.* Cambridge University Press.

Wenger, E. (2002). *Cultivating communities of practice: A field guide to managing.* Harvard.

Wertsch, J. V. (1991). *Voices of the mind: A sociocultural approach to mediated action.* Cambridge, MA: Harvard University Press.

YouTube. (2007). *Web 2.0...The machine is using us.* YouTube. Retrieved February 9, 2007, from http://www.youtube.com/watch?v=6gmP4nk0EOE

Section V
Implications of Social Information Technology in Education

Chapter XVIII
Cultural Variables and Instructional Engineering

Christine Simard
Télé-université (TÉLUQ), Canada

Josianne Basque
Télé-université (TÉLUQ), Canada

ABSTRACT

This chapter discusses how cultural variables can be taken into account when designing computer-based learning environments (CLEs). Its purpose is to identify concrete recommendations to guide instructional engineering of computer-based learning for diverse cultures through a review of the literature on the subject. First, this chapter describes the background in which such recommendations have emerged, and identifies some of the issues underlying instructional design for diverse cultures. Then it introduces models and guidelines on how cultural variables can be taken into account when designing CLEs. Specific recommendations are organized using a method of instructional engineering for CLEs called MISA (Paquette, 2003) as a frame of reference. This is followed by a discussion on future trends and future research directions.

INTRODUCTION

Corporate providers and educational institutions are competing in the global education and training services market. Computer-based learning environments (CLEs) are becoming a commodity marketed across nations and cultures. Educators at all educational levels and training professionals who design these systems face the challenge of meeting the needs of culturally diverse learners. More than ever, they need sound methodologies and guidelines for developing CLEs that address cultural diversity issues and meet learners' requirements.

The goal of this chapter is to report recommendations to guide instructional engineering for diverse cultures, which are suggested by diverse authors in the field of educational technology. The frame of reference used to synthesize and organize these recommendations is based on a method of instructional engineering for CLEs called *MISA*[1] (Paquette, 2003).

This chapter is divided into four sections, followed by a conclusion. In the first section, we describe the methodology used to search and select the documents reviewed. We also examine the context in which the culturally sensitive instructional design recommendations are emerging and identify some underlying issues. In the second section, we introduce some models and guidelines intended to assist the instructional designer in addressing cultural variables. Then, we use the six phases and the four axis of MISA as a framework to report specific instructional design recommendations found in the literature. The third section identifies future trends that may influence the instructional design of culturally sensitive CLEs. The fourth section identifies future research directions. In conclusion, we synthesize recommendation highlights.

BACKGROUND

Scope and Limitations

This literature review focuses on documents published over the last decade, and comprises theoretical essays, research papers, case studies, promotional materials originating from both corporate and institutional education providers, and so forth. We searched on Web engines such as Copernic and Google, as well as educational literature databases (e.g., ERIC) and specialized bibliographical databases available through university libraries. Our search descriptors included French and English keywords such as culture, learning, instructional design, and so forth.

About 300 documents identified during that initial step were reviewed, and helped focus the

research on specific researchers, organizations, and conferences. Helpful resources included sites such as:

- Institute of Educational Technology (IET) at Open University
- Australasian Society for Computers in Learning in Tertiary Education
- Center for Enhancing Learning and Teaching at Charles Sturt University
- Department of Educational Technologies at Twente University

The following criteria were used to select about 60 documents for detailed analysis: (a) the document attempts to answer the question of how cultural variables can guide the instructional engineering of computer-based learning, (b) the author or organization is recognized in the field, (c) the document focuses on adult education issues, (d) the document provides a variety of perspectives and viewpoints.

Computer-based learning is defined here very broadly, as any electronically mediated learning, either Web-based or not, and distant or not. Collis and Remmers (in McLoughlin & Oliver, 2000) define two categories of Web sites that have cross-cultural implications: (1) sites designed to address one context and culture, but visited by other cultures; and (2) sites designed specifically for cross-cultural participation. We suggest that CLEs can be classified similarly, and both categories have been considered in our review.

So far, very little has been written about emerging models or guidelines to address cultural diversity in instructional design. Even fewer attempts have been made to organize recommendations within a specific framework or method.

Context

In 2000, the Australian Flexible Learning Framework was established to meet the rapidly increasing demand for flexible learning and e-learning from industry, enterprise, and clients. Funded by the Australian Government and all States and Territories, it has provided direct funding and support to more than 20,000 vocational education and training (VET) practitioners. The Framework stresses the importance of considering culture. "Cultural considerations are important in any teaching design. Teaching across cultures from one place to another, or to different cultures in one setting or dispersed across different geographical locations, presents particular challenges" (Backroad Connections, 2004a, p. 2). Many authors also argue that cultural variables must be considered when designing CLEs (Backroad Connections Pty Ltd., 2002, 2004a; Conner, 2000; Downey, Cordova-Wentling, Wentling, & Wadsworth, 2004; Dunn & Marinetti, 2006; Goodear, 2001; Henderson, 2006; Sabin & Ahern, 2002; Subramony, 2004; Wang & Reeves, 2006).

The issue of cultural influence on instructional systems is becoming one of the most important challenges faced by developers of e-learning products (Dunn & Marinetti, 2006). How to address it, however, is a relatively new field of research. Concerns about the neglect of culture by providers of educational products appeared in the literature in the 1990s (Bates, 1999; Gayol & Schied, 1997; Gunawardena, Lowe, & Anderson, 1997; Henderson, 1996; McIsaac & Gunawardera, 1996). Years later, many researchers still deplore the scarcity of research on the subject (Moore, Shattuck, & Al-Harti, 2006; Taylor, 2005), particularly the "few personal accounts and scant empirical research, especially in the field of e-learning" (Edmundston, 2006, p. IX) and the "paucity of reseach that systematically analyzes culture-related variables to suggest design guidelines for culture-related, flexible, on-line learning environments" (Seufert, 2002, p. 412).

Nevertheless, some recommendations on how to design culturally sensitive CLEs began to appear in the educational technology literature in the last years. Before reporting these recommendations, we assess the context in which they emerge with the following questions: Why the interest now? Who is interested? What is the literature about?

Why is Interest in Integrating Cultural Variables into Instructional Engineering on the Rise?

Two main reasons seem to explain the current rise in the interest in integrating cultural variables into the instructional engineering of CLEs. First, CLE providers are concerned about the instructional effectiveness of their products in global markets. Thomas, Mitchell, and Joseph (2002) argue that the consequences of not directly addressing culture in the design of instruction include the production of ineffective instructional products, the underuse of potentially effective products, culturally insensitive products, and products that are deemed overtly culturally offensive by some members of certain populations. Dunn and Marinetti (2003a) also claim that "the lack of cultural adaptation is a leading reason why e-learning fails to work for a globally distributed audience" (p. 1).

Second, the CLE providers that currently dominate the international market want to avoid the potential financial consequences of not adequately serving emerging markets, such as Asia. A larger proportion of corporate learning is being delivered via technology to more and more countries (Dunn & Marinetti, 2003a), and tertiary education providers are moving into the international realm to increase revenues (Bates, 1999; Mannan, 2005). The design of CLEs is highly dominated by a few Western and English-speaking countries comprising Britain, Australia, and North America (United States and Canada), which we shall refer to as BANA. The domination of BANA is challenged, particularly in the Indian and Chinese markets. Asia holds 56% of the world population; it represents 36% of current users of Internet, with a 245% growth since the year 2000. That is just the tip of the iceberg, since only 10% of Asians currently have access to the Internet (*Internet Usage in Asia*, n.d.). Concerns with the needs of learners from Asia (Backroad Connections, 2004b; Chan, 2002; Chen, Mashhadi, Ang, & Harkrider, 1999; McCarty, 2006; Wong & Trinidad, 2004) can best be understood in light of those numbers. As Internet use in Asia continues to grow exponentially, so too will the potential market for Web-based education in Asian countries.

Who is Interested in Culturally Based Instructional Engineering of CLEs?

The bulk of the literature reviewed originates from BANA. The United States is the number one producer of CLEs. The demographic and linguistic composition of population in this country is changing rapidly, with Hispanics now comprising 20% of the total population, outnumbering Afro-Americans as the largest minority group. Literature on cultural variables addresses: (a) concerns with minority populations; and (b) marketing of American postsecondary educational products to other countries. Many American-based private sector providers who thrived in the unilingual English e-training market now promote solutions that take cultural variables into account (Conner, 2000; Marcus & Gould, 2001; McBrien, 2005), opening offices in diverse countries and using local experts as spokespeople.

Australia's fourth most important export is education (Goodear, 2001). The country occupies a unique geopolitical position: English speaking and built on Anglo-Saxon traditions, it is surrounded by Asian countries. Australian policy makers are proactive, with initiatives such as the Australian Quality Training Framework of the Australian National Training Authority, which requires training to be equitable to all persons, taking into account cultural and linguistic needs (Goodear, 2001). Australia's objective is to become the world leader in designing and facilitating flexible vocational training that is sensitive to the cultural needs of the global e-learning market (Goodear, 2001).

Britain's Open University was the first university dedicated to distance education. Other universities worldwide have modeled themselves on this successful stronghold of the Anglo-Saxon tradition in education. Not surprinsigly, several instructional designers associated with Open University have discussed linguistic and cultural issues surrounding the teaching and assessment of students who are distributed globally. Mayor and Swann (2002) focus on the problems and possibilities of using English for the design of teaching and assessment materials. Goodfellow, Lea, Gonzalez, and Mason (2001) investigate how cultural and linguistic differences manifest themselves in global online learning environments.

Canada is officially bilingual and can target international English-speaking as well as French-speaking markets. Translation and adaptation of materials from one official language to the other are current practices. Canadian universities' involvement in global education often takes the form of collaborative projects, such as the Masters in Education Technology program partnership between the University of British Columbia and Mexico's Monterrey Institute of Technology (Bates, 1999). Canadian West coast institutions are targeting the Asian educational market.

What is the Literature Concerning Cultural Variables and the Instructional Engineering of CLEs About?

Literature concerning cultural variables and the instructional engineering of CLEs includes discussions about definitions of culture and models of cultural variables, learning styles based on culture, power relationships associated with cultural issues, learning theories and instructional approaches, world citizenship and cultural awareness, language, and the culture of the designer.

Definition of Culture and Models of Cultural Variables

Such discussions usually precede the examination of the influence of cultural variables on learner's behaviour or the identification of recommendations on ways to address them. The three models of national cultural characteristics most often referred to are Holfstede's (1980/2001), Trompenaars's (1993), and Hall's and Hall's (1990). Holfstede's model (1980/2001) identifies five national cultural dimensions: (1) power distance; how different societies handle inequalities in areas such as prestige, wealth, and power; (2) individualism vs. collectivism; (3) masculinity vs. feminity; (4) long- vs. short-term orientation; how different societies deal with persistence and thrift to personal stability and respect for traditions; and (5) uncertainty avoidance; how different societies cope with the uncertainty of the future through the domains of technology, law, and religion.

Trompenaars (1993, 2004) introduces a seven-dimension model of culture: (1) universalism-particularism; do people tend to follow standardized rules or do they prefer a flexible approach to unique situations? (2) individualism-communitarianism, (3) specific-diffuse; do people have a low or high degree of involvement in personal relationships? (4) neutral-affective; do people control their emotions or display them overtly? (5) achievement-ascription; are peoples' status and power based on performance or more likely to be determined by the school they went to, their age, gender, and family background? (6) sequential-synchronic; do people organize their time by doing one task at a time, or by multitasking? and (7) internal-external control.

In Hall's and Hall's (1990) model of culture, cultures of the world can be compared on a scale from high to low context. In high-context cultures (Japanese, Arabic, and Mediterranean), people have extensive information networks, and interaction between people does not require much background information. Conversely, in low-context cultures (North American, Northern European, etc.), interaction requires detailed background information, since many aspects of life are compartmentalized. Holfstede's model is

the most frequently mentioned framework (Wang & Reeves, 2006).

Limitations of Learning Styles Based on Culture

Goodfellow and Hewling (2005) argue that generalizations about cultural learning styles are of limited value because: (1) individual members of national groups do not necessarily exhibit the characteristics of the collective; (2) there is a danger of conceptualizing culture as a normative dimension, and (3) identifying the locus of cultural difference in learners who are in some way marked as "other" with respect to an assumed norm risks causing the very problem that it is intended to address. Indeed, many researchers caution against the danger of stereotyping learners (Henderson, 2006; Marcus & Gould, 2001; McLoughlin, 2006; Subramony, 2004).

Power Relationships Associated with Cultural Issues

Some discussions focus on issues of global cultural domination and cultural postcolonianism (Edwards, 2002; Gayol & Schied, 1997; Kinuthia, 2006; Mannan, 2005). For example, Mannan (2005) argues that globalization "facilitates the reproduction of cultural capital of the dominant nations that are exporting knowledge and skills and threatens and sometimes destroys the identities and values of cultures and traditions of recipient nations" (p. 1).

Learning Theories and Instructional Approaches

Discussions focus here on the issue of whether learning theories derived from American and European culture implemented in learning environments conflict with the values of the growing number of learners from different cultures (Catterick, 2006; Moore, Shattuck, & Al-Harti, 2006). While many remain convinced that constructivist design principles and instructional methods best address issues of cultural variables in instructional design (McCarty, 2006; McLoughlin & Oliver, 2000), others question their universal relevance (Catterick, 2006; Henderson, 2006; Moore, Shattuck, & Al-Harti, 2006). Catterick (2006) identifies three possible responses to cultural diversity: (1) non-accommodation response, based on the notion that BANA's teaching approaches and educational philosophies have been developed for "sound" reasons and need not be modified to accommodate differences in the educational culture; (2) intervention response, which is quite similar to non-accomodation response, except that differences in the educational culture are acknowledged and partly addressed; or (3) modification response, based on the notion that the educational philosophies that inform teaching appoaches in BANA countries need to be re-evaluated and possibly modified.

World Citizenship and Cultural Awareness

Discussions around CLEs designed for intercultural participation sometimes include implicit or explicit goals, such as preparing individuals for global economy and world citizenship by developing cultural awareness and sensitivity (Bates, 1999; Cifuentes & Murphy, 2000; Goodear, 2001; Olaniran, 2006; Palaiologou, 2006). Some maintain that cultural diversity enriches the coconstruction of knowledge, as it enhances the level of divergence amongst learners (Cifuentes & Murphy, 2000; Coulibaly, 2005; Eberle & Childress, 2006). Multicultural education (Gorski, 2005) seems to have influenced the discourse surrounding intercultural participation in CLEs.

Language

The issue of language appears frequently in the literature, as the international delivery of distance education is dominated by the English language (Bates, 1999). Language differences are important and disadvantage students working in another language when they have to contribute in collaborative assignments or discussion forums (Bates,

1999; Morse, 2003). "Given that computed-mediated communication is a textual (electronic) rather than a visual (face-to-face) medium, meaning must be carried by the language itself rather than relying on the environmental context as the means of communication and/or interpretation" (Morse, 2003, p. 41). Since 92% of the world population does not speak English (Conner, 2000), and 57% of Internet users are native speakers of a language other than English, language issues are not likely to disappear.

Culture of the Designer

Instructional systems are shaped by the culture in which they are developed (Dunn & Marinetti, 2006; Mcloughlin & Oliver, 2000). When the schemata of the learner and of the instructional designer do not correspond, the result is what Wilson termed "cultural discontinuities" (Goodear, 2001).

Much of the literature concerning cultural variables and the instructional engineering of CLEs focuses on these subjects. Existing literature yields few, if any, specific recommendations on how to address cultural variables. However, as we shall see in the next section, some resources are becoming available.

CULTURAL VARIABLES AND INSTRUCTIONAL ENGINEERING

Overview of Models and Guidelines

Although models and guidelines are emerging to assist the instructional designer in addressing cultural variables, they are often built on opposing underlying assumptions. The question that arises is: Should models guiding the development of CLEs be tailored to address specific cultural variables or, on the contrary, be designed to cater to most learners' cultural needs? We shall use that distinction to introduce the models and guidelines documents that we reviewed.

Approaches in which Materials are Produced in Ways which Encourage and/or Facilitate Local Adaptation

Seven models or guidelines documents using this more popular approach were identified. Following is a brief description of each of them.

Hendersons's theoretical "Multiple Cultural Model of Instructional Design" aims at providing the rationale and strategies for creating and adapting e-learning resources for local, national, and international e-learning (1996, 2006).

In their "Model of Flexible Learning in a Web-Based Environment," McLoughlin and Oliver (2000) and McLoughlin and Gower (2000) propose design guidelines for flexible and culturally responsive Web design. Their work is based on the analysis of a project using Henderson's model for developing culturally appropriate online courses for indigenous learners in Australia.

Goodear's "Framework of Review" (2001) describes issues to consider in developing culturally sensitive flexible learning models (FLM), particularly for online learning. Goodear recommends the use of Khan's (2000) Web-based learning framework.

Zahedi, Van Pelt, and Song (2001) propose a conceptual framework exploring differences in how people from diverse cultural backgrounds and with diverse individual characteristics might perceive and use Web documents. The conceptual framework is based on Holftede's model.

First published in 2003 (2003a, 2003b), Dunn and Marinetti's "Guideline for the Selection for Adaptation Strategies and Decision Support Tool" aims at assisting the instructional designer to select an appropriate adaptation strategy: (a) translation only; (b) localization – translation and some content adaptation (such as context and examples); (c) modularization – more content adaptation (some of which may be modular) and adaptation of instructional strategy (such as reordering of material, using alternative media, etc.); or (d) origination – a significant proportion of the content and of the instructional strategy is unique to the culture in which the CLE is used and may require an alternative course architecture.

Recently, Dunn and Marinetti (2006) proposed a tool to support the selection of specific learning strategies, based on understanding of cultural values. It uses Reigeluth's and Moore's framework for comparing and selecting instructional strategies by mapping the identified learning-related norms and preferences of specific cultures against specific learning strategies and theories.

Burn's and Thongprasert's (2005) "Strategic Framework for Successful VED (Virtual Education Delivery) Implementation" is used to determine the specific factors that influence online learning environments in other cultural contexts. It is based on the authors' study examining critical factors for implementing VED in Thailand.

Finally, Edmundston (2006) provides guidelines for evaluating existing e-learning courses and for matching them to the cultural profiles of targeted learners. The author's "Cultural Adapation Process (CAP) Model" has nine dimensions and integrates Marinetti and Dunn's guidelines, Holfstede's cultural dimensions and Henderson's multiple cultural model.

Approaches in which Materials are Produced so that They Can Be Used in Any Context

Here is a brief description of the six models and guidelines associated with this approach found in the literature review.

Collis (1999) proposes design guidelines to adapt Web-based, course-support sites to different expectations and learners preferences, especially those related to culture.

Slay's (2002) "Theoretical Framework for Designing Learning for Multicultural Settings" examines human activity within a learning environment as a system and uses a systematic approach (guided by the application of Kline's (1995) systems theory[2]) to analyze the role of culture within it.

Sabin's and Ahern's (2002) approach is based on the work of Samovar, Porter, and Stefani (1998), and aims at integrating cultural differences within traditional instructional design methodologies, such as Gagné's nine events of instruction.

In their "Universal Design for Learning (UDL)", Eberle and Childress (2006) provide a guide for designing and delivering UDL-based online learning for culturally-diverse learners. It uses Rose's and Meyer's (2000, 2002) recommendations for various instructional techniques and teaching strategies, based upon brain networking theory.

McLouglin's (2006) "Cross-Cultural Teaching Ladder" is a three-level model or holistic framework for the development of collaborative e-learning environments appropriate for culturally diverse learners. It links activity design, learner needs and pedagogy.

Finally, Gunawardena, Wilson, and Nolla (2003) propose a two-part design framework: the first part describes the institutional context, and the second part describes issues related to online course design. It uses the amoeba as a metaphor for an adaptive, meaningful, organic, environmentally based architecture for culturally relevant course design. The framework takes into consideration the works of Collis (1999), Marcus and Gould (2001), and Chen et al. (1999).

Overview of MISA (Engineering Method for Instructional Systems)

MISA is an instructional engineering method particularly useful for the design of CLEs. It was designed by Paquette (2003) at the LICEF Research Center at Télé-université in Montreal. MISA incorporates aspects of systems theory, instructional design, software engineering, and knowledge engineering. "The main goal of the method is to provide an operational base for the cognitivist and constructivist theories of learning" (Paquette, 2003, p. 115). As such, it may not be free from bias.

MISA divides the instructional engineering process in six main phases, which are quite similar to the phases of the classical ADDIE instructional design model (Analysis, Design, Development, Implementation and Evaluation). The first phase (Analysis) is divided into two phases in MISA, called "Problem Definition" (Phase 1) and "Preliminary Analysis" (Phase 2). The Design phase is also subdivided into two MISA phases, called "Architecture design" (Phase 3, which corresponds to the macro-design of CLEs) and "Learning Material Design" (Phase 4, which corresponds to the micro-design of each learning material integrated into CLEs: text, audio, video, graphics, etc.). The fifth phase of MISA combines the Development and Validation phases of the ADDIE model, because those processes are usually iterative. However, since MISA was developed exclusively for instructional designers, this fifth phase includes only the *planning* of the development and validation processes. The sixth and final phase of MISA (called Delivery Plan) is also limited to the planning of the implementation process, and does not include this process itself.

Thus, Paquette (2002) did not consider the operationalization of the development, implementation and delivery of CLEs as being instructional designers' tasks. Instead, other actors (media specialists, technologists, learning environment managers, etc.) complete this work, although an individual may carry out the instructional design "role" and these other roles. In other words, the MISA process stops where the learning system delivery begins.

One main point of originality of MISA is that it suggests progressive and parallel elaboration of four main "axis" of the CLE during the instructional engineering process (see Table 1): the *Knowledge* Axis, the *Instructional* Axis, the *Media* Axis, and the *Delivery* Axis. The Knowledge Axis refers to the identification of the targeted knowledge of different types (*concepts, procedures, principles, and facts*) and the specification of competencies that learners will develop when interacting with the CLE. The Instructional Axis refers to the elaboration of the learning scenario that the learners will follow in the CLE and the associated teaching scenario that the instructor will implement. The Media Axis concerns the format of the CLE interface and the different learning resources integrated in the CLE. Finally, the Delivery Axis refers to the description of the technological and organizational infrastructure needed to implement the CLE and the different actors' roles during the actual implementation (or delivery) phase.

When progressing along the phases of the MISA, and at the crossroads of the six phases and the four axis, the instructional designer produces a series of "documentation elements" (DEs). Examples of DEs include "Target Audiences," "Target Competencies," "Knowledge Model," "Instructional Scenarios," and so forth. For complex CLEs, the instructional designer could produce up to 35 DEs, but for simple CLEs, a smaller number

of core DEs would be produced. As illustrated in Table 1, when communicating the results of the instructional design process, the instructional designer can group the DEs produced either by phases or by axis.

To develop each axis, the instructional designer is invited to use a methodology based on a graphical object-typed modeling technique (Paquette, 2002), borrowed and adapted both from knowledge representation techniques used in artifical intelligence and from concept mapping technique.

Recommendations Found in the Literature

This section uses the six phases and the four axis of MISA as a frame of reference to organize recommendations concerning cultural variables that may guide instructional designers in their role as defined by MISA. Our purpose is to contribute to the identification of concrete recommendations

Table 1. Phases, Axis, and Documentation Elements[3] of the MISA (Adapted from Paquette, 2003)

Phase 1 Training Problem Definition		Phase 2 Preliminary Solution	Phase 3 Design of the Instructional Architecture	Phase 4 Design of Learning Materials	Phase 5 Production and Validation of Learning Materials	Phase 6 Planning of the Learning System Delivery	
100 Training Framework of the Organization 102 Objectives of the Project	Knowledge Axis	210 Knowledge Orientation Principles 212 – Knowledge Model 214 Target Competencies	310 Learning Unit Content	410 Content of Learning Instruments		610 Knowledge and Competency Management	Knowledge Model
104 Target Audiences 106 Current Context	Instructional Axis	220 Instructional Orientation Principles 222 Learning Event Network (LEN) 224 Learning Unit (LU) Properties	320 Instructional Scenarios 322 Propreties of Learning Activities	420 Propreties of Learning Instruments and Guides		620 Actors and Group Management	Instructional Model
108 Documented Resources	Media Axis	230 Material Orientation Principles	330 Development Infrastructure	430 List of Learning Materials 432 Learning Material Models 434 Media Elements 436 Source Documents		630 Learning System and Resources Management	Media Model
	Delivery Axis	240 Delivery Orientation Principles 242 Cost -Benefit Analysis	340 Delivery Planning	440 Delivery Model 442 Actors and Materials Packages 444 Tools and Means of Communication 446 Delivery Services and Locations	540 Assessment Planning for the Learning System 542 Revision Log	640 Maintenance and Quality Management	Delivery Model
Problem Definition Report		Preliminary Analysis Report	Architecture Report	Design BluePrint	Production and Validation Plan	Delivery Plan	

to guide instructional engineering of CLEs for diverse cultures by providing an overview of those currently found in the literature. We did not include recommendations that touch upon aspects addressed through standard use of MISA (and most ID methods), but rather focused on those recommendations specifically aimed at addressing cultural variables. We neither support nor reject these recommendations, and we are fully aware that some may conflict with others. Contradictions are the common lot of new, ill-defined knowledge domains.

MISA Phase 1: Define the Training Problem

- Assess market size (Burn & Thongprasert, 2005) and determine if the CLE will be internationalized (McBrien, 2005).
- Decide whether to use a model such as Trompenaar's (1993), Hall's and Hall's (1990), or Holfstede's (1980/2001) to guide the analysis of the target population.
- Determine what kind of learning environment is most familiar to target populations (Mannan, 2005; McLoughlin & Gower, 2000; Olaniran 2006), assess the value of education in the culture (Eberle & Childress, 2006; Wang & Reeves, 2006), particularly the attitude towards virtual education delivery (Burn & Thongprasert, 2005).
- Determine who uses computers in that society (Slay, 2002) as well as the technical infrastructure available to the learner and location: work, home, or cybercafe (Conner, 2000; Mannan, 2005; McIsaac & Gunawardera, 1996; Olaniran, 2006; Treuhaft, 2000; Wang & Reeves, 2006).
- Identify etiquette customs and traditions (Henderson, 2006).
- Identify cultural practices associated with gender issues in the target population society (Eberle & Childress, 2006; Henderson, 2006; Slay, 2002).

- Determine learner's view of time (Coulibayi, 2005; McLoughlin & Gower, 2000) and assess the amount of time available for learning (Conner, 2000; Coulibayi, 2005).
- Assess expectations regarding the role of the teacher and teacher-student relationship (Bates, 1999; Downey & al., 2004; McIsaac & Gunawardera, 1996; McLoughlin & Gower, 2000; Olaniran, 2006; Wang & Reeves, 2006).
- Determine which language(s) are spoken, as well as the skill level for each of them in the target population (McBrien, 2005). Clarify the level of language skills required to use the CLE (Bentley, Vawn Tinney, & Howe Chia, 2005; Treuhaft, 2000) and identify the need for translation (Eberle & Childress, 2006).
- Assess staff competencies in the area of intercultural communication and address their training needs (Cifuentes & Murphy, 2000; Goodear, 2001; Holzl, 1999; McIsaac & Gunawardera, 1996).
- Identify educational partners from the local culture (Bates, 1999; Cifuentes & Murphy, 2000; Goodear, 2001) and if required, recommend training of local experts to research, design, and implement the learning system (McIsaac & Gunawardera, 1996).
- Decide whether to use an approach in which materials are produced in ways that encourage and/or facilitate local adaptation, or one in which materials are produced so that they can be used in any context. If using an adaptation approach, consider defining strategy using Dunn's and Marinetti's (2006) "Guideline for the Selection for Adaptation Strategies."
- Decide which models and guidelines described earlier in the chapter will best assist in addressing cultural variables through the ID process.
- Adopt one of Catterick's (2006) three possible responses to cultural diversity: (1) non-

accommodation response, (2) intervention response, or (3) modification response.

- Determine whether the use of learning objects[4] would be an appropriate solution to address cultural variables, as they may allow for reusability from one cultural group to another, as long as they share cultural variables (Dunn & Marinetti, 2003a, 2003b, 2006; Goodear, 2001).

MISA Phase 2: Propose a Preliminary Solution

Instructional Axis

- Create opportunities for the cultural diversity of the participants to be explored (Eberle & Childress, 2006; Goodear, 2001), such as enabling learners to create resources and to add culturally relevant sources of information (Holzl, 1999; McLoughlin & Oliver, 2000).
- Design authentic learning activities and tasks aligned with the learners' existing skills and the values of their communities (McLoughlin & Oliver, 2000; Wang & Reeves, 2006).
- Pay attention to differences in instructional methods, which may vary from country to country (see example in McBrien, 2005).
- Include examples from indigenous and ethnic minorities as regular content (Henderson, 2006).
- Do not include examples that refer to alcohol, sex, religion, politics, the human body, or animals (McBrien, 2005).
- If learners are "low context" (Hall & Hall, 1990), inform learner of objectives, including information that may seem obvious; gain attention with possible loud, flashy methods; stimulate recall of prior knowledge by continually raising past discussion items and topics; present material so users have the option of reading through all of it; enhance retention and transfer by providing

few examples, and review what has been learned in the instruction (Sabin & Ahern, 2002).

- If learners are "high context" (Hall & Hall, 1990), briefly discuss objectives; gain attention in subtle ways, for example, startling facts; stimulate recall by asking questions and including intermediate quiz type assignments; present materials so users can skim for key concepts; provide concrete examples of how the information can be applied to actual work (Sabin & Ahern, 2002).
- Create multiple channels for communication between learners and teachers, some of which should be private (Cifuentes & Murphy, 2000; Eberle & Childress, 2006; Holzl, 1999; McLoughlin & Oliver, 2000) and in-between learners (Collis, 1999; Goodear, 2001; Wang & Reeves, 2006), including discussion forums in local language (Bates, 1999).

Media Axis

- Select the instructional medium carefully (Ali, 2006; Mannan, 2005), particularly because of the costs associated with modifications. Eberle and Childress (2006) caution against the cost of modifying videos.
- Provide a wide range of media, which can include face-to-face and paper-based support (Goodear, 2001), even when assigned readings are provided in electronic formats (Morse, 2003).

MISA Phase 3: Design the Instructional Architecture

Instructional Axis

- Provide a teacher's guide, which may be different depending on countries, languages, and culture types (Olaniran, 2006).
- Provide a learner's guide with specific guidelines for assignments that clearly

communicate the aims, objectives, and requirements (McLoughlin & Oliver, 2000). The guide should also include a guide for online communication (Goodear, 2001) and explicitly describe the educational values embedded in the course design, examples and strategies (Bentley et al., 2005).

- Include a self-assessment test on proficiency for the language used in the CLE.

Media Axis

- Work with community artists and designers to design the user interface and navigation features (McLoughlin & Gower, 2000). Let cultural variables inform the design of the user interface (see examples in Marcus & Gould, 2001).
- Pay attention to the position of navigation controls: right-hand Web navigation for those whose writing systems are right to left (Henderson, 2006).

MISA Phase 4: Design and Deliver Instructional Materials

Knowledge Axis

- Use simple sentences, particularly if the CLE is written in the learners' second language (Bentley et al., 2005; Eberle & Childress, 2006; McBrien, 2005; Treuhaft, 2000; Wang & Reeves, 2006), use the active voice (McBrien, 2005) and avoid colloquialism, humour or jargon (Bentley et al., 2005; Conner, 2000; Goodear, 2001; McBrien, 2005).

Media Axis

- Ensure high quality translation (Henderson, 2006) and use comments to provide context for translators (McBrien, 2005).
- Avoid using pictures of people from specific cultures (Eberle & Childress, 2006).
- Replace simple visual materials such as icons, sounds, and menus with localized words or symbols (Olaniran, 2006), or use

signs and symbols to facilitate mediation with, and integration of, knowledge (Gannon Cook & Crawford, 2006), or keep icons generic (Eberle & Childress, 2006; McBrien, 2005).

- Provide technological tools to encourage "multi-vocality," for example, machine translators, international keyboards, and virtual teachers (Goodear, 2001).

MISA Phase 5: Build and Validate Materials

Delivery axis

- Include representatives of the target population(s) in the test team (McBrien, 2005).

MISA Phase 6: Plan the Learning System Delivery

Instructional Axis

- Respect various e-learners' traditions and customs (Eberle & Childress, 2006) by not scheduling assignment dates during religious observances (Henderson, 2006).

Delivery Axis

- Emphasize human mediation, such as ensuring quality facilitation of computer-mediated communication. In some CLEs, this may include providing onsite course facilitators of the same culture as learners to take care of technical matters, assist students in communication and course organization, and explain content (Ali, 2006; Facey, 2001). If direct human mediation is unavailable because learners interact in a virtual meeting place, use a computerized social agent to play the role of host and provide "ongoing, in-context help in forming social relationships and building common ground between visitors" (Nakanishi, Isbister, Ishida, & Nass, 2004).

We were able to associate a significant number of recommendations from the literature with each of the six phases of MISA. This process highlighted the importance of considering culture, especially during the initial analysis, at Phase 1. We also noticed that some recommendations could not be integrated into the existing "documentation elements" (DEs) usually produced during MISA, indicating a need to make some modifications to the method if we want to make it more culturally sensitive.

FUTURE TRENDS

The identification of concrete recommendations to guide instructional engineering for diverse cultures is a new field of concern, in which many research issues are emerging. Which of them will most influence the instructional design of CLEs over the next decade? Following is an analysis of emerging and future trends and issues to watch for:

- **Emerging instructional engineering expertise in non-BANA countries.** Will instructional designers, particularly in Asia and Africa, raise issues and contribute through their practice to changes in the field of instructional engineering?
- **Culture of the instructional designer?** To deal with the affect the designer's culture may have on the instructional engineering process, Bates (1999) suggests the development of ID training that focuses on design issues for programs being delivered internationally. In an experiment conducted by Faiola and Matei (2005), users performed information seeking faster when using Web content created by designers from their own culture. This area of research raises the issue of who should design what for whom... Are local instructional designers better suited to develop culturally relevant CLEs? If so, what are the implications for BANA producers?

- **Cost and development time issues.** The strongest belief around e-learning is that it does save money, while addressing cultural diversity in the initial stage of a project is perceived as being very expensive (Conner, 2000). Will enough CLEs be built, considering cultural variables from the start, to provide a basis for comparison in cost and development time? Most e-learning is currently developed using the adaptation strategy called localization. Will that change? At what cost?
- **Dominant approach to culturally sensitive instructional engineering.** Which emerging model or guideline will be most influential? Will new ones be developed? Will adaptation or generalised approaches (Backroad Connections Pty Ltd, 2002, 2004a) dominate? Which of Catterick's (2006) three possible responses to cultural diversity will impose itself? Non-accommodation response, intervention response, or modification response?

FUTURE RESEARCH DIRECTIONS

Methodological Shortcomings

We agree with Bannan-Riltand (2003) that more sound design-based research studies are needed to build the foundation of a robust framework to guide instructional design. Current methodological shortcomings should be addressed particularly in regards to subject sampling. Therefore, we recommend that future research addresses the following:

- Absence of a control group
- Absence of reciprocity (for example, numerous studies of Asian learners using Western CLEs, but none about Western learners using Eastern CLEs)

- Small size of samples (some studies rely on a sample smaller than 10!)
- Over-representation of ESL (English as a Second Language) students and indigeneous learners as subjects
- Lack of distinction between students living in different cultures, in different countries, and students from different cultures, living in the same country. For example, in Faiola's and Matei's experiment (2005), Chinese students living in the U.S. are treated as if they were living in their homeland.

Information Sources

Instructional engineering should also be informed by sources other than the actual three models of national cultural characteristics. Sources could include research conducted with adult learners in multicultural classrooms, multicultural education (Gorski, 2005), and ethnocomputing, which is the study of the design, implementation, and evaluation of human-computer interactions that are targeted towards a specific cultural demographic (for examples, see the Institute for African-American Electronic Culture (IAAEC) at http://www.iaaec.com, and Hall, 2006). Another potentially relevant source of information is the research done by Katagiri, Nass, and Takeuchi (2001), which suggests that people treat computers using the norms for treating people within their culture. Human-Computer Interaction (HCI) research may also provide some guidance, including a study by Kamppuri, Tedre, and Tukiainen (2006) on the meaning of culture in interface design, the interplay of culture and technology, and methods of cross-cultural design.

Learning Object Approaches

Dunn's and Marinetti's (2003a, 2003b, 2006) methodolody, which incorporates cultural orientation theories, has already been adopted by the Australian Flexible Learning Framework (Goodear, 2001). Could learning objects, as Palaiologou (2006) maintains, have the potential to make culturally acceptable information accessible to all students, regardless of their ethnocultural background?

CONCLUSION

Research into cultural variables and the instructional engineering of computer-based learning is a relatively new and emerging field. Whether they be corporations, institutions, or entire countries, current and aspiring education and training services providers are concerned with both the effectiveness of learning and the financial consequences of not meeting the needs of learners from diverse cultures. The tremenduous potential of a globalized educational market, particularly in Asia, fuels the interest in cultural variables and learning.

Literature on the subject is often based on models of national cultural characteristics, such as those developed by Holfstede (1980/2001), Trompenaar (1993), and Hall and Hall (1990). Issues discussed in the literature include power relationships, relevance of learning theories and instructional approaches, underlying agendas of world citizenship and cultural awareness, language differences, and the impact of the designer's culture. Most of the literature to date comes from BANA countries.

So far, no framework to guide instructional design has demonstrated its adequacy to meet pedagogical, cost, and development goals. However, some models and guidelines are emerging to assist instructional designers, which we described briefly. We have used a method of engineering for instructional systems called MISA to organize recommendations found in the literature. We conclude with the following summary:

- Know your learners and their context and culture

- Consider cultural diversity from the start
- Be aware of your own cultural biases
- Use culturally informed instructional strategy
- Use human mediation (facilitation of computer-mediated communication and/or onsite facilitation) to ensure cultural inclusivity;
- Favor partnerhips and transfer of know-how. Involve your partners (learners, teachers and other local stakeholders) from the start and at every phase
- Provide many different forms of support to teachers and learners: guides, communication tools, and so forth
- Be aware and use recommendations coming from culturally informed HCI research
- Be aware and use recommendations coming from developers' experience

Although not specifically designed for this purpose, MISA provides a means of organizing recommendations related to cultural variables throughout the instructional engineering process. In the process, we noticed that some recommendations for Phase 1 could not be integrated into the usual "documentation elements" (DEs) produced during that phase. Therefore, to ensure that issues related to cultural variables are fully considered during Phase 1, a new DE should be added. Areas for which recommendations could not be found may also indicate a need for further research. Hopefully, this effort will contribute to the identification of concrete recommendations to guide the instructional engineering of computer-based learning for diverse cultures and provide insights into the constant transformation of the social aspects of technology and culture.

REFERENCES

Ali, A. (2006). Modern technology and mass education: A case study of a global virtual learning system. In A. Edmundston (Ed.), *Globalized e-learning cultural challenges* (pp. 327-339). Hershey, PA: Idea Group Inc.

Backroad Connections Pty Ltd 2002 (Ed.). (2004a). *Cross-cultural issues in content development and teaching online (version 2.00)*. Australian flexible framework quick guides series, Australian National Training Authority. Retrieved June 29, 2006, from http://pre2005.flexiblelearning.net.au/guides/crosscultural.pdf

Backroad Connections Pty Ltd 2002 (Ed.). (2004b). *Globalisation/Internationalisation of online content and teaching*. Australian flexible framework quick guides series, Australian National Training Authority. Retrieved June 29, 2006, from http://pre2005.flexiblelearning.net.au/guides/international.pdf

Bannan-Ritland, B. (2003). The role of design in research: The interactive learning design framework. *Educational Researcher, 32*(1), 21-24.

Bates, T. (1999). *Cultural and ethical issues in international distance education*. Paper presented at the Engaging Partnerships, Collaboration and Partnership in Distance Education UBC/CREAD Conference, Vancouver, Canada. Retrieved November 5, 2006, from http://www.tonybates.ca/papers/cread.html

Bentley, P. H., Vawn Tinney, M., & Howe Chia, B. (2005). Intercultural Internet-based learning: Know your audience amd what it values. *ETR&D, 53*(2), 117-127.

Burn, J., & Thongprasert, N. (2005). A culture-based model for strategic implementation of virtual education delivery. *International Journal of Education and Development Using ICT, 1*(1). Retrieved October 11, 2006, from http://ijedict.dec.uwi.edu/viewarticle.php?id=17&layout=html

Catterick, D. (2006). Do the philosophical foundations of online learning disadvantage non-Western students? In A. Edmundston (Ed.), *Globalized e-learning cultural challenges* (pp. 116-129). Hershey, PA: Idea Group Inc.

Chan, B. (2002). A study of the relationship between tutor's personality and teaching effectiveness: Does culture make a difference? *International Review of Research in Open and Distance Learning, 3*(2), 1-21.

Chen, A., Mashhadi, A., Ang, D., & Harkrider, N. (1999). Cultural issues in the design of technology-enhanced learning systems. *British Journal of Educational Technology, 30*(3), 217-230.

Cifuentes, L., & Murphy, K. L. (2000). Cultural connections: A model for eliminating boundaries and crossing borders. *Quarterly Review of Research on Distance Education (inaugural issue), 1*(1), 17-30.

Collis, B. (1999). Designing for differences: Cultural issues in the design of WWW-based course-support sites. *British Journal of Educational Technology, 30*(3), 201-215.

Conner, M. (2000). Global implications of elearning. *LiNE Zine, 2*(1). Retrieved May 14, 2006, from http://linezine.com/2.1/features/mcgie.htm

Coulibaly, B. (2005). Multiculturalité et apprentissage collaboratif assisté par ordinateur (ACAO): L'exemple du DESS UTICEF. *TICE et Développement, 1.* Retrieved May 20, 2006, from http://www.revue-tice.info/document.php

Downey, S., Cordova-Wentling, R. M., Wentling, T., & Wadsworth, A. (2004*). The relationship between national culture and the usability of an e-learning system.* Retrieved December 1, 2006, from http://www.learning.ncsa.uiuc.edu/downey/docs/AHRD2004-downey_cordova-wentling-wentling-wadsworth.pdf

Dunn, P., & Marinetti, A. (2003a). Cultural adaptation: Necessity for global elearning. *LiNE Zine, 7*(2). Retrieved May 16, 2006, from http://www.linezine.com/7.2/articles/pdamca.htm

Dunn, P., & Marinetti, A. (2003b). *E-learning and national culture.* Retrieved May 16, 2006, from http://www.trainingfoundation.com/articles/default.asp?PageID=1266

Dunn, P., & Marinetti, A. (2006). Beyond localization: Effective learning strategies for cross-cultural e-learning. In A. Edmundston (Ed.), *Globalized e-learning cultural challenges* (pp. 223-238). Hershey, PA: Idea Group Inc.

Eberle, J. H., & Childress, M. D. (2006). Universal design for culturally diverse online learning. In A. Edmundston (Ed.), *Globalized e-learning cultural challenges* (pp. 239-254). Hershey, PA: Idea Group Inc.

Edmundston, A. (2006). The cultural adapation process (cap) model: Designing e-learning for another culture. In A. Edmundston (Ed.), *Globalized e-learning cultural challenges* (pp. 267-290). Hershey, PA: Idea Group Inc.

Edmundston, A. (Ed.). (2006). *Globalized e-learning cultural challenges.* Hershey, PA: Idea Group Inc.

Edwards, R. (2002). Distribution and interconnectedness. The globalisation of education. In M. R. Lea & K. Nicoll (Eds.), *Distributed learning: Social and cultural approaches to practice* (pp. 98-110). London: Routledge.

Facey, E. E. (2001). First nations and education by Internet: The path forward, or back? *Journal of Distance Education/Revue de l'enseignement à distance, 16*(1). Retrieved August 30, 2006, from http://cade.athabascau.ca/vol16.1/facey.html

Faiola, A., & Matei, S. A. (2005). Cultural cognitive style and Web design: Beyond a behavioral inquiry into computer-mediated communication. *Journal of Computer-Mediated Communication, 11*(1). Retrieved October 8, 2006, from http://jcmc.indiana.edu/vol11/issue1/faiola.html

Fay, R., & Hill, M. (2003). Educating language teachers through distance learning: The need for culturally appropriate DL methodology. *Open Learning, 18*(1), 9-27

Gannon Cook, R., & Crawford, C. M. (2006). What can cave walls teach us? In A. Edmundston

(Ed.), *Globalized e-learning cultural challenges* (pp. 187-208). Hershey, PA: Idea Group Inc.

Gayol, Y., & Schied, F. (1997). Cultural imperialism in the virtual classroom: Critical pedagogy in transnational distance education. *ICDE Conference Proceedings: The new learning environment: A global perspective.* Retrieved June 29, 2006, from http://www.geocities.com/athens/olympus/9260/culture.html?200629

Goodear, L. (2001). *Presentation of findings 2001 flexible learning leaders professional development activity. Cultural diversity and flexible learning.* Australian National Training Authority. Retrieved October 8, 2006, from http://www.flexiblelearning.net.au/leaders/events/pastevents/2001/statepres01/papers/l_goodear.Pdf

Goodfellow, R., & Hewling, A. (2005). Re-conceptualising culture in virtual learning environments: From an "essentialist" to a "negotiated" perspective. *E-Learning, 2(4),* 356-368. Retrieved October 8, 2006, from http://www.wwwords.co.uk/ELEA/content/pdfs/2/issue2_4.asp#5

Goodfellow, R., Lea, M., Gonzalez, F., & Mason, R. (2001). Opportunity and e-quality: Intercultural and linguistic issues in global online learning. *Distance Education, 22*(1), 65-84.

Gorski, P. (2005). *Multicultural education and the Internet: Intersections and integrations.* Boston, Toronto: McGraw-Hill.

Gunawardena, C. N., Lowe, C. A., & Anderson, T. (1997). Analysis of a global online debate and the development of an interaction analysis model for examining social construction of knowledge in computer conferencing. *Journal of Educational Computing Research, 17*(4), 397-431.

Gunawardena, C., Wilson, P., & Nolla, A. (2003). Culture and online education. In M. Moore & W. Anderson (Eds.), *Handbook of Distance Education* (pp. 753-775). Mahwah, NJ: Lawrence Erlbaum Assoc.

Hall, A. (2006). Who's learning? Responding to the needs of a culturally diverse world of online learners. In Markauskaite, L., Goodyear, P. & Reimann. P. (Eds.), *Proceedings of the 23rd annual conference of the Australasian Society for Computers in Learning in Tertiary Education: Who's learning? Whose technology?* Sydney: Sydney University Press. Retrieved December 15, 2006, from http://www.ascilite.org.au/conferences/sydney06/proceeding/pdf_papers/p138.pdf

Hall, E. T., & Hall, M. R. (1990). *Understanding cultural differences.* Yarmouth, MA: Intercultural Press Inc.

Henderson, L. (1996). Instructional design of interactive multimedia: A cultural critique. *ETR&D, 44*(3), 85-104.

Henderson, L. (2006). Theorizing a multiple cultures instructional design model for e-learning and e-teaching. In A. Edmundston (Ed.), *Globalized e-learning cultural challenges* (pp. 130-153). Hershey, PA: Idea Group Inc.

Hewett, T. T., Baecker, R., Card, S., Carey, T., Gasen, J., Mantei, M., Perlmen, G., Strong, G., & Verplank, W. (1996). *ACM SIGCHI Curriculum for Human-Computer Interaction.* Retrieved December 26, 2006, from http://sigchi.org/cdg/index.html

Holfstede, G. (1980, 2001). *Culture's consequences. Comparing values, behaviors, institutions, and organizations across nation.* (2nd ed.). Thousand Oaks, London, New Delhi: Sage Publications.

Holliday, A. R. (1994). *Appropriate methodology and social context.* Glasgow, UK: Cambridge University Press.

Holzl, A. (1999). *Designing for diversity within online learning environments.* Paper presented at the Australasian Society for Computers in Learning in Tertiary Education Conference, Brisbane, Australia. Retrieved June 29, 2006, from http://

www.ascilite.org.au/conferences/brisbane99/papers/holzl.pdf

Internet usage in Asia. (n.d.). Retrieved October 22, 2006, from http://www.internetworldstats.com/stats3.htm

Kamppuri, M., Tedre, M., & Tukianien, M. (2006). *Towards the sixth level in interface design: Understanding culture.* Proceedings of the CHI-SA 2006, 5th Conference on Human Computer Interaction in Southern Africa, Cape Town, South Africa, January 25th-27th 2006 (pp. 69-74). Retrieved December 1, 2006, from http://www.tedre.name/pg_research.html

Katagiri, Y., Nass, C., & Takeuchi, Y. (2001). Cross-cultural studies of the computers are social actors paradigm: The case of reciprocity. In M. J. Smith, G. Salvendy, D. Harris, & R. Koubek (Eds.), *Usability evaluation and interface design: Cognitive engineering, intelligent agents, and virtual* (pp. 1558-1562). Mahwah, NJ: Lawrence Erlbaum Associates.

Khan, B. H. (2000). *A framework for open, flexible and distributed learning.* Paper presented at TEND 2000, Crossroads of the New Millenium. Retrieved December 1, 2006, from http://www.eric.ed.gov/ERICWebPortal/Home.portal

Kinuthia, W. (2006). African education perspectives on culture and e-learning. In A. Edmundston (Ed.), *Globalized e-learning cultural challenges* (pp. 1-17). Hershey, PA: Idea Group Inc.

Kline, S. J. (1995). *Conceptual foundations for multidisciplinary thinking.* Stanford, CA: Stanford University Press.

Mannan, A. (2005). *Open and distance education in developing countries and globalisation: Facing the challenges.* Paper presented at the ICDE 2005 Conference, New Delhi, India. Retrieved June 29, 2006, from http://www.ignou.ac.in/ICDE2005/PDFs/theme1pdf/theme1_17.pdf

Marcus, A., & Gould, E. W. (2001). *Cultural dimensions and global Web user-interface design: What? So what? Now what?* Retrieved August 26, 2006, from http://www.amanda.com

Mayor, B., & Swann, J. (2002). The English language and "global" teaching. In M. Lea and K. Nicoll (Eds.), *Distributed learning: Social and cultural approaches to practice* (pp. 111-130). London: Routledge.

McBrien, K. (2005). *Developing localization friendly e-learning.* Retrieved July 20, 2006, from http://www.chinaonlineedu.com/yuanwen/special.asp?id=122

McCarty, S. (2006). Theorizing and realizing the globalized classroom. In A. Edmundston, (Ed.), *Globalized e-learning cultural challenges,* (pp. 90-115). Hershey, PA: Idea Group, Inc.

McIsaac, M. S., & Gunawardera, C. N. (1996). Distance education. In D. H. Jonassen (Ed.), *Handbook of research for educational communications and technology* (pp. 403-437). New York: Simon & Schuster MacMillan.

McLoughlin, C. (2006). Adapting e-learning across cultural boundaries: A framework for quality learning, pedagogy, and interaction. In A. Edmundston (Ed.), *Globalized e-learning cultural challenges* (pp. 223-238). Hershey, PA: Idea Group Inc.

McLoughlin, C., & Gower, G. (2000). *Indigenous learners on-line: A model for flexible learning in an innovative Web-based environment.* Paper presented at the Australian Indigenous Education Conference, Freemantle, Australia.

McLoughlin, C., & Oliver, R. (2000). Instructional design for cultural difference: A case study of the indigenous online learning in a tertiary context. *Australian Journal of Educational Technology,* 16(1), 58-72. Retrieved June 29, 2006, from http://www.ascilite.org.au/ajet/ajet16/mcloughlin.html

Moore, M. G., Shattuck, K., & Al-Harthi, A. (2006). Cultures meeting cultures in online distance education. *Journal of e-Learning and Knowledge Society. The Italian e-Learning Association Journal, 1*(2), 187-208. Retrieved September 29, 2006, from http://www.je-lks.it/archive/02_05/Methodologies1.html

Morse, K. (2003). Does one size fit all? Exploring asynchronous learning in a multicultural environment. *JALN, 7*(1), 37-55. Retrieved July 28, 2006, from http://www.sloan-c.org/publications/jaln/v7n1/index.asp

Nakanishi, H., Isbister, K., Ishida, T., & Nass, C. (2004). Designing a social agent for a virtual meeting space. In R. Trappl & S. Payr (Eds.), *Agent culture: Designing virtual characters for a multi-cultural world* (pp. 245-266). Hillsdale, NJ: Lawrence Erlbaum Associates.

Olaniran, B. (2006). Challenges to implementing e-learning in lesser-developed countries. In A. Edmundston (Ed.), *Globalized e-learning cultural challenges* (pp. 18-34). Hershey, PA: Idea Group Inc.

Palaiologou, N. (2006). Intercultural dimensions in the information society: Reflections on designing and developing culturally-oriented learning. In A. Edmundston (Ed.), *Globalized e-learning cultural challenges* (pp. 74-88). Hershey, PA: Idea Group Inc.

Paquette, G. (2002). *Modélisation des connaissances et des compétences.* Sainte-Foy (Québec): Presses de l'Université du Québec.

Paquette, G. (2003). *Instructional engineering in networked environments.* San Francisco: Pfeiffer/Wiley Publishing Co.

Rose, D. H., & Meyer, A. (2000). Universal design for learning: Associate editor column. *Journal of Special Education Technology, 15*(1). Retrieved December 28, 2006, from http://jset.unlv.edu/15.1/asseds/rose.html

Rose, D. H., & Meyer, A. (2002). *Teaching every student in the digital age.* Alexandria, VA: Association for Supervision and Curriculum Development.

Saba, F. (1994). From development communication to systems thinking: A postmodern analysis of distance education in the international arena. In M. Thompson (Ed.), *Internationalism in distance education: A vision for higher education* (pp. 107-114), American Center for the Study of Distance Education Research Monograph No. 10, Pennsylvania State University.

Saba, F. (2003). Distance education theory, methodology, and epistemology: A pragmatic paradigm. In M. G. Moore, & W. G. Anderson (Eds.), *Handbook of distance education* (pp. 3-20). Mahwah, NJ: Lawrence Erlbaum Associates, Publishers.

Sabin, C., & Ahern, T. C. (2002). *Instructional design and culturally diverse learners.* Paper presented at the 32nd ASEE/IEEE Frontiers in Education Conference, November 6-9, Boston, Ma, 2002. Retrieved September 27, 2006, from http://fie.engrng.pitt.edu/fie2002/

Samovar L. A., Porter R. E., & Stefani L. A. (1998). *Communication between cultures.* Belmont, CA: Wadsworth Publishing Company.

Seufert, S. (2002). Cultural perspectives. In H. H. Adelsberger, B. Collis, & J. M. Pawlowski (Eds.), *Handbook on information technologies for education and training* (pp. 411-21). New-York: Springer.

Slay, J. (2002). Human activity systems: A theoretical framework for designing learning for multicultural settings. *Educational Technology & Society, 5*(1), 93-99. Retrieved June 29, 2006, from http://ifets.ieee.org/periodical/vol_1_2002/slay.html

Subramony, D. P. (2004). Instructional technologists' inattention to issues of cultural diversity among learners. *Educational Technology*, *44*(4), 19-24.

Taylor, B. C. (2005*). Virtual kaleidoscopes: Socio-cultural implications for distance learning*. Paper presented at the 21st Annual Conference on Distance Teaching and Learning. Retrieved September 27, 2006, from http://www.uwex.edu/disted/conference/Resource_library/shared_space.cfm?main=search

Thomas, M., Mitchell, M., & Joseph, R. (2002). The third dimension of ADDIE: A cultural embrace. *TechTrends*, *46*(2), 40-45.

Treuhaft, J. D. (2000). Global online learning among asia-pacific economies: Lessons learned. *Journal of Educational Media*, *25*(1), 51-55. Retrieved July 12, 2006, from http://www.col.org/tel99/acrobat/treuhaft.pdf

Trompenaars, F. (1993). *Riding the waves of culture*. London: Nicholas Brearley Publishing Ltd.

Trompenaars, F., & Woolliams, P. (2004). *Marketing across cultures*. Chichester: Capstone Publishing Ltd.

Wang, C.-M., & Reeves, T. C. (2006). The meaning of culture in online education: Implications for teaching, learning, and design. In A. Edmundston (Ed.), *Globalized e-learning cultural challenges* (pp. 1-17). Hershey, PA: Idea Group Inc.

Wiley, D. A. (2002). Connecting learning objects to instructional design theory: A definition, a metaphor, and a taxonomy. In D.A. Wiley, *The Instructional Use of Learning Objects* (pp. 1-35). Retrieved December 8, 2006, from http://reusability.org/read/chapters/wiley.doc

Wong, L. F., & Trinidad, S. G. (2004). Using Web-based distance learning to reduce cultural distance. *The Journal of Interactive Distance Online Learning*, *3*(1), 1-13.

Zahedi, F., van Pelt, W. V., & Song, J. (2001). A conceptual framework for international Web design. *IEEE Transactions on professional Communication*, *44*(2), 83-103.

ADDITIONAL READING

Bentley, J. P. H., & Tinney, M. V. (2003). *Does culture influence learning? A report on trends in learning styles and preferences across cultures*. Paper presented at the annual conference of the Association of Educational Communication & Technology, Anaheim, CA.

Carr-Chellman, A. A. (Ed.) (2005). *International perspectives oneE-learning: Rhetoric and realities*. Thousand Oaks, CA: Sage.

Chase, M., Macfadyen, L., Reeder, K., & Roche, J. (2002). Intercultural challenges in networked learning: Hard technologies meet soft skills. *First Monday*, *7*(8). Retrieved April 8, 2007, from http://firstmonday.org/issues/issue7_8/chase/index.html

Chavan, A. L. (2005). *Another culture, another method*. Paper presented at the 11th International Conference on Human-Computer Interaction, Las Vegas, Nevada, United States, July 22-27.

Cyr, D., & Trevor-Smith, H. (2004). Localization of Web design: An empirical comparison of German, Japanese, and United States Web site characteristics. *Journal of the American Society for Information Science & Technology*, *55*(13), 1199-1208.

Hancock, J., Barnhard, S., Cox, P., & Faldasz, D. (2005). The global needs assessment: Instructional design considerations for a global community. *AACE Journal*, *13*(1), 65-72.

Holfstede, G. (1986). Cultural differences in teaching and learning. *International Journal of Intercultural Relations*, *10*, 301-320.

Holmes, G. (2002). The importance of culture when creating audio-enhanced, Web-based instruction. *TechTrends*, *46*(2), 56-61

Honold, P. (2000). Culture and context: An empirical study for the developement of a framework for the elicitation of cultural influence in product usage. *The International Journal of Human-Computer Interaction*, *12*, 327-345.

Horton, W. (2000). *Designing Web-based training*. New York: John Wiley & Sons.

Keller, J. M., & Suzuki, K. (2004). Learner motivation and e-learning design: A multinationally validated process. *Journal of Educational Media*, *29*(3), 229-239.

Kurzel, F., & Slay, J. (2002). *Towards an adaptive multimedia learning environment: An Australian solution to cross-cultural and offshore delivery issues*. Paper presented at INC2002, Plymouth, UK. Retrieved on April 8, 2007, from http://www.informingscience.org/proceedings/IS2002Proceedings/papers/Kurzel89Towar.pdf

Lim, D. 2004. Cross-cultural differences in online learning motivation. *Educational Media International*, *41*(2), 163-175.

Lipton, R. (2002). *Designing across cultures – How to create effective graphics for diverse ethnic groups*. Cincinnati, OH: F&W Publications.

Lum, L. (2006). Internationally educated health professionals: A distance education multiple cultures model. *Education and Training*, *48*(2/3), 112-126.

Macfayden, L. P. (2004). Internet mediated communication at the cultural interface. In C. Ghaoui (Ed.), *Encyclopedia of Human-Computer Interaction*. Hershey, PA: The Idea Group.

Macfadyen, L., Chase, M., Reeder, K., & Roche, J. (2003). *Matches and mismatches in intercultural learning: Designing and moderating an online intercultural course*. Paper presented at the UNESCO Conference on International and Intercultural Education, Jyvaskyla, Finland.

Olaniran, B. A. (2004). Computer-mediated communication in cross-cultural virtual groups. In G. M. Chen & W. J. Starosta (Eds.), *Dialogue among diversities* (pp. 142-166). Washington, DC: National Communication Association.

Onibere, E. A., Morgan, S., Busang, E. M., & Mpoeleng, D. (2000). Human computer interface design issues for a multicultural multilingual English speaking country - Botswana. *The Inderdisciplinary Journal of Human-Computer Interaction*, *4*(13), 497-512.

Pincas, A. (2001). Culture, cognition and communication in global education. *Distance Education*, *22*(1), 30-51.

Rogers, P. C., Graham, C. R., & Mayes, C. T. (2006). *Cultural competence and instructional design: Exploration research into the delivery of online instruction cross-culturally*. Paper presented at the 6th International Conference on Cultural Attitudes towards Technology and Communication, Tartu, Estonia.

Rose, E. (2005). Cultural studies in instructional design: Building a bridge to practice. *Educational Technology*, *45*(March-April), 5-10.

Singh, N., & Pereira, A. (2005). *The culturally customized Web site – Customizing Web sites for the global marketplace*. Burlington, MA: Elsevier Butterworth-Heinneman.

Smith, P. J., & Smith, S. N. (2002). *Supporting Chinese distance learners through computer-mediated communication - Revisiting Salmon's model*. Paper presented at the International Conference of Computer Support for Collaborative Learning 2002, Boulder, Co.

Sudweeks, F., & Ess, C. (2002). *Cultural attitudes towards technology and communication*. Paper presented at the 3rd International Conference on Cultural Attitudes towards Technology and Communication, Montreal, Canada (pp. 69-88).

Thomas, M. K. (2003). Designer's dilemmas: The tripartheid responsibility of the instructional designer. *TechTrends*, *47*(6), 34.

Wilson, M. S. (2001). Cultural considerations in online instruction and learning. *Distance Education*, *22*(1), 52-62.

Zhang, J. X. (2001). Cultural diversity in instructional design. *International Journal of Instructional Media*, *28*(3), 299-307.

ENDNOTES

1. *MISA* is a French acronym for *Méthode d'ingénierie d'un système d'apprentissage*, which could be translated into "Engineering Method for Instructional Systems." This method was developed at the LICEF (*Laboratoire en informatique cognitive et environnements de formation*) Research Center of the Télé-Université of the University of Quebec in Montreal, Canada (TÉLUQ). The LICEF is dedicated to research in the field of cognitive informatics and training environments.

2. Kline (1995) identifies three foundational perspectives that are helpful in considering a complex system: 1) a synoptic view, which is an overview with a top-down approach; 2) a piecewise view, which identifies and examines the smallest portions of a system; and 3) a structural view, which provides details on how each piece fits together within a particular system.

3. The number of the DE is composed of three digits. The first one refers to the phase. The second one refers to the axis ("0" for the first phase, as it is not related to any axis). The third digit is an even number attributed to the ED as a unique identifier.

4. Wiley (2002) defines a learning object as "any digital resource that can be reused to support learning" (p. 7). It includes "anything that can be delivered across the network on demand, be it large or small. Examples of smaller reusable digital resources include digital images or photos, live data feeds (like stock tickers), live or prerecorded video or audio snippets, small bits of text, animations, and smaller Web-delivered applications, like a Java calculator. Examples of larger reusable digital resources include entire Web pages that combine text, images, and other media or applications to deliver complete experiences, such as a complete instructional event." (p. 7)

Chapter XIX
Technology and Continuing Professional Education:
The Reality Beyond the Hype

Maggie McPherson
University of Leeds, UK

Miguel Baptista Nunes
University of Sheffield, UK

John Sandars
University of Leeds, UK

Christine Kell
University of Sheffield, UK

ABSTRACT

Social Information Technology (SIT) can allow individuals, dispersed both in time and place, to connect via the Internet. Consequently, the use of online networks is very appealing to Continuing Professional Education (CPE) providers. However, our findings seem to have revealed an underlying reality overshadowed by this hype. Our experience, as both providers and researchers of online CPE to a range of healthcare workers, suggests that the reality of online networks is often far different from the planned learning objectives. In fact, we believe that learning in CPE must be assumed to be much more then the attainment of intangible concepts. Acquisition of static facts are useless if the learners do not have the understanding to apply them in apposite contexts and organisational settings. The use of new Web 2.0 approaches, such as social bookmarking and social networking, may well be an exciting potential development, but if busy professionals are to use SITs as an integral part of their daily personal and professional lives, further research into factors that facilitate and inhibit such usage is required.

INTRODUCTION

There is an increasing emphasis on technology to enhanced learning for professional education. The main drivers have come from commercial providers of e-learning products and professional organisations trying to make the most of current trends and fads. Sometimes this drive has resulted in national policies that are supported by Government, such as the recent e-learning strategy that has been proposed for the National Health Service in the United Kingdom (UK).

Continuing Professional Education (CPE) has the aim of developing personal and professional skills so that individuals are able to deal with the wide range of problems that they face in their day-to-day work. This requires a constant renewal of knowledge and skills, especially the tacit dimension that is gained through experience. Technology Enhanced Learning (TEL) approaches seem ideal for collaborative and cooperative learning approaches, and allow for tacit knowledge to be shared by professionals who are unable to meet face-to-face. Social information technology can easily allow widely dispersed individuals, both in time and place, to be connected through the Internet, and the vision of online networks has a seductive appeal to providers of CPE.

However, the vast majority of andragogical models for TEL in continuing professional education appear to be largely based on hype and reuse of traditional and very objectivist models. Whilst there has been large capital investment in structured multimedia products that provide sequential instruction and explicit knowledge based skills, however, it is very often the lack of tacit knowledge that hinders the acquisition of these skills.

Having performed several studies and several literature reviews of the use of TEL for healthcare professionals in the UK (Kell, 2006; Sandars & Langlois, 2005; Sandars & Langlois, 2006; Sandars & Walsh, 2004), our findings have highlighted the fact that there is an underlying reality that appears to have been overshadowed by this hype. In fact, our experience, as both providers and researchers of online CPE to a range of healthcare workers, suggests that the reality of online networks is often far different from the planned learning objectives. Common themes emerging from all of these studies include a lack of confidence, competence, contextualisation, and connectivity that are essential for individual professionals who wish to make effective use of TEL. These professionals, who are working within a wider organisational context, often appear to lack holistic views of the organisational context, inter-professional perspectives and the necessary tacit knowledge provided by years of work in the health system.

In this chapter, we will describe the potential of Social Information Technologies (SITs) for online CPE, and identify the main driving forces. We will highlight the important findings from our experience and research of online CPE, particularly within the health service, but the discussion will also be informed by the authors experience in other areas of CPE, such as the IT and Information sectors. In fact, our motivation in writing this chapter was in part to raise awareness of the importance of the major differences between policy and the reality of the context of professional practice and online CPE, and to propose recommendations that can inform future policy and practice. Thus, although the illustrations will be largely based on our studies of CPE for healthcare professionals in the UK, we believe that our study and findings can be generalised to other professions and to other contexts.

CONTINUING PROFESSIONAL EDUCATION

Since CPE is a fairly complex concept, before we can discuss the appropriateness of SITs for healthcare professionals, we need to clarify what we mean by this term. Weingand (1999) defined CPE as:

Education that takes place once professional quali-fication is achieved, with the intent of maintaining competence and/or learning new skills.

In trying to further describe this very complex concept, this author decomposed its parts into its most specific components as follows:

- **Continuing:** To go on with a particular action or in a particular condition; persist; to exist over a prolonged period; last;
- **Professional:** Of, relating to, engaged in, or suitable for a profession; engaged in a specific activity as a source of livelihood; performed by persons receiving pay; having great skill or experience in a particular field or activity;
- **Education:** The knowledge or skill obtained or developed by a learning process;
- **Continuing education:** An educational program that brings participants up to date in a particular area of knowledge or skills.

However, as noted by McPherson and Nunes (2002), professional education encompasses two different and distinguishable very complex components within the fields of educational studies: Continuing Professional Development (CPD) and Continuing Professional Education (CPE), both of which have been extensively and separately studied and researched. In fact, whilst CPE could be considered as a subset of CPD, it is structured with the formalism inherent to an educational programme. Therefore, although Weingand's (1999) definition is quite straightforward and logical, it is probably not sufficient to really allow an understanding of the complexity of CPE in this day and age.

The Nature of CPD

CPD is, in itself, no longer a synonym for traditional training. In fact, CPD nowadays has a much wider remit, which includes informal learning both in the workplace and in the general broader social environments away from the organisation. Until the late 1990s, the Healthcare Profession in the UK relied on what was termed Continuing Medical Education (CME). This was based on the acquisition of medical skills and knowledge through expert lectures on a specific medical subject; complemented by reading of medical journals and books (Kell & McPherson, 2005). More recently, the emphasis has moved from this pattern of subject-based skills acquisition to a more personal focus on the needs of the individual, and the process of professional learning and development was aligned with other professions through the use of the term CPD, defined as:

A process of lifelong learning for all individuals and teams which meets the needs of patients and delivers the health outcomes and healthcare priorities of the NHS and which enables professionals to expand and fulfil their potential. (Department of Health, 1998:42)

Some of the differences between these two paradigms have been discussed by Burrows (2003), who contrasted "Old CME" with "New CPD," as shown in Table 1.

As an example of the impact of this new paradigm, from 2004, the old system by which General Practitioners (GP) in the UK received remuneration in the form of a Post Graduate Education Allowance (PGEA) in exchange for completing 30 hours of postgraduate education sessions, has been replaced by a system of annual appraisal and Personal Development Plans (PDP) based on agreement with an accredited appraiser, as indicated in the "License to Practise and Revalidation for Doctors" published by the General Medical Council (2003). UK medical doctors are now obliged to maintain evidence of learning and reflection, which will be used to inform annual appraisal. Additionally, revalidation for a licence to practice will be required every 5 years. The exact form this will take is yet to be decided.

Table 1: Contrasting old CME and CPD, adapted from Burrows (2003).

	Old CME	New CPD
Setting	Hospital/PGMC based	Practice/personal based
Framework	PGEA	PDPs
Delivery	Lectures Refresher courses	Small-group discussion Multidisciplinary learning
Influences	Pharmaceutical sponsorship	Educational theory
Drivers	Specialists' messages to GPs	GPs' learning needs
Strengths	Expert resource	Relevance to practice
Availability	Local programmes Random uptake	Internet, journals Planned activity

This perspective on CPD is not confined to the healthcare profession. For example, it is clearly reflected in the following definition, which, according to Lorriman (1997), has been generally accepted by The (UK) Engineering Council's members:

The systematic maintenance, improvement and broadening of knowledge and skills and the development of personal qualities necessary for the execution of professional and technical duties throughout the individual's working life. (Lorriman, 1997:2)

Therefore, CPD is necessarily more than just the acquisition of technical and professional skills in a formal and structured setting. It encompasses the acquisition of tacit knowledge and personal skills that are often organisational related and only acquired through social interaction and negotiation.

The Nature of CPE

The role of Higher Education (HE) and Further Education (FE) institutions in CPD, that is CPE, has hitherto been extremely structured and formal. As Kell (2006) describes, CPE for health professionals has traditionally been performed in a didactic manner and the stereotypical ethos clearly objectivist with a focus on:

- Narrow medical subjects
- Experts distilling wisdom to passive "learners"
- Didactic delivery
- Passive reception of knowledge
- Uni-professional events
- Credit points by hours of attendance

Hence, CPE in the health sector in the UK has been closely subject based and consisting mainly of face-to-face (f2f) lectures and tutorials. Davis *et al.* (Davis, Thomson, Oxman, & Haynes, 1995) reported in the *Journal of the American Medical Association* on a systematic review of the effect of continuing medical education strategies, pointing to the deficiencies of the traditional approaches of CPE for health professionals, known as CME. Here a systematic review of Randomised Controlled Trials (RCT) in the literature was done, relating to how effective CME strategies were in bringing about both physician and health care outcome improvement. Their criteria for inclusion were met by 99 studies, 35 of which focussed on family physicians or GPs. Although 70% of interventions were effective in demonstrating a change in physician performance, only 48% of those aimed at improving health care outcomes produced a positive change. They found a variable effect on both performance and health care outcomes, with formal conferences lasting 1 day or less generally effecting no change. More effective methods included reminders, patient-mediated interventions, outreach visits, opinion leaders, and multifaceted activities. Less effective methods included audit with feedback and educational materials; least effective of all were widely used methods such as conferences. Within the study limitations, Davis *et al.* (1995) also point out that the focus on RCTs led to exclusion of the results of qualitative research methods that would afford additional valuable insights into physician behavioural change. In the final section of their chapter, Davis *et al.* (1995) suggest a full research agenda is needed, which should include more qualitative methods to elucidate physicians' perceptions regarding learning and change.

Oxman, *et al.* (Oxman, Thomson, Davis, & Haynes, 1995) performed a similar systematic review of 102 trials of intervention to improve professional practice from 1970-1993, and they concluded:

There are no 'magic bullets' for improving the quality of health care, but there are a wide range of interventions available that, if used appropriately, could lead to important improvements in professional practice and patient outcomes. (Oxman *et al.*, 1995: 1423)

This paper went on to suggest that the use of conferences or unsolicited material sent by mail, showed little effect on changing professional behaviour or improving health outcomes. Moderately effective interventions included outreach visits, and the use of local opinion leaders. These reduced the incidence of inappropriate performance in the range of 20% to 50%.

Both studies mentioned the need for caution in accepting their findings as they had included studies with a great variety of approaches, so no firm conclusions about the effects of specific interventions could be drawn.

Further work by Davis *et al.* (1999) attempted to: "review, collate, and interpret the effect of formal CME interventions on physician performance and health care outcomes." Here, findings suggested that although traditional lecture-based didactic methods could bring about change in knowledge skills or attitudes, there was no evidence of changed performance or health care outcomes. However, interactive techniques, such as case discussion, role-play, and hands on practice sessions (especially if they were sequenced), seemed to have more impact. At the same time, these authors advised caution in interpreting the results due to the possibilities of publication bias, limited numbers of randomised controlled trials, and possible flaws in the process of study selection, even though three independent reviewers were involved. Similar cautions were also noted in the two previous studies (Davis *et al.*, 1995; Oxman *et al.* 1995). Therefore, and despite evidence pointing to deficiencies in this approach:

... continuing education of health professionals remains dominated by the 'day in medicine,' when physicians assemble to hear a full day of lectures on a particular topic from academic specialists. (Norman, 2002, p. 1561)

Furthermore, Burrows (2003) states that rank and file healthcare practitioners have not wholeheartedly embraced the necessary changes, and continue to seek after traditional forms of CME. This is also discussed by other authors such as Calman (1998) and Ramsay *et al.* (Ramsey, Pitts, While, Attwood, Wood, & Curtis, 2003).

Therefore, and taking into account the definition of CPD presented, there is a need to change the perception of CPE, its objectives, planned learning outcomes, and andragogical approaches. This is evident in the extended definition proposed by Calman (1998:5):

There was consensus that continuing professional development in primary care should be purposeful, patient-centred and educationally effective. It should integrate consumer and patient interests with those of the NHS both nationally and locally and be constructed in such a way as to encourage team working within primary care and facilitate the appropriate adaptability of professional roles. Resource constraints should not be used as an excuse for neglecting continuing professional development, particularly in the sense that CPD should be personal and developmental. Artificial barriers between academics and non-academics should go and participation should be universal. (Calman, 1998:5)

This definition suggests a change of focus on both educational objectives and andragogical approaches. Professor Pringle, in his foreword to "Continuing Professional Development in Primary Care: Making it Happen" by Wakley, Chambers, and Field (2000), further suggests that the identification of educational needs should be performed by the health practitioner, and should result in changes in practice and behaviours:

...the recognition of educational need; the meeting of that need by the best available means (which might still include the traditional lecture); and the outcome is change in practice and patient care. (Pringle, 2000: v)

Therefore, the objectivist classroom model, although useful in some circumstances, may not always be appropriate. This idea is expanded by Burrows (2003) who proposes specific andragogical contextualised approaches for CPE:

...based on sound educational principles, such as being relevant to problems encountered at work, based on identified learning need, directed by the learner, shared with peers, using reflection, recording and evaluating outcomes. (Burrows, 2003: 411)

This type of approach to CPE can clearly not be supported by traditional classroom approaches alone. Furthermore, it requires more constructivist approaches to learning focused on collaborative learning, social negotiation of meanings, and active reflection on both practical and theoretical knowledge. SITs and Internet 2.0 technologies may play a crucial role in this new approach to CPE when combined with traditional approaches. These blended approaches are certainly well suited to support individual health practitioners to meet their identified learning needs. This stance received support from the UK Department of Health in section 5.9 of "Continuing Professional Development Quality in the New NHS," where the role of information technology in the delivery of CPE was emphasised as follows:

IT supports work-based learning and provides access to learning resources. It is a vital component of a modern managed approach to CPD...For clinicians, developing a deeper understanding of the use of information management in clinical practice will be an increasingly important part of CPD. (Department of Health, 1998: 5.9)

However, these blended approaches will present significant challenges in terms of the pedagogical/andragogical approaches and models to be adopted, as well as the necessary tutoring and learning skills that are implicit in the use of SITs in educational settings. In order to define andragogical models for CPE, it is necessary to discuss and establish the type of learning that occurs in this complex process.

NEW MODELS FOR CPE

In general terms, learning in CPE can be seen as a series of activities that promote acquisition of high-level knowledge (McPherson & Nunes, 2004, p. 41). However, both the nature of this knowledge, and the way that this knowledge is to be acquired, is changing due to the impacts of new technologies, namely SITs and Web 2.0. In fact, as early as 1997, the EC Study Group on Education and Training (1997) considered that the exponential development of new information technologies (IT) would lead to profound transformations in education and training. This Study Group foresaw that a new paradigm would overturn educational processes and methods, educational actor's roles and positions, and even the very concept of education. While this has not yet fully transpired, there are clear signs and indications that changes are taking place, including in CPE.

However, more importantly, the European Commission Study Group on Education and Training (1997) identified the need for a transition from objective to constructed knowledge that concurs with the views of CPE, as discussed. Accordingly, CPE should focus on developing problem-solving skills and social-communicative competencies, and requires new andragogical models that imply "a fundamental shift from the 'once in a lifetime' approach to higher education to one of educational progression linked to a process of continuous personal and professional development" (DES UK White Paper on the Future of Higher Education, 2003).

Therefore, learning in CPE must be assumed to be much more then the acquisition of inert and abstract concepts (e.g., decontextualised definitions, processes, and routines) that are of no use if the learner does not have the understanding to apply them in appropriate contexts and organisational settings (Nunes, 2003). Consequently, the aim in CPE must be to develop the learner's critical faculties, understanding, and independence of thought, in addition to the gathering of theoretical facts and concepts (Anderson, 1997).

Thus, and as discussed, this view of CPE implies the rejection of the classical tradition of transferring some body of knowledge in the form of unchangeable and authoritarian ideas, concepts, or definitions to the learner, as defended by the objectivist school of thought (McPherson

& Nunes, 2004, p. 41). According to this objectivist view, concepts are considered external to the learner and received through a process of communication.

This objectivist view of learning prevails even today in many universities and healthcare educational environments. This stance on learning was further developed and defended by the behaviourist school of thought. Behaviourist theories of learning do not attempt to account for any mental processes that occur in learning, the emphasis being on what the learner does in response to the knowledge transferred into her/him and passively accepted. Thus, this process focuses on behaviour and its modifications, rather than on cognitive or mental processes that facilitate learning (e.g., constructing, reflecting, or planning). This view of learning embodies a strongly individualistic conception of learning, in the sense that the individual behaviour is modified due to presentation of stimuli from the learning environment. Behaviourism embodies a model of the learner as a solitary striver for understanding (Jones & Mercer, 1993) and acquisition of knowledge as an abstract Platonic form (Laurillard, 1993).

However, CPE, as discussed, implies a learning process that is assumed to be much more than passive reception and acquisition of knowledge. The way learners handle knowledge is what really concerns academics (Laurillard, 1993). Knowledge has a contextualised character, which means that it cannot be separated from the situations in which it is used. When learning occurs in isolation it remains inert, that is, the learner has the information available in memory, but never recognises when it is relevant (CTGV, 1991). Acquisition of concepts is of no use if the learner cannot apply those concepts and transfer knowledge across different settings (Nunes, 1999).

Therefore, CPE in the healthcare sector involves the acquisition of high-level skills of critical thinking and problem solving in addition to the gathering of facts and concepts. Learning consists of a process of construction of knowledge and the development of reflexive awareness, where the individual is an active processor of information (Nunes, 2003). Learning occurs through interaction with rich learning environments, and results from engaging in authentic activities, and social interaction and negotiation. This view reflects the constructivist learning theory and in terms of CPE, is rooted on the following main assumptions:

- Learning must be situated in the domain of the use and the learning activities must match the complexity of that domain.
- Learning must contain both direct experience of the world and the reflection on that experience that will produce the intended way of representing it.
- Learners must be provided with the opportunity to explore *multiple perspectives* on an issue, that is, one activity is not enough to acquire a comprehensive view of a particular concept.

Situated learning raises another important issue in constructivist learning, that is, the way an individual learns, and the cognitive resources that are called upon, depend on the nature of the learning situation and previous learning activities (Hammond, 1992). Moreover, it is important to note that any learning activity in a particular domain is framed by its culture (Brown, Collins, & Duguid, 1989). This is of foremost importance in the healthcare sector, and implies that meaning and purpose are socially constructed through negotiations among present and past members of that society. That is, learning happens in a social context, and conceptual growth comes from sharing of perspectives and testing of ideas with others. Learning, in the sense of reaching common understandings and shared meanings, results from social interaction and negotiation with peers and tutors. The construction of knowledge by individual learners is based on the processes of interaction with peers, facilitators, and experts. Conceptions and ideas are compared, confronted,

and discussed through this interaction process. In the process, all actors modify their views to finally achieve a common understanding (Nunes, 2003). This means that SITs become paramount to support these learning communities and sustain interactions and negotiation of meanings for prolonged periods of time, long after the actual formal CPE has taken place.

However, the use of these SITs requires new forms of communication, learning, and interacting that are often not part of the set of skills developed by both tutors and learners.

NEW SKILLS FOR TUTORING WITH SITs

As discussed by McPherson et al. (McPherson, Nunes, & Zafeiriou, 2003), online tutoring and leadership has been widely considered as a crucial factor in the success of computer-mediated collaborative learning activities, as supported by SITs. Different and alternative names have been used in the literature referring to the role of the tutor in online interaction, such as coach (Murphy, Drabier, & Epps,, 1998), leader (Hotte & Pierre, 2002), tutor (Gerrard, 2002), moderator (Berge 1995; Feenberg, 1986; Kerr, 1986; Salmon, 2000), facilitator (Berge, 1992; Collison, Elbaum, Haavind, & Tinker, 2000; Marjanovic, 1999), motivator, mentor, mediator, and even production coordinator (English & Yazdani, 1999).

Nevertheless, most studies focus on online tutoring, as provided by an assigned e-moderator (Salmon, 2000, p. 7-11). These moderators were divided into institutional interveners, appointed interveners, and natural interveners by Hotte and Pierre (2002), that is, tutors, experts, and learners. This chapter focuses on the institutional interveners, that is, the academic tutors that support the CPE students throughout their learning process. In fact, by making the decision to adopt SITs for their online learning delivery, educationalists will need to reevaluate their roles as academic tutors, since familiar face-to-face teaching solutions may not work in an online learning environment (McPherson & Nunes, 2004).

As McMann (1994) points out, roles that have to be performed as part of e-tutors' tasks are actually not very dissimilar in nature in relation to the traditional face-to-face tasks. Nevertheless, there are significant differences that were identified from the very start of e-learning as a delivery mode. Authors, such as Mason (1991), discussed the roles of e-tutors as involving responsibilities at both technical and educational level. Mason (1991) focused on the discussion of the educational role of the online moderator that involves three categories: the organisational, the social, and the intellectual. McPherson and Nunes (2004), based on a thorough literature review, further developed this characterization and identified four main e-tutor roles:

- **Pedagogical or Intellectual Roles:** These are some of the most important roles in the use of SITs (Paulsen, 1995). The e-tutor uses questions and probes for student responses that focus discussions on critical concepts, principles, and skills (Zafeiriou, 2000, p. 67). These roles may include a number of tasks such as opening the discussions, focusing on relevant content and issues, intervening in order to promote interest and productive conversation, guiding and maintaining students' involvement in discussions, and summarising debates. Additionally, these roles may encompass directing and focusing discussions on vital points (Davie, 1989), synthesising points made by the participants (Hiltz, 1988), and providing summaries and interpreting online discussions (Feenberg, 1986).

- **Social Roles:** These involve the creation of friendly and comfortable social environments in which students feel that learning is possible. McMann (1994) considered the social role to be one of the key critical success factors in online learning. In this context, e-tutors are responsible for guaranteeing opportunities for participants to introduce themselves; identifying and dealing with lurkers who are reticent and sometimes reluctant to participate; ensuring that appropriate communication takes place; taking into consideration cultural and ethnic backgrounds by minimising humoristic, offensive, and disruptive behaviour; promoting interactivity between students; and finally, dealing with flaming, should this occur, by reminding participants of the appropriate netiquette.

- **Managerial or Organisational Roles:** These involve setting learning objectives; establishing agendas for the learning activities; timetabling learning activities and tasks; clarifying procedural rules and decision-making norms (Mason, 1991; Paulsen, 1995). These roles also include encouraging participants to be clear, responding to the participants' contributions, being patient, following the flow of the conversation and encouraging comments, synchronising, handling overload of information, encouraging participation, and ending the sessions (Zafeiriou, 2000, p. 67).

- **Technical Roles:** These are possibly the most daunting for some of the less technophile academics, and involve becoming familiar, comfortable, and competent with the SITs and other software that compose the e-learning environment. Additionally, this type of role includes supporting the students in becoming competent and comfortable themselves (McCreary, 1990) by providing technical guidance such as offering study guides, directions, and feedback on technical problems, ensuring that time to harness the ICT systems is made available, and encouraging peer learning.

From this characterisation, and according to McPherson and Nunes (2004), although similar in many respects to face-to-face (f2f) delivery, tutoring with SITs differs in a number of ways:

- Places greater emphasis on written skills
- Produces a more formal tone
- Does not follow a linear conversation but instead promotes multiple conversations
- Does not confine teaching to specific times
- Places greater emphasis on student-student learning
- Requires teachers to develop new ways of encouraging participation
- Requires teachers to assess the worth of online contributions

Therefore, even for the more experienced and talented of f2f tutors, there is much knowledge to be acquired about the skills required for learning supported by SITs. Consequently, the e-tutor must, in addition to the subject matter expertise and traditional pedagogical training, be able to demonstrate additional skills (Nunes & McPherson, 2004), such as an ability to:

- Plan and organise delivery by clearly specifying learning objectives and outcomes
- Set learning agendas and providing leadership and scaffolding in learning activities
- Welcome and embrace diversity of learning outcomes, attitudes, and styles
- Adapt supporting styles to the needs of individual participants
- Provide advice on different levels of access to learning materials according to the needs of individual participants
- Create an atmosphere of collaborative learning of which the e-tutor him/herself is often an integral part
- Be able to cope with and resolve online conferencing conflicts and difficult behaviours

- Encourage active construction of knowledge by being actively involved in discussions, activities, and debates
- Develop and implement methods for learner feedback and reinforcement
- Present advance organisers into the content materials and advice on learning pace so as to avoid cognitive overload and information anxiety

This new set of skills poses particularly difficult challenges in the selection of online tutors. In fact, subject matter expertise is usually certified by either academic institutions or professional bodies, thus, making it easy for selectors to identify suitable candidates. Similarly, traditional educational qualifications are easily recognised. However, e-tutors require the additional and crucial set of skills described, which makes it very difficult for selectors to choose appropriately qualified candidates to fill this role.

NEW SKILLS FOR LEARNING WITH SITs

However, it not enough that tutors are equipped with appropriate skills for online tutoring, the learners also need preparation. Due to the hype associated with online learning, CPE learners often feel compelled to engage with these new environments, without being properly equipped with the basic skills required to be successful (Nunes, McPherson, & Rico,, 2000a). In fact, adult students are expected to develop high cognitive skills such as negotiation of meaning, long-life learning, reflective analysis, and metacognition without being properly trained in low-level skills, such as the basic use of computer-mediated technology, online social skills, online etiquette, Web navigation, and Web searching. These skills were identified by Nunes et al. (Nunes, McPherson, & Rico, 2000b) as Networked Information and Communication Literacy Skills (NICLS). These skills are not only required to succeed in the on-line learning environment to which learners are exposed, but are also fast becoming an essential part of all aspects of daily networked activity (McPherson & Nunes, 2004).

In the future, these basic NICLS will be addressed and acquired at lower levels of the educational system, namely at primary school levels (Madden et al., 2007). However, most students enrolling in CPE courses nowadays are adults, having only acquired the traditional basic educational skills: reading, writing, spelling, handwriting and numeracy (Bramley, 1991). Unfortunately, these are insufficient skills to learn effectively in a learning environment supported by SITs (Madden et al., 2007).

NICLS complement the traditional basic skills with a new set of information and communication literacy skills. Information literacy includes recognising information needs, distinguishing ways of addressing gaps, constructing strategies of locating information, locating and accessing information, comparing and evaluating information, as well as organising, applying, and synthesising information (Webber & Johnston, 2000). Additionally, the limitations and affordances of conferencing technologies require adaptations and changes in human behaviour for successful communication to take place (Musselbrook, McAteer, Crook, McCloud, & Tholmy,, 2000). The skills required to undertake such a change when communicating online form what can be considered communication literacy as suggested by Pincas (2000). The conjunction of these two new types of literacy form what Nunes et al (2000b) identified as NICLS.

One of the greatest benefits of SITs is its ability to liberate educational delivery from the constraints of time and distance. However, when considering the use of these technologies, there is the need to prepare students to use these new social technologies in the context of learning. For successful communication to take place, the introduction of SITs into the learning environment generally requires changes and adaptations in human behaviour (Carr, 2000; Musselbrook et al., 2000). Authors, such as Rutter et al. (Rutter, Stephenson, and Dewey, 1981) argued that the lack of social cues such as audio and visual information, usually present in face-to-face (f2f), could hinder communication and disrupt the learning process. Therefore, and as proposed by McPherson and Nunes (2004, p. 84), CPE learners should be aware of crucial social factors involved in using SITs such as ignoring social boundaries, dealing with self-disclosure, flaming, guiding behaviour, adding cues to the communication (emoticons), and online etiquette (netiquette).

CPE learners must acquire NICLS before actually engaging with any online learning activity. Failure to address this issue in online learning, leads to much frustration for the learners, and eventually to lower levels of success for the on-line learning courses (Hara & Kling, 1999). In sum, NICLS can clearly be divided into two main categories: CMC and information skills. CMC skills are related to the interaction of the student with the learning community and information skills are related with problems of information anxiety and overload, as well as access to the learning resources.

CONCLUSION

A key aspect of the everyday work of professionals in healthcare environments is dealing with a range of complex and undifferentiated problems. The application of knowledge to help in this problem solving is essential, and the work of Polanyi (1967) has emphasised the important dimensions of the required knowledge. Polanyi (1958) describes two main dimensions of knowledge: explicit and tacit.

Explicit knowledge can be regarded as knowledge that is codified and made easily available through books, guidelines, and protocols. This is often presented as "evidence," and is the foundation of evidence-based medicine. This notion has tended to dominate healthcare, both policy and practice. Explicit knowledge could perhaps be acquired through traditional objectivist teaching and learning.

Tacit knowledge is gained through daily experience by being immersed in practice, and is shared between individuals when they meet. This knowledge is especially useful for decision making since it recognises the nuances of applying evidence that is based on populations rather than individuals. Tacit knowledge requires social negotiation of meanings, that is, interaction and discussion of concepts and solutions between peers within contextualised learning activities. This sharing of tacit knowledge is an essential aspect of both professional decision making and CPE. This has been recognised for centuries and has been part of the traditional services of most professional organisations, with the provision of opportunities for face-to-face meetings between colleagues, such as conferences and study groups. However, the pattern of work has changed for many professionals, and these are deceasing opportunities to meet face-to-face. The response has been to offer online opportunities, and these have been provided in the main by healthcare providers (such as the NHS) and professional organisations (such as BMA or academic colleges). This online provision is within a much wider social and political arena in which technology has been proposed as a way to communicate between individuals. This requires a constructivist approach supported by SITs.

The potential benefits of SITs have been heavily marketed as the new way of the Information Age. It is seductive to think that professionals can share tacit knowledge any time and any place. Widely distributed individuals, both geographically and in time, can be united and in learning. This vision is even more seductive, and there is hype about the development of online communities of practice, with the expectation that professionals will form close-knit groups in which there is extensive collaborative learning and sharing of tacit knowledge. However, this deduction has led to important failures, disappointments, and frustrations. In fact, neglecting to identify the new challenges posed by SITs has led to numerous forays into the unknown and into blind alleys. SITs in CPE require new tutoring and learning skills and understandings that need to be acquired before starting the learning process.

Therefore, we propose the following recommendations that should be addressed if the potential of social information technology for healthcare CPE is to be realised:

1. A developmental approach to design and development using action research should be adopted; McPherson and Nunes (2004) propose the EMAR model as a process of applying action research to CPE postgraduate programmes. This model contextualises traditional models of action research into educational design and development, and aims at guiding and supporting practitioners during the different stages of the process.

2. A systematic approach to evaluation of the learning phenomenon within a wider sociopolitical context should be embedded in the design and development process; a model that may be of particular use has been activity system analysis, as proposed by Mwanza (2002). This model is based on an activity theory perspective, and situates the interactivity of healthcare professionals and social information technology within a wider sociopolitical perspective.

3. Consider the use of newer more socially oriented forms of SITs; in recent years, there has been a phenomenal and increasing use of newer types of social software outside CPE, especially by young persons. These include blogs, file sharing, social bookmarking, and social networks. To date, there has been little use of this software for CPE, but there is potential that they can lead to more effec-

tive communication, and also collaborative learning, between healthcare professionals (Sandars, 2006).

Finally, the use of Web 2.0 encompasses the newer forms of social networked applications. Web 2.0 is predicated upon the principle that the use of the Internet is changing from one that is directed at the production of content to one that supports the active participation of members and the sharing of knowledge. There are major implications for CPE since it recognises that knowledge cannot be easily packaged into comprehensive and predetermined learning programmes. The role of the tutor also significantly changes from a provider of knowledge to a skilful facilitator who orchestrates the various resources and guides the learner through the maze. Learning becomes a process in which widely dispersed knowledge, especially tacit, is shared and collected, with the result that there is a shared individual and collective knowledge about an aspect of professional practice. The significant advantage of this coalescence approach to CPE is that it allows for rapid learning of useful knowledge that is directly situated in professional practice.

FUTURE RESEARCH DIRECTIONS

We suggest that further research in the use of SIT for CPE should be highly practical and related to the problems that have been identified in the previous research. The ultimate goal for all CPE is to improve the service that the professional provides, and this has obvious implications for the role and impact of all professions for the wider Society.

Most of the existing approaches to online collaborative learning for CPE have used first-generation SIT, such as discussion boards or e-mail. All of these approaches can be perceived as formal and imposed upon the learner. Recently, Web

2.0 methods of SIT, such as Webs, blogs, social network, and social bookmarks, have started to be widely used, mainly for informal learning. Research into how busy professionals are developing their own opportunities to share knowledge using these new SIT approaches would be useful.

The usual approach to online collaborative learning for CPE is to provide the technology and expect learners to use it. However, it may be that the identification of existing informal networks or communities, with subsequent support by SIT, would be more effective. Research into differences between created and emergent networks or communities is recommended.

The vision of vibrant communities, especially communities of practice, requires a high degree of mutuality and emotional involvement by the members of these communities. The present research suggests that some learners in CPE do not wish to engage in this depth of investment, both time and emotional. Nardi et al. (Nardi, Whittaker, & Schwarz, 2002) proposed the concept of intensional networks in which individuals develop multiple personal networks dependent on their particular needs, whether they are for information, support, opinion, or sharing of past experiences. Further research is recommended on how professionals create their own intensional networks for CPE, and to develop methods that allow individuals to maintain and balance their various intensional networks so that they can be quickly and effectively utilised. An exciting future development may be the use of new Web 2.0 approaches, such as social bookmarking and social networking.

The previous research has highlighted the importance of the wider organisational context in the success of SIT for CPE. Further research is recommended in the identification and understanding of the factors that facilitate and inhibit busy professionals to use SIT as an integral part of their busy daily personal and professional lives.

REFERENCES

Anderson, T. (1997). Integrating lectures and electronic course materials. *Innovations in Education and Training International, 34,* 24-31.

Berge, Z. L. (1992). *The role of the moderator in a scholarly discussion group (SDG).* Retrieved July 10, 2007, from http://www.emoderators.com/moderators/zlbmod.html

Berge, Z. L. (1995). Facilitating computer conferencing: Recommendations from the field. *Educational Technology, 35,* 22-30.

Bramley, G. (1991). *Adult literacy: Basic skills and libraries.* London: Library Association Publishing Limited.

Brown, J., Collins, A., & Duguid P. (1989). Situated cognition and the culture of learning. *Education Researcher, 18,* 10-12.

Burrows, P. (2003). Continuing professional development: Filling the gap between learning needs and learning experience. *Education for Primary Care, 14,* 411-413.

Calman, K. (1998). *A review of continuing professional development in general practice. Report by the Chief Medical Officer.* London: Department of Health.

Carr, S. (2000). Learning to communicate online is a challenge for new distance-ed students. *The Chronicle of Higher Education.* Retrieved July 12, 2007, from http://chronicle.com/free/2000/01/2000011301u.htm

Collison, G., Elbaum, B., Haavind, S., & Tinker, R. (2000). *Facilitating online learning: Effective strategies for moderators.* Madison, WI: Atwood Publishing.

Cognition and Technology Group at Vanderbilt University. (1991). Technology and the design of generative learning environments (pp.77-89). In T. Duffy & D. Jonassen (Eds.), *Constructivism and the technology of instruction: A conversation.* NJ: Lawrence Erlbaum Associates.

Davie, L. (1989). Facilitation techniques for the online tutor. In R. Mason & A. R. Kaye (Eds.), *Mindweave: Communication, computers and communication.* Oxford: Pergamon.

Davis, D., Thomson, M. A., Oxman, A. D., & Haynes, B. (1995). Changing physician performance: A systematic review of the effect of continuing medical education strategies. *The Journal of the American Medical Association, 274,* 700-705.

Department for Education and Skills. (2003). *Education and skills: The future of higher education (UK Government White Paper).* Norwich, UK: Cabinet Office. Department of Health. (1998). *A first class service – Quality in the new NHS.* London: The Stationary Office.

EC Study Group on Education and Training. (1997). *Accomplishing Europe through education and training.* Luxembourg: Office for Official Publications of the European Communities.

English, S., & Yazdani, M. (1999). Computer supported cooperative learning in a virtual university. *Journal of Computer Assisted Learning, 15,* 2-13.

Feenberg, A. (1986). Network design: An operational manual for computer conferencing. *IEEE Transactions on Professional Communications, 29,* 2-7.

General Medical Council. (2003). *Licence to practise and revalidation for doctors.* London: GMC.

Gerrard, C. (2002). Promoting best practice for e-tutoring through staff development. In *Proceedings of Networked Learning 2002: Third International Conference, Lancaster University and University of Sheffield, March 26-28th.*

Hammond, N. (1992). Tailoring hypertext for the learner (pp.149-160). In P. Kommers, D. Jonassen, & J. Mayes (Eds.), *Cognitive tools for learning.* Berlin: Springer Verlag.

Hara, N., & Kling, R. (1999). Students' frustrations with a Web-based distance education course. *First Monday, 4.* Retrieved July 12, 2007, from http://www.firstmonday.org/issues/issue4_12/hara/index.html

Hiltz, S. R. (1988). Productivity enhancement from computer-mediated communication: A systems contingency approach. *Communications of the ACM, 31,* 1438-1454.

Hotte, R., & Pierre, S. (2002). Leadership and conflict management support in a cooperative tele-learning environment. *International Journal on e-Learning, 1*(2), 46-59. Retrieved 10/03/2003, from http://www-icdl.open.ac.uk/

Jones, A., & Mercer, N. (1993). Theories of learning and information technology. In P. Scrimshaw (Ed.), *Language, classroom and computers,* (pp. 11-26). London: Routledge.

Kell, C. (2006). *Continuing professional development for general practitioners: Is eLearning an option?* MPhil Thesis. Sheffield, UK: Department of Information Studies, University of Sheffield.

Kerr, E. B. (1986). Electronic leadership: A guide to moderating online conferences. *IEEE Transactions on Professional Communication, 29,* 12-18.

Laurillard, D. (1993). *Rethinking university teaching: A framework for the effective use of educational technology.* New York: Routledge.

Lorriman, J. (1997). *Continuing professional development: A practical approach.* London: IET.

Madden, A. D., Baptista Nunes, J. M., McPherson, M., Ford, N. J., & Miller D. (2007). Mind the gap! New 'literacies' create new divides. In L. Tomei, (Ed.), *Integrating information and communica-tions technologies into the classroom,* (pp. 231-249). Hershey, PA: Idea Group.

Marjanovic, O. (1999). Learning and teaching in a synchronous collaborative environment. *Journal of Computer Assisted Learning, 15,* 129-38. Retrieved July 12, 2007, from http://www-icdl.open.ac.uk/

Mason, R. (1991). Moderating educational computer conferencing. *DEOSNEWS, 1*(19). Retrieved July 12, 2007, from http://www.emoderators.com/papers/mason.html

McCreary, E. (1990). Three behavioral models for computer mediated vommunications. In L. Harasim (Ed.), *Online education — Perspectives on a new environment.* New York, NY: Praeger Publishing.

McMann, G. W. (1994). The changing role of moderation in computer mediated conferencing. In *Proceedings of the Distance Learning Research Conference,* San Antonio, TX, April 27-29 (pp. 159-166).

McPherson, M. A., & Nunes, J. M. (2002). Supporting educational management through action research. *International Journal of Educational Management, 16,* 300-308.

McPherson, M. A., & Nunes, J. M. (2004). *Developing innovation in online learning: An action research framework.* London: RoutledgeFalmer.

McPherson, M. A., Nunes, J. M., & Zafeiriou, G. (2003). New tutoring skills for online learning: Are e-tutors adequately prepared for e-learning delivery? In *Proceedings of EDEN 2003 The Quality Dialogue; Integrating Quality Cultures in Flexible, Distance and e-learning,* 15-18 June 2003, Rodos Palace Hotel, Rhodes, Greece, (pp. 347-350).

Murphy, K. L, Drabier, R., & Epps, M. L. (1998). A constructivist look at interaction and collaboration via computer conferencing. *International Journal of Educational Telecommunications 4,* 237-261.

Musselbrook, K., McAteer, E., Crook, C., Mc-Cloud, H., & Tholmy, A. (2000). Learning networks and communication skills. *Association for Learning Technology Journal, 8*, 71-80.

Mwanza, D. (2002). *Towards an activity-oriented design method for HCI research and practice.* PhD Thesis. The Open University, UK.

Nardi, B., Whittaker, S., & Schwarz, H. (2002). NetWORKers and their activity in intensional networks. *Computer Supported Cooperative Work 11*, 205–242.

Norman, G. (2002). Research in medical education: Three decades of progress. *British Medical Journal, 324*, 1560-1562.

Nunes, J. M. (1999). *The experiential dual layer model (EDLM): A conceptual model integrating a constructivist theoretical approach to academic learning with the process of hypermedia design.* Sheffield: PhD Thesis, University of Sheffield, Department of Information Studies.

Nunes, J. M. (2003). Constructivism vs. objectivism: Where is the difference for designers of e-learning environments. In Keynote Address to the *E-Learning: Principles and Practice Research Seminar*, 22nd April 2003. Lismullin, co. Meath, Ireland.

Nunes, J. M., McPherson, M. A., & Rico, M. (2000a). Instructional design of a networked learning skills module for Web-based collaborative distance learning. In *Proceedings of the European Conference on Web-Based Learning Environments (WBLE 2000)*, 2000, Faculty of Engineering, University of Porto, Portugal, June 5-6th 2000, (pp.95-103).

Nunes, J. M.; McPherson, M., & Rico, M. (2000b). Design and development of a networked learning skills module for Web-based collaborative distance learning. In *Proceedings of 1st ODL International Workshop*, 2000, Universidad Politécnica de Valencia, Centro de Formación de Postgrado, Valencia, Spain, 19-21 July 2000, (pp, 117-131).

Oxman, A. D., Thomson, M. A. Davis, D. A., & Haynes, R. B. (1995). No magic bullets: A systematic review of 102 trials of intervention to improve professional practice. *Canadian Medical Association Journal, 153*, 1423-1431.

Paulsen, M. F. (1995). Moderating educational computer conferences. In Z. L. Berge & M. P. Collins (Eds.), *Computer mediated communication and the online classroom in distance education* (pp. 81-90). Cresskill, NJ, Hampton Press.

Pincas, A. (2000). New literacies and future educational culture. *Association for Learning Technology Journal, 8*, 69-79.

Polanyi, M. (1958, 1998). *Personal knowledge. Towards a post critical philosophy.* London: Routledge.

Polanyi, M. (1967). *The tacit dimension*, New York: Anchor Books.

Pringle, (2000). Foreword. In Wakley, Chambers, & Field (Eds.), *Continuing professional development in primary care: Making it happen,* (p.v.).

Ramsay, R., Pitts, J., While, R., Attwood, M., Wood, V. & Curtis, A. (2003). Factors that helped and hindered undertaking practice professional development plans and personal development plans. *Education for Primary Care, 14*, 166-177.

Rutter, D. R. Stephenson, E. A., & Dewey, M. E. (1981). Visual communication and the content and style of communication. *British Journal of Social Psychology, 20*, 41-52.

Salmon, G. (2000). *E-moderating: The key to teaching and learning online.* London: Kogan Page, Ltd.

Sandars J. (2006). The net generation: A challenge for work based learning. *Work Based Learning in Primary Care, 4*, 215-222.

Sandars, J., & Langlois, M. (2005). Online learning networks for general practitioners: Evaluation of a pilot project. *Education for Primary Care, 16*, 688-696.

Sandars, J., & Langlois, M. (2006). Online collaborative learning for healthcare continuing professional development: Lessons from the recent literature. *Education for Primary Care 17*, 584-592.

Sandars, J., & Walsh, K. (2004). E- learning for general practitioners: Lessons from the recent literature. *Work based learning in primary care, 2*, 305-314.

Wakley, G., Chambers, R., & Field, S. (2000). *Continuing professional development in primary care.* Oxford: Radcliffe Medical Press.

Webber, S., & Johnston, B. (2000). Conceptions of information literacy: New perspectives and implications. *Journal of Information Science, 26*, 381-397.

Weingand, D. (1999). Describing the elephant: What is continuing professional education? In *Proceedings of the 65th IFLA Council and General Conference Bangkok*, Thailand, 20-28 August. Retrieved July 12, 2007, from http://www.ifla.org/IV/ifla65/papers/089-104e.htm

Zafeiriou, G. (2000). *Students' perceptions of issues arising from and factors influencing group interaction in computer conferencing: A grounded theory approach.* PhD. Thesis. Sheffield, UK: Department of Information Studies, University of Sheffield.

ADDITIONAL READING

Kell, C., & McPherson, M. A. (2005). An investigation using Delphi into whether e-learning can meet the continuing professional development needs of general practitioners. In A. Brown & Remenyi, (Eds.), *Proceedings of the 4th European Conference on Research Methodology for Business and Management Studies* (pp. 225-234), 21-22 April 2005, Université Paris-Dauphine, Paris, France.

Kell, C., & McPherson, M. A. (2006). E–learning for general practitioners/family physicians: Barriers and enablers. In V. Uskov (Ed.), *Proceedings of the Web Based Education Conference,* January 23-25, 2006, Puerto Vallarta, Mexico.

Sandars, J. (2005). Work-based learning: A social network perspective. *Work based learning in primary care, 3*, 4-12.

Sandars, J. (Ed.). (2006). *e-Learning for GP educators.* Abingdon: Radcliffe Medical Publishing.

Sandars, J. (2006). The net generation: A challenge for work based learning. *Work based learning in primary care, 4*(3), 215-222.

Sandars, J. (2006). Twelve tips for effective online discussions in continuing medical education. *Medical Teacher, 28*, 591 –593.

Sandars, J. (2007). Developing a virtual personal network. *BMJ Careers 13 Jan*, 13-15.

Sandars, J. (2007). The potential of blogs and wikis in healthcare education. *Education for Primary Care, 18*, 16-21.

Sandars, J. (2007). Online communities for healthcare professionals: When hype meets reality. *Health Information on the Internet, 56*, 3-4.

Sandars, J., & Langlois, M. (2005). E-learning and the educator in primary care: Responding to the challenge. *Education for Primary Care, 16*, 129-133.

Sandars, J., & Walsh, K. (2005). There's never been a better time to e-communicate. *BMJ Careers, 331*, 265-266.

Chapter XX
Investigating and Encouraging Student Nurses' ICT Engagement

Michael R. Johnson
Cardiff University, UK

ABSTRACT

Higher education institutions rely increasingly on information and communications technology (ICT) to provide learning opportunities. Written to support this enterprise, the Guidelines for Networked Learning in Higher Education (Goodyear & NLinHE Team, 2001) carefully blend theory and practice to provide a wealth of sound advice for course design teams. The focus is on "promoting connections" that directly relate to learning. However, in nursing, 6 years after the Guidelines were published, levels of students' skills and engagement with ICT remain problematic, which undermines attempts to deploy networked learning. I argue that for such initiatives to succeed, other, more foundational connections need also to be promoted. I focus on some of the factors that contribute to student nurses' ICT non-engagement: gender, caring, professional identity, and knowledge work. Finally, I explain how some of the barriers identified can be overcome through integrating ICT. HE programs can provide students with meaningful encounters with ICT in the different elements of a course: curriculum, teaching methods, and assessment, as well as informal learning through online forums. If successful, this integration can promote the students' development of working knowledge in ICT, and increase the chances of their engagement in networked learning and evidence-based practice.

The JISC (Joint Information Systems Committee) funded "Effective networked learning in higher education: notes and guidelines" (hereafter simply the "Guidelines") was written "to support teachers in higher education who are thinking seriously about making use of networked learning" (Guidelines p .4). Since the Guidelines were published, learning technologies such as virtual learning environments (VLE) have been deployed throughout Further and Higher education in the United Kingdom (Joint Information Systems Committee, 2004). The Guidelines' "language, constructs, models, theoretical insights and evidence" (Guidelines p. 5) are as needful today as ever.

Networked learning is defined in the Guidelines as: "Learning in which information and communications technology (ICT) is used to promote connections: between one learner and other learners, between learners and tutors; between a learning community and its learning resources." (Guidelines p. 9)

The loose coupling of technology to student activity, implied by the central notion of *promoting connections*, is well suited to study at university, with its climate of autonomous learning. However, technological "solutions" bring their own layers of complexity and, in spite of their being extremely well informed, the Guidelines do not sufficiently promote connections of a more foundational nature, that is, access to and engagement with ICT *in the minds and lives of students*. In my experience with student nurses, sociocultural factors are more powerful than the most well-informed learning designs in deciding the fate of networked learning initiatives. With much rhetoric touting the benefits of ICT to learning, it can be difficult for course designers to resist investing technology *per se* with deterministic power (Jones, 2002). E-learning, in particular, is regularly portrayed as having the potential to enhance learning, motivate learners, and cater for widening access and participation, and so forth. (Department for Education and Skills, 2005). As with antecedent learning technologies, ICT generated excitement and expectations far beyond its capacity to deliver (Cuban, 2001; Ludvigsen, 2006). However, Goodyear (1998) argues that Universities have *not* invested in computers on primarily educational grounds. Rather, the proliferation of computers in the wider world of work makes their absence unthinkable in universities, dominated as they are by knowledge work. Thus the "project world view" that characterized UK government investment in learning technology (e.g., the Teaching and Learning Technology Programme) did not catalyze widespread uptake. Not that a project approach *per se* is to blame, the Guidelines themselves suggest a project lifecycle approach to course development. These "organizational fictions" are necessary to bring a complex goal to fruition. The Guidelines enact Goodyear's (1998) environment-centered approach in the Pedagogical Framework, which chimes in with the underlying innovation process in higher education. Universities have proved to be remarkably adaptable where the purpose of the innovation has been central to their mission (Goodyear, 1998). Without such a central motive force, mere enthusiasm about the advantages of computer use will not be sufficient to promulgate learning technologies, especially when built on the assumption that students will engage with computers in a moderately straightforward way. In my role as ICT lecturer, it used to surprise me that not everyone shared the same blasé attitude to using ICT as I do. Many of the ICT workshops I ran were poorly attended, and a significant proportion of those who did come did not even know their log in details. It would be easy to fall in with uninformed prejudice and write off nurses as technophobic, but the reasons for non-engagement are more complex and, moreover, usually rational. For example, Donald Norman is scathing towards hardware and software designers for accentuating the mismatch between "rampant featurism" and the practical needs of users (Cuban, 2001; Norman, 1999). At the most prosaic and yet telling level, Neil Selwyn *et al.*(Selwyn, Gorard,

& Furlong, 2006) found that many people simply did not need ICT to carry on their daily lives, and so did not engage with it. The following section presents four aspects of student nurses that plausibly contribute to their lack of engagement with ICT. This is not a trivial matter since it unhinges two important outcomes of their course. Firstly, to be equipped with the ICT skills necessary to become "fit for practice." This includes the need to engage with ICT for "evidence-based practice" and electronic care and patient record systems. Secondly, to participate fully in networked learning on their course and into a future of lifelong learning. Professional development budget-cuts make practice areas less able to release staff for study leave increasing the demand for "flexible" e-learning courses that require staff to study in their own time.

Selwyn offers three options when faced with non-engagement (Selwyn, 2003):

1. Restructuring of HE around ICT
2. Realistically embedding ICT within existing practices in HE
3. Accepting the status quo

This chapter goes on to describe how student engagement can be maximized if courses are designed to maximize the "impact, meaning and consequences of ICT use" (Selwyn et al., 2006, p. 24).

BACKGROUND: NURSING, STUDENT NURSES, AND ICT

In this section, I present and discuss four sociocultural factors that influence student nurses use of ICT.

Caring and Technology

Nursing has been defined by the Royal College of Nursing (RCN) (Royal College of Nursing, 2003) as:

The use of clinical judgment in the provision of care to enable people to improve, maintain, or recover health, to cope with health problems, and to achieve the best possible quality of life, whatever their disease or disability, until death. (Royal College of Nursing, 2003, p. 3)

The essence of the "provision of care" consists in "having an eye" for when it is appropriate to counterpoint routine "doing for," with shafts of individual attention, "being with" the patient (Freshwater & Biley, 2005). The daily mix of routine administrative and managerial tasks cut directly across the moral obligation of "emotional intimacy" with patients that is continually reinforced by the vivid and poignant stories told to demark a good nurse from a bad one (Freshwater & Biley, 2005). Technological expertise, and so forth, may be far more appropriate for the patient's immediate needs than emotional intimacy *per se*. For example, emotional intimacy could be *dangerous* where a mentally ill patient is being detained in a secure unit, or distinctly *one way* where a patient is comatose on an intensive care bed. Yet, in contrast to "the little things" never forgotten, the "touches of compassion" that aid recovery, the overwhelming majority of activities around the boundaries of caregiving amount to little more than "hygiene factors" in the eyes of healthcare consumers, that is, their absence is noticed whereas their presence is assumed. Musk (2004) cites two studies which showed that "patients rarely noted the nurse's technical competence [i.e., with clinical or therapeutic technologies], more commonly noticing the nurse's personal qualities, including smiling, taking time, understanding, and listening."

For an alternative view, Allen's work (Allen, 2001) portrays nurses as "organisational glue" holding the health service together. This shift in focus from the individual to the workforce does not hold the same potential for sustaining romantic narratives of nursing. Her ethnographic work, and subsequent literature review (Allen, 2004), draws upon Andrew Abbott's analysis of the tensions that arise between a society's shared ideals and a profession's lived experience of praxis. This is particularly the case in nursing as it is currently being evolved. Through recent NHS initiatives, Agenda for Change and the Knowledge and Skills Framework, NHS employers are "able to design jobs around patient and staff needs" (NHS Employers, 2005). New roles, such as nurse prescribing, consultant nurse, and advanced nurse practitioner, have sought to alleviate some of the NHS's workforce tensions, moving work traditionally done by doctors to nurses. In turn, this shifts more of the burden of providing "basic care" to unqualified nursing assistants and away from nurses *per se*. Dissonance between shared ideals about direct caregiving, often cited as what attracted nurses to the profession (Spouse, 2000), and what nursing is becoming, may make staff resistant to anything that further blurs the boundaries of their role. The rise of information systems in healthcare holds clear potential for this, where feeding the demands of audit shifts the carer's role towards one of managing health information. As Bloomfield and McLean put it:

...a tension between the demands of form filling and the established requirements of situated professional practice. On the one hand, we have the imperative of gaining information for the purposes of instituting/following the CPA [Care Programme Approach – a clinical audit project], managing it and rendering it accountable—in other words, activities of categorizing and coding that we might describe as belonging to the order of information. On the other, we have the clinical knowledge and experience of the practitioner—that is, the embodied and situated order of professional practice. (Bloomfield & McLean, 2002, p. 74)

Timmons (2003) studied nurses resistance of an ICT-based care-planning system. Nurses objected to the way the system pulled them away from the patients; lacked sophistication in its reification of their preferred [Roper, Logan, and Tierney] model of care; detracted from individualized care; and degraded their [nursing] skills.

Objections to the technology's infringement of caring are countered at the highest levels by an "ICT empowerment rhetoric," as manifested in an NHS Wales flyer (2004): addressed to nurses, it states that, "Properly trained to use the new systems, you should find that you are spending less time in front of technology and more time where you are most valuable; with your patients."

Thus, training in ICT is positioned as advantageous precisely because it will facilitate the nurse in carrying forward their core activity, and free them up from that which is on the periphery. Furthermore, the phrase "in front of the technology" is pejorative, implying inactivity, as one would slump "in front of the television" after a hard day. Extended sedentary computer-based work may also be perceived to be at odds with the caring role, given that "nurses provide or supervise around 80% of hands-on patient care in the NHS." (Royal College of Nursing, 2006b, p. 6) In light of the nature of this workload, appearing to linger at the computer may arouse resentment from peers and senior staff, especially given the ambiguity of apparent use afforded by computers, that is, that users can quickly and unobtrusively switch between work and leisure applications. That fear was somewhat allayed by Morris-Docker *et al.* (Morris-Docker, Tod, Harrison, Wolstenholme, & Black, 2004), who found that when ward-based nurses were given computers with unrestricted Internet access, they managed their use around busy periods. The study acknowledged some limitations, for example, individuals allowed others to use their log ins, however, no consideration was given to bias incurred through subjects' free access to the Internet, something common in higher education but rare in the NHS.

A recent leaflet by the RCN (Royal College of Nursing, 2006a) is squarely aimed at positioning ICT at the heart of caregiving: "There are still nurses who believe ICT has very little to do with nursing, but nothing could be further from the truth... In reality, ICT is primarily about managing information, which is central to nursing practice."

Objections to the role of ICT in nursing are thus portrayed as Luddite and irrational. It is questionable how many nurses would agree that managing information is "central to nursing practice." Buller and Butterworth's (2001) research generated a grounded model of expert nursing practice, where managing information is, at best, *implied* in the themes of planning, auditing and educating.

Gender and ICT

If gender does predict engagement with ICT, then this has a major bearing on our present investigation. Student nurses are predominantly female: the UCAS (Universities & Colleges Admissions Service) figures bear this out. Applications for entry to a Nursing Degree program in Wales for 2004 totaled 1,343, with 1,218 women (91%) and just 125 men. Furthermore, "nursing is women's work": nursing is imbued with values and tasks that have been identified with roles traditionally occupied by women (Meachin & Webb, 1996).

How gender relates to computer use is a complex, controversial, and emotive topic that divides expert and lay opinion (see Gunn, French, MacLeod, McSporran, & Conole, 2002; Gunn, French, McLeod, McSporran, & Conole, 2002; Hughes, 2002). When Neil Selwyn fed back evidence of gender effects in the students he had interviewed, their ICT teacher flatly denied the finding (Selwyn, 2002, p.166). Moule (2003) concludes that the balance of evidence lies with those, like Wishart and Ward (2002, p. 234), who find males more confident and engaged with ICT, possessing greater social capital for ICT, and so forth. A recent poll found that women are more likely than men to express a lack of confidence about using the Internet (45% vs. 30%) (MORI Social Research Institute, 2005). Furthermore, national figures from 2001 (Figure 1) show a pattern of decreasing use by age, with just 63% of women in the 25-44 who had ever used the Internet. This age group is significant for nursing students, since UCAS figures show the preregistration nursing intake is bimodal for age (Figure 2).

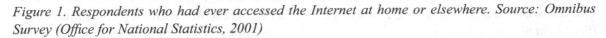

Figure 1. Respondents who had ever accessed the Internet at home or elsewhere. Source: Omnibus Survey (Office for National Statistics, 2001)

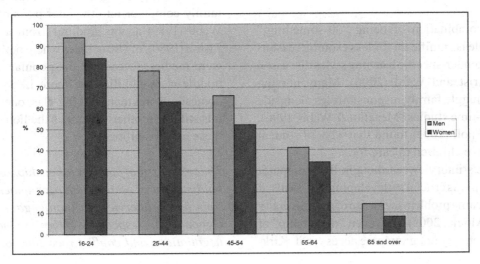

Figure 2. Bar chart of 2004 applications for Nursing, Psychology and Medicine in Wales (source: UCAS)

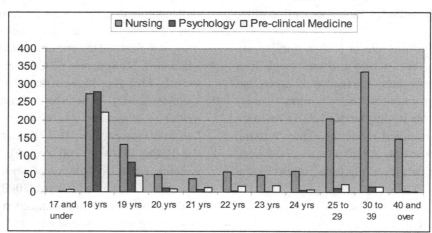

Gilchrist and Ward (2006) argue that since many nursing students are older, they will not have had so much (if any) ICT at school. However, school leavers are not necessarily any more confident users at 18:

We had a computer course in school, I was always way behind then, instead of listening I was play-ing the 'worm game' [on the computer]... it was either doing that or RE [religious education]... sometimes we did stuff but nothing I remember. (Selwyn et al., 2006, p. 164)

The combination of being "30-something" and female is significant for less esoteric reasons than the gender-specific learning styles discussed by Gilchrist and Ward (2006). Many nursing students juggle family responsibilities alongside their full-time studies (Meachin & Webb, 1996). A MORI poll (2003) found that 42% of student nurses have children to care for.

Moule's interviewees thought that computer ownership was crucial to developing ICT skills; it also overcame problems with use of the university system (Moule, 2003). However, "ownership" of a computer may not guarantee access to it. Kirk-wood and Price (2005, p. 265) claim that "male students are likely to report using their *own* equip-ment, while females often report using a *family* resource" (see also Cockcroft, 1994).

Once the computer comes into the home, it may not visit for long before being abducted, infested by viruses, or simply stolen. One student informed me that her partner had suddenly moved out, taking the entire computer system with them. Homemaking responsibilities constrain students' ability to choose when they attempt academic work, often pushing unhindered access to the family computer into the later parts of the day. Webb (1989) adapts findings from a study by Elston (1980), of 400 couples where both partners were medics, to counter the popular myth that middle-class families are more likely to share domestic chores than working-class ones. In 2006, it is still the mother who takes the lion's share of these responsibilities:

The complexity of family relationships and house-hold structures were crucial for understanding some female interviewees' (non)engagement with computers... – especially in terms of the familial negotiations and conflict regarding ownership, control and spatial positioning of computers in the home as well as the 'guilt' of spending time on the home computer at the expense of other members of the family. (Selwyn et al., 2006, p. 120)

Children can make assertive demands on the family computer, whether for schoolwork, gaming, or networking with friends. If the domestic home is the nursing student's main learning place, undisturbed use at *any* time of the day may be difficult to secure (Selwyn et al., 2006).

Kirkwood and Price (2005) analyzed data from Open University students' questionnaires, and mention health and social welfare courses as of particular concern regarding their limited access to computers (see also Breen, Lindsay, Jenkins, & Smith, 2001; Wishart & Ward, 2002), or where the computer tended to be of a lower specification.

However, even when access and ability may be presumed, "making sense of and acting upon the 'meaning' of technology in their everyday lives appeared to lie at the heart of why many of our interviewees were not making use of computers or the Internet." (Selwyn et al., 2006, p. 181)

Professional Identity

According to Fagermoen:

Professional identity refers to the nurse's conception of what it means to be and act as a nurse... as such it serves as a basic frame of reference in the nurse's deliberation and enactment in nursing practice influencing what are seen as relevant problems, goals and approaches. (Fagermoen, 1997, p. 435)

Names are one of the most important social markers for individual and group identity (Giddens, 1997, p. 582). Nursing has:

certain social values and needs, a lengthy and required education, a code of ethics, a mechanism

for self-regulation, research-based theoretical frameworks as bases for practice, a common identity and distinctive subculture, and members who are motivated by altruism and committed to the profession. (MacIntosh, 2003, p. 739)

To practice in the UK, a nurse has qualified for entry on the publicly accessible register maintained by the Nursing and Midwifery Council (NMC). The nurse will have undertaken 4,600 hours of study over 3 years: 50% practice and 50% theory (Nursing and Midwifery Council, 2004).

Students are allocated a single personal tutor throughout the 3 years at university, and although each new placement brings a new mentor, these experienced nurses directly supervise the student over a period of up to 8 weeks. Thusly, *practice* hours contribute an immersive experience for the formation of a student nurse's professional identity, each placement being an authentic site of their potential future employment, populated by *bona fide* members of the aspirant's community of practice.

Although graduates "soon realize that there is more to being professional than completing their initial education" (MacIntosh, 2003, p. 739), and while Spouse's study (2000) cautions that students do not passively adopt the norms and mores of the practice areas they experience, the alignment, or even subordination, of their own values and beliefs about nursing with the ones they experience while on placement are a key part of the whole enterprise of becoming a nurse.

What values and beliefs do students encounter on placement that could affect their engagement with ICT? Nurses use ICT for obtaining patients' test results, care planning, entering audit information, researching the evidence for a given treatment, and communicating with other healthcare professionals, as well as other more personal interests like reading job adverts (Morris-Docker et al., 2004). However, Brooks and Scott (2006, p. 85) assert that, "studies concerned with attitudes to computers and tools, such as the Internet, suggest that nurses' professional use and acceptance of the value of computers to their professional practice is lower than for other professional communities."

Even if students are enthusiastic to learn about the application of ICT in clinical areas, they tend to have very limited access to computers in these contexts (Moule, 2003). Wishart and Ward (2002, p. 236) agree, adding that, where computer use does occur, it is still common for students to observe apprehension about them among the clinical staff they encounter.

A report sponsored by the NHS Information Authority (NHS Information Authority, 2004) presents readers with an unlikely scenario: "I want you to imagine if you can…" The nurse is then depicted flowing effortlessly through an episode of care facilitated by a series of efficient and successful forays to the computer: for test results, and so forth. However, the focus group data shattered this vision: "The entire group indicated a problem with the basic IT skill level of most staff; comments such as 'I think we would have to start with how to turn the computer on' were common." (NHS Information Authority, 2004, p. 11)

More worrying still was that e-learning, thought to be "ripe for development," was one of the reports' main hopes for closing the reality gap. In often strongly hierarchical healthcare settings, students may find it difficult or undesirable to challenge more senior staff's abilities and attitudes towards computers. The 39-year-old nurse interviewed in Selwyn *et al.*'s research viewed computers as irrelevant to her work: "Behind her dismissal of the technology, it seemed to us, was a view that the technology was not central to her professionalism." (Selwyn et al., 2006, p. 130). The technology was resented for the way it de-skilled the nurse or else meant that the management had yet another way of keeping tabs on her performance. Another comment from this individual emphasized that if a technology could value and support the nurse's professionalism, then

it would be welcomed. She warmly envisioned a "network of medical knowledge" that would allow sharing knowledge, rather than being dictated to by what the computer "thought" was the correct action to take.

It seems ironic that something approximating to this vision of a nursing knowledge nirvana already exists in electronic bibliographic databases. Another of Selwyn's nurse interviewees found these resources invaluable while studying as a full-time graduate student, although "some of the [other] students didn't get on with it" (Selwyn et al., 2006, p. 115).

The Access to Knowledge project (A2K)[1] was to provide an electronic library of healthcare knowledge to all healthcare staff in Wales (NHS Wales, 2005). This has since been abandoned and funds used to provide staff with the Map of Medicine[2] instead. Improving access to resources also requires equipping staff with skills to evaluate and use that knowledge. I was reminded of Goodyear and Jones' (2003, p. 40) account of their evaluation of a group of government funded e-learning projects: "Many were driven by the beliefs about improved access to electronic content… where content was conjured up in the hope that *somehow* it may prove useful." Without some hegemonic imperative to require use of these resources, individuals are unlikely to make the quantum leap into the kinds of meaningful use envisaged by the project objectives.

Knowledge Work

To what extent is nursing knowledge work? Given that much research activity hinges on IT use, could this be a cause for engagement with IT? In 1972, Archie Cochrane called for healthcare to be "evidence-based" (Chalmers, 2006), and the Briggs Report challenged nursing to become research-based (Department of Health and Social Security, 1972). Since then, the transition of Nursing into higher education in the early 1990s (Burke, 2006) and the objective of becoming an all-degree entry profession by 2004 (Royal College of Nursing, 2006b) recognized the power vested in "academic" knowledge and its utility in bolstering Nursing's status among the other healthcare professions. However, debate around Nursing's status as an academic profession continues (McKenna, Thompson, Watson, & Norman, 2006) and although Beverly Malone, the RCN's former General Secretary, wanted research to be part of a nurse's job description, her organization was unable to find it an explicit place in their definition of nursing (McClimens, 2003). There may be greater social capital in what Blackler (1995) calls "embrained knowledge," but none of the 18 final-year preregistration nurses interviewed by Pateman and Jinks (1999) were contemplating research careers. Apart from a handful of students, the vast majority saw themselves as research *users* at most, which is all their curriculum requires. Veeramah (2004) suggests that where a degree program pays attention to research topics (e.g., critiquing, methods, etc.), students *are* being equipped to use these skills to maintain the currency of their knowledge and deploy evidence-based practice. The subjects, recent nursing graduates, described many barriers to their utilization of research, for example, a lack of time to read research (73%), resistance to change by others (38%), limited access to relevant research findings (37%). Such barriers are deeply seated within organizational cultures, and it is perhaps unreasonable to expect novices entering the profession to overhaul them. Indeed, it is likely that a student's apprehension of these barriers while on clinical placements act as a "reality check," inhibiting their ownership of research as part of a fundamental nursing skill-set.

Having bought into the need for evidence in clinical decision making, nursing theorists are having to untangle themselves from the trappings of a "biomedical model" that discounts professional expertise in favor of experimental studies, especially randomized controlled trials (RCT) (McKenna, Cutcliffe, & McKenna, 2000;

McSherry, Simmons, & Abbot, 2002). Freshwater (2004) argues for a widening of the definition of evidenced-based care to include expert opinion while McKenna (2004), partly to highlight implicit reductionism, turns the putative hierarchy of evidence (Gray, 2001) on its head, putting "expert opinion" at the top and "results of quantitative research" at the bottom. This highlights the sheer level of alienation between nursing and biomedical epistemologies, and it is the latter that the increasingly ICT-mediated peer-reviewed literature has privileged. Even the predominantly nursing-based JBI (Joanna Briggs Institute) regards "the results of well designed research studies grounded in any methodological position as providing more vigorous evidence than anecdotes or personal opinion" (Joanna Briggs Institute, 2006). Nevertheless, for nurses to perform at the highest levels, the nursing theorists mentioned do advocate a melding of research evidence with nurses' "expertise" (Benner, 1984); so, the role for ICT is obvious enough, as a portal to the tools of research (e.g., bibliographic databases and online journals), but the time-consuming and complex nature of working with these resources, per se, in a bustling under-resourced practice area should not be underestimated. It is not surprising to read that the qualified nurses' Internet search strategies observed by Morris-Docker *et al.* (2004) were often unsophisticated. Recognizing that existing staff were not receiving the same ICT learning opportunities as new entrants had, the NHS Executive sponsored "Learning to Manage Health Information," which sought to establish a core framework in health informatics development for all clinical health professionals. This was endorsed by a range of statutory and professional bodies, including the UKCC (the United Kingdom Central Council for Nursing, Midwifery and Health Visiting was replaced in 2002 by the Nursing and Midwifery Council or NMC) and the RCN. Section 5 lists 13 computer skills that *all* healthcare staff should acquire via professional development, for example:

4. Search a simple database, and
5. Undertake searches and access relevant sites on the World Wide Web and relevant health related databases. (e.g., Medline, CINAHL).

This advice was reviewed by the further publication "Moving Ahead" (NHS Information Authority, 2002), which delegated the learning and assessment of basic ICT skills to the European Computing Driving License (ECDL), which all NHS staff were recently expected to pursue. The ECDL is a basic ICT-skills qualification consisting of seven modules (http://www.ecdl.nhs.uk). Module 7 covers the same ground as the Learning to Manage Skills 4 and 5, yet this could only suffice as a platform for further development if nurses are to achieve competence in the more elaborate information literacy skills, as required by the evidence-based practice agenda. The Chartered Institute of Library and Information Professionals (CILIP, 2005) defines information literacy as: "Knowing when and why you need information, where to find it, and how to evaluate, use and communicate it in an ethical manner."

Survey data (NHS Connecting for Health, 2005) has been published to show that many nurses have benefited from passing the ECDL through having more time and being less dependant on asking for IT help. Compared with the routine retrieval of test results or updating medical records (which is the focus of a new stand-alone "ECDL Health Unit"), information literacy incurs a far heavier cognitive and ICT-skills burden that ECDL does not address.

Thus, in spite of arguments for student nurses to own information skills, including associated ICT skills, as part of their basic skill set, a student's inclination to engage with ICT is undermined from many directions:

Nursing, it seems, not only suffers from an absence of appropriate systems targeted to meet their professional needs, but barriers of time, access, workload and attitude may also prevent nurses

from embracing computer use as a medium for knowledge work and knowledge transfer. (Brooks & Scott, 2006, p. 85)

MAXIMIZING ENGAGEMENT

As Selwyn *et al.* argue, "engagement with ICTs is based around a complex mixture of social, psychological, economic and, above all, pragmatic reasons" (2006, p. 23). For each student, these reasons, which vary over time, make it more or less likely that they will decide to engage with ICT. This chapter sets out how I have implemented networked learning that *promotes connections* of ICT engagement in students' minds and lives, as well as those which directly relate to learning. This has required drawing upon and enacting best practice about learning in higher education and how people become fluent with ICT.

Best Practice in Learning in Higher Education

The Guidelines' authors seek to help readers reify their own "pedagogical framework" without strongly prescribing what should fill its parts. Readers are tasked with reviewing the presentation of current alternative views on the purpose of higher education, how students learn, and so forth. The authors' ideals are clear, especially when reviewing other work, in particular by Peter Goodyear (1998).

Epistemic Fluency

Epistemic fluency acknowledges various types and qualities of knowledge (de Jong & Ferguson-Hessler, 1996) that learners should become fluent at manipulating. This is best achieved through careful task formulation aimed at equipping learners with the ability to select an appropriate epistemic form or game (Morrison & Collins, 1996) to address the challenges facing them in academia, or the world of work, where the requirement to engage in knowledge work is increasing. Epistemic fluency is seen as key to a graduate's transformative potential, arguably their most significant transferrable skill:

Learners must learn how to take more control of their learning, how to make smooth transitions between abstract knowledge and concrete applications, how to integrate domain-specific knowledge with the skills needed to render it articulate and applicable. (Guidelines p. 61)

Guided Construction

Tracing a path from transmissive forms of learning and constructivism, the Guidelines explain guided construction using Tom Shuell's (1992) aspects of learning, as active, individual, cumulative, self regulated and goal orientated. These are well illustrated in the way the Guidelines provide readers with tasks to complete following each section. Pettigrew and Elliott's "Student IT Skills" (1999) takes a similar approach, recommending readers to reflect on, evaluate, and plot their own approach to learning.

Learning is Social and Situated

According to Brown *et al.* (Brown, Collins, & Duguid,1989), all learning is conditioned by the context in which it takes place. The traditional site of ICT skills training, the ICT lab, may not be optimal for learning ICT, unless that which is learned closely resembles the essence of the activity where the knowledge and experience is to be enacted. When there is a large contextual difference, for example, between home and university computers, students may struggle to transfer what they have learned between sites. In the Guidelines, the social element is clear from the definition: promoting connections between "one learner and other learners, between learners and tutors; between a learning community and

its learning resources." The place of technology is therefore to facilitate education that is believed to be "fundamentally conversational" (Selwyn et al., 2006, p. 29), as Säljö concludes:

The creation of knowledge is essentially a matter of learning to argue, and no technology will ever replace the need for learners to participate in ongoing conversations with partners sharing interests and commitments. Technology should not be seen as replacing such communication but rather as providing a resource for supporting it.

It then behooves teachers to bring these elements of theory, together with the components of the learning system, curriculum, teaching methods, and assessment procedures, into "constructive alignment" in order to promote deep learning (Biggs, 2003). Problem Based Learning (PBL) offers much potential for aligned teaching (Biggs, 2003) and so, a recent example of this is described towards the end of the section.

Best Practice on Learning to Use ICT

The Quality Assurance Agency for Higher Education (QAA) subject benchmark statements require all graduates to "demonstrate an ability to engage with technology, particularly the effective and efficient use of information and communication technology." (Quality Assurance Agency, 2001). Allan Martin (2002) charts the brief history of ICT use and learning in higher education and suggests three stages: mastery, applications, and reflective. While the applications stage was about enabling learners to become more *efficient*, for example, by knowing *how* to create a presentation (ECDL hails from this stage), the reflective stage is about *effectiveness*, avoiding "death by PowerPoint" through good design (Shepherd, 2004). It positions learners amidst their community of "apprentice knowledge workers" (Goodyear, 1998). Working knowledge in information fluency is valued and engendered through discussion and the performance of information mapping, seeking, and appraisal that is closely related to course assessments. Lev Vygotsky's zone of proximal development (ZPD) (1978) is helpful in understanding the tutor's role and the importance of collaboration in ICT lab workshops. ZPD is a complex concept that is frequently misunderstood as unidirectional scaffolding by the more competent other, that is, the teacher providing assistance just beyond the learner's ability (Tudge & Scrimsher, 2000). According to Tudge and Scrimsher, the misunderstanding is partly due to the English rendering of the Russian *obuchenie* as "instruction" *or* "learning," which ignores the dialectic aspect of the word. We are closer to

Vygotsky's original meaning if we restate "good learning is that which is in advance of development" as, "good *teaching/learning* is that which is in advance of development" (Vygotsky, 1978, p. 89). If we take the reference to time in the word "advance" in a looser sense, it could also imply deeper familiarity with the knowledge landscape, as well as affectively pushing learning beyond the "comfort zone." The ZPD is a most fruitful "space" for learning through a meeting of minds, where although one is more advanced than another, *each mind may be more advanced in their own way*. Each can assist the other in exploring the knowledge landscape, shaping, and being shaped by each other's interactions.

Table 1. A list of core ICT heuristics and concepts

1	Work out your support network: who can help you best with what?
2	Learn about "backing up" and versioning: delete nothing, version it instead.
3	Error messages: Try and act on their advice but if you don't understand what to do, guess, and learn from what happens next.
4	If something goes wrong, don't blame yourself – it's usually the computer's fault.
5	If something doesn't work or is taking too long, be pragmatic, find another way – there usually is one.
6	In design, simplicity is genius: ICT allows you to be creative but that may just waste time and/or obstruct your message.
7	If you forget how to do something use a program's help system to remind yourself.
8	A key function of computers is that they are good at storing, managing, and searching for information. What are the implications of this?
9	ICT is made up of files: learning to manage files is key.
10	Typing is still an important skill: Use a "learn to type" program to gain efficiency and confidence.
11	Copy and paste: it works between applications although Paste Special, unformatted text is useful to avoid carrying over the formatting.
12	Become familiar with these four shortcuts (there are more): ⊞+e (Windows Explorer)or ⊞+d (show desktop), Ctrl&c (copy) Ctrl&v (paste).
13	Right click to access task specific functions (e.g., open link in new browser).
14	ICT cannot be trusted.
15	Everything is owned by someone (beware of copyright)
16	Never use the space bar to align text – use tabs, indents, or a table instead. Find out about these from the help system.
17	Use heading styles in Word (enables table of contents, document map, etc.)

A recent ICT-lab session was entirely based around a collaborative task where pairs of students search for Web sites relevent to their module themes, critique them, and post their comments to an online forum in the VLE. ICT learning outcomes for the session were limited to just one or two hints aimed at making their browser use more effective: *right-clicking* on a link to open it in a new browser and *copy and paste* between windows/applications. Students are actively encouraged to help each other learn these operations. These two ICT hints stem from a limited number of core ICT concepts and heuristics I have identified, around which "working knowledge" can coalesse (see Table 1). Bransford *et al.* (2000, p. 9) use a similar term, *usable knowledge*: "expert knowledge is connected and organised around important concepts; it is 'conditionalized' to specify the contexts in which it is applicable." (Bransford et al., 2000, p. 9)

Tagging these concepts on to epistemic tasks that are closely related to course outcomes, while avoiding the intellectual overhead of technical computer knowledge wherever possible, promotes purposeful engagement during the class and after it. This mimics the way that many people learn ICT skills autonomously. Furthermore, designing for a "loose coupling" (Guidelines p. 55) between the set task and its performance allows students the flexibility to experiment, which students acknowledge is vital in learning to use a computer (Moule, 2003; Selwyn, Marriott, & Marriott, 2000). Moule's nursing students expressed initial intimidation and a lack of time and inclination to experiment, making it even more important to build in time for, sanction, and demonstrate this in lab-based sessions. I agree with Dutton that "the Internet is an experience technology" (in Selwyn et al., 2006, p. 195). By "playing" with ICT, the student is behaving "beyond his average age, above his daily behaviour" (Vygotsky, 1978, p. 102). The student ventures beyond the known, beyond their current ability, like Hill and Plath's "teacherless" shellfish divers (Hill & Plath, 1998), whose *bodies*

learned to negotiate the seabed, the lab becomes a "learn-place," where "moneyed knowledge" of ways to enhance summative assignments and make working on them more efficient, provides a worthwhile motive of learning activities.

Building the Bricolage

A bricolage of ICT incidences reflects the way people achieve and maintain fluency in ICT through an assortment of experiences that may include formal ICT lab-based training sessions, but is in no way limited to that (Selwyn et al., 2006, p. 172). An ICT bricolage does not privilege the formality, degree of success, personal involvement, availability or quality of support, and so forth, that define each ICT experience. Some people's lives do not have a critical mass of ICT experiences necessary to maintain adequate levels of working knowledge. Indeed, this may create a vicious circle: the minimal ICT experiences they do have are stressful because they lack working knowledge, which further undermines the development of fluency.

In addressing student non-engagement, Neil Selwyn (2003) suggests three options:

1. **Restructuring of HE around ICT:** Making ICT engagement unavoidable through, for example, requiring the completion of assessments to be mediated through computers. However, such a "strategy of compulsion can be strongly argued to be of limited long-term effect" (Selwyn, 2002, p. 115) in the same way as knowledge memorized for exams.

2. **Realistically embedding ICT within existing practices in HE:** To minimize the rejection of learning technologies, using them to "supplement and complement existing curricular processes" (*ibid*), thus providing meaningful and successful instances of ICT use.

3. **Accepting the status quo:** Recognizing that ICT is as fragmented and ineffectively used

as any other learning resource, this option requires staff to adjust their expectations accordingly.

Referring to Figure 3, even though John is a further cognitive, and perhaps physical, distance from engaging than Janet, *requiring* them to do so when the logic is compelling, *helping* them to do so when it is relevant, and *letting* them chart their own route when they opt out of other technological aspects of the course, is entirely consistent with adult education (Rogers, 2004; Selwyn, 2003). It behooves course designers to choose carefully which activities should be attributed what level of compulsion, and endeavor to promote connections in John's mind and life so that his decision *to* engage in *any* of these activities is easier to make and carry out. The outcome is similar to the integration of ICT into curricula advocated by many authors (Dearing,

1997; Gwinnett & Massie, 1987; Hodgson, McCartan, Hare, Clayphan, & Jezierski, 1995; Maier & Warren, 2000; Wharrad, Clifford, Horsburgh, Ketefian, & Lee, 2002).

Microsoft Word for Web Page Creation

Jonassen (1996) argues that instructional designers should take advantage of the relative strengths of human and machine: ICT is a powerful tool for the storage, management, search, and retrieval of information, which the human mind is not as good at. Instead, humans have powerful faculties of problem solving and intuition that are difficult to implement via computers. Therefore, computers are best used to facilitate knowledge construction rather than take the tutor's role in providing knowledge, albeit interactively: "When learners use multimedia to build knowledge bases, they function as *knowledge engineers* rather than

Figure 3. Two students in different proximity to engaging with ICT (arrows representing differing strengths of factors which distance students from engaging with ICT)

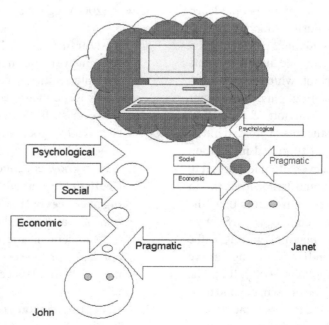

knowledge receivers." (Jonassen, 2001, p. 60, emphasis added)

Teachers keep some of the most powerful learning experiences to themselves when they design and deliver episodes of "passive reception" learning (Shuell, 1992). The continuous refreshing or manipulation of knowledge to develop or maintain teaching materials is an activity that students can also benefit from by performing knowledge construction through epistemic tasks. Clever task *design* and the facilitative actions of an attendant pedagogue are vital to support learning, since there is a danger that apprentice "knowledge engineers" will lose sight of the learning trajectory in the process of artefact production (Bransford et al., 2000, p. 13). The Guidelines recommend making the technology invisible, "so that everyone concentrates on the academic or other learning task at hand" (Guidelines, 2001, p. 131). Confining the software platform to generic IT knowledge working tools, a word processor, Internet browser, and e-mail client, gives the nearest approximation to "invisible" for everyone. Furthermore, as the Guidelines warn... "Technology which enforces an unacceptably restricted interpretation of the task will be rejected by its intended users." (Guidelines p. 48)

Generic ICT tools not only afford much flexibility in the completion of tasks, but gaining a deeper understanding of their applicability and facilities *through use* is not the wasted investment it might be with more niche software. They are, as Goodyear points out, the mainstream "tools of the trade" of their academic discipline or intended profession.' (1998, p. 5)

Hyperlinks are the core technology of the Web, and merely typing them in and pressing the space bar is sufficient to invoke their automatic creation in MS Word. This keeps the technical level required to complete the task as low as possible, while still enabling students to generate a functioning "Web page." It also provides scope for more IT-fluent students to express their creativity. The facilitator's role is to help students

understand and focus on the epistemic task, and to actively offer technical assistance.

Late in 2004, a team of lecturers wanted to deliver learning outcomes via problem based learning (PBL) mediated through ICT. For the tutors, this project was something of a "bridgehead" towards updating teaching practice in the School. John Biggs advocates PBL as particularly appropriate for developing professional skills because, "the student is required to base decisions in knowledge, to hypothesise, to justify, to evaluate and to reformulate, all of which are the kinds of cognitive activities that are required in professional practice." (Biggs, 2003, p. 213)

The project team believed that PBL was a useful high-level pedagogic strategy, but that they were too few to facilitate small groups in a cohort of 120 students. It was hoped that ICT would overcome the numerical imbalence through efficiency gains, for example, negating the need to travel and meet in a fixed time and place. Tutors were also keen to encourage students in using ICT, and agreed that the PBL activity would culminate with each group, presenting a coauthored Web page at a "mini-conference."

Students had already been put into groups for a previous module's activity, and these were recycled for the PBL. Numbering between four and six students, each group was provided with a private VLE (Blackboard) space, which offered them a discussion list, a file drop-box, an online chat area, and a means of e-mailing group members. The 8 available weeks were divided up into three triggers that were published in meetings between the tutor team and the whole cohort (see Figure 4). Triggers were also timed to be released automatically via Blackboard. Student PBL groups were expected to explore the implications of these, and post their response to the online drop-box on the last day before the next trigger. Their allocated tutor gave feedback via the group's online forum.

A "PBL coffee room" online forum was also available to all. It was well used, allowing everyone

Figure 4. One of the slides used to introduce the BSS PBL

How will this PBL be organised?

Week	Activity
One	Receive background information and trigger one
Two	Upload 'work in progress'. Receive online supervision
Three	Receive trigger two. Upload completed work for trigger one. Receive online supervision.
Four	Upload 'work in progress'. Receive online supervision.
Five	Receive trigger three. Upload completed work for trigger two. Receive online supervision.
Six	Upload 'work in progress'. Receive online supervision. Finalise your web based 'posters'
Seven	Present your work in the 'poster presentations' day.
Eight	Well earned break!

involved to share experiences, comment on the process, or even ask other groups for help.

Students information fluency development was supported through lectures, written guidance, and workshops on Web page searching, critiquing, and creation.

A PBL marking grid was devised to correspond with the validated summative assessment marking grids, so strengthening any future case for wider adoption. The one difference was where "Presentation" criteria were substituted for "Design/Technology," which was reworded. Group-work was recognized through peer assessment. The marks for the presentation formed 80% of each individual's score, and the remaining 20% was allocated by aggregating marks that individuals awarded for each group member on the basis of their contribution to the group work. This was done through a peer marking grid that was collected from groups on presentation day at the end of their viva with the paired tutor markers. This process prompted varied reactions, with some groups agreeing to give everyone the same top marks while others took the chance to vent their frustrations over members who had made no contribution. One student refused to participate

altogether, judging the process to be subversive.

All the marks, peer and group, were collated and e-mailed such that each student received an individualized breakdown of their marks and markers comments. In stark contrast to usual marking procedure, all the marking was completed on one day and feedback was returned electronically within the same week.

Students' PBL work was done in addition to work that counted towards their degree classification. In spite of this, tutors were amazed at the quality of work presented. The fact that nearly every student came to the presentation event was also pleasing, affected, no doubt, by the fact that failing to attend would mean having to make good all the theory hours allocated to group work during the previous 8 weeks (the normal register signing process was suspended until the presentation day). Evaluation data showed that students were annoyed that the work did not count towards their degree. They were also upset by "freeloaders" in the groups, and the timing of the PBL; they wanted more of it earlier in the course. Students also wanted freedom to choose their own groups, and some felt the marking "viva" was too short and did not do justice to their efforts. All of these issues can be corrected in further itterations of the PBL. There were hardly any concerns voiced over the technology.

For "bricolage building," the PBL intervention required and promoted meaningful engagement via ICT from all students, while allowing them significant freedom over the extent and manner of their engagement, that is, over and above the baseline of obtaining feedback on their weekly trigger responses, presenting their final work, reading their results, and being awarded their attendance hours.

FUTURE TRENDS

In higher education, the Net is closing in on non-users. As universities seek to leverage their huge investment in ICT, core processes, from enrollment to photocopying, are becoming "computer clad." Nevertheless, to the chagrin of technophile colleagues, 5 years from now, I still expect to meet some highly strategic non-users who continue to survive on their course by technological proxy (Selwyn et al., 2006, p. 167), relying on others to mediate the benefits of computer use, by typing essays, printing handouts from the VLE, even performing bibliographic searches for them.

In spite of the increasing ubiquity of ICT in clinical areas, computer-inhospitable cultures may be challenging to overhaul. Managers and educationalists must ensure that ICT interventions are a good fit with the actual needs and practices of users. Promising online tools, such as the Map of Medicine[2], will be underused unless they can be embedded in a culture that supports and enacts a dialectic vision of learning and practice, where each routinely informs and shapes the other.

FUTURE RESEARCH DIRECTIONS

Failing to fully engage with ICT may not "hamper successful living in contemporary society" (Sel-

wyn et al., 2006, p. 190), but the implications of non-engagement by specific professional groups is worthy of further investigation. For example, to what extent does non-engagement undermine the "evidence-based practice" (EBP) vision? A key ethic of EBP is that patients have the right to the best treatment. By failing to connect with or heed the advice of relevant evidence, harmful culturally ensconced "folklore-based" health interventions may continue to be enacted. Although the precise nature of evidence-based practice is contested, it does require practitioners to combine contextual expertise with the best available published research. ICT is the portal to this reified knowledge. EBP therefore hinges on practitioners' uninhibited access to ICT, a "critical mass" of information skills, and the potential for the ongoing development of finesse in handling the knowledge worker's ICT toolset.

Non-engagement also diminishes the potential worth of networked learning interventions, especially forms of computer-mediated communication that rely on sustained participation to perpetuate fruitful online discourse and dialogue. Answering Goodyear's call (Goodyear, 1998), "Social IT" could investigate the ergonomics of these environments, for example, the presence and strength of factors such as the four inhibitors described earlier in this chapter. One promising theoretical lens for this is activity theory (AT), which offers an analysis of individual and collective activity within a sociohistorical context (Bedney, Seglin, & Meister, 2000; Kaptelinin & Nardi, 2006).

CONCLUSION

Eight years ago, in the face of ongoing NHS ICT initiatives, Sinclair and Gardner (1999, p. 1443) warned that: "Preparing nurses for this information-based hi-tech health service is a major priority for all involved in their education and training." This was reaffirmed recently by the RCN (2006b,

p. 10): "Information technology is key to future health care and the aspirations of the future patient. Nurse Education must be able to support the development of skills in this arena."

As the rhetoric rumbles on, the onus for delivering an ICT-literate workforce lies squarely and awkwardly on the shoulders of education providers; an invidious position in the face of monolithic organizational cultures. Scholarly advice that aims to promote meaningful engagement with ICT, such the Guidelines, is undermined by the fact that technology use in 2007 is more like a *chain of weak links* than a chain *with* a weakest link, an opprobrium too often and too easily applied to human users. The Guidelines' authors do not expect non-use, or else merely pathologize it. As time passes, the "problem" will cease to exist. Selwyn reviews five types of discourse that have sought to account and prescribe for non-use of ICT, all based around a "deficit model": "where non-use of technology is due to shortfalls in cognition, personality, knowledge, resourcing, social situation or personal ideology." (Selwyn, 2003, p. 13) He asserts the more positive and realistic notion that individuals have technological *careers*, moving in and out of non-use (Selwyn, 2003). In this case, higher education and clinical sites, their processes and values, need to address their own issues of non-use by ensuring that their environments and cultures are times of moving *into* meaningful use, not *out* of it. I described how integrating ICT with PBL could provide a way of encouraging this in higher education. However, the trajectory plotted for student nurses by their experience in practice areas rarely encourages their engagement with ICT.

I have argued that the introduction of ICT has challenged Nursing's professional identity, even its epistemology. Without adequate freedoms in terms of time with and access to ICT, anything more than routine data entry and collection is ruled out in the daily milieu of care giving. To counter this, "there is a need for educators and managers to aim for an implicit and explicit acculturation of regularly accessing, sharing and critically evaluating evidence to influence individual and team practice." (Gulati, 2006, p. 27)

ACKNOWLEDGMENT

I would like to thank Neil Selwyn, whose insightful work has been vital to support some of this chapter's key arguments.

REFERENCES

Allen, D. (2001). *The changing shape of nursing practice: The role of nurses in the hospital division of labour.* London: Routledge.

Allen, D. (2004). Rereading nursing and rewriting practice: Towards an empirically based reformulation of the nursing mandate. *Nursing Inquiry, 11*(4), 271-283.

Bedney, G. Z., Seglin, M. H., & Meister, D. (2000). Activity theory: History, research and application. *Theoretical Issues in Ergonomics Science, 1*(2), 168-206.

Benner, P. E. (1984). *From novice to expert: Excellence and power in clinical nursing practice.* Menlo Park, CA.: Addison-Wesley Pub. Co., Nursing Division.

Biggs, J. B. (2003). *Teaching for quality learning at university: What the student does* (2nd ed.). Philadelphia, PA: Society for Research into Higher Education: Open University Press.

Blackler, F. (1995). Knowledge, knowledge work and organizations: An overview and interpretation. *Organization Studies, 6*, 1021-1046.

Bloomfield, B. P., & McLean, C. (2002). Beyond the walls of the asylum: Information and organization in the provision of community mental health services. *Information and Organization, 13*, 53–84.

Bransford, J. D., National Research Council (U.S.), Committee on Developments in the Science of Learning; National Research Council (U.S.), Committee on Learning Research and Educational Practice. (2000). *How people learn: Brain, mind, experience, and school* (Expanded ed.). Washington, DC: National Academy Press.

Breen, R., Lindsay, R., Jenkins, A., & Smith, P. (2001). The role of information and communication technologies in a university learning environment. *Studies in Higher Education, 26*(1), 95-114.

Brooks, F., & Scott, P. (2006). Knowledge work in nursing and midwifery: An evaluation through computer-mediated communication. *International Journal of Nursing Studies–97, 43*, 83-97.

Brown, J., Collins, A., & Duguid, P. (1989). Situated cognition and the culture of learning. *Educational Researcher, 18*(1), 32-42.

Buller, S., & Butterworth, T. (2001). Skilled nursing practice - A qualitative study of the elements of nursing. *International Journal of Nursing Studies, 38*(4), 405-417.

Burke, L. M. (2006). The process of integration of schools of nursing into higher education. *Nurse Education Today, 26*, 63-70.

Chalmers, I. (2006). *Archie Cochrane (1909-1988).* Retrieved 11 April 2007, 2007, from http://www.jameslindlibrary.org

Chartered Institute of Library and Information Professionals. (2005). *Information literacy: definition.* Retrieved 21 June, 2005, from http://www.cilip.org.uk/professionalguidance/informationliteracy/definition/

Cockcroft, S. (1994, 27 May 1998). *The effects of gender and computer access on computer literacy scores among first year undergraduates.* Retrieved 25 April, 2005, from http://www.is.cityu.edu.hk/Research/WorkingPapers/paper/9410.pdf

Cuban, L. (2001). *Oversold and underused: Computers in the classroom.* Cambridge, MA: Harvard University Press.

Dearing, R. (1997). *Higher education in the learning society: Report of the National Committee.* London: National Committee of Inquiry into Higher Education,.

de Jong, T., & Ferguson-Hessler, M. (1996). Types and qualities of knowledge. *Educational Psychologist, 31*(2), 105-113.

Department for Education and Skills. (2005). *Harnessing technology: Transforming learning and children's services.* Nottingham: DfES Publications.

Department of Health and Social Security. (1972). *Report of the Committee of Nursing* (No. 5155). London: HMSO.

Elston, M. A. (1980). Medicine: Half our future doctors? In R. Silverstone & A. Ward (Eds.), *Careers of Professional Women.* Croom Helm.

Fagermoen, M. S. (1997). Professional identity: Values embedded in meaningful nursing practice. *Journal of Advanced Nursing, 25*, 434-441.

Freshwater, D. (2004). Aesthetics and evidence-based practice in nursing: An oxymoron? *International Journal of Human Caring, 8*(2), 8-12.

Freshwater, D., & Biley, F. C. (2005). Heart of the matter: Dawn Freshwater and Francis Biley analyse what some believe is the most fundamental nursing value--caring. *Nursing Standard, 19*(20), 14-15.

Giddens, A. (1997). *Sociology* (3rd ed.). Cambridge: Polity Press.

Gilchrist, M., & Ward, R. (2006). Facilitating access to online learning. In S. Glen & P. Moule (Eds.), *E-learning in nursing.* Basingstoke: Palgrave Macmillan.

Goodyear, P. (1998). *New technology in higher education: Understanding the innovation process.* Retrieved 3 December, 2006, from http://tinyurl.com/yn4qw2

Goodyear, P., & Jones, C. (2003). Implicit theories of learning and change: Their role in the development of e-learning environments for higher education. In S. Naidu (Ed.), *Learning & teaching with technology.* London; Sterling, VA: Kogan Page.

Goodyear, P., & NLinHE Team. (2001). *Effective networked learning in higher education: Notes and guidelines.* Retrieved 14 January, 2001, from http://csalt.lancs.ac.uk/jisc/advice.htm

Gray, J. A. M. (2001). *Evidence-based health care: How to make health policy and management decisions.* Edinburgh: Churchill Livingstone.

Gulati, S. (2006). Applications of new technologies. In S. Glen & P. Moule (Eds.), *E-learning in nursing* (pp. 138). Basingstoke: Palgrave Macmillan.

Gunn, C., French, S., MacLeod, H., McSporran, M., & Conole, G. (2002). A response to the critique of gender issues in computer-supported learning. *Alt-J - Association for Learning Technology Journal, 10*(2), 80-82.

Gunn, C., French, S., McLeod, H., McSporran, M., & Conole, G. (2002). Gender issues in computer-supported learning. *Alt-J - Association for Learning Technology Journal, 10*(1), 32-44.

Gwinnett, A., & Massie, S. (1987). Integrating computers into the curriculum (2): Transforming a concept into a working tool. *Nurse Education Today, 7*(3), 116-119.

Hill, J., & Plath, D. (1998). Moneyed knowledge: How women become commercial shellfish divers. In J. Singleton (Ed.), *Learning in likely places: Varieties of apprenticeship in Japan* (pp. 211-225). Cambridge: Cambridge University Press.

Hodgson, M., McCartan, A., Hare, C., Clayphan, R., & Jezierski, G. (1995). *Teaching and learning in higher education: The integrative use of IT within the institutional context.* Durham: University of Durham.

Hughes, G. (2002). Gender issues in computer-supported learning: What we can learn from the gender, science and technology literature. *Alt-J - Association for Learning Technology Journal, 10*(2), 77-79.

Joanna Briggs Institute. (2006, 22 December 2006). *Systematic reviews - The review process.* Retrieved 11 April 2007, 2007, from http://www.joannabriggs.edu.au/pubs/approach.php

Joint Information Systems Committee. (2004). *Effective practice with e-learning.* Retrieved 27 January, 2005, from http://www.jisc.ac.uk/elearning_pedagogy.html

Jonassen, D. H. (1996). *Computers in the classroom: Mindtools for critical thinking.* Englewood Cliffs, NJ: Merrill, Prentice Hall.

Jonassen, D. H. (2001). Chapter 3: Learning from, in and with multimedia: An ecological psychology perspective. In S. Dijkstra & D. H. Jonassen (Eds.), *Multimedia learning: Results and perspectives.* Frankfurt am Main - New York: Peter Lang.

Jones, C. (2002, March 26th - 28th). *Is there a policy for networked learning?* Paper presented at the Networked Learning Conference 2002, University of Sheffield.

Kaptelinin, V., & Nardi, B. A. (2006). *Acting with technology: Activity theory and interaction design.* Cambridge, MA: The MIT Press.

Kirkwood, A., & Price, L. (2005). Learners and learning in the twenty-first century: What do we know about students' attitudes towards and experiences of information and communication technologies that will help us design courses? *Studies in Higher Education, 30*(3), 257-274.

Ludvigsen, S. R. (2006, 10-12 April 2006). *Learning and the use of ICT in higher education. Expectations and results.* Paper presented at the 5th International Conference on Networked Learning, Lancaster.

MacIntosh, J. (2003). Reworking professional nursing identity. *Western Journal of Nursing Research,, 25*(6), 725-741.

Maier, P., & Warren, A. (2000). *Integr@ting technology in learning & teaching: A practical guide for educators.* London: Kogan Page.

Martin, A. (2002). *Concepts of ICT literacy in higher education.* Retrieved 19 April, 2006, from http://www.citscapes.ac.uk/citscapes/products/backgroundreports/files/concepts_ict_HE.pdf

McClimens, A. (2003). A bad idea, by definition: Defining Nursing risks pleasing no one. *Nursing Standard, 17*(35), 25(21).

McKenna, H. (2004, 12 May 2004). *Evidence based practice: Does profusion of evidence mean confusion in practice.* Paper presented at the RCN Congress 2004, Harrogate, UK.

McKenna, H., Cutcliffe, J., & McKenna, P. (2000). Evidence-based practice: Demolishing some myths. *Nursing Standard, 14*(16), 39-42.

McKenna, H., Thompson, D., Watson, R., & Norman, I. (2006). The good old days of nurse training: Rose-tinted or jaundiced view? (Editorial). *International Journal of Nursing Studies, 43*(2), 135-137.

McSherry, R., Simmons, M., & Abbot, P. (2002). *Evidence-informed nursing: A guide for clinical nurses.* London: Routledge.

Meachin, K., & Webb, C. (1996). Training to do women's work in a man's world. *Nurse Education Today, 16*(3), 180-188.

MORI. (2003). *Student nurses: The pressure of work.* Retrieved 6 June, 2006, from http://www.mori.com/polls/2003/rcn1.shtml

MORI Social Research Institute. (2005, 17 January 2005). *Understanding the audience: Research study conducted for the Common Information Environment (CIE) group.* Retrieved 3 February, 2005, from http://www.common-info.org.uk/audienceresearch.shtml

Morris-Docker, S. B., Tod, A., Harrison, J. M., Wolstenholme, D., & Black, R. (2004). Nurses' use of the Internet in clinical ward settings. *Journal of Advanced Nursing, 48*(2), 157-166.

Morrison, D., & Collins, A. (1996). Epistemic fluency and constructivist learning environments. In B. Wilson (Ed.), *Constructivist learning environments.* Englewood Cliffs, NJ: Educational Technology Press.

Moule, P. (2003). ICT: A social justice approach to exploring user issues? *Nurse Education Today, 23*(7), 530-536.

Musk, A. (2004). Proficiency with technology and the expression of caring: Can we reconcile these polarised views? *International Journal for Human Caring, 8*(2), 13-20.

NHS Connecting for Health. (2005). *Health informatics programme basic IT skills programme (ECDL) NHS survey results.* London: Department of Health.

NHS Employers. (2005, 14 December 2005). *What is agenda for change?* Retrieved 14 August, 2006, from http://www.nhsemployers.org/pay-conditions/pay-conditions-199.cfm

NHS Information Authority. (2002). *Learning to manage health information - A theme for clinical education: Moving ahead.* Birmingham: NHS Information Authority.

NHS Information Authority. (2004). *Health informatics education and development for clinical professionals: Making progress?* Wigan: NHS Information Authority.

NHS Wales. (2004). *Basic information technology skills standard for NHS Wales - http://www. wales.nhs.uk/ecdl. Implementing the European Computer Driving Licence (ECDL®) Nurses, Midwives and Health Visitors.* Retrieved 2 July 2005, 2005, from http://www.wales.nhs.uk/ecdl

NHS Wales. (2005). *Informing healthcare projects: Access to knowledge (A2K).* Retrieved 7 July, 2005, from http://www.wales.nhs.uk/ihc/informing_healthcare_project.cfm?project=a2k

Norman, D. (1999). *The invisible computer: Why good products can fail, the personal computer is so complex, and information appliances are the solution.* Cambridge, MA: MIT Press.

Nursing and Midwifery Council. (2004). *Standards of proficiency for preregistration nursing education.* Retrieved 11 August, 2006, from http://www.nmc-uk.org

Office for National Statistics. (2001). *Omnibus survey.* Retrieved 30 November, 2006, from http://www.statistics.gov.uk/StatBase/Expodata/Spreadsheets/D5200.xls

Pateman, B., & Jinks, A. M. (1999). Stories or snapshots? A study directed at comparing qualitative and quantitative approaches to curriculum evaluation. *Nurse Education Today, 19*, 62-70.

Pettigrew, M., & Elliott, D. (1999). *Student IT skills.* Aldershot: Gower.

Quality Assurance Agency. (2001). *Subject benchmark statements: Healthcare programmes - Nursing.* Retrieved 2 July, 2005, from http://www. qaa.ac.uk/academicinfrastructure/benchmark/health/nursing.pdf

Rogers, J. (2004). *Adults learning*: Oxford University Press.

Royal College of Nursing. (2003). *Defining nursing.* Retrieved 6 June, 2005, from http://www.rcn. org.uk/downloads/definingnursing/definingnursing-a4.pdf

Royal College of Nursing. (2006a). *E-health: Putting information at the heart of nursing care.* Retrieved 2 June, 2006, from http://www.rcn.org.uk/information

Royal College of Nursing. (2006b). *The future nurse: The future for nurse education, a discussion paper.* London: Royal College of Nursing.

Selwyn, N. (2002). *Telling tales on technology: Qualitative studies in technology and education.* Aldershot: Ashgate Publishing Limited.

Selwyn, N. (2003, October 2003). *Understanding students' (non)use of information and communications technology in university.* Retrieved 22 May, 2006, from http://www.cf.ac.uk/socsi

Selwyn, N., Gorard, S., & Furlong, J. (2006). *Adult learning in the digital age: Information technology and the learning society.* Abingdon: Routledge.

Selwyn, N., Marriott, N., & Marriott, P. (2000). Net gains or net pains? Business student's use of the Internet. *Higher Education Quarterly, 54*(2), 166-186.

Shepherd, C. (2004). *The new IT training.* Retrieved 20 April, 2006, from http://www.trainingfoundation.com

Shuell, T. (1992). Designing instructional computing systems for meaningful learning. In M. Jones & P. Winne (Eds.), *Adaptive learning environments.* New York: Springer Verlag.

Sinclair, M., & Gardner, J. (1999). Planning for information technology key skills in nurse education. *Journal of Advanced Nursing, 30*(6), 1441-1450.

Spouse, J. (2000). An impossible dream? Images of nursing held by preregistration students and their effect on sustaining motivation to become nurses. *Journal of Advanced Nursing, 32*(3), 730-739.

Timmons, S. (2003). Nurses resisting information technology. *Nursing Inquiry, 10*(4), 257-269.

Tudge, J., & Scrimsher, S. (2000). Lev Vygotsky. In B. J. Zimmerman & D. H. Schunk (Eds.), *Educational psychology: A century of contributions*. Mahwah NJ: Lawrence Erlbaum Associates.

Veeramah, V. (2004). Utilization of research findings by graduate nurses and midwives. *Journal of Advanced Nursing, 47*(2), 183-191.

Vygotsky, L. S. (1978). *Mind in society: The development of higher psychological processes*. Cambridge, MA: Harvard University Press.

Webb, M. (1989). Sex and gender in the labour market. In I. Reid & E. Stratta (Eds.), *Sex differences in Britain* (2nd ed.), (pp. xi,321p323cm. Aldershot: Gower.

Wharrad, H., Clifford, C., Horsburgh, M., Ketefian, S., & Lee, J. (2002). Global network explores diversity and opportunity in nurse education. *Nurse Education Today, 22*, 15-23.

Wishart, J., & Ward, R. (2002). Individual differences in nurse and teacher training students' attitudes toward and use of information technology. *Nurse Education Today, 22*(3), 231-240.

ADDITIONAL READING

Brosnan, M. (1998). *Technophobia: The psychological impact of information technology*. London: Routledge.

Goodyear, P. (1998). *New technology in higher education: Understanding the innovation process*. Lancaster University. Retrieved 3 December, 2006, from http://tinyurl.com/yn4qw2

Goodyear, P., & NLinHE Team. (2001). *Effective networked learning in higher education: Notes and guidelines*. Retrieved 14 January, 2001, from http://csalt.lancs.ac.uk/jisc/advice.htm

Gulati, S. (2006). Applications of new technologies. In S. Glen & P. Moule (Eds.), *E-learning in nursing* (pp. 138). Basingstoke: Palgrave Macmillan.

Harris, S., (2004). Activity theory: Introduction & background. Retrieved from http://case.glam.ac.uk/CASE/StaffPages/SteveHarris/Research/AT.html

Kaptelinin, V., & Nardi, B. A. (2006). *Acting with technology: Activity theory and interaction design*. Cambridge, MA: The MIT Press.

Networked Learning Conference Proceedings. (2002, 2004, 2006). Retrieved from http://www.networkedlearningconference.org.uk

Pettigrew, M., & Elliott, D. (1999). *Student IT skills*. Aldershot: Gower.

Selwyn, N. (2002). *Telling tales on technology: Qualitative studies in technology and education*. Aldershot: Ashgate Publishing Limited.

Selwyn, N. (2003, October 2003). Understanding students' (non)use of information and communications technology in university. *Working Papers* Retrieved 22 May, 2006, from http://www.cf.ac.uk/socsi

Selwyn, N., Gorard, S., & Furlong, J. (2006). *Adult learning in the digital age: Information technology and the learning society*. Abingdon: Routledge.

ENDNOTES

1   A2K was a major strand of the Welsh Assembly Government funded (£88 million over 3 years) "Informing Healthcare" project, which aims "to create a set of information and infrastructure services that enable the provision of integrated person-based information that can be used to integrate patient care across the NHS in Wales and with Social Care." (NHS Wales 2005a)

2   http://www.medictomedic.com/mom/national_stage/index.html - "provides over 250 evidence-based clinical care pathways in an interactive and user-friendly web based tool"

Chapter XXI
Social Implications of Three Different Models of Distributed Learning

Robin Mason
The Open University, UK

Frank Rennie
Lews Castle College, UHI, UK

ABSTRACT

Distributed universities that use technology to support a social mission are a new phenomenon reflecting changing demands on higher education and the availability of new, facilitative technologies. This chapter describes three different models of distributing education to achieve different social missions: a distance teaching university (The UK Open University), a multicampus higher education institute servicing remote and rural areas in the Highlands and Islands of Scotland (UHI Millennium Institute), and a new university in Greece spread over five small islands (University of the Aegean). The chapter considers the different social missions and the ways in which the choice of technologies supports distributed teaching and research. International activities are also described and future trends considered. An initial typology for considering institutions of distributed learning is proposed.

INTRODUCTION

This chapter considers the social implications of three quite different institutional models for providing flexible higher education. Different technologies, different aspects of flexibility, and different venues for learning account for the variation in the models described. These, in turn, reflect different cultural imperatives and have different implications for learners.

The three institutions studied in this chapter are:

1. **The UK Open University (OU)**, which is a mass distance-education institution set up originally by a Labour Government to provide a second chance for the many UK adults who had no opportunity to attend university at the age of 18.

2. The very new **UHI Millennium Institute (UHI)**, which has been set up to provide higher education for people in rural and remote areas in the Highlands and Islands of Scotland.

3. **The University of the Aegean (UA)**, located on five different islands in the Aegean Sea and established as the first Greek University to fully utilise Information and Communication Technologies (ICT) in its everyday activities, and thus, implementing the Information Society in Greek higher education.

As the notion of a distributed university is central to the underlying model of these institutions, the chapter begins with a discussion about this vexed term. The focus then moves to an analysis of the differences resulting from the three models described, using the categories: social imperatives, technologies, and international activities. The chapter concludes with a look forward at some future trends of these three institutions. The objective throughout the chapter is to highlight the ways in which the social and cultural mission of these institutions has led to the development of different models. The social implications of the establishment and growth of an institution of higher education in a region may be distinct but as this chapter indicates, they may also be overlapping. Considerable academic analysis has been undertaken recently to investigate the relationship between "knowledge laboratories" and regional economies, and shows the interrelationship between social implications and the establishment of an institution of higher education (Cooke & Piccaluga, 2004).

BACKGROUND

The term "distributed," in relation to education, particularly higher education, encompasses a number of different practices. For some the term is synonymous with distance education and e-learning (Oblinger, Barone, & Hawkins, 2001); others prefer to distinguish between these terms. For example, according to the Web site of Tarleton State University (2004):

Although the phrases "distributed education" and "distance education" are often used interchangeably, distributed education has a broader meaning. The primary characteristic of distance education is that learning takes place independently of place and time, allowing students to absorb the content from a distance. On the other hand, the principal goal of distributed education is to customize learning environments to better-fit different learning styles, whether students are on or off campus. In this new pedagogical model, students are encouraged to learn in an interactive and collaborative environment.

Distance education is a subset of distributed learning, focusing on students who may be separated in time and space from their peers and the instructor. Distributed education can occur either on or off campus, providing students with greater flexibility and eliminating time as a barrier to learning. A common feature of both distance and distributed learning is technology. Regardless of whether students are on campus or online, there are many implications of integrating technology into education, i.e., in making learning distributed. (p.1)

"Blended learning" is another term that encompasses a range of different practices. Usually it refers to learning that combines face-to-face teaching with online resources. The learners may be full-time campus students, or they may be located partially on campus and partially at a distance. Although these terms are always changing in their application, it might be fairly safe to say that distributed education is commonly used for the teaching model or means of a university, whereas blended learning tends to be used at a course level to describe particular design components.

As these descriptions make clear, technologies of varying sorts are a central component in the practice of distributed education. In this chapter, we show how the choice of technologies reflects a different model of distributed education and even more significantly, a different social mission.

SOCIAL IMPERATIVES

It is significant that all three of these institutions are very young (post 1960s), and all three have a social mission inherent in their structure. However, the use of different technologies means that different aspects of a social mission are addressed.

The Open University

The OU aims to provide higher education to those who do not necessarily have the usual university entrance qualifications. By careful course design and student support, the University concentrates on the "output" rather than the "input." It is thus "open" to people who have not succeeded in secondary education. The University began in the early 1970s by providing high quality print-based materials to learners that they could study in between employment and family obligations. Tutor support by telephone and face-to-face meetings at Study Centres provided the necessary interactive component of the mix.

As ownership and facility with personal computers has grown, the University has moved some of its content and much of its tutor support online. Students all over Europe study the courses and sit exams at local centres. Students need not meet face-to-face at all, though increasingly synchronous and asynchronous technologies for interaction provide a form of virtual meeting.

Flexibility for students is the watchword of this model.

The University of the Highlands and Islands Millennium Institute

UHI has focused on bringing higher education opportunities to people in remote locations, so that they do not need to leave home. As a federated network of 15 existing colleges and research centres, it is spread over a very wide geographical area with the second lowest population density in Europe. There is no other university located within this region. UHI offers access courses in further education and vocational training, right through to undergraduate and postgraduate degrees. There is some specialisation of subjects by the different colleges, but most degree courses are delivered jointly across the UHI network. This means that the aim of networked courses is to ensure that wherever the student is located, a range of courses can be studied. In short, "the course comes to the student, not the student to the course." The key characteristic of UHI is therefore the networking of courses, such that students in any location can study any course offered using a range of advanced technologies. Rather than concentrating the economic benefits of a university in one location, the UHI model distributes the benefits and acts as a multiplier for local economies. Furthermore, UHI aims to be responsive to the local context in its choice of curriculum and research focus. Examples of this would include the Masters Degree on Managing Sustainable Rural/Mountain Development and the undergraduate programmes in Gaelic and North Atlantic Studies, or Rural Health. The aims of the UHI are simple to articulate, but difficult to accomplish in practice. The main aims (in no particular order of priority) could be summarised (Rennie, 2000) as:

- To provide a seamless lifelong education at all levels of study from vocational short courses to advanced research and study.

- To reduce the out-migration of young people in search of Higher Education by providing a quality local alternative.
- To attract inward investment and human resource potential to the area with a focus on the Higher Education needs of the region.
- To stimulate local employment and local GDP through greater engagement in the knowledge industry.
- To provide a focus for research and development that is relevant to the Highlands and Islands of Scotland and the communities which inhabit this region.

University of the Aegean

The University of the Aegean has chosen a different model to protect and enhance the environment of its remote islands. Different faculties of the University are located on one of five islands, and students choosing that discipline move to the island for the duration of their studies. The presence of students stimulates local business and provides a new community focus. For example, the School of the Environment is located on the island of Lesbos, while the Department of Shipping, Trade and Transport is based on Chios. Research in these focus areas is equally as important as teaching at UA and conferences are a regular feature of UA activity. Again, this has positive impacts on island life.

Blended learning describes the pedagogical approach of UA as face-to-face lecturing is combined with online resources and social networking. In addition, the University emphasizes the development and promotion of new disciplines and curricula that adhere to the needs of contemporary Greek society. For example, biodiversity, conservation, and environmental studies are a major focus and so are ICT, computer studies, and security systems.

SOCIAL AFFECTS

As in many other countries, Europe has moved away from manual labour as the bedrock of the economy in favour of a "knowledge economy." This, in turn, puts greater pressure on education, and particularly higher education, to deliver the kind of workers that are required in a knowledge economy. Typical skills demanded by many employers are ease with a range of computer software, communication, and team-working skills, including those in a distributed environment, as well as critical and analytical ability to work with large amounts of information. Many professions have become degree-only entry, and many require regular updating. At the same time, some jobs have become location independent, allowing more and more people to live in remote locations and work from home or local hubs. All of these trends empower distributed universities particularly, and the three described here meet these requirements in different ways. In each of these three institutions, there is a social and/or cultural imperative, that is explicit in the creation of the institution and its operational remit. For example, over the last 30 years, the Open University has empowered a whole generation of people to obtain degrees without moving or giving up their jobs. The UHI has substantially reduced the need for people in rural locations of the Highlands and Islands of Scotland to leave home in order to gain higher level qualifications. The University of the Aegean has made a significant contribution to the sustainability of small Greek islands as well as to the outputs of local research.

APPROPRIATE TECHNOLOGIES

Web-based technologies underpin the educational experience of all three institutes, not surprisingly. Supporting courses with online resources, online interaction, and tutor contact is now a standard feature of all Western universities, whether the institution teaches largely at a distance, face-to-face, or a blend of the two (Paulsen, n.d.) Because the OU is primarily a distance-teaching university, it has invested considerable resource into developing technologies for supporting students studying individually in their own home: online library facilities, teleconferencing, online activities, and Web-based assessment processes. Increasingly, courses are using blogging, wikis, and e-portfolios, in order to provide students with a rich experience of intellectual life and social networking (Mason, 2006). Through extensive questionnaires (now often online), students provide information about their means and time of access, ownership of technology, training needs, and interest in using technology in their learning. Through extensive training, OU tutors are given the skills and support to interact with students online, to manage discussion forums, and to provide useful comments on students' online assignments. Through its Knowledge Media Institute, the OU has developed leading edge technologies to support local communities, schools, and heritage sites. For example, it has developed a facility called Open Guide for the area where the headquarters of the University is based:

The Open Guide to Milton Keynes is part of the OpenGuides network of free, community-maintained wiki guidebooks to places around the world. Anyone is free to contribute, whether it's by writing new articles or editing existing articles. The OpenGuides are developed with the Semantic Web in mind; metadata is organised to allow easy machine-readable output, in order to enable reusage by other Web services.

The guide has been set up to investigate the application of semantic Web technologies in a locality based resource, to provide a service to the local Milton Keynes community, and to explore the possibilities of wiki based social software. (Gaved, Heath, & Eisenstadt, 2006, p. 1)

It has also worked with Bletchley Park, a local heritage site that was the WWII location of the code-breaking section called Station X. A Mobile Information Service has been developed as a ubiquitous unobtrusive technology to support post-visit support of its online museum resources (Mulholland, Collins, & Zdrahal, 2005).

UHI makes use of similar technologies as their students are frequently located in remote areas of the Highlands or Islands. However, UHI has invested in a network of over 100 local learning centres across the region, where students can go to access course materials and receive support from the local learning facilitator. These local learning centres range from simple access to a computer and desk space in the premises of a local organisation (e.g., a school, community hall, or the office of a voluntary body) to sophisticated, purpose-built learning centres with dedicated classrooms, IT access, a small library, and perhaps local staff. In some cases, the local learning centres have been built by the Academic Partners of the UHI (the constituent colleges and research centres), while other learning centres are housed in premises leased from community organisations or the Local Authority. Many small communities seem to regard the location of a local learning centre in their village as a key factor in local economic and social rejuvenation. No doubt the economics and value of running a local learning centre will change over time, particularly as broadband access becomes more ubiquitous and affordable, and as learners obtain better access to online resources and communications applications from their own homes, perhaps the value of the local learning centre will become more important as a study space and a social space to meet with other local learners, but this is for the future. The UHI has invested heavily in developing a range of learning resources and ways of communications that allow learners to be spread over a wide geographical area, and also to utilise a variety of technologies that suit their skills and lifestyles, such as print,

VLE, audioconferencing, videoconferencing, skype, and face-to-face tutorials.

In addition, UHI has invested in videoconferencing as a major technology to link the various colleges both as a teaching medium and as an administrative link. UHI is currently the heaviest user of videoconferencing for higher education use in the European Union, and accounts for more than half of all the use for educational purposes in the UK. Most of the big committees of the UHI, from the Executive Board, through the research committee, quality assurance committee, to the network teams of academics at each of the 15 Academic Partners, will routinely conduct their regular meetings by videoconference. In addition, many courses include some subject tuition, research seminars, and/or presentations using the videoconference system. An interesting spin-off on this heavy utilisation has been the adoption of videoconference technology by other agencies and government departments in the region, as well as a number of community and voluntary organisations seeking to make use of the UHI videoconference network to link with their own geographically dispersed collaborators.

Unlike the OU and UHI, the University of the Aegean is primarily a face-to-face teaching institution. However, because the University is distributed over five islands, it has also installed a satellite-based videoconferencing network to link the campuses administratively, and to provide a unifying role coordinating the parts into a whole. Teaching, research, and administration of the University are intentionally decentralized, so that the University reflects the geographically fragmented structure of the Greek Archipelago. In addition, computer labs for student access to online resources provide the backbone of the technology support for learning. UA aims to be a student-facing institution that prepares young scientists and citizens of the future. It is proud of its ability to remain at the cutting edge of technology development, as well as to provide these opportunities for small Greek islands that would

otherwise suffer the common fate of migration to the mainland. For example, local personnel are hired to manage the computer labs and local people are given access to the labs for their own use.

UA also has a mission to conduct Mediterranean-centred research, and it does this across all disciplines. For example, research projects are conducted in the history, archaeology, and culture of the Aegean, and in the sciences, projects are underway in biodiversity, environmental impact of human activities, regional development, and environmental engineering. The major research topics of the Laboratory of Biogeography and Cultural Ecology include plant and insect biogeography in the Mediterranean area, pollination ecology, structure and function of Mediterranean scrub communities, biodiversity conservation, species rarity and isolation, life strategies of Mediterranean plants, habitat fragmentation, study and sustainable land use of Mediterranean landscapes. These research projects are all underpinned by communication technologies, laboratories, and scientific fieldwork.

All three institutes are enthusiastic users of technology to support students, to conduct research, and to develop culturally appropriate relationships.

INTERNATIONAL ACTIVITIES

With all three institutes, there is an international dimension to their social mission, though again, these take very different forms.

The Open University promotes educational opportunity and social justice by providing high-quality university education to all who wish to realise their ambitions and fulfill their potential. This aspect of the OU's mission explains why the University that was founded to tackle inequality of opportunity in the UK is just as intent on addressing such issues on a global scale:

Universal Primary Education is one of the key United Nations Millennium Development Goals, but in many African countries AIDS has severely reduced the number of teachers. Often the teachers that remain have received little teacher training. The Open University's Digital Education Enhancement Project (DEEP) and Teacher Education in Sub-Saharan Africa (TESSA) projects work in collaboration with African schools and communities. They provide this much-needed teacher training that can provide young Africans with the essential skills needed to become active and valued members of their community, able to develop their own solutions to the challenges they face. (Gourley, 2005, p. 1)

In addition, the Open University is extending its commitment to sharing knowledge with partners from the developing world, and has launched a new *International Fellowship Programme*, whereby successful applicants are funded to come to the OU for several months to work on mutually relevant projects. Furthermore, the OU is a major provider of course content to a number of start-up universities. For example, the Arab Open University is currently using a range of OU courses in Technology, Social Science, Business, Arts, and Mathematics. The OU provides support, training, and through its Validation Services, offers UK qualifications to Arab students. The OU has had similar arrangements in Singapore, Hong Kong, and Eastern Europe.

The UHI has Memoranda of Understanding with Cape Breton, the University of the Arctic, and the Royal University of Bhutan, among others, and the particular model of a federated university institution based upon the networking of geographically dispersed, independent colleges/research centres has attracted worldwide interest. The current structure of the UHI is a response to the particular constraints and opportunities of the geography and social history of the Highlands and Islands of Scotland, and the UHI has responded to this in its aim of being "for the region and of the

region." The enthusiastic adoption by UHI of new technologies to deliver educational resources and support learners in a very wide variety of situations and locations has been enormously aided by state and regional development agencies investing in new buildings and high-performance telecommunications infrastructure. From the beginning, the creation of the UHI has been seen as an educational initiative with very strong economic and social development potential for the whole of the Highlands and Islands (Rennie, 2000), and has sought to capitalise on the establishment of a university across the region to serve as a critical driver of wider regional development (Cooke & Piccaluga, 2004).

The University of the Aegean is obliged by charter to teach in Greek. This obviously limits some of their international activities, for example, the popular process of attracting foreign students, although UA does attract expatriate Greek speakers to study on the islands. The School of Humanities runs intensive summer programs for international students wanting to study the Greek language and civilization. Subjects covered include Greek Art and Archaeology, Greek philosophers, ethnography, Olympic games, and Greek dances. UA also takes part in many European-funded research and development projects. One example is the Asia-Link Programme, in which UA partnered with the OU and UHI to exchange information and provide hands-on training for university staff from two Less Developed Countries in Asia. UA provided the 15 delegates from the Royal University of Bhutan and Tribhuvan University in Nepal with individual lab space to access an online course, take part in workshops and discussions, as well as to have a guided tour around the island of Samos.

FUTURE TRENDS

Unlike many traditional, established universities, the three institutes described here have a strong social mission. Being new institutes, they are also less entrenched in long-standing ways of operating. Consequently, their future visions tend to focus on a willingness to be responsive, flexible, and adaptable to new technologies, new opportunities, and even new kinds of students. The University of the Aegean, for example, is aiming for permission to teach some courses in English, in order to be more responsive to international interest in Aegean studies and Greek culture. The Open University is responding to the new fee regulations in the UK by opening its doors to the 18–25 year old market, for whom amassing large debts at a campus university is less appealing than getting a degree whilst working. UHI lays great emphasis on the flexibility for learners, not only geographically and utilising diverse communications media, but also at all levels of study from basic access courses, through vocational training and Further Education, to higher level degrees, postgraduate studies, and postdoctoral work.

The advent of social networking provides new opportunities for all three institutes. One particular aspect of note is the idea of student-produced content. For the OU, which sees the internationally recognised quality of its existing content as one of its major strengths, this presents a conundrum. However, the University has developed a major new initiative called OpenLearn, whereby OU content from across the curriculum is made freely available online under the Creative Commons License (see http://openlearn.open.ac.uk/). More than just course content, OpenLearn provides teachers and learners with tools to organise their learning and to communicate with other learners. The UHI has chosen a very diverse mix of learning styles and educational resources that allows flexibility for the complete spectrum from specialised face-to-face courses delivered largely in one locality, through various types of blended delivery, to specialised courses that are almost entirely delivered online over the Internet. Over time, it is anticipated that the majority of courses will be "blended learning" that combines a wide

variety of ways for learners to study and to communicate with their tutors without necessarily being required to move home from the location where they normally live and work.

TYPOLOGY OF DISTRIBUTED EDUCATION MODELS

There may be a case for proposing a broad typology for the manner in which educational institutions engage with distributed learning. This typology is not meant to imply a value to the style of distributed learning that an institution has adopted, simply that institutions have evolved different permutations of distributed learning to best suit their socioeconomic situation and the needs of their learners. This typology can be based upon the two key characteristics of distributed learning, namely the geographic distribution of learners and the pedagogical distribution of educational resources across a range of media (see figure below). In this simple typology, the OU and the UHI are both in the high section on the basis of the level of their interaction with learners over a wide geographical area, generally studying at some distance from the tutor. The University of Aegean, on the other hand, despite being distributed as an institution, has a low level of geographical distribution and networking in our typology, as students are expected to travel to the island on which the Department offering their course is based.

In a similar manner, the three institutions that we have described in this chapter can be distinguished on the basis of the extent to which they have utilised communications technologies in the learning. The University of Aegean has so far employed distributed learning mainly in support of face-to-face tuition that is located in conventional settings, and is not generally networked between locations. The OU is primarily a university for distance learning (originally print based but now extending to other media) with face-to-face only used for occasional Study Centre meetings. The UHI is evolving a complex mix in which the permutations of the "blend" by which distributed learning is delivered will vary considerably for different subject areas, different levels of study, and different aspirations of the learners. This is a difficult area to categorise dogmatically, and to a large extent, it will be driven by the preferences of the learner community.

Examples of distributed institutions in the fourth quadrant of Figure 1, that is, highly distributed use of media, but low geographical distribution of students, would be the following:

1. **UOC:** The Open University of Catalonia headquartered in Barcelona, which makes extensive use of information and communications technologies (ICT), allowing students, professors, and administrators to interact and cooperate through a Virtual Campus, constituting a university community that uses the Internet to create, structure, share, and disseminate knowledge. Its social mission is to contribute to the projection of Catalan culture and the Catalan university around the world.

2. **The University of Akureyri** in northern Iceland also uses Web technologies to provide higher education to students in a small geographical area in Iceland. Its social mission includes conducting locally relevant research on topics such as tourism and the food industry. Although the majority of its courses are conducted in Icelandic, it aims to attract international students and where sufficient numbers exist, courses can be taught in English.

FUTURE RESEARCH DIRECTIONS

Considerable interest has been shown in promoting universities as centres of regional economic regeneration. What evidence is there for this assumption? How can the impact of the university be separated from other local factors? The intention is that the research generated by the university will spin off into new venture companies, local businesses, and patents. This attracts other businesses that perceive benefits in being near to innovation and new ways of working. What incentives are

Figure 1. Typology of distributed learning

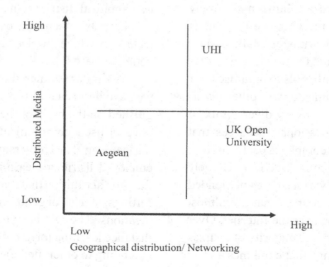

required to stimulate this? When are constraints useful and when are they an impediment? In this digital age, there is an interest in centralising the function of the task but decentralising the location of the task. In other words, the staff may not need to be colocated or could be based anywhere in the regional network. Is there added value in distributing expertise around a network or is work more effective with colocation?

In particular, how do regional nodes with a particular expertise collaborate with and benefit from other regional partners?

Of the three university models described in this chapter, both University of the Aegean and UHI are examples of distributed research networks, although they function differently. The Open University, on the other hand, despite being the premier distance education facility in the UK, carries out most of its research at a central location. The OU has demonstrated the benefits of transformational changes in students' lives across the country and beyond. This kind of transformational impact should now be extended to research outputs, projects, and findings; taking them out of the cloister and into the community. This is the intention at UHI, which at the strategic level, is being encouraged by the regional development agency to nurture nodes of specialist research areas, for example, rural health, renewable energies, and marine science. Can these research nodes be networked as effectively as a centralised research hub? The hypothesis is that by each campus developing its own speciality, the benefits can be spread more widely over the region. For example, can research students be distributed at other locations than the primary research node? Are there benefits of cross-fertilisation by researchers NOT being gathered in one location? How best can distributed research students be supported?

One of the added benefits to local communities of these distributed nodes is their ability to support a variety of regional functions, for example,

summer schools, conferences, out-of-term accommodation, and other local services. This is a key feature of the University of the Aegean model. How should the local community insure that the university addresses regional needs? What are the key indicators of successful integration of the university into the local economy?

These and other related research questions are fundamental to a research agenda that seeks to address the role of universities in economic and social regeneration.

CONCLUSION

The location of students as they study with the university is one element in the three models described here. Allowing students the greatest amount of flexibility as to where and when they study is important to the OU model; staying in their home areas is important for UHI; and contributing to small island communities is the key factor in UA. These models are sustained by different (though now overlapping) technologies. A global or at least international dimension is important for all modern universities, and the three described here have again chosen different methods of implementing this.

As societies evolve and technologies are developed, distributed education is beginning to rival campus-based education, particularly amongst newly established universities. The typology developed in this chapter is only one way of categorising institutions; others might focus on mission (local or global), or on types of technologies (Web or videoconferencing), or on the study context of students (home, study centre, or campus). The three institutions described here were chosen because they illustrate different ways in which a social mission defines the teaching model.

REFERENCES

Cooke, P., & Piccaluga, A. (Eds.). (2004). *Regional economies as knowledge laboratories*. Cheltenham, Glos: Edward Elgar Publishing.

Gaved, M., Heath, T., & Eisenstadt, M. (2006). *Wikis of locality: Insights from the OpenGuides*. 2006 International Symposium on Wikis (WikiSym2006), Odense, Denmark. Retrieved December 21, 2006, from http://kmi.open.ac.uk/projects/hot.cfm?name=Open%20Guide%20to%20Milton%20Keynes

Gourley, B. (2005). *The Open University in Africa*. Milton Keynes: The Open University. Retrieved November 10, 2006, from http://www.open2.net/development/ouandafrica.html

Greener, I., & Perriton, L. (2005). The political economy of networked learning communities in higher education. *Studies in Higher Education. 30*(1), 67-79.

Lamb, B. (2004). Wide open spaces: Wikis, ready or not. *EDUCAUSE Review, 39*(5), 36-48.

Mason, R. (2006). Holistic course design using learning objects. *IJLT, 2*(2/3), 203-215.

Mayes, T. (2002). The technology of learning in a social world. In R. Harrison et al., (Eds.), *Supporting lifelong learning, vol. 1, Perspectives on learning*. London: Routledge Falmer.

Miller, M., & Lu, M. (2003). Serving non-traditional students in e-learning environments: Building successful communities in the virtual campus. *Education Media International, 40*(1-2), 163-9.

Moloney, J., & Tello, S. (2003). Principles for building success in online education. *Syllabus*, February 2003, 17-18.

Mulholland, P., Collins, T., & Zdrahal, Z. (2005). Bletchley Park text: Using mobile and semantic Web technologies to support the post-visit use of online museum resources. *Journal of Interactive Media in Education, 24*. Retrieved December 27, 2006, from http://jime.open.ac.uk/2005/24/mulholland-2005-24.html

Oblinger, D., Barone, C., & Hawkins, B. (2001). *Distributed education and its challenges: An overview*. Washington, D.C.: American Council on Education. Retrieved November 10, 2006, from http://www.acenet.edu/bookstore/pdf/distributed-learning/distributed-learning-01.pdf

Paulsen, M. F. (n.d.). *An international analysis of Web-based education*. Bekkestua, Norway: NKI Fjernundervisning. Retrieved November 10, 2006, from http://www.nettskolen.com/pub/artikkel.xsql?artid=131

Rennie, F. W. (2000). The importance of the University of the Highlands and Islands Project in regional development in NW Scotland. In J. G. Allansson & I. R. Edvardsson (Eds.), *Community viability, rapid change, and socioecological futures*. Akureyri: University of Akureyri and the Stefansson Arctic Institute.

Tarleton State University. (2004). *About distributed education, What is distributed education?* Tarleton, TX: Tarleton State University. Retrieved November 10, 2006, from http://online.tarleton.edu/dist_distr_ed.htm

ADDITIONAL READING

Arundel, A., & Geuna, A. (2001). Does proximity matter for knowledge transfer from public institutes and universities to firms? *Science and Technology Policy Research*, electronic working paper series paper no. 73. Retrieved April 04, 2007, from http://www.sussex.ac.uk/spru/1-6-1-2-1.html

Berge, Z. (Ed.). (2000). *Sustaining distance training: Integrating learning technologies into the fabric of the enterprise*. Hoboken, NJ: John Wiley & Sons.

Bowman, M. (1999). *What is distributed learning?* Technical Sheet 2(1). Retrieved April 04, 2007, from http://techcollab.csumb.edu/techsheet2.1/distributed.html

Chung, Q. B. (2005). Sage on the stage in the digital age: The role of online lecture in distance learning. *The Electronic J. of e-Learning, 3*(1), 1-14. Retrieved April 04, 2007, from http://www.ejel.org/volume-3/v3-i1/v3-i1-art1-chung.pdf

Dede, C. (2004). An intellectual journey from distance education to distributed learning. In G. Kearsley (Ed.), *Online learning: Personal reflections on the transformation of education.* Educational Technology Publications. Retrieved April 04, 2007, from http://home.sprynet.com/~gkearsley/History/OLHistory_contents.htm

Huffaker, D. (2004). The educated blogger: Using Weblogs to promote literacy in the classroom. *First Monday, 9*(6). Retrieved April 04, 2007, from www.firstmonday.dk/issues/issue9_6/huffaker/index.html

Lefoe, G., Gunn, C., & Hedberg, J. (2002). Recommendations for teaching in a distributed learning environment: The students' perspective. *Australian Journal of Educational Technology, 18*(1), 40-56.

Mason, R., & Rennie, F. (2004). Broadband: A solution for rural e-learning? *International Review of Research in Open and Distance Learning, 5*(1). Retrieved April 04, 2007, from http://www.irrodl.org/index.php/irrodl/article/view/173/255

Mason, R., & Rennie, F. (2006). *eLearning: The key concepts.* London: Routledge.

Mayes, J. T. (2001). Quality in an e-University. *Assessment and Evaluation in Higher Education, 26*(5), 465-73.

Preece, J. (2002). Supporting community and building social capital. *Communications of the ACM, 45*(4), 37-9.

Ramsden, P. (1992) *Learning to teach in Higher Education.* London: Routledge.

Rennie, F. (2003). The use of flexible learning resources for geographically distributed rural students. *Distance Education, 24*(1), 25-39.

Rennie, F., & Mason, R. (2004). *The connecticon: Learning for the connected generation.* Greenwich, CT: Information Age Publishing.

Ryan, S., Scott, B., Freeman, H., & Patel, D. (2000). *The virtual university. The Internet and resource-based learning.* London: Kogan Page.

Selwyn, N., & Gorard, S. (2004). Exploring the role of ICT in facilitating adult informal learning. *Education, Communication and Information, 4*(2/3, July/Nov).

Weller, M., Pegler, C., & Mason, R. (2005). Use of innovative technologies on an e-learning course. *The Internet and Higher Education, 8*(1), 61-71.

Wheeler, S. (2001). Information and communication technologies and the changing role of the teacher. *Journal of Educational Media, 26*(1), 7-17.

Whitworth, A. (2005). The politics of virtual learning environments: Environmental change, conflict and e-learning. *British Journal of Educational Technology, 36*(4), 685-692.

Williams, R. (2003). Integrating distributed learning with just-in-context Knowledge Management. *Electronic J. of e-Learning, 1*(1), 45-50. Retrieved April 04, 2007, from http://www.ejel.org/volume-1-issue-1/issue1-art6.htm

Wolf, A. (2002). *Does education matter? Myths about education and economic growth.* London: Penguin Books.

Chapter XXII
Sociotechnical System Design for Learning:
Bridging the Digital Divide with CompILE

Benjamin E. Erlandson
Arizona State University, USA

ABSTRACT

CompILE is a sociotechnical "comprehensive interactive learning environment" system for personal knowledge management and visualization that represents the growing collective knowledge an individual gathers throughout his or her lifespan. A network of intelligent agents connects the user and his or her inhabited knowledge space to external information sources and a multitude of fellow users. Following a brief perspective on educational technology, concepts of human-computer interaction, and a description of CompILE, this chapter will introduce CompILE as a sociotechnical system supported by an enriched design process. From an educational perspective, CompILE can bridge the digital divide by creating community, embracing culture, and promoting a learning society.

INTRODUCTION

This chapter begins with a brief perspective on educational technology, concepts of human-computer interaction, and a description of the *Comp*rehensive *I*nteractive *L*earning *E*nvironment (CompILE) as a knowledge management system controlled using a network of intelligent software agents. Strategies for bridging the digital

divide using CompILE will be presented using the four-part framework of the "Wheel of Policy Instruments" constructed by van Dijk (2005).

The effect of CompILE on society will be approached from the standpoint of lifelong learning and usability engineering. CompILE will create a sense of community via participatory research, scenario-based design, and heuristic evaluation. In terms of culture, CompILE will rely heavily upon ethnography to refine its ability to facilitate cross-cultural communication, and a distinct effort to achieve functional beauty as an interactive system should help its participants achieve a higher level of appreciation for the aesthetics of "culture" from a philosophical perspective. Globalization can be addressed by CompILE in terms of ubiquitous computing, the mobile user, visual literacy, and just-in-time translation. The chapter will conclude with a description of CompILE as a hybrid entity, and the essence of CompILE as a sociotechnical system.

This chapter has two specific objectives:

- Introducing CompILE as a sociotechnical system supported by an enriched design process
- Using CompILE to bridge the digital divide by creating community, embracing culture, and promoting a learning society.

BACKGROUND

One trait of humans that makes us advanced social creatures is our ability to create artificial devices or artifacts that expand our capabilities (Norman, 1993). Throughout history, many of these artifacts have been perceived as the final piece to the ultimate puzzle of technological advancement; the last thing humans would create to meet all their future needs. The automobile, the airplane, the telephone, the television, the microwave, the Internet; the list goes on. While no single invention can actually be that final puzzle piece, major technological advancements cannot be denied as a driving force of society. Norman (1993) agrees, noting the essential nature of technology for growth of human knowledge and mental capabilities.

An important consideration to be made when designing any new interface is the anticipated impact it will have on human activity. In fact, most significant consequences of design are based on impact to human activity. In an effort to reduce occurrence of these consequences, the design process should include a well-managed team of participants with a variety of knowledge and skills, willing to completely deconstruct any particular problem that may arise (Carroll, 1991). Why are these consequences so important? These consequences have the power to make technology completely redundant, existing merely for entertainment.

This breakpoint of redundancy is paramount in education, which, upon clarification, is essentially a purposed form of communication between one or more individuals, intended to facilitate learning and knowledge construction. Using a learning-centric approach, the application of technology to the processes of teaching and learning can be seen as an amplification of the channels of communication. There is no point in seeking to improve the educational communication process with technology if all efforts result in glamorous toys with no effect beyond distraction. Computers cannot be placed in schools for an administration to show that it is on the forefront with cutting-edge educational technology. Technology must be carefully integrated with curricula to be used as tools, or artifacts, fundamental to the learning process.

This concept extends beyond the classroom geographically and temporally. Students using the technology must be wholly engaged in the content of the curriculum, using the technology as a mechanism of that engagement. Kling (2000) reinforces this notion of engagement when describing such an application of technology as the development of a "sociotechnical system," or an information technology system that cannot separate its existence from the social context of its users. Once this point of engagement is reached, the technology available today and tomorrow can create amazing opportunities for experience and growth within and beyond the classroom. To reach this point, a sociotechnical system must be designed and developed, with an eye toward the inseparable bond between human, machine, and use.

HUMAN-COMPUTER INTERACTION

There are four main sources of knowledge underlying information systems design: (1) systematic empirical evidence of user-interface relations, (2) models and theories of human cognition and artificial systems, (3) field studies of how humans cope with tasks in real-world settings, and (4) specific work domain knowledge derived from textbooks, interviews with experts, and analytical methods such as task analysis (Rasmussen, Anderson, & Bernsen, 1991). The diversity of these sources underscores the interdisciplinary nature of the studies and practices involved with human-computer interaction (HCI), including but not limited to the natural sciences, engineering, the social sciences, and humanities.

One might assume that the foundations of HCI are purely objective, due to the binary nature of information systems. Computers are objective machines based on logic, but humans are interacting with them; this completely unbalances the equation. HCI research and development must take into account human knowledge, decision-making and planning, current mental representations of the user based on causal and intentional relationships, and the fact that interactive behavior is influenced by the environment in which it takes place (Bechtel, 1997; Gifford, 1997; Sommer, 1969).

It is increasingly inadequate for system designers to consider the modules of the information system in isolation from each other (Rasmussen et al, 1991). Increasingly numerous applications working in seamless integration on the same computer (and across networks) becomes more feasible with each new cycle in computer processing technology. Modules can no longer be designed around the requirements of a narrow group of users (Rasmussen et al, 1991). As greater

numbers of users become cognizant of the true potential of personal computing, the "narrow" user groups formerly associated with modules and applications in information systems are expanding rapidly. The expansion presents an enormous challenge to designers; accounting for so much more variety when building interfaces for their products. Accounting for variety involves the careful specification of user communities in tandem with a thorough identification of tasks. With novice users, the most success with this dual process can be found through reliance on several measurable criteria: time taken to learn specific functions, speed of task performance, rate of human error, subjective user satisfaction, and human retention of functions over time (Shneiderman, 1993).

The less time users must spend learning a system, the more time they can spend being productive. In man-made environments (interfaces), there are two phases of activity: adaptation and adapted. During adaptation, a user's activity is being guided by exploratory behavior. Once adapted, a user's behavioral patterns have reached a state of equilibrium, or a *satisfactory state of transparency* between user input and system output (Rasmussen et al., 1991). The characteristics of any particular workplace and the type of work being done determine the priority of the two phases.

COMPREHENSIVE INTERACTIVE LEARNING ENVIRONMENTS

The "workplace" of most interest to those designing interfaces for educational technology would be the transitioning traditional classroom, which can be propelled beyond the 21st century with CompILE. CompILE relies heavily upon provision of access to information to all students at all stages of the educational process, as well as continual facilitation of mediated communication between humans and machines. This is accomplished through a network of intelligent agents whose existence is focused entirely upon two processes: (1) facilitation of learning for the user and (2) constantly learning about the user. These two processes are inseparable, as an integral part of the agents' facilitation of learning processes for each user is learning the "quirks" of each user's processes in situations of learning (both formal and informal). To create a personal knowledge management system, agents must know the personality of the user almost better than the user knows himself or herself.

As a system for personal knowledge management and visualization, CompILE can be considered an inhabited information space, or IIS (Snowdon, Churchill, & Frécon, 2004), that represents the growing collective knowledge an individual gathers throughout his or her lifespan. To be more specific, CompILE connects the user and his or her *inhabited knowledge space* (IKS). This IKS can be navigated individually by the user or collaboratively with additional individuals. Any number of interfaces could be used to access this IKS. Most of these interfaces would function as intermediaries between the internal knowledge architecture, external information sources, the user(s), and associated intelligent agents.

These agents can permanently link education and technology into a symbiotic relationship. Agents have become fairly reliable forms of autonomous software, intertwined more actively with the social lives of humans than any technology ever before, playing "an increasingly critical role in the organization, in particular the self-organization, of social life" (Brown & Duguid, 2000). Education is a highly socialized activity, with constant interaction between people a fundamental part of learning. A positive attribute of software agents is their ability to deal with the increasingly intimidating amounts of information that people are forced to deal with on a daily basis (Brown & Duguid, 2000). This ability would enable agents to assist students with keeping track of much larger amounts of information.

Agents that exist today (mainly for consumer purposes) can be broken down into three categories: information brokering, product brokering, and merchant brokering. Information brokers are agents that gather information from a wide variety of resources, and perform operations with the gathered information. Product broker agents are designed to track their owner's history (usually shopping habits) and alert that person to the availability of particular products in various venues. Agents that perform merchant brokering are essentially price comparison agents, trying to find the best possible "buy" for their owner. No successful negotiation agents (a fourth category) have ever been created (Brown & Duguid, 2000). Humans negotiate through nonverbal behavior in order to accommodate themselves to one another; constructing and adjusting the social fabric, but software agents have yet to be built with this capacity.

Information brokering agents would have the most direct crossover into education, being resourceful for students, teachers, and administrators; taking the form of research agents. Product brokering agents would translate to learning agents, tracking learning styles and suggesting individual supplements and alternative approaches to the basic curriculum for each student. Merchant brokering agents would not necessarily be feasible in an educational environment on a regular basis, but a similar concept can be realized in terms of brokering a user's time. Time management agents can assist the user by calculating approximate durations for activities, with a focus on multitasking and efficiency. Negotiation agents are an integral part of the CompILE system, facilitating intercommunication amongst all types of participants, with the agents dutifully negotiating with each other on the users' behaviors as the users themselves go about their daily routines. As a networked system of these four types of agents, CompILE could prove to be a vital instrument to help our society bridge the "digital divide."

THE DIGITAL DIVIDE: WHEEL OF POLICY INSTRUMENTS

Van Dijk (2005) addresses the "digital divide" with a four-part strategy called the "Wheel of Policy Instruments," which denotes four perspectives for access to information and communication technology (ICT): motivational, material, skills, and usage. Motivational access features increasing surplus values and user-friendliness of ICTs, organizing user trust by regulation, promoting useful applications of ICTs, and providing specific services for underserved groups. In terms of surplus value and user-friendliness, every use of CompILE must be beneficial for the user, with little or no margin for "user errors" that do nothing but frustrate the user, decreasing user confidence in the reliability of the CompILE system. Additionally, certain agents can focus upon the "add-on value" of a user's current actions within CompILE, giving suggestions for efficiency that the user may or may not have noticed; thus, increasing the surplus value of the system.

Regulation and promotion of ICTs can be seen as a symbiotic relationship. Government and corporate institutions can work together to promote useful applications of CompILE by upholding regulations in an open, trustworthy manner that promotes the benefits of CompILE (and other applications and services) to the user. A democratic, user-centric approach to legislation of regulations can serve as a valuable promotional tool as well. CompILE can help eliminate "underserved groups" using special agents designed to find information and services specifically targeted to the individual demographics of the agents' owner/user, such as cultural groups, gender- and age-specific information, or sociopolitical, health, and spiritual or secular information.

Material access features universal service, access to basic provisions, promotion of broadband access, support of competition, interconnectivity amongst media, conditional subsidies to lagging groups, and creation of public access points. As insinuated, much of materials access improvement involves government and corporate institutions cooperating to provide equal access to ICT services for all citizens. A good start would be the deprivatization of broadband Internet access into a public utility, much like public water and sewer service or electricity co-ops. Furthermore, public access points for broadband Internet connectivity (both wired and wireless) would be a fundamental element for the complete operation of CompILE. A combination of passive RFID tags and agents would allow for user identity and seamless integration from one access point to another, with just-in-time delivery of information to the user. This should all be available free of charge as part of a public broadband infrastructure.

Skills access features connecting all schools, libraries, hospitals, and cultural centers, adapting curricula for operational, instrumental, and strategic skills, creating better educational software and better digital teaching skills, teaching both basic and advanced skills to everyone, extending adult education to learning digital skills, and an emphasis upon distance education at home and in local classes or meetings. Adaptation of curricula for operational, instrumental, and strategic ICT skills would help users "meet" advancing technology at a "middle ground" of usability and user-friendliness. This should also lead to an increased knowledge base and skill sets for those who will be maintaining and supporting the CompILE system on a regular basis.

CompILE can reduce the need for purposed standalone educational software applications by providing such a dynamic, comprehensive digital teaching and learning environment. Additionally, CompILE can improve digital teaching skills with the assistance of special agents for preservice teachers while they are still in training. These agents can be carried over with these teachers into the in-service environment for professional development to expand technological skills and knowledge.

As opposed to a somewhat narrowed emphasis on "distance education" at home and in local classes, an emphasis should be made on a broader inclusion of self-paced, asynchronous collateral/supplemental learning and inquiry. The path of learning should extend throughout the waking hours of each individual's day. The formation of networked learning groups could supplement the current formal education system, leading to a "cottage industry" of sorts in the field of education and training. CompILE could facilitate these encounters both synchronously and asynchronously, both in-person and across distances via ICTs.

Usage access features support for learning on the job and at home, more hardware and software designed for underserved groups, special content for minorities and socially deprived groups, open access to all public and scientific information and major cultural events, support for competition in software and services, promotion of open-source software, lifelong learning and circulation of applications in jobs and education, and the full integration of ICTs into social and user environments. The success of CompILE depends (perhaps most heavily) upon open access to all public and scientific information. This information *must* be available to all who wish to learn, reflecting back upon the users' trust of the system—CompILE's agents must be able to deliver *all* the pertinent information related to a subject of inquiry. Also, upon completion of an initial performance or showing, major cultural events should be released into the public domain. The option should be available for immediate, free access to any cultural event, in appropriate digital format via the Internet.

The CompILE application will be open source software. With the source code available for public development, advanced users would be able to modify CompILE with add-ons or "plug-ins" that can increase the benefits of CompILE use. Similar to other open source software projects, these add-ons will be shared with other users across the Internet. In addition to extending the basic internal functionality of the main CompILE application, the add-ons would allow CompILE to communicate with an increasing number of current (and future) software applications. This would allow for a much fuller integration of ICTs into social and user environments, based on the intended widespread use of CompILE as a tool set for learning. The increased user-friendliness and surplus value realized with better communication between CompILE, and other applications would promote lifelong learning and the circulation of useful software applications in jobs and education.

CompILE AND SOCIETY

The concept of "lifelong learning" has its official origination in the 1973 UNESCO "Faure Report" (Faure, Herrera, Kaddoura, Lopos, Petrovsky, Rahnema, & Ward, 1972), which indicates the world's transition to a "learning society" and a "knowledge economy." Since then, many definitions of lifelong learning have surfaced. Smith and Spurling (1999) approach lifelong learning from a holistic perspective, with empirical and moral elements. Concerned with the scope of lifelong learning, the empirical element includes continuity, intention, and unfolding strategy as keys to the learning process. The moral element deals with the character of the learner, in terms of personal and social commitment, respect of others, and respect of the truth. Most importantly, Smith and Spurling give a wide berth to the activities that fall within the realm of lifelong learning, including formal, informal, and self-directed learning.

Crick (2005) hints toward the autonomy of the learner, noting that learning and metacognition are activities that we must do for ourselves, leading to a stronger self-awareness of and responsibility for learning. Fischer (2001) maintains that the arena for lifelong learning is highly contextualized and driven by the specific yet flexible demands of these situations of context. Considering the wide range of learning activities, learner autonomy, and highly contextual situations of learning, it's no surprise that humans must embrace the concept of a "learning society."

One approach to understanding this concept of a "learning society" is in terms of a social learning system, which can be understood as a "constellation" of communities of practice (Wenger, 2000). However, from a sociopolitical perspective, Lambeir (2005) suggests that "lifelong learning has become a new kind of power mechanism," highlighting two important trends: (1) a shift from a "knowledge-based" society to an information society, with learning having an emphasis upon the retrieval, dissemination, and evaluation of information; and (2) the increasing autonomy of the learner. With or without consideration of the politics involved, how can technology be applied to such a socially expansive concept?

The Open University Knowledge Network is under development as a software environment for lifelong learners' community knowledge network, based on Wenger's community of practice framework (McAndrew, Clow, Taylor, & Aczel, 2004). The designers chose to use evolutionary design methods, building only essential elements into the software, to be improved with user feedback. From their experiences with the OU Knowledge Network, they conclude that knowledge management software is an excellent tool for the collection of resources and experiences within a community, *only* if great care is taken when introducing the system and in *maintaining existing work practices.*

Koper and Tattersall (2004) note four main characteristics of lifelong learning to be considered when developing ICT support networks:

- Self-direction of learners
- Mobile access to distributed information
- Heterogeneity of learners
- Necessity for the maintenance of individual records of growth in competence

Their "Learning Network" (Koper & Sloep, 2003), developed exclusively with open source software, is currently in the pilot stages, also at the Open University of the Netherlands. Designed to support "seamless, ubiquitous access" to learning facilities at work, home, and schools, this architecture helps lower the access barriers to lifelong learning (Koper & Tattersall, 2004).

Two crucial areas of research taking place simultaneously at the Center for Lifelong Learning and Design (L^3D) are knowledge-based systems (KBS) and human-computer communication (HCC), with the idea that success cannot fully be realized in either area without substantial progress in the other (Fischer, 2001). All of these projects surrounding the application of technology in support of lifelong learning have similar indications, working with information, autonomy and heterogeneity of the learner, improvement through user feedback, maintaining existing work practices, and the inseparability of KBS and HCC, lead to a necessary focus upon the absolute importance of the usability of applied technology.

USABILITY

There are five distinct attributes of usability: learnability, efficiency, memorability, errors, and satisfaction. An interface should be simple enough to learn that users can quickly become productive with the application. Efficiency is also essential, as a user should be able to maintain high levels of productivity with the application upon learning the interface. The interface should be easy to remember, so those users that are not constantly in contact with the application can easily reorient themselves when necessary. User error should be kept to a minimum, and errors that are unavoidable should have easy avenues of recovery. The interface should be enjoyable for the user, creating a sense of satisfaction with the application (Nielsen, 1993).

The "common sense" foundation of usability makes it quite easy for a designer to forget the actual level of importance that usability has in the design process. The concepts become second nature, and because of this may become "second-rate." Also, it may seem as though an interface designer for a fairly complex system would have to choose between ease of use (learnability) and productivity (efficiency). This choice can be avoided by providing multiple interaction styles along with user action accelerators (Nielsen, 1993). Through a purposed focus upon multiple interaction styles, accelerators, or both, CompILE must compensate completely for learnability *and* efficiency. Not only should this focus increase endearment of the user population to CompILE, it should create a general increase in the appreciation of the usability design process amongst members of this user community.

CompILE AND COMMUNITY

The discovery-based design process inherent in sociotechnical systems effectively integrates the designers as participants within the system itself. This integration indicates a need for change within educational research as well. Geelan (2006) would agree, noting that the time has come for drastic changes in the methods of educational research, with the need for a highly participatory approach. This can be accomplished with an appropriate combination of scenario-based design, heuristic evaluation, and a better understanding of individual human participatory roles within CompILE.

SCENARIO-BASED DESIGN

While most engineering methods seek to control the complexity and fluidity of design using filtering and decomposition techniques, scenario-based design techniques seek to exploit the complexity and fluidity of design by learning more about the structure and dynamics of the problem domain. This process of exploitation promotes diverse views of the situation at hand, as well as intimate interaction with the concrete elements of that problem domain (Carroll, 2000). To exemplify this scenario-based process, consider an ambitious educational administration that wishes to implement CompILE across its entire school system. The problem domain of CompILE consists of all the individual schools within the system and the "usual" issues that these separate schools face: curricular consistency, communication, funding, staffing, regulations, parental involvement, and so forth.

There are two fundamental premises of the scenario-based approach that make it such an attractive design option. First, descriptions of how people accomplish tasks are a primary working design representation. Second, each context in which humans experience and act provides detailed constraint for the development and application of information technologies (Carroll, 2000). Considering these two premises, it is easy to see how a scenario-based approach for designing CompILE would radically differ from the same type of approach for designing an accident prevention program for a nuclear power plant.

Scenarios are contexts of interaction that highlight key aspects of a particular problem domain or system: goals suggested by the appearance and behavior of the system; what people try to do with the system; what procedures are adopted or not adopted, carried out successfully or erroneously; and reflections of system participants. In addition, these scenarios are comprised of four characteristic elements: setting, or the place and its props; agents/actors, or the people operating within the system; goals/objectives, or the changes an agent/actor wishes to achieve in the circumstances of the setting; and plot, including sequences of actions and events that can facilitate, obstruct, or be irrelevant to the given goals/objectives (Carroll, 2000).

Creating and using scenarios pushes designers beyond simple static answers. The emphasis on raising questions makes it easier for designers to integrate reflection and action into their own design practice. The process creates constant integration between the designers and the constituents of the problem domain by evoking reflection, contrasting the simultaneously concrete and flexible nature of scenarios, promoting work orientation, and melding abstraction with categorization. Scenarios also allow analysts and designers to visually sketch interactions in order to probe relationships (Carroll, 2000). It is precisely the nuances revealed through these questions and sketches that hold the keys to progress within the design of a system like CompILE. In addition, much of the reflection/action paradox is resolved by scenarios, as they provide a language for action that invokes reflection (Carroll, 2000). For example, a designer concerned with the implementation of stand-alone Web-browsing functionality within the global navigation menu of the CompILE interface would have a much easier time making a primary decision if he or she knew the current classroom dynamic between students, teachers, and the integration of Web content as a daily part of the curriculum.

Scenarios of use reconcile concreteness and flexibility by embodying concrete design actions that evoke concrete move testing by designers, and by facilitating open-ended exploration of design requirements and possibilities (Carroll, 2000). This approach is perfect for a project such as CompILE, because many decisions would be cut-and-dry, based on preceding projects within the same vein, but the specific needs of any school system would call for the refreshment of open-ended exploration. Exploration of this nature would help avoid overapplication of technology, as would the practical approach to interface use and analysis; heuristic evaluation.

HEURISTIC EVALUATION

Heuristic evaluation is the process of a person viewing an interface and making value judgments based on the 10 heuristics of usability, using his or her own common sense or intuition. Nielsen (1993) provides the following 10 heuristics of usability:

- Simple and natural dialog
- Speak the users' language
- Minimize user memory load
- Consistency
- Feedback
- Clearly marked exits
- Shortcuts
- Good error messages
- Error prevention
- Help and documentation

One of the best ways to find mistakes and problems in interfaces is to "use" the interface and look for them. Evaluators should work individually, only communicating after completion, including written or recorded reports following inspection (Nielsen, 1993). This lowers the probability of biased evaluations. For CompILE, individualized evaluation might not work, since students would be using the interface in close proximity to each other within the classroom environment. Even though the results would likely be biased for these group evaluation sessions, the bias itself would be an integral part of the feedback loop in designing CompILE. Examining "off-line" communication between students would be essential for creating seamless computerized intercommunication functionality.

Observers are a necessity for evaluating CompILE, since the evaluators would include young children, incapable of successfully completing comprehensive written evaluations. However, the "observer method" would still have its shortcomings, as much of the responsibility for interface content analysis still falls upon the evaluator. Due to the inexperience that most children would have with such an evaluation, the fact that observers are free to give ample hints for interface operation would be crucial to successful testing of CompILE. The short attention spans of most school-aged children combined with the complex nature of the CompILE interface would necessitate the series of short, small-scope evaluation sessions (as opposed to one marathon session). The product of a heuristic evaluation of any interface is a list of problems about that interface, directly referencing the 10 heuristics. When designers receive the report, the dots between problem and solution are mostly connected.

Unfortunately, many children might have difficulty remembering the 10 heuristics. There are at least three solutions to compensate for this difficulty: (1) place posters or reference cards of the heuristics near the child evaluator; (2) provide simple training for any child who would be heuristically evaluating the interface; or (3) create a third role within the evaluation process, a "supporter." A supporter would be an observer with more "clout," helping the child with his or her analysis as opposed to merely recording it. However, this supporter role does not have to be entirely fulfilled by humans. Supporters could manifest as "quality feedback" agents, similar to many software applications already in existence. Instead of the typical reactionary role that most of these quality feedback agents play, CompILE's supporter agents would assume a highly proactive role, providing an almost constant link between the users (from all roles of participation) and the processes of scenario-based design and heuristic evaluation.

ROLES OF PARTICIPATION

How can these agents specifically benefit the current and future individuals involved in the educational system: students, teachers, parents, administrators, researchers, and designers? Students could benefit from research agents, tutoring agents, archival agents, and communication agents. Research agents could constantly scour the infinite resources of the World Wide Web, reporting back to the student (or another agent) whenever any relative information is discovered. Tutoring agents would be highly customizable personal agents that grow with the student. Much like the aforementioned product brokering agents, these personal tutoring agents would remember the learning history of the student, keeping track of patterns of learning. This would enable the tutor to create a custom-built learning package that would cater directly to the child's learning style.

Archival agents could track the student throughout the day, digesting every idea communicated (and piece of work created) by the student into a digital archive. In the CompILE environment, every interaction in the classroom would be recorded in digital format. These records would be readily available, produced quickly and quietly by the archival agents. If a student cannot remember exactly what a teacher said or wrote at the beginning of the day, he or she would no longer need to worry, with everything available on a permanent basis. Issues of storage would need to be considered, but a half-sufficient remedy could be the use of a single storage facility (accessible by all the students in the class) for all in-class communication. Communication agents representing each student could queue up for the teacher, and he or she could answer the questions in the order in which they were received. This would work much like the "spooling" process for a networked printer. A student could place the requests and continue working on some other task while his or her communication agent representative waited to be served.

The teacher could employ several intelligent teaching assistant agents to deal with the overload of student questions. Many students would likely repeat the same question, so one of these assistant agents could be created specifically to tackle this issue, essentially replicating the teacher's original answer for each of the students. Teachers could employ grading agents to assist them with grading exams, especially the objective evaluations. This portion of the grading process could be an automatic function of CompILE, with the teacher's "grading" agents merely collecting the data from the system for the teacher's records. Observational agents that track the student's progress and individual learning styles could compare notes with the teacher's lesson plan preparation agents (primarily used like research agents) to create customized lessons for the class that compensated for each student's current position within the learning spectrum. It is even possible that these agents could continue working while the lesson is being presented, providing real-time diagnostics for the teacher, giving him or her the ability to change the speed or direction of the lesson on the fly!

As parents would have easy, secure access to CompILE, teachers could send conference requests via agents. As opposed to unanswered e-mails or phone calls that might have arrived at a time inconvenient to the parent, agents would be willing to wait indefinitely for a response, dutifully delivering it back to the teacher immediately upon receipt. Parents could also create agents to request progress reports on their children, or to create conferencing agents of their own, if they wished to speak with the teacher. Messenger agents could provide a way for parents to alert their children (and the teachers and administration) to any sudden change of plans that might arise on any particular day. This would be particularly helpful if the family has more than one child in the same school system, but different facilities (one in elementary school, one in middle school), or in entirely different systems. One agent could carry the message to all the different constituents involved.

In addition to progress report agents, parents could create agents that gathered their children's homework assignments for the day (or week), creating a chart for easy time management,

helping the children finish their homework efficiently and effectively. The homework agents could also serve as tutoring assistance agents, gathering information to assist the parent who might need a "refresher" on the fundamentals to be learned in the homework. These agents could report back to the teacher on the following day, giving a brief evaluation of the previous evening's proceedings.

Administrators would have many uses for agents. In addition to agents already mentioned, the administration could employ agents to monitor teachers, creating periodical "evaluations" that indicate the progress of the students; one indication of the teacher's ability to teach. Financial agents could help the administration cope with more political issues, such as which departments need more funding for equipment or textbooks, with research agents in turn scouring the resources of the Internet for the best options. Communication agents could serve the administration by contacting other school systems with similar demographic issues and comparing notes.

Researchers could employ the assistance of statistical agents that would perform data collection, sorting, and statistical analysis. Observation agents could continually observe the actions of different types of participants, searching for recognizable patterns of use of the CompILE system. As with administrators, communication agents could assist researchers by linking to the research taking place at other school systems with similar and different circumstances, performing trend comparisons and facilitating the collaboration of researchers on pertinent issues.

Design teams could rely heavily upon testing agents for the initial alpha testing of upgrades and new modules to be added to the CompILE application tool set, as the purpose of alpha testing is to find all possible ways to "break" software, and agents are the perfect digital drones for simulating endless combinations of user actions in an organized fashion. Role-playing agents could assist designers by demonstrating alternative solutions in the scenario-based design approach. Documentation agents could be responsible for tracking and archiving each iteration within the design team's process, allowing for appropriate reflection upon completion of a project.

Special care should be given when CompILE is implemented to prevent oversaturation of agents within the "cybersphere." Most agents should be able to multitask. Or it is possible that the better solution would involve millions of minimalist agents designed to complete one simple task and dispose of themselves. In either case, the possibilities abound for agent use in education, and the main purpose of their existence should be to allow humans to perform their roles in a manner that embodies valid participation in the educational community. Additionally, the persistence of researchers and designers "on the scene" in schools should raise the comfort level of other participants (especially children) due to familiarity. Perhaps increased exposure to research and design processes for other participant roles would cause an increased general appreciation of these processes. More importantly, though, researchers would likely gain more honest insight into participant processes, especially on the qualitative level.

CompILE AND CULTURE

Ethnography is the process of identifying the customs, habits, and key differences between different races, cultures, and groups of people. Due to its small focus and personalized nature, ethnography is known for its rich descriptions providing historical depth and contextual perspective, tracing social processes within groups (Howard, 2002). The rich descriptions and contextual perspective can provide the foundation for the new form of education that accommodates comprehensive interactive learning environments. In terms of communication, ethnography is concerned with patterns and functions of communication, the nature and definition of speech community, the components of communicative competence, and linguistic and social universals and inequalities (Saville-Troike, 2003).

Patterns of communication exist on the societal, group, and individual level. The interconnectedness of these patterns largely affects the roles of individuals in society in general, as well as within an educational setting. If a person was unaware that the patterns differ from one group of people to the next, it would be easy to misunderstand the implications of a particular attempt at communication by someone from a different group or culture. The fact that our schools are becoming increasingly multicultural opens a floodgate of potential misconception.

The classroom can be viewed as a model for societal structure in the sense that it can serve as a microcosm of the communicative situations that exist in our society. Considering this, the need for more attentiveness to the context of the discourse makes sense, but is not always possible at the time the discourse takes place. Teachers have too many other things to think about, and the context of discourse cannot possibly always be their main concern. Teachers can have more time to explain the context of discourse to students, thanks to the streamlined efficiency of CompILE. Addressing this context "in the moment" can reinforce an open-mindedness in students that leads to a broader appreciation of all cultures.

In addition to a broader appreciation of the diversity of human cultures, CompILE can also foster an overall appreciation for "culture" from a more philosophical perspective, one that considers aesthetic beauty. Adler (1981) refers to the subjective side of beauty as "enjoyable beauty," and the objectivity of beauty as "admirable beauty." Gelernter (1998) takes the concept of admirable beauty and refines it into a more fitting term for the technological world: "machine beauty," which can be considered a keen symmetry of simplicity and power. Conceptually, CompILE exemplifies this marriage of simplicity and power, providing access to so much information in such an organized, efficient way. However, its development falls under the shadow of the "beauty paradox": (1) most computer technologists are oblivious to beauty; (2) the best are obsessed with it; (3) the public has a love-hate relationship with beauty in computing; (4) beauty is the most important quality that exists in the computer world, when all is said and done (Gelernter, 1998). The subjectivity of the love-hate relationship between users and computers is the biggest hindrance to the development of simple yet powerful applications such as CompILE. An application can be admirably beautiful to all its users, but some will not experience its enjoyable beauty, at first. A deeper appreciation for the admirable beauty can lead to a newfound appreciation and enjoyment.

FUTURE TRENDS: CompILE AND GLOBALIZATION

The globalization of our learning society will come about with the increased ubiquity of ICTs (including those yet to be realized), which is leading to the disappearance of the traditional "brick-and-mortar classroom space." CompILE must be designed in a way to facilitate participants' responses to this removal in a seamless, "beautiful" manner. A core of visual communication and literacy (Dondis, 1973), backed by a network of translation agents, will advance the intercultural community that would thrive in this global learning society, based entirely upon open access to information by all participants.

As mobile inhabitants of a global society, lifelong learners should not be held stationary by any sociotechnical system. A learner must be able to collaborate effectively, sharing the contents of his or her IKS with others using a sophisticated visualization interface. As we begin working across national and cultural boundaries with higher frequency, verbal communication in a "common language" might not resonate clearly, but recognition of patterns in other's knowledge

spaces, using basic elements of visual form could transcend this issue altogether. If we as a society were to become visually literate, would a common "visual language" lead to better understanding, communication, and cooperative learning? Perhaps this visual communication process could initially be augmented by translation agents, a specialized form of negotiation agents that augment the verbal communication between people who cannot find a common spoken language between them. These agents would be reliant upon the advent of highly accurate voice recognition technology, and instantaneous translation would be paramount to provide seamless assistance during conversation.

CONCLUSION

As a sociotechnical system, CompILE must manifest as a hybrid system in at least two ways. First, its users, in all forms of participation, would in fact be de facto designers. Second, CompILE would combine reality and virtual environments in a manner conducive to constructive learning practices, taking full advantages of the added dimensionality provided by this combination. Imagine a learner interested in Greek civilization, standing in modern-day Greece, able to augment his or her current visual field with images of classic Greek structures overlaid precisely upon those structures in their current form. Upon the request of the user, these augmenting images could animate, showing the degradation of the structures over time, highlighting access to information about specific historic events that had direct impact on the process. This is just one example of how CompILE could embody the careful integration of ICT as a tool fundamental to the learning process.

The agents of CompILE can help promote higher levels of information literacy amongst its users, which in time should lead to a more informed consumer society, which will provide society with a more appropriate mindset to create community, embrace all cultures, and become a true learning society. The CompILE system, obviously, is a continuous work in progress, still in its infancy. Much more discussion must take place concerning theories and applications as a continuing predevelopment phase. It is precisely such a discussion, as well as the continued involvement in its design and development, that will empower users of CompILE to cross the digital divide.

REFERENCES

Adler, M. J. (1981). *Six great ideas*. New York: Simon & Schuster.

Bechtel, R. B. (1997). *Environment & behavior: An introduction*. Thousand Oaks, CA: Sage.

Brown, J. S., & Duguid, P. (2000). *The social life of information*. Boston: Harvard Business School Press.

Carroll, J. M. (1991). *Designing interaction: Psychology at the human-computer interface*. New York: Cambridge University Press.

Carroll, J. M. (2000). *Making use: Scenario-based design of human-computer interactions*. Cambridge: MIT Press.

Crick, R. D. (2005). Being a learner: A virtue for the 21st century. *British Journal of Educational Studies, 53*(3).

Dondis, D. A. (1973). *A primer of visual literacy*. Cambridge: MIT Press.

Faure, E., Herrera, F., Kaddoura, A.-R., Lopos, H., Petrovsky, A. V., Rahnema, M., & Ward, F. C. (1972). *Learning to be: The world of education today and tomorrow*. Paris: UNESCO.

Fischer, G. (n.d.). Introduction to *L³D*. Retrieved December, 2006, from http://l3d.cs.colorado.edu/introduction.html

Fischer, G. (2001). Lifelong learning and its support with new media. In N. J. Smelser & P. B. Baltes (Eds), *International encyclopedia of social and behavioral sciences*. Amsterdam: Elsevier.

Geelan, D. (2006). *Undead theories: Constructivism, eclecticism and research in education*. Rotterdam: Sense Publishers.

Gelernter, D. (1998). *Machine beauty: Elegance and the heart of technology*. New York: Basic Books.

Gifford, R. (1997). *Environmental psychology: Principles and practice* (2nd ed.). Boston: Allyn and Bacon.

Howard, P. N. (2002). Network ethnography and the hypermedia organization: New media, new organizations, new methods. *New Media and Society, 4*.

Kling, R. (2000). Learning about information technologies and social change: The contribution of social informatics. *The Information Society, 16*(3).

Koper, E. J. R., & Sloep, P. (2003). *Learning networks: Connecting people, organizations, autonomous agents and learning resources to establish the emergence of effective lifelong learning*. Heerlen: The Open University of the Netherlands.

Koper, E. J. R., & Tattersall, C. (2004). New directions for lifelong learning using network technologies. *British Journal of Educational Technology, 35*(6).

Lambeir, B. (2005). Education as liberation: The politics and techniques of lifelong learning. *Educational Philosophy and Theory, 37*(3).

Marks, W., & Dulaney, C. L. (1998). Visual information processing on the World Wide Web. In C. Forsythe, E. Grose, & J. Ratner (Eds.), *Human factors and Web development*. Mahwah, NJ: Lawrence Erlbaum.

McAndrew, P., Clow, D., Taylor, J., & Aczel, J. (2004). The evolutionary design of a knowledge network to support knowledge management and sharing for lifelong learning. *British Journal of Educational Technology, 35*(6).

Nielsen, J. (1993). *Usability engineering.* San Diego, CA: Morgan Kaufman.

Norman, D. A. (1993). *Things that make us smart.* Reading, MA: Addison-Wesley.

Rasmussen, J., Anderson, H. B., & Bernsen, N. O. (Eds.). (1991). *Human-computer interaction.* Hillsdale, NJ: Lawrence Erlbaum.

Saville-Troike, M. (2003). *The ethnography of communication: An introduction.* (3rd ed.). Malden, MA: Blackwell.

Shneiderman, B. (Ed.). (1993). *Sparks of innovation in human-computer interaction.* Norwood, NJ: Ablex.

Smith, J., & Spurling, A. (1999). *Lifelong learning: Riding the tiger.* London: Cassell.

Snowdon, D. N., Churchill, E. F., & Frécon, E. (2004). *Inhabited information spaces: Living with your data.* New York: Springer.

Sommer, R. (1969). *Personal spaces: The behavioral basis of design.* Englewood Cliffs, NJ: Prentice Hall.

van Dijk, J. A. G. M., (2005). *The deepening divide: Inequality in the information society.* Thousand Oaks, CA: Sage.

Wenger, E. (2000). Communities of practice: The key to knowledge strategy. In E. Lesser, M. Fontaine, & J. Slusher, (Eds.), *Knowledge and communities,* (pp. 3-20). Oxford: Butterworth-Heinemann.

Chapter XXIII
Structural Coupling as a Foundation for Instructional Design

Jeanette Bopry
National Institute of Education, Nayang Technological University, Singapore

Donald J. Cunningham
USF St. Petersburg, USA

ABSTRACT

In this chapter, we describe an alternative to the cognitive and neo-behavioral views of learning that currently dominate the field of instructional design and development. Founded in the work of Chilean biologists Humberto Maturana and Francisco Varela, this view questions the fundamental notions that the environment can actually be "instructive" and that instruction can be prescribed to change learners in predictable ways. Instead we offer a proscriptive model of instructional design, one that embeds the process in the basic foundation that learners are organizationally closed, structurally determined, and coupled with their environment. Instead of threatening the field of instructional design, as some writers have expressed, we argue that this approach actually "sets it free"!

INTRODUCTION

A hallmark of traditional models of learning and cognition is that they assume that culture, in general, and knowledge, in particular, is external to the learner and can be objectively specified (e.g., by task analyses, schema, semantic networks, production systems, etc.). That is, they rely on the existence of information "objects" that can be passed through mental structures by cognitive mechanisms in an analogous way that a message flows through a telephone wire. The process of learning becomes one of mapping this external knowledge into some form of internal representation that more or less approximates the external "objects." To see if the transmission process has been successful, we check the match between the student's cognitive representation and the knowledge as previously defined. The learner learns by acquiring or being directed by the culture to behave in new ways. Thus one may say that the interactions between the learner and the environment are instructional: The environment instructs the learner. Most self-described constructivists hold the position that while knowledge is constructed, information is still received from the environment in this manner. This places those constructivists well within this same tradition.

In this chapter, we will explore the consequences of a position that takes quite a different point of view of the teaching-learning process, one that questions the very notion that culture/environment can be "instructive" in any real sense of that word. We will draw upon the writings of the Chilean biologists, Humberto Maturana and Francisco Varela. Our purpose is not simply to reject other positions, but mainly to assess the implications of this view for existing and possible new instructional systems. In other words, would instructional design and the use of technology look different based upon Maturana's notion of autopoiesis? In what way can we design instruction that is synomorphic[1] with this process? But first, a few words about Maturana.

BACKGROUND

Two Questions: What is a Living System? How Does Perception Work?

At this point the reader must be warned that terminology plays an important role in the story we will tell. For example, most scientists, biologists included, use the terms organization and structure interchangeably. However, Maturana found that he had to make a logical distinction between the two in order to solve the problem of what makes a living system a living system. Maturana has always been very conscious of the terminology he uses because any given language limits what may be said. Terminology will be discussed in a later section of this chapter.

As an instructor of biology interested primarily in perception, Maturana found that he was constantly faced with some variant on the following question from his students: "What is proper to living systems that had its origin when they originated, and has remained invariant since then in the succession of their generations?" (Maturana, 1980, p. xii). This was turned into his initial driving question: "What is the organization of the living?" (p. xii). There are, of course, lists of the characteristics of living systems, and we can recognize whether a system is living, but this is different from saying that we *know* what a living system is; that we can identify the invariant feature of living systems around which natural selection operates (Maturana, 1980). After years of research and thought, Maturana concluded that the single most important characteristic that distinguishes the living from the non-living, in regard to their unitary character, is *autopoiesis* (a term he coined to differentiate what he was saying from the more general term, autonomy). In brief, a living unity is self-producing; it produces within itself all its own components, everything it needs to stay alive. This is his answer to the first question. The prototypical example is the cell. Self-production means that the living system does not depend upon an external environment for any of its components. The boundaries of the living system separate it from its medium, it does not import any necessary components; it produces them all, including its boundaries. The living system has no function or purpose other than to keep itself alive.

Following his own particular interests, Maturana's second driving question became "What takes place in the phenomenon of perception?" The two questions began as parallel interests, but rapidly converged. His investigation into perception, particularly color vision led him to realize that experience of color could not be accounted for by the presence or absence of particular wavelengths of light in the world. An orange is experienced as the same color whether viewed under sunlight or under fluorescent light. Illuminating an object with a pink light may result in a green shadow even in the absence of wavelengths of light associated with green. While Maturana's research group could not correlate activity in the retina with physical stimuli, they could correlate it with the color experience of the subject. Perception could not be seen as the mapping of some external reality onto the nervous system, it had to originate with the nervous system itself.

What startled him is that the only way to account for what they were learning about perception was if the nervous system were informationally closed, allowing for no inputs or outputs. There could be no taking in of information; the nervous system is not instructed by the environment, it interprets stimuli and makes meaning of those interpretations. Maturana states:

What was still more fundamental was the discovery that one had to close off the nervous system to account for its operation, and that perception should not be viewed as a grasping of an external reality, but rather as the specification of one, because no distinction was possible between perception and hallucination in the operation of the nervous system as a closed network. (1980, p. xv)

Again the circular, organizational closure is apparent. The nervous system is a closed system of neuronal activity: The firing of neurons leads to the firing of other neurons ad infinitum. So both questions have lead to answers that involve organizational closure, or autonomous systems. Both the cell and the nervous systems are examples of autonomous systems; the cell is a member of a subset of autonomous systems that are also autopoietic. In contrast, an *allonomous* system has a linear or open organization and allows inputs to and outputs from the system. An example of a system that is not autonomous is the heart; it is organization based on the input and output of blood. It exists to serve the rest of the body, not itself. Designed systems are usually input/output systems that function to serve human needs. On the other hand, many non-living systems exhibit organizational closure, and are therefore autonomous. Varela (1979) lists language, calculations of all types, and natural social groups as examples of autonomous systems. This remarkable concept has had an impact on fields as diverse as sociology, the law, and family therapy.

MAIN FOCUS OF THE CHAPTER

Main Concepts and Their Implications

Because Maturana was introducing new concepts he had to be particularly careful about terminology. We have already introduced the reader to autopoiesis, a term that was coined to avoid confusion between living systems and other types of autonomous systems. We have also hinted at a distinction between organization and structure. Terminology is important because the original concepts inherent in this theory provide the grounding from which we draw implications for education, instructional design, and for the uses of technology.

The Distinction Between Organization and Structure

Lakoff and Johnson (1999) discuss a number of metaphors that undergird the way we think about the world. One of the metaphors they highlight is that organization is physical structure. What interests us is that many people, including scientists, do not consider this a metaphor at all. Science textbooks may use the terms interchangeably.

It seems that the transparency of this metaphor may have blinded us to a distinction that must be made in order to understand the nature of living systems and, indeed, any systems that "seem to have a life of their own." To understand autonomous systems theory, one must be able to make a distinction between the two concepts. To be concise, organization is an abstraction that is expressed through a structure. We never see the color blue independent of some object that is blue: blue car, blue sky, blue light, and so on. Organization is similar in that it does not exist except as an expression of some physical structure, but it is not the physical structure any more than blue is the car. However, organization is more essential to a system than color is to an object. While structure gives an entity physical presence in the world, organization gives it its identity. Think of something as simple as a square; then, think of how many different physical manifestations a square can take. Each of these manifestations is a structure, what they share is their organization: Squares are closed geometric figures consisting of four sides of equal length, with all adjacent sides meeting at right angles. We can create squares of brick, of plastic, of wood, and so on. We can replace one side of our wood square with a length of plastic and still have a square. However, if we alter the length of one of the sides or change the degree of one of the angles, the square ceases to exist. Organization is not the physical structure itself; it is how the structure is put together.

Organization and structure have different implications for systems: While organization provides the system with its identity; structure determines how the system will interact with its environment. Both are necessary, but in very different ways. There are important concepts associated with organization and structure that we need to take into consideration: organizational closure, structural determination, and structural coupling.

Organizational Closure and Conservation of Identity

Loss of autopoietic organization in a system is death. To remain alive it must conserve its organization. In fact, one of the interesting things about autonomous systems in general is that they will struggle to conserve their organization, their identity. Some instructional designers may find solace in this, given the resistance to change they regularly encounter!

For organizational closure to come about two things are required: a network of components that through their interactions "...recursively regenerate the network of interactions that produced them;" and that "...realize the network as a unity in the space in which the components exist by constituting and specifying the unity's boundaries as a cleavage from the background" (Varela, 1981, p. 15). For an observer to define a system as organizationally closed, it is necessary that this cleavage from the background coincide with the boundaries within which the recursive regeneration of interactions operates:

Organizational closure ... arises through the circular concatenation of processes to constitute an interdependent network. Once this circularity arises, the processes constitute a self-computing organization, which attains coherence through its own operation, and not through the intervention of contingencies from the ambient. (Varela, 1981, p. 16)

Language is an example of such a system. We cannot communicate about language except through language; further, every time we use language we contribute to its continuing existence. Anthony Giddens (1984) argues the same about social structure; it is both the medium and the outcome of social practices: once again, a closed or circular organization. By engaging in social practices, we ensure the continuing existence of the social structure.

At this point, we would like to turn to important concepts related to structure, the physical form a system takes. Recall that we stated earlier that structure determines the way a system will interact with the environment. In fact, structural determination has very important implications within this theory. The other concept related to structure that we ought to consider is structural coupling. These concepts complement one another.

Structural Determination

Systems may undergo change without loss of identity; change may even be necessary in order to maintain that identity. Changes in the structure of a unity can come from two sources: its internal dynamics and continuous interactions with an environment (Maturana & Varela, 1992). Both types of interaction are determined by its structure. A system only engages in the kinds of interactions its structure makes possible. Although we may not think about it in these terms, we intuitively treat everything we come into contact with as if it were structurally determined. You get into your car, press the accelerator, and turn the key. If nothing happens, you will not blame your foot, nor will you blame the key. Instead, you will look for a mechanical (structural) problem with the car. Disease may result in internal dynamics that can change the structure we inhabit; learning is another form of internal dynamic that may result in structural change. Our feet may change shape because of the shoes we wear. There is a range of possible changes that any system may undergo. These changes are determined by the structure of the system. Some of these potential changes are destructive to the system, or to the identity of the system. Autonomous systems will subordinate changes to the maintenance of the organization; they attempt to maintain their identity. Structural determination is an aspect of our commonsense

approach to everyday life (Maturana & Varela, 1992). Any stimulus from the environment is interpreted by the system, and whatever change ensues is a response to that interpretation. This stimulus is referred to as a perturbation.

The distinction between a system that interprets perturbations, and compensates for deformations to its sensory systems, and a system that accepts inputs from the environment and outputs to the environment is crucial. The second kind of system, referred to Heinz Von Foerster (1981) as a trivial machine, is instructed by its environment, and derives its identity from these instructions, which determine the transformations that will take place within the system. In other words, input determines output in a predictable manner. The computer is an excellent example of a trivial machine. It is, unfortunately, also the primary metaphor of mind in cognitive psychology, the dominant psychological theory in education today. We suggest that many of our strategies of instruction, many of our models of instructional design treat learners as trivial machines. This is, after all, the assumption on which prescription is based, that we can predict output based on input. When we do this, we place ourselves at the center of the learner's cognition (Maturana, 1974). We treat learners as extensions of our own cognition. This approach is inherently oppressive (Maturana, 1974). We need strategies that place learners at the center of their own cognition.

Wait, you may be saying, if we are structurally determined and informationally closed, then how in the world do we communicate with one another? If all is interpretation, if there is no transmission of information or meaning between individuals, are not we all living in solipsistic dreams? If the nervous system is informationally closed, without inputs and outputs, unable to distinguish between hallucination and perception, how can we even function? How do we survive in a world full of real dangers? The answer to these objections can be found in structural coupling.

Structural Coupling

Structural coupling is a relationship between two entities that allows both to maintain their organization even while engaging in recurrent interactions over time. It is, in effect, adaptation. Let us return to an example we used earlier: We can say that our shoes and our feet are structurally coupled because both change over time to conform to each other, and neither suffers loss of identity in the process; shoes can be pretty beaten up and still remain shoes. As the ancient practice of foot binding shows, even feet can undergo significant change without loss of identity. Living systems can become structurally coupled to one another: Families are made up of structurally coupled individuals, people who share a history of interaction; pet owners are structurally coupled to their pets.

That organisms be structurally coupled to their environment is a requirement for survival. Structural coupling within social groupings also contributes to survival because the group contributes to the survival of the individual. While structural coupling with an environment is also called adaptation, structural coupling that is species wide and takes place over generations is evolution.

Guddemi (2000) suggests that structural coupling works through mechanisms of predictive regularity: (1) things that look alike are alike; (2) if two things regularly appear together and we see one, then we can expect to see the other; and, (3) when we speak to you, you will behave in a way that allows us to know you understand.

Klaus Krippendorff (1994) has created a model of communication based upon the ideas of structural coupling and structural determination. According to this model, communication is a matter of believing that we understand one another until it is demonstrated that in fact there has been a breakdown in communication. As long as our interlocutor behaves in the manner we expect, we do not question the process. When something

unexpected happens, then a process of negotiation of meaning begins. Maintaining the sense that we are communicating is a matter of keeping the conversation going without breakdown.

A lot a space has been devoted to organization and structure because the changes that an autonomous system undergoes are meaningful only in relation to what does not change. Invariance/change is the organization/structure duality. The system must change constantly while conserving its organization. So what does all this have to do with cognition and learning? According to Varela (1979), "the specification of a cognitive domain is the propensity of every autonomous system endowed with structural plasticity" (p. 260). This means that the emergence of an autonomous system is also the specification of a cognitive domain. Structural change in such a system generates information. "How a system establishes its identity (its autonomy) correlates with how it generates information: The mechanisms of identity are interwoven with the mechanisms of knowledge" (p. 261). Structural change in a cognitive domain is information. When an autonomous system recognizes and is able to recursively interact with these structural changes (i.e., treat them as meaningful) two things happen: language emerges and with it another phenomenon, the observer. All human beings are observers.

Effective Action

Effective action is the final important concept that we will discuss. Its meaning should be obvious, its importance may be less so. This theory pulls the rug out from under the belief that the environment instructs our nervous system in such a manner that it generates internal representations of that environment. The representational position is that the primary way we interact with the world is by acting upon an internal representation. Such a position considers the nervous system as an allonomous (input/output) system, and therefore, instructable. Such systems manipulate symbols syntactically, just as computers do. It is no accident that the primary metaphor of the representational position is the computer. The alternative that we are presenting here, enaction, is the position that we interact with the world directly through action. The advantage of this position is that it can account for common sense, something that the representational position cannot. Meaning is provided by the structure of the system itself, which operates semantically rather than syntactically. The import of structural determination is that perception, information, and meaning are all constructions of the cognitive system. To suggest, as many so-called moderate constructivists do, that we construct meaning, based on information input to our sensory systems, is, from this position, self-contradictory. It treats the nervous system as allonomous in terms of information, but autonomous in terms of meaning. In contrast, the enactive position never treats living systems as trivial machines.

Enaction provides support for interpretive approaches. For example, it is consistent with the idea that meaning is provided by the receiver rather than the sender of a message (senders are receivers of their own messages as well). The emphasis is placed on readers rather than authors as the source for meaning of text.

Enaction supports both cognitive and social constructivist positions. When representation ceases to play the central role, intelligence becomes the capacity to enter a shared world of meaning rather than the capacity to solve a problem via some internal algorithm. We can join existing worlds of meaning or join with others to create new worlds of meaning; that is, enaction focuses on creating joint understandings rather than manipulating systems according to internal rules to solve problems. Entering a shared world of meaning is metaphorically a conversation; maintaining the continued integrity of that world requires the ability to keep the conversation going. The conversation, rather than the computer, is the primary metaphor of enaction.

Enaction has resulted in a number practical applications. Maturana's work has been applied effectively in the area of family therapy; and, it has had an impact on Luhmann's sociological theory. It has also had an impact in the field of artificial intelligence. Rodney Brook's robots, called creatures, are created by layering simple programs one on top of another. The Mars Rover and the small disc shaped automatic vacuum sweeper are both examples of practical developments consistent with this position (Brooks, 2002). Let us turn next to how we can apply this theory in educational technology areas.

FUTURE TRENDS

Principles for Action

In this section of the chapter, we will discuss two basic approaches that comport with this theoretical framework. First, an alternative to prescriptive design in the form of proscription will be described, and then we will discuss a change in emphasis from the development of instructional processes to the development of learning environments.

Proscription, an Alternative Logic to Prescription

Early in this chapter, we brought up the idea that instruction, in the sense that the environment instructs the nervous system, was problematic. The idea that we can prescriptively design instruction is based on the belief that it is possible to predict a learner's behavior or output, based on inputs that we control. Maturana has convincingly argued against this. He believes that we cannot determine a student's learning, that is, directly produce the behaviors we want, when we want them. Students actively construct their own cognition as determined by their own structural states.

When we engage in prescription, we treat learners as trivial machines (input - output devices).

Maturana (1974) argues that when we engage in prescription, we deny learners a place at the center of their own cognition, treating them instead as extensions of our own cognition. This brings an ethical dimension to our decision-making process about instructional strategies. When we believe we are doing a pretty good job of instructing, students may simply be accommodating to the situation in which they find themselves, acting in the way they think we want them to act (i.e., in terms of the world that we have brought forth with them) so as to conserve structural coupling and adaptation. Students may find it more efficacious to structurally couple with the teacher or with peers than with the material that the teacher intends them to learn. In order to provide for a situation in which the learner is the center of his or her own cognition we need to consider a different logic for design than prescription.

The basic idea behind *proscription* is that instead of determining what a learner will do, you determine what they will not do; constrain their actions rather than determine them. Varela, Thompson, and Rosch (1991) recommend proscriptive logic as a viable alternative to prescriptive logic for describing change in nature:

The first step is to switch from a prescriptive logic to a proscriptive one, that is, from the idea that what is not allowed is forbidden to the idea that what is not forbidden is allowed. In the context of evolution this shift means that we remove selection as a prescriptive process that guides and instructs in the task of improving fitness. In contrast, in a proscriptive context natural selection can be seen to operate, but in a modified sense: selection discards what is not compatible with survival and reproduction. Organisms and the population offer variety; natural selection guarantees only that what ensues satisfies the two basic constraints of survival and reproduction. (Varela, Thompson, & Rosch, 1991, p. 195)

These two constraints still allow for a wide range of diversity in nature, just look about you.

What about human activity systems? What makes a given culture distinct if not the form of life experience offered its members? While rites and rituals may be prescriptive in nature, we suggest that the primary means by which members are enculturated is through the proscription of certain kinds of experience. What we do not experience, what we have never had the opportunity to construct, falls outside our sense of reality and our sense of identity as a member of a particular culture. No culture can prescribe what experiences all its members have but, it can establish taboos or experiences that are not allowed, or even more effectively, cultures can simply ignore the possibility of certain experiences. Monster sighting has little place in mainstream American culture, but may be accepted in some Native American cultures. Any given language allows speakers to construct sentences never before spoken, any language provides opportunity for individual styles of expression or idiolect, yet there are things that cannot be expressed in English, for example, that can be expressed in German. Originality and diversity within constraint are characteristic of natural human activity systems.

Let us say that you, as an educator, are aware that there are seven ways of approaching a given task or solving a given problem, four which will be successful and three of which will not. If you follow a prescriptive logic, you are likely to provide learners the algorithm for the approach with which you are most familiar or most comfortable. If instead, you follow a proscriptive logic, you would be more likely to warn students that there are many ways of reaching the objective and many ways to fail. Some of the ways to fail are a, b, and c. You tell them what to avoid doing rather than what to do. This immediately makes visible something that is hidden in a prescriptive approach, what is not allowed. It makes what is not allowed available for critical analysis. Why is it not allowed? Why does it not work? The educational advantage of a proscriptive approach is that it permits students to find the path to the solution that is best suited to their own understanding of the task or problem. This should provide the teacher who engages in observation with a rich set of information about the thinking of his or her students. It provides students an opportunity to share their perspectives with their peers, reinforcing the idea of multiple viable perspectives. It also has the potential to expand the teacher's subject matter knowledge base. Learners are likely to find additional ways to fail that the teacher has not anticipated, and possibly additional and uniquely new ways to succeed. So, not only does proscription enhance diversity in practice, it also encourages creativity. These are two values to which much lip service is given in our educational system, but which are systematically obstructed through the practice of prescription.

Enaction foregrounds the concept of creativity: "Context and common sense are not residual artifacts that can be progressively eliminated by the discovery of more sophisticated rules. They are in fact the very essence of creative cognition" (Varela, 1992, p. 252). Context provides the constraints that must be negotiated by the learner in a given situation. Common sense is the ability to maintain a history of effective action even while the obstacles or constraints that one encounters change. The advantage of proscription is that it provides a humanistic alternative to design by prescription; it promotes diversity within constraints, and facilitates creativity. Design from this perspective is grounded in the local community and maintains the flavor of this community.

A proscriptive approach does not lend itself to the nice neat models for design preferred by many educational technologists. The design process is a creative one. This process is not prescriptive, yet it works within constraints. Bereiter (1993) describes design as iterations of applications of constraints to a problem space. Each iteration builds upon the previous one and gradually the problem space narrows down to a solution. The eventual solution may not become apparent until fairly late in the process. Both rapid collaborative prototyping and design-based research follow this general pattern. From the perspective of enaction, there is continual tension between the designer's vision, which may be undergoing continuous revision and the constraints within the environment, which may also be changing; this fits with the actual experience of designers, if not with the ideal suggested by prescriptive models. If we consider design a form of structural coupling, where everyone involved in the interaction is structurally determined, then it becomes apparent why: Designers can only trigger changes in the environment, they cannot determine them.

That said, designers will make choices that impose constraints on the problem space, and will effectively orient the forms of interactions that their clients may engage in. For example, designers of learning environments must choose the extent to which an experience will be grounded in the community of learners and to what extent it will be grounded in the community of practice. When the choice favors the former, some form of social system design is implicated, when the latter is chosen focus is on the adaptation of learners into an already existing community. For the learner, the opportunity to create new worlds of meaning within the already existing community of practice is remote; however, the opportunity to create new worlds of meaning within the community of learners is immediate. Technological environments facilitate community building. They make possible opportunities for the creation of communities that could otherwise not exist, communities of people separated by time and distance, for example, or communities of people with very specialized interests. We shall turn, then, to the issue of designing environments, given our perspective.

Design of Environments

In essence, learning from our perspective is seen as adaptation, effective action within an environment, or continuous structural change while conserving organization (identity). In other words, learning takes place through structural coupling. This leads to the conclusion that learners need some appropriate other with which to couple, some other living or nonliving system.

So, the issue of design becomes one of creating cultures and environments that facilitate learning by students. Efran and Lukens (1985, p.23) highlight Maturana's belief that instruction in the traditional sense is simply not possible. They suggest that "you do not change organisms—you design an environment in which organisms thrive, respond, and change themselves." Within the enactive perspective, problem solving is rejected as the highest form of intelligence. Instead, that place is reserved for the ability to join ongoing worlds of meaning or create new worlds of meaning. The importance of new technologies becomes salient: New technologies, virtual spaces, open new opportunities for the creation of community that would otherwise not exist. The ability to connect with people that would otherwise be inaccessible to you creates spaces in which worlds of meaning may be created or extended. Science students can have direct access to professionals in fields that before were mediated solely through the classroom teacher. YouTube is an example of a space that allows for the coconstruction of community. The Internet provides space for circumventing roadblocks to one to one, one to many, and many to one forms of communication.

Such environments need to take the *embodied* nature of cognition into account. Maturana and Varela (1980, 1992) divide experience into two types of activity: non-reflective activity that resembles the thrownness borrowed by Winograd and Flores (1986) from Heidegger; and reflective activity, the domain of description and the observer (similar to Heidegger's *Dasein*). Bopry

(2005) further divides reflective experience into observation (first order description) and description (second-order description). Observation is primarily experienced as an individual activity; description involves the observer in the act of communication through language. Non-reflective activity is the brute fact of existence, of being thrown into the world. This is the sense of being part of a river of sensory perturbation, within which effective action is demonstrated by continued survival. The observer exists in the domain of language and both observation and description are considered aspects of the observer. These levels are independent cognitive domains. While each emerges from the level subordinate to it, they do not intersect. Our experience of an event is distinct from our observation of our experience and different again from our description to a friend of the experience. There is no correspondence (as there would be if correspondence theory held up) between the experience, the observation, and the description. Higher levels of experience cannot be reduced to lower levels of experience.

The implication for the design of environments, therefore, is that they need to be calibrated in such a way as to provide depth of experience to learners. The most memorable experiences penetrate all levels. If it is not possible to provide an experience that exploits all levels, then we suggest you try to provide as deep an experience as possible. For example, one could choose primary sources over secondary sources since the former are more likely to generate vicarious experience than the latter. Learners should be provided opportunities for the observation of processes as these are generally easy to arrange and more efficacious than providing only the descriptions of someone who has engaged in these processes. Designs that emphasize sensory and emotional experience need to consider observation, reflection, and description. Conversely, designs focused on exercising the skills required in the descriptive domain need to consider reflection, observation, and phenomenal experience. In those circumstances where all levels of experience can be exploited, each should make a contribution to achieving the overarching goal (Bopry & Hedberg, 2005).

The issue of scaffolding becomes more complex as it will need to be provided at each level of experience and different levels will make different demands on the teacher. Learners can be debriefed about their observations of their own sensory/emotional experiences as well as their observations of others engaged a shared learning activity. They can also be asked to reflect upon how and why they chose to describe, explain, or represent their experience in a particular manner. A more complete discussion of this topic can be found in Bopry and Hedberg (2005).

The learning environment can be designed to facilitate a form of play: In some privileged conditions, two or more organisms can disengage from the demands of immediate adaptation to their shared environment and relate to each other as if they constituted a "world of their own." (Guddemi, 2000, p. 139) This world of their own will not surprise them with threatening actions, but does allow experimentation with various forms of structural coupling. It provides a shared environment that allows learners to coordinate their activities, to work together and to communicate about shared experiences. Effective cooperative work requires learners be cocoupled to a shared environment or work domain, the embodied nature of which needs to be taken into consideration. The metaphors we use in communication are extensions of this embodiment.

An Example

As an example of the design approach we advocate in this chapter, we offer the Inquiry Learning Forum (ILF, see Barab, Makinster, Moore, & Cunningham, 2001). The ILF, originally funded by the National Science Foundation, is a Web-based professional development system designed to support a community (currently 6,800 registered members) of in-service and preservice

secondary mathematics and science teachers sharing, improving, and creating inquiry-based pedagogical practices (see http://ilf.crlt.indiana. edu/). The design centered on the vision of a community in which teachers can virtually visit each other's classrooms to observe, reflect, and discuss approaches to teaching mathematics and science topics; share teaching practices and experiences with other teachers, explore inquiry-based teaching, view lesson plans, student work, and resources, make connections to national and state standards, and reflect on their own teaching. Tools for project–centered, online collaboration are available as well as models for learning how to teach from an inquiry perspective. While developed primarily for Indiana math and science teachers, the ILF is open to all teachers, school administrators, university faculty, and preservice education students interested in inquiry-based teaching and learning.

The ILF consists of a variety of Web-based structures, all related to encouraging online collaboration. The ILF Web site is designed around a school metaphor. When you enter the ILF you are able to visit several "rooms" typical of any school building. Within these spaces you can obtain or share lesson plans, view video examples of teachers, engage in online discussions, and work online with groups focused around a particular topic or idea. The home screen of the ILF is shown in Figure 1 (see the last page of this narrative section) in which the classrooms are available through the Classrooms space. When an ILF member selects a specific classroom lesson (see Figure 2 on the last page of this narrative section for a sample classroom) they can view seven to eight video segments of the implemented lesson. Additionally, they can access an overview of the lesson, reflective commentary from the teachers, descriptions of activities, lesson plans, students' examples and connections with both state and national standards. The ILF Web site serves as a tool for developing and improving teaching practice as well as advancing community and individual reflection. Through observation, discussion, and reflection, each participant can find his or her own path to continued professional growth and development.

A primary area of interest in the ILF is the Collaboratory, a space in which groups of teachers can come together in an online space around some collective experience and/or curricular interest. Each group within the Collaboratory is referred to as an Inquiry Circle and the contents of the Inquiry Circle are only visible to its members. Each Inquiry Circle space enables teachers to (a) organize the ILF classrooms, resources, and create discussion forums that are of interest to this group, (b) share announcements, ideas, Web links, and electronic documents, (c) collaboratively create and edit documents, and (d) organize the efforts and interests of this group as they use this space as a way to keep in touch.

There are also five other spaces designed to support the professional development needs of ILF teachers. The ILF Office is the place where new participants can secure a password (the site is password protected), get help with technology, or make suggestions. The Lounge contains general asynchronous discussion forums that are not tied to a particular classroom. The Inquiry Lab is a series of professional development activities that members can use to address their current professional development needs. These activities may be modified and adopted for use by preservice classes and professional development groups. The Library is an online database of member-contributed lessons, ideas, and resources. Members can access links to a variety of resources and reference materials of interest, including teaching resource materials (software, other classroom artifacts like the graphing calculator, manipulatives, sensory probes), state and national standards, grants, applied research and theory, relevant state initiatives, and other materials the ILF teachers identify as relevant. Finally, My Desk is the teacher's desk (since entry into ILF is password protected, My Desk is a personalized space of the person who

logged in) in which she can store bookmarks to resources and classrooms that are of personal relevance and return to those at a later visit. The owner can also maintain a journal that they can later email to any ILF member, a useful feature in preservice classes.

Notice that in all of this design, we are in no way prescribing a best way to teach, the so-called "best practices." We do proscribe certain pedagogies that are incompatible with inquiry learning (e.g., the ubiquitous display and reading of PowerPoint slides to students), but stress that there are many good ways to teach the lessons on display. Our participants are supported by viewing teachers who are more or less successful, discussing these practices with colleagues and the teacher in the video, inspecting artifacts, and so forth as they construct their own "best" practice.

The example we have provided is used for the professional development of educators, however, by using different metaphors to structure the virtual space we belive that this basic structure would serve to support professional development in a variety of fields.

FUTURE RESEARCH DIRECTIONS

New technologies, virtual spaces, open new opportunities for the creation of community that would otherwise not exist. This suggests a number of questions: What are the affordances of a given technology within specific contexts? How do these affordances interact with individual and group identities? What forms of structural coupling can be observed within given spaces?

More generally, what forms do organizational closure take (both in terms of individual identity and group identity) within various contexts? How does closure determine which forms of change a given system will be receptive to and which it will reject?

Within educational technology, there is a legitimate question of whether this approach leads to a research program that can develop improved models of instructional design or whether the very existence of traditional instructional design is threatened. Winn (1989, p.40) expresses this sentiment this way: "Indeed, the very idea that instruction can be designed in the first place must be abandoned unless one subscribes to the belief that how students will react to instruction can be predicted with reasonable accuracy." But the fact that humans are informationally closed need not inevitably lead to the notion that they can not be "influenced," and influenced in predictable ways. The ideas underlying constructivism, for example, suggest that we shift from designing environments that *instruct* to designing environments that *influence* the structure of autopoietic unities in ways that conserve organization and adaptation. Thus, while the organization of, say, the human nervous system is fixed, its interconnectivity allows for nearly infinite structural flexibility. Through structural coupling with its environment (that includes other beings), the organism literally brings forth the world in which it finds itself, a world constrained by the organization of the environment and by its own organization. But within those limits, an incredible variety of worlds are possible.

Knuth and Cunningham (1993) have listed seven principles of constructivism that are compatible with this position:

1. All knowledge is constructed
2. Many worlds are possible, hence there will be multiple perspectives
3. Knowledge is effective action
4. Human learning is embedded within social coupling
5. Knowing is not sign dependent
6. World views can be explored and changed with tools
7. Knowing how we know is the ultimate human accomplishment

If these are taken as proscriptions, then they all provide testable hypotheses for further research to determine the many ways that compatible instruction can be designed. Knuth and Cunningham (1993) lay out some of these possibilities and we think you can think of many more. The message is actually one of optimism for the field of instructional design, not abandonment. The only thing you must abandon is the notion that there is a single best way to design instruction. This position sets you free!

CONCLUSION

In this chapter, we have described an alternative to the representational position that dominates cognitive psychology. This position is supported by research in biology, neurophysiology, and immunology. It has been developed over the decades since the 1960s, when many of these ideas were first published as research reports at Heinz Von Foerster's Biological Computing Laboratory at the University of Illinois–Urbana. This position has implications for our understanding of communication, learning, and instruction. It provides a warrant for constructivist practices. For readers wishing to continue to read in this literature, the essential source for information on autopoiesis is Maturana and Varela (1980), for autonomous systems theory, Varela (1979), and for enaction, Varela, Thompson, and Rosch (1991). Maturana and Varela (1992) provide an accessible introduction to many of these ideas.

REFERENCES

Barab, S., Makinster, J., Moore, J., & Cunningham, D.J. (2001). Designing and building an online community: The struggle to support sociability in the Inquiry Learning Forum. *Educational Technology Research and Development, 49,* 71-96.

Bereiter, C. (1993). *Surpassing ourselves.* Peru, IL: Open Court Publishing.

Bopry, J. (2005). Levels of experience: An exploration for learning design. *Educational Media International, 42*(1), 83-89.

Bopry, J., & Hedberg, J. (2005). Designing encounters for meaningful experience, with lessons from J. K. Rowling. *Educational Media International, 42*(1), 91-105.

Brooks, R. A. (2002). *Flesh and machines: How robots will change us*. New York: Pantheon.

Efran, J., & Luken, M. D. (1985). The world according to Humberto Maturana. *Family Therapy Networker, 9*, 22-25, 27-28, 72-75.

Giddens, A. (1984). *The constitution of society*. Berkeley, CA: The University of California Press.

Guddemi, P. (2000). Autopoiesis, semiosis, and cocoupling: A relational language for describing communication and adaptation. *Cybernetics & Human Knowing, 7*(2-3), 127-145.

Krippendorff, K. (1994). A recursive thoery of communication. In D. Crowley & D. Mitchell (Eds.), *Communication theory today* (pp. 78-104). Stanford, CA: Stanford University Press.

Knuth, R. A., & Cunningham, D. J. (1993). Tools for constructivism. In T. Duffy, J. Lowyck, & D. Jonassen (Eds.), *The design of constructivist learning environments: Implications for Instructional design and the use of technology* (pp. 163-188). NATO ASI Series F: Computer and Systems Sciences (Vol. 105). Berlin: Springer Verlag.

Lakoff, G., & Johnson, M. (1999). *Philosophy in the flesh*. New York: Basic Books.

Maturana, H. R. (1974). Coginitive strategies. In H. Von Foerster (Ed.), *Cybernetics of cybernetics* (pp. 457-469). Urbana, IL: Biological Computer Library, University of Illinois.

Maturana, H. R. (1980). Introduction. In H. Maturana & F. Varela, *Autopoiesis and cognition: The realization of the living* (pp. xi-xxx). Dordrecht: D. Reidel.

Maturana, H. R., & Varela, F. J. (1980). *Autopoiesis and cognition: The realization of the living*. Dordrecht: D. Reidel.

Maturana, H. R., & Varela, F. J. (1992). *The tree of knowledge* (rev. ed). Boston: Shambhala.

Pink, S. (2001). *Doing visual ethnography*. London: Sage.

Pink, S. (2006). *The future of visual anthropology: Engaging the senses*. London: Routledge.

Varela, F. J. (1979). *Principles of biological autonomy*. New York: North Holland.

Varela, F. J. (1981) Autonomy and autopoiesis. In G. Roth & H. Schwegler (Eds.), *Self-organizing systems* (pp. 14-23). Frankfort: Campus Verlag.

Varela, F. J., Thompson, E., & Rosch, E. (1991). *The embodied mind*. Cambridge, MA: The MIT Press.

Varela, F. J. (1992). Whence perceptual meaning? A cartography of current ideas. In F. J. Varela & J. Dupuy (Eds.), *Understanding origins* (pp. 234-271). Dordrecht: Kluwer.

Von Foerster, H. (1981). Perception of the future and the future of perception. In *Observing Systems* (pp. 192-210). Seaside, CA: Intersystems.

Winn, W. (1989). Towards a rationale and theoretical basis for educational technology. *Educational Technology Research and Development, 37*, 35-46.

Winograd, T., & Flores, F. (1986). *Understanding computers and cognition*. Norwood, NJ: Ablex.

ADDITIONAL READING

Essential Readings

Maturana, H. R., & Varela, F. J. (1980). *Autopoiesis and cognition: The realization of the living*. Dordrecht: D. Reidel.

Maturana, H. R., & Varela, F. J. (1992). *The tree of knowledge* (rev. ed). Boston: Shambhala.

Varela, F. J. (1979). *Principles of biological autonomy.* New York: North Holland.

Varela, F. J., Thompson, E., & Rosch, E. (1991). *The embodied mind.* Cambridge, MA: The MIT Press.

Other Useful Readings

Bopry, J. (2006). Providing a warrant for constructivist practice: The contribution of Francisco Varela. In J. L. Kincheloe & R. A. Horn (Eds.), *The Praeger handbook of education and psychology, 4,* 474-484). Westport, CT: Praeger.

Bopry, J., & Brier, S. (2001). *The ages of Francisco Varela.* Special issue of *Cybernetics and Human Knowing, 9*(2). Exeter: Imprint Academic.

Bunnell, P. (2004). Reflections on the ontology of observing. *Cybernetics and Human Knowing, 11*(4), 72-84.

Bunnell, P., & Forsythe, K. (2001). The chain of hearts: Practical biology for intelligent behavior. In B. Hocking, J. Haskell, & W. Linds (Eds.), *Unfolding bodymind* (pp. 152-169). Brandon, VT: Foundation for Educational Renewal.

Cunningham, D. J. (1992). Everything said is said by someone. *Educational Psychology Review, 4*(2), 261-269.

Dorsey, L. T., Goodrum, D. A., & Schwen, T. M. (1997). Rapid collaborative prototyping as an instructional development paradigm. In C. R. Dills & A. J. Romiszowski (Eds.), *Instructional development paradigms* (pp. 445-466). Englewood Cliffs, NJ: Educational Technology Publications.

Freire, P. (1970). *The pedagogy of the oppressed* (M. B. Ramos, Trans.). New York: Continuum.

Giddens, A. (1979). *Central problems in social theory.* Berkeley: University of California Press.

Giddens, A. (1991). *Modernity and self-identity.* Stanford, CA: Stanford University Press.

Glasersfeld, E. von (1995). *Radical constructivism.* London: The Falmer Press.

Graham, P., & McKenna, B. J. (2000). A theoretical and analytical synthesis of autopoiesis and sociolinguistics for the study of organisational communication. *Social Semiotics, 10*(1), 49-59.

Guddemi, P. (2000). Autopoiesis, semeiosis, and cocoupling: A relational language for describing communication and adaptation. *Cybernetics & Human Knowing, 7*(2-3), 127-145.

Heidegger, M. (1962). *Being and time.* New York: Harper & Row.

Johnson, M. (1987). *The body in the mind.* Chicago: University of Chicago Press.

Luhmann, N. (1984). *Social systems.* Stanford, CA: Stanford University Press.

Luhmann, N. (1990). *Essays on self-reference.* New York: Columbia University Press.

Lyon, P. (2004). Autopoiesis and knowing: Reflections on Maturana's biogenic explanation of cognition. *Cybernetics and Human Knowing, 11*(4), 21-46.

Maturana, H. R. (1980). Man and society. In F. Benseler, P. M. Hejl, & W. K. Köck (Eds.), *Autopoiesis, communication and society* (pp. 11-31). Frankfurt: Campus Verlag.

Maturana, H. R. (1988). Reality: The search for objectivity or the quest for a compelling argument. *The Irish Journal of Psychology, 9*(1), 25-82.

Maturana, H. R. (1991). Science and daily life: The ontology of scientific explanations. In F. Steier (Ed.), *Research and reflexivity* (pp. 30-52). London: Sage.

Maturana, H. R., & Poerksen, B. (2004). Varieties of objectivity. *Cybernetics and Human Knowing, 11*(4), 63-71.

Maturana, H. R., & Zöller, G. V. (in press). *The origin of humanness in the biology of love* (P. Bunnell, Ed.). Exeter: Imprint Academic.

Petitot, J., Varela, F., Pachoud, B., & Roy, J. M. (Eds.). (1999). *Naturalizing phenomenology: Contemporary issues in phenomenology and cognitive science,* Stanford: Stanford University Press.

Reddy, K. (1993). The conduit metaphor: A case of frame conflict in our language about language. In A. Ortony (Ed.), *Foundations of communication theory* (2nd ed.), (pp. 164-201). New York: Harper & Row.

Russell, D., & Ison, R. (2004). Maturana's intellectual contribution: A choreography of conversation and action. *Cybernetics and Human Knowing, 11*(2), 72-84.

Schön, D. A. (1983). *The reflective practitioner.* New York: Basic Books.

Schön, D. A. (1987). *Educating the reflective practitioner.* San Francisco: Jossey-Bass.

Teubner, G. (1993). *Law as an autopoietic system.* Oxford: Blackwell.

Varela, F. J. (1981). Autonomy and autopoiesis. In G. Roth & H. Schwegler (Eds.), *Self-organizing systems* (pp. 14-23). Frankfurt: Campus Verlag.

Varela, F. J. (1981). Describing the logic of the living. In M. Zeleny (Ed.), *Autopoiesis, A theory of living organization* (pp. 36-48). New York: North Holland.

Varela, F. J. (1984). Living ways of sense-making: A middle path. In P. Livingstone (Ed.), *Order and disorder* (pp. 208-224). Saratoga, CA: ANMA Libri.

Varela, F. J. (1997). *Sleeping, dreaming, and dying: An exploration of consciousness with the Dalai Lama,* Boston: Wisdom Publications.

Varela, F. J. (1999). *Ethical know-how: Action, wisdom, and cognition.* Stanford, CA: Stanford University Press.

Von Foerster, H. (2003). *Understanding understanding: Essays on cybernetics and cognition.* New York: Springer.

Whitaker, R. (2004). Thanks for the magic, Humberto. *Cybernetics and Human Knowing, 11*(4), 93-97.

Winn, W. (1993). A constructivist critique of the assumptions of instructional design. In T. M. Duffy, J. Lowyck, & D. H. Jonassen (Eds.), *Designing environments for constructive learning* (pp. 189-212). NATO ASI Series F: Computer ande Systems Sciences, Vol. 105. Berlin: Springer Verlag.

Winograd, T., & Flores, F. (1986). *Understanding computers and cognition.* Norwood, NJ: Ablex.

ENDNOTE

[1] Synomorphy means that there is a closeness of fit between two entities. For example, a shoe is synomorphic with a foot or a glove with a hand.

APPENDIX

Figure 1. ILF Welcome Screen

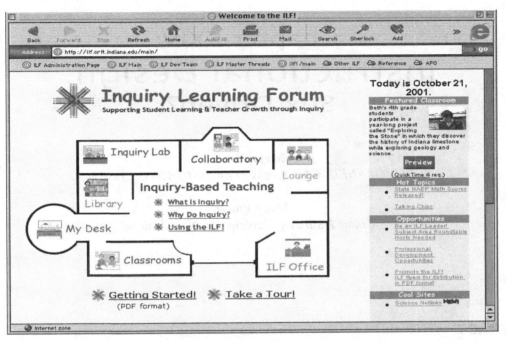

Figure 2. Sample ILF Classroom Page

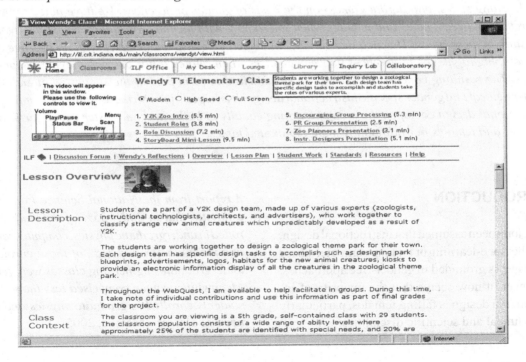

Chapter XXIV
Instructional Design:
Sex Driven?

Maja Pivec
FH JOANNEUM, University of Applied Sciences, Austria

Mary Panko
Unitec Institute of Technology, New Zealand

ABSTRACT

In this chapter, we have analysed three main aspects of instructional design (online learning communities, learning styles, and digital games) on the basis of gender preferences. We have noted the visible differences between males and females when interacting with technology, and reviewed the available literature in these areas. The included survey, conducted on males and females with an average age of 21 years, highlights the preferences between genders when related to the use and playing of computer games. The resulting conclusions have been summarized to form part of the suggested guidelines for gender neutral and gender specific instructional design. It is hoped that with these guidelines, appropriate instructional design can open the area of learning equally to both sexes and foster equal participation of males and females in traditionally male-dominated topics.

INTRODUCTION

It has long been assumed that instructional design, whether for e-learning or for non-computer-based teaching, is grounded in gender-free approaches. However, it now seems that the majority of instructional design is failing females, particularly in technical and scientific disciplines:

A report from the National Science Foundation estimates that in 2001, 35% of the students enrolled in undergraduate physics, computer science, and math classes and 16% of those enrolled in undergraduate engineering classes were female. Meanwhile, women comprised less than 10% of students enrolled in graduate physics and engineering classes. (Malone, 2005)

Currently several European countries as well as The United States of America are attempting to redress this balance in order to encourage more girls to study in these male dominated areas.

Before this can be done, it is important to consider what are the educational motivators and the inhibitors for both genders.

Extensive research has taken place in area of instructional design (Taylor, 1996) but generally this has been looked at from a male perspective, even if this has not been acknowledged. We hope that the contribution this chapter will make to the design of e-learning will improve this situation and allow designers to recognise that there are potentially different motivations between the two genders.

INSTRUCTIONAL DESIGN AND GENDER

"Instruction" is what instructors do (e.g., a music instructor), and is mostly focused on training, whereas 'Design' stands for creativity for example, an environmental designer focuses on creating the external ambience. Thus Instructional Design can be viewed as process of designing the learning experiences for learners. If we accept that Instructional Design is a system of procedures for developing educational and teaching programmes in a consistent and reliable fashion (Reiser & Dempsy, 2001), it should also be consistent for the gender of the target audience.

Based on the decades of studies related to gender and software design, Huff (2002) argues that the instructional design of teaching programmes designed for males had game characteristics like competition, time pressure, and were focussed on hand-eye coordination. Application for females looked like goal-based learning tools, that is, drill and practice programs including conversation features. Most interesting is the further result of the study, what was claimed as gender unspecified

instructional design had characteristics of typical design for boys in particular:

Programs designed for 'students in general' were really programs designed for boys. Interestingly, 80% of the designers of our programs were female, many of whom expressed concern that educational software was male-biased. (Huff, 2002, p. 113)

Gorizz and Medina (2000) state that game designers have to create compelling content while at the same time understanding the context of use and societal attitudes of computer usage to be able to address girls and boys. Only when using true gender-neutral content, both genders are equally reached.

Klawe (2002) argues that there is still a surprisingly big gender difference in comprehending interaction and occupation with computers as "mainly a boy-thing." This reflects on the dominance of software and games for boys as well as on their physical access to computers. According to Huff (2002), gender-influenced instructional design mirrors the experience of interacting with the software, especially when the software is used in public. The participant experiences visible stress when interacting with the software created for the other gender.

A person's beliefs about his or her capabilities are a significant part of self-knowledge. (Lester & Brown, 2004, p. 4)

The central question therefore is, what is gender appropriate instructional design?

The focus of gender appropriate instructional design considers how we may offer the same topic to both genders while also creating suitable learning experience for females.

Respect and accommodate differences in preference in activities and usage styles of computers whether gender based or not.

Provide gender inclusive curriculum and teaching so that all children can develop confidence and understanding of appropriate computer science concepts and skills (including programming). (Klawe, 2002, p. 17)

Research shows that gender differences are observed when males and females are using computers together in mixed groups, caused mainly due to the male dominance. Nevertheless one can provide equal opportunities for girls integrating a variety of activities thus supporting the difference in the use of computers between boys and girls. As outlined in Ching, Kafai, and Marshall (2000), introducing negotiating spaces in the mixed teamwork, team members can explore their various approaches, roles, and establish differences in their concepts, fostering at the same time increasing participation of girls. This relates to the findings of Bates and Norton (2002), who assert that the strong motivations behind the participation of woman in education are self-fulfilment and self-esteem. Therefore, according to Lester and Brown (2004), it is very important to include verbal positive feedback in the learning process, to support the shaping of self-perception of their computing capabilities by the learners.

LEARNING COMMUNITIES AND GENDER

A gender-sympathetic approach to design creates collaborative and supportive environments that acknowledge the contributions of others; value the holistic approach of connecting the cognitive and affective, the mind and the body; and the political and the personal. (Campbell, 2000, p. 138)

In the field of online learning the concept of "learning communities" has been an increasingly popular idea since the start of the 1990s (Palloff & Pratt, 1999), becoming almost a mantra with many online educators. Although contextually

differing in nature, overall these communities are seen as creating "the socially constructed meaning that is the hallmark of a constructivist classroom in which active learning is taking place" (p.32). As such, they are generally regarded as gender-free environments where learning occurs in an atmosphere of high-level social connection. But the question needs to be raised as to whether this is an equally successful approach for men as for women.

Palloff and Pratt (p. 26) also emphasise that, "In distance education, attention needs to be paid to the developing sense of community within the group of participants in order for the learning process to be successful." This humanistic orientation to the nature of online activities gives rise to recommendations for online teachers to make space for personal issues to encourage the sense of community for all their students, whether male or female. These spaces can be of varied types, for example some online teachers (often known as e-moderators in this context) develop a one-to-one chat area for individual reflection, while others rely on the scaffolding role of the teacher, and opportunities for social interaction, dialogue, and collaboration among students in asynchronous discussions. Some online educators might simply communicate with their students through e-mail or via phone conversations.

Regardless of type, all these examples of online learning environments are normally regarded as gender-free environments where learning occurs in an atmosphere of high-level social connection. Nevertheless, studies of varied responses related to gender (Ayerson & Reed, 1995; Fahy & Ally, 2005; Herring, 2003) have already revealed that men and women react differently in computer-mediated communication (CMC), with women preferring to be less confrontational during debate. In other words, could the relationship-dependent characteristics of online learning communities might be generally more appropriate for women than for men?

To examine this question, it is first necessary to explore the nature of learning communities and then relate the characteristics of these contexts to the learning approaches of recognised in men and women.

The development or organisation of a learning community in the adult education field has a number of similarities to the models of communities of professional practice originally outlined by Lave and Wenger (1991). Collectively this entails the shifting of learning from the individual, to that gained by participating within a wider group in which knowledge is generated and shared within a social and cultural context. Wenger (2001, n.p.) has recently indicated the overlap between communities of practice and learning communities as:

Communities of practice are formed by people who engage in a process of collective learning in a shared domain of human endeavor: a tribe learning to survive, a band of artists seeking new forms of expression, a group of engineers working on similar problems, a clique of pupils defining their identity in the school, a network of surgeons exploring novel techniques, a gathering of first-time managers helping each other cope.

In relation to a specifically educational environment, Wenger (2001, n.p.) makes the point that the process of learning is not restricted to the classroom or course objectives but is part of a broader learning system:

It is life itself that is the main learning event. Schools, classrooms, and training sessions still have a role to play in this vision, but they have to be in the service of the learning that happens in the world.

Put another way, the learning community is situational, socially based, and forms part of a pattern of life-long learning.

Buysse, Sparkman, and Wesley (2003, p.267) reach a similar conclusion and hypothesise that such a framework must have two central tenets:

a. Knowledge is situated in experience
b. Experience is understood through critical reflection with others who share this experience ... or who have similar, if not identical, issues and concerns.

Buysse and her colleagues suggest a number of circumstances under which these reflections could occur, one of which involves peers engaging in discourse to analyse problems and consider alternative viewpoints. It is in this area that the community of practice model closely overlaps the online learning community in which the majority of learning management systems, such as WebCT or Blackboard, provide environments for learners to synchronously or asynchronously debate and explore course topics.

Online discussion forums, with their emphasis on collaborative learning, might seem to provide an environment more conducive to female relationship building than to male learning styles. This concept can be examined through the lens of an intellectual development model of women's learning developed by Belenky and her colleagues (1986/1997). This model proposed that women's learning positions evolved from Silent Receiver through Subjective and then Procedural Knower, sometimes reaching the stage of Constructivist. When Belenky's model is applied to online discussions (see Table 1), it appears likely that some women are quite capable of flourishing in a collaborative environment, but others will only be able to survive the community of learners if the "rules" are clearly explained in advance, often by an authority figure. Regrettably, the silent learner is likely to find herself lost in the absence of information transfer taking place. To counteract this possibility, Campbell (2000) recommends that a high level of moderator support is provided and that online contributions be anonymous. At the

Table 1. Women's intellectual positions in relation to discussion forums (based loosely on Belenky et al, 1986)

Intellectual position	Characteristics	Discussion forum consequences
Silent learning	Receives information passively, dualist beliefs. Respects authority.	Unhappy to explore non-determined topics.
Subjective knowing	Dualist beliefs, but internally validated.	Certain of own ideas and unhappy with opposing concepts.
Procedural knowing	Knowledge reflectively and systematically analysed:	Requires discussion structure to be detailed.
a) Separate	Carries out processes of critical analysis, only within boundaries of established system,	Complies with requirements but reluctant to criticise peers.
b) Connected	Uses personal experience and forbearance, plus analysis.	Expresses interest and empathy. Will discuss topics deeply when trust established.
Constructed knowing	Reclaiming the self. The knower's own perspective.	Passionate participant, openly reflecting on own and others experiences.

same time, the subjective learner may also rapidly lose interest in the opposing ideas of others, particular ones expressed by the moderator, as she regards knowledge as either true or false, her own viewpoint being the overriding one. For this group Campbell makes a number of suggestions, including the introduction of female role models, and modelling critical thinking in the context of relational knowing (2000, p. 143).

Women who have achieved Procedural knowing or who have become Constructivist learners are the most likely to take part in discussion and gain from the shared experiences of the learning community.

The variations in the needs and responses of women highlight the requirement for care in the design and facilitation of the discussion forum for both women and men.

That the discussion forum context could also be uncomfortable to men was reinforced recently to one of the authors of this chapter during an attempt to create an online learning community with a group of 14 adult educators at the start

of a discussion forum series. Following a well-established procedure, the group of both sexes were encouraged to introduce themselves to one another online using a structured process. They were asked to post a digital picture of themselves, and include some personal details, as well as family images if they felt comfortable doing this. Suggestions were made about the sort of information they might consider posting, such as hobbies, children, or some topic they might feel passionate about. In addition, they were asked to outline what their expectations were for the course and a few notes about the area of teaching each came from. The e-moderator provided a model by posting a picture of herself with her puppy and added some snippets of both family and professional details.

On previous occasions this process had generally a high level of success, both socially and practically. The group become acquainted with each other and recognised the diverse experiences each member brought to the learning community, as well as having an opportunity to practise basic techniques of posting and replying.

All seemed to go well and most members of the group, both male and female, got into the spirit of the first discussion. Further discussion topics, which focussed more specifically on the learners'/community's experiences in relation to course content, were engaged with at a generally high level of learning, debate growing from shared knowledge and alternative perceptions. One man, however, did not participate and gradually withdrew from the course. When questioned later he explained that it had been the introductory discussion that had deterred him. He described himself as a very private person who did not wish to reveal personal information, or want to hear it from others. This was the first time we came to have doubts about the mantra of a learning community as an ideal situation for all learners and the matter of gender involvement raised.

Following the theme of the learning community described, the question remains: how are women likely to view tutor encouragement to participate and interact? Eager to join a community of learners or reluctant to "speak out" in public? On reflection, the opportunity to develop an online community of learners through the judicious use of discussion forums might be seen as a rare case of female bias in instructional design but only if e-moderated with empathy.

LEARNING STYLES AND GENDER

Within a student-centred model of teaching the concept of learning styles is intimately related to that of Instructional design. This relationship enables the course designer to allow for the different learning needs of the students and amend the nature of the course according to those needs. A large number of different learning style analyses have been applied to determine the particular nature of students in different learning environments (Coffield, Moseley, Hall, & Ecclestone, 2004). And although frequently the analysis does not record the gender of the students questioned,

there are a number of examples where this has been reported on, particularly in the area of online learning.

Examined through Kolb's cognitive model (Kolb, 2000), learners are identified as having strengths with four learning modes. These are: Concrete Experience (feeling), Reflective Observation (watching), Abstract Conceptualisation (thinking), and Active Experimentation (doing). When Garland and Martin (2005) applied this model to 168 university students enrolled across a mixture of face-to-face and online courses, they concluded that, "learning style characteristics of the online student are different from the learning style of the student enrolled in the traditional face-to-face course" (p.77). From this they recommended that online developers needed to include a diversity of components in a course that would complement variety of learning styles and promote learner engagement.

In particular, Garland (2003) has reported that there are differences between the level of engagement for the online male and online female students. Her study found that there was a significant difference between the way male and female students viewed the computer. Garland's subsequent research indicates that male students saw it as a tool to gain power, speed, infinite wisdom, and the ability to control, while females saw it as a device for connected learning, emphasising relationships, empathy, and cooperation. "The implications for online course designers are significant. When designing online courses the learning style and gender of all students must be considered."

Once again the Kolb cognitive learning style model of learning styles has been used by Fahy and Ally (2005), but their research showed no significant difference between the responses of women and men. They suggest that the reason for this was due to their discussion being e-moderated and the pattern provided a model for all the participants to follow. Although a few other studies on learning styles have employed alternative models such as the Myers Briggs personality approach, the majority of learning style studies have adopted a cognitive model. It might be argued that this would not suit women learners coming from the silent or subjective positions, and so it is recommended that further research is carried out into the preferences of women learners in technological areas, already a domain festooned with male symbolism.

GAMES AND GENDER

Game design is a market driven process and the majority of game designers are males (DIGRA, 2005). Male designers design games for male players, focussing on sex, violence, speed, and "on the edge" behaviours. The idea behind most games is competition and the concept of winning. However, some games do attract females. Women get more enthusiastic playing multiplayer games where social interaction, emotions or challenge are in foreground. Numbers of women are playing social games such as SIMS and SIMS 2, and puzzle games.

Another type of games popular with women is digital pets, where a player, that is, pet owner, has to feed, play with, and keep the pet happy. The 1997 burst of Tamagotchi was followed recently by big successes of Nintendogs, with over 4 million units sold in one year, 2 million of them in Europe. The statistics showed that female gamers accounted for 40% on Nintendogs sales. Nintendogs is a game based on touch screen and is focus on emotional bonding with the player.

At the FH JOANNEUM in Austria, 47 2nd year students of Information Design were surveyed about their preferences and experiences with computer games. We wanted to analyse motivation for playing "games for males" and establish differences in females' preferences, thus projecting these into requirements for designing "games for females." [For details of the questionnaire and results, see appendix]

Total respondents	-	47	
Males	-	21	
Females	-	26	
Average age (M& F)	-	21	
Males			
Gamers	-	17	(80%)
Non-Gamers	-	4	(20%)
Females			
Gamers	-	15	(58%)
Non-Gamers	-	11	(42%)

The differences between the responses of the genders became clear straight away when asked why they played computer games. While the majority in both groups stated that the played "for fun," 40% of the males indicated that competition and socialising was an important motivator while the girls did not rate competition as a driving force. Instead, 28% of the girls stated that they played to "waste time" although 29% of the girls stated that they used computer games as a learning tool. Indeed, half of the female respondents listed that games were a waste of time, with 40% stating that they had no interest. The remainder stated that they preferred real face to face people contact to technology.

This difference was also identified when the preferred game types were examined, males ranked First-Person Shooters (FPS) and Real Time Strategy (RTS) games, closely followed by Role Playing Games (RPG) and Adventure games. At least 90% of the preferred games were War games of some kind—FPS, RTS, or RPG. Females preferred Adventure games and Puzzle games, with War games being the least preferred.

This survey shows that the common attraction for both genders to play computer games is fun and entertainment or relaxation. With 54% female players the survey confirms the increasing presence of females in this previously male dominated domain, as reported often in the literature (Dickey, 2006; Gorriz & Medina, 2000). Males see online games as a social event and a way of communication. Both genders see computer games as a leisure time activity. Nevertheless some females see also the learning benefits of games.

Adventure games are genre preferred by both genders, followed by RTS games. Puzzle games were female only, and FPS games were male only. The results correlate with previous surveys on play pattern preferences by girls, carried out by US game producer and publisher Purple Moon (bought by Matel), that girls prefer using the puzzle-solving skills over the training of hand-eye coordination. War games are definitely preferred by males, and not preferred by females; hence competition and winning have strong presence in this type of games and relate to male motivators for playing games. Equal percentage from both genders dislikes sport games what makes us conclude that sport games are an area related to the personal affinity to sport.

The survey indicated that puzzle games are amongst preferred games (60%) only by female players. Interestingly, males perceive "train your brain" type of game as being no fun. And fun is the major reason why they play computer games. In contrast to males, more than half of females (54%) play games similar to train your brain.

Examples of merging adventure game type with puzzles are edutainment games produced by Heureka-Klett publisher (or TIVOLA for the US market). Their puzzle-adventure game is aimed for self-directed learning in various topics, for example, chemistry, physics, math, computer science, history, and so forth. At the beginning of the game, the player is immersed in a mystery and challenged to solve it. With the presence of mystery, subtle competition, and problem solving, both genders are reached. The puzzles being part of the story, that is, "disguised" in the fantasy are obviously presented also for the male players in a compelling way to play the game.

The only game that was listed as preferred for both genders was "Monkey Island," a cartoon adventure game with humour. Despite the common belief that SIMS2 and puzzle games are gender neutral, that is, preferred by both genders, this survey shows otherwise. SIMS2 is preferred by female players and listed by 50% of the male players as least popular game. That can be interpreted with motivation why they play; hence, females want an overall good time, open end, and exploration while playing games, whereas for male players competition is motivation to play. These findings are supported by the work of Gorriz and Medina, (2000, 47):

Girls often identify with characters in video games and mimic the main character. They like to act out other lives but prefer to do so in familiar surroundings with characters that behave like people they know.

Girls don't put a large emphasis on whether they've completed a stage before moving on as today's computer games typically do. Rather, they move freely in the game, without necessarily finishing or winning a stage.

As the focus of interests changes throughout the lifetime, and being a student brings new social context, responsibilities, and higher workload into the foreground, most of the students stated that they do not play computer games due to lack of time. Females perceived playing computer games also as a waste of time. Non-players outlined that they prefer to socialise and meet friend face to face over the virtual environment.

GUIDELINES FOR GENDER APPROPRIATE DESIGN

Based on the thorough literature survey in areas like instructional design, learning communities, and games related to gender as well as the carried out poll, conclusions in form of guidelines for gender-appropriate design are outlined.

The survey showed that humor is an element that both genders respond to extremely well. When we are creating content or learning situations appealing for both gender, we should include and/or base it on humour.

When creating content, designers have to be aware of different preferences of feedback sound and music. As reported by Gorriz and Medina (2000), repetitive sounds are appreciated by males and not accepted by females. Rich texture and good audio quality are appreciated by females.

When taking the behaviour and preferences of girl gamers into account and transforming them to the guidelines of female-oriented instructional design, one should consider creation of goal-based collaborative learning environments, where communication and intensive interaction among learners are in the foreground. The learning situations are preferably based on stories and fantasy that contributes to the motivation of the learners and fosters their immersion. This leads also to the better efficiency in learning.

Advantages of virtual environment (VE) like massive multiplayer online games or virtual worlds such as Second Life are complex social interactions and the opportunity to do and experience things that are less accessible in the real world. Having possibility of experiencing virtual sky dives or being part of activities otherwise unavailable could be used as additional challenge to self-directed and explorative learning. In such environments players/learners have control over their character and can freely interact with their environment. Thus, they can make decisions and experience consequences of their actions. It is also possible to take various roles, for example, very often the avatar has other characteristics and sex as the player in reality. By means of various virtual experiences girls (and boys) can improve their self-reflection and self esteem.

Despite being well accepted, the VEs are in their early stage. The majority of e-learning is still carried out in the classical learning environments like Moodle, with content repositories and forums. Few isolated progressive solutions merge Moodle and VE components. For all these systems, classical e-learning paradigms apply, outlined at the beginning of this chapter. Observations from learning communities and learning styles and gender suggest following guidelines for encouraging female participation:

1. In online discussions, the e-moderator to initially lead the way in responses at a collegial level to provide a model for cautious participators.
2. The e-moderator to provide expert references to support both Subjective and Procedural knowers.
3. To encourage the growth of a learning community information sharing should be encouraged in a way which supports individuals without letting them feel exposed to excessive public gaze.

Research reported by Pivec and Baumann (2004) showed that personalisation of the learning environments is very important feature by the younger generation. On one hand, this could be connected to the shift of mobile phone paradigm of various covers into the virtual world. On the other hand, personalisation gives opportunity to show the creativity of the users and introduces the notion of ownership into the e-learning.

CONCLUSION

This chapter has looked at learning communities and learning styles, and identified that while females should not be stereotyped into rigid categories, with no overlaps with males, there are sufficient overall differences in their approaches to learning technologies that only appropriate instructional design can open this area of learning equally to both sexes. When games styles are added to the mix, it is clear that there are significantly different motivational factors based on personality differences.

We identified gender neutral elements and features like humor and personalization that are equally important and appreciated by males and females. By introducing these elements in the e-learning we can expect more participation and enthusiasm in the learning situations.

Having in mind visible gender differences in interaction and behavior when using the computers and software, we can create a variety of gender appropriate content, thus fostering equal participation of males and females in different (also male dominated) learning topics.

REFERENCES

Ayerson, D. J., & Reed, W. M. (1995-1996). Effects of learning styles, programming, and gender on computer anxiety. *The Journal of Research on Computing in Education, 28*(2), 148-161.

Bates, M. J., & Norton, S. (2002). Educating Rita: An examination of the female life course and the influence on women's participation in higher education. *New Horizons, 16*, 3, 4-11.

Belenky, M. F., Clinchy, B. M., Goldberger, N. R., & Tarule, J. M. (1986/1997). *Women's ways of knowing, The development of self, voice and mind.*: BasicBooks.

Buysse, V., Sparkman, K. L., & Wesley, P. W. (2003). Communities of practice: Connecting what we know with what we do. *Council for Exceptional Children, 69*(3), 263-277.

Campbell, K. (2000). Gender and educational technologies: Relational frameworks for learning design. *Journal of Educational Multimedia and Hypermedia, 9*(1), 131-149. Retrieved January 29, 2007, from http://www.aace.org/dl/files/JEMH/JEMH-09-02-131.pdf

Carswell, L., Thomas, P., Petre, M., Price, B., & Richards, M. (2000). Distance education via the Internet: The student experience. *British Journal of Educational Technology, 31*(1), 29-46.

Ching, C. C., Kafai, Y. B., & Marshall, S. (2000). Spaces for change: Gender and technology access in collaborative software design projects. *Journal for Science Education and Technology, 9*(1), 45-56.

Coffield, F., Moseley, D., Hall, E., & Ecclestone, K. (2004). *Learning styles and pedagogy in post16 learning.* London: Learning and Skills Research Centre.

Dickey, M., (2006). Girl gamers: The controversy of girl games and the relevance of female-oriented game design for instructional design. *BJET, 37*(5), 785 - 793

DIGRA (Digital Game Research Association). (2005). *Special event, developers in play: Changing views on game creation* (industry panel). Retrieved September 15, 2006, from http://www.gamesconference.org/digra2005/features.php

Fahy, P. J., & Ally, M. (2005). Student learning style and asynchronous computer-mediated conferencing (CMC) interaction. *The American Journal of Distance Education, 19*(1), 5-22.

Garland, D. (2003) *Characteristics of the online student: A study of learning styles, learner engagement and gender.* Annual Meeting of the University Continuing Education Association, Chicago, March 28-30.

Garland D., & Martin B., N. (2005). Do gender and learning style play a role in how online courses should be designed? *Journal of Online Interactive Learning, 4*(2). Retrieved January 29, 2007, from http://www.ncolr.org/jiol/issues/viewarticle.cfm?volID=4&IssueID=15&ArticleID=68

Gorizz C. M., & Medina C., (2000). Engaging girls with computers through software games. *Communications of the ACM, 43*(1), 42 – 49.

Herring, S. C. (2003). *Gender and power in online communication.* In J. Holmes & M. Meyerhoff (Eds.), *The handbook of language and gender* (pp. 202-228). Oxford: Blackwell.

Huff, C. 2002. Gender, software design, and occupational equity. *SIGCSE Bull., 34*(2), 112-115.

Klawe, M. (2002). Girls, boys, and computers. *SIGCSE Bull., 34*(2), 16-17.

Kolb, D. (2000). *Facilitator's guide to learning.* Boston, MA: Hay/McBer Training Resources Group.

Lave, J., & Wenger, E. (1991). *Situated learning: Legitimate peripheral participation.* Cambridge: Cambridge University Press.

Lester, C. Y., & Brown, M. (2004). Creating gender parity: An instruction aide's influence. *Journal of Educational Resources in Computing, 4*(1), 5.

Malone, Z. (2005). Pushing girls toward science. *Edwardsville Intelligencer* (IL) (09/05/05). Retrieved January 29, 2007, from http://technews. acm.org/articles/2005-7/0907w.html#item4

Palloff, R. M., & Pratt, K. (1999). *Building learning communities in cyberspace: Effective strategies for the online classroom.* San Francisco: Jossey-Bass Inc.

Pivec, M., & Baumann, K. (2004). The role of adaptation and personalisation in classroom-based learning and in e-learning. *Special Issue of J.UCS, Human Issues in Implementing eLearning Technology, 10*(1), 73-89. Retrieved January 29, 2007, from http://www.jucs.org/jucs_10_1/

Reiser, R., & Dempsy, J. (Eds). (2001). *Trends and issues in instruction design and technology.* Englewood Cliffs, NJ: Prentice Hall.

Taylor, P. G. (1996). Pedagogical challenges to open learning: Looking to borderline issues. In E. McWilliam & P. G. Taylor (Eds.), *Pedagogy, technology, and the body* (vol. 29), (pp. 59-77). New York: Peter Lang.

Wenger, E. (2001). *Supporting communities of practice: A survey of community-oriented technologies.* Retrieved January 29, 2007, from http://www.ewenger.com/tech

APPENDIX

Questionnaire About Your Experiences with Computer Games

	Questions	*Results*
1.	Age:	
2.	Gender: (Male / Female)	
3.	Do you play computer games? YES / NO **(If NO please see question 11.)**	
4.	Why do you play computer games?	**Males** 60% play for "fun," some listed fun and relaxation. The remainder was equally divided amongst "competition" and "socialising". **Females** 72% play for "fun," some listed fun and relaxation. The other 28% suggested they played to waste time.
5.	Which genre(s) do you play? (to define genres see Computer and video game genres) http://en.wikipedia.org/wiki/Video_game_genre)	**Males** The two top equal genres were First-Person Shooters (FPS) and Real Time Strategy (RTS) games. These were closely followed by Role Playing Games (RPG) and Adventure games. **Females** The two top equal genres were Adventure games and Puzzle games. These were closely followed by and Real Time Strategy (RTS) games.
6.	Which is your most popular game? a) Why?	**Males** Most popular game title was mixed but 90% of them "War" games of some kind – FPS, RTS, or RPG. **Females** Most popular game title (30%) was SIMS2, but in generally 60% of females played puzzle games of various titles.
7.	Which is your least popular game? a) Why?	**Males** Least popular game (50%) was SIMS2, 30% sports games of some kind, and the remainder were non-specific. **Females** Least popular game (50%) were "War" games of various types, 30% sports games of some kind, and the remainder were non-specific.

continued on following page

	Questions	Results
8.	Do you play puzzle type games (such as "train your brain" "PQ") or other similar games? a) Why?	**Males** Yes - 3 (18%) No - 14 (82%) **Females** Yes - 8 (54%) No - 7 (46%)
9.	What would motivate you to play such games?	**Males** If it was "Fun" 70% Had more time 15% If they had better gameplay 15% **Females** If it was "Fun" 25% Had more time 25% If they had better gameplay 25% Better value for money 25%
10.	Please list any advantages you can see in playing computer games.	**Males** Generally to have "fun" and relax (64%), but also for socialising (Online games). **Females** To have "fun" and relax (37%), but also for learning (29%). One female student also listed "escapism," the only student of either gender to do so.
11.	Why do you not like computer games?	**Males** All respondents listed "no time." **Females** Half of the respondents listed that games were a waste of time, with 40% stating that they had no interest. The remainder stated that they preferred real face to face people contact to technology.

Compilation of References

A Report Prepared for Asia Pacific Foundation. (2002). *Asia-Pacific e-commerce: B2B & B2C*. Retrieved from http://www.gii.co.jp/english/em11033_asia_ec_toc. html

Abbas, N. (2005). *Mapping Michel Serres*. Ann Arbor: University of Michigan Press.

Abbate J. (1999). *Inventing the Internet*. Cambridge, MA: MIT Press

Abbott, J. (Ed.) (2004). *The political economy of the Internet in Asia and the Pacific: Digital divides, economic competitiveness, and security challenges*. Westport, CT: Praeger.

Abrams, D., Baecker, R., & Chignell, M. (1998). Information archiving with bookmarks: Personal Web space construction and organization. In *CHI '98: Proceedings of the SIGCHI Conference on Human Factors in Computing Systems* (pp. 41-48). New York, NY: ACM Press/A-W Publishing Co.

Achterhuis, H. (Ed.) (2001). *American philosophy of technology: The empirical turn*. Bloomington, IN: Indiana University Press.

Adam, A. (2004). Gender and computer ethics. In R. A. Spinello & H. T. Tavani, (Eds.), *Readings in cyberethics* (2nd ed.) (pp. 67-80). Sudbury, MA: Jones and Bartlett.

Adams, J. (2005). White supremacists, oppositional culture and the World Wide Web. *Social Forces, 84*(2), 759-778.

Adams, T. (1987). Dementia is a family affair. *Community Outlook*, 7-8.

Adler, M. J. (1981). *Six great ideas*. New York: Simon & Schuster.

Adler, M. J., & van Doren, C. (1972). *How to read a book*. NY: Simon & Shuster.

Adler, P., & Kwon, S.-W. (2002). Social capital: Prospects for a new concept. *Academy of Management Review, 27*(1), 17–40. Retrieved from http://www.uky. edu/~skwon2/Social%20capital.pdf

Adorno, T. W. (1981). *Prisms* (1st MIT Press ed.). Cambridge, MA: MIT Press.

Adrianson, L. (2001). Gender and computer-mediated communication: Group processes in problem solving. *Computers in Human Behaviour, 17*, 71-94.

Agosti, M. (1996). An overview of hypertext. In M. Agosti & A. F. Smeaton, *Information retrieval and hypertext* (pp. 27–47). Dordrecht: Kluwer Academic Publishers.

Agosti, M., & Ferro, N. (2005). Annotations as context for searching documents. In *CoLIS '05: Proceedings of the 5th International Conference on Conceptions of Library and Information Sciences* (pp. 155-170). *LNCS, 3507*. Springer.

Agosti, M., & Melucci, M. (2000). Information retrieval on the Web. In M. Agosti, F. Crestani, & G. Pasi (Eds.), *ESSIR 2000, Lecture Notes in Computer Science 1980* (pp. 242–285). Berlin: Springer Verlag.

Agosti, M., & Smeaton, A. F. (1996). *Information retrieval and hypertext*. Dordrecht: Kluwer Academic Publishers.

Agre, P. E. (1994). Surveillance and capture: Two models of privacy. *The Information Society, 10*(2), 101-127.

Agre, P. E. (2002). Cyberspace as American culture. *Science as Culture, 11*(2), 171-189.

Aiello, J. R. (1993). Computer-based monitoring: electronic surveillance and its effects. *Journal of Applied Social Psychology, 23*(7), 499-601.

Ajzen, I., & Fishbein, (1988). *Attitudes, personality, and behavior*. Chicago, IL: Dorsey Press.

Akbar, M. J. (2003). *India, the siege within: Challenges to a nation's unity*. New Delhi: Rolli.

Akgunduz, H., Oral B., & Avanoglu, Y. (2006). Bilgisayar oyunlari ve internet sitelerinde sanal şiddet öğelerinin değerlendirilmesi. *Milli Eğitim Dergisi, 71*, 67-82.

Akyay, S. (2004). Internet kafelerin çocuklar üzerine etkileri, *Çağın Polisi Dergisi, 3*(32).

Alexa. (2007). *Results for Wikipedia*. Retrieved February 7, 2007, from http://www.alexa.com/search?q=wikipedia

Ali, A. (2006). Modern technology and mass education: A case study of a global virtual learning system. In A. Edmundston (Ed.), *Globalized e-learning cultural challenges* (pp. 327-339). Hershey, PA: Idea Group Inc.

Allen, D. (2001). *The changing shape of nursing practice: The role of nurses in the hospital division of labour*. London: Routledge.

Allen, D. (2004). Rereading nursing and rewriting practice: Towards an empirically based reformulation of the nursing mandate. *Nursing Inquiry, 11*(4), 271-283.

Allen, J. (1993). Groupware and social reality. *Computers and Society, 2*, 23-28.

Allen, K., & Rainie, L. (2002). Parents online. *Pew Internet & American life project*. Retrieved 12 October 2004, from http://www.pewinternet.org/

Allport, G. W. (1954). *The nature of prejudice*. Cambridge, MA: Addison-Wesley.

Almeida, P. D., & Lichbach, M. I. (2003). To the Internet, From the Internet: Comparative media coverage of transnational protests. *Mobilization: An International Journal, 8*(3), 249-272.

Altman, I., & Chemers, M. (1980). *Culture and environment*. Monterey, CA: Brooks/Cole Publishing.

AMA. (2001 & 2005). 2001 and 2005 *AMA survey: Workplace monitoring and surveillance*. Retrieved from www.amanet.org/research/archive_2001_1999.htm

American Association of University Women (2000). *Tech-savvy: Educating girls in the new computer age*. Washington, DC: American Association of University Women Foundation. Retrieved December 1, 2006 from http://www.aauw.org/member_center/publications/TechSavvy/TechSavvy.pdf

Amstrong, P. (1999). Information privacy concerns, procedural fairness and impersonal trust: An empirical investigation. *Organ. Sci., 10*(1), 105-121.

Anderson, D. M., & Haddad, C. J. (2005). Gender, voice, and learning in online course environments, *JALN, 9*(1), 3-14.

Anderson, T. (1997). Integrating lectures and electronic course materials. *Innovations in Education and Training International, 34*, 24-31.

Andic, Y. (2002). İnternet cafeler nereye gidiyor? VIII. "Türkiye'de Internet" Konferansı, İstanbul, Turkey.

anon. (2004). *The social report*. Wellington, New Zealand.

Ara, C. T. (2006). To spy, or not to spy. *National Underwritter Life & Health*. Aug. 21/28, 58.

Aranowitz, S. (Ed.) (1996). *Technoscience and cyberculture*. NY: Routledge.

Armstrong, J. (2000, 2004). Web grrrls, guerrilla tactics: Young feminism on the Web. In D. Gauntlett & R. Horsley (Eds.), *Web.Studies* (pp.92-102). New York, NY: Oxford University Press.

Armstrong, R., Freitag, D., & Joachims, T. (1995). Webwatcher: Machine learning and hypertext, In *Proceedings of the 1995 AAAI Spring Symposium on Information Gathering from Heterogeneous, Distributed Environments.* Palo Alto, CA: Stanford University.

Arquilla, J., & Ronfeldt, D. (2001). Emergence and influence of the Zapatista social netwar. In D. Ronfeldt & J. Arquilla (Eds.). *Networks and netwars: The future of terror, crime, and militancy* (pp. 171-199). Santa Monica, CA: RAND.

Arundel, A., & Geuna, A. (2001). Does proximity matter for knowledge transfer from public institutes and universities to firms? *Science and Technology Policy Research,* electronic working paper series paper no. 73. Retrieved April 04, 2007, from http://www.sussex.ac.uk/spru/1-6-1-2-1.html

Assad, M. L. (1999). *Reading with Michel Serres: An encounter with time.* State University of New York Press.

Assay, N. M. (2005). Open source and the commodity urge: Disruptive models for a disruptive development process. In C. DiBona, D. Cooper, & M. Stone (Eds.), *Open sources 2.0: The continuing evolution.* London: O'Reilly. Retrieved from http://www.open-bar.org/docs/matt_asay_open_source_chapter_11-2004.pdf

Atan, H., Sulaiman, F., Rahman, Z. A., & Idrus, R. M. (2002). Gender differences in availability, Internet access and rate of usage of computers among distance education learners. *Education Media International, 39*(3/4), 205-210.

Attali, J. (1985). *Noise: The political economy of music.* Minneapolis: University of Minnesota Press.

Atton, C. (2004). *An alternative Internet: Radical media, politics and creativity.* Edinburgh: Edinburgh University Press.

Aust, R., Newberry, B., O'Brien, J., & Thomas, J. (2005). Learning generation: Fostering innovation with tomorrow's teachers and technology. *Journal of Technology and Teacher Education, 13*(2), 167-195.

Axelrod, R. (1984). *The evolution of co-operation.* London: Penguin Books.

Axelrod, R. (Ed.) (1997). *The complexity of cooperation.* Princeton University Press.

Ayers, M. D. (2003). Comparing collective identity in online and off-line feminist activists. In M. McCaughey & M. D. Ayers (Eds.), *Cyberactivism: Online activism in theory and practice* (pp.145-164). New York: Routledge.

Ayerson, D. J., & Reed, W. M. (1995-1996). Effects of learning styles, programming, and gender on computer anxiety. *The Journal of Research on Computing in Education, 28*(2), 148-161.

Baasa, S. (2003). *A gift of fire: Social, legal, and ethical issues in computing* (2nd ed.). Upper Saddle River, NJ: Prentice Hall.

Backroad Connections Pty Ltd 2002 (Ed.). (2004). *Crosscultural issues in content development and teaching online (version 2.00).* Australian flexible framework quick guides series, Australian National Training Authority. Retrieved June 29, 2006, from http://pre2005.flexiblelearning.net.au/guides/crosscultural.pdf

Backroad Connections Pty Ltd 2002 (Ed.). (2004). *Globalisation/Internationalisation of online content and teaching.* Australian flexible framework quick guides series, Australian National Training Authority. Retrieved June 29, 2006, from http://pre2005.flexiblelearning.net.au/guides/international.pdf

Baeza-Yates, R., & Ribeiro-Neto, B. (1999). *Modern information retrieval.* Addison Wesley.

Bailey, J. E., & Pearson, S. W. (1983). Development of a tool for measuring and analysing computer user satisfaction. *Management Science, 29*(5), 530-545.

Bair, J. H., (1989). Supporting cooperative work with computers: Addressing meeting mania. *IEEE Computer,* (4), 208-217.

Bakardjieva, M. (2005). *Internet society: The Internet in everyday life.* Thousand Oaks, CA: Sage Publications.

Baker, E. (2000). *Child residency litigation: Processes and effects.* Paper presented at the Family futures: issues in research and policy 7th Australian Institute of Family Studies Conference, Sydney, July.

Balabanovic, M., & Shoham, Y. (1997). Fab: Content-based, collaborative recommendations. *Communications of the ACM, 40*(3), 66–72.

Ball, H. (2004). *The USA Patriot Act: A reference handbook* (Contemporary World Issues). Santa Barbara, CA: ABC-CLIO.

Ballantine, J., Levy, M., & Powell, P. (1998). Evaluating information systems in small and medium sized enterprises: issues and evidence. *European Journal of Information Systems, 7*(4), 241-251.

Bandyopadhyaya, J. (1987). *The making of India's foreign policy*. New Delhi: Allied Publishers Private Ltd.

Bannan-Ritland, B. (2003). The role of design in research: The interactive learning design framework. *Educational Researcher, 32*(1), 21-24.

Barab, S., Makinster, J., Moore, J., & Cunningham, D.J. (2001). Designing and building an online community: The struggle to support sociability in the Inquiry Learning Forum. *Educational Technology Research and Development, 49*, 71-96.

Barber, B. (1983). *The logic and limits of trust*. New Burnswick, NJ: Rutgers University Press.

Bargh, J. A., & McKenna, K. Y. A. (2004). The Internet and social life. *Annual Review of Psychology, 55*, 573-590.

Barker, L. J., & Aspray, W. (2006). The state of research on girls and IT. In J. M. Cohoon & W. Aspray (Eds.), *Women and information technology* (pp. 3-54).Cambridge, MA: The MIT Press.

Barlow, J., Bayer, S., & Curry, R. (2006). Implementing complex innovations in fluid multistakeholder environments: Experiences of "telecare". *Technovation, 26*(3), 396-406.

Baroudi, J. J., & Orlikowski, W. J. (1988). A short-form measure of user information satisfaction: A psychometric evaluation and notes on use. *Journal of Management Information Systems, 4*(Spring), 44-59.

Barrett, E., & Lally, V. (1999). Gender differences in an online learning environment. *Journal of Computer Assisted Learning, 15*, 48-60.

Barrett, R., Maglio, P. P., & Kellem D. C. (1997). How to personalize the Web. In *International ACM Conference on Human Factors and Computing Systems (CHI)*, Atlanta Georgia (pp 75-82).

Bartlett, M. (2002). Paradigms of online peace activism. *Peace Review: A Journal of Social Justice, 14*(1), 121-128.

Bärwolff, M. (2006). Tight prior open source equilibrium. *FirstMonday, 11*(1). Retrieved from http://www.firstmonday.org/issues/issue11_1/barwolff/index.html

Basham, A. L. (1967). *The wonder that was India*. London: Sidgwick & Jackson.

Bates, M. J., & Norton, S. (2002). Educating Rita: An examination of the female life course and the influence on women's participation in higher education. *New Horizons, 16*, 3, 4-11.

Bates, T. (1999). *Cultural and ethical issues in international distance education*. Paper presented at the Engaging Partnerships, Collaboration and Partnership in Distance Education UBC/CREAD Conference, Vancouver, Canada. Retrieved November 5, 2006, from http://www.tonybates.ca/papers/cread.html

Baum, E. (1989). A proposal for more powerful learning algorithms. *Neural Computation, 1*, 201-207.

Bauwens, M. (2005). 1000 days of theory: The political economy of peer production. *CTheory*, td026. Retrieved April 1, 2007 from http://www.ctheory.net/articles.aspdx?id=499

Beal, T. (2000). SMEs and the World Wide Web: Opportunities and prospects. In A. M. A. (Ed.) *Small and medium enterprises in Asia Pacific; Vol. III: Development prospects* (pp. 102-134). Nova Science, Commack, New York.

Beamish, A. (2004) The city in cyberspace. In S. Graham (Ed.) *The cybercities reader* (pp. 273-281). NY: Routledge.

Bechtel, R. B. (1997). *Environment & behavior: An introduction.* Thousand Oaks, CA: Sage.

Beck, U. (1992). *Risk society.* London: Sage.

Becker, H. J. (2000). Who's wired and who's not: Children's access to and use of computer technology. *The Future of Children* (Fall/Winter), 44-75. Retrieved from http://www.futureofchildren.org

Beckles, C.A. (2001). Africa: New realities and hopes. *Journal of Black Studies, 31*(3), 311-324.

Bedney, G. Z., Seglin, M. H., & Meister, D. (2000). Activity theory: History, research and application. *Theoretical Issues in Ergonomics Science, 1*(2), 168-206.

Beenen, G., Ling, K., Wang, X., Chang, K., Frankowski, D., Resnick, P., & Kraut, R. E. (2004). Using social psychology to motivate contributions to online communities. In *CSCW '04: Proceedings of the 2004 ACM conference on Computer Supported Cooperative Work* (pp. 212–221). New York, NY: ACM Press.

Belenky, M. F., Clinchy, B. M., Goldberger, N. R., & Tarule, J. M. (1986/1997). *Women's ways of knowing, The development of self, voice and mind.*: BasicBooks.

Belkin, N. J., & Croft, W. B. (1992). Information filtering and information retrieval: Two sides of the same coin? *Communication of the ACM, 35*(12), 29-38.

Bell, D. (1987). *And we are not saved: The elusive quest for racial justice.* New York: BasicBooks.

Bellamy, C., & Taylor, J. (1998). *Governing in the Information Age.* Buckingham: Open University Press.

Bellman, S., Johnson, E., Kobrin, S., & Lohse, G. (2004). International differences in information privacy concerns: A global survey of consumers. *Information Society, 20*(5), 313-324.

Benford, R. D., & Snow, D. A. (2000). Framing processes and social movements: An overview and assessment. *Annual Review of Sociology, 26,* 611-639.

Benford, S., Snowdon, D, Greenhalgh, C., Knox, I., & Brown, C. (1995). VR-Vibe: A virtual environment for cooperative information retrieval. *EuroGraphics, 14*(3), 349–360.

Benjamin, W. (1986). The work of art in the age of mechanical reproduction (H. Zohn, Trans.). In H. Arendt (Ed.), *Illuminations.* New York: Harcourt Brace.

Benkler, Y. (2002). Coase's penguin, or, Linux and the nature of the firm. *Yale Law Journal, 112*(3), 369–446.

Benkler, Y. (2004). Sharing nicely: On shareable goods and the emergence of sharing as a modality of economic production. *Yale Law Journal, 114*(2), 273–358. Retrieved from http://www.yalelawjournal.org/pdf/114-2/Benkler_FINAL_YLJ114-2.pdf

Benkler, Y. (2006). *The wealth of networks: How social production transforms markets and freedom.* Yale University Press. Retrieved from http://www.benkler.org/Benkler_Wealth_Of_Networks.pdf

Benner, P. E. (1984). *From novice to expert: Excellence and power in clinical nursing practice.* Menlo Park, CA.: Addison-Wesley Pub. Co., Nursing Division.

Bennet, M., Swaney, D., & Talbot, D. (2003). *The Samoan Islands.* Retrieved 11 November, 2004, from http://www.lonelyplanet.com/destinations/pacific/american_samoa/culture.htm

Bennett, W. L. (2003). Communicating global activism: Strengths and vulnerabilities of networked politics. *Information, Communication & Society, 6*(2), 143-168.

Bentley, J. P. H., & Tinney, M. V. (2003). *Does culture influence learning? A report on trends in learning styles and preferences across cultures.* Paper presented at the annual conference of the Association of Educational Communication & Technology, Anaheim, CA.

Bentley, P. H., Vawn Tinney, M., & Howe Chia, B. (2005). Intercultural Internet-based learning: Know your audience amd what it values. *ETR&D, 53*(2), 117-127.

Bentz, V. M., & Shapiro, J. J. (1998). Quantitative and behavioural inquiry, action research, and evaluation research. In *Mindful inquiry in social research* (pp. 121-127). Thousand Oaks: Sage.

Bereiter, C. (1993). *Surpassing ourselves*. Peru, IL: Open Court Publishing.

Berge, Z. (Ed.). (2000). *Sustaining distance training: Integrating learning technologies into the fabric of the enterprise*. Hoboken, NJ: John Wiley & Sons.

Berge, Z. L. (1992). *The role of the moderator in a scholarly discussion group (SDG)*. Retrieved July 10, 2007, from http://www.emoderators.com/moderators/zlbmod.html

Berge, Z. L. (1995). Facilitating computer conferencing: Recommendations from the field. *Educational Technology, 35*, 22-30.

Bergerson, S. (2006). *Fragments of development: Nation, gender and the space of modernity*. Ann Arbor, MI: University of Michigan Press.

Bergman, M. K. (2001). The Deep Web: Surfacing the hidden value. *Journal of Electronic Publishing from the University of Michigan*. Retrieved January 10, 2007, from http://www.press.umich.edu/jep/07-01/bergman.html

Berscheid, E. (1977). Privacy: A hidden variable in experimental social psychology. *Journal of Social Issues, 33*(3), 85-101.

Bessen, J. E. (2005). *Open source software: Free provision of complex public goods* (Working Paper). Research on Innovation. Retrieved from http://ssrn.com/abstract=588763

Best, S., & Kellners, D. (2001). *The postmodern adventure: Science, technology, and cultural studies at the Third Millenium*. NY: The Guilford Press.

Bezroukov, N. (1999b). A second look at the cathedral and the bazaar [Electronic Version]. *First Monday, 4*(12). Retrieved March, 15, 2007, from http://firstmonday.org/issues/issue4_12/bezroukov/index.html.

Bharat, K., & Henzinger, M. (1998). Improved algorithms for topic distillation in a hyperlinked environment. In *Proceedings of the 21ᵗʰ Annual International ACM SIGIR Conference on Research and Development in Information Retrieval, Distributed Retrieval* (pp. 104-111).

Bies, R. J., & Tripp, T. M. (1996). Beyond distrust: Getting even and the need for revenge. In R. Kramer & T. Tyler (Eds.), *Trust in organizations: Frontiers of theory and research* (pp. 246-260). Thousand Oaks, CA: Sage.

Biggs, J. B. (2003). *Teaching for quality learning at university: What the student does* (2nd ed.). Phildelphia, PA: Society for Research into Higher Education: Open University Press.

Bijker, W. E. (1992). *Shaping technology/building society: Studies in sociotechnical change*. Cambridge, MA: MIT Press.

Bijker, W. E. (1995). *Of bicycles, bakelites and bulbs: Toward a theory of sociotechnical change*. Cambridge, MA: MIT Press.

Bijker, W. E., Hughes, T., & Pinch, T. (Eds.) (1987). *The social construction of technological systems: New directions in the sociology and history of technology*. Cambridge, MA: MIT Press.

Bikson, T. K., & Gutek, B. (1984). *Implementation of office automation*. Santa Monica, CA: Rand Corporation.

Bimber, B. (1998). The Internet and political transformation: Populism, community, and accelerated pluralism. *Polity, 31*(1), 133-160.

Bimber, B., Flanagin, A. J., & Stohl, C. (2005). Reconceptualizing collective action in the contemporary media environment. *Communication Theory, 15*(4), 365-388.

Birsch, D. (2004). Moral responsibility for harm caused by computer system failures. *Ethics and Information Technology, 6*(4), 233-245.

Blackler, F. (1995). Knowledge, knowledge work and organizations: An overview and interpretation. *Organization Studies, 6*, 1021-1046.

Blili, S., Raymond, L., & Rivard, S. (1998). Impact of task uncertainty, end-user involvement, and competence on the success of end-user computing. *Information & Management, 33*, 137-153.

Blitz, J., Hope, K., & White, D. (1999). Mediterranean trio see millennium bug as problem for manana. *Financial Times,* November 12.

Bloomfield, B. P., & McLean, C. (2002). Beyond the walls of the asylum: Information and organization in the provision of community mental health services. *Information and Organization, 13,* 53–84.

Bolter, J. D. (1984). *Turing's man: Western culture in the computer age.* Chapel Hill, NC: University of North Carolina Press.

Bonk, C. J. (2001). *Online teaching in an online world.* Bloomington, IN: CourseShare.com.

Bonk, C. J., & Cunningham, D. J. (1998). Searching for learner-centered, constructivist, and sociocultural components of collaborative educational learning tools. In C. J. Bonk & K. S. Kim (Eds.), *Electronic collaborators: Learner-centered technologies for literacy, apprenticeship, and discourse* (pp. 25-50). NJ: Erlbaum.

Bonk, C. J., & Kim, K. A. (1998). Extending sociocultural theory to adult learning. In M. C. Smith & T. Pourchot (Ed.), *Adult learning and development: Perspectives from educational psychology* (pp. 67-88). Lawrence Erlbaum Associates.

Bonk, C. J., Wisher, R. A., & Nigrelli, M. L. (2004). Learning communities, communities of practice: Principles, technologies, and examples. In K. Littleton, D. Miell & D. Faulkner (Eds.), *Learning to collaborate, collaborating to learn* (pp. 199-219). Hauppauge, NY: Nova Science Publishers.

Booker, L., Goldberg, D., & Holland, J. (1989). Classifier systems and genetic algorithms. *Artificial Intelligence Journal, 40,* 235-282.

Bopry, J. (2005). Levels of experience: An exploration for learning design. *Educational Media International, 42*(1), 83-89.

Bopry, J. (2006). Providing a warrant for constructivist practice: The contribution of Francisco Varela. In J. L. Kincheloe & R. A. Horn (Eds.), *The Praeger handbook of education and psychology, 4,* 474-484). Westport, CT: Praeger.

Bopry, J., & Brier, S. (2001). *The ages of Francisco Varela.* Special issue of *Cybernetics and Human Knowing, 9*(2). Exeter: Imprint Academic.

Bopry, J., & Hedberg, J. (2005). Designing encounters for meaningful experience, with lessons from J. K. Rowling. *Educational Media International, 42*(1), 91-105.

Bottraud, J. C., Bisson, G., & Bruandet, M. F. (2003). An adaptive information research personnal assistant. In *Proceedings of the Workshop AI2IA (Artificial Intelligence, Information Access and Mobile Computing) IJCAI.*

Bouthors, V., & Dedieu, O. (1999). *Pharos, a cooperative infrastructure for Web knowledge sharing.* Technical report num. 3679, Institut de Recherche en Informatique et en Automatique (INRIA).

Bowen et al (1999), Low tech culture may prove region's Y2K saviour. *Financial Times,* November 30.

Bowles, S. (2004). *Microeconomics: Behavior, institutions, and evolution.* Princeton University Press.

Bowman, M. (1999). *What is distributed learning?* Technical Sheet 2(1). Retrieved April 04, 2007, from http://techcollab.csumb.edu/techsheet2.1/distributed.html

Bowyer, K. (Ed). (2001). *Ethics and computing: Living responsibility in a computerized world* (2nd ed.). New York: IEEE Press.

Boyd, A. (2003). The Web requires the movement. *The Nation.* Retrieved October 31, 2006 from http://www.thenation.com/doc.mhtml?i=20030804&c=1&s=boyd

Boyle, J. (2000). Cruel, mean, or lavish? Economic analysis, price discrimination and digital intellectual property. *Vanderbilt Law Review, 53*(6), 2007–39.

Bramley, G. (1991). *Adult literacy: Basic skills and libraries.* London: Library Association Publishing Limited.

Bransford, J. D., National Research Council (U.S.), Committee on Developments in the Science of Learning; National Research Council (U.S.), Committee on Learning Research and Educational Practice. (2000). *How people learn: Brain, mind, experience, and school* (Expanded ed.). Washington, DC: National Academy Press.

Brecht, B. (1932). Der Rundfunk als Kommunikationsapparat. *Blätter des Hessischen Landestheaters*(16). (Excerpt of English translation titled "The Radio as an Apparatus of Communication." Retrieved from http://www.medienkunstnetz.de/source-text/8/

Breen, R., Lindsay, R., Jenkins, A., & Smith, P. (2001). The role of information and communication technologies in a university learning environment. *Studies in Higher Education, 26*(1), 95-114.

Breese, J. S., Heckerman, D., & Kadie, C. (1998). Empirical analysis of predictive algorithms for collaborative filtering. In *Proceedings of 14th Conference on Uncertainty in Artificial Intelligence* (UAI'98), Wisconsin (pp. 43-52).

Brewer, M. B. (1979). In-group bias in the minimal intergroup situation. A cognitive motivational analysis. *Psychological Bulletin, 86*, 307-324.

Brewer, M. B. (1999). The psychology of prejudice: In-group love or out-group hate?*Journal of Social Issues, 55*(3), 429-444.

Brey, P. (2005). Freedom and privacy in ambient intelligence. *Ethics and Information Technology, 7*(3), 157-166.

Brey, P. (Ed.). (2005). *Surveillance and privacy.* Special Issue of *Ethics and Information Technology, 7*(4). Dordrecht, The Netherlands: Springer.

Bridges.org. (2003/2004). *Spanning the digital divide: Understanding and tackling the issues.* Retrieved 31/10/2004, from http://www.bridges.org/spanning/summary.html

Brignall, T. W., & Valey, T. V. (2005). The impact of Internet communications on social interaction. *Sociological Spectrum, 25*, 335-348.

Brin, S., & Page, L. (1998). The anatomy of a large-scale hypertextual Web search engine. In *Proceedings of the 7th International World Wide Web Conference* (WWW7) (pp. 107-117).

British Computer Society. (2001). *Code of Conduct,* Version 2.0, MTG/CODE/292/1201.

Bronowski, J. (1956). *Science and human values.* New York: Harper & Row.

Bronson, M. (1998). The impact of psychological gender, gender-related perceptions, significant others, and the introducer of technology upon computer anxiety among students. *Journal of Educational Computing Research, 18*(1), 63-78.

Brooks Jr., F. P. (1995). *The mythical man-month: Essays on software engineering – anniversary edition.* Reading: Addison-Wesley. (First published in 1975.)

Brooks, F., & Scott, P. (2006). Knowledge work in nursing and midwifery: An evaluation through computer-mediated communication. *International Journal of Nursing Studies–97, 43*, 83-97.

Brooks, R. A. (2002). *Flesh and machines: How robots will change us.* New York: Pantheon.

Broos, A. (2005). Gender and information and communication technologies (ICT) anxiety: Male self-assurance and female hesitation. *Cyberpsychology & Behavior, 8*(10), 21-31.

Broos, A., & Roe, K. (2006). The digital divide in the playstation generation: Self-efficacy, locus of control and ICT adoption among adolescents. *Poetics, 34*, 306-317.

Brosnan, M. (1998). *Technophobia: The psychological impact of information technology.* London: Routledge.

Brosnan, M., & Lee, W. (1998). A cross-cultural comparison of gender differences in computer attitudes and anxieties: The United Kingdom and Hong Kong. *Computers in Human Behaviour, 14*(4), 559-577.

Brown, B., Green, N., & Harper, R. (Eds.). (2001). *Wireless world: Social and interactive aspects of the mobile age.* Cologne: Springer-Verlag.

Brown, J. S. (2006). *Relearning learning—Applying the long tail to learning.* Presentation at MIT iCampus. Retrieved February 9, 2007, from http://www.mitworld.mit.edu/video/419

Brown, J. S. (Ed.). (1997). *Seeing differently: Insights into innovation.* Cambridge, MA: Harvard Business Review Book.

Brown, J. S., & Duguid, P. (2000). *The social life of information.* Boston: Harvard Business School Press.

Brown, J. S., & Duguid, P. (Eds.). (2000). *The social life of information.* Cambridge, MA: Harvard Business School Press.

Brown, J., Collins, A., & Duguid P. (1989). Situated cognition and the culture of learning. *Education Researcher, 18,* 10-12.

Brown, S. D. (1999). *Caught up in the rapture: Serres translates Mandlebrot.* Retrieved May 12, 2007, from http://www.keele.ac.uk/depts/stt/cstt2/comp/rapture.htm

Bruckman, A. (2002). Studying the amateur artist: A perspective on disguising data collected in human subjects research on the Internet. *Ethics and Information Technology, 4*(3), 217-231.

Bruns, A., & Humphreys, S. (2005). *Wikis in teaching and assessment: The M/Cyclopedia project.* Paper presented at the WikiSym 2005. Retrieved February 5, 2007, from http://www.wikisym.org/ws2005/proceedings/paper-03.pdf

Brunt, L. (2006). *Mapping NZ family violence research.* Social Science Research Centre, University of Canterbury.

Bryant, S. L., Forte, A., & Bruckman, A. (2005). Becoming Wikipedian: Transformation of participation in a collaborative online encyclopedia. In M. Pendergast, K. Schmidt, G. Mark, & M. Acherman (Eds.), *Proceedings of the 2005 International ACM SIGGROUP Conference on Supporting Group Work,* GROUP 2005, Sanibel Island, FL, November 6-9 (pp. 1-10). Retrieved February 7, 2007, from http://www-static.cc.gatech.edu/~aforte/BryantForteBruckBecomingWikipedian.pdf

Brynjolfsson, E. (1993). The productivity paradox of information technology. *Association for Computer Machinery. Communications of the ACM, 36*(12), 67-71.

Brynjolfsson, E. (1996). Paradox lost? Firm-level evidence on the returns to information systems spending. *Management Science, 42*(4), 541 - 558.

Buckingham, D. (2000). *After the death of childhood: Growing up in the age of electronic media.* London, UK: Polity.

Budzik, J., & Hammond, K. (1999). *Watson: Anticipating and contextualizing information needs.* Annual Meeting of the American Society for Information Science (ASIS), Washington.

Buie, J. (Date unknown). *Virtual families and friends.* Retrieved 23 September, 2004, from http://www.virtualfamiliesandfriends.com/

Bull, M. (2004). Sound connections: An aural epistemology of proximity and distance in urban culture. *Environment & Planning D: Society & Space, 22(*1), 103-116.

Buller, S., & Butterworth, T. (2001). Skilled nursing practice - A qualitative study of the elements of nursing. *International Journal of Nursing Studies, 38*(4), 405-417.

Bunnell, P. (2004). Reflections on the ontology of observing. *Cybernetics and Human Knowing, 11*(4), 72-84.

Bunnell, P., & Forsythe, K. (2001). The chain of hearts: Practical biology for intelligent behavior. In B. Hocking, J. Haskell, & W. Linds (Eds.), *Unfolding bodymind* (pp. 152-169). Brandon, VT: Foundation for Educational Renewal.

Bunzl, J. (2001). *The simultaneous policy: An insider's guide to saving humanity and the planet.* New European Publications.

Burby, L. N. (2001). *Together time.* Retrieved 25 September, 2004, from http://www.divorceinteractive.com/consumer/RelationshipArticle.asp?ID=50

Burkart, P. (2005). Loose integration in the popular music industry. *Popular Music & Society, 28*(4), 489-500.

Burke, L. M. (2006). The process of integration of schools of nursing into higher education. *Nurse Education Today, 26,* 63-70.

Burn, J., & Thongprasert, N. (2005). A culture-based model for strategic implementation of virtual education delivery. *International Journal of Education and Development Using ICT, 1*(1). Retrieved October 11, 2006, from http://ijedict.dec.uwi.edu/viewarticle.php?id=17&layout=html

Burrows, P. (2003). Continuing professional development: Filling the gap between learning needs and learning experience. *Education for Primary Care, 14*, 411-413.

Buysse, V., Sparkman, K. L., & Wesley, P. W. (2003). Communities of practice: Connecting what we know with what we do. *Council for Exceptional Children, 69*(3), 263-277.

Cabanac, G., Chevalier, M., Chrisment, C., & Julien, C. (2005). A social validation of collaborative annotations on digital documents. In J.-F. Boujut (Ed.), *International Workshop on Annotation for Collaboration* (pp. 31-40). Paris: Programme société de l'information, CNRS.

Cagiltay, K. (2005). *Türkiye intenet'i büyüme eğilimleri*. X. "Türkiye'de Internet" Konferansı, İstanbul, Turkey.

Callon, M., Law, J., & Rip, A. (1996). *Mapping the dynamics of science and technology: Sociology of science in the real world*. Houndsmills, Basingstore, Hampshire: Macmillan.

Calman, K. (1998). *A review of continuing professional development in general practice. Report by the Chief Medical Officer*. London: Department of Health.

Cambridge Reports. (1989). Technology and consumers: Jobs, education, privacy. *Bulletin on Consumer Opinion*, (157).

Campbell, J. E. (2004). *Getting it on online. Cyberspace, gay male sexuality and embodied identity*. Binghamton, NY: The Harrington Park Press.

Campbell, K. (2000). Gender and educational technologies: Relational frameworks for learning design. *Journal of Educational Multimedia and Hypermedia, 9*(1), 131-149. Retrieved January 29, 2007, from http://www.aace.org/dl/files/JEMH/JEMH-09-02-131.pdf

Campus Technology (2006, October 10). News Update: MIT launches center for Collective (Wiki) intelligence. *Campus Technology*. Retrieved February 2, 2007, from http://campustechnology.com/news_article.asp?id=19384&typeid=150

Campus Technology (2006, October 10). News update: Stanford debuts Wiki of all things Stanford. *Campus Technology*. Retrieved February 2, 2007, from http://campustechnology.com/news_article.asp?id=19384&typeid=150

Campus Technology (2007, January 30). News update: MIT, Wharton to publish collaborative textbook by Wiki. *Campus Technology*. Retrieved February 2, 2007, from http://campustechnology.com/news_article.asp?id=20096&typeid=150

Carr, S. (2000). Learning to communicate online is a challenge for new distance-ed students. *The Chronicle of Higher Education*. Retrieved July 12, 2007, from http://chronicle.com/free/2000/01/2000011301u.htm

Carr-Chellman, A. A. (Ed.) (2005). *International perspectives one-learning: Rhetoric and realities*. Thousand Oaks, CA: Sage.

Carrière, J., & Kazman, R. (1997). WebQuery: Searching and visualizing the Web through connectivity. In *Proceedings of the 6th International World Wide Web Conference* (WWW6) (pp. 701-711).

Carroll, J. M. & Rosson, M. B. (2007). Participatory design in community informatics. *Design Studies, 1*(3), 243-261.

Carroll, J. M. (1991). *Designing interaction: Psychology at the human-computer interface*. New York: Cambridge University Press.

Carroll, J. M. (2000). *Making use: Scenario-based design of human-computer interactions*. Cambridge: MIT Press.

Carswell, L., Thomas, P., Petre, M., Price, B., & Richards, M. (2000). Distance education via the Internet: The student experience. *British Journal of Educational Technology, 31*(1), 29-46.

Carty, V., & Onyett, J. (2006). Protest, cyberactivism and new social movements: The reemergence of the peace movement post 9/11. *Social Movement Studies, 5*(3), 229-249.

Cashmore, J. (2003). Chidren's participation in family law matters. In C. Hallett & A. Prout (Eds.), *Hearing voices of children* (pp. 158-176). London: RoutledgeFalmer.

Castells, M. (1999). *Information technology, globalisation and social development.* Geneva: The United Nations Research Institute for Social Development .

Castells, M. (2000). Towards a sociology of the network society. *Contemporary Sociology, 29*(5), 693-699.

Castells, M. (2001). *The Internet galaxy: Reflections on the Internet, business, and society.* New York, NY: Oxford University Press.

Castells, M. (2003). *The oower of identity.* Malden, MA: Blackwell Publishing.

Castells, M., & Hall, P. (1994). *Technopoles of the world.* London: Routledge.

Castells, M., Fernandez-Ardevol, M., Qiu, J. L., & Sey, A. (2007). *Mobile communication and society: A global perspective.* Cambridge, MA: MIT Press.

Catterick, D. (2006). Do the philosophical foundations of online learning disadvantage non-Western students? In A. Edmundston (Ed.), *Globalized e-learning cultural challenges* (pp. 116-129). Hershey, PA: Idea Group Inc.

CERT. (2004). *2004 E-Crime Watch Survey.* Pittsburg, PA: Carnegie Mellon University.

Chalmers, I. (2006). *Archie Cochrane (1909-1988).* Retrieved 11 April 2007, 2007, from http://www.james-lindlibrary.org

Chan, B. (2002). A study of the relationship between tutor's personality and teaching effectiveness: Does culture make a difference? *International Review of Research in Open and Distance Learning, 3*(2), 1-21.

Chandra, S. (2002). Information in a networked world: The Indian perspective. *International Information & Library Review, 34*(3), 235-246.

Chant, C. (1999). *The pre-industrial cities and technology reader.* London: Routledge.

Chartered Institute of Library and Information Professionals. (2005). *Information literacy: definition.* Retrieved 21 June, 2005, from http://www.cilip.org.uk/professionalguidance/informationliteracy/definition/

Chase, M., Macfadyen, L., Reeder, K., & Roche, J. (2002). Intercultural challenges in networked learning: Hard technologies meet soft skills. *First Monday, 7*(8). Retrieved April 8, 2007, from http://firstmonday.org/issues/issue7_8/chase/index.html

Chavan, A. L. (2005). *Another culture, another method.* Paper presented at the 11th International Conference on Human-Computer Interaction, Las Vegas, Nevada, United States, July 22-27.

Chen, A., Mashhadi, A., Ang, D., & Harkrider, N. (1999). Cultural issues in the design of technology-enhanced learning systems. *British Journal of Educational Technology, 30*(3), 217-230.

Chen, A.Y., Mashhadi, A., Ang, D., & Harkrider, N. (1999). Cultural issues in the design of technology-enhanced learning systems. *British Journal of Educational Technology, 30*(3), 217-230.

Chen, C. (1999). The StarWalker virtual environment - An integrative design for social navigation. *Human-Computer Interaction: Communication, Cooperation, & Application Design, Proceedings of HCI International '99, the 8th International Conference on Human-Computer Interaction, 2* (pp. 207-211).

Chen, C. (2006). *Information visualization – Beyond the horizon.* Springer.

Chesbrough, H. W. (2003). *Open innovation: The new imperative for creating and profiting from technology.* Harvard Business School Press.

Chevalier, M., Chrisment, C., & Julien, C. (2004). Helping people searching the Web: Towards an adaptive and a social system. In P. Asaias & N. Karmakar (Eds.), *IADIS/WWW Internet 2004.*

Ching, C. C., Kafai, Y. B., & Marshall, S. (2000). Spaces for change: Gender and technology access in collaborative software design projects. *Journal for Science Education and Technology, 9*(1), 45–56.

Cho, Y. H., Kyeong, J., & Kim, S. H. (2002). A personalized recommender system based on Web usage mining and decision tree induction. *Expert System with Applications, 23*(3), 329 –342.

Chow-White, P. (2006). Race, gender and sex on the net: Semantic networks of selling and storytelling. *Media, Culture & Society, 28*(6), 883-905.

Christensen, R., Knezek, G., & Overall, T. (2005). Transition points for the gender gap in computer enjoyment. *Journal of Research on Technology in Education, 18*(1), 23-37.

Chung, Q. B. (2005). Sage on the stage in the digital age: The role of online lecture in distance learning. *The Electronic J. of e-Learning, 3*(1), 1-14. Retrieved April 04, 2007, from http://www.ejel.org/volume-3/v3-i1/v3-i1-art1-chung.pdf

CIA, (2004). *The World FactBook,* Retrieved October 31, 2006 from https://www.cia.gov/cia/publications/factbook/index.html

Cialdini, R. B. (1996). Social influence and the triple tumor structure of organizational dishonesty. In D. M. Messick & A. E. Tenbrunsel (Eds.), *Codes of conduct: Behavioral research into business ethics* (pp. 44-58). New York: Russell Sage Foundation.

Ciffolilli, A. (2003). Phantom authority, self-selective recruitment and retention of members in virtual communities: The case of Wikipedia [Electronic Version]. *First Monday, 8*(12). Retrieved February 10, 2007, from http://firstmonday.org/issues/issue8_12/ciffolilli/index.html

Cifuentes, L., & Murphy, K. L. (2000). Cultural connections: A model for eliminating boundaries and crossing borders. *Quarterly Review of Research on Distance Education (inaugural issue), 1*(1), 17-30.

Clarke, L. (2005). *Worst cases: Terror and catastrophe in the popular imagination.* Chicago: University of Chicago Press.

Clement, A., Gurstein, M., Longford, G., et al. (2004). The Canadian Research Alliance for Community Innovation and Networking (CRACIN). *Journal of Community Informatics, 1*(1), 7-20.

Cm 4703. (2000). *Modernising government in action: Realising the benefits of Y2K.* London: HMSO.

Coase, R. H.(1937). The nature of the firm. *Economica, 4,* 386–405.

Cockcroft, S. (1994, 27 May 1998). *The effects of gender and computer access on computer literacy scores among first year undergraduates.* Retrieved 25 April, 2005, from http://www.is.cityu.edu.hk/Research/WorkingPapers/paper/9410.pdf

Cody, W. K. (2003). Nursing theory as a guide to practice. *Nursing Science Quarterly, 16*(3), 225-231.

Coffield, F., Moseley, D., Hall, E., & Ecclestone, K. (2004). *Learning styles and pedagogy in post16 learning.* London: Learning and Skills Research Centre.

Cognition and Technology Group at Vanderbilt University. (1991). Technology and the design of generative learning environments (pp.77-89). In T. Duffy & D. Jonassen (Eds.), *Constructivism and the technology of instruction: A conversation.* NJ: Lawrence Erlbaum Associates.

Cohen, J. (1988). *Statistical power analysis for the behavioural sciences* (2nd edition). New York: Academic Press.

Cohen, J. (1992). A power primer. *Psychological Bulletin, 112*(1), 155-159.

Cole, M., & Engestrom, Y. (1997). A cultural-historical approach to distributed cognition. In G. Salomon (Ed.), *Distributed cognitions: Psychological and educational considerations* (pp. 1-46). Cambridge, UK: Cambridge University Press.

Cole, R. S., & Crawford, T. (2007). *Building peace through information and communications technologies.* Retrieved on June 22, 2007 from http://www.idealware.org/printable.php?page=/articles/peace_through_ICTs.php

Coles, R. (1993). *The call of service: A witness to idealism.* Mariner Books.

Colley, A. (2003). Gender differences in adolescents' perceptions of the best and worst aspects of computing at school. *Computers in Human Behaviour, 19,* 673-682.

Colley, A., & Comber, C. (2003). Age and gender differences in computer use and attitudes among secondary school students: what has changed? *Educational Research, 45*(2), 155-165.

Collins, R. (1981). On the microfoundations of macrosociology. *American Journal of Sociology, 86,* 948-1014.

Collis, B. (1999). Designing for differences: Cultural issues in the design of WWW-based course-support sites. *British Journal of Educational Technology, 30*(3), 201-215.

Collison, G., Elbaum, B., Haavind, S., & Tinker, R. (2000). *Facilitating online learning: Effective strategies for moderators.* Madison, WI: Atwood Publishing.

Comber, C., Colley, A., Hargreaves, D. J., & Dorn, L. (1997). The effects of age, gender and computer experience upon computer attitudes. *Educational Research Volume, 39*(2), 123-133.

Conner, M. (2000). Global implications of elearning. *LiNE Zine, 2*(1). Retrieved May 14, 2006, from http://linezine.com/2.1/features/mcgie.htm

Connor, S. (1999). *Michel Serres' five senses.* Retrieved May 12, 2007, from http://www.bbk.ac.uk/english/skc/5senses.htm

Cooke, P., & Piccaluga, A. (Eds.). (2004). *Regional economies as knowledge laboratories.* Cheltenham, Glos: Edward Elgar Publishing.

Cooney, E. (2006). *Communication in cyberspace: Attachment styles as a mediator of self-disclosure.* Dissertation defense presented at the Department of Developmental Psychology, Graduate Center, City University of New York, Friday, August 18, 2006.

Corbett, D., Wilson, B., & Williams, B. (2002). *Effort and excellence in urban classrooms: Expecting—and getting—success with all students.* New York, NY: Teachers College Press.

Couffou, A. (1997). Year 2000 risks: What are the consequences of technology failure? Statement of Hearing Testimony before Subcommittee on Technology and Subcommittee on Government Management, Information and Technology. March 20. Washington DC: GPO.

Couldry, N. (2000, 2004) The digital divide. In D. Gauntlett & R. Horsley (Eds.), *Web. Studies* (pp.185-194). New York, NY: Oxford University Press.

Coulibaly, B. (2005). Multiculturalité et apprentissage collaboratif assisté par ordinateur (ACAO): L'exemple du DESS UTICEF. *TICE et Développement,* 1. Retrieved May 20, 2006, from http://www.revue-tice.info/document.php

Coyne, R., & Wiszniewski, D. (2000). Technical deceits: Critical theory, hermeneutics and the ethics of information technology. *International Journal of Design Sciences and Technology, 8*(1), 9-18.

Coyne, R., McMeel, D., & Parker, M. (2005) *Places to think with: Non-place and situated mobile working.* Edinburgh: Working Paper, Architecture ACE, The University of Edinburgh.

Cragg, P. B., & King, M. (1993). Small firms computing: Motivators and inhibitors. *MIS Quarterly, 17*(1), 47-60.

Cresser, F., Gunn, L., & Balme, H. (2001). Women's experiences of online e-zine publications. *Media, Culture & Society, 23*(4), 457-473.

Cresswell, J. B. (2003). *Research design: Qualitative, quantitative, and mixed methods approaches* (2nd ed.). Thousand Oaks, CA: Sage.

Crick, R. D. (2005). Being a learner: A virtue for the 21st century. *British Journal of Educational Studies, 53*(3).

Crombie, G., Abarbanel, T., & Trinneer, A. (2002). All-female classes in high school computer science: Positive effects in three years of data. *Journal of Educational Computing Research, 27*(4), 383-407.

CSO. (2006). *2006 E-Crime Watch Survey from CSO magazine.* Retrieved February 10, 2007, from http://www2.csoonline.html/info/release.html?CID=24531

Cuban, L. (2001). *Oversold and underused: Computers in the classroom.* Cambridge, MA: Harvard University Press.

Cunliffe, B. (2001). *The extraordinary voyage of Pytheas the Greek.* Penguin.

Cunningham, D. J. (1992). Everything said is said by someone. *Educational Psychology Review, 4*(2), 261-269.

Cutting, D. R., Karger, D. R., & Pederson, J. O. (1993). Constant interaction-time scatter/gather browsing of very large document collections. In *14th International ACM SIGIR Conference on Research and Development in Information Retrieval* (pp 121-131).

Cyert, R. M., & March, J.G. (1963). *A behavioral theory of the firm.* Englewood Cliffs, NJ: Prentice-Hall.

Cyr, D., & Trevor-Smith, H. (2004). Localization of Web design: An empirical comparison of German, Japanese, and United States Web site characteristics. *Journal of the American Society for Information Science & Technology, 55*(13), 1199-1208.

Dale, C., & Adamson, G. (1998-1999). *A Michel Serres interview.* Retrieved May 12, 2007, from http://www.thepander.co.nz/culture/mserres5.php

Dalle, J.-M., & David, P. A. (2005). Allocation of software development resources in open source production mode. *Perspectives on free and open source software* (pp. 297–328). Cambridge, MA: The MIT Press. Retrieved from http://mitpress.mit.edu/books/chapters/0262562278.pdf

Danitz, T., & Strobel, W. P. (1999). The Internet's impact on activism: The case of Burma. *Studies in Conflict and Terrorism, 22*, 257-269.

Darling-Hammond, L. (1997). *The right to learn: A blueprint for creating schools that work.* San Francisco, CA: Jossey-Bass Publishers.

Daryl, G. N., Tipton F. M., & Jeretta, H. N. (2006). E-monitoring in the workplace: Privacy, legislation, and surveillance software. *Communications of the ACM, 49*(8), 73-77.

Davie, L. (1989). Facilitation techniques for the online tutor. In R. Mason & A. R. Kaye (Eds.), *Mindweave: Communication, computers and communication.* Oxford: Pergamon.

Davis, D., Thomson, M. A., Oxman, A. D., & Haynes, B. (1995). Changing physician performance: A systematic review of the effect of continuing medical education strategies. *The Journal of the American Medical Association, 274*, 700-705.

Davis, F. D. (1989). Perceived usefulness, perceived ease of use, and user acceptance of information technology. *MIS Quarterly 13*(September), 318-340.

Davis, S., Elin, L., & Reeher, G. (2002). *The Internet's power to change political apathy into civic action.* Cambridge, MA: Westview Press.

Day, P., & Schuler, D. (Eds.) (2004). *Community practice in the network society: Local action/global interaction.* New York, NY: Routledge.

De George, R. T. (2003). *Ethics of information technology and business.* Malden, MA: Blackwell Publishers.

de Jong, T., & Ferguson-Hessler, M. (1996). Types and qualities of knowledge. *Educational Psychologist, 31*(2), 105-113.

De Pree Jr., C., & Jude, R. (2006). Who's reading your office e-mail? Is that legal? *Strategic Finance, 87*(10), 45-47.

Dearing, R. (1997). *Higher education in the learning society: Report of the National Committee.* London: National Committee of Inquiry into Higher Education,.

deBeer, J. F. (2005). The role of levies in Canada's digital music marketplace. *Canadian Journal of Law & Technology, 4*(3), 15.

DeCerteau, M. (1985). Practices of space. In M. Blonsky (Ed.), *On signs* (pp.122-145). Baltimore, MD: The John Hopkins University Press.

Dede, C. (2004). An intellectual journey from distance education to distributed learning. In G. Kearsley (Ed.), *Online learning: Personal reflections on the transformation of education*. Educational Technology Publications. Retrieved April 04, 2007, from http://home.sprynet. com/~gkearsley/History/OLHistory_contents.htm

Deflem, M. (1996). Introduction: Law in Habermas's Theory of Communicative Action. In M. Deflem (Ed.), *Habermas: Modernity and law* (pp. 1-20). London: Sage.

Delgado, R. (Ed.) (1995). *Critical race theory: The cutting edge*. Philadelphia: Temple University Press.

DeLone, W. H. (1988). Determinants of success for computer usage in small business. *MIS Quarterly, 12*(1), 51-61.

DeLone, W. H., & McLean, E. R. (1992). Information systems success: The quest for the dependent variable. *Information Systems Research, 3*(1), 60-94.

DeLone, W. H., & McLean, E. R. (2003). The DeLone and McLean Model of Information Systems success: A ten-year update. *Journal of Management Information Systems, 19*(4), 9-30.

Demil, B., & Lecocq, X. (2003). *Neither market nor hierarchy or network: The emerging bazaar governance*. Retrieved from http://opensource.mit.edu

Denning, P. J. (2004). The social life of innovation: The profession of IT. *Communications of the ACM, 47*(4), 15–19.

Department for Education and Skills. (2003). *Education and skills: The future of higher education (UK Government White Paper)*. Norwich, UK: Cabinet Office. Department of Health. (1998). *A first class service – Quality in the new NHS*. London: The Stationary Office.

Department for Education and Skills. (2005). *Harnessing technology: Transforming learning and children's services*. Nottingham: DfES Publications.

Department of Health and Social Security. (1972). *Report of the Committee of Nursing* (No. 5155). London: HMSO.

Desilets, A., Paquet, S., & Vinson, N. G. (2005). *Are Wikis usable?* Paper presented at the WikiSym 2005. Retrieved February 26, 2006, from http://www.wikisym. org/ws2005/proceedings/paper-01.pdf

Deutsch, M. (1973). *The resolution of conflict: Constructive and destructive processes*. New Haven, CT: Yale University Press.

Deuze, M. (2006). Collaboration, participation and the media. *New Media & Society, 8*(4), 691-698.

Dewan, P. (1999). A technical overview of CSCW. Tutorial. *ACM Computer-Supported Cooperative Work (CSCW'98)*, Seattle.

Dhillon, G. (1999). Managing and controlling computer misuse. *Information Management & Computer Security, 7*(5): 171-175.

Dhillon, G. (2001). Violation of safeguards by trusted personnel and understanding related information security concerns. *Computer & Security, 20*(2), 165-172.

Dhillon, G., & Backhouse, J. (1996). Risks in the use of information technology within organizations. *International Journal of Information Management, 16*(1), 65-74.

Dhillon, G., & Backhouse, J. (2000). Information system security management in the new millennium. *Communications of the ACM, 43*(7), 125-128.

Dhillon, G., & Moores, S. (2001). Computer crimes: Theorizing about the enemy within. *Computers & Security, 20*(8), 715-723.

Dhillon, G., & Torkzadeh, G. (2006). Value focused assessment of information system security in organizations. *Information Systems Journal, 16*(3), 391-392.

Di Scipio, A. (1998). Questions concerning music technology: From Heidegger's view to Feenberg's subversive rationalization. *Switch*, (4).

Di Scipio, A. (1998). *Towards a critical theory of (music) technology. Computer music and subversive rationalization*. Retrieved from http://xoomer.alice.it/adiscipi/tct(m)t.htm

Diani, M. (2000). Social movement networks: Virtual and real. *Information, Communication and Society, 3*(3), 386-401.

Dickey, M., (2006). Girl gamers: The controversy of girl games and the relevance of female-oriented game design for instructional design. *BJET, 37*(5), 785 - 793

Diettrich, D., & Himma, K. E. (2005). Active response to computer intrusion. In H. Bidgoli (Ed.), *The handbook of information security*. Hoboken, NJ: John Wiley & Sons Inc.

DIGRA (Digital Game Research Association). (2005). *Special event, developers in play: Changing views on game creation* (industry panel). Retrieved September 15, 2006, from http://www.gamesconference.org/digra2005/features.php

Dinev, T., Bellotto, M., Hart, P., & Russo, V. (2006). Privacy calculus model in e-commerce - A study of Italy and the United States. *European Journal of Information Systems, 15*(4), 389-402.

Divers-Stamnes, A. C. (2002). Oppression and resultant violence in the inner city: Causes, effects on students, and responsibilities of educators. In L. A. Catelli & A. C. Diver-Stamnes (Eds.), *Commitment to excellence*. (pp. 267-286). Cresskill, NJ: Hampton Press Inc.

Dodge, M., & Kitchin, R. (2001). *Mapping cyberspace*. London: Routledge.

Doll, W., & Torkzadeh, G. (1988). The measurement of end user computing satisfaction. *MIS Quarterly, 12*(2), 259-274.

Dömel, P. (1994). Webmap - A graphical hypertext navigation tool. *2nd International World Wide Web Conference* (pp. 785-798).

Dondis, D. A. (1973). *A primer of visual literacy*. Cambridge: MIT Press.

Doney, P. M., Cannon, J. P., & Mullen, M. R. (1998). Understanding the influence of national culture on the development of trust. *Academy of Management Review, 23*, 601-620.

Dorsey, L. T., Goodrum, D. A., & Schwen, T. M. (1997). Rapid collaborative prototyping as an instructional development paradigm. In C. R. Dills & A. J. Romiszowski (Eds.), *Instructional development paradigms* (pp. 445-466). Englewood Cliffs, NJ: Educational Technology Publications.

Dos Santos, B. L. (2003). Information technology investments: Characteristics, choices, market risk and value. *Information Systems Frontiers, 5*(3), 289-301.

Dourish, P., & Anderson, K. (2006). Collective information practice: Exploring privacy and security as social and cultural phenomena. *Human-Computer Interaction, 21*(3), 319-342.

Downey, S., Cordova-Wentling, R. M., Wentling, T., & Wadsworth, A. (2004*). The relationship between national culture and the usability of an e-learning system*. Retrieved December 1, 2006, from http://www.learning.ncsa.uiuc.edu/downey/docs/AHRD2004-downey_cordova-wentling-wentling-wadsworth.pdf

Dragulanescu, N. (2002). Social impact of the "Digital Divide" in a central-eastern European country. *International Information & Library Review, 34*(2), 139-151.

Dreilinger, D., & Howe, A. E. (1997). Experiences with selecting search engines using metasearch. *ACM Transactions on Information Systems, 15*(3), 195 –222.

Dunn, P., & Marinetti, A. (2003). Cultural adaptation: Necessity for global elearning. *LiNE Zine, 7*(2). Retrieved May 16, 2006, from http://www.linezine.com/7.2/articles/pdamca.htm

Dunn, P., & Marinetti, A. (2003). *E-learning and national culture*. Retrieved May 16, 2006, from http://www.trainingfoundation.com/articles/default.asp?PageID=1266

Dunn, P., & Marinetti, A. (2006). Beyond localization: Effective learning strategies for cross-cultural e-learning. In A. Edmundston (Ed.), *Globalized e-learning cultural challenges* (pp. 223-238). Hershey, PA: Idea Group Inc.

Dunn, R., & Griggs, S. A. (1995). *Multiculturalism and learning style: Teaching and counseling adolescent.* Westport, CT: Praeger.

Durndell, A., & Haag, Z. (2002). Computer self efficacy, computer anxiety, attitude towards the Internet and reported experience with the Internet, by gender, in an east European sample. *Computers in Human Behaviour, 18,* 521-535.

Durndell, A., & Thomson, K. (1997). Gender and computing: A decade of change. *Computers & Education, 28*(1), 1-9.

Durndell, A., Haag, Z., & Laithwaite, H. (2000). Computer self efficacy and gender: a cross cultural study of Scotland and Romania. *Personality and Individual Differences, 28,* 1037-1044.

Duska, R. (1991). Whistle-blowing and employee loyalty. In D. G. Johnson (Ed.), *Ethical issues in engineering* (pp. 241-247). Englewood Cliffs, NJ: Prentice Hall.

Dutta, A. (1999). The physical infrastructure for electronic commerce in developing nations: Historic trends and the impacts of privatization. *International Journal of Electronic Commerce, 2*(1), 63-82.

Dutton, W. H., Kahin, B., O'Callaghan, R., & Wyckoff, A. W. (Eds.). (2005). *Transforming enterprise: The economic and social implications of information technology.* Cambridge, MA: MIT Press.

Dyson, F. (2003). Technology and social justice. In M. E. Winston & R. O. Edelbach (Eds.), *Society, ethics, and technology* (pp. 126-136). Belmont, CA: Wadsworth Group, Thomson Learning.

Ebare, S. (2003). *The computerization of practice in peripheral music communities.* Unpublished M.A., Simon Fraser University, Burnaby.

Ebare, S. (2004). Digital music and subculture: Sharing files, sharing styles. *First Monday, 9*(2).

Eberle, J. H., & Childress, M. D. (2006). Universal design for culturally diverse online learning. In A. Edmundston (Ed.), *Globalized e-learning cultural challenges* (pp. 239-254). Hershey, PA: Idea Group Inc.

EC Study Group on Education and Training. (1997). *Accomplishing Europe through education and training.* Luxembourg: Office for Official Publications of the European Communities.

Economic Intelligence Unit. (2001). Pyramid research e-readiness rankings. Retrieved from http://www.ebusinessforum.com

Edmundston, A. (2006). The cultural adapation process (cap) model: Designing e-learning for another culture. In A. Edmundston (Ed.), *Globalized e-learning cultural challenges* (pp. 267-290). Hershey, PA: Idea Group Inc.

Edmundston, A. (Ed.). (2006). *Globalized e-learning cultural challenges.* Hershey, PA: Idea Group Inc.

Edwards, R. (2002). Distribution and interconnectedness. The globalisation of education. In M. R. Lea & K. Nicoll (Eds.), *Distributed learning: Social and cultural approaches to practice* (pp. 98-110). Londres: Routledge.

Efran, J., & Luken, M. D. (1985). The world according to Humberto Maturana. *Family Therapy Networker, 9,* 22-25, 27-28, 72-75.

Ekeh, P. P. (1974). *Social exchange theory: The two traditions.* Cambridge, MA: Harvard University Press.

Ellickson, R. C.(1991). *Order without law: How neighbors settle disputes.* Harvard University Press.

Elliot, G., & Starkings, S. (1998). Information systems and infomation technology. In G. Black & S. Wall (Eds.), *Business information technology systems, theory and practice* (pp. 16-19). London: Longman.

Elsberry, R. B. (1999). The spying game: How safe are your secrets? *Office Systems,* September.

Elston, M. A. (1980). Medicine: Half our future doctors? In R. Silverstone & A. Ward (Eds.), *Careers of Professional Women.* Croom Helm.

Emigh, W., & Herring, S. C. (2005). Collaborative authoring on the Web: A genre analysis of online encyclopedias. *Proceedings of the 38th Hawai'i International Conference on System Sciences (HICSS-38).* Los Alamitos: IEEE

Press. Retrieved February 3, 2007, from http://ella.slis.indiana.edu/~herring/wiki.pdf

Engel, A., & Van Den Broeck, C. (2001). *Statistical mechanics of learning*. Cambridge University Press.

English, S., & Yazdani, M. (1999). Computer supported cooperative learning in a virtual university. *Journal of Computer Assisted Learning, 15*, 2-13.

Enoch, Y., & Soker, Z. (2006). Age, gender, ethnicity and the digital divide: University students' use of Web-based instruction. *Open Learning, 21*(2), 99-110.

Eriksen, T. H. (2001). *Small places, large issues*. Pluto Press.

Erikson, K. (2005). Epilogue: The geography of disaster. In N. Foner (Ed.), *Wounded city: The social impact of 9/11*. NY: Russell Sage Foundation.

Etzioni, A. (2004) *How patriotic is the Patriot Act?: Freedom vs. security in the Age of Terrorism*. New York, NY: Routledge.

Evans, P. (2006, January/February). The Wiki factor. *BizEd*, 28-32.

Facey, E. E. (2001). First nations and education by Internet: The path forward, or back? *Journal of Distance Education/Revue de l'enseignement à distance, 16*(1). Retrieved August 30, 2006, from http://cade.athabascau.ca/vol16.1/facey.html

Fagermoen, M. S. (1997). Professional identity: Values embedded in meaningful nursing practice. *Journal of Advanced Nursing, 25*, 434-441.

Fahmi, I. (2002). The Indonesian Digital Library Network is born to struggle with the digital divide. *International Information & Library Review, 34*(2), 153-174.

Fahy, P. J., & Ally, M. (2005). Student learning style and asynchronous computer-mediated conferencing (CMC) interaction. *The American Journal of Distance Education, 19*(1), 5-22.

Faiola, A., & Matei, S. A. (2005). Cultural cognitive style and Web design: Beyond a behavioral inquiry into computer-mediated communication. *Journal of Computer-Mediated Communication, 11*(1). Retrieved October 8, 2006, from http://jcmc.indiana.edu/vol11/issue1/faiola.html

Fan, T., & Li, Y. (2005). Gender issues and computers: College computer science education in Taiwan. *Computer & Education, 44*, 285-300.

Farkas, D. K., & Farkas, J. B. (2002). *Principles of Web design*. New York, NY: The Allyn & Bacon.

Faure, E., Herrera, F., Kaddoura, A.-R., Lopos, H., Petrovsky, A. V., Rahnema, M., & Ward, F. C. (1972). *Learning to be: The world of education today and tomorrow*. Paris: UNESCO.

Fay, R., & Hill, M. (2003). Educating language teachers through distance learning: The need for culturally appropriate DL methodology. *Open Learning, 18*(1), 9-27

Federal Bureau of Investigation, United States Department of Justice. (February 24, December 18, 2003). *Carnivore/DCS 1000 Report to Congress*.

Feenberg, A. (1986). Network design: An operational manual for computer conferencing. *IEEE Transactions on Professional Communications, 29*, 2-7.

Feenberg, A. (1995). Subversive rationalization: Technology, power, and democracy. *Technology and the Politics of Knowledge*, 3-22.

Feenberg, A. (1999). *Questioning technology*. London; New York: Routledge.

Feenberg, A. (2002). Democratic rationalization: Technology, power and freedom. *Dogma*. Retrieved November 26, 2006, from http://dogma.free.fr/txt/AF_democratic-rationalization.htm

Feenberg, A. (2002). *Transforming technology*. Oxford: Oxford University Press.

Feenberg, A. (2003). *What is philosophy of technology?* Lecture for the Komaba undergraduates, June, 2003. Retrieved January 20, 2007, from http://www-rohan.sdsu.edu/faculty/feenberg/komaba.htm

Feenberg, A., & Feenberg, A. (2002). *Transforming technology: A critical theory revisited*. Oxford; New York, NY: Oxford University Press.

Fehr, E., & Gächter, S. (2000). Fairness and retaliation: The economics of reciprocity. *The Journal of Economic Perspectives, 14*(3), 159–181. Retrieved from http://e-collection.ethbib.ethz.ch/ecol-pool/incoll/incoll_553.pdf

Fehr, E., and Falk, A. (2001). *Psychological foundations of incentives* (Working Paper No. 95). Institute for Empirical Research in Economics of the University of Zurich.

Felten, E. W. (2003). A skeptical view of DRM and fair use. *Communications of the ACM, 46*(4), 56-59.

Fernback, J. (2007). Beyond the diluted community concept: A symbolic interactionist perspective on online social relations. *New Media and Society, 9*(1), 49-69.

Fichter, D. (2006). Using Wikis to support online collaboration in libraries. *Information Outlook, 10*(1), 30-31.

Fidel, R., Bruce, H., Pejtersen, A. M., Dumais, S., Grudin, J., & Poltrock, S. (2000). Collaborative information retrieval (CIR). *The New Review of Information Behaviour Research* (pp. 235-247).

Fielden, K., & Goldson, J. (2005). *Hearing their voices: ICT-enabled communication in the Family Court.* Paper presented at the CIRN2005: The second annual conference of the Community Informatics Network, Capetown.

Fielden, K., & Malcolm, P. (2006). *Feasibility and evaluation: Critical early research steps.* Presented at the 3rd Qualit Conference, Brisbane.

Finkelstein, A. (2000). Y2K: A retrospective view. Retrieved from http://www.cs.ucl.ac.uk/Staff/A.Finkelstein, originally published in *Computing and Control Engineering Journal, 11*(N4), 156-159.

Fischer, G. (2001). Lifelong learning and its support with new media. In N. J. Smelser & P. B. Baltes (Eds), *International encyclopedia of social and behavioral sciences.* Amsterdam: Elsevier.

Fischer, G. (n.d.). Introduction to L^3D. Retrieved December, 2006, from http://l3d.cs.colorado.edu/introduction.html

Fischer, L.. (1989). *Life of Mahatma Gandhi.* Norwalk, CT.: Easton Press.

Fiske, A. P. (1993). *Structures of social life.* NY: Free Press.

Fitzpatrick, H., & Hardman, M. (2000). Mediated activity in the primary classroom: Girls, boys and computers. *Learning and Instruction, 19*, 431-446.

Fortunati, L. (2002). The mobile phone: Towards new categories of social relations. *Information, Communications and Society, 5* (4), 513-28.

Fraenkel, A. S., & Klein, S. T. (1999). Information retrieval from annotated texts. *J. Am. Soc. Inf. Sci., 50*(10), 845-854.

Frampton, K., Spector, A., & Rosman, L. R. (Eds.). (1998). *Technology, place and architecture.* The Jerusalem Seminar in Architecture. NY: Rizzoli.

Freire, P. (1970). *The pedagogy of the oppressed* (M. B. Ramos, Trans.). New York: Continuum.

Freshwater, D. (2004). Aesthetics and evidence-based practice in nursing: An oxymoron? *International Journal of Human Caring, 8*(2), 8-12.

Freshwater, D., & Biley, F. C. (2005). Heart of the matter: Dawn Freshwater and Francis Biley analyse what some believe is the most fundamental nursing value--caring. *Nursing Standard, 19*(20), 14-15.

Fried, C. (1990). Privacy: A rational context. In M. D. Ermann, M. B. William, & C. Gutierrez (Eds.), *Computers, ethics, and society* (pp. 51-67). New York: Oxford University Press.

Friedman, M. (1962). *Capitalism and freedom.* Chicago: The University of Chicago Press.

Friedman, T. L. (2005). *The world is flat: A brief history of the twenty-first century.* NY: Farrar, Straus, and Giroux.

Frischmann, B. M. (2004). *An economic theory of infrastructure and sustainable infrastructure commons.* SSRN Electronic Library. Retrieved from http://papers.ssrn.com/sol3/papers.cfm?abstract_id=588424

Frith, S. (1986). Art versus technology: The strange case of popular music. *Media, Culture and Society, 8*(3), 263-279.

Frommholz, I., & Fuhr, N. (2006). Probabilistic, object-oriented logics for annotation-based retrieval in digital libraries. In *JCDL '06: Proceedings of the 6th ACM/IEEE-CS Joint Conference on Digital Libraries* (pp. 55-64). New York: ACM Press.

Fukuyama, F. (1995). *Trust: The social virtues and the creation of prosperity.* New York: Macmillan.

Gadamer, H-G. (2004). *Truth and method.* London: Continuum Publishing Group.

Galliers, R. D. (1992). Choosing information systems research approaches. In R. D. Galliers (Ed.), *Information systems research: Issues, methods and practical guidelines.* Oxford: Blackwell Scientific Publications.

Galusky, W. (2003). Identifying with information: Citizen empowerment, the Internet, and the environmental anti-toxins movement. In M. McCaughey & M. D. Ayers (Eds.), *Cyberactivism: Online activism in theory and practice* (pp. 185-205). New York: Routledge.

Gambetta, D. (1988). *Trust: Making and breaking cooperative relations.* New York: Basil Blackwell.

Gamson, W. (1975). *The strategy of social protest* (2nd ed.). Belmont, CA: Wadsworth Publishing.

Gamson, W. A., Croteau, D., Hoynes, W., & Sasson, T. (1992). Media images and the social construction of reality. *Annual Reviews of Sociology, 18*, 373-393.

Gannon Cook, R., & Crawford, C. M. (2006). What can cave walls teach us? In A. Edmundston (Ed.), *Globalized e-learning cultural challenges* (pp. 187-208). Hershey, PA: Idea Group Inc.

Garfield, E. (1972). Citation analysis as a tool in journal evaluation. *Science, 178*(4060), 471-479. Retrieved from http://www.garfield.library.upenn.edu/essays/V1p527y1962-73.pdf

Garfinkel, S. L. (2003). Leaderless resistance today. *First Monday, 8*(3), Retrieved October 31, 2006 from http://www.firstmonday.dk/issues/issue8_3/garfinkel/index.html

Garland D., & Martin B., N. (2005). Do gender and learning style play a role in how online courses should be designed? *Journal of Online Interactive Learning, 4*(2). Retrieved January 29, 2007, from http://www.ncolr.org/jiol/issues/viewarticle.cfm?volID=4&IssueID=15&ArticleID=68

Garland, D. (2003) *Characteristics of the online student: A study of learning styles, learner engagement and gender.* Annual Meeting of the University Continuing Education Association, Chicago, March 28-30.

Garland, K. J., & Noyes, J. M. (2004). Computer experience: A poor predictor of computer attitudes. *Computers in Human Behaviour, 20*, 823-840.

Garlick, M. (2005). A review of Creative Commons and Science Commons. *EDUCAUSE Review, 40*(5), 78-79.

Garrett, R. K. (2006). Protest in an information society: A review of literature on social movements and new ICTs. *Information, Communication & Society, 9*(2), 202-224.

Gaved, M., Heath, T., & Eisenstadt, M. (2006). *Wikis of locality: Insights from the OpenGuides.* 2006 International Symposium on Wikis (WikiSym2006), Odense, Denmark. Retrieved December 21, 2006, from http://kmi.open.ac.uk/projects/hot.cfm?name=Open%20Guide%20to%20Milton%20Keynes

Gayol, Y., & Schied, F. (1997). Cultural imperialism in the virtual classroom: Critical pedagogy in transnational distance education. *ICDE Conference Proceedings: The new learning environment: A global perspective.* Retrieved June 29, 2006, from http://www.geocities.com/athens/olympus/9260/culture.html?200629

Geelan, D. (2006). *Undead theories: Constructivism, eclecticism and research in education.* Rotterdam: Sense Publishers.

Gehring, R. A. (2005). The institutionalization of open source. *Poiesis und Praxis, 4*(1), 54–73.

Gelernter, D. (1998). *Machine beauty: Elegance and the heart of technology*. New York: Basic Books.

General Accounting Office. (1998). *FAA computer systems: Limited progress on year 2000 issue increases risk dramatically*. GAO/AIMD-98-45. January 30. Washington, DC.

General Accounting Office. (1998). *Year 2000 computing crisis: Progress made at labor, but key systems at risk*. GAO/T-AIMD-98-303. September 17. Washington, DC.

General Medical Council. (2003). *Licence to practise and revalidation for doctors*. London: GMC.

George, C., & Chandak, N. (2006). Issues and challenges in securing interoperability of DRM systems in the digital music market. *International Review of Law, Computers & Technology, 20*(3), 271-285.

Gerder, L. I. (Ed.). (2005). *The Patriot Act*. (Opposing Viewpoints Series). Farmington Hills, MI: Greenhaven Press.

Gerrard, C. (2002). Promoting best practice for e-tutoring through staff development. In *Proceedings of Networked Learning 2002: Third International Conference, Lancaster University and University of Sheffield, March 26-28th*.

Ghosh, R. A., et al. (2006). *Economic impact of open source software on innovation and the competitiveness of the information and communication technologies (ICT) sector in the EU* (Final Report, Contract ENTR/04/112). UNU-MERIT. (Prepared for European Communities). Retrieved from http://ec.europa.eu/enterprise/ict/policy/doc/2006-11-20-flossimpact.pdf

Giacalong, R., & Greenberg, J. (1997). *Antisocial behavior in organizations*. Thousand Oaks, CA: Sage.

Gibson, D., Heitor, M. & Ibarra-Yunez, A. (Eds.) *Learning and knowledge for the network society*. West Lafayette, IN: Purdue University Press.

Giddens, A. (1979). *Central problems in social theory*. Berkeley: University of California Press.

Giddens, A. (1984). *The constitution of society*. Berkeley, CA: The University of California Press.

Giddens, A. (1991). *Modernity and self-identity*. Stanford, CA: Stanford University Press.

Giddens, A. (1997). *Sociology* (3rd ed.). Cambridge: Polity Press.

Giddens, A. (2002). The consequences of modernity. In Calhoun, Gerteis, Moody, Pfaff, & Virk (Eds.), *Contemporary sociological theory*, (pp. 244-255).

Gifford, R. (1997). *Environmental psychology: Principles and practice* (2nd ed.). Boston: Allyn and Bacon.

Gilchrist, M., & Ward, R. (2006). Facilitating access to online learning. In S. Glen & P. Moule (Eds.), *E-learning in nursing*. Basingstoke: Palgrave Macmillan.

Giles, J. (2005). Internet encyclopaedias go head to head [Electronic Version]. *Nature*, 438, 900-901. Retrieved December 15, 2005 from http://www.nature.com/nature/journal/v438/n7070/full/438900a.html

Gillespie, T. (2004). Copyright and commerce: The DMCA, trusted systems, and the stabilization of distribution. *Information Society, 20*(4), 239-254.

Gillespie, T. (2006). Designed to 'effectively frustrate': Copyright, technology and the agency of users. *New Media & Society, 8*(4), 651-669.

Girard, B. (2005). Internet, radio and network extensioin. In A. K. Mohan & W. H. Melody (Eds.), *Stimulating investment in network development: Roles for regulators*. Report on the World Dialogue on Regulation. Retrieved from http://www.regulateonline.org

Gjedde, L. (2005). Designing for learning in narrative multimedia environments. In S. Mishra & R. C. Sharma (Eds.) *Interactive multimedia in education and training*, (pp. 101 – 111). Hershey, PA: Idea Group.

Glasersfeld, E. von (1995). *Radical constructivism*. London: The Falmer Press.

Godoy D., & Amandi A. (2006). Modeling user interests by conceptual clustering. *Information Systems, 31*(4), 247–265.

Goffman, E. (1967). *Interaction ritual: Essays on face-to-face behavior*. New York: Pantheon Books.

GOI. (1999). *National Task Force on Information Technology and Software Development: IT Action Plan Part III – Long Term National IT Policy*. New Delhi: Government of India. Retrieved from http://it-taskforce.nic.in/actplan3/

GOI. (2003). *v2020: Vision 2020 report*. Retrieved from http://planningcommission.nic.in/reports/genrep/bk-pap2020/1_bg2020.pdf

Goldberg, D., Nichols, D., Oki, B. M., & Terry, D. (1992). Using collaborative filtering to weave an information tapestry. *Communication of the ACM, Information Filtering, 35*(12), 61–70.

Golder, S. A., & Huberman, B. A. (2006). Usage patterns of collaborative tagging systems. *Journal of Information Science, 32*(2), 198-208.

Goldson, J. (2004). Children's voices: Optimizing the opportunities for inclusion. *Social Work Now, January*, 5-9.

Goldstein, J., & Puntambekar, S. (2004). *Journal of Social Science Education and Technology, 13*(4), 505-522.

Gomez, J. (2002). *Internet politics: Surveillance and intimidation in Singapore*. Singapore: Think Centre.

Good, N., Schafer, J., Konstan, J., Borchers, A., Sarwar, B., Herlocker, J., & Riedl, J. (1999). Combining collaborative filtering with personnal agents for better recommendations. In *Proceeding of AAAI, AAAI Press, 35*, 439-446.

Goodear, L. (2001). *Presentation of findings 2001 flexible learning leaders professional development activity. Cultural diversity and flexible learning*. Australian National Training Authority. Retrieved October 8, 2006, from http://www.flexiblelearning.net.au/leaders/events/pastevents/2001/statepres01/papers/1_goodear.Pdf

Goodfellow, R., & Hewling, A. (2005). Re-conceptualising culture in virtual learning environments: From an "essentialist" to a "negotiated" perspective. *E-Learning, 2(4)*, 356-368. Retrieved October 8, 2006, from

http://www.wwwords.co.uk/ELEA/content/pdfs/2/issue2_4.asp#5

Goodfellow, R., Lea, M., Gonzalez, F., & Mason, R. (2001). Opportunity and e-quality: Intercultural and linguistic issues in global online learning. *Distance Education, 22*(1), 65-84.

Goodyear, P. (1998). *New technology in higher education: Understanding the innovation process*. Lancaster University. Retrieved 3 December, 2006, from http://tinyurl.com/yn4qw2

Goodyear, P., & Jones, C. (2003). Implicit theories of learning and change: Their role in the development of e-learning environments for higher education. In S. Naidu (Ed.), *Learning & teaching with technology*. London; Sterling, VA: Kogan Page.

Goodyear, P., & NLinHE Team. (2001). *Effective networked learning in higher education: Notes and guidelines*. Retrieved 14 January, 2001, from http://csalt.lancs.ac.uk/jisc/advice.htm

Goodyear, P., & NLinHE Team. (2001). *Effective networked learning in higher education: Notes and guidelines*. Retrieved 14 January, 2001, from http://csalt.lancs.ac.uk/jisc/advice.htm

Gopinath, S. (2005). Ringtones, or the auditory logic of globalization. *First Monday, 10*(12).

Gordon, L. A., Loeb, M. P., Lucyshyn, W., & Richardson, R. (2005). *2005 CSI/FBI computer crime and security survey*. Computer Security Institute.

Gorizz C. M., & Medina C., (2000). Engaging girls with computers through software games. *Communications of the ACM, 43*(1), 42 – 49.

Gorski, P. (2005). *Multicultural education and the Internet: Intersections and integrations*. Boston, Toronto: McGraw-Hill.

Gotterbarn, D. (1995). Computer ethics: Responsibility regained. In D. G. Johnson & H. Nissenbaum (Eds.), *Computers, ethics and social values*. Englewood Cliff, NJ: Prentice Hall.

Gouchenour, P. H. (2006). Distributed communities and nodal subjects. *New Media and Society, 8*(1), 33-51.

Gourley, B. (2005). *The Open University in Africa.* Milton Keynes: The Open University. Retrieved November 10, 2006, from http://www.open2.net/development/ouandafrica.html

Government Accountability Office. (2005). *Critical infrastructure protection: Department of Homeland Security faces challenges in fulfilling cybersecurity responsibilities.* GAO-05-434. May. Washington DC.

Graham, P., & McKenna, B. J. (2000). A theoretical and analytical synthesis of autopoiesis and sociolinguistics for the study of organisational communication. *Social Semiotics, 10*(1), 49-59.

Graham, S. (Ed.) (2004). *The Cybercities Reader.* London: Routledge.

Graham, S., & Marvin, S. (2001). *Splintering urbanism: Network infrastructures, technological mobilities and the urban condition.* NY: Routledge.

Grand, S., von Krogh, G., Leonard, D., & Swap, W. (2004). Resource allocation beyond firm boundaries: A multi-level model for open source innovation. *Long Range Planning, 37,* 591–610.

Gravano, L., Garcia-Molina, H., & Tomasic, A. (1999). GloSS: Text-source discovery over the Internet. *ACM Transactions on Database Systems, 24*(2), 229-264.

Gray, J. A. M. (2001). *Evidence-based health care: How to make health policy and management decisions.* Edinburgh: Churchill Livingstone.

Greener, I., & Perriton, L. (2005). The political economy of networked learning communities in higher education. *Studies in Higher Education. 30*(1), 67-79.

Gresham-Lancaster, S. (1998). The aesthetics and history of the hub: The effects of changing technology on network computer music. *Leonardo Music Journal, 8*(1), 39.

Grossman, L. (2006/2007). You: Time Magazine Person of the Year. *Time Magazine, 168*(26), 38-41. December 25, 2006/January 1, 2007.

Grossman, L. (2006/2007). Power to the people. *Time Magazine Person of the Year, 168*(26), 42-47, 50, 53-56, 58.

Grossman, S. J., & Hart, O. D. (1986). The costs and benefits of ownership: A theory of vertical and lateral integration. *Journal of Political Economy, 94*(4), 691–719.

Grover, V., Jeoung, S. R., & Segars, A. J. (1998). Information systems effectiveness: The construct space and patterns of application. *Information & Management, 31*(4), 177-191.

Guddemi, P. (2000). Autopoiesis, semeiosis, and cocoupling: A relational language for describing communication and adaptation. *Cybernetics & Human Knowing, 7*(2-3), 127-145.

Gudykunst, W. B., & Ting-Toomey, S. (1988). *Culture and interpersonal communication.* Newbury Park, CA: Sage.

Guillen, M., & Suarez, S. (2005). Explaining the global digital divide: Economic, political and sociological drivers of cross-national Internet use. *Social Forces, 84*(2), 681-708.

Guiller, J., & Durndell, A. (2006). "I totally agree with you": Gender interactions in educational online discussion groups. *Journal of Computer-Assisted Learning, 2*(5), 368-381.

Gulati, S. (2006). Applications of new technologies. In S. Glen & P. Moule (Eds.), *E-learning in nursing* (pp. 138). Basingstoke: Palgrave Macmillan.

Gunawardena, C. N., Lowe, C. A., & Anderson, T. (1997). Analysis of a global online debate and the development of an interaction analysis model for examining social construction of knowledge in computer conferencing. *Journal of Educational Computing Research, 17*(4), 397-431.

Gunawardena, C. N., Wilson, P. L., & Nolla, A. C. (2003). Culture and online education. In M. G. Moore & W. G. Anderson (Eds.), *Handbook of distance education.* Mahwah, NJ: Lawrence Erlbaum Assoc.

Gunn, C., French, S., MacLeod, H., McSporran, M., & Conole, G. (2002). A response to the critique of gender issues in computer-supported learning. *Alt-J - Association for Learning Technology Journal, 10*(2), 80-82.

Gunn, C., French, S., McLeod, H., McSporran, M., & Conole, G. (2002). Gender issues in computer-supported learning. *Alt-J - Association for Learning Technology Journal, 10*(1), 32-44.

Gurol, M., & Sevindik, T. (2007). Profile of Internet café users in Turkey. *Telematics and Informatics, 24,* 59–68.

Gurstein, M. (2003). Effective use: A community informatics strategy beyond the Digital Divide. *Firstmonday.* Retrieved 10 February 2004, from http://www.firstmonday.dk/issues/issues8_12/gurstein/

GVU. (1999). *10th WWW user survey. Graphic, visualisation & usability center (GVU).* Retrieved January 10, 2007, from http://www.gvu.gatech.edu/user_surveys/survey-1998-10/

Gwinnett, A., & Massie, S. (1987). Integrating computers into the curriculum (2): Transforming a concept into a working tool. *Nurse Education Today, 7*(3), 116-119.

Haase, P., Stojanovic, N., Sure, Y., & Völker, J. (2005). On personalized information retrieval in semantics-based peer-to-peer systems. In *Proceedings of the BTW-Workshop "WebDB Meets IR."* Retrieved January 10, 2007, from http://www.aifb.uni-karlsruhe.de/WBS/ysu/publications/2005_webdbir.pdf

Habermas, J. (1971). Technology and science as "Ideology" (J. J. Shapiro, Trans.). In J. Habermas (Ed.), *Toward a rational society; student protest, science, and politics* (pp. 81-122). Beacon Press.

Habermas, J. (1987). *The theory of communicative action, Volume 2, System and lifeworld: A critique of functionalist reason.* Boston, MA: Beacon Press.

Habermas, J. (1996). *The structural transformation of the public sphere: An inquiry into a category of bourgeois society.* Great Britain: Polity Press.

Hall, A. (2006). Who's learning? Responding to the needs of a culturally diverse world of online learners. In Markauskaite, L., Goodyear, P. & Reimann. P. (Eds.), *Proceedings of the 23rd annual conference of the Australasian Society for Computers in Learning in Tertiary Education: Who's learning? Whose technology?* Sydney: Sydney University Press. Retrieved December 15, 2006, from http://www.ascilite.org.au/conferences/sydney06/proceeding/pdf_papers/p138.pdf

Hall, B. (1997). *Testimony to Government Management, Information and Technology Subcommittee.* March 20.

Hall, B. (2006). Five innovation technologies. *Chief Learning Officer, 5*(7), 13. Retrieved February 2, 2007, from http://www.clomedia.com/content/templates/clo_article.asp?articleid=1443&zoneid=190

Hall, E. T. (1984). *The dance of life: The other dimension of time.* Garden City, N.Y., Anchor Press/Doubleday.

Hall, E. T., & Hall, M. R. (1990). *Understanding cultural differences.* Yarmouth, MA: Intercultural Press Inc.

Hallett, C., & Prout, A. (Eds.). (2003). *Hearing the voices of children: Social policy for a new century.* London: RoutledgeFalmer.

Hammond, N. (1992). Tailoring hypertext for the learner (pp.149-160). In P. Kommers, D. Jonassen, & J. Mayes (Eds.), *Cognitive tools for learning.* Berlin: Springer Verlag.

Hammond, T., Hannay, T., Lund, B., & Scott, J. (2005). Social bookmarking tools (I): A general review. *D-Lib Magazine, 11*(4).

Hancock, J., Barnhard, S., Cox, P., & Faldasz, D. (2005). The global needs assessment: Instructional design considerations for a global community. *AACE Journal, 13*(1), 65-72.

Hands, J. (2006). Civil society, cosmopolitics and the net: The legacy of 15 February 2003. *Information, Communication & Society, 9*(2), 225-243.

Hannerz, U. (1997). Scenarios for peripheral cultures. In A. King (Ed.), *Culture, globalization and the world-system: Contemporary conditions for the representations of identity* (pp. 107-128). Minneapolis, MN: University of Minnesota Press.

Hansen, P., & Järvelin, K. (2005). Collaborative information retrieval in an information-intensive domain. *Information Processing & Management Journal, 41*(2005), 1101 –1119.

Hara, N., & Estrada, Z. (2005). Analyzing the mobilization of grassroots activities via the internet: a case study. *Journal of Information Science, 31*(6), 503-514.

Hara, N., & Kling, R. (1999). Students' frustrations with a Web-based distance education course. *First Monday, 4.* Retrieved July 12, 2007, from http://www.firstmonday. org/issues/issue4_12/hara/index.html

Haraway, D. (1991). *Simians, Cyborgs, and Women: The reinvention of nature.* NY: Routledge.

Harding, S. (1998). *Is science multicultural? Postcolonialism, Feminism, and Epistemologies.* Bloomington: Indiana University Press.

Hardt, M., & Negri, A. (2000). *Empire.* Cambridge, MA: Harvard University Press.

Harrington, S. J. (1996). The effect of codes of ethics and personal denial of responsibility on computer abuse judgments and intentions. *MIS Quarterly, 20*(3), 257-278.

Harris, S. E., & Katz, J. L. (1991). Firm size and the information intensity of life insurers. *MIS Quarterly, 15*(3), 333-352.

Harris, S., (2004). Activity theory: Introduction & background. Retrieved from http://case.glam.ac.uk/CASE/ StaffPages/SteveHarris/Research/AT.html

Hars, A., & Ou, S. (2001). *Working for free? motivations of participating in open source projects.* (Proceedings of the 34th Hawaii International Conference on System Sciences.) Retrieved from http://csdl.computer.org/comp/ proceedings/hicss/2001/0981/07/09817014.pdf

Hart, O. D., & Moore, J. (1988). Incomplete contracts and renegotiation. *Econometrica, 56*(4), 755–785.

Harvey, D. (1990). *The condition of postmodernity.* Cambridge, MA: Blackwell.

Hascoët, M. (2000). A user interface combining navigation aids. In *Proceedings of the 11ᵗʰ International ACM Hypertext Conference* (pp 224-225).

Hasdell, P. (2002). *Mediated spaces.* Retrieved December 16, 2006, from http://www.arch.kth.se/mediatedspaces/ mediatedspaces.pdf

Hauffe, H. (1994). Is citation analysis a tool for evaluation of scientific contributions? In *13ᵗʰ Winterworkshop on Biochemical and Clinical Aspects of Pteridines.* Retrieved January 10, 2007, from http://www.uibk.ac.at/ub/ueber_uns/ publikationen/hauffe_is_citation_analysis_a_tool. html

Hayes, J. R., & Flower, L. S. (1986). Writing research and the writer. *American Psychologist, 41*(10), 1106-1113.

Hayles, N. K. (1984). *How we became posthuman: Virtual bodies, in Cybernetics, Literature, and Informatics.* Chicago: University of Chicago Press.

Heeks, R. (1999). *Reinventing government in the information age: International practice in IT-tenable public sector reform.* NY: Routledge.

Heidegger, M. (1962). *Being and time.* New York: Harper & Row.

Heidegger, M. (1977). *The question concerning technology, and other essays* (W. Lovitt, Trans. 1st ed.). New York: Harper & Row.

Heinssen, R. K., Glass, C. R., Knight, L. A. (1987). Assessing computer anxiety: Development and validation of the computer anxiety rating scale. *Comput. Human Behavior, 3*(2) 49-59.

Helweg-Larsen, M., & Sheppard, J. A. (2001). Do moderators of the optimistic bias affect personal or target risk estimates? A review of the literature. *Personality and Social Psychology Review, 5*(1), 74-95.

Henderson, L. (1996). Instructional design of interactive multimedia: A cultural critique. *ETR&D, 44*(3), 85-104.

Henderson, L. (2006). Theorizing a multiple cultures instructional design model for e-learning and e-teaching.

In A. Edmundston (Ed.), *Globalized e-learning cultural challenges* (pp. 130-153). Hershey,PA: Idea Group Inc.

Hennion, A. (1989). An intermediary between production and consumption: The producer of popular music. *Science, Technology, & Human Values, 14*(4), 400-424.

Hennion, A. (2001). Music lovers: Taste as performance. *Theory, Culture & Society, 18*(5), 1.

Herlocker, J. L., Konstan, A. J., Borchers, A., & Riedl, J. (1999). An algorithmic framework for performing collaborative filtering. In *Proceedings of the 22nd International ACM Conference on Research and Development in Information Retrieval* (SIGIR'99) (pp. 230-237).

Herlocker, J. L., Konstan, A. J., Terveen, L., & Riedl, J. (2004). Evaluating collaborative filtering recommender systems. *ACM Transactions on Information Systems (TOIS), 22* (1), 5-53.

Herring, S. C. (2003). *Gender and power in online communication*. In J. Holmes & M. Meyerhoff (Eds.), *The handbook of language and gender* (pp. 202-228). Oxford: Blackwell.

Hess, D. J. (2005). Technology- and product-oriented movements: Approximating social movement. *Science, Technology & Human Values, 30*, 515-535.

Hetzler, B., Harris, W. M., Havre, S., & Whitney P. (1999). Visualizing the full spectrum of document relationships. In *5th International Conference of the International Society for Knowledge Organization (ISKO)* (pp. 168–175).

Hewett, T. T., Baecker, R., Card, S., Carey, T., Gasen, J., Mantei, M., Perlmen, G., Strong, G., & Verplank, W. (1996). *ACM SIGCHI Curriculum for Human-Computer Interaction*. Retrieved December 26, 2006, from http://sigchi.org/cdg/index.html

Hickey, H. (2007). *Mobile phones facilitate romance in modern India*. Retrieved on June 23, 2007 from http://uwnews.org/article.asp?articleid=30477

Hill, J., & Plath, D. (1998). Moneyed knowledge: How women become commercial shellfish divers. In J. Singleton (Ed.), *Learning in likely places: Varieties of apprenticeship in Japan* (pp. 211-225). Cambridge: Cambridge University Press.

Hills, J. (2006). What's new? War, censorship and global transmission. From the Telegraph to the Internet. *The International Communication Gazette, 68*(3), 195-216.

Hiltz, S. R. (1988). Productivity enhancement from computer-mediated communication: A systems contingency approach. *Communications of the ACM, 31*, 1438-1454.

Hinchcliffe, S. M. (Ed.). (1989). *Nursing practice and health care*, (1st ed. only). London: Edward Arnold.

Hippel, E. Von. (2005). *Democratizing innovation*. Cambridge, MA: MIT Press. Retrieved from http://web.mit.edu/evhippel/www/democ.htm

Hodgson, M., McCartan, A., Hare, C., Clayphan, R., & Jezierski, G. (1995). *Teaching and learning in higher education: The integrative use of IT within the institutional context*. Durham: University of Durham.

Hoffman, D. L., & Novak, T. P. (1999) Marcos Peralta, building consumer trust online, *Communications of the ACM, 42*(4), 80-85.

Hoffman, D. L., Novak, T. P., & Venkatesh, A. (2004). Has the Internet become indispensable? *Communication of the ACM, 47*(7), 37-42.

Hoffman, T. (1999). Y2K failures have hit 75% of US firms. *Computerworld*, August 16, 33:33.

Hofstede, G. (1980). *Culture's consequences: International differences in work-related values*. Newbury Park, CA: Sage.

Hofstede, G. (1991). Culture and organizations: Software of the mind. *Journal of Applied Social Psychology, 23*(7), 499-507.

Hofstede, G. (1991). *Cultures and organizations: Software of the mind*. London: McGraw-Hill U.K.

Hofstede, G. (1991). Levels of culture. In *Cultures and organizations. Software of the mind* (pp. 3-18). London: McGraw-Hill.

Hogan, R., & Hogan, J. (1994). The mask of integrity. Pp. 107-125 In T. Sarbin, R. Carney, & C. Eoyang (Eds.), *Citizen espionage: Studies in trust and betrayal.* Westport, CT: Praeger.

Holfstede, G. (1980, 2001). *Culture's consequences. Comparing values, behaviors, institutions, and organizations across nation.* (2nd ed.). Thousand Oaks, London, New Delhi: Sage Publications.

Holfstede, G. (1986). Cultural differences in teaching and learning. *International Journal of Intercultural Relations, 10*, 301-320.

Holliday, A. R. (1994). *Appropriate methodology and social context.* Glasgow, UK: Cambridge University Press.

Holmes, G. (2002). The importance of culture when creating audio-enhanced, Web-based instruction. *TechTrends, 46*(2), 56-61

Hölscher, C., & Strube, G. (2000). Web search behavior of Internet experts and newbies. In *Proceedings of the 9th International World Wide Web Conference on Computer Networks: The International Journal of Computer and Telecommunications Networking* (pp. 337-346). Amsterdam: North-Holland Publishing Co.

Holzl, A. (1999). *Designing for diversity within online learning environments.* Paper presented at the Australasian Society for Computers in Learning in Tertiary Education Conference, Brisbane, Australia. Retrieved June 29, 2006, from http://www.ascilite.org.au/conferences/brisbane99/papers/holzl.pdf

Honegger, B. D. (2005). *Wikis – A rapidly growing phenomenon in the German-speaking school community.* Paper presented at the WikiSym 2005. Retrieved February 5, 2007, from http://www.wikisym.org/ws2005/proceedings/paper-10.pdf

Hong, J., & Huang, L. (2005). A split and swaying approach to building information society: The case of Internet cafes in China. *Telematics and Informatics, 22*, 377–393.

Honold, P. (2000). Culture and context: An empirical study for the developement of a framework for the elicitation of cultural influence in product usage. *The International Journal of Human-Computer Interaction, 12*, 327-345.

Hood, C. (1996). Where extremes meet: SPRAT vs. SHARK in public risk management. In C. Hood and D. Jones (Eds), *Accident and design.* London: UCL.

Hood, C., Rothstein, H., & Baldwin, R. (2001). *The government of risk: Understanding risk regulation regimes.* Oxford: Oxford University Press.

Hornborg, A. (2001). *The power of the machine: Global inequalities of economy, technology, and environment.* New York: Altamira Press.

Hosmer, L. T. (1995). Trust: The connecting link between organization theory and philosophical ethics. *Academy of Management Review, 20,* 379-403.

Hotte, R., & Pierre, S. (2002). Leadership and conflict management support in a cooperative tele-learning environment. *International Journal on e-Learning, 1*(2), 46-59. Retrieved 10/03/2003, from http://www-icdl.open.ac.uk/

House of Commons Library. (1998). *The millennium bug.* Research Paper: 98/72. London.

Howard, P. N. (2002). Network ethnography and the hypermedia organization: New media, new organizations, new methods. *New Media and Society, 4.*

Howe, J. (2006/2007). Your Web, your way. Time Magazine Person of the Year. *Time Magazine Person of the Year, 168*(26), 60-61. Lamb, B. (2004). Wide open spaces: Wikis, ready or not. *EDUCAUSE Review, 39*(5), 36-48. Retrieved February 26, 2006, from http://www.educause.edu/ir/library/pdf/erm0452.pdf

Huff, C. 2002. Gender, software design, and occupational equity. *SIGCSE Bull., 34*(2), 112-115.

Huffaker, D. (2004). The educated blogger: Using Weblogs to promote literacy in the classroom. *First Monday, 9*(6). Retrieved April 04, 2007, from www.firstmonday.dk/issues/issue9_6/huffaker/index.html

Hughes, E. (1958). *Men and their work.* New York: Free Press.

Hughes, G. (2002). Gender issues in computer-supported learning: What we can learn from the gender, science and technology literature. *Alt-J - Association for Learning Technology Journal, 10*(2), 77-79.

Hunt, S. A., & Benford, R. D. (1994). Identity talk in the peace and justice movement. *Journal of Contemporary Ethnography, 22*(4), 488-517.

Hussin, H., King, M., & Cragg., P. (2002). IT alignment in small firms. *European Journal of Information Systems, 11*(1), 108-127.

Ide, E. (1971). New experiments in information retrieval. In G. Salton, (Ed.), *The SMART retrieval system – Experiments in automatic document processing* (pp. 337–354). Englewood Cliffs, NJ: Prentice Hall, Inc.

Idrus, R. M., & Sharma, R. (2007). *Leveling the information field via interactive technologies.* Paper presented at the Academic Conference on Information Revolution and Cultural Integration in East Asia, 25-26 January 2007, Vietnam National University, Ho Chi Minh City, Vietnam

Illich, I. (1974). *Energy and equity.* London: Marion Boyars Publishers Inc.

Inal, Y. & Cagiltay, K. (2005). *Turkish elementary school students' computer game play characteristics.* BILTEK 2005 International Cognition Congress, Eskişehir, Turkey.

Ingham, G. (2004). The emergence of capitalist credit money. In L. R. Wray (Ed.), *Credit and state theories of money: The contributions of a. mitchell innes* (p. 173-222). Cheltenham: Edward Elgar.

Inglehart, R. (1989). *Culture shift in advanced industrial society.* Princeton, NJ: Princeton University Press.

Innes, A. (1914). The credit theory of money. *Banking Law Journal, 31*, 151–168.

International Finance Corporation. (2002). *E-commerce readiness assessment of selected South Pacific economies.* International Finance Corporation.

International Finance Corporation. (2004). *SME definition.* Retrieved 12 March 2004, from http://www2.ifc.org/sme/html/sme_definitions.html

Internet usage in Asia. (n.d.). Retrieved October 22, 2006, from http://www.internetworldstats.com/stats3.htm

Ishida, T. (1969). Beyond traditional concepts of peace in different cultures. *Journal of Peace Research, 6*(2), 133-145.

Ives, B. (1994). Probing the productivity paradox. *MIS Quarterly, 18*(2).

Jack, A. (1999). Level of Russian IT lessens year 2000 fears: Moscow has been late in putting together some moderate Y2K defences. *Financial Times,* November 26.

Jackson, H. J. (2002). *Marginalia: Readers writing in books.* Yale University Press.

Jackson, L. A., Ervin, K. S., Gardner, P. D., & Schmitt, N. (2001). Gender and the Internet: Women communicating and men searching. *Sex Roles, 44*(5), 363-379.

Jackson, M. (2002). Using technology to add new dimensions to the nightly call home. *New York Times,* 22 October.

Jacobs, J. (1961). *The death and life of great American cities.* NY: Vintage Book.

Jaczynski M., & Trousse B. (1997). Broadway: A World Wide Web browsing advisor reusing past navigations from a group of users. In *Proceedings of the 3rd UK Case-Based Reasoning Workshop (UKCBR '97).*

Jaeger, C., Webler, T., Rosa, E., & Renn, O. (2001). *Risk, uncertainty and rational action.* London: Earthscan.

Jansen, B. J., Spink, A., & Saracevic. T. (2000). Real life, real users and reals needs: A study and analysis of users queries on the Web. *Information Processing & Management Journal, 36*(2), 207–227.

Jasola, S., & Sharma, R. (2005). Open and distance education through wireless mobile Internet: A learning model. *International Journal of Instructional Technology and Distance Learning, 2*(9), 35-47. Retrieved from http://www.itdl.org/Journal/Sep_05/article04.htm

Javalgi, R. G., Wickramasinghe, N., Scherer, R. F., & Sharma, S. K. (2005). An assessment and strategic guidelines for developing e-commerce in the Asia-Pacific region. *International Journal of Management, 22*(4), 523-531.

Javalgi, R.G., & Ramsey, R. (2001). Strategic issues of e-commerce as an alternative global distribution system. *International Marketing Review, 18*, 376-391.

Jenkins, H. (2006). *Convergence culture: Where old and new media collide.* New York: New York University Press.

Jenkins, H., Seawell, B., & Thorburn, D. (2003). *Democracy and new media.* Cambridge, MA: MIT Press.

Jenkins, T. L. (2003). Black Futurists in the information age. In A. H. Teich (Ed.), *Technology and the future.* Belmont, CA: Wadsworth/Thomson.

Jensen, A., & McKee, L. (2003). *Children and the changing family: Between transformation and negotiation.* London: RoutledgeFalmer.

Jenson, J., deCastell, S., & Bryson, M. (2003). Girl talk: Gender, equity, and identity discourses in a school-based computer culture. *Women's Studies International Forum, 26*(6), 561-573.

Jin, H., Ning, X., & Chen, H. (2006). Efficient search for peer-to-peer information retrieval using semantic small world. In *Proceedings of the 15th International Conference on World Wide Web* (pp. 1003-1004). NY: ACM Press.

Jin, R., Chai, J. Y., & Si, L., (2004). An automatic weighting scheme for collaborative filtering. In *Proceedings of the 27th International ACM Conference on Research and Development in Information Retrieval.* SIGIR'04 (pp. 337-344).

Joanna Briggs Institute. (2006, 22 December 2006). *Systematic reviews - The review process.* Retrieved 11 April 2007, 2007, from http://www.joannabriggs.edu.au/pubs/approach.php

Johnson, D. K. (2004). *The Cold War persecution of gays and lesbians in the Federal Government.* Chicago, MI: University of Chicago Press.

Johnson, M. (1987). *The body in the mind.* Chicago: University of Chicago Press.

Johnson, P. (2002). New technology tools for human development? Towards policy and practice for knowledge societies in Southern Africa. *Compare, 32*(2), 381-389.

Johnson, R. (2005). *The evolution of family violence criminal courts in New Zealand.* Police Executive Conference, Nelson. Retrieved December 18, 2006, from http://www.police.govt.nz/events/2005/ngakia-kia-puawai/johnson-on-evolution-of-family-violence-courts-in-nz.pdf

Johnston, H., & Klandermans, B. (1995). *Social movements and culture.* Minneapolis, MN: University of Minnesota Press.

Joiner R., Gavin J, Brosnan M, Crook C., Duffield, J., Durndell A., Maras P., Miller J., Scott, A. J., & Lovatt P. (2005). Gender, Internet identification, and Internet anxiety: Correlates of Internet use. *Cyberpsychology and Behavior, 8*(4), 373-380.

Joiner, R. W. (1998). The effect of gender on children's software preferences. *Journal of Computer Assisted Learning, 14*, 195-198.

Join-Lambert, L., Klein, P., & Serres, M. (1997). Interview. Superhighways for all: Knowledge's redemption. *Revue Quart Monde, 1*,163. Retrieved May 12 2007, from http://www.nettime.org/Lists-Archives/nettime-l-9810/msg00137.html

Joint Information Systems Committee. (2004). *Effective practice with e-learning.* Retrieved 27 January, 2005, from http://www.jisc.ac.uk/elearning_pedagogy.html

Jonassen, D. H. (1996). *Computers in the classroom: Mindtools for critical thinking.* Englewood Cliffs, NJ: Merrill, Prentice Hall.

Jonassen, D. H. (2001). Chapter 3: Learning from, in and with multimedia: An ecological psychology perspective. In S. Dijkstra & D. H. Jonassen (Eds.), *Multimedia learning: Results and perspectives.* Frankfurt am Main - New York: Peter Lang.

Jones, A., & Mercer, N. (1993). Theories of learning and information technology. In P. Scrimshaw (Ed.),

Language, classroom and computers, (pp. 11-26). London: Routledge.

Jones, C. (2002, March 26th - 28th). *Is there a policy for networked learning?* Paper presented at the Networked Learning Conference 2002, University of Sheffield.

Jones, P. (1996). Humans, information, and science. *Journal of Advanced Nursing,* 591-598.

Jones, P. (1998). *Hodges' health career care domains model.* Retrieved May 12, 2007, from http://www.p-jones.demon.co.uk

Jones, P. (2000). *Hodges' health career care domains model, structural assumptions.* Retrieved May 12, 2007, from http://www.p-jones.demon.co.uk/theory.html

Jones, P. (2000). *Hodges' health career care domains model, theoretical assumptions.* Retrieved May 12, 2007, from http://www.p-jones.demon.co.uk/struct.html

Jones, P. (2004). Viewpoint: Can informatics and holistic multidisciplinary care be harmonised? *British Journal of Healthcare Computing & Information Management, 21*(6), 17-18.

Jones, P. (2004). *The four care domains: Situations worthy of research.* Conference: Building & Bridging Community Networks: Knowledge, Innovation & Diversity through Communication, Brighton, UK. Retrieved May 7, 2007, from http://www.comminit.com/healthecomm/planning.php?showdetails=318

Jones, R. (2005). Entertaining code: File sharing, digital rights management regimes, and criminological theories of compliance. *International Review of Law, Computers & Technology, 19*(3), 287-303.

Jones, S. (2000). Music and the Internet. *Popular Music, 19*(2), 217.

Jones, W., Phuwanartnurak, A. J., Gill, R., & Bruce, H. (2005). Don't take my folders away!: Organizing personal information to get things done. In *CHI '05: CHI '05 extended abstracts on Human factors in computing systems* (pp. 1505-1508). New York, NY: ACM Press.

Judd, C. M., & Park, B. (1988). Out-group homogeneity: Judgments of variability at the individual and group levels. *Journal of Personality and Social Psychology, 54*(5), 778-788.

Julien, O. (1999). The diverting of musical technology by rock musicians: The example of double-tracking. *Popular Music, 18*(3), 357.

Jussawalia, M., & Taylor, R. (Eds.) (2003). *Information technology parks of the Asia Pacific: Lessons for the regional digital divide.* New York, NY: M. e. Sharpe.

Kagami, M., Tsuji, M., & Giovannetti, E. (Eds.) (2004). *Information technology policy and the digital divide: Lessons for developing countries.* Northhampton, MA: Edward Elgar.

Kahan, J., Koivunen, M.-R., Prud'Hommeaux, E., & Swick, R. R. (2002). Annotea: An open rdf infrastructure for shared Web annotations. *Computer Networks, 32*(5), 589-608.

Kahn, R., & Kellner, D. (2004). New media and Internet activism: From the 'Battle of Seattle' to blogging. *New Media and Society, 6*(1), 87-95.

Kamppuri, M., Tedre, M., & Tukianien, M. (2006). *Towards the sixth level in interface design: Understanding culture.* Proceedings of the CHI-SA 2006, 5th Conference on Human Computer Interaction in Southern Africa, Cape Town, South Africa, January 25th-27th 2006 (pp. 69-74). Retrieved December 1, 2006, from http://www.tedre.name/pg_research.html

Kaplan, B., & Duchon, D. (1988). Combining qualitative and quantitative methods in information systems research: A case study. *MIS Quarterly, 12*(4), 362-377.

Kaptelinin, V., & Nardi, B. A. (2006). *Acting with technology: Activity theory and interaction design.* Cambridge, MA: The MIT Press.

Karamuftuoglu, M., (1999). Collaborative information retrieval: Towards a social informatics view of IR interaction. *Journal of the American Society for Information Science, 49*(12), 1070–1080.

Karavidas, M., Lim, N. K., & Katsikas, S. L. (2005). The effects of computers on older adult users. *Computers in Human Behaviour, 21*, 697-711.

Katagiri, Y., Nass, C., & Takeuchi, Y. (2001). Cross-cultural studies of the computers are social actors paradigm: The case of reciprocity. In M. J. Smith, G. Salvendy, D. Harris, & R. Koubek (Eds.), *Usability evaluation and interface design: Cognitive engineering, intelligent agents, and virtual* (pp. 1558-1562). Mahwah, NJ: Lawrence Erlbaum Associates.

Katz, J. E. (Ed.). (2003). *Machines that become us: The social context of personal communication technology.* New Brunswick, NJ and London: Transaction Publishers.

Katz, J., & Askhus, M. (Eds.) (2002). The mobile phone: Towards new categories of social relations, Information. *Communication and Society, 5* (4), 513-28.

Katz, J., & Askhus, M. (Eds.). (2002). *Perpetual contact: Mobile communication, private talk, performance.* Cambridge: Cambridge University Press.

Katz, M. (2004). *Capturing sound: How technology has changed music.* Berkeley, CA; London: University of California Press.

Kautz, H., Selman, B., & Shah, M. (1997). ReferralWeb: Combining social networks and collaborative filtering. *Commun. ACM, 40*(3), 63–65.

Kawachi, P. (2005). Computers, multimedia and e-learning. In Reddi, U. V. & Mishra, S. (Eds). *Perspectives on distance education: Educational media in Asia* (pp. 97-122). Vancouver: Commonwealth of Learning.

Kawachi, P., Sharma, R. C., & Mishra, S. (2004). E-learning technologies in Asia. Asian Journal of Distance Education, *2*(2). Retrieved from http://www.asianjde.org/

Kay, R. H. (1992). An analysis of methods used to examine gender differences in computer-related behaviour. *Journal of Educational Computing Research, 8*(3), 323-336.

Kay, R. H. (2006). Addressing gender differences in computer ability, attitudes and use: The laptop effect.

Journal of Educational Computing Research, 34(2), 187-211.

Kaye, J. J., Vertesi, J., Avery, S., Dafoe, A., David, S., Onaga, L., Rosero, I., & Pinch, T. (2006). To have and to hold: Exploring the personal archive. In *CHI '06: Proceedings of the SIGCHI conference on Human Factors in computing systems* (pp. 275-284). New York, NY: ACM Press.

Keeble, L., & Loader, B. (Eds.) (2001). *Community informatics: Shaping computer-mediated social relations.* London: Routledge.

Keefe, P. (1983). Computer crime insurance available-for a price. *Computerworld, 31*, 20-21.

Keen, P. G. W. (1980). *Reference disciplines and a cumulative tradition.* Paper presented at the International Conference of Information Systems.

Kell, C. (2006). *Continuing professional development for general practitioners: Is eLearning an option?* MPhil Thesis. Sheffield, UK: Department of Information Studies, University of Sheffield.

Kell, C., & McPherson, M. A. (2005). An investigation using Delphi into whether e-learning can meet the continuing professional development needs of general practitioners. In A. Brown & Remenyi, (Eds.), *Proceedings of the 4th European Conference on Research Methodology for Business and Management Studies* (pp. 225-234), 21-22 April 2005, Université Paris-Dauphine, Paris, France.

Kell, C., & McPherson, M. A. (2006). E-learning for general practitioners/family physicians: Barriers and enablers. In V. Uskov (Ed.), *Proceedings of the Web Based Education Conference,* January 23-25, 2006, Puerto Vallarta, Mexico.

Keller, J. M., & Suzuki, K. (2004). Learner motivation and e-learning design: A multinationally validated process. *Journal of Educational Media, 29*(3), 229-239.

Keller, R. M., Wolfe, S. R., Chen, J. R., Rabinowitz, J. L., & Mathe, N. (1997). A bookmarking service for organizing and sharing URLs. In *Selected papers from the 6th*

International Conference on World Wide Web (pp. 1103-1114). Essex, UK: Elsevier Science Publishers Ltd.

Kellner, D. (Ed.). (1998). *Technology, war and fascism: Collected papers of Herbert Marcuse, Volume 1.* NY: Routledge.

Kelvin, P. (1973). A socio-psychological examination of privacy. *British Journal of Social Clinical Psychology, 12*(3), 248-261.

Kendall, G. (1999). Pop music: Authenticity, creativity and technology. *Social Alternatives, 18*(2), 25.

Keniston, K., & Kumar, D. (Eds.) (2004). *IT experience in India: Bridging the digital divide.* Thousand Oaks, CA: SAGE Publications.

Kennedy, S. (2006). *Small, smart, stealthy.* Paper presented at the Architecture and Situated Technologies Conference, The Urban Center, New York, NY.

Kerr, E. B. (1986). Electronic leadership: A guide to moderating online conferences. *IEEE Transactions on Professional Communication, 29*, 12-18.

Kerr, O. S. (2003). Internet surveillance law after The USA PARIOT Act: The big brother that isn't. *Northwestern University Law Review, 97*(2), 607-673.

Khan, B. H. (2000). *A framework for open, flexible and distributed learning.* Paper presented at TEND 2000, Crossroads of the New Millenium. Retrieved December 1, 2006, from http://www.eric.ed.gov/ERICWebPortal/Home.portal

Kheifets, L. Hester, G., & Banerjee, G. (2001). The precautionary principle and EMF: Implementation and evaluation. *The Journal of Risk Research, 4*(2),113-125.

Kidd, D. (2003). Indymedia.org: A new communications commons. In M. McCaughey & M. D. Ayers (Eds.), *Cyberactivism: Online activism in theory and practice.* London. Routledge.

Kim, K. K. (1989). User satisfaction: A synthesis of three different perspectives. *Journal of Information Systems, 3*(Fall), 1-12.

Kimberly, J. R., & Evanisko, M. J. (1981). Organizational innovation: The influence of individual, organizational, and contextual factors on hospital adoption of technological and administrative innovations. *Academy of Management Journal, 24*(4), 689-713.

Kimborough, D. R. (1999). Online chat room tutorial – An unusual gender bias in computer use. *Journal of Science Education and Technology, 8*(3), 227-234.

King, J., Bond, T., & Blandford, S. (2002). An investigation of computer anxiety by gender and grade. *Computers in Human Behaviour, 18*, 69-84.

Kinuthia, W. (2006). African education perspectives on culture and e-learning. In A. Edmundston (Ed.), *Globalized e-learning cultural challenges* (pp. 1-17). Hershey, PA: Idea Group Inc.

Kirkwood, A., & Price, L. (2005). Learners and learning in the twenty-first century: What do we know about students' attitudes towards and experiences of information and communication technologies that will help us design courses? *Studies in Higher Education, 30*(3), 257-274.

Kizza, J. M. (2003). *Ethical and social issues in the Information Age* (2nd ed.). New York: Springer-Verlag.

Klawe, M. (2002). Girls, boys, and computers. *SIGCSE Bull., 34*(2), 16-17.

Kleinberg, J. M. (1999). Authoritative sources in a hyperlinked environment. In *Proceedings of the 19th Annual ACM-SIAM Symposium on Discrete Algorithms* (pp. 668-677).

Klemm, F., & Aberer, K. (2005). Aggregation of a term vocabulary for peer-to-peer information retrieval: A DHT stress test. In *Proceedings of the Third International Workshop on Databases, Information Systems and Peer-to-Peer Computing* (DBISP2P 2005).

Kline, R., & Pinch, T. (1999). The social construction of technology. In D. Mackenzie & J. Wajcman (Eds.), *The social shaping of technology* (pp. 113-115). Buckingham, UK: Open University Press.

Kline, S. J. (1995). *Concpetual foundations for multidisciplinary thinking.* Stanford, CA: Stanford University Press.

Kling, R. (2000). Learning about information technologies and social change: The contribution of social informatics. *The Information Society, 16*(3).

Kling, R., Rosenbaum, H., & Sawyer, S. (2005). Understanding and communicating social informatics. *Information Today.*

Knuth, R. A., & Cunningham, D. J. (1993). Tools for constructivism. In T. Duffy, J. Lowyck, & D. Jonassen (Eds.), *The design of constructivist learning environments: Implications for Instructional design and the use of technology* (pp. 163-188). NATO ASI Series F: Computer and Systems Sciences (Vol. 105). Berlin: Springer Verlag.

Kolb, D. (2000). *Facilitator's guide to learning.* Boston, MA: Hay/McBer Training Resources Group.

Konstan, J. A., Miller, B. N., Maltz, D., Herlocker, J. L., Gordon, L. R., & Riedl, J. (1997). Grouplens: Applying collaborative filtering to usenet news. *Communications of the ACM, 40*(3), 77–87.

Koper, E. J. R., & Sloep, P. (2003). *Learning networks: Connecting people, organizations, autonomous agents and learning resources to establish the emergence of effective lifelong learning.* Heerlen: The Open University of the Netherlands.

Koper, E. J. R., & Tattersall, C. (2004). New directions for lifelong learning using network technologies. *British Journal of Educational Technology, 35*(6).

Korfhage, R. R. (1997). *Information storage and retrieval.* Wiley computer publishing.

Korfiatis, N., Poulos, M., & Bokos, G. (2006). Evaluating authoritative sources using social networks: An insight from wikipedia. *Online Information Review, 30*(3). Retrieved February 4, 2007, from http://www.korfiatis.info/papers/OISJournal_final.pdf

Kozma, R., McGhee, R., & Quellmalz, E. (2004). Closing the digital divide: Evaluation of the World Links program. *International Journal of Educational Development, 24*(4), 361-381.

Kozol, J. (1991). *Savage inequalities: Children in America's schools.* New York: Crown.

Kramer, R. M., & Tyler, T. R. (1996). *Trust in organizations: Frontiers of theory and research.* Thousand Oaks, CA: Sage.

Kramer, R. M., & Wei, J. (1999). Social uncertainty and the problem of trust in social groups: The social self in doubt. In T. M. Tyler & R. M. Kramer, & O. P. John (Eds.), *The psychology of the social self* (pp. 145-168). Mahwah, NJ: Lawrence Erlbaum Associates.

Krippendorff, K. (1994). A recursive thoery of communication. In D. Crowley & D. Mitchell (Eds.), *Communication theory today* (pp. 78-104). Stanford, CA: Stanford University Press.

Krishnamurthy, S. (2002). Cave or community? An empirical examination of 100 mature open source projects. *First Monday, 7*(6). Retrieved from http://www.firstmonday.org/issues/issue7_6/krishnamurthy/

Krulwich, B. (1997). Lifestyle finder: Intelligent user profiling using large-scale demographic data. *AI Magazine, 18*(2), 37-45.

Kurzel, F., & Slay, J. (2002). *Towards an adaptive multimedia learning environment: An Australian solution to cross-cultural and offshore delivery issues.* Paper presented at INC2002, Plymouth, UK. Retrieved on April 8, 2007, from http://www.informingscience.org/proceedings/IS2002Proceedings/papers/Kurze189Towar.pdf

Kwok, S. H. (2006). P2P searching trends: 2002-2004. *Information Management and Processing Journal, 42*(1), 237-247.

La Porte, T. R., & Consolini, P. (1991). Working in practice but not in theory: Theoretical challenges of high reliability organizations. *Journal of Public Administration Research and Theory, 1*, 19-47.

Ladd, J. (1989). Computer and moral responsibility: A framework for ethical analysis. In C. Gould (Ed.), *The information Web: Ethical and social implications of computer networking.* Boulder, CO: Westview Press.

Ladd, J. (1991). Collective and individual moral responsibility in engineering: Some questions. In D. G. Johnson (Ed.), *Ethical issues in engineering* (pp. 26-39). Englewood Cliffs, NJ: Prentice Hall.

Lægran, A. S. (2002). The petrol station and the Internet café: Rural technospaces for youth. *Journal of Rural Studies, 18,* 157–168.

Lakoff, G., & Johnson, M. (1999). *Philosophy in the flesh.* New York: Basic Books.

Lamb, B. (2004). Wide open spaces: Wikis, ready or not. *EDUCAUSE Review, 39*(5), 36-48.

Lamb, R., & Kling, R. F. (2002). *From users to social actors: Reconceptualizing socially rich interaction through information and communication technology.* Retrieved January 23, 2004, from http://www.slis.indiana.edu/CSI/WP/WP02-11B.html

Lambeir, B. (2005). Education as liberation: The politics and techniques of lifelong learning. *Educational Philosophy and Theory, 37*(3).

Langer, J. A., & Applebee, A. A. (1987). *How writing shapes thinking.* Urbana, IL: National Council of Teachers of English.

Lanthier, R. P., & Windham, R. C. (2004). Internet use and college adjustment: The moderating role of gender. *Computers in Human Behaviour, 20,* 591-606.

Latham, R., & Sassen, S. (Eds.) (2005). *Digital formations: IT and new architectures in the global realm.* Princeton, NJ: Princeton University Press.

Latour, B. (1983). Give me a laboratory and I will raise the world. In K. D. Knorr-Cetina & M. J.Mulkay (Eds.), *Science observed* (pp. 141-170). Beverly Hills: Sage.

Latour, B. (1992). Where are the missing masses: Sociology of a few mundane artefacts. . In W. Bijker & J. E. Law (Eds.), *Shaping technology/building society: Studies in sociotechnical change* (pp. 225-259). Cambridge, MA: MIT Press.

Latour, B. (1993). *We have never been modern.* Cambridge, MA: Harvard University Press.

Latour, B. (1996). *Aramis or the love of technology.* Boston.: Harvard University Press.

Latour, B., & Wiebel, P. (2005). *Making things public: Atmospheres of democracy.* Cambridge, MA: MIT Press.

Laudon, K, & Laudon, J. (2004). *Managing the digital firm* (8th ed.). Upper Saddle River, NJ: Prentice-Hall.

Laufer. R. S., & Wolfe, M. (1997). Privacy as a concept and a social issue: A multidimensional developmental rheory. *Journal of Social Issues, 33*(3), 22-41.

Laurillard, D. (1993). *Rethinking university teaching: A framework for the effective use of educational technology.* New York: Routledge.

Lauwers, J. C., & Lentz, L. A. (1990). Collaboration awareness in support of collaboration transparency: Requirements for the next generation of shared Windows systems. In *Conference on Computer Human Interaction CHI'90* (pp. 303-311).

Lave, J., & Wenger, E. (1991). *Situated learning: Legitimate peripheral participation.* Cambridge, UK: Cambridge University Press.

Law, J. (2002). *Aircraft stories: Decentering the object in technoscience.* Durham, NC: Duke University Press.

Lawrence et al. v. Texas, 539 U.S. 558. (2003).

Lax, S. (2000, 2004). The Internet and democracy. In D. Gauntlett & R. Horsley (Eds.), *Web.Studies* (pp. 217-229). New York, NY: Oxford University Press.

Lax, S. (Ed.) (2001). *Access denied in the information age.* New York, NY: Palgrave.

Le Grand, B., & Soto, M. (2005). Topic maps, RDF graphs and ontologies visualization. In V. Geroimenko & C. Chen (Eds.), *Visualizing the semantic Web* (2nd ed.). Springer.

Lechner, F. L., & Boli, J. (2004). *The globalization reader* (2nd. ed.). New York: Blackwell.

Lee, A. C. K. (2003). Undergraduate students' gender difference in IT skill and attitudes. *Journal of Computer Assisted Learning, 19*(4), 488-500.

Lee, C. S. (2001). Modeling the business value of information technology. *Information & Management, 39*(3), 191-210.

Lee, H., & Liebenau, J. (1996). In what way are information systems social systems? A critique from sociology. *Proceedings of the First UK Academy for Information Systems Conference.* Cranfield School of Management, Cranfield, Bedford.

Lee, J. (February 23, 2003). Critical mass: How protesters mobilized so many and so nimbly. *New York Times,* WK 3.

Lee, S., Moisa, N., & Weiss, M. (2003). *Open source as a signalling device: An economic analysis* (Discussion Paper No. 03-20). German Economic Association of Business Administration e. V. Retrieved from http://www.whu.edu/orga/geaba/Papers/2003/GEABA-DP03-20.pdf

Lefoe, G., Gunn, C., & Hedberg, J. (2002). Recommendations for teaching in a distributed learning environment: The students' perspective. *Australian Journal of Educational Technology, 18*(1), 40-56.

LeLoup, J. W., & Ponterio, R. (1998). Using WWW multimedia in the foreign language classroom: Is this for me? *Language Learning & Technology, 2*(1), 4-10. Retrieved from http://llt.msu.edu/vol2num1/Onthenet/

Leonard, J., Davis, J. E., & Sidler, J. L. (2005). Cultural relevance and computer-assisted instruction. *Journal of Research on Technology in Education, 37*(3), 263-284.

Leouski, A. V., & Croft, W. B. (1996). *An evaluation of techniques for clustering search results, Technical Report IR-76.*

Lerner, J., & Tirole, J. (2002). Some simple economics of open source. *Journal of Industrial Economics, 50*(2), 197-234. (The working paper from 2000 is available from http://www.people.hbs.edu/jlerner/simple.pdf)

Lessig, L. (1999). *Code and other laws of cyberspace.* Basic Books.

Lessig, L. (2002). *The future of ideas: The fate of the commons in a connected world.* New York: Vintage Books.

Lessig, L. (2004). *Free culture: How big media uses technology and the law to lock down culture and control creativity.* Penguin Books. Retrieved from http://www.free-culture.cc/

Lessig, L. (2005). Creatives face a closed net. *Financial Times.* Retrieved February 14, 2007, from http://www.ft.com/cms/s/d55dfe52-77d2-11da-9670-0000779e2340.html

Lester, C. Y., & Brown, M. (2004). Creating gender parity: An instruction aide's influence. *Journal of Educational Resources in Computing, 4*(1), 5.

Leuf, B., & Cunningham, W. (2001). *The Wiki way: Quick collaboration on the Web.* Addison Wesley Longman.

Levin, B. (2002). Cyberhate: A legal and historical analysis of extremists' use of computer networks in America. *American Behavioral Scientists, 45*(6), 958-988.

Lewicki, R. J., & Bunker, B. B. (1996). Developing and maintaining trust in work relationships. In R. Kramer & T. Tyler (Eds.), *Trust in organizations: Frontiers of theory and research,* (pp. 14-139). Thousand Oaks, CA: Sage.

Leyshon, A. (2001). Time-space (and digital) compression: Software formats, musical networks, and the reorganisation of the music industry. *Environment and Planning A, 33*(1), 49-77.

Leyshon, A., Webb, P., French, S., Thrift, N., & Crewe, L. (2005). On the reproduction of the musical economy after the Internet. *Media, Culture & Society, 27*(2), 177-209.

Li, N., & Kirkup, G. (2007). Gender and cultural difference in Internet use: A study of China and the UK. *Computers & Education, 48,* 301-317.

Lieberman, H. (1995). Letizia: An agent that assists Web browsing. *In Proceedings of the IJCAI* (pp. 924-929).

Light, J. (1999). From city space to cyberspace. In M. Crang, P. Crang, & J. May (Eds.), *Virtual geographies: Bodies, space and relations* (pp. 109-130). New York: Routledge.

Light, P., Littleton, K., Bale, S., Joiner, R., & Messer, D. (2000). Gender and social comparison effects in computer-based problem solving. *Learning and Instruction, 10*, 483-496.

Lightfoot, J. M. (2006). A comparative analysis of e-mail and face-to-face communication in an educational environment. *Internet and Higher Education, 9*, 217-227.

Lih, A. (2004). *Wikipedia as participatory journalism: Reliable sources? Metrics for evaluating collaborative media as a news resource.* Paper presented at the 5th International Symposium on Online Journalism, April 16-17, UT Austin.

Lim, D. 2004. Cross-cultural differences in online learning motivation. *Educational Media International, 41*(2), 163-175.

Lin, M. (2006). *Sharing knowledge and building community: A narrative of the formation, development, and sustainability of OOPS.* Unpublished dissertation, University of Houston, Houston, TX.

Lin, M., & Lee, M. (2006). E-learning localized: The case of the OOPS project. In A. Edmundson (Ed.), *Globalization in education: Improving education quality through cross-cultural dialogue* (pp. 168-186). Hershey, PA: Idea Group.

Ling, K., Beenen, G., Ludford, P., Wang, X., Chang, K., Li, X., Cosley, D., Frankowski, D., Rashid, L. T. A. M., Resnick, P., & Kraut, R. (2005). Using social psychology to motivate contributions to online communities. *Journal of Computer-Mediated Communication, 10*(4), 10.

Lio, E. D., Fraboni, L., & Leo, T. (2005). *TWiki-based facilitation in a newly formed academic community of practice.* Paper presented at the WikiSym 2005. Retrieved February 5, 2007, from http://www.wikisym. org/ws2005/proceedings/paper-09.pdf

Lipton, R. (2002). *Designing across cultures – How to create effective graphics for diverse ethnic groups.* Cincinnati, OH: F&W Publications.

Liu, M. (1993). The complexities of citation practice: A review of citation studies. *Journal of Documentation, 49*(4), 370–408.

Loch, K. D., Carr, H. H, & Wartentin, M. E. (1992). Threats to information systems: Today's reality, yesterday's understanding. *MIS Quarterly, 17*(2), 173-186.

Locke, L. F., Spirduso, W. W., & Silverman, S. J. (1992). Research proposals: Function and content. In R. D. Galliers (Ed.), *Information systems research: Issues methods and guidelines.* Oxford: Blackwell Scientific Publications.

Longford, G. (2005). Pedagogies of digital citizenship and the politics of code. *Techné: Research in Philosophy and Technology, 9*(1).

Looney, S. (2004). Civic participation and the Internet. *LBJ Journal of Public Affairs, 14*, 49-61.

Lopez, A. D., Mathers, C. D., Ezzati, M., Jamison, D. T., & Murray, C .J. L. (2006). Global and regional burden of disease and risk factors, 2001: Systematic analysis of population health data. *The Lancet, 367*(9524), 1747-1757.

Lorriman, J. (1997). *Continuing professional development: A practical approach.* London: IET.

Lu, L. T. (2006). The relationship between cultural distance and performance in international joint ventures: A critique and ideas for further research. *International Journal of Management, 23*(3), 436-446.

Lu, Y. H. (2005). Privacy and data privacy issues in contemporary China. *Ethics and Information Technology, 7*(1), 7-15.

Lucas, H. C. 1975. *Why information systems fail.* New York: Columbia University Press.

Ludvigsen, S. R. (2006, 10-12 April 2006). *Learning and the use of ICT in higher education. Expectations and results.* Paper presented at the 5th International Conference on Networked Learning, Lancaster.

Luhmann, N. (1984). *Social systems.* Stanford, CA: Stanford University Press.

Luhmann, N. (1990). *Essays on self-reference.* New York: Columbia University Press.

Luke, T. (2004). The co-existence of cyborgs, humachines, and environments in postmodernity: Getting over the end of nature. In S. Graham (Ed.), *Cybercities reader*. London: Routledge.

Lund, B., Hammond, T., Flack, M., & Hannay, T. (2005). Social bookmarking tools (II): A case study - Connotea. *D-Lib Magazine, 11*(4).

Lyon, P. (2004). Autopoiesis and knowing: Reflections on Maturana's biogenic explanation of cognition. *Cybernetics and Human Knowing, 11*(4), 21-46.

Macfadyen, L., Chase, M., Reeder, K., & Roche, J. (2003). *Matches and mismatches in intercultural learning: Designing and moderating an online intercultural course*. Paper presented at the UNESCO Conference on International and Intercultural Education, Jyvaskyla, Finland.

Macfayden, L. P. (2004). Internet mediated communication at the cultural interface. In C. Ghaoui (Ed.), *Encyclopedia of Human-Computer Interaction*. Hershey, PA: The Idea Group.

MacIntosh, J. (2003). Reworking professional nursing identity. *Western Journal of Nursing Research,, 25*(6), 725-741.

Mack, R. L. (2001). *The digital divide: Standing at the intersection of race & technology*. Durham, NC: Carolina Academic Press.

Maclean, C. (2005). Family violence court at Manukau is called both 'therapeutic and punitive.' *Auckland District Law Society Newsletter*.

Madden, A. D., Baptista Nunes, J. M., McPherson, M., Ford, N. J., & Miller D. (2007). Mind the gap! New 'literacies' create new divides. In L. Tomei, (Ed.), *Integrating information and communications technologies into the classroom*, (pp. 231-249). Hershey, PA: Idea Group.

Madden, M. (2004). *Artists, musicians and the Internet*: Pew Internet & American Life Project.

Maglio, P. P., Barrett, R., Campbell, C. S., & Selker, T. (2000). SUITOR: An attentive information system. *International ACM Conference on Intelligent User Interfaces (IUI)* (pp. 169-176).

Maier, P., & Warren, A. (2000). *Integr@ting technology in learning & teaching: A practical guide for educators*. London: Kogan Page.

Malinowski, B. (1922). *Argonauts of the western pacific: An account of native enterprise and adventure in the archipelagoes of melanesian new guinea*. London: Routledge & Kegan Paul.

Malone, T. W., Grant, K. R., Turbak, F. A., Brobst, S. A., & Cohen M. D. (1987). Intelligent information sharing systems. *Communications of the ACM, 30*(5), 390–402.

Malone, Z. (2005). Pushing girls toward science. *Edwardsville Intelligencer* (IL) (09/05/05). Retrieved January 29, 2007, from http://technews.acm.org/articles/2005-7/0907w.html#item4

Manion, M., & Evan, W. (2000). The Y2K problem and professional responsibility: A retrospective analysis. *Technology in Society, 22*(3), 361-387.

Manjul. T. (2005). *From women's media to rural media*. Retrieved June 24, 2007, from http://www.indiatogether.org/2005/jun/med-rurmedia.htm

Mann, C., & Stewart, F. (2000a). *Internet communication and qualitative research: A handbook for researching online*. Thousand Oaks, CA: Sage Publication.

Mannan, A. (2005). *Open and distance education in developing countries and globalisation: Facing the challenges*. Paper presented at the ICDE 2005 Conference, New Delhi, India. Retrieved June 29, 2006, from http://www.ignou.ac.in/ICDE2005/PDFs/theme1pdf/theme1_17.pdf

Mansfield, J. (2005). The global musical subject, curriculum and Heidegger's questioning concerning technology. *Educational Philosophy & Theory, 37*(1), 133-148.

Marcus, A., & Gould, E. W. (2001). *Cultural dimensions and global Web user-interface design: What? So what? Now what?* Retrieved August 26, 2006, from http://www.amanda.com

Marcuse, H. (2004). Social implications of technology. In D. M. Kaplan (Ed.), *Readings in the philosophy of technology* (pp. 63-87). New York: Rowman & Littlefield Publishers, Inc.

Margetts, H. (1999). *Information technology in government: Britain and America.* London: Routledge.

Marjanovic, O. (1999). Learning and teaching in a synchronous collaborative environment. *Journal of Computer Assisted Learning, 15,* 129-38. Retrieved July 12, 2007, from http://www-icdl.open.ac.uk/

Markoff, J. (2006). Entrepreneurs see a Web guided by common sense. *The New-York Times,* November 12, 2006.

Marks, W., & Dulaney, C. L. (1998). Visual information processing on the World Wide Web. In C. Forsythe, E. Grose, & J. Ratner (Eds.), *Human factors and Web development.* Mahwah, NJ: Lawrence Erlbaum.

Marontate, J. (2005). Digital recording and the reconfiguration of music as performance. *American Behavioral Scientist, 48*(11), 1422-1438.

Marshall, C. C., & Brush, A. J. B. (2004). Exploring the relationship between personal and public annotations. In *JCDL '04: Proceedings of the 4th ACM/IEEE-CS Joint Conference on Digital Librarie,* (pp. 349–357). New York, NY: ACM Press.

Marshall, C. C., (1999). Toward an ecology of hypertext annotation. In *HYPERTEXT '98: Proceedings of the 9th ACM conference on Hypertext and hypermedia* (pp. 40-49). New York, NY: ACM Press.

Martin, A. (2002). *Concepts of ICT literacy in higher education.* Retrieved 19 April, 2006, from http://www.citscapes.ac.uk/citscapes/products/backgroundreports/files/concepts_ict_HE.pdf

Martin, S. (2003). Working online - developing online support groups for stepfamilies. In *Australian Institute of Family Studies Conference.* Canberra.

Martinez-Torres, M. E., (2001). Civil society, the Internet, and the Zapatistas. *Peace Review, 13*(3), 347-355.

Mason, R. (1991). Moderating educational computer conferencing. *DEOSNEWS, 1*(19). Retrieved July 12, 2007, from http://www.emoderators.com/papers/mason.html

Mason, R. (2006). Holistic course design using learning objects. *IJLT, 2*(2/3), 203-215.

Mason, R. O. (1986). Four ethical issues of the Information Age. *MIS Quarterly,* 10(1), 4-12.

Mason, R., & Rennie, F. (2004). Broadband: A solution for rural e-learning? *International Review of Research in Open and Distance Learning, 5*(1). Retrieved April 04, 2007, from http://www.irrodl.org/index.php/irrodl/article/view/173/255

Mason, R., & Rennie, F. (2006). *eLearning: The key concepts.* London: Routledge.

Mathison, S. (2005). *Digital dividends for the poor.* ICT for Poverty Reduction in Asia. Global Knowledge Parternership.

Matsuhashi, A. (Ed.). (1987). *Writing in real time: Modelling production processes.* Norwood, NJ: Ablex Publishing Corporation.

Matsumoto, D. (1996). *Culture and psychology.* Pacific Grove, CA: Brooks/Cole Pub. Co.

Maturana, H. R. (1974). Coginitive strategies. In H. Von Foerster (Ed.), *Cybernetics of cybernetic*s (pp. 457-469). Urbana, IL: Biological Computer Library, University of Illinois.

Maturana, H. R. (1980). Introduction. In H. Maturana & F. Varela, *Autopoiesis and cognition: The realization of the living* (pp. xi-xxx). Dordrecht: D. Reidel.

Maturana, H. R. (1980). Man and society. In F. Benseler, P. M. Hejl, & W. K. Köck (Eds.), *Autopoiesis, communication and society* (pp. 11-31). Frankfurt: Campus Verlag.

Maturana, H. R. (1988). Reality: The search for objectivity or the quest for a compelling argument. *The Irish Journal of Psychology, 9*(1), 25-82.

Maturana, H. R. (1991). Science and daily life: The ontology of scientific explanations. In F. Steier (Ed.), *Research and reflexivity* (pp. 30-52). London: Sage.

Maturana, H. R., & Poerksen, B. (2004). Varieties of objectivity. *Cybernetics and Human Knowing, 11*(4), 63-71.

Maturana, H. R., & Varela, F. J. (1980). *Autopoiesis and cognition: The realization of the living.* Dordrecht: D. Reidel.

Maturana, H. R., & Varela, F. J. (1992). *The tree of knowledge* (rev. ed). Boston: Shambhala.

Maturana, H. R., & Zöller, G. V. (in press). *The origin of humanness in the biology of love* (P. Bunnell, Ed.). Exeter: Imprint Academic.

Mayer, R., Davis, J., & Schoormann, F. D. (1995). An integrative model of organizational trust. *Academy of Management Review, 20,* 709-734.

Mayer-Smith, J., Pedretti, E., & Woodrow, J. (2000) Closing of the gender gap in technology enriched science education: A case study. *Computers & Education, 35,* 51-63.

Mayes, J. T. (2001). Quality in an e-University. *Assessment and Evaluation in Higher Education, 26*(5), 465-73.

Mayes, T. (2002). The technology of learning in a social world. In R. Harrison et al., (Eds.), *Supporting lifelong learning, vol. 1, Perspectives on learning.* London: Routledge Falmer.

Mayor, B., & Swann, J. (2002). The English language and "global" teaching. In M. Lea and K. Nicoll (Eds.), *Distributed learning: Social and cultural approaches to practice* (pp. 111-130). Londres: Routledge.

McAdam, D., McCarthy, J. D., & Zald, M. N. (1996). Introduction: Opportunities, mobilizing structures, and framing processes—toward a synthetic, comparative perspective on social movements. In McAdam, McCarthy, and Zald (Eds.) *Comparative perspectives on social movements* (1-20). New York: Cambridge University Press.

McAndrew, P., Clow, D., Taylor, J., & Aczel, J. (2004). The evolutionary design of a knowledge network to support knowledge management and sharing for lifelong learning. *British Journal of Educational Technology, 35*(6).

McBrien, K. (2005). *Developing localization friendly e-learning.* Retrieved July 20, 2006, from http://www.chinaonlineedu.com/yuanwen/special.asp?id=122

McCabe, M. (1992). Human factors aspects of user interface design. *Engineering Computing Newsletter,* SERC #38, 4-5.

McCarthy, J. D., & Zald, M. N. (1977). Resource mobilization and social movements: A partial theory. *American Journal of Sociology, 82*(May), 1212–1239.

McCaughey, M., & Ayers, M. D. (Eds.) (2003). *Cyberactivism: Online activism in theory and practice.* New York: Routledge.

McClimens, A. (2003). A bad idea, by definition: Defining Nursing risks pleasing no one. *Nursing Standard, 17*(35), 25(21).

McCourt, T. (2005). Collecting music in the digital realm. *Popular Music & Society, 28*(2), 249-252.

McCreary, E. (1990). Three behavioral models for computer mediated vommunications. In L. Harasim (Ed.), *Online education—Perspectives on a new environment.* New York, NY: Praeger Publishing.

McDowell, S. D. (1998). Regionalism and National Communications Policies: Canada and the United States in North American Telecommunications Governance. *Working Paper No. 9.* Retrieved December 1, 2006, from http://www.fis.utoronto.ca/research/iprp/publications/wp/wp9.html

McHenry, R. (2004). *The faith-based encyclopedia.* Retrieved February 10, 2005, from http://tcsdaily.com/article.aspx?id=111504A

McIlroy, D., Bunting, B., Tierney, K., & Gordon, M. (2001). The relation of gender and background experience to self-reported computing anxieties and cognitions. *Computers in Human Behaviour, 17,* 21-33.

McIntosh, J. (2000). Child inclusive divorce mediation: Report on a qualitative study. *Mediation Quarterly, 18*(1), 55-69.

McIsaac, M. S., & Gunawardera, C. N. (1996). Distance education. In D. H. Jonassen (Ed.), *Handbook of research for educational communications and technology* (pp. 403-437). New York: Simon & Schuster MacMillan.

McKenna, H. (2004, 12 May 2004). *Evidence based practice: Does profusion of evidence mean confusion in practice.* Paper presented at the RCN Congress 2004, Harrogate, UK.

McKenna, H., Cutcliffe, J., & McKenna, P. (2000). Evidence-based practice: Demolishing some myths. *Nursing Standard, 14*(16), 39-42.

McKenna, H., Thompson, D., Watson, R., & Norman, I. (2006). The good old days of nurse training: Rose-tinted or jaundiced view? (Editorial). *International Journal of Nursing Studies, 43*(2), 135-137.

McKierman, G. (2005). WikimediaWorlds Part I: Wikipedia. *Library Hi Tech News, 22*(8), 46-54.

McLoughlin, C. (1999). Culturally responsive technology use: Developing an online community of learners. *British Journal of Educational Technology, 30*(3), 231-243.

McLoughlin, C. (2006). Adapting e-learning across cultural boundaries: A framework for quality learning, pedagogy, and interaction. In A. Edmundston (Ed.), *Globalized e-learning cultural challenges* (pp. 223-238). Hershey, PA: Idea Group Inc.

McLoughlin, C., & Gower, G. (2000). *Indigenous learners on-line: A model for flexible learning in an innovative Web-based environment.* Paper presented at the Australian Indigenous Education Conference, Freemantle, Australia.

McLoughlin, C., & Oliver, R. (2000). Instructional design for cultural difference: A case study of the indigenous online learning in a tertiary context. *Australian Journal of Educational Technology, 16*(1), 58-72. Retrieved June 29, 2006, from http://www.ascilite.org.au/ajet/ajet16/mcloughlin.html

McMann, G. W. (1994). The changing role of moderation in computer mediated conferencing. In *Proceedings of the Distance Learning Research Conference*, San Antonio, TX, April 27-29 (pp. 159-166).

McMurdo, G. (1997). Cyberporn and communication decency. *Journal of Information Science, 23*(1), 81-90.

McPherson, M. A., & Nunes, J. M. (2002). Supporting educational management through action research. *International Journal of Educational Management, 16*, 300-308.

McPherson, M. A., & Nunes, J. M. (2004). *Developing innovation in online learning: An action research framework.* London: RoutledgeFalmer.

McPherson, M. A., Nunes, J. M., & Zafeiriou, G. (2003). New tutoring skills for online learning: Are e-tutors adequately prepared for e-learning delivery? In *Proceedings of EDEN 2003 The Quality Dialogue; Integrating Quality Cultures in Flexible, Distance and e-learning*, 15-18 June 2003, Rodos Palace Hotel, Rhodes, Greece, (pp. 347-350).

McSherry, R., Simmons, M., & Abbot, P. (2002). *Evidence-informed nursing: A guide for clinical nurses.* London: Routledge.

Meachin, K., & Webb, C. (1996). Training to do women's work in a man's world. *Nurse Education Today, 16*(3), 180-188.

Mechkour, M., Harper, D. J., & Muresan G., (1999). The Webcluster project: Using clustering for mediating access to the World Wide Web. In *Proceedings of the 21st International ACM SIGIR Conference on Research and development in Information Retrieval* (pp. 357-358), August 24-28, 1998.

Medawar, P. (1984). *The limits of science.* Oxford, Oxford University Press.

Meier, D. (1995). *The power of their ideas.* Boston, MA: Beacon Press.

Memmi, D., & Nérot, O. (2003). Building virtual communitites for information retrieval. In Favela & D. Decouchant (Eds), *GroupWare: Design, implementation and use.* Berlin: Springer.

Mercier, E. M., Baron, B., & O'Connor, K. M. (2006). Images of self and others as computer users: The role of gender and experience. *Journal of Computer Assisted Learning, 22*, 335-348.

Meredyth, D., & Ewing, S. (2003). Social capital and wired communities: A case study. In *Australian Insititute of Family Studies Conference*. Canberra.

Merges, R. P. (2004). *A new dynamism in the public domain* (Boalt Working Papers in Public Law No. 65). UC Berkeley, Boalt Hall. Retrieved from http://papers.ssrn.com/sol3/papers.cfm?abstract_id=558751

Midgley, M. (2003). *Myths we live by*. Routledge.

Milberg, S. J., Burke, S. J., Smith, H. J., & Kaliman, E. A. (1995). Values, personal information, privacy concerns, and regulatory approaches. *Communications of the ACM, 38*(12), 65-74.

Millen, D. R., Feinberg, J., & Kerr, B. (2006). Dogear: Social bookmarking in the enterprise. In *CHI '06: Proceedings of the SIGCHI Conference on Human Factors in Computing Systems* (pp. 111-120). New York, NY: ACM Press.

Miller, A. (1982). Computers and privacy. In W. M. Hoffman & J. M. Moore (Eds.), *Ethics and the management of computer technology*. Cambridge, MA: Oelgeschlager, Gunn, and Hain Publishers, Inc.

Miller, L. M., Schweingruber, H., & Brandenburg, C. L. (2001). Middle school students' technology practices and preferences: Re-examining gender differences. *Journal of Educational Multimedia and Hypermedia, 10*(2), 125-140.

Miller, M., & Lu, M. (2003). Serving non-traditional students in e-learning environments: Building successful communities in the virtual campus. *Education Media International, 40*(1-2), 163-9.

Milojicic, D. S., Kalogeraki, V., Lukose, R., Nagaraja, K., Pruyne, J., Richard, B., Rollins, S., & Xu., Z. (2002). *Peer-to-peer computing*. Technical Report HPL-2002-57, HP Lab.

Mishra, S. (1999). An empirical analysis of interactivity in teleconference. Indian *Journal of Open Learning, 8*(3), 243-253.

Mishra, S., & Sharma, R. C. (2004). Multimedia: Meeting the challenge of cultures and languages. *Distance Learning Link*. Retrieved September 28, 2004, from http://www.idea-group.com/downloads/pdf/DLL.pdf

Mishra, S., & Sharma, R. C. (2005). Development of e-learning in India. *University News, 43*(11), 9 – 15.

Mitechell, W. J. (2003). *The cyborg self and the networked city*. Cambridge, MA: MIT Press.

Mitnick, K. (2003). *The art of deception*. New York, NY: John Wiley & Sons.

Moloney, J., & Tello, S. (2003). Principles for building success in online education. *Syllabus*, February 2003, 17-18.

Montaner, M., Lopez, B., & Rosa, J. L. D. L. (2003). A taxonomy of recommender agents on the Internet. *Artificial Intelligence Review, 19*, 285-330.

Moore, M. G., Shattuck, K., & Al-Harthi, A. (2006). Cultures meeting cultures in online distance education. *Journal of e-Learning and Knowledge Society. The Italian e-Learning Association Journal, 1*(2), 187-208. Retrieved September 29, 2006, from http://www.je-lks.it/archive/02_05/Methodologies1.html

MORI Social Research Institute. (2005, 17 January 2005). *Understanding the audience: Research study conducted for the Common Information Environment (CIE) group*. Retrieved 3 February, 2005, from http://www.common-info.org.uk/audienceresearch.shtml

MORI. (2003). *Student nurses: The pressure of work*. Retrieved 6 June, 2006, from http://www.mori.com/polls/2003/rcn1.shtml

Morris, J. H., & Moberg, D. J. (1994). Work organizations as contexts for trust and betrayal. Pp. 163-187 In T. Sarbin, R. Carney, & C. Eoyang (Eds.), *Citizen espionage: Studies in trust and betrayal*. Westport, CT: Praeger.

Morris-Docker, S. B., Tod, A., Harrison, J. M., Wolstenholme, D., & Black, R. (2004). Nurses' use of the Internet in clinical ward settings. *Journal of Advanced Nursing, 48*(2), 157-166.

Morrison, D., & Collins, A. (1996). Epistemic fluency and constructivist learning environments. In B. Wilson

(Ed.), *Constructivist learning environments.* Englewood Cliffs, NJ: Educational Technology Press.

Morse, K. (2003). Does one size fit all? Exploring asynchronous learning in a multicultural environment. *JALN,* 7(1), 37-55. Retrieved July 28, 2006, from http://www. sloan-c.org/publications/jaln/v7n1/index.asp

Mosco, V. (1996). *The political economy of communication: Rethinking and renewal.* London; Thousand Oaks, CA: SAGE Publications.

Mosco, V. (2000). Webs of myth and power: Connectivity and the new computer technopolis. In A. Herman & T. Swiss (Eds.), *The world wide web and contemporary cultural theory* (pp. 37-60). New York: Routledge.

Mossberger, K., Tolbert, C., & Stansbury, M. (2003). *Virtual inequality: Beyond the digital divide.* Washington, D.C.: Georgetown University Press.

Moule, P. (2003). ICT: A social justice approach to exploring user issues? *Nurse Education Today, 23*(7), 530-536.

Mukhopadhyay, T., Vicinanza, S. S., & Prietula, M. J. (1992). Examining the feasibility of a case-based reasoning model for software and effort estimation. *MIS Quarterly, 16*(2), 155-171.

Mulholland, P., Collins, T., & Zdrahal, Z. (2005). Bletchley Park text: Using mobile and semantic Web technologies to support the post-visit use of online museum resources. *Journal of Interactive Media in Education, 24.* Retrieved December 27, 2006, from http://jime.open. ac.uk/2005/24/mulholland-2005-24.html

Mumford, E. (1995). *Effective systems design and requirement analysis: The ETHICS approach.* Basingstoke, UK: Macmillan Press.

Mumford, E. (1996). *Systems design ethical tools for ethical change.* Macmillan.

Murphy, K. L, Drabier, R., & Epps, M. L. (1998). A constructivist look at interaction and collaboration via computer conferencing. *International Journal of Educational Telecommunications 4,* 237-261.

Musk, A. (2004). Proficiency with technology and the expression of caring: Can we reconcile these polarised views? *International Journal for Human Caring, 8*(2), 13-20.

Musselbrook, K., McAteer, E., Crook, C., McCloud, H., & Tholmy, A. (2000). Learning networks and communication skills. *Association for Learning Technology Journal, 8,* 71-80.

Mwanza, D. (2002). *Towards an activity-oriented design method for HCI research and practice.* PhD Thesis. The Open University, UK.

Mwesige, P. G. (2004). Cyber elites: A survey of Internet café users in Uganda. *Telematics and Informatics, 21,* 83–101.

Nadeem, M. F., Ramin, T., & Jitka, S. (2006) E-mails in the workplace: The electronic equivalent of 'DNA' evidence. *The Journal of American Academy of Business, 8*(2), 71-78.

Nakanishi, H., Isbister, K., Ishida, T., & Nass, C. (2004). Designing a social agent for a virtual meeting space. In R. Trappl & S. Payr (Eds.), *Agent culture: Designing virtual characters for a multi-cultural world* (pp. 245-266). Hillsdale, NJ: Lawrence Erlbaum Associates.

Nardi, B. A., Schiano, D. J., & Gumbrecht, M. (2004). Blogging as social activity, or would you let 900 million people read your diary? *Proceedings of the 2004 ACM conference on Computer Supported Cooperative Work,* 222-231.

Nardi, B., Whittaker, S., & Schwarz, H. (2002). NetWORKers and their activity in intensional networks. *Computer Supported Cooperative Work 11,* 205–242.

National Institute of Standards and Technology. (2001). *Risk management guide for information technology systems.* Special Publication 800-30. Washington DC: GPO.

Negus, K. (1992). *Producing pop: Culture and conflict in the popular music industry.* London; New York: E. Arnold.

Negus, K. (1995). Where the mystical meets the market: Creativity and commerce in the production of popular music. *Sociological Review, 43*(2), 316-341.

Nehru, J.. (1946). *The discovery of India* (Calcutta: The Signet Press). (Reprint. New Delhi, Oxford University Press), 2003.

Networked Learning Conference Proceedings. (2002, 2004, 2006). Retrieved from http://www.networkedlearningconference.org.uk

Neustadt, R. E., & Fineberg, H. (1983). *The epidemic that never was: Policy-Making and the swine flu scare.* New York: Vintage Books.

Neuwirth, C., Kaufer, D., Chimera, R., & Gillespie, T. (1987). *The notes program: A hypertext application for writing from source texts.* Paper presented at Hypertext '87, Chapel Hill, NC.

Nevárez, J. (2005). *Culture and empire in the global city: Urban development initiaves and the transformation of Harlem.* Retrieved November 13, 2007, from http://orsp.kean.edu/communications/documents/Denis%20Klein

Newell, P. B. (1998). Across-cultural comparison of privacy definitions and functions: A systems approach. *Journal of Environmental Psychology. 18*, 367-371.

NHS Connecting for Health. (2005). *Health informatics programme basic IT skills programme (ECDL) NHS survey results.* London: Department of Health.

NHS Employers. (2005, 14 December 2005). *What is agenda for change?* Retrieved 14 August, 2006, from http://www.nhsemployers.org/pay-conditions/pay-conditions-199.cfm

NHS Information Authority. (2002). *Learning to manage health information - A theme for clinical education: Moving ahead.* Birmingham: NHS Information Authority.

NHS Information Authority. (2004). *Health informatics education and development for clinical professionals: Making progress?* Wigan: NHS Information Authority.

NHS Wales. (2004). *Basic information technology skills standard for NHS Wales - http://www.wales.nhs.uk/ecdl. Implementing the European Computer Driving Licence (ECDL®) Nurses, Midwives and Health Visitors.* Retrieved 2 July 2005, 2005, from http://www.wales.nhs.uk/ecdl

NHS Wales. (2005). *Informing healthcare projects: Access to knowledge (A2K).* Retrieved 7 July, 2005, from http://www.wales.nhs.uk/ihc/informing_healthcare_project.cfm?project=a2k

Nielsen, J. (1993). *Usability engineering.* San Diego, CA: Morgan Kaufman.

Nissenbaum, H. (1998). Protecting privacy in an Information Age. *Law and Philosophy, 17*, 559-596.

Noack, D. (1999). *Nearly a third of firms monitor works online.* Retrieved from http://www.apbnews.com/safetycenter/business/1999/11/11/vaultsurvey1111_01.html

Noguera, P. A. (2003). *City schools and the American dream.* New York, NY: Teachers College Press.

Nord, G. D., McCubbins, T,. & Nord, J. H. (2006). E-monitoring in the workplace; privacy, legislation, and surveillance software. *Communications of the ACM, 49*(8), 72-77.

Norman, D. (1999). *The invisible computer: Why good products can fail, the personal computer is so complex, and information appliances are the solution.* Cambridge, MA: MIT Press.

Norman, D. A. (1988). *The design of everyday things.* New York: Basic Books.

Norman, D. A. (1993). *Things that make us smart.* Reading, MA: Addison-Wesley.

Norman, G. (2002). Research in medical education: Three decades of progress. *British Medical Journal, 324*, 1560-1562.

Norris, P. (2001). *Digital divide: Civic engagement, information poverty, and the Internet worldwide.* New York, NY: Cambridge University Press.

North, A. S., & Noyes, J. M. (2002). Gender influences on children's computer attitudes and cognitions. *Computers in Human Behaviour, 18*, 135-150.

Northouse, P. G. (2003). *Leadership: Theory and practice.* Sage Publications Ltd.

Nulens, G. (Ed.) (2001). *The digital divide in developing countries: Towards an information society in Africa.* Brussels: VUB Brussels University Press.

Nunes, J. M. (1999). *The experiential dual layer model (EDLM): A conceptual model integrating a constructivist theoretical approach to academic learning with the process of hypermedia design.* Sheffield: PhD Thesis, University of Sheffield, Department of Information Studies.

Nunes, J. M. (2003). Constructivism vs. objectivism: Where is the difference for designers of e-learning environments. In Keynote Address to the *E-Learning: Principles and Practice Research Seminar*, 22nd April 2003. Lismullin, co. Meath, Ireland.

Nunes, J. M., McPherson, M. A., & Rico, M. (2000). Instructional design of a networked learning skills module for Web-based collaborative distance learning. In *Proceedings of the European Conference on Web-Based Learning Environments (WBLE 2000)*, 2000, Faculty of Engineering, University of Porto, Portugal, June 5-6th 2000, (pp.95-103).

Nunes, J. M.; McPherson, M., & Rico, M. (2000). Design and development of a networked learning skills module for Web-based collaborative distance learning. In *Proceedings of 1st ODL International Workshop*, 2000, Universidad Politécnica de Valencia, Centro de Formación de Postgrado, Valencia, Spain, 19-21 July 2000, (pp, 117-131).

Nursing and Midwifery Council. (2004). *Standards of proficiency for preregistration nursing education.* Retrieved 11 August, 2006, from http://www.nmc-uk.org

Nye, D. (1994). *American technological sublime.* Cambridge, MA: MIT Press.

Nye, D. (1997). *Narratives and spaces: Technology and the construction of American culture.* UK: University of Exeter Press.

Nye, D. (2006). *Technology matters: Questions to live with.* Cambridge, MA: MIT Press.

O'Hara, K., & Brown, B. (2006). *Consuming music together: Social and collaborative aspects of music consumption technologies* (K. O'Hara & B. Brown, Trans.). Dordrecht: Springer.

O'Neil, D. (2002). Assessing community informatics: A review of methodological approaches for evaluating community networks and community technology centres. *Internet Research, 12*(1), 76-102.

O'Neill, R., & Colley, A. (2006). Gender and status effects in student e-mails to staff. *Journal of Computer Assisted Learning, 22*, 360-367.

O'Rourke, M. (2005). Data secured? Taking on cyberthievery. *Risk Management*, Oct.

Oblinger, D., Barone, C., & Hawkins, B. (2001). *Distributed education and its challenges: An overview.* Washington, D.C.: American Council on Education. Retrieved November 10, 2006, from http://www.acenet. edu/bookstore/pdf/distributed-learning/distributed-learning-01.pdf

Odasz, F. (n.d.) *Realizing cultural sovereignty through Internet applications.* Retrieved October 14, 2004, from http://lone-eagles.com/sovereignty.htm

Office for National Statistics. (2001). *Omnibus survey.* Retrieved 30 November, 2006, from http://www.statistics. gov.uk/StatBase/Expodata/Spreadsheets/D5200.xls

Office of Management and Budget. (1997). *Progress on Year 2000 conversion.* Washington, DC: GPO. November 15.

Office of Management and Budget. (1998). *Progress on Year 2000 conversion.* Washington, DC: GPO. May 15.

Office of Management and Budget. (1998). *Progress on Year 2000 conversion.* Washington, DC: GPO. August 15.

Office of Management and Budget. (1999). *Progress on year 2000 conversion*. Washington, DC: GPO. December 14.

Ogawa, S., & Piller, F. T. (2006). Collective customer commitment: Reducing the risks of new product development. *MIT Sloan Management Review, 47*(2), 65–72. Retrieved from http://sloanreview.mit.edu/smr/issue/2006/winter/14/

Ogburn, W. F. (1966). *Social change with respect to cultural and original nature*. New York: Dell.

Okin, J. R. (2005). *The Internet revolution: The not-for-dummies guide to the history, technology, and use of the Internet*. Winter Harbor, ME: Ironbound Press.

Olaniran, B. (2006). Challenges to implementing e-learning in lesser-developed countries. In A. Edmundston (Ed.), *Globalized e-learning cultural challenges* (pp. 18-34). Hershey, PA: Idea Group Inc.

Olaniran, B. A. (2004). Computer-mediated communication in cross-cultural virtual groups. In G. M. Chen & W. J. Starosta (Eds.), *Dialogue among diversities* (pp. 142-166). Washington, DC: National Communication Association.

Oliver, P. E., & Johnston, H. (2000). What a good idea! Frames and ideologies in social movement research. Mobilization: An international journal. 5(1), 37-54.

Oliver, P. E., & Maney, G. M. (2000). Political processes and local newspaper coverage of protest events: From selection bias to triadic interactions. *American Journal of Sociology, 106*(2), 463-505.

Olsen, D. R. J., Taufer, T., & Fails, J. A. (2004). ScreenCrayons: Annotating anything. In *UIST '04: Proceedings of the 17th Annual ACM symposium on User Interface Software and Technology* (pp. 165-174). New York, NY: ACM Press.

Olutimayin, J. (2002). Adopting modern information technology in the South Pacific: A process of development, preservation, or underdevelopment of the culture? *The Electronic Journal of Information Systems in Developing Countries, 9*(3), 1-12.

OMB. (2006). *Report to Congress on Federal Government Information Security Reform*. Office of Management and Budget.

Omnibus Crime Control and Safe Streets Act of 1968 42 U.S.C. § 3789D

Omotayo, B. O. (2006). A survey of Internet access and usage among undergraduates in an African university. *The International Information & Library Review, 38*, 215–224.

Ong, C., & Lai, J. (2006). Gender differences in perceptions and relationships among dominants of e-learning acceptance. *Computers in Human Behavior, 22*, 816-829.

Onibere, E. A., Morgan, S., Busang, E. M., & Mpoeleng, D. (2000). Human computer interface design issues for a multicultural multilingual English speaking country - Botswana. *The Inderdisciplinary Journal of Human-Computer Interaction, 4*(13), 497-512.

Ono, H., & Zavodny, M. (2003). Gender and the Internet. *Social Science Quarterly, 84*(1), 111-121.

Orlikowski, W. J., & Baroudi, J. J. (1991). Studying information technology in organizations. *Information Systems Research, 2*(1), 1-28.

Orlowski, A. (2005). Wikipedia founder admits to serious quality problems [Electronic Version]. *The Register*. Retrieved February 10, 2006 from http://www.theregister.co.uk/2005/10/18/wikipedia_quality_problem/

Ory, J. O., Bullock, C., & Burnaska, K. (1997). Gender similarity in the use of and attitudes about ALN in a university setting. *JALN, 1*(1), 39-51.

Osterloh, M., Rota, S., & Kuster, B. (2002). *Open source software production: Climbing on the shoulders of giants* (Working Paper). The University of Zurich. Retrieved from http://opensource.mit.edu/papers/osterlohrotakuster.pdf

Osterweigel, A., Littleton, K., & Light, P. (2004). Understanding computer-related attitudes through an idiographic analysis of gender- and self-representations. *Learning and Instruction, 14*, 215-233.

Oudshoorn, N., Pinch, T. J., & Books24x7 Inc. (2005). *How users matter: The co-construction of users and technology.* 1st MIT press paperback. From http://www.lib.sfu.ca/cgi-bin/validate/books24x7.cgi?bookid=12347

Oxley, J. E. & Yeung, B. (2001). E-commerce readiness: Institutional environment and international competitiveness. *Journal of International Business Studies, 32*(4), 705-723.

Oxman, A. D., Thomson, M. A. Davis, D. A., & Haynes, R. B. (1995). No magic bullets: A systematic review of 102 trials of intervention to improve professional practice. *Canadian Medical Association Journal, 153*, 1423-1431.

Pacific Enterprise Development Facility, & International Finance Corporation. (2003). *SME Business Survey, Country Report - Samoa. Summary of Findings.*

Pacific Enterprise Development Facility, & International Finance Corporation. (2003). *SME Business Survey. Pacific Region. Summary of Findings and Country Reports.*

Packer, G. (March 9, 2003). Smart-mobbing the war. Eli Pariser and other young antiwar organizers are the first to be using wired technologies as weapons. *New York Times Magazine.* Section 6, p. 46.

Palaiologou, N. (2006). Intercultural dimensions in the information society: Reflections on designing and developing culturally-oriented learning. In A. Edmundston (Ed.), *Globalized e-learning cultural challenges* (pp. 74-88). Hershey, PA: Idea Group Inc.

Palloff, R. M., & Pratt, K. (1999). *Building learning communities in cyberspace: Effective strategies for the online classroom.* San Francisco: Jossey-Bass Inc.

Palloff, R., & Pratt, K. (2005). *Collaborating online: Learning together in community.* San Francisco, CA: Jossey-Bass.

Panagariya, A. (2000). E-commerce, WTO and developing countries. *The World Economy, 23*(8), 959-978.

Paoletti, J. (1997). The gendering of infants' and toddlers' clothing in America. In K. Martinez & K. Ames (Eds.), *The material culture of gender/the gender of material culture.* Wilmington, DE: Henry Francis du Pont Winterhur Museum.

Papastergiou, M., & Solomonidou, C. (2005). Gender issues in Internet access and favourite Internet activities among Greek high school pupils inside and outside school. *Computers & Education, 44*, 377–393.

Paquette, G. (2002). *Modélisation des connaissances et des compétences.* Sainte-Foy (Québec): Presses de l'Université du Québec.

Paquette, G. (2003). *Instructional engineering in networked environments.* San Francisco: Pfeiffer/Wiley Publishing Co.

Parasuraman, S., & Igbaria, M. (1990). An examination of gender differences in the determinants of computer anxiety and attitudes toward microcomputers among managers. *Internal J. Man-Machine Stud., 2*(3), 327-340.

Parayil, G. (Ed.) (2006). *Political economy and information capitalism in India: Digital divide, development and equity.* New York, NY: Palgrave Macmillan.

Parenti, C. (2003). *The soft cage: Surveillance in America from slavery to the war on terror.* New York, NY: Basic Books.

Parsons T. (1951). *The social system.* Glencoe, IL: The Free Press.

Parvez, Z., & Ahmed, P. (2006). Towards building an integrated perspective on e-democracy. *Information, Communication & Society, 9*(5), 612-632.

Passig, D., & Levin, H. (1999). Gender interest difficulties with multimedia learning interfaces. *Computers in Human Behaviour, 15*, 173-183.

Pateman, B., & Jinks, A. M. (1999). Stories or snapshots? A study directed at comparing qualitative and quantitative approaches to curriculum evaluation. *Nurse Education Today, 19*, 62-70.

Paulos, E., & Jenkins, T. (2005). *Urban probes: Encountering our emerging urban atmospheres.* Retrieved

December 5, 2006, from http://berkeley.intelresearch.net/Paulos/Pubs/Papers/Urban%Probes%20(CHI%202005).pdf

Paulsen, M. F. (1995). Moderating educational computer conferences. In Z. L. Berge & M. P. Collins (Eds.), *Computer mediated communication and the online classroom in distance education* (pp. 81-90). Cresskill, NJ, Hampton Press.

Paulsen, M. F. (n.d.). *An international analysis of Web-based education*. Bekkestua, Norway: NKI Fjernunder-visning. Retrieved November 10, 2006, from http://www.nettskolen.com/pub/artikkel.xsql?artid=131

Payne, P. (2002). *Long-distance Mom*. Paper presented at the AFCC Conference: New Horizons for Families, Courts and Communities.

Pazzani, M. (1999). A framework for collaborative, content-based and demographic filtering. *Artificial Intelligence Review, 13*(5-6), 393-408.

Pazzani, M., Muramatsu, J. and Billsus, D., (1996). Syskill & Webert: Identifying interesting Web sites. In *Proceedings of the Thirteenth National Conference on Artificial Intelligence* (pp. 54-61).

Pea, R. D. (1996). Practices of distributed intelligence and designs for education. In G. Salomon (Ed.), *Distributed cognitions: Psychological and educational considerations* (pp. 47-87). New York: Cambridge University Press.

Pejtersen, A. M., & Fidel, R. (1999). *A framework for centred evaluation and design: a case study of information retrieval on the Web*. Working paper for mira workshop, Grenoble, France. Retrieved January 10, 2007, from http://www.dcs.gla.ac.uk/mira/workshops/nancy/amprf.html

Pemberton, D., Rodden, T., & Procter, R. (2000). GroupMark: A WWW recommander system combining coopérative and information filtering. In *Proceedings of the 6th ERCIM Workshop "User Interfaces for All"*.

Perrons, D. (2004). *Globalization and social change: People and places in a divided world*. New York, NY: Routledge.

Perrow, C. (1999). *Normal accidents: Living with high-risk technologies*. Princeton: Princeton University Press.

Pervan, G. P., & Klass, D. J. (1992). The use and misuse of statistical methods in information systems research. In R. Galliers (Ed.), *Information systems research: Issues, methods and practical guidelines*. Oxford: Blackwell Scientific Publications.

Petitot, J., Varela, F., Pachoud, B., & Roy, J. M. (Eds.). (1999). *Naturalizing phenomenology: Contemporary issues in phenomenology and cognitive science*, Stanford: Stanford University Press.

Petrie, S. J. (1997). Indecent proposals: How each branch of the federal government overstepped its institutional authority in the development of Internet obscenity law. *Stanford Law Review, 49*(3), 637-665.

Pettigrew, M., & Elliott, D. (1999). *Student IT skills*. Aldershot: Gower.

Pfeil, U., Zaphiris, P., & Ang, C. S. (2006). Cultural differences in collaborative authoring of Wikipedia. *Journal of Computer-Mediated Communication, 12*(1), article 5. Retrieved February 7, 2007, from http://jcmc.indiana.edu/vol12/issue1/pfeil.html

Pidgeon, J. (2003). *Family pathways - Towards an integrated family law system in Australia*. Paper presented at the Children's Issues Centre's Fifth Child and Family Policy Conference: Joined Up Services; Linking Together for Children and Families, Dunedin.

Pincas, A. (2000). New literacies and future educational culture. *Association for Learning Technology Journal, 8*, 69-79.

Pincas, A. (2001). Culture, cognition and communication in global education. *Distance Education, 22*(1), 30-51.

Pinch, T. J., & Bijsterveld, K. (2003). Should one applaud? *Technology & Culture, 44*(3), 536.

Pinch, T. J., & Trocco, F. (2002). *Analog days: The invention and impact of the Moog synthesizer*. Cambridge, MA: Harvard University Press.

Pinch, T., & Bijsterveld, K. (2004). Sound studies: New technologies and music. *Social Studies of Science (Sage), 34*(5), 635-648.

Pink, S. (2001). *Doing visual ethnography*. London: Sage.

Pink, S. (2006). *The future of visual anthropology: Engaging the senses*. London: Routledge.

Pitt, L. F., Watson, R. T., & Kavan, C. B. (1995). Service quality: A measure of information systems effectiveness. *MIS Quarterly, 19*(2), 173-188.

Pivec, M., & Baumann, K. (2004). The role of adaptation and personalisation in classroom-based learning and in e-learning. *Special Issue of J.UCS, Human Issues in Implementing eLearning Technology, 10*(1), 73-89. Retrieved January 29, 2007, from http://www.jucs.org/jucs_10_1/

Polanyi, M. (1958, 1998). *Personal knowledge. Towards a post critical philosophy*. London: Routledge.

Polanyi, M. (1967). *The tacit dimension*, New York: Anchor Books.

Porta, D. D., & Diani, M. (1999). *Social movements: An introduction*. Malden, MA: Blackwell.

Porter, M. (1998). Clusters and the new economics of competition. *Harvard Business Review, 76*(6), 77-91.

Poster, M. (1997). Cyberdemocracy: Internet in the public sphere. In D. Porter (Ed.), *Internet culture*. New York: Routledge.

Postmes, T., & Brunsting, S. (2002). Collective action in the age of the Internet: Mass communication and online mobilization. *Social Science Computer Review, 20*(3), 290-301.

Powell, G. C. (1997). On being culturally sensitive instructional designer and educator. *Educational Technology, 37*(2), 6-14.

Power, M. (2004). *The risk management of everything*. London: Demos.

Preece, J. (2002). Supporting community and building social capital. *Communications of the ACM, 45*(4), 37-9.

Prekop, P. (2002). A qualitative study of collaborative information seeking. *Journal of Documentation, 58*(5), 533–547.

Prensky, M. (2001). Digital natives, digital immigrants. *On the Horizon, 9*(5).

President's Council on Year 2000 Conversion. (2000). *The journey to Y2K: Final report*. Retrieved October 2004, from http://www.y2k.gov/docs/lastrep3.htm

Price, L. (2006). Gender differences and similarities in online course: Challenging stereotypical views of women. *Journal of Computer Assisted Learning, 22*, 349-359.

Price, M. N., Schilit, B. N., & Golovchinsky, G., (1999). Xlibris: The active reading machine. In *CHI'98 Conference Summary on Human Factors in Computing Systems* (pp. 22-23). ACM Press.

Priddat, B. P. (2006). *Open Source als Produktion von Transformationsgütern*. In B. Lutterbeck, Bärwolff, M., & Gehring, R. A. (Eds.), *Open source jahrbuch 2006. Zwischen softwareentwicklung und gesellschaftsmodell* (pp. 109–121). Berlin: Lehmanns Media. Retrieved from http://www.opensourcejahrbuch.de

Pringle, (2000). Foreword. In Wakley, Chambers, & Field (Eds.), *Continuing professional development in primary care: Making it happen*, (p.v.).

Prior, J., & Rodgers, B. (2001). *Children in changing families: Life after parental separation*. Oxford: Blackwell.

Pruitt-Mentle, D. (2003). *Cultural dimensions of multimedia: Design for instruction*. Presentation made at NECC conference, Seattle. Retrieved from http://edtechoutreach.umd.edu/Presentations/NECC2003/2003_presentation_v2.ppt

Purcell, F. (1999). *E-commerce adoption and SMEs in developing countries of the Pacific. An exploratory study of SMEs in Samoa*. Unpublished exploratory case study, Victoria University of Wellington, Wellington.

Purcell, F., & Toland, J. (2002). *Information & communications technology in the South Pacific: Shrinking the barriers of distance.* Foundation for Development Cooperation.

Purcell, F., & Toland, J. (2004). Electronic commerce for the South Pacific: A review of e-readiness. *Electronic Commerce Research, 4*, 241-262.

Putnam, R. D. (2000). *Bowling alone: The collapse and revival of American community.* New York: Simon & Schuster.

Quality Assurance Agency. (2001). *Subject benchmark statements: Healthcare programmes - Nursing.* Retrieved 2 July, 2005, from http://www.qaa.ac.uk/academicinfrastructure/benchmark/health/nursing.pdf

Quiggin, J. (2005). The Y2K scare: Causes, costs and cures. *Australian Journal of Public Administration, 64*(3), 46-55.

Quigley, K. (2004). The Emperor's new computers: Y2K (re)visited. *Public Administration, 82*, 4.

Quigley, K. F. (2005). Bug reactions: Considering US government and UK government Y2K operations in light of media coverage and public opinion. *Health, Risk & Society, 7*(3), 267-291.

Rachels, J. (1995). Why privacy is important. In D. G. Johnson & H. Nissenbaum (Eds.), *Computers, ethics, and social values* (pp. 351-357). Englewood Cliffs, NJ: Prentice Hall.

Rackow, S. H. (2002). How the USA Patriot Act will permit governmental infringement upon the privacy of Americans in the name of intelligence investigations. *University of Pennsylvania Law Review, 150*(5), 1651-1696.

Rahman, H. (Ed.) (2006). *Enpowering marginal communities with information networking.* Hershey, PA: Idea Group Publishing.

Rai, A., Lang, S. S., & Welker, R. B. (2002). Assessing the validity of IS success models: An empirical test and theoretical analysis. *Information Systems Research, 13*(1), 50-69.

Rai, A., Patnayakuni, R., & Patnayakuni, N. (1997). Technology investment and business performance. *Association for Computer Machinery. Communications of the ACM, 40*(7), 89-97.

Ramsay, R., Pitts, J., While, R., Attwood, M., Wood, V. & Curtis, A. (2003). Factors that helped and hindered undertaking practice professional development plans and personal development plans. *Education for Primary Care, 14*, 166-177.

Ramsden, P. (1992) *Learning to teach in Higher Education.* London: Routledge.

Rasmussen, J., Anderson, H. B., & Bernsen, N. O. (Eds.). (1991). *Human-computer interaction.* Hillsdale, NJ: Lawrence Erlbaum.

Ray, C. M., Sormunen, C., & Harris, T. M. (1999). Men's and women's attitudes towards computer technology: A comparison. *Office Systems Research Journal, 17*(1), 1-8.

Raymond, E. S. (2000). *The cathedral and the bazaar.* Retrieved March 10, 2007, from http://www.catb.org/~esr/writings/cathedral-bazaar/cathedral-bazaar/

Raymond, E. S. (2001). *The cathedral and the bazaar: Musings on Linux and open source by an accidental revolutionary.* Cambridge, MA: O'Reilly.

Raymond, E. S. (1999). The revenge of the hackers. In C. DiBona, S. Ockman, & M. Stone (Eds.), *Open sources: Voices from the open source revolution.* London: O'Reilly. Retrieved from http://www.oreilly.de/catalog/opensources/book/raymond2.html

Raymond, L. (1987). Validating and applying user satisfaction as a measure of MIS success in small organizations. *Information & Management, 12*, 173-179.

Reddy, K. (1993). The conduit metaphor: A case of frame conflict in our language about language. In A. Ortony (Ed.), *Foundations of communication theory* (2nd ed.), (pp. 164-201). New York: Harper & Row.

Rees, J., Bandyopadhyay, S., & Spafford, E. (2003). PFIRES: A policy framework for information security. *Communications of the ACM, 46*(7), 101-106.

Reeves, T. C. (1997). An evaluator looks at cultural diversity. *Educational Technology, 37*(2), 27-31.

Reid, R. C., & Pascalev, M. (2002). Strategic and ethical issues in outsourcing information technology. In A. Salehnia (Ed.), *Ethical issues of information systems* (pp. 232-248). Hershey, PA: IRM Press.

Reiffenstein, T. (2006). Codification, patents and the geography of knowledge transfer in the electronic musical instrument industry. *Canadian Geographer, 50*(3), 298-318.

Reiser, R., & Dempsy, J. (Eds). (2001). *Trends and issues in instruction design and technology.* Englewood Cliffs, NJ: Prentice Hall.

Rennie, F. (2003). The use of flexible learning resources for geographically distributed rural students. *Distance Education, 24*(1), 25-39.

Rennie, F. W. (2000). The importance of the University of the Highlands and Islands Project in regional development in NW Scotland. In J. G. Allansson & I. R. Edvardsson (Eds.), *Community viability, rapid change, and socioecological futures.* Akureyri: University of Akureyri and the Stefansson Arctic Institute.

Rennie, F., & Mason, R. (2004). *The connecticon: Learning for the connected generation.* Greenwich, CT: Information Age Publishing.

Reno, Attorney General of the United States et al. v. American Civil Liberties Union et al., 96 U.S. 511. (1997).

Reuters (2007). Publisher launches it's first "wiki" novel. *Yahoo News.* Retrieved February 5, 2007, from http://news.yahoo.com/s/nm/20070201/tc_nm/penguin_wiki_dc_4

Rheingold, H. (2000). *The virtual community: Homesteading on the electronic frontier.* Cambridge, MA: MIT Press.

Rheingold, H. (2000). *Tools for thought: The history and future of mind-expanding technology.* Cambridge, MA: MIT Press.

Richards, R. (2006). Users, interactivity and generation. *New Media & Society, 8*(4), 531-550.

Rieff, D. (2002). *A bed for the night, humanitarianism in crisis.* Vintage.

Roberts, G., K., & Steadman, P. (1999). *American cities and technology: Wilderness to wired city.* London: Routledge.

Robertson, R. (2001). *Comments on the "global triad" and "glocalization."* Retrieved October 31, 2006, from http://www2.kokugakuin.ac.jp/ijcc/wp/global/15robertson.html

Robins, K., & Webster, F. (1999). *Times of technoculture.* NY: Worth Publishers.

Robinson, R. (2000). *The debt: What America owes to Blacks.* New York: Dutton.

Rocchio, J. J. (1971). Relevance feedback in information retrieval. In G. Salton (Ed.), *The SMART retrieval system - Experiments in automatic document processing* (pp. 313-323). Englewood Cliffs, NJ: Prentice Hall, Inc.

Rochlin, G. (1997). *Trapped inside the net: The unanticipated consequences of computerization.* Princeton: Princeton University Press.

Rodan, G. (1998). The Internet and political control in Singapore. *Political Science Quarterly, 113*(1), 63-89.

Rogers, J. (2004). *Adults learning*: Oxford University Press.

Rogers, P. C., Graham, C. R., & Mayes, C. T. (2006). *Cultural competence and instructional design: Exploration research into the delivery of online instruction cross-culturally.* Paper presented at the 4th International Conference on Cultural Attitudes towards Technology and Communication, Tartu, Estonia.

Rogoff, B. (1990). *Apprenticeship in thinking: Cognitive development in social context.* New York, NY: Oxford University Press.

Romer, P. M. (1990). Endogenous technological change. *Journal of Political Economy, 98*(5), 71–102.

Ronfeldt, D., & Arquilla, J. (Eds.). (2001). *Networks and netwars: The future of terror, crime, and militancy.* Santa Monica, CA: RAND.

Rosch, E. (1981). *Prototype classification and logical classification: The two systems.* In E. Scholnick (Ed.), *New trends in conceptual representation.* Hillsdale, NJ: Erlbaum.

Röscheisen, M., Mogensen, C., & Winograd, T. (1994). *Shared Web annotations as a platform for third-party value-added, information providers : Architecture, protocols, & usage examples.* Technical report CSDTR/DLTR, Stanford, CA.

Rose, D. H., & Meyer, A. (2000). Universal design for learning: Associate editor column. *Journal of Special Education Technology, 15*(1). Retrieved December 28, 2006, from http://jset.unlv.edu/15.1/asseds/rose.html

Rose, D. H., & Meyer, A. (2002). *Teaching every student in the digital age.* Alexandria, VA: Association for Supervision and Curriculum Development.

Rose, E. (2005). Cultural studies in instructional design: Building a bridge to practice. *Educational Technology, 45*(March-April), 5-10.

Rosenberg, S. (2007). *Dreaming in code: Two dozen programmers, three years, 4,732 bugs, and one quest for transcendent software.* Crown Publishers.

Rosenthal, C. (2005). Making science and technology results public: A sociology of demos. In B. Latour & P. Weibel (Eds.), *Making things public: Atmospheres of democracy* (pp. 346-348). Germany: ZKM/Center for Art and Media Karlsruhe & Cambridge, MA: MIT Press.

Rosenthal, D. A. (2003). Intrusion detection technology: Leveraging the organization's security posture. *Information Systems Management, 19*, 35-44.

Rosenzweig, R. (2006). Can history be open source: Wikipedia and the future of the past. *The Journal of American History, 93*(1), 117-146. Retrieved February 4, 2007, from http://chnm.gmu.edu/resources/essays/d/42

Ross, A. (1991). *Strange weather: Culture, science, and technology in the age of limits.* New York: Verso Books.

Ross, A. (1998). *Science wars.* Durham, NC: Duke University Press.

Rothenberg, D. (1993). *Hand's end: Technology and the limits of nature.* Berkeley, CA: University of California Press.

Royal College of Nursing. (2003). *Defining nursing.* Retrieved 6 June, 2005, from http://www.rcn.org.uk/downloads/definingnursing/definingnursing-a4.pdf

Royal College of Nursing. (2006). *E-health: Putting information at the heart of nursing care.* Retrieved 2 June, 2006, from http://www.rcn.org.uk/information

Royal College of Nursing. (2006). *The future nurse: The future for nurse education, a discussion paper.* London: Royal College of Nursing.

Roztocki, N., & Weistroffer, H. R. (2004). Evaluating information technologies in emerging economies using activity based costing. *Electronic Journal of Information Systems in Developing Countries, 19*(2), 1-6.

Rücker, J., & Polanco, M. J. (1997). Siteseer: Personalized navigation for the Web. *Communications of the ACM, 40*(3), 73–75.

Russell, D., & Ison, R. (2004). Maturana's intellectual contribution: A choreography of conversation and action. *Cybernetics and Human Knowing, 11*(2), 72-84.

Rutter, D. R. Stephenson, E. A., & Dewey, M. E. (1981). Visual communication and the content and style of communication. *British Journal of Social Psychology, 20*, 41-52.

Ryan, S., Scott, B., Freeman, H., & Patel, D. (2000). *The virtual university. The Internet and resource-based learning.* London: Kogan Page.

Saba, F. (1994). From development communication to systems thinking: A postmodern analysis of distance education in the international arena. In M. Thompson (Ed.), *Internationalism in distance education: A vision for higher education* (pp. 107-114), American Center for the Study of Distance Education Research Monograph No. 10, Pennsylvania State University.

Saba, F. (2003). Distance education theory, methodology, and epistemology: A pragmatic paradigm. In M. G. Moore, & W. G. Anderson (Eds.), *Handbook of distance education* (pp. 3-20). Mahwah, NJ: Lawrence Erlbaum Associates, Publishers.

Sabin, C., & Ahern, T. C. (2002). *Instructional design and culturally diverse learners*. Paper presented at the 32nd ASEE/IEEE Frontiers in Education Conference, November 6-9, Boston, Ma, 2002. Retrieved September 27, 2006, from http://fie.engrng.pitt.edu/fie2002/

Sagan, S. (1993). *The limits of safety: Organizations, accidents and nuclear weapons*. Princeton: Princeton University Press.

Sajjapanroj, S., Bonk, C. J., Lee, M., & Lin, M.-F. G. (2007). *The challenges and successes of Wikibookian experts and Wikibook novices: Classroom and community perspectives*. Paper presented at the American Educational Research Association, Chicago, IL.

Salmon, G. (2000). *E-moderating: The key to teaching and learning online*. London: Kogan Page, Ltd.

Salomon (Ed.). (1993). *Distributed cognitions: Psychological and educational considerations* (pp. 47–87). New York: Cambridge University Press.

Salomon, G. (1988). AI in reverse: Computer tools that turn cognitive. *Journal of Educational Computing Research, 4*(2), 123-139.

Salter, L. (2003). Democracy, new social movements, and the Internet: A Habermasian analysis. In M. McCaughey, & M. Ayers (Eds.), *Cyberactivism: Online activism in theory and practice*. New York, NY: Routledge.

Salton, G., & Buckley, C. (1990). Improving retrieval performance by relevance feedback. *Journal of the American Society for Information Science, 41*(4), 288–297.

Samovar L. A., Porter R. E., & Stefani L. A. (1998). *Communication between cultures*. Belmont, CA: Wadsworth Publishing Company.

Samuelson, P., & Scotchmer, S. (2002). The law and economics of reverse engineering. *The Yale Law Journal, 111*, 1575–1663.

Samulowitz M., Michahelles F., & Linhoff-Popien C. (2001). Capeus: An architecture for context-aware selection and execution of services. In *New developments in distributed applications and interoperable systems* (pp. 23–39).

Sandars, J. (2005). Work-based learning: A social network perspective. *Work based learning in primary care, 3*, 4-12.

Sandars, J. (2006). The net generation: A challenge for work based learning. *Work based learning in primary care, 4*(3), 215-222.

Sandars, J. (2006). Twelve tips for effective online discussions in continuing medical education. *Medical Teacher, 28*, 591 –593.

Sandars, J. (2007). Developing a virtual personal network. *BMJ Careers 13 Jan*, 13-15.

Sandars, J. (2007). Online communities for healthcare professionals: When hype meets reality. *Health Information on the Internet, 56*, 3-4.

Sandars, J. (2007). The potential of blogs and wikis in healthcare education. *Education for Primary Care, 18*, 16-21.

Sandars, J. (Ed.). (2006). *e-Learning for GP educators*. Abingdon: Radcliffe Medical Publishing.

Sandars, J., & Langlois, M. (2005). E-learning and the educator in primary care: Responding to the challenge. *Education for Primary Care, 16*, 129-133.

Sandars, J., & Langlois, M. (2005). Online learning networks for general practitioners: Evaluation of a pilot project. *Education for Primary Care, 16*, 688-696.

Sandars, J., & Langlois, M. (2006). Online collaborative learning for healthcare continuing professional development: Lessons from the recent literature. *Education for Primary Care 17*, 584-592.

Sandars, J., & Walsh, K. (2004). E- learning for general practitioners: Lessons from the recent literature. *Work based learning in primary care, 2*, 305-314.

Sandars, J., & Walsh, K. (2005). There's never been a better time to e-communicate. *BMJ Careers, 331,* 265-266.

Sanders, J. (2006). Gender and technology: A research review. In C. Skelton, B. Francis, & L. Smulyan (Eds.), *Handbook of Gender and Education*. London: Sage.

Sanger, L. (2004). *Why Wikipedia must jettison its anti-elitism*. Retrieved February 10, 2006, from http://kuro-5hin.org/story/2004/12/30/142458/25

Sannomiya, T., Amagasa, T., Yoshikawa, M., & Uemura, S. (2001). A framework for sharing personal annotations on Web resources using XML. In *ITVE '01: Proceedings of the Workshop on Information Technology for Virtual Enterprises* (pp. 40-48). Washington, DC: IEEE Computer Society.

Sassen, S. (1991). *The global city: New York, London, Tokyo*. Princeton, NJ: Princeton University Press.

Saville-Troike, M. (2003). *The ethnography of communication: An introduction*. (3rd ed.). Malden, MA: Blackwell.

Savoy, J., & Picard, J. (2001). Retrieval effectiveness on the Web. *Information Processing & Management Journal, 37*(4), 543–569.

Sawyer, S. (2005). Social informatics: Overview, principles and opportunities. *Bulletin of the American Society for Information Science and Technology, 31*(5).

Sax, L. J., Ceja, M., & Teranishi, R. T. (2001). Technological preparedness among entering freshmen: The role of race, class, and gender. *Journal of Educational Computing Research, 24*(4), 363-383.

Scanlan, Robinson, Douglas, & Murch. (2003). *Divorcing children: Children's experience of their parents' divorce*. London: Jessica Kingsley Publishers.

Scardamalia, M., & Bereiter, C. (1986). Research on written composition. In M. C. Wittrock (Ed.), *Handbook of research on teaching*. (3rd ed.), (pp. 778-803). New York: Macmillan Education Ltd.

Schachaf, P., & Hara, N. (2006). *Beyond vandalism: Trolls in Wikipedia*. Presentation at the Rob Kling Center for Social Informatics, School of Library and Information Science, Indiana University, Bloomington, IN.

Scheppler, B. (2005). *The USA PATRIOT Act: Antiterror legislation in response to 9/11*. New York, NY: Rosen Central.

Schlosser, F. (2007). Can managers use handheld technologies to support salespeople? *Qualitative Market Research, 10*(2), 183-198.

Scholz, T. (2006). *Overture, Architecture and Situated Technologies Conference*, The Urban Center, New York, NY.

Schön, D. A. (1983). *The reflective practitioner*. New York: Basic Books.

Schön, D. A. (1987). *Educating the reflective practitioner*. San Francisco: Jossey-Bass.

Schrage, M. (1990). *Shared minds: The technologies of collaboration*. New York: Random House.

Schulman, A. (2001). *One-third of U.S. online workforce under Internet/e-mail surveillance*. Retrieved from http://www.privacyfoundation.gov/workplace/technology/extent.asp

Schultz, J. (2001). *Long distance families · Discussion on how to use the Internet to maintain and nurture long-distance relationships*. Retrieved 23 September, 2004, from http://groups.yahoo.com/group/longdistancefamilies/message/152

Schumacher, P., & Morahan-Martin, J. (2001). Gender, Internet and computer attitudes and experiences. *Computers in Human Behaviour, 17*, 95-110.

Seddon, P. B. (1997). A respecification and extension of the DeLone and McLean model of IS success. *Information Systems Research, 8*(3), 240-253.

Seddon, P. B., Staples, S., Paynayakuni, R., & Bowtell, M. (1999). Dimensions of information systems success. *Communications of AIS, 2*(3).

Sehmel, H. (2004). How a small environmental group uses the Web to inform and promote action: A content analysis. In A. Scharl (Ed.), *Environmental online communication*. London: Springer.

Seibt, D. (1979). User and specialist evaluation of system development. In Sijthoff & Nordhoff (Eds.), *Design and implementation of computer-based information systems* (pp. 24-32). Germantown, MD.

Sellen, A. J., & Harper, R. H., (2003). *The myth of the paperless office*. Cambridge, MA: MIT Press.

Selwyn, N. (2002). *Telling tales on technology: Qualitative studies in technology and education*. Aldershot: Ashgate Publishing Limited.

Selwyn, N. (2003, October 2003). Understanding students' (non)use of information and communications technology in university. *Working Papers*. Retrieved 22 May, 2006, from http://www.cf.ac.uk/socsi

Selwyn, N., & Gorard, S. (2004). Exploring the role of ICT in facilitating adult informal learning. *Education, Communication and Information, 4*(2/3, July/Nov).

Selwyn, N., Gorard, S., & Furlong, J. (2006). *Adult learning in the digital age: Information technology and the learning society*. Abingdon: Routledge.

Selwyn, N., Marriott, N., & Marriott, P. (2000). Net gains or net pains? Business student's use of the Internet. *Higher Education Quarterly, 54*(2), 166-186.

Serres, M. (1977). *The birth of physics*. Clinamen Press.

Serres, M. (1981). *Rome: The book of foundations*. Ann Arbor, MI: University of Michigan Press.

Serres, M. (1995). *Conversations on science, culture, and time*. Ann Arbor, MI: University of Michigan Press.

Serres, M. (1995). *Genesis*. Ann Arbor, MI: University of Michigan Press. p.6.

Serres, M. (1995). *The natural contract*. Ann ARbor, MI: University of Michigan Press.

Serres, M. (1997). *The troubadour of knowledge*. Ann Arbor, MI: University of Michigan Press.

Seufert, S. (2002). Cultural perspectives. In H. H. Adelsberger, B. Collis, & J. M. Pawlowski (Eds.), *Handbook on information technologies for education and training* (pp. 411-21). New-York: Springer.

Shah, J., White, G., & Cook, J. (2007). Privacy protection overseas as perceived by USA-based professionals. *Journal of Global Information Management, 15*(1), 68-82.

Shapira, B., Shoval, P., & Hanani, U. (1997). Stereotypes in information filtering systems. *Information Processing & Management, 33*(3), 273–287.

Shapiro, C., & Varian, H. R. (1999). *Information rules: A strategic guide to the network economy*. Harvard: Harvard Business School Press.

Shapka, J. D., & Ferrari, M. (2003). Computer-related attitudes and actions of teacher candidates. *Computers in Human Behaviour, 19*, 319-334.

Sharma, C., & Maindiratta, Y. R. (2005). Reconciling culture and technology in India. Retrieved on 24 June 2007 from http://www.centerdigitalgov.com/international/story.php?docid=92645

Sharma, R. (2006). EDUSAT: Taking Indian distance education to new frontiers. *Distance Learning Link*, Jan-June 2006, 6-8.: Information Science Publishing.

Sharma, R. C. (2002). Interactive radio counselling in distance education. *University News, 40*(10), 8-11.

Shashaani, L., & Khalili, A. (2001). Gender and computers: Similarities and differences in Iranian college students' attitudes toward computers. *Computers & Education, 37*, 363-375.

Shaw, G., & Marlow, N. (1999). The role of student learning styles, gender, attitudes and perceptions on information and communication technology assisted learning. *Computers & Education, 33*, 223-234.

Shayo, C., Guthrie, R., & Igbaria, M. (1999). Exploring the measurement of end user computing success. *Journal of End User Computing, 11*(1), 5.

Sheikh, S. (2004). *In the place of the public sphere? Or the world of fragments*. Lecture given at the Multicultural Centre, Botkyrka.

Shepherd, C. (2004). *The new IT training*. Retrieved 20 April, 2006, from http://www.trainingfoundation.com

Shneiderman, B. (1999). *Designing the user interface*. Addison-Wesley.

Shneiderman, B. (Ed.). (1993). *Sparks of innovation in human-computer interaction*. Norwood, NJ: Ablex.

Short, J. R., & Kim, Y. (1999). *Globalization and city*. Essex, England: Longman.

Shuell, T. (1992). Designing instructional computing systems for meaningful learning. In M. Jones & P. Winne (Eds.), *Adaptive learning environments*. New York: Springer Verlag.

Sidler, G., Scott A., & Wolf H. (1997). Collaborative browsing in the World Wide Web. In *Proceedings of the 8th Joint European Networking Conference*.

Siegrist, M., Keller, C., & Kiers, H. A. L. (2005). A new look at the psychometric paradigm of perception of hazards. *Risk Analysis, 25*(1), 211-222.

Sinclair, M., & Gardner, J. (1999). Planning for information technology key skills in nurse education. *Journal of Advanced Nursing, 30*(6), 1441-1450.

Singh, J. (2002). From atoms to bits: Consequences of the emerging digital divide in India. *International Information & Library Review, 34*(2), 187-200.

Singh, K. P. (2003). *Multimedia and e-learning: A new direction for productivity* (pp. 96-100).

Singh, N., & Pereira, A. (2005). *The culturally customized Web site – Customizing Web sites for the global marketplace*. Burlington, MA: Elsevier Butterworth-Heinneman.

Sjoberg, L. (1999). Risk perception by the public and by experts: A dilemma in risk management. *Research in Human Ecology, 2*(2), 1-9.

Slater, H. (2006). Towards agonism – Moishe's postpone's time, labour and social domination. *MuteBeta: Culture and politics after the net*. Retrieved November 16, 2006, from http://metamute.org/en/node/8081/print

Slay, J. (2002). Human activity systems: A theoretical framework for designing learning for multicultural settings. *Educational Technology & Society, 5*(1), 93-99. Retrieved June 29, 2006, from http://ifets.ieee.org/periodical/vol_1_2002/slay.html

Slovic, P. (1987). Perception of risk. *Science, 236*, 280-285.

Slovic, P. (1998). Do adolescent smokers know the risks? *Duke Law Review, 47*(6), 1133-1141.

Slovic, P., Fischhoff, B., & Lichtenstein, S. (1976). Cognitive processes and societal risk taking. Pp. 165-184 In J. S. C. J. W. Payen (Ed.), *Cognition and social behavior*. Potomac, MD: Lawrence Erlbaum Associates.

Slovic, P., Fischhoff, B., & Lichtenstein, S. (1978). Accident probabilities and seat belt usage: A psychological perspective. *Accident Analysis and Prevention, 10*, 281-285.

Slovic, P., Fischhoff, B., & Lichtenstein, S. (1979). Rating the risks. *Environment, 21*(3), 14-39.

Smeets, E. (2005). Does ICT contribute to powerful learning environments in primary education? *Computers & Education, 44*, 343-355.

Smith, A., Taylor, N., & Gollop, M. (Eds.). (2000). *Children's voices. Research, policy and practice*. Auckland, NZ: Pearson Education.

Smith, B. (2004). *Parent-child contact and post-separation parenting arrangements* Canberra: Research Report No.9 Australian Institute of Family Studies.

Smith, H. J. (1994). *Managing privacy: Information technology and organizational America*. Chapel Hill, NC: University of North Carolina Press.

Smith, H. J., Milberg, S. J., & Burke, S. J. (1996). Information privacy: Measuring individuals' concerns about organizational practices. *MIS Quart. 20*(2), 167-196.

Smith, H. J., Milberg. S. J., & Kallman, E. A. (1995). *Privacy practices around the world: An empirical study*. Working paper. Washington, D.C.: Georgetown University.

Smith, J., & Spurling, A. (1999). *Lifelong learning: Riding the tiger.* London: Cassell.

Smith, M. S., Seifert, J. W., McLoughlin, G. J., & Moteff, J. DF. (2002). The Internet and the USA PATRIOT Act: Potential implications for electronic privacy, security, commerce, and government. *Congressional Research Service Report for Congress.* Retrieved December 1st, 2006, from http://www.epic.org/privacy/terrorism/usa-patriot/RL31289.pdf

Smith, P. J., & Smith, S. N. (2002). *Supporting Chinese distance learners through computer-mediated communication - Revisiting Salmon's model.* Paper presented at the International Conference of Computer Support for Collaborative Learning 2002, Boulder, Co.

Smith, R., & Buckman, R. (1999). Wall Street deploys troops to battle Y2K: Command centre, jets, extra toilets are at the ready. *Wall Street Journal,* December 22.

Smithson, S., & Hirschheim, R. (1998). Analysing information systems evaluation: Another look at an old problem. *European Journal of Information Systems, 7*(3), 158-174.

Snow, D. A., Rochford, B., Worden, S. K., & Benford, R. D. (1986). Frame alignment processes, micromobilization, and movement participation. *American Sociological Review, 51*(4), 464-481.

Snowdon, D. N., Churchill, E. F., & Frécon, E. (2004). *Inhabited information spaces: Living with your data.* New York: Springer.

Soares, A., Farhangmehr, M., & Shoham, A. (2007). Hofstede's dimensions of culture in international marketing studies. *Journal of Business Research, 60*(3), 277-284.

Solomon, G., & Allen, N. J. (2003). Introduction: Educational technology and equity. In G. Solomon, N. J. Allen, & P. Resta (Eds.), *Toward digital equity: Bridging the divide in education.* (pp. xvii-xxiv). Boston, MA: Pearson Education Group, Inc.

Solvberg, A. (2002). Gender differences in computer-related control beliefs and home computer use. *Scandinavian Journal of Educational Research, 46*(4), 410-426.

Sommer, R. (1969). *Personal spaces: The behavioral basis of design.* Englewood Cliffs, NJ: Prentice Hall.

Sonnenwald, D., & Pierce, L. G. (2000). Information behaviour in dynamic group work contexts: Interwoven situational awareness dense social networks and contested collaboration in command and control. *Information Processing and Managemnt. 36*(3), 461–479.

Souzis, A. (2005). Building a semantic Wiki. *IEEE Intelligent Systems, 20*(5), 87-91.

Spence, A. M. (1973). Job market signaling. *Quarterly Journal of Economics, 87,* 355–374.

Spinney, L. (2005). How time flies. *The Guardian.*

Spouse, J. (2000). An impossible dream? Images of nursing held by preregistration students and their effect on sustaining motivation to become nurses. *Journal of Advanced Nursing, 32*(3), 730-739.

Stahl, B. (2004). *Responsible management of information systems.* Hershey, PA: Idea Group Publishers.

Stallman, R. (2007). Warum "Open Source" das wesentliche von "Freier Software" verdeckt. In Lutterbeck, B. Bärwolff, M., & Gehring, R. A. (Eds.), *Open source jahrbuch 2007. Zwischen freier software und gesellschaftsmodell,* (pp. 1–7). Berlin: Lehmanns Media. Retrieved from http://www.opensourcejahrbuch.de

Stallman, R. M. (1992). *Why software should be free.* Retrieved from http://www.fsf.org.philosophy/should-befree.html

Stallman, R. M. (1999). The GNU operating system and the free software movement. In C. DiBona, S. Ockman, & M. Stone, (Eds.), *Open sources: Voices from the open source revolution* (pp. 53–70). London: O'Reilly. Retrieved from http://www.oreilly.de/catalog/opensources/book/stallman.html

Staples, W. G. (1997). *The culture of surveillance: Discipline and social control in the United States.* New York, NY: St Martin's Press.

Stewart, K. A., & Segars, A. H. (2002). An empirical examination of the concern for information privacy instrument. *Information Systems Research, 13*(1), 33-49.

Stone, D. L. (1986). Relationship between introversion/ extraversion, values regarding control over information, and perceptions of invasion of privacy. *Perceptual and Motor Skills, 62*(2), 371-376.

Stone, E. F., & Stone, D. L. (1990). Privacy in organizations: Theoretical issues, research findings, and protection mechanisms In K. M. Rowland & G. R. Ferris (Eds.), *Research in personnel and human resources management, 8*, 349-411.Greenwich, CT: JAI Press.

Stone, E. F., Gardner, D. G., Gueutal, H. G., & McClure, S. (1983). A field experiment comparing information-privacy values, beliefs, and attitudes across several types of organizations. *Journal of Applied Psychology, 68*(3), 459-468.

Strahilevitz, L. (2007). Wealth without markets. *Yale Law Journal, 116*. Retrieved from http://papers.ssrn.com/sol3/papers.cfm?abstract_id=946479

Straub, D. (1990). Effective IS security: An empirical study. *Information Systems Research, 1*(3), 255-276.

Straub, D. W., Jr., & Collins, R. W. (1990). Key information liability issues facing managers: Software piracy, proprietary databases, and individual rights to privacy. *MIS Quarterly, 14*(2), 142-156.

Straub, D., & Nance,W. (1990). Discovering and discipling computer abuse in organizations: A field study. *MIS Quarterly, 14*(2), 45-60.

Straub, D., & Welke, R. (1998). Coping with systems risk: Security planning models for management decision making. *MIS Quarterly, 22*(4), 441-469.

Strickland, L. H. (1958). Surveillance and trust. *Journal of Personality, 26*, 200-215.

Subramony, D. P. (2004). Instructional technologists' inattention to issues of cultural diversity among learners. *Educational Technology, 44*(4), 19-24.

Sudweeks, F., & Ess, C. (2002). *Cultural attitudes towards technology and communication*. Paper presented at the 3rd International Conference on Cultural Attitudes towards Technology and Communication, Montreal, Canada (pp. 69-88).

Sugumaran, V., & Arogyaswamy, B. (2003/2004). Measuring IT performance "contingency" variables and value modes. *The Journal of Computer Information Systems, 44*(2), 79-86.

Sumner, W. G. (1906). *Folkways*. New York: Ginn.

Sunstein, C. (2005). *Laws of fear: Beyond the Precautionary Principle*. Cambridge: Cambridge University Press.

Surowiecki, J. (2005). *The wisdom of crowds*. NY: Anchor.

Sussman, N. M., & Tyson, D. H. (2000). Sex and power: Gender differences in computer-mediated interactions. *Computers in Human Behaviour, 16*, 381-394.

Suzman, M. (1999), World is mostly ready for Y2K. *Financial Times*, December 30.

Swartz, J. (2005). 2005 worst year for breaches of computer security. *USA Today*.

Székely, M. (2006). Pushing the popular, or, toward a compositional popular aesthetics. *Popular Music & Society, 29*(1), 91-108.

Tabak, F., & Smith, W. (2005). Privacy and electronic monitoring in the workplace: A model of managerial cognition and relational trust development. *Employee Responsibilities and Rights Journal, 17*(3), 173-189.

Taipale, K. (1998). Technological change and the fate of the public realm. In K. Frampton (Ed.), *Technology, place and architecture* (pp. 194-199). The Jerusalem Seminar in Architecture, NY: Rizzoli International Publications.

Talja, S. (2002). Information sharing in academic communities: Types and levels of collaboration in information seeking and use. *New Review of Information Behaviour Research, 3*, 143-159.

Tapp, P., & Henaghan, M. (2000). Family law: Conceptions of children and children's voices- the implications of Article 12 of the United Nations convention on the rights of the child. In A. Smith, N. Taylor & M. Gollop (Eds.),

Children's voices. Research, Policy and Practice. (pp. 132-145). Auckland, New Zealand: Pearson Education.

Tarleton State University. (2004). *About distributed education, What is distributed education?* Tarleton, TX: Tarleton State University. Retrieved November 10, 2006, from http://online.tarleton.edu/dist_distr_ed.htm

Tarrow, S. (1998). *Power in movement: Social movements and contentious politics* (2nd ed.). Cambridge: Cambridge University Press.

Taylor, B. C. (2005*). Virtual kaleidoscopes: Socio-cultural implications for distance learning.* Paper presented at the 21ˢᵗ Annual Conference on Distance Teaching and Learning. Retrieved September 27, 2006, from http://www.uwex.edu/disted/conference/Resource_library/shared_space.cfm?main=search

Taylor, N. J., Smith, A. B., & Tapp, P. (Eds.). (2001).*Childhood and family law: The rights and views of children.* Dunedin: Children's Issues Centre.

Taylor, P. G. (1996). Pedagogical challenges to open learning: Looking to borderline issues. In E. McWilliam & P. G. Taylor (Eds.), *Pedagogy, technology, and the body* (vol. 29), (pp. 59-77). New York: Peter Lang.

Taylor, R. (2006). *Management perception of unintentional information security risks.* International Conference on Information Systems, Milwaukee, WI. December 10-13, 2006.

Taylor, W., & Yu, X. (Eds.) (2003). *Closing the digital divide: Transforming regional economies and communities with information technology.* Westport, CT: Praeger.

Taylor-Gooby, P. (2004). *Psychology, social psychology and risk.* Working paper. Social contexts and responses to risk network, University of Kent at Canterbury. Retrieved from http://www.kent.ac.uk/scarr/papers/papers.htm

Teevan, J., Dumais, S. T., & Horvitz, E. (2005). Personalizing search via automated analysis of interests and activities. In *Proceedings of the 28ᵗʰ Annual International ACM SIGIR Conference on Research and Development in Information Retrieval* (pp. 449-456). ACM Press.

Teich, A. H. (2003). *Technology and the future* (9ᵗʰ ed.). London: Thomson Wadsworth.

Temperton, V. M. et al., (Eds.) (2004). *Assembly rules and restoration ecology: Bridging the gap between theory and practice.* Washington, Island Press.

Tenner, E. (2003). *Our own devices: The past and future of body technology* . NY: Vintage Books.

Teubner, G. (1993). *Law as an autopoietic system.* Oxford: Blackwell.

Thayer, S. E., & Ray, S. (2006). Online communication preferences across age, gender, and duration of Internet use. *CyberPsychology & Behavior, 9*(4), 432-440.

Théberge, P. (1997). *Any sound you can imagine: Making music/consuming technology.* Hanover, NH: Wesleyan University Press: University Press of New England.

Theberge, P. (2004). The network studio: Historical and technological paths to a new ideal in music making. *Social Studies of Science, 34*(5), 759-781.

Thiel, U., Brocks, H., Frommholz, I., Dirsch-Weigand, A., Keiper, J., Stein, A., & Neuhold, E. J. (2004). COLLATE - A collaboratory supporting research on historic European films. *Int. J. Digit. Libr.,* I(1), 8-12.

Thomas, M. K. (2003). Designer's dilemmas: The tripartheid responsibility of the instructional designer. *TechTrends, 47*(6), 34.

Thomas, M., Mitchell, M., & Joseph, R. (2002). The third dimension of ADDIE: A cultural embrace. *TechTrends, 46*(2), 40-45.

Thompson, P. B. (2001). Privacy, secrecy, and security. *Ethics and Information Technology, 3*(1), 22-35.

Thong, J. Y. L., Yap, C.-S., & Raman, K. S. (1993). *Top management support in small business information systems implementation: How important is it?* Paper presented at the Special Interest Group on Computer Personnel Research Annual Conference. Conference on Computer Personnel Research, St. Louis, Missouri, USA.

Thong, J. Y. L., Yap, C-S., & Raman, K. S. (1996). Top management support, external expertise in information systems implementation in small businesses. *Information Systems Research, 7*(2), 248-267.

Tiene, D. (2002). Addressing the global digital divide and its impact on educational opportunity. *Educational Media International, 39*(3-4), 211-222.

Tiene, D. (2004). Bridging the digital divide in the schools of developing countries. *International Journal of Instructional Media, 31*(1).

Time Magazine. (2006/2007). *Time Magazine Person of the Year, 168*(26), December 25, 2006/January 1, 2007.

Timmons, S. (2003). Nurses resisting information technology. *Nursing Inquiry, 10*(4), 257-269.

Tindale, R. S., & Kameda, T. (2000). "Social sharedness" as a unifying theme for information processing in groups. *Group Processes & Intergroup Relations, 3*(2), 123-140.

Todman, J. (2000). Gender differences in computer anxiety among university entrants since 1992. *Computers & Education, 34*, 27-35.

Todman, J., & Day, K. (2006). Computer anxiety: The role of psychological gender. *Computers in Human Behavior, 22*, 856-869.

Tolchinsky, P. D., McCuddy, M. K., Adams, J., Ganster, D. C., Woodman, R. W., & Fromkin, H. L. (1981). Employee perceptions of invasion of privacy: A field simulation experiment. *Journal of Applied Psychology, 66*(3), 308-313.

Treuhaft, J. D. (2000). Global online learning among asia-pacific economies: Lessons learned. *Journal of Educational Media, 25*(1), 51-55. Retrieved July 12, 2006, from http://www.col.org/tel99/acrobat/treuhaft.pdf

Trompenaars, F. (1993). *Riding the waves of culture.* London: Nicholas Brearley Publishing Ltd.

Trompenaars, F., & Woolliams, P. (2004). *Marketing across cultures.* Chichester: Capstone Publishing Ltd.

Tsai, C., Lin, S. S. J., & Tsai, M. (2001). Developing an Internet attitude scale for high school students. *Computers & Education, 37*, 41-51.

Tudge, J., & Scrimsher, S. (2000). Lev Vygotsky. In B. J. Zimmerman & D. H. Schunk (Eds.), *Educational psychology: A century of contributions*. Mahwah NJ: Lawrence Erlbaum Associates.

Tuomi, I. (2003). *Networks of innovation*. Oxford: Oxford University Press.

U.S. Department of Commerce. (2002). *A nation online: How Americans are expanding their use of the Internet.* Retrieved from http://www.ntia.doc.gov/ntiahome/dn/

United States Senate Special Committee on the Year 2000 Technology Problem. (2000). *Y2K aftermath – A crisis averted* (Final Committee Report). Retrieved October 2004, from http://www.senate.gov

Uniting and Strengthening America by Providing Appropriate Tools Required to Intercept and Obstruct Terrorism (USA PATRIOT Act), HR 3162 RDS. (2001).

Urbaczewski, A., & Jessup, L. (2002). Does electronic monitoring of employee Internet usage work? *Communications of the ACM, 45*(1), 80-84.

Uribe, S., & Marino, R. J. (2006). Internet and information technology use by dental students in Chile. *Eur J Dent Educ, 10*, 162–168.

US Department of Justice, Office of Legislative Affairs, Office of the Assistant Attorney General, Washington, DC 20530. (2006). *Foreign Intelligence Surveillance Act 2005 Annual Report.*

USA Today. (2006). *Questions and answers about the NSA phone record program.*

US-Canada Power System Outage Task Force. (2004). *Final report on the August 14 2003 blackout in the United States and Canada: Causes and recommendations.* Published jointly by the US Government and the Government of Canada. Retrieved October 2005, from http://reports.energy.gov

Utne, L. (2006). To wikifinity and beyond! [Electronic Version]. *Utne Magazine*. Retrieved April 29, 2006 from http://www.utne.com/issues/2006_133/view/11894-1.html

Valentine, S. (2004). *E-powering the people: South Africa's Smart Access Project*. Washington, D.C.: Council on Library and Information Resources. Retrieved from http://www.clir.org/pubs/reports/pub125/pub125.pdf

van de Donk, W., Loader, B. D., Nihon, P. G., & Rucht, D. (Eds.). (2004). *Cyberprotest: New media, citizens and social movements*. London; New York: Routledge.

van Dijk, J. A. G. M., (2005). *The deepening divide: Inequality in the information society*. Thousand Oaks, CA: Sage.

Varela, F. J. (1979). *Principles of biological autonomy*. New York: North Holland.

Varela, F. J. (1981) Autonomy and autopoiesis. In G. Roth & H. Schwegler (Eds.), *Self-organizing systems* (pp. 14-23). Frankfort: Campus Verlag.

Varela, F. J. (1981). Describing the logic of the living. In M. Zeleny (Ed.), *Autopoiesis, A theory of living organization* (pp. 36-48). New York: North Holland.

Varela, F. J. (1984). Living ways of sense-making: A middle path. In P. Livingstone (Ed.), *Order and disorder* (pp. 208-224). Saratoga, CA: ANMA Libri.

Varela, F. J. (1992). Whence perceptual meaning? A cartography of current ideas. In F. J. Varela & J. Dupuy (Eds.), *Understanding origins* (pp. 234-271). Dordrecht: Kluwer.

Varela, F. J. (1997). *Sleeping, dreaming, and dying: An exploration of consciousness with the Dalai Lama*, Boston: Wisdom Publications.

Varela, F. J. (1999). *Ethical know-how: Action, wisdom, and cognition*. Stanford, CA: Stanford University Press.

Varela, F. J., Thompson, E., & Rosch, E. (1991). *The embodied mind*. Cambridge, MA: The MIT Press.

Varnelis, K. (2006). *The network city: Emergent urbanism in contemporary life*. Retrieved November 6, 2006, from http://varnelis.net/books/networkcity/proposal

Vaughan, D. (1996). *The Challenger launch decision: Risky technology, culture, and deviance at NASA*. Chicago: University of Chicago Press.

Vedder, A. H. (2004). KDD, privacy, individuality, and fairness. In R. A. Spinello & H. Tavani (Eds.), *Readings in cyberethcis* (2nd ed.) (pp. 462-470). Sudbury, MA: Jones and Bartlett.

Veeramah, V. (2004). Utilization of research findings by graduate nurses and midwives. *Journal of Advanced Nursing, 47*(2), 183-191.

Vegh, S. (2003). Classifying forms of online activism: The case of cyberprotests against the World Bank. In M. McCaughey & M. D. Ayers (Eds.), *Cyberactivism: Online activism in theory and practice* (pp. 71-95). New York: Routledge.

Venkatraman, N. (1997). Beyond outsourcing: IT resources as a value center. *Sloan Management Review*, 51-64.

Vidal, R. V. V. (2006). *Creative and participative problem solving – The art and the science, informatics and mathematical modelling*. Technical University of Denmark. Retrieved from http://www2.imm.dtu.dk/ vvv/CPPS/

Viégas, F. B., Wattenberg, M., & Dave, K. (2004). Studying cooperation and conflict between authors with history flow visualizations. In E. Dykstra-Erickson & M. Tscheligi (Eds.), *Proceedings from ACM CHI 2004 Conference on Human Factors in Computing Systems* (pp. 575-582). Vienna, Austria. Retrieved February 3, 2007, from http://web.media.mit.edu/~fviegas/papers/history_flow.pdf

Virilio, P. (2000). *The information bomb*. London: Verso.

Volman, M., Eck, E., Heemskerk, I., & Kuiper, E. (2005). New technologies, new differences. Gender and ethnic differences in pupils' use of ICT in primary and secondary education. *Computers & Education, 45*, 35-55.

Volti, R. (2001). *Society and technological change*. New York: Worth.

Von Foerster, H. (1981). Perception of the future and the future of perception. In *Observing Systems* (pp. 192-210). Seaside, CA: Intersystems.

Von Foerster, H. (2003). *Understanding understanding: Essays on cybernetics and cognition*. New York: Springer.

Voss, J. (2005). Measuring wikipedia [Electronic Version]. *Proceedings for International Society for Scientometrics and Informetrics*. Retrieved February 10, 2007 from http://eprints.rclis.org/archive/00003610/01/MeasuringWikipedia2005.pdf

Voyles, M., & Williams, A. (2004). Gender differences in attributions and behaviour in a technology classroom. *Journal of Computers in Mathematics and Science Teaching, 23*(3), 233-256.

Vyas, R. V., Sharma, R. C., & Kumar, A. (2002). Educational radio in India. *Turkish Online Journal of Distance Education, 3*(3). Retrieved from http://tojde.anadolu.edu.tr/tojde7/articles/educationalradio.htm

Vyas, R. V., Sharma, R. C., & Kumar, A.. (2002). Educational television in India. *Turkish Online Journal of Distance Education, 3*(4). Retrieved from http://tojde.anadolu.edu.tr/tojde8/articles/educationaltv.htm

Vygotsky, L. S. (1978). *Mind in society: The development of higher psychological processes*. Cambridge, MA: Harvard University Press.

Wagner, C., & Bolloju, N. (2005). Supporting knowledge management in organization with conversational technologies: Discussion forums, Weblogs, and wikis. *Journal of Database Management, 16*(2), i-viii.

Wahid, F., Furuholt, B., & Kristiansen, S. (2006). Internet for development? Patterns of use among Internet café customers in Indonesia. *Information Development, 22*(4), 278-291.

Wahlberg, A., & Sjoberg, L. (2000). Risk perception and the media. *Journal of Risk Research, 3*(1), 31-50.

Waite, S. J., Wheeler, S., & Bromfield, C. (2007). Our flexible friend: The implications of individual differences for information technology teaching. *Computers & Education, 48*, 80-99.

Wakley, G., Chambers, R., & Field, S. (2000). *Continuing professional development in primary care*. Oxford: Radcliffe Medical Press.

Walsham, G., Symons, V., & Waema, T. (1990). Information systems as social systems: Implications for developing countries. In S. Bhatnagar & N. Bjorn-Andersen (Eds.), *Information Technology in Developing Countries*, (pp. 51-61). Amsterdam: Elsevier Science Publishers.

Wang, C.-M., & Reeves, T. C. (2006). The meaning of culture in online education: Implications for teaching, learning, and design. In A. Edmundston (Ed.), *Globalized e-learning cultural challenges* (pp. 1-17). Hershey, PA: Idea Group Inc.

Warf, B., & Grimes J. (1997). Counterhegemonic discourses and the Internet. *Geographical Review, 87*(2), 259-274.

Warren, C., & Laslett, B. (1977). Privacy and secrecy: A conceptual comparison. *Journal of Social Issues, 33*(3), 43-51.

Warschauer, M. (2003). *Technology and social inclusion: Rethinking the digital divide*. Cambridge, MA: MIT Press.

Wasserman, S., & Faust, K. (1994). *Social network analysis – Methods and application*. Cambridge University Press.

Watkins, W. H. (2001). *The White architects of Black education: Ideology and power in America, 1865-1954*. New York: Teachers College Press.

Weatherall, A., & Ramsay, A. (2006). *New communication technologies and family life*. Wellington: Blue Skies Fund. Retrieved December 18, 2006, from http://www.nzfamilies.org.nz/download/blueskies-weatherall.pdf

Webb, M. (1989). Sex and gender in the labour market. In I. Reid & E. Stratta (Eds.), *Sex differences in Britain* (2nd ed.), (pp. xi,321p323cm. Aldershot: Gower.

Webber, S., & Johnston, B. (2000). Conceptions of information literacy: New perspectives and implications. *Journal of Information Science, 26*, 381-397.

Weber, S. (2004). *The success of open source.* Harvard University Press.

Wegner, E. (1996). *Communities of practice: Learning meaning and identity.* Cambridge: Cambridge University Press.

Wei, R., & Lo, V.H. (2006). Staying connected while on the move: Cell phone use and social connectedness. *New Media and Society, 8*(1), 53-72.

Weik, K., & Roberts, K. (1993). Collective mind in organizations: Heedful interrelating on flight decks. *Administrative Science Quarterly, 38*(3), 357-381.

Weingand, D. (1999). Describing the elephant: What is continuing professional education? In *Proceedings of the 65th IFLA Council and General Conference Bangkok,* Thailand, 20-28 August. Retrieved July 12, 2007, from http://www.ifla.org/IV/ifla65/papers/089-104e.htm

Weller, M., Pegler, C., & Mason, R. (2005). Use of innovative technologies on an e-learning course. *The Internet and Higher Education, 8*(1), 61-71.

Wellman, B., Quan-Haase, A., Boase, J., & Chen, W. (2003). The social affordances of the Internet for networked individualism. *Journal of Computer Mediated Communication, 8*(3). Retrieved November 12, 2006, from http://jcmc.indiana.edu/vol8/issue3/wellman.html

Wen, H. J. & Gershuny, P. (2005). Computer-based monitoring in the American workplace: Surveillance technologies and legal challenges. *Human Systems Management, 24*(2), 165-173.

Wenger, E. (1998). *Communities of practice: Learning, meaning, and identity.* Cambridge University Press.

Wenger, E. (2000). Communities of practice: The key to knowledge strategy. In E. Lesser, M. Fontaine, & J. Slusher, (Eds.), *Knowledge and communities,* (pp. 3-20). Oxford: Butterworth-Heinemann.

Wenger, E. (2001). *Supporting communities of practice: A survey of community-oriented technologies.* Retrieved January 29, 2007, from http://www.ewenger.com/tech

Wenger, E. (2002). *Cultivating communities of practice: A field guide to managing.* Harvard.

Wertsch, J. V. (1991). *Voices of the mind: A sociocultural approach to mediated action.* Cambridge, MA: Harvard University Press.

Westbrook, L. (1994). Qualitative research methods: A review of major stages, data analysis techniques, and quality controls. *Library & Information Science Research, 16*(3), 241-254.

Westby, D. L. (2002). Strategic imperative, ideology, and frame. *Mobilization, 7*(3), 287-304.

Westin, A. F. (1967). *Privacy and freedom.* New York: Atheneum.

Westin, A. F. (1992). Two key factors that belong in a macroergonomics analysis of electronic performance monitoring: Employee perceptions of fairness and the climate of organizational trust or distrust. *Applied Ergonomics, 23*(1): 35-42.

Wexelblat, A., & Pattie M. (1999). Footprints: History-rich tools for information foraging. ACM SIGCHI Conference on Human Factors in Computing Systems. In *CHI'99 Proceedings.* ACM Press.

Wharrad, H., Clifford, C., Horsburgh, M., Ketefian, S., & Lee, J. (2002). Global network explores diversity and opportunity in nurse education. *Nurse Education Today, 22,* 15-23.

Wheeler, D. L. (2003). The Internet and youth subculture in Kuwait. *Journal of Computer-Mediated Communication, 8*(2).

Wheeler, J., & Aoyama, Y. (Eds.). (1999). *Fractured geographies: Cities in the telecommunications age.* NY: Routledge.

Wheeler, S. (2001). Information and communication technologies and the changing role of the teacher. *Journal of Educational Media, 26*(1), 7-17.

Whitaker, R. (2004). Thanks for the magic, Humberto. *Cybernetics and Human Knowing, 11*(4), 93-97.

White, M. P., Eiser, J. P., & Harris, P. R. (2004). Risk perceptions of mobile phone use while driving. *Risk Analysis, 24*(2), 323-334.

Whitley, B. E., Jr. (1997). Gender differences in computer-related attitudes and behaviors: A metaanalysis. *Computers in Human Behavior, 13*, 1-22.

Whitworth, A. (2005). The politics of virtual learning environments: Environmental change, conflict and e-learning. *British Journal of Educational Technology, 36*(4), 685-692.

Wikibooks (2007). *Wikibooks: History of Wikibooks.* Retrieved February 9, 2007, from http://en.wikibooks.org/wiki/Wikibooks:History_of_Wikibooks

Wikibooks (2007). *Wikibooks: Statistics.* Retrieved February 9, 2007, from http://en.wikibooks.org/wiki/Special:Statistics

Wikibooks (2007). *Wikibooks: Wikijunior.* Retrieved February 16, 2007, from http://en.wikibooks.org/wiki/Wikijunior

Wikipedia (2007). *Wikipedia: Larry Sanger.* Retrieved February 7, 2007, from http://en.wikipedia.org/wiki/Larry_Sanger

Wikipedia (2007). *Wikipedia: List of Wikipedias.* Retrieved February 7, 2007, from http://meta.wikimedia.org/wiki/List_of_Wikipedias#All_Wikipedias_ordered_by_number_of_articles

Wikipedia (2007). *Wikipedia: Main page.* Retrieved February 7, 2007, from http://en.wikipedia.org/wiki/Main_Page

Wikipedia (2007). *Wikipedia: Statistics.* Retrieved February 9, 2007, from http://en.wikipedia.org/wiki/Special:Statistics

Wikipedia (2007). *Wikipedia: Wikipedians.* Retrieved February 4, 2007, from http://en.wikipedia.org/wiki/Wikipedia:Wikipedians

Wikiquotes (2007). *Wikiquotes: Main page.* Retrieved February 16, 2007, from http://en.wikiquote.org/wiki/Main_Page

Wiktionary (2007). *Wiktionary: Main page.* Retrieved February 16, 2007, from http://en.wiktionary.org/wiki/Main_Page

Wilber, K. (2000). *Integral psychology: Consciousness, spirit, psychology, therapy.* Shambhala Publications.

Wiley, D. A. (2002). Connecting learning objects to instructional design theory: A definition, a metaphor, and a taxonomy. In D.A. Wiley, *The Instructional Use of Learning Objects* (pp. 1-35). Retrieved December 8, 2006, from http://reusability.org/read/chapters/wiley.doc

Williams, & Shauf, M. S. (Eds.). *Computers, ethics, and society* (2nd ed.) (pp. 3-19). New York: Oxford University Press.

Williams, R. (2003). Integrating distributed learning with just-in-context Knowledge Management. *Electronic J. of e-Learning, 1*(1), 45-50. Retrieved April 04, 2007, from http://www.ejel.org/volume-1-issue-1/issue1-art6.htm

Wilson, E. O. (1998). *Consilience: The unity of knowledge.* Abacus.

Wilson, M. S. (2001). Cultural considerations in online instruction and learning. *Distance Education, 22*(1), 52-62.

Wilson, W. J. (1996). *When work disappears: The world of the new urban poor.* New York, NY: Vintage Books.

Winn, W. (1989). Towards a rationale and theoretical basis for educational technology. *Educational Technology Research and Development, 37*, 35-46.

Winn, W. (1993). A constructivist critique of the assumptions of instructional design. In T. M. Duffy, J. Lowyck, & D. H. Jonassen (Eds.), *Designing environments for constructive learning* (pp. 189-212). NATO ASI Series F: Computer ande Systems Sciences, Vol. 105. Berlin: Springer Verlag.

Winner, L. (1986). *The whale and the reactor: A search for limits in an age of high technology.* Chicago: University of Chicago Press.

Winograd, T., & Flores, F. (1986). *Understanding computers and cognition*. Norwood, NJ: Ablex.

Wirth, L. (1996). Urbanism as a way of life. In R. LeGates & F. Stout (Eds.), *The city reader* (pp. 189-197). London: Routledge.

Wishart, J., & Ward, R. (2002). Individual differences in nurse and teacher training students' attitudes toward and use of information technology. *Nurse Education Today, 22*(3), 231-240.

Wolf, A. (2002). *Does education matter? Myths about education and economic growth*. London: Penguin Books.

Wolfe, J. L., & Neuwirth, C. M. (2001). From the margins to the center - The future of annotation. *Journal of Business and Technical Communication, 15*(3), 333–371.

Wong, L. F., & Trinidad, S. G. (2004). Using Web-based distance learning to reduce cultural distance. *The Journal of Interactive Distance Online Learning, 3*(1), 1-13.

Wood, A., Drew, N., Beale, R., & Hendley, B. (1995). Hyperspace: Web browsing with visualisation. In *Proceedings of the 3rd International World Wide Web Conference (WWW3)* (pp. 21-25).

Woodworth, G. M. (2004). Hackers, users, and suits: Napster and representations of identity. *Popular Music & Society, 27*(2), 161-184.

Worchel, P. (1979). Trust and distrust. In W. G. Austin & S. Worchel (Eds.), *The social psychology of intergroup relations*. Belmont, CA: Wadsworth.

Wray, R. (2004). Mobiles to let parents keep a track on children. *The Guardian, 25 September*.

Wu, D., & Hiltz, S. R. (2004). Predicting learning from asynchronous online discussions. *JALN, 8*(2), 139-152.

Wu, J., & Aberer, K. (2004). Using SiteRank for decentralized computation of Web document ranking. In *Adaptive hypermedia and adaptive Web-based systems, LNCS 3137*: 265-274.

Wu, X., Zhang, L., & Yu, Y. (2006). Exploring social annotations for the semantic Web. In *WWW '06: Proceedings of the 15th International Conference on World Wide Web* (pp. 417–426). New York, NY: ACM Press.

Yager, R. R. (2002). Fuzzy logic methods in recommender systems. *Fuzzy sets and Systems, 136*(2), 133–149.

Yang, B., & Garcia-Molina, H. (2002). Improving search in peer-to-peer networks. In *Proceedings of the 22nd International Conference on Distributed Computing Systems* (pp. 5-14).

Yesil, B. (2003). Internet café as battlefied: State control over Internet cafés in Turkey and the lack of popular resistance. *The Journal of Popular Culture, 37*(1), 12-127.

Yoshii, R., Katada, F., Alsadeqi, F., & Zhang, F. (2003). Reaching students of many languages and cultures. *Proceedings of the EDMEDIA Conference*, AACE.

Young, B. J. (2000). Gender differences in student attitudes toward computers. *Journal of Research on Computing in Education, 33*(2), 204-216.

YouTube. (2007). *Web 2.0...The machine is using us*. YouTube. Retrieved February 9, 2007, from http://www.youtube.com/watch?v=6gmP4nk0EOE

Yúdice, G. (2003). The expediency of culture. Raleigh, NC: Duke University Press.

Yuen, A. H. K. (2002). Gender differences in teacher computer acceptance. *Journal of Technology and Teacher Education, 10*(3), 365-382.

Zack, M. A. (1993). Interactivity and communication mode choice in ongoing management groups. *Information Systems Research, 4*(3), 207-239.

Zafeiriou, G. (2000). *Students' perceptions of issues arising from and factors influencing group interaction in computer conferencing: A grounded theory approach*. PhD. Thesis. Sheffield, UK: Department of Information Studies, University of Sheffield.

Zahedi, F., van Pelt, W. V., & Song, J. (2001). A conceptual framework for international Web design. *IEEE Transactions on professional Communication, 44*(2), 83-103.

Zamir, O. (1999). *Visualisation of search results in document retrieval systems*. General Examination, University of Washington, 1998.

Zandpour, F., Campos, V., Catalano, J., Chang, C, Cho, Y, Hoobyar, R., Jiang, H., Lin, M, Madrid, S., Scheideler, P., & Osborn, S. (1994). Global research and local touch: achieving cultural fitness in TV advertising. *Journal of Advertising Research, 34*(5), 35-63.

Zhang, J. X. (2001). Cultural diversity in instructional design. *International Journal of Instructional Media, 28*(3), 299-307.

Zhang, Y. (2005). Age, gender, and Internet attitudes among employees in the business world. *Computers in Human Behaviour, 21*, 1-10.

Zubin, J., & Spring, B. (1977). Vulnerability - A new view of schizophrenia. *Journal of Abnormal Psychology, 86*(2), 103-124.

Zuboff, S. (1988). *In the age of the smart machine: The future of work and power.* New York: Basic Books.

Zuo, J., & Benford, R. D. (1995). Mobilization processes and the 1989 Chinese democracy movement. *The Sociological Quarterly, 36*, 131-156.

About the Contributors

Zehra Akyol is a doctoral student and research assistant in the Department of Computer Education and Instructional Technology of the Middle East Technical University, Ankara, Turkey. Her research and interest focus on distance education; social, cultural and cognitive aspects of distance teaching and learning, new learning environments for distance education, and cultural aspects of technology applications in education.

Matthias Bärwolff has been working as a research assistant at Technische Universität Berlin since he completed his master's thesis at Bournemouth University, UK. His current research focus lies with the diverse subject fields related to open source, network, and Internet economics as well as institutional economics. Aside from this, Matthias is editor of the *Open Source Jahrbuch* series, a German language comprehensive annual overview of current dynamics and trends in open source, open access, and other related fields. Hands-on experience in diverse computer science matters and Web design complement his academic background.

Josianne Basque, PhD in Psychology, is a professor in Educational Technology at the Télé-université, which is a French-Canadian distance education university associated with the University of Québec in Montreal. She has designed many web-based courses in the field of instructional design, cognitive science and learning, and computer-based learning. She is also a researcher at the LICEF Research Center (Laboratory of Cognitive Informatics and Training Environments) at Télé-université. Her research interests include distance education, computer-supported co-construction of knowledge, self-regulation of learning and knowledge modeling techniques for learning, knowledge management and instructional design. For more information, visit www.teluq.uqam.ca/~jbasque.

Curt Bonk received his master's and PhD degrees in educational psychology from the University of Wisconsin. He is professor of Instructional Systems Technology in the School of Education at Indiana University and adjunct in the School of Informatics. He has received the CyberStar Award from the Indiana Information Technology Association, the Most Outstanding Achievement Award from the U.S. Distance Learning Association, and the Most Innovative Teaching in a Distance Education Program Award from the State of Indiana. Curt has given hundreds of talks around the globe related to online teaching and learning. In addition, he has nearly 200 publications on topics such as online learning pedagogy, massive multiplayer online gaming, wikibooks, blogging, open source software, collaborative technologies, and synchronous and asynchronous computer conferencing. His "Handbook of Blended Learning Environments: Global Perspectives, Local Designs," was published by Pfeiffer in 2006. Curt is President of CourseShare and SurveyShare (see http://mypage.iu.edu/~cjbonk/; e-mail: cjbonk@indiana.edu).

Jeanette Bopry is an Assistant Professor in Learning Sciences and Technologies Academic Group, National Institute of Education, Nanyang Technological University. She is also the faculty researcher in Learning Sciences Lab. Jeanette received her doctoral degree in Instructional Systems Technology from Indiana University. She is affiliated with the American Society for Cybernetics, the International Society for the Systems Sciences, the Semiotic Society of America, and the International Semiotics Institute. She is Associate Editor of the peer-reviewed journal *Cybernetics and Human Knowing*, and has coedited three books.

Guillaume Cabanac is a PhD candidate in computer science at the University Paul Sabatier of Toulouse III. He conducts research within the Toulouse Computing Research Laboratory (IRIT - UMR 5505). It concerns information systems; he currently works on digital document-related activities, especially annotation.

Jengchung V. Chen, PhD, is an assistant professor of the Institute of Telecommunications Management at National Cheng Kung University. His research interests are information ethics, information assurance, and electronic commerce. He has 20 articles published/accepted in refereed journals in these fields. Dr. Chen is the director of Digital Convergence Management Research Center.

Max Chevalier is associate professor in computer science at the University Paul Sabatier of Toulouse III. His research addresses user-centered approaches in information systems like personalization, visual information retrieval interface, social computing. He conducts research on these topics within the Toulouse Computing Research Laboratory (IRIT - UMR 5505).

Claude Chrisment is currently professor of computer science at the University Paul Sabatier of Toulouse III. He is also codirector of the Toulouse Computing Research Laboratory (IRIT - UMR 5505). He serves as the head of the Generalized Information Systems (SIG) research team. His research addresses different aspects of Information Systems like databases.

Donald J. Cunningham, PhD is Barbara Jacobs Chair in Education and Technology and a member of the faculties of Education, Cognitive Science, Semiotic Studies and Informatics at Indiana University, Bloomington. He was the Director of the Center for Research on Learning and Technology from January 2000 to December 2002 and Director of the Center for Applied Semiotics from September 1998 to August 2004. He teaches graduate courses and seminars in the learning, cognition, and instruction program in the Department of Counseling and Educational Psychology, and is a founding member of the new PhD program in Learning Science. During the 1990-1991 academic year he was Garfield Weston Visiting Professor at the University of Ulster at Coleraine, where he collaborated with the Language Development and Hypermedia Research Group. From May of 1992 to August of 1994, he was Professor and Head of the Department of Learning, Development and Communication at the University of New England, Armidale, Australia where he founded the Centre for Research into the Educational Application of Multimedia. He pursues an active program of research and development in computer-mediated instruction, and is a leading contributor to the development of semiotic/constructivist theories of learning and instruction.

Marc (Jung-Whan) de Jong is a PhD candidate in Sociology at the University of Southern California. He is currently working on his dissertation, which examines the influences of gender and sexuality on racialization processes in the United States, the Netherlands, and the United Kingdom post 9/11. His research interests center on the impact of new media technologies (especially the Internet) on social diversity and political activism; representations of minority groups in mass media; moral panics; constructions of crime and morality; and gender and violence. Because of his multicultural upbringing and academic background (he received degrees from the Universities of Amsterdam and London), Marc's research focus tends to be global in perspective.

Orhan Erden was born in Ankara in 1969. He graduated from the Industrial Technology Education Department of the Faculty of Industrial Arts Education, Gazi University in 1991. He completed his master's degree in 1996 and his doctorate degree in 2001 on Industrial Technology Education Institute of Science, at Gazi University. He served as teacher during the period 1991-1996. During 1996-2001 he served as research assistant in the Industrial Technology Education Department of Gazi University and as of the year 2002, he began to work as a lecturer in the same department. He is married and has two children.

Benjamin E. Erlandson is currently a doctoral student in the educational technology program at Arizona State University. His research focuses upon cognitive theories of multimedia learning, factors of learner motivation, and principles of design for a multitude of virtual learning environments. He hopes to apply all of his findings toward the improvement of informal learning environments and opportunities for lifelong learning. His academic background centers upon the design, production, and theories of multimedia, as he holds both baccalaureate and master's degrees in the multimedia arts and sciences. In addition to his academic pursuits, including teaching several university courses in the past few years, he has an extensive background in production and consulting work with several institutions, including the Boston Medical Center and the Library of Congress.

Kay Fielden is an associate professor in Computing in the School of Computing and Information Technology, Unitec Institute of Technology, Auckland, New Zealand. She is also the research leader for the school, mentors staff research, supervises postgraduate students and teaches postgraduate research methods. Her own research interests are grounded in qualitative research and systems thinking.

Noriko Hara, PhD, is an assistant professor of Information Science in the School of Library and Information Science at Indiana University, Bloomington. In addition, she is the codirector of the new Graduate Certificate in Information Architecture (GCIA) program. Her work is primarily in Social Informatics. Her focus is on communities of practice, knowledge management, online learning, and e-democracy. In addition, she is also a fellow of the Rob Kling Center for Social Informatics. She served the ASIS&T (American Society for Information Science & Technology) Special Interest Group on Social Informatics (SIG-SI) as a cochair.

Jean Hebert is a doctoral candidate and a researcher in the School of Communications at the Simon Fraser University in Vancouver, Canada, where he researches online music with the Centre for Policy Research on Science and Technology.

Val Hooper has been lecturing for nearly two decades in diverse areas including Information Systems Management; Electronic commerce; Brand Management; Economics; Strategic Management; Marketing Management; and Research Methodology. In 2004 she was awarded the Victoria University of Wellington Teaching Excellence Award. She has also practised widely as a management and specialist consultant in both developed and developing countries, with clients emanating from a range of industries including industrial engineering, agricultural engineering, a university consortium, a national health research council, and the tobacco industry. Val obtained her PhD in Information Systems from Victoria University, and her current research focuses on the strategic alignment between IS and marketing, and the impact of that alignment on marketing performance and business performance. Further research interests include all areas pertaining to the strategic application of IS to business performance, to e-commerce, and to m-commerce.

Yavuz Inal is a doctoral student and research assistant in the Computer Education and Instructional Technology, Middle East Technical University, Ankara, Turkey. His research and interests focus on game-based learning, cross-cultural aspects of computer games, flow experiences, ideological frameworks in games, localization of games, avatars in game-like learning environments, and new media use for societies. Web address: http://www.metu.edu.tr/~yinal/

Christine Julien is assistant professor in computer science at the University of Toulouse 3 (France) since 1989, and carries out her research at the Toulouse Computing Research Laboratory (IRIT - UMR 5505). She initially worked in document engineering and particularly in structured documents and hypertext documents. Her current works are oriented on personalized information access on the Web using social approaches.

Mike Johnson has enjoyed 10 years supporting staff and students use of ICT at Cardiff University, where he has been a lecturer in Cardiff School of Nursing and Midwifery since 2001. In 2006 he gained an MSc in Advanced Learning Technology with the renowned Centre for Studies in Advanced Learning Technology, Lancaster University (England). He has reviewed articles and books for the British Journal of Educational Technology since 2003. Research interests include learning technology, networked learning, *non-use* of information technology, computer-mediated communication, and Activity Theory.

Peter Jones, RMN, RGN, CPN(Cert.), BA(Hons), PGCE, PG(Dip.) COPE – has worked in the UK within mental health nursing services for the NHS since 1977. Based in the NW of England, his training includes mental health and general nursing, community mental health, and specialist therapy interventions using cognitive and psychosocial therapies. Since the early 1980s an interest in informatics saw the production of several computer-aided learning packages. In the mid-1990s this interest was formally recognised with a BA (Hons.) in computing and philosophy. Independent studies during the past decade have sought to publicize Hodges' model, a conceptual framework to communities beyond health and social care. This effort is ongoing through a Web site, blog, and the chapter to be found in this volume. A further chapter is in preparation on Hodges' model and sociotechnical structures. Peter is married to Christine; they have three children Daniel, Matthew, and Bethany.

Robin Kay has published over 30 articles in the area of computers in education, presented numerous papers at 15 international conferences, is a reviewer for five prominent computer education journals, and has taught computers, mathematics, and technology for over 18 years at the high school, college, and university level. Current projects include research on laptop use in teacher education, learning objects, audience response systems, gender differences in computer-related behaviour, discussion-board use, emotions and the use of computers, and factors that influence how students learn with technology. He completed his PhD in Cognitive Science (Educational Psychology) at the University of Toronto, where he also earned his master's degree in Computer Applications in Education. He is currently an Assistant Professor in the Faculty of Education at the University of Ontario Institute of Technology in Oshawa, Canada.

Christine Kell is Postgraduate Researcher and General Practitioner in the Department of Information Studies, University of Sheffield.

Patricia Randolph Leigh is associate professor of Curriculum and Instruction at Iowa State University and is affiliated with the Center for Technology in Learning and Teaching (CTLT) within the College of Human Sciences. Dr. Leigh teaches courses in instructional technology, educational foundations, curriculum theory, and multicultural education. Her research scholarship focuses on the equality of educational opportunities afforded underserved children as she examines, from an historical perspective, the impact of economic discrimination and residential segregation upon their public schooling. Within her investigations, Dr. Leigh also explores issues of technology and digital equity and the use of technology to promote multicultural and culturally relevant pedagogy.

Meng-Fen Grace Lin is a postdoctoral fellow at the University of Houston. She has degrees in Management Information System and Computer Science, and has worked in the computer industry prior to obtaining her EdD in Instructional Technology. She currently is an adjunct lecturer at both the University of Houston in Houston, Texas and National Taitung University, Taiwan. Her research interests include online community, open education resources (OER), and social learning theories. Her e-mail address is grace.mf.lin@gmail.com.

Robin Mason is professor of Educational Technology at The Open University, UK. Her work spans teaching, research, and scholarship in the area of e-learning, including online and distance education. She is coauthor of *Elearning: The Key Concepts* (Routledge, 2006), *The Educational Potential of e-Portfolios: Supporting Personal Development and Reflective Learning* (Routledge, 2007), and *The e-Learning Handbook: Social Networking for Education* (Routledge, forthcoming). She is the leader of several European Union-funded projects with universities in developing countries using open content to produce locally appropriate course material.

Maggie McPherson is a senior lecturer MA ICT in Education and member of ICT in Education Research Group at the University of Leeds. Her research interests e-Learning, IT/IS Management, and e-Society/eGovernment issues.

Sanjaya Mishra holds a PhD in library and information science in the area of library networks. He has been a teacher of communication technology to distance educators. He has been involved in successful implementation of many multimedia and Internet-based courses. With professional training in distance education, television production, and multimedia, he is actively involved in collaboration at international level. At present, he is reader in distance education at the staff training and research institute of distance education, Indira Gandhi National Open University, New Delhi. He also served (2001-2003) the Commonwealth Educational Media Centre for Asia at New Delhi as a program officer, where he conducted a number of workshops on "multimedia" and "e-learning" in the Asian region. He has served as consultant to UNESCO, UN-ESCAP, World Bank, and the Commonwealth of Learning. He was book review editor of *Indian Journal of Open Learning* from 1997-2000

Julia Nevárez obtained her PhD in Environmental Psychology at the Graduate Center of the City University of New York and is Assistant Professor in the Sociology and Anthropology Department at Kean University, New Jersey. She has been past Chair of the Environmental Design Research Association and Cochair of the Faculty Seminar at Kean University. Her interdisciplinary work focuses on urban space and globalization, public space, and technoculture. More specifically, she is interested in the transformations of urban space, urban development, and technology that affect social relations in the city. Her most recent publications analyze the aesthetics of order in Central Park, NY; the social content of urban screens in Times Square as part of the urban development initiatives implemented there; and agoraphobia as an urban condition examined through the conceptualization of Bachelard's "felicitous space." She is currently working as editor of the book "On global grounds: Urban change and globalization."

Miguel Baptista Nunes, PhD, is a Lecturer in Information Management in the Department of Information Studies at the University of Sheffield. His teaching and research interests are in the areas of Information Systems, Instructional Systems Design, Database Design, and Information Management.

Mary Panko directs a professional development programme at UNITEC Institute of Technology - the Graduate Diploma in Higher Education, which is designed to develop effective and critically reflective practitioners from a variety of adult and tertiary settings. Her research has focussed on individuals' teaching perspectives, particularly in online environments. Her previous experience ranges from training leader in the tertiary education, lecturing to coordinating the Interactive Learning Centre at the Robert Gordon University. Mary is member of Editorial Board of *Journal of Distant Learning*. In 1998 she received the British Council Award.

Maja Pivec, PhD, is professor of Game Based Learning and Learning with Multimedia at the University of Applied Sciences FH JOANNEUM in Graz, Austria. For her research achievements, Maja Pivec received, in the year 2001, Herta Firnberg Award (Austria) in the field of computer science. In 2003 she was awarded by European Science Foundation in the form of a grant for an interdisciplinary workshop organisation in the field of affective and emotional aspects of human-computer interaction, with emphasis on game-based learning and innovative learning approaches. She is coordinator, scientific leader, or partner in several EU or national-founded projects. She is editor and coeditor of two book publications in the area of innovative learning approaches. She is guest editor of *British Journal of Educational Technology*, Special issue on learning from games, May 2007. Her research work is published and presented at more than 70 international conferences and publications.

Kevin Quigley is an assistant professor at the Dalhousie University in Halifax, Nova Scotia, Canada. He recently completed a postdoctoral fellowship from the Economic and Social Research Council at the

University of Edinburgh. His areas of expertise include public sector risk management, critical infrastructure protection, and comparative public administration. His research specializes in public sector risk and crisis management, strategic management, and critical infrastructure protection. He is particularly interested in research methods that employ interdisciplinary and comparative approaches.

Frank Rennie is the Head of Research and Post-graduate Development at Lews Castle College, and Course Leader of the MSc in Managing Sustainable Rural Development at the UHI Millennium Institute in the Highlands and Islands of Scotland. His research interests lie in the general areas of rural and community development, especially in community-based approaches to integrated sustainable development. Recent work has been on new approaches to online education and distributed learning on and in rural communities. He is an advisor to several government programs and committees and is a Fellow of a number of learned societies. Frank has been involved in developing and delivering various combinations of distributed learning solutions (with a particular emphasis on networked solutions for rural areas) with colleges and university partners in Europe, Amazonia, Asia, and New Zealand. He has published a wide range of materials related to rural issues and is a regular keynote speaker at international conferences. For further details see http://www.lews.uhi.ac.uk/Research/StafRecl.htm.

Suthiporn Sajjapanroj is a doctoral student in curriculum studies with a minor in inquiry methodology at Indiana University. She has an undergraduate degree in Business Administration with finance major and master's degree in Computers and Engineering Management from her home country of Thailand. She received the Outstanding Performance Honor in the completion of her master's subjects. Before pursuing her study in PhD, Suthiporn worked as an academic staff in the Institution for the Promotion of Teaching Science and Technology, Thailand. She also has diverse work experience in banking systems, human resource management, and software training. She is now working on her dissertation. Her current research interests are student collaboration, teacher professional development, emerging technologies, and learning in a sociocultural context. She can be reached at ssajjapa@indiana.edu.

John Sandars is a senior lecturer in Community Based and Medical Education. His research interest is in e-learning, especially the use of newer technologies, such as blogs and podcasting, to enhance the student learning experience. He is particularly interested in online networks that link healthcare professionals. He has published extensively in the areas of elearning

Pnina Shachaf is an assistant professor of Library and Information Science in the School of Library and Information Science (SLIS) at Indiana University, Bloomington (IUB). Her research areas focus on computer-mediated communication, international and comparative librarianship, ethics, and evaluation of library services.

Ramesh Sharma holds a PhD in Education in the area of Educational Technology and is currently working as Regional Director in Indira Gandhi National Open University (IGNOU). He has been a teacher trainer and has taught Educational Technology, Educational Research and Statistics, Educational Measurement and Evaluation, Special Education, Psychodynamics of Mental Health Courses. He has conducted many Human Development training programmes for the in- and preservice teachers. He had established a Centre of ICT in the College he was working. He is a member of many committees on implementation of technology in the Open University. His areas of specialization include staff development, online learning, student support services in open and distance learning, and teacher education. He is a member of Advisory Group meeting on Human Resources Development for the United Nations Conference on Trade and Development (UNCTAD). He is the coeditor of *Asian Journal of Distance Education* (http://www.ASIANJDE.org). In addition to these, he is/has been on the Editorial Advisory Board of *International Review of Research in Open and Distance Learning*, online journal published by Athabasca University, Canada, http://www.irrodl.org, and *Turkish Online Journal of Distance Education* published by Anadolu University, Turkey (http://tojde.anadolu.edu.tr). He was on the Editorial Advisory Board of *Distance Education* (http://www.tandf.co.uk/journals/carfax/01587919.html); *Indian Journal of Open Learning* published by IGNOU. He has coauthored a book on distance education research, coedited a book entitled *Interactive Multimedia in Education and Training* and *Cases on Global E-Learning Practices: Successes and Pitfalls* (both from Idea Group, USA). He is also an Advisory Board Member and author for the *Encyclopedia of Distance Learning* (four-volume set) released by Idea Group Publishing. (www.igi-global.com)

Christine Simard holds a diploma in information technology and computer-based learning environments. She is an Education Specialist at the Télé-université. She has worked with organizations such as Reitmans Canada, Loblaws, BBM (Broadcast Bureau of Measurement) and La Puce – a non-profit community training organization.

Chantal Soule-Dupuy received the PhD degree in computer science from the University of Toulouse 3 (France) in 1990. She is currently Professor of computer science at the University of Toulouse 1 and serves as the head of the Department of Computer Science (since November 2003). Her recent research addresses information modeling and retrieval in digital libraries, personalized, and social search. She conducts and supervises research on these topics within the Toulouse Computing Research Laboratory (IRIT - UMR 5505).

J. Michael Tarn is an associate professor of the Department of Business Information Systems at Western Michigan University. Dr. Tarn's areas of expertise include network security, data communication management, Internet research, integrative systems design, international MIS, decision support systems, client-server database design, business forecasting, and critical systems management. He has published over 60 research articles in refereed journals, book chapters, and refereed conference proceedings in these areas. Dr. Tarn is the coordinator of Telecommunications & Information Management (TIM) Program.

Richard Taylor is a PhD candidate at the University of Houston. Before entering academia, he spent over 15 years in the business industry working as a systems engineer and a technology executive. He has been a frequent speaker at conferences, primarily in the financial services industry, presenting lectures on topics such as information security, technology ethics, and e-commerce. His academic work can be seen in the *Communications of the Association for Information Systems*, *Proceedings of American Conference for Information Systems*, and *Proceeding of the International Conference for Information Systems*. Upon completion of his doctorate, he plans to continue his career in academia, focusing his teaching and research efforts on information security and technology ethics.

Pascaline Tchienehom received the PhD degree in computer science from the University of Toulouse I in 2006. Her research addresses user and information modeling via an interoperable and flexible profile. She applies her work in the information retrieval field.

Filifotu Vaai was born in Samoa, on January 17th, 1984. After growing up in Samoa, she graduated in December, 2004 from Victoria University of Wellington, New Zealand with a Bachelor of Commerce and Administration (BCA) with majors in Electronic Commerce and Commercial Law. In May 2005 she graduated with a BCA with Honours in Information Systems. Since May 2005, Filifotu has worked as a business analyst for SamoaTel, the largest telecommunications provider in Samoa. Her research interests include information systems in small businesses in the South Pacific, telecommunications policy in the Pacific, and trust in virtual teams. She is currently studying for her Master's in Communications, with a focus in Telecommunications at the University of Hawaii under a research scholarship from the East West Center in Honolulu, Hawaii. An avid sportwoman, Filifotu has represented Samoa in netball, and enjoys rugby, swimming, and Polynesian dance.

Index